The Glories of War

By

Charles P. Poland Jr.

First published by AuthorHouse 07/26/06

ISBN: 1-4184-5973-9 (e-book)
ISBN: 1-4184-4066-3 (Paperback)
ISBN: 1-4184-4067-1 (Dust Jacket)

Library of Congress Control Number: 2004090892

Printed in the United States of America
Bloomington, IN

This book is printed on acid free paper.

The Glories of War

Small Battles
and Early Heroes of 1861

Charles P. Poland Jr.

To my beautiful wife,
Betty, for her devotion
and tireless effort in
what had to seem like
endless work in the
creation of this book

Table of Contents

Illustrations

MAPS

PREFACE

The American Civil War is a fascinating subject. It is the most dramatic as well as arguably the most pivotal period in American history. Countless volumes on major battles and political and military figures make it the most-written-about period of the nation's history. New volumes continue to flood bookstores: books dealing with social aspects of the lives of soldiers and civilians, specialized studies providing more details about major battles and primary figures, and works covering lesser battles and persons that had previously received little attention.

This volume is an overview of a sizable part of the war. It is a study of the Union invasions of the Old Dominion during 1861. The Union invaded along four corridors, and this military action often had a traumatic impact upon civilians. Maps using configurations are designed to aid the reader in remembering the areas and nature of military activity. Special attention has been given to western Virginia, an area that has received limited consideration.

Most of the combat of 1861, with the exception of Bull Run, involved small battles and innumerable skirmishes. These would be dwarfed by the numbers of men and size of battles of subsequent years. Although earlier battles were of far less consequence and significance than later mammoth bloodbaths, participants in small battles and skirmishes faced the same danger of being wounded, suffering, and dying as those in larger conflicts. These and other horrifying military experiences soon disillusioned many young men who had volunteered to participate in what they believed would be the "glories of war" for a "noble cause." The result often was discontentment. Like a strong undertow, dissatisfaction drowned the excitement for and the romantic view of the war and replaced them with problems of morale and behavior that challenged leaders of both sides, leaders already grappling with sundry difficulties in fighting a war.

ACKNOWLEDGMENTS

To my loving wife, who typed and edited the original draft from my difficult scrawl, I owe an unpayable debt. Her unwavering support was undaunted by heart surgery that interrupted my work. She informed the surgeon, "I greatly hope you bring his body through the operation without impairment, but you must keep his mind undamaged. He has a book to finish!" Special thanks to Bryce A. Suderow, whose knowledge of the Civil War and unparalleled ability to obtain much of the vast sources needed were crucial in the making of this book. An enormous debt of gratitude is owed Jennifer Hornsby for the cheerful and expert editing of this volume. Thanks also to Debi Blum for ably typing the final draft, the advise of Lina B. Burton, and to my daughters, Elisa Poland-McMahon, for traveling great distances to type part of the original draft, and Lynette Poland-Lucas, for her support.

Encouragement was also received from my colleagues Dr. Wallace Hutcheon and Dr. Terry Alford and former student and superb historian Dr. Ethan Rafuse. Two young and very capable historians, former students of whom I am proud, Alan McClarnand and Charles T. Harrell, provided helpful material.

I am grateful to the knowledgeable E. B. Vandiver III for piquing my interest about West Virginia and for the encouragement of a host of students, most of whom have finished school and have successful and distinguished careers. They have followed me on field trips over dusty roads not only to sites of events covered in this book but also to sites along the entire eastern theater of the war. During the two and a half decades of offering Civil War field-trip courses and traveling approximately 25,000 miles, many have been engaging companions. Among the hundreds who have taken my field-trip courses, the following have been participants for one to two decades: Arch Scurlock, E. B. Vandiver III, John M. Atkinson, John Briar III, Janice Magnuson, Linda Javins, and the late Elfrida Martin. Among others of faithful years of study and travel: Pam Unger, Alan McClarnand, John Campbell, John Grimes, Shirley Suski, Fred R. Pitman Jr., Lakhwant S. Aulahk, Frank Woods, Bill Anderson, Leona Stich, Gina Goodman, John Watson, John Ortega, Vern Bettencourt, Charles Harrell, Carlos Sutton, and the late Randolph F. Caldwell, Jr., Jim Dacey and Jack Wamsley.

Additionally, I have benefited from having possession of the late Sam Neal's extensive Civil War collection, which includes much of Douglas Southall Freeman's library. Ownership of the Neal collection was made possible by the benevolence of my mother, Ina B. Poland, and Doug Neal, a friend and colleague. David Myles graciously provided access to Myles Knob. Others have granted permission to quote passages from their works: Nancy Chappelear Baird, Mary H. Lancaster, Greenwood Publication Group, and the West Virginia Division of Culture and History.

To the librarians and personnel in a host of public and private depositories, including those at colleges, universities, state libraries, the Library of Congress, National Archives, and National Battlefield Parks, I owe a debt of gratitude.

PART I

THE EASTERN INVASION CORRIDOR

CHAPTER I

HIS BLOOD CRIES FOR VENGEANCE: ELMER ELLSWORTH

From May through December 1861 the realities of combat challenged the antebellum view of war held by Americans. This was true for civilians, soldiers, and officers. They found that war was not as simplistic or glorious as many had assumed. Commanders applied strategies and tactics of the Napoleonic era that, in 1861, were often outdated by recent technology. Grand battle plans for glorious victories were rarely implemented as designed; untrained men and inexperienced officers proved to be ill-prepared for the tasks they faced. Press coverage of the first year of the war, of even the smallest skirmishes, was extensive, and at times, events were hyperbolically depicted as heroic. Similar combat actions later in the war would be considered commonplace.

Union strategy and Confederate responses would determine the location of the theaters of war and battle sites. The South maintained that she was out of the Union, so it was up to Lincoln and the North to take the offense in the war to try to keep the South in the Union. Federal strategies evolved to accomplish this, including the blockading of the southern Atlantic coast of the Confederacy. In the West the Union's major objective was to split the Confederacy by gaining control of the Mississippi River. A secondary goal in this theater was to break the Allegheny barrier by gaining control of key routes through the mountains that separated the eastern and western theaters. East of the Appalachians the primary goal was to capture Richmond, the Confederate capital. This goal made Virginia the heart of the fighting in the eastern theater of the war. The Old Dominion would become the scene of 2,154 military events—more than any other state—out of the 10,455 military actions of varying types and size occurring during the war[1].

With Richmond its primary target in the eastern theater, the Union developed, based on geographical factors and the location of key rail communications, four major invasion routes into Virginia: from Washington into northern Virginia; from Washington up the peninsula between the James and York Rivers to Richmond; from Maryland into the lower Shenandoah Valley; and crossing the Ohio River into Virginia.

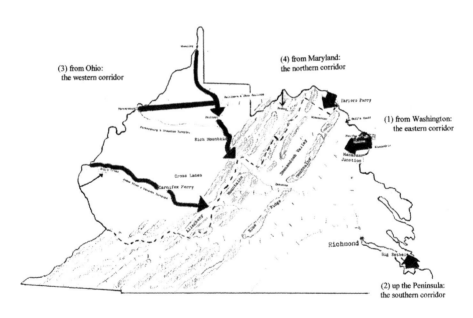

THE FOUR INVASION CORRIDORS INTO VIRGINIA: 1861

ELMER ELLSWORTH: A LITTLE MAN WITH BIG IDEAS

The most immediate problem facing the Lincoln administration from April 17, 1861, when the Virginia convention voted for secession, through May 23, when the state held a referendum on secession, was the security of Washington. A number of the Federal military leaders did not believe the flooding of the town with military units from the North made Washington safe from attack. Some of these leaders felt the Virginia shore of the Potomac, especially the high ground across from the District, must be immediately seized. Only two miles from government buildings in Washington lay Arlington Heights, the site of Robert E. Lee's home and the potential location for enemy artillery that could batter government structures in the District. Therefore, land on the Virginia shore needed to be taken. Redoubts or earthworks would also be constructed south of the Potomac in order to secure these bridges to Washington: Long Bridge, Chain Bridge, and the aqueduct that carried the Chesapeake and Ohio Canal over the river from Georgetown. Another crucial target was Alexandria, about seven miles from Washington. Occupation of this old port town was vital to protect and control the navigation of the Potomac.

For weeks prior to Virginia's secession, nightly in Washington, the militia guarded government buildings and stationed men at the northern end of the Potomac bridges to prevent any sneak attacks from the Old Dominion. Lincoln waited until the people of Virginia voted on the referendum on secession before moving Federal troops into northern Virginia. The eventual seizure of Alexandria would create the first heroes of the war, Elmer Ellsworth from the North and James W. Jackson, a Southerner. Both, depending on the location of the commentator, would be called either martyr or villain.

Citizens who remained in Washington started feeling safer as the militia arrived from the North from the end of April into May, overwhelming their city. Washington was unprepared for the new arrivals. Temporary shelter was found in government buildings, including the Capitol. Later soldiers were sent to camps scattered in and around the city. Urgently needed food and supplies were rushed

5

to the District. By rail and boat came everything from blankets to beef cattle. The latter were pastured on the grounds of the Smithsonian Institution and the Washington Monument. One herd fell into the canal. It took a day and half to get them out, and six cattle drowned. Many of the items sold to the War Department by profiteering contractors were of shabby quality. Blankets, uniforms, shoes, and knapsacks were of such inferior quality that they soon fell apart.

Colonel Elmer Ephraim Ellsworth
Commander of the New York Fire Zouaves,
close friend of the Lincolns and first martyred hero of the war.
(Courtesy of the Library of Congress)

Citizens' nervousness of the previous months and the current problems of mobilization, procurement, and the realities of war were seemly veiled behind a festive atmosphere in Washington. Civilians eagerly watched parades and visited camp sites to listen to concerts and singing or to view military drills. To many, the events seemed like a "grand gala."

Some Yankee soldiers arrived in the District dressed in blue, and others, in gray. Some came in civilian clothing and in need of weapons. They were from all walks of life, of different economic, social, and educational backgrounds. The soldiers of the First Rhode Island were wealthy society men and were commanded by an impressive-looking colonel, Ambrose E. Burnside. Others were less refined, such as the rowdy members of the Eleventh New York Regiment, who were raised from the New York Fire Department and were known as the Fire Zouaves. Their garish uniforms were as brazen as their behavior. They complained about bypassing Baltimore and being sent to Washington by way of Annapolis. "We would have gone through Baltimore like a dose of salts," one Zouave bragged to a newspaper reporter. Once in D.C., they were sheltered in the House of Representatives, where one of their favorite amusements (and a popular amusement of the regiments that were billeted in Senate chambers) was to hold mock legislative sessions.

Strange scenes, described by the Alexandria *Gazette,* included soldiers' pretending they were legislators amidst the food supplies of beef, bacon, ham, mutton, bags of pepper and salt, all piled upon the carpeted floor. Knapsacks, belts with cartridge boxes, and bayonet scabbards were draped upon "rich and costly bronze ornaments, upon gas chandeliers, and the...brackets that held back the silk and lace curtains," according to the newspaper. Some precautions were taken to protect the premises. "All the statuary in the halls of the capitol and in the old rotunda" were boxed. The pictures were covered with protective planks. The building's porticoes were "barricaded to the height of about eight feet." The iron plates for the "new dome were used for the breastworks," and behind them were barrels of cement and "piles of stone and timber forming an impenetrable barrier."[2]

The wild behavior of the Fire Zouaves soon became an engaging topic for gossip and newspaper columns. Select members of the regiment displayed their enthusiasm, athleticism, and efficiency in fighting fires by saving Willard's Hotel from the flames that were consuming a nearby building. (Willard's was an important caravansary and meeting place of prominent politicos and the elite.) Some found the pranks and irresponsible acts of the Zouaves

7

amusing. The soldiers walked around the unfinished dome at 200 feet up, dangled from ropes, charged meals, cigars, and boots to Jeff Davis and Old Abe, chased secessionists, and frightened elderly ladies. Single women were horrified by rumored stories, read in newspapers, of a Zouave's role in the "frightful seduction" of a young woman, who, it was later revealed, had "been a most yielding seducee, offering to settle the matter for 25 dollars." The rowdy behavior by the Zouaves soon led to complaints, which forced their commander, Colonel Elmer Ellsworth, to expel and send home six of the worst offenders. But the colonel remained steadfastly proud of the remaining 1,094 men and took great delight in daily marching them "down Pennsylvania Avenue and past the White House," where the Lincoln family eagerly watched them.[3]

The Zouaves were also proud of their diminutive "Little Colonel" in his mid-twenties, whose personal magnetism made them eager to respond to his leadership. In many ways he was their antithesis. Unlike the rowdy and often undisciplined men he commanded, Ellsworth was deeply moral and self-controlled, always adhering to a childhood pledge never to allow liquor to touch his lips. He was also a romantic and idealist who liked to read aloud these lines from the Victorian English poet Alfred Tennyson, expressing the heroic and knightly duty of man:

> To break the heathen and uphold the Christ,
> To ride abroad redressing human wrongs,
> To speak no slander, no, nor listen to it,
> To lead sweet lives in purest chastity,
> To love one maiden only, cleave to her,
> And worship her by years of noble deeds.[4]

Born during the depression of 1837, Ellsworth had known poverty as a child and again as a young adult. At age eighteen he struggled to survive on his own by doing odd jobs. After settling in Chicago, Ellsworth tenaciously endured an austere life as a store clerk. After working for hours, he assiduously studied law, spent the night on a store floor, and subsisted for long periods on a meager diet of bread and water.[5] At times, the lack of nutrition was so debilitating that Ellsworth was near starvation; he suffered from nausea and the inability to concentrate. Such hard times somehow did not shake his conviction that an indomitable willpower can overcome great obstacles—including the lack of nourishment. While Ellsworth underestimated the importance of food for good health, he espoused the necessity of proper ventilation. He opposed sleeping with the windows closed, so Elmer, the renter, devised a novel solution to having sashes stuck down from years of inactivity. He would stand ten paces from the window and empty his revolver, leaving holes in the glass the size of fifty-cent pieces. This practice did not endear him to landlords.

He instructed the teenage girl he planned to marry, Caroline ("Carrie") Spafford, on a variety of subjects. And through his "courtship by correspondence," he informed her of the virtues of fresh air and exercise and the evils of tight corsets. Women's fascination with tight-laced corsets was, in Ellsworth's view, a "most pernicious habit."

In the late 1850's, after several years of a meager existence, young Ellsworth found fame and adulation. By rigorous training every night from seven to midnight, he transformed an inept cadet company into national champions. He and the Ellsworth Zouaves would later tour the country, performing impressive and precise maneuvers and drills for thousands of spectators.

For a brief time, Ellsworth had been a law student in the office of Lincoln and Herndon. Elmer was not a particularly adept student of law, as he lost legal papers and some of Lincoln's speeches. Nevertheless, Abraham Lincoln became extremely fond of the energetic and personable youth with the fascination for weapons. The future president felt the lad had great potential to be an outstanding military leader, and he called Ellsworth "the greatest little man I ever met." Lincoln was also impressed by Ellsworth's loyalty. The youth vigorously campaigned for his mentor and was later responsible for the president-elect's safety, accompanying him on the eleven-day journey to Washington. Next to Lincoln, Ellsworth was the most famous person on the train. Once in the capital city, Ellsworth became a close friend of the entire first family. His frequent visits to the White House were eagerly awaited, but on one occasion, a visit led to Ellsworth's contracting measles from the Lincoln boys, Willie and Tad. A more welcomed consequence of his visits was the continued friendship with the Lincolns, and also that of John Nicolay and John Hay, the president's private secretaries.[6]

Despite having been befriended by the president, Ellsworth struggled to advance his career while in Washington. He was unsuccessful in lobbying for the establishment of a bureau of militia, which he wanted to head. Thwarted—by the seniority system—in obtaining a commission greater than lieutenant, Ellsworth went to New York, raised a regiment from firemen, and returned with them to Washington. His fame brought immediate attention to his unit, the Eleventh New York. Despite the embarrassing indiscretions of some of Ellsworth's men, public interest in the Zouave regiment continued to grow. Zouave dolls, dressed in scarlet trousers and blue jackets, appeared on the market. One was given to Willie and Tad as a gift. Their fascination with Ellsworth's regiment led them, with their playmates, to form a company of "Mrs. Lincoln's Zouaves." Tad even had his picture taken in a small Zouave uniform provided by his indulgent parents. While the kids played soldier, newspapers ran ads for Ellsworth's *Manual of Arms,* originally published in 1858; the ads proclaimed it the "best book" for young recruits to learn how to be soldiers. Colonel Ellsworth now seemed to be in the right place at the right time.[7]

JAMES W. JACKSON: RESOLUTE AND DEFIANT

In Alexandria, across the Potomac from the capital, there was a taunting and irritating symbol: a large Confederate flag fluttering from a staff that rose from the roof of the Marshall Hotel. Apparently this flag was visible to the naked eye from Washington. Lincoln's secretaries, Nicolay and Hay, maintained the "rebel flag" was "in plain view from the windows of the Executive Mansion in Washington." They, the Lincoln family, Ellsworth, and others saw it, no doubt with feelings of righteous indignation. The "tycoon," Hay's "affectionate nickname" for Lincoln, reportedly stated that the flag was an insult. Ellsworth shared his opinion. The raising of this flag on April 17, the day Virginia's convention voted to secede, soon received considerable attention in newspapers throughout the North. But Lincoln would take no action against Virginia or to remove the "obnoxious" banner of defiance that fluttered virtually in the face of the Federal government until after the voters of Virginia cast their ballots on the matter of secession.[8]

The town that displayed the offending flag sat about a half-dozen miles south of Washington and across the Potomac. Alexandria was founded in 1749 as a port for the tobacco trade and was nearly a half-century older than the capital city. In 1860 its population of 9,000 was approximately one-seventh of Washington's 61,000 inhabitants; these numbers would be drastically altered by mobilization and war.[9] Alexandria's genesis and economic life were sparked by the Potomac River. (Though despite the economic benevolence of the river, the decade before the Civil War saw over sixty people finding "a watery grave." Some were murdered, others committed suicide, but most drowned by accident.[10])

By the mid-nineteenth century the Potomac at Alexandria was described as "nearly a mile wide, and affords a commodious harbor for ships of the largest tonnage. It is also a place where shipbuilding is carried on to some extent. The town is a convenient place to export products from Virginia." Trade at Alexandria was "materially increased by the recent opening of the canal to Georgetown, intersecting the Chesapeake and Ohio Canal and a railroad (Orange

11

and Alexandria) ninety miles long," extending to Gordonsville and the Virginia Central Railroad, as pointed out by the Chicago *Tribune*. "This connection is a most important one to the South, as the line extends...through the southern States to Montgomery and Mobile and connects with branch lines to almost every prominent southern city and port."[11]

Turnpikes also connected Alexandria with the interior of Virginia. These were supplemented by an additional rail line, the Alexandria, Loudoun, and Hampshire, that reached Leesburg, a short distance to the west. When the war started, Alexandria was described as "regularly laid out" and "gas lighted." The streets were paved with oval stones that often weighed sixty pounds or more. The stones had been dredged from the Potomac River and brought to shore as ship's ballast. Angry citizens damned the condition of the town's roads, as they were frequently in need of repair, at times causing both horse and man to struggle over them. Shortly before the war, a citizen of the town lamented the plight of passengers "whose heads were in danger as the stage bounced over huge boulders" and "pitied the noble horses as they dragged along at a slow pace often staggering as they would put a foot by accident in a deep rut."[12]

Numerous homes, twelve churches, three banks, two newspaper officers, hostelries, and businesses of varying historical significance lined these cobblestone thoroughfares. A few of the more noteworthy structures were the City Hotel of Gadsby's Tavern, known for superior accommodations and food; the Carlyle House, the town's governor's mansion and General Edward Braddock's headquarters for a time during the French and Indian War; and Christ Church, where George Washington and, later, Robert E. Lee were parishioners. It was in this church where Lee, whose boyhood home was in Alexandria, married Mary Custis, the reputed step-great-granddaughter of George Washington. Lesser-known buildings included a three-story brick hostelry constructed during the late 1700's on a street corner. In this structure the first martyrs of the Civil War would die. The building was known as the Marshall House, in honor of Chief Justice John Marshall. When the Civil War started, the proprietor was a rabid supporter of the Confederacy, a man in his late thirties or early forties, James W. Jackson.[13]

Unlike the diminutive Elmer Ellsworth, whom he would confront in the Marshall House, Jackson was a powerful six-footer.

Both were resolute men, but Jackson was more so. The sternness and grimness of his expression were an outward indication of an obstinate determination, a characteristic that would lead to his death. This native of Fairfax County, Virginia, was not normally a disagreeable or mean person, and he befriended those who did not offend him. For instance, Jackson once helped a youth he met by chance while hunting. Jackson adjusted the sights on the young man's musket and taught him to kill squirrels by "barking" (which involved aiming underneath the squirrel so the bullet penetrated the tree bark, but not the carcass of the animal, who would be killed by concussion—it was no small feat). Jackson shared half his kill with his new friend, whose erring marksmanship prevented him from bagging anything.

After he moved to Alexandria, Jackson befriended a former Spanish employee who was left behind at Fairfax Court House. He visited and saw that the man—who had been beset by illness and excessive drink and been abandoned by others—was cared for. If a kindly and loyal friend, Jackson was a terrible and unyielding enemy, especially to those who sullied his name or that of the South. A Kentucky priest who tried unsuccessfully to block Jackson's marriage by appealing to the bride's father was soon confronted by the uncompromising groom. When the Catholic cleric denied his role, Jackson supposedly demanded that the priest state his position in a note and send it to Jackson's father-in-law. When the clergyman refused, he was given the ultimatum of sending the explanation or receiving a thrashing. The priest took off his robe and fought. At first he was a tough adversary, but after a long and bloody encounter, the priest did indeed suffer a terrible beating. So severe was the thrashing that the priest obtained a warrant and sent a posse after Jackson. The Virginian proved to be more than the pursuers wanted to confront.

Jackson returned from Kentucky to Fairfax County with his new bride. There he farmed and, later, managed hotels. In 1858 he leased a structure in Fairfax Court House with the ironic name Union Hotel. Early in 1861 he rented the Marshall House after moving to Alexandria.

James W. Jackson
Indomitable, villain to Northerners and martyr to Southerners.
(Courtesy of the Alexandria Library, Lloyd House)

The brief biography of Jackson printed a year after his death describes him as foremost among "custodians" of the honor and rights of Virginia and the South. According to his biographer, Jackson felt that "true sons of the South" must ferret out those who were disloyal and see that offenders were punished. "During the spring of 1860," Thomas Crux, a "Yankee" resident of Fairfax, was such an offender. According to Jackson, Crux was "uttering incendiary language" and, in northern Virginia, distributing "incendiary literature," including Hinton R. Helper's *Impending Crisis*.[14] Helper, a native of North

Carolina, had authored a book published in New York in 1857. He tried to prove through statistics that the South was vastly inferior to the North because slavery had impoverished and degraded the South. "Slavery destroys, or vitiates, or pollutes whatever it touches," Helper wrote. According to Helper, slavery had reduced the South to "literary pauperism" and "sunk a large majority" of Southern whites "in galling poverty and ignorance." Helper proposed to stop this decline with "the abolishment of slavery."[15] The circulation of this scathing tract motivated Jackson and a friend to plan the capture of Crux and bring him to justice for violating Virginia's law banning the distribution of *The Impending Crisis* in the state. After a spirited chase across the Long Bridge into Washington, Crux was seized and turned over to the authorities in Fairfax County. Crux posted $2,500 in bail and fled from the state, forfeiting the money but escaping prosecution.

When Lincoln received the Republican nomination for the presidency, James Jackson immediately became a secessionist. His biographer wrote that Jackson was further annoyed when "a party of miserable Black Republicans" in a neighboring county raised a flag in Occoquan, Virginia, in honor of the Illinoisan's candidacy. Jackson rode to Prince William County and joined irate citizens of the county in marching to remove what Jackson thought of as "the flaunting nuisance." Jackson, the outsider, took an ax, cut down the flagpole, and brought the offending flag back as a trophy to his residence at Fairfax Court House.[16] The business cards the Marshall House proprietor had printed in early 1861 show his dedication to the Confederate cause:

> MARSHALL HOUSE
> James W. Jackson, Proprietor
> Corner of Pitt and King sts.
> Alexandria, Virginia
> Virginia is determined and will conquer under the command
> of Jeff. Davis

In light of his allegiance, it is not surprising that Jackson would be among the first to fly the Confederate flag. The enormous emblem, eighteen feet long and thirteen feet, four inches, wide, was raised over the Marshall House as part of the movement of Southern defiance that accelerated after Lincoln's call for volunteers. The bunting flag that was flown in Alexandria was designed by a town citizen, Charles M. Taylor, who solicited $30 from other residents so John W. Padgett could be hired to make the emblem. Padgett's wife and sister-in-law made the flag, working on it up to the time it was taken to the Marshall House. Jackson was eager for the flag to fly over his establishment. A forty-foot pole was placed through a trapdoor on the roof, with the bottom of the pole resting on the attic floor for support. Around 4:00 P.M. on April 17 the flag was raised. It fluttered in the brisk northwest wind as a large crowd watched, shouted, and cheered approval, punctuated by the firing of a cannon. During this time Taylor claimed he told Jackson, "I want you to defend this flag." To this, Jackson is said to have responded, "If the flag ever comes down, it will come down over my dead body."[17]

The day after the Confederate flag was hoisted over the Marshall House, the Alexandria militia, the nucleus of what would become the Seventeenth Virginia Infantry, was mobilized. The town militia was joined by four companies from across the river in Washington. All were billeted in Alexandria. Some stayed in the Marshall House, whose proprietor, James Jackson, despite having received a lieutenant's commission from the governor to raise an artillery battery, had been unsuccessful in his attempts to form a unit.

Militiamen in Alexandria spent much of a typical day grumbling about hearing reveille at five in the morning, as well as about the many roll calls and the intermittent drills that led to sore feet. They would be arguing over who was winning the poker game when their diversion would be so rudely interrupted at 9:00 at night by tattoo and orders for all lights out. Inexperience and unwillingness to follow orders sometimes led to confusion and conflict. A misinterpretation of an order caused Alexandria troops to be moved miles west of town before the error was discovered and corrected. Later in the month of May, Colonel Algernon S. Taylor, in violation of orders, but fearing his men were no match for the Federals who could cross the river at any time, evacuated the militia from Alexandria. Angry superiors replaced Taylor for having left Alexandria unprotected from invasion; the Federal gunboat of Fort Sumter fame, the USS *Pawnee,* had been nearby in the river since April 27, with her Dahlgrens pointed menacingly at the town.[18] Taylor's replacement, Colonel George H. Terrett, proved to be a no-nonsense officer. When some of his men attempted to serenade him, he ordered them to leave. When they refused, he called the guards, and a melee ensued, with the musicians smashing their cornet, banjo, bass, and flute upon the guards—benefiting neither the heads of the arresting soldiers nor the condition of the musical instruments. There were more tranquil and enjoyable movements: some of the young women continually provided food for sentries, and the owner of a brewery kept "drinkables" available for the men at any hour in the vestibule of his home.[19]

James Jackson and fellow Alexandrians were jubilant on the night of May 23. Voters of their state had ratified secession. Alexandrians had given their approval by voting: 958 for leaving the Union, and 106 against. It was a time to celebrate. Town citizens serenaded their local members of the Confederate state legislature, who won their elections that day. Jackson, one of the leaders of the celebration, concluded the joyous occasion by bringing many of the revelers back to the Marshall House to continue the festivities. Around "11 o'clock the party broke up and the music ceased." Jackson went to bed content over political developments.[20]

Details of what followed the next day vary, especially concerning the fatal shootings of Ellsworth and Jackson. Ellsworth seemed to have had a premonition that he would die, but it is not clear what Jackson felt. He expected the "Yankees" to come, and he prepared to resist them. One account tells of Jackson's boldness in borrowing a "small four pound cannon from some friends in Alexandria," that had been used "almost from time immemorial to fire 4th of July salutes." Residents claimed to have seen the artillery piece behind a screen in the backyard of the Marshall House. Jackson stated he later loaded the piece to the muzzle with nails and scrap iron. Some claimed he had it put under the front steps of the hotel and had an artillery officer point it upward so he could to rake the hotel's entrance, hallway, and office if Federal soldiers should enter the hotel. When the local artillery officer pointed out to Jackson that such an act "would be folly" as he would most certainly be killed, Jackson supposedly replied, "I have not a long time to live anyhow, and if I can kill fifteen or twenty Yankees, I'll be willing to die."[21]

Charles P. Poland Jr.

FIRST INVASION: THE FEDERALS MOVE
ON ALEXANDRIA

While Jackson lay asleep in his inn for the last time, across the Potomac, the man he would soon kill was preparing his "Pet Lambs" to move to Alexandria. Ellsworth informed the Fire Zouaves they would be taken by steamer to Alexandria during the night. Once there, they must act with restraint and "kindness unless" forced "to use violence." Finally he told them, "Go to your tents, lie down and take your rest till two o'clock, when the boat will arrive and we go forward to victory or death." Few slept, in nervous anticipation. Instead they talked, laughed, and sang patriotic songs. Their "little Colonel" spent much of his time darting about the camp that the Eleventh New York had occupied since their move from the capitol. It was known as Camp Lincoln and was located on Giesboro Point, about four miles from the White House. Ellsworth seemed jovial, joking with those around him. At about midnight he took the time to write two moving letters, one to Carrie Spafford, the woman he planned to marry, and another to his parents. He warned them that something might happen to him at Alexandria, but said they must always remember his great love for them. If something happened to him, he wrote, they must "cherish the consolation" that he was "engaged in the performance of a great sacred duty" and was "perfectly content to accept whatever" his "fortune may be." More than a month earlier, as Lincoln had been planning to send supplies to Fort Sumter, Ellsworth—while still in bed recovering from the measles—had expressed the same fatalistic view to his good friend John Hay: "You know I have a great work to do, to which my life is pledged; I am the only earthly stay of my parents; there is a young woman whose happiness I regard as dearer than my own; yet I could ask no better death than to fall next week before Sumter."

Ellsworth carefully chose his attire for the trip to Alexandria. He remarked to one of his captains that he was selecting "clothes in which he was to die"; he had a feeling that in the next few hours, his country would require him to give his life. He pinned a gold badge on his chest, which was symbolic of his romanticized Victorian view of war and of his belief that it was a man's noble duty to sacrifice his life

18

for his country. Inscribed in Latin on the emblem was the phrase "Not for ourselves alone but for country."[22]

A reporter witnessed three steamboats appearing near Camp Lincoln at 2:00 A.M. The night was still and clear, he observed, "and the moon so full and lustrous" it illuminated the men, who moved toward the "long lines of rowboats at the water's edge," which would carry them to the steamers. He continued: "the vivid costumes of the men—come wrapped from head to foot in the great red blankets, but most of them clad [in uniforms]"; "the peaks of the tents...all glowing like huge lanterns from the fires within them; the glittering rows of rifles and sabers; the woods and hills, and the placid river, which here meet in exquisite proportion, enfolding all—and all these suffused with the broad moonlight" created an unforgettable scene. In less than two hours, all 1,000 men were aboard three steamers.[23]

The Fire Zouaves' trip down and across the river was only one of a four-pronged movement of Federals invading Virginia. Cavalry crossed Chain Bridge; infantry stomped across the Aqueduct and over rickety Long Bridge to secure the high ground and bridge entrances south of the Potomac. They met virtually no Southern resistance. The 500 or so Virginia militia were no match for the Union force of 15,000 that swarmed across the river. When informed by a Federal navy officer from the *Pawnee,* who arrived in Alexandria at 5:30 A.M. under a flag of truce, that they would be given until 9:00 that morning to leave town, Colonel Terrett and his Virginia force eagerly consented. Federals came to Alexandria by 9:00 A.M., capturing thirty-five cavalrymen and prompting secessionists to claim that they had known all along that the Northern forces' movement was a deceitful Yankee attempt to trap them.[24]

At the same time as the landing of Ellsworth's regiment at Alexandria, the First Michigan Infantry, which had crossed over Long Bridge, entered the town from the north. The immediate targets for the more than 2,000 men in both units were the two railroads and the telegraph—the town's communication with the rest of the South. While a company of Zouaves went to tear up the tracks leading to Manassas, Ellsworth led a small force toward the telegraph office to cut the wires. He never arrived. Noticing the Confederate flag atop the Marshall House, he seemed to have impetuously entered the three-story structure, accompanied by his small squad, a chaplain, a newspaper reporter for the New York *Tribune,* and the regiment's secretary.[25]

Ellsworth rapidly ascended to the roof of the inn and cut down the "Secessionist" flag as several of the men with him watched. They proceeded down the steps, led by corporal Francis Brownell, with Ellsworth following closely, while folding the flag. As they neared a landing, James Jackson sprang forward and fired one shot at close range from his double-barreled shotgun at the intruder who carried the Confederate flag. The buckshot ripped through Ellsworth's rib cage, penetrating his chest. His body dropped heavily from the steps, face forward on the floor. Jackson then fired at Brownell, but the corporal had knocked away the barrel of the shotgun, causing the shot to miss the intended victim by only inches and to strike, according to a reporter, the "panels and wainscoting of a door, behind which housed sleeping lodgers." Brownell fired his musket almost "simultaneously with Jackson's second shot," wrote the reporter. The contents from the Zouave's musket struck Jackson in the middle of his face at the bridge of his nose, causing a ghastly wound that an eyewitness, Edward House, claimed was too appalling to describe. As Jackson fell to the floor, Brownell bayoneted him.

These events happened in a matter of seconds. Confusion and fear consumed those in the hotel. Those who had accompanied Ellsworth were horrified by what had happened to their colonel and were distrusting of the curious patrons who suddenly appeared from their rooms and, as rapidly, disappeared when frightened by the Federals' threats to shoot them.[26] Ellsworth, wrote a reporter, "had fallen on his face and the streams of blood that flowed from his wound had literally flooded the way." The chaplain gently turned the body over, and Edward House stooped and called Ellsworth's name, thinking he might have heard an inarticulate murmur. He had not. Ellsworth had died instantly.

The shot had ripped through the left part of Ellsworth's chest, broken a rib, passed through the left lung, shredded the aorta, and lodged in the spine.[27] Henry J. Winser, a New York *Times* correspondent who left the paper to become Ellsworth's private secretary, stated that he and House "lifted the body with all the care" they "could apply, and laid it upon a bed in a room near by." A short time later, while still under the traumatic influence of having seen Ellsworth's and Jackson's violent deaths, House described the scene for the *Tribune*'s readers, attempting to find meaning in Ellsworth's actions and death. He wrote: "The rebel flag, stained with his blood, and purified by this contact from the baseness of its former meaning, It laid at his feet, It was at first difficult to discover the precise locality…[of Ellsworth's] wound for all parts of his coat were equally saturated with blood." The report continued: "By cautiously loosening the belt and unbuttoning the coat, we found where the shot had penetrated. None of us had any medical knowledge, but we saw all hope [was gone]." "Nevertheless it seemed proper to summon the surgeon as speedily as possible." House and the others were torn between wanting to send for the doctor and feeling isolated in a hostile town while fearing an ambush and feeling afraid of leaving Ellsworth's body unguarded. They waited until reinforcements arrived.[28]

Finally, reinforcements came, accompanied by a surgeon, who confirmed that "Ellsworth was no more." House, the reporter, remembered the dead colonel's orders to cut the wires at the telegraph office and led a squad of Zouaves there. Upon returning to the hotel, House witnessed what he called "a terrible scene." He saw a "woman run from a lower room to the stairway where the body" of Jackson lay. Recognizing it, the woman "cried aloud with an agony so heart-rending that no person could witness it without emotion. She flung her arms in the air, struck her brow madly, and seemed in every way utterly abandoned to desolation and frenzy." Despite the presence of strangers, she yielded "to her own frantic despair" and was "wild almost to insanity." It was her husband who lay in a pool of blood on the floor with a bullet hole in his face. Amazingly, Susan Jackson did not reproach the intruders for what they had done, but "seemed sensible," according to House, "to assurance that the safety of her children, for whom she expressed fears, could not possibly be endangered."[29]

Winser gave the New York *Times* firsthand information, and the paper presented detailed accounts of events after Ellsworth's death. "As the morning advanced, the townspeople began to gather" near the Marshall House. A Zouave guard was posted to prevent anyone from entering or leaving the hotel. Guests could not leave, and even Jackson's sister was not allowed to enter. The Union soldiers in charge did not want news of what had happened in the hotel on that Friday morning to reach the rest of the Zouave regiment or the townspeople for fear of what either might do. Nevertheless, rumors were swirling outside the house. Jackson's sister was heard to remark as she walked away, "Of course they wouldn't shoot a man dead in his own house about a bit of bunting."

Soon after the surgeon made arrangements to move Ellsworth's body, it was covered. The body was wrapped in one of the Zouaves' scarlet blankets, placed on an unhinged door to be used as a makeshift litter, and carried to a steamer, the *James Guy,* in the harbor. In Ellsworth's pocket remained a picture of the young woman he planned to marry, Carrie Spafford, and the two letters written hours earlier, one to Carrie and the other to his parents, which told them he would likely be killed.

In the meantime, across the river at the Naval Yard, men anxiously waited to be called as reinforcements. Word came before breakfast that Alexandria had been taken without a fight. With the good news came relief and rejoicing. Then, an hour later, the same people watched the *James Guy* approach with a flag flying at half-mast. Aboard was Ellsworth's body. Joy shifted to grief and anger. Union troops on both sides of the Potomac talked of revenge. That night, the Zouaves were kept aboard ship to prevent them from torching Alexandria.

The body of the little colonel was taken to a dark-brown engine house, where six flags covered the windows. Inside, the corpse lay on two doors in the middle of the building, the face blackened by death, described by the New York *Times* reporter as having "[hair] a distracted mess, but the remains still dressed, except for the coat which lay near by with a hole through the chest above the medal" worn above the heart. One sock was worn inside out, as Ellsworth had put it on in a hurry before his trip to Alexandria. Two surgeons performed an autopsy before turning over the body to the undertaker. They found that the contents of the shotgun had entered in the left chest, causing a lacerated wound about an inch and three-quarters in diameter, fracturing the third rib, passing through the lung, and lacerating part of the aorta.[30]

FIRST HERO AND FIRST VILLAIN

As the news of Ellsworth's death spread, church bells tolled and flags were lowered. All the firehouses of the city were draped in mourning. After the embalmment, Ellsworth's body temporarily lay in state in the engine house where the remains were first taken. The body was encased in a metallic coffin with silver mountings and a lid with a glass cover so the face and chest could be viewed. Zouaves hobbled forward from their sickbeds to pay their respects to their former commander. Later that afternoon, the grief-stricken president and his wife stared at the still remains. While there, Lincoln uttered in a broken voice, "My boy! My boy! Was it necessary this sacrifice should be made."[31]

According to witnesses Jackson's body, at 2:00 P.M. of May 24, "was still laying where he had been killed." Later it was removed to a nearby room, where it was prepared for burial and dressed in an artillery officer's uniform. A private funeral was held, attended only by the family, but friends and townspeople still came to pay their respects. One elderly man cut off locks of Jackson's hair, wrapped them up, and muttered, "Let this be remembered as coming from the head of the first man who shed his blood in the cause of Southern independence."[32] Another townsman, Richard L. Carnes, after viewing Jackson in his coffin, observed a pool of blood still on the landing. Carnes dipped his handkerchief in it to preserve as "a relic of the first blood shed in defense of the Confederate Flag."[33] The town coroner's inquest agreed that Jackson's impetuous act was justified. It ruled Jackson had been "killed by an armed force of Federal troops while in defense of his hotel and private rights."[34]

Treatment of the Jackson family by Federal troops was called sympathetic by the Northern press. Friends of Jackson described the behavior of the Zouave as shockingly barbaric. Acts might well have been embellished by rumors, as stories were told of the corpse's being "pinned to the floor by a bayonet," prevented from being removed "for five hours," and robbed of "keys and money." The widow and children were forced to stay in a room where they could hear taunting threats about cutting the body "into bits," insensitive shouts "to stop their howling" when they cried, and orders to leave the premises—

until town officials intervened. Jackson's family was also told to leave "the house before five o'clock that afternoon or have the corpse" cast "into the street." On leaving Alexandria the next morning, the hack and hearse were frequently stopped, and threats were heaped upon the grieving wife, three children, and a sister.

Witnesses claimed that Jackson's body was first carried to Fairfax Court House, and from there, to his mother's home on the Georgetown and Leesburg Turnpike, where it was interred. When the corpse approached Fairfax Court House, the courthouse bell tolled, and citizens and soldiers set out, according to Jackson's biographer, "to receive the cortege, and meeting it about a mile from the village, lined the road on both sides, and with uncovered heads, suffered it to pass through their lines, then followed on in solemn procession." When Jackson's body arrived at this mother's McLean home, it was met by a large crowd. There, the biographer wrote, "the grief of his eldest daughter...broke forth in most pitiable vehemence. She raised the head from the coffin, which was opened at her request, and embracing it and uttering the pathetic entreaties, and only with difficulty removed. The service was performed by...an old church-elder of the neighborhood." The biographer continued: "When he had finished, he raised his hands, gazing into the grave" and earnestly exclaiming, "Would to God it were my son!"[35]

The South embraced the recalcitrant and impetuous Jackson as her first martyred hero of the war. Throughout the South, newspapers reported, Jackson's death became a symbol of what the war was about: the defense of home and country against a tyrannical foe "whose feet pollute" their land in a "war of subjugation." Jackson was nominated to head a list of Virginia martyrs. He was eulogized in poetry that helped lift him to the status of a hero and martyr. A South Carolinian praised Jackson in a verse entitled, "Stand by Your Flag," and a Georgian's poet penned "Jackson, Our First Martyr." Subscriptions were raised throughout the South for the relief of the wife and three daughters of the dead innkeeper. Boys and girls from a private school in Charleston South Carolina, gave $6.25 to the Jackson Fund. Merchants of the city subscribed $100 toward the support of the family of their "heroic Jackson." The money was "invested in Confederate State bonds for the benefit of the family." In Memphis, Tennessee, $948 was subscribed for their support.[36]

Back at the spot where Jackson was killed, Federal soldiers occupied the Marshall House, including the office, which was now used by the provost marshal. The house immediately became a tourist attraction for Northern soldiers, newspaper reporters, and souvenir hunters who wanted mementos of the place where Ellsworth had died. Objects with Ellsworth's blood on them were the first to go, including the oilcloth in the hall and on the stairs. It was cut up into pieces, some with blood as "thick as a knife blade," according to witnesses. Several papers ran stories about the fall of the Marshall House, telling how eager scavengers clipped off the railing and cut up the floor where Ellsworth fell. "That being demolished—entirely cut away— they attacked indiscriminately the whole house and furniture, took pieces of the flagpole and cut into the studding behind the plastered walls." Some of the town citizens attempted to save the furniture by "packing it all in one room, but Union soldiers would not protect it," so by June 7, two weeks after Ellsworth's and Jackson's deaths, the "house, furniture, and all were in common ruin."[37]

As the South mourned for Jackson, the North grieved over the loss of Ellsworth. Flags were lowered throughout the North and as far south as Louisville and Jeffersonville, Kentucky, in respect for the "Boy Colonel." Extensive and descriptive newspaper coverage had spread the details of the Zouave leader's death throughout the North. The New York *Tribune* devoted virtually the entire front page of its Sunday, May 26, 1861, issue to the subject, including a large picture of the slain Ellsworth. In this and other editions of the *Tribune,* as well as in other papers, there were detailed accounts of the "Martyr of Alexandria's…Assassination and Murder," along with the denunciation and description of his killer as a vicious and depraved creature.[38] Citizens of Mechanicville, New York, Ellsworth's native town, were especially hurt and outraged by the news of the colonel's demise. Residents there became greatly agitated when a Dutch peddler named Wallam, who was a Southern sympathizer, said he felt the shooting of Ellsworth was justified. Wallam was given twenty minutes by the residents to get out of town. He left with "the band playing the 'Rogue's March'" and was ordered, as reported in the New York *Tribune,* never to return.[39]

Others vented their anger at the town of Alexandria and wanted retribution. The New York *Tribune* wanted "a heavy fine of $2,000 to $3,000 imposed on the town." "If it failed to pay, that portion of the city where the foul crime occurred should be leveled to the ground."

Furthermore, the *Tribune* contended, "Let barbarians be taught that we are in earnest: that since they have invoked war they shall have war—rigorous, unrelenting, but honorable war, that shuns alike the secret poison and the assassins arm, and will punish unsparingly the use of either." The Chicago *Democrat*'s account of Ellsworth's death was written in a manner the Richmond *Enquirer* called an "indignant howl." The Chicago paper maintained it was the second time Virginia had snuffed out the life of a brave man who "dare fight for freedom." First they hung Brown, and then they shot Ellsworth. The newspaper proclaimed: "How much longer is this damnable system of human oppression to be allowed existence? Why not now sweep it away, at once and forever, before it murders anymore brave and good men? Away with it!"[40]

The day after Ellsworth's death, citizens from Illinois met at the Willard Hotel in Washington and formed a committee to raise funds to remove Ellsworth's "aged parents" from "want."[41] Subscriptions for the Ellsworth Fund were collected in other Northern cities and towns. The men at the Willard Hotel also voted that "a banner should be presented" to Ellsworth's Zouave regiment, "by the citizens of Illinois, in which should be interwoven some of Col. Ellsworth's hair, with an appropriate motto." One newspaper reported that "pieces of the planking of the stairway" of the Marshall House sold in Chicago for "one dollar per square inch."[42]

The same day Jackson's body was laid to rest, May 25, there began a series of more elaborate ceremonies that accompanied the journey of Ellsworth's remains from the capital city to its final resting place upon the hill high above his boyhood town, Mechanicville, New York. Government, Army, and Navy leaders assembled in the White House for a morning service. Among the dignitaries who filed pass the bier was the elderly, distinguished General Winfield Scott. He paused reflectively at the casket. Young Julia Taft placed a wreath of white roses on Ellsworth's chest, but seeing the lifeless form made her sick and faint. Shortly after 11:00 A.M., President and Mrs. Lincoln entered the East Room and were seated near the foot of the coffin.

After the White House ceremonies, a large funeral procession escorted the body to the rail depot. A great throng crowded

Pennsylvania Avenue to watch as line after line of soldiers marched by, followed by Ellsworth's saddled but riderless horse, which led the way for four white horses pulling the hearse. Then came carriages carrying the president, members of his cabinet, and pallbearers. Upon arriving at the depot, the bells tolled as the body was placed on a special train for New York City. There it would lie in state at the Astor House and City Hall before going to Albany and Mechanicville. Ellsworth's parents, upon seeing their son's body for the first time, at the Astor House, kissed the pale and cold, still lips. They were overcome with grief and had to be led from the room.[43] All of New York wore a badge of mourning. Flags were at half-mast, and crepe draped the buildings, including the interior and exterior of the Astor House, where there was displayed over the entrance a large sable banner emblazoned with bearing the words "Ellsworth, May 24, 1861." Even statues of Washington in the city "wore the mantle of a pallbearer," according to New York papers, while at an engine house near Broadway, a banner was displayed that reflected the anger of the firemen. The banner was inscribed, "Ellsworth, 'His blood cries for vengeance.'"[44]

The lying in state, the viewing by thousands who filed pass the casket, the funerals, and the long processions of dignitaries in late May 1861 are, in retrospect, sad, eerie scenes that would be repeated four years later after Lincoln's assassination.[45] Ellsworth's death led to the North's first national mourning of the war; Lincoln's would be her last.

A conspicuous figure in all the Ellsworth viewing, funerals, and processions was Francis Brownell. Now the secondary hero of the tragedy, he was given the title of Ellsworth's Avenger. At all the occasions of mourning, Brownell dressed in his Zouave uniform and carried the musket and bayonet that had taken Jackson's life as well as the Confederate flag that had cost Ellsworth his. Earlier, parts of the bloodstained emblem had been cut away by relic-seeking Zouaves.[46] Absent from all the ceremonies for Ellsworth was his eighteen-year-old fiancée, Carrie Spafford. She was prevented from traveling because of an injury to her ankle, as well as prostration from grief.[47]

The images of Ellsworth and Jackson were reversed in the North and South. Each adoringly embraced one and bitterly denounced the other. Both sides acted in a similar way toward their slain heroes. Both established funds for surviving members of the deceased families. Poems were written about their bravery and sacrifice while condemning their counterparts. Some lamented Ellsworth's death as robbing the Union of a military genius who would have risen to be the top military commander. Babies were named after him; enlistment increased; and Zouave regiments were formed, including the Forty-fifth New York, whose members called themselves Ellsworth's Avengers. Special memorial envelopes circulated through the mail, with Ellsworth's picture on the left-hand side and a caption under it that frequently read, "Remember Ellsworth." Many Northern streets and towns and a fort in Alexandria were named in his honor.[48]

Temporarily, the stories and accounts of the deaths of Ellsworth and Jackson tended to overshadow Union military achievements. Federal troops for the first time had penetrated the boundary of a seceded state and occupied their first Confederate city while increasing the security of their own capital city. This had been achieved without confronting Confederate resistance.[49] The three fatalities of this invasion were all involved in incidental events that were not vital to obtaining the primary military objectives. All three deaths resulted from incidents involving a flag: the taking, defending, and raising of colors. Ellsworth and Jackson died over the Confederate banner, while a Union sailor from the *Pawnee* lost his life while attempting to fix a halyard on the Alexandria city-hall flagpole. The hapless seaman had climbed the pole to make repairs so the U.S. flag could be raised over the Federally occupied town, when he lost his balance and fell, sustaining fatal injuries.[50]

During the emotional climate of the start of the war, any rashness, folly, or military insignificance associated with the last acts of Ellsworth and Jackson did not matter. Although not the first to die in the war, they became symbols of the first shedding blood. News of their fates rocketed throughout the North and South, and they were seen as exemplars of boldness and bravery in war. Personal and family tragedy was transcended by the nobler and higher meaning of dying for one's country. They became a rallying point, the martyred first sacrifices of war. Their fate was a prelude of things to come—events that would eclipse their stories and dim the memory of their fate.

[1] E. B. Long, *The Civil War Day by Day,* 719.

[2] Leech, *Reveille* in Washington, 73-74; Randall, *Colonel Elmer Ellsworth,* 237-39.

[3] Leech, *Reveille in Washington,* 66-73.

[4] Carl Sandburg, *Abraham Lincoln: The War Years* (New York: Harcourt, Brace & Company, 1937), vol I, 37.

[5] W. Bums Jones Jr., "The Marshall House Incident," *Northern Virginia Heritage* (February, 1988), 4.

[6] Ellsworth had his girlfriend Carrie's letters sent in care of J. G. Nicolay at the executive mansion. Ellsworth was afraid her letters might be lost in the "avalanche of mail" sent to the Zouave regiment.

[7] Randall, *Colonel Elmer Ellsworth,* 10-15, 27, 130-41, 147-51, 205, 221-25, 241-45; Sandburg, *Abraham Lincoln: The War Years,* vol. I, 36-37.

[8] Randall, *Colonel Elmer Ellsworth,* 225, 245; William M. Glasgow Jr., *Northern Virginia's Own: The 17th Virginia Regiment, Confederate States Army* (Alexandria, Va.: Gobill, 1989), 42-43.

[9] Glasgow, *Northern Virginia's Own,* 1; C. B. Rose Jr., *Arlington County, Virginia* (Arlington, Va.: Arlington Historical Society, 1976), 7; William F. Smith and T. Michael Miller, *A Seaport Saga: Portrait of Old Alexandria, Virginia* (Norfolk, Va.: Donning, 1989), 7-9, 13-14, 51. From 1801 to 1847 Alexandria and Arlington were part of the District of Columbia. Virginia ceded them to the federal government, who, after forty-six years, retroceded them back to the Old Dominion.

[10] Alexandria *Gazette,* April 19, 1861.

[11] Chicago *Tribune,* May 30, 1861.

[12] Alexandria *Gazette,* June 18, 1858; Smith and Miller, *A Seaport Saga,* 90-91, 120.

[13] Smith and Miller, *A Seaport Saga,* 19, 36, 38-39, 41-49, 83-87. The Marshall House was first known as the Washington Tavern. Later the name was changed to Franklin House, and upon the death of John Marshall in 1835, to the Marshall House.

[14] *Life of James W. Jackson: The Alexandria Hero, the Slayer of Ellsworth, the First Martyr in the Cause of Southern Independence* (Richmond, Va.: West & Johnson 1862), 11-23.

[15] Hinton Rowan Helper, *The Impending Crisis of the South: How to Meet It* (New York: Burdick Brothers, 1857), 25, 34, 404-13.

[16] *Life of James W. Jackson,* 22-25.

[17] Fairfax *Herald,* April 28, 1905. The forty-foot pole was called the democratic pole. It had earlier been used at election time to endorse a political candidate. Taylor later claimed the Alexandria flag was the first to have thirteen stars for the seceded states. In reality, eleven states seceded, including Arkansas, North Carolina, and Tennessee. These three seceded during the month of May, weeks after the Confederate flag was raised in Alexandria. In *Life of James W. Jackson,* published in 1862, the author writes that Jackson took down the flag each time an additional state seceded and added a star to it. The actual work on the Alexandria flag was done by Mrs. Libby Ann Padgett and her sister, Miss S. M. Graham. Mrs. Padgett also made a Confederate flag during the spring of 1861 for Fairfax Court House.

[18] The New York *Times* on May 20, 1861 ran a headline "Laughable Stampede of the Alexandrians." The paper went on to report that with the arrival of the *Pawnee* hundreds of families fled the city.

[19] Glasgow, *Northern Virginia's Own*, 26-38, 42; Alexander Hunter, *Johnny Reb and Billy Yank* (New York: Neale, 1905), 16-35; George Wise, *History of the Seventeenth Virginia Infantry* (Baltimore, Md.: Kelly, Piet & Co., 1870), 7-15.

[20] *Life of James W. Jackson*, 29-30; Smith and Miller, *A Seaport Saga*, 83

[21] Glasgow, *Northern Virginia's Own*, 44; *Life of James W. Jackson*, 43.

[22] Randall, *Colonel Elmer Ellsworth*, 247, 252-54.

[23] New York *Tribune*, May 26, 1861; Randall, *Colonel Elmer Ellsworth*, 255. The three steamboats *James Guy, Baltimore*, and *Mount Vernon* were commanded by Captain Dahlgen, who was in charge of the Navy Yard.

[24] *OR*, ser. 1, vol. 2, 37-41; Glasgow, *Northern Virginia's Own*, 40-41; Baltimore *Republican*, May 25, 1861; New York *Tribune*, June 1, 1861. As Ball's cavalry was being captured, the rest of the Virginians hastily marched up Duke Street and half a mile west of the depot, where Colonel Terrett had ordered the train to wait. The Virginians boarded cars to Manassas Junction. Federal infantry regiments that crossed Long Bridge were the Seventh and Twenty-fifth New York, Third New Jersey, and First Michigan, plus a cavalry company and an artillery battery. The Fifth, Fourteenth, Twenty-eighth, and Sixty-ninth New York infantry regiments, along with a company of cavalry and battery of artillery, crossed over the aqueduct.

[25] The motives given for Ellsworth's entering the Marshall House vary. Some say it was a spontaneous act; others, a resolve set before the occupation of Alexandria. Others say the colonel had been heading to the telegraph office, but upon seeing the flag, he went to seize it. An officer insisted that Ellsworth went to the roof to get a view of the town, then, as an afterthought, cut down the flag. Stories later circulated in Alexandria that Ellsworth had promised Mrs. Lincoln he would remove the flag. Before going to the Marshall House, James Jackson was awakened by the soldiers marching in the street or the noise Ellsworth and his companions made ascending to the roof. Once in the attic they climbed a ladder to the roof. The Marshall House must have been full: two boarders sleeping in the attic were startled by Union soldiers climbing to and from the roof.

[26] W. Bums Jones, Jr., "The Marshall House Incident," *Northern Virginia Heritage*, (February 1988); New York *Tribune*, May 26, 1861.

[27] New York *Times*, May 27, 1861.

[28] New York *Tribune*, May 26, 1861. Before entering the Marshall House, Ellsworth sent a sergeant for reinforcements. They took the wrong street to the Marshall House, delaying their arrival.

[29] Ibid. Jackson had fallen, clutching his shotgun, which was soon removed. House maintained the two dead men had contrasting expressions. Ellsworth'—excepting the pallor due to the loss of blood—was "beautifully natural." Jackson, on the other hand, "wore the most revolting expression of rage and hatred" that House had ever seen. Other details seem to have become garbled by confusion, time, and rumor. They vary as follows: Jackson was awakened by marching troops and was present as Ellsworth entered the inn. When Ellsworth asked him who put the flag on the

roof, Jackson is supposed to have replied that he did not know since he was only a border. Others claim Jackson was awakened by the noise of Ellsworth and others ascending to the roof and did not see Ellsworth and his party (the number varies from one to a company) until he shot the colonel. Accounts of the shooting scene vary. Some claim (perhaps accurately) that no statements were made by the mortally shot Ellsworth and Jackson. Other claim they witnessed these situations: (1) Ellsworth, as soon as he was shot, exclaimed "My God;" (2) Padgett, the maker of the controversial flag, went to the second floor of the hotel. There he saw Jackson, in his nightshirt, coming out of his second-story bedroom, asking "What is all the noise about?" Padgett was said to have told him, "They are taking down your flag." Jackson was said to have gotten his gun immediately, then waited on the second-floor landing. (Sketches of the scene show Jackson fully dressed.) (3) Another scenario has Ellsworth coming down the steps saying, "I have a trophy." Then Jackson stepped forward saying, "And you are mine." Other varied details have Jackson taking the flag from Ellsworth before being shot and bayoneted. Some say Jackson was repeatedly bayoneted and stabbed by several men who had difficulty removing a Bowie knife with saw-tooth ridges. Allegedly it was this knife that one of Jackson's children saw; she ran to her mother exclaiming that her daddy was on the floor "with broomsticks sticking out all over him."

[30] New York *Times*, May 27, 1861. "A *post mortem* examination was made by the Assistant-Surgeon of the Seventy-first Regiment and the Assistant-Surgeon of the Navy Yard." They found "the contents of the gun entered the chest, a little to the left of the breast bone, between the second and fourth ribs…fracturing the third rib, passing through the left lung, lacerating the arch of the aorta and its branches; the heart and pericardum were not wounded. The slugs lodged in the spine, fracturing the third and fourth vertebra and the third rib."

[31] Boston *Post*, May 25, 1861; Chicago *Tribune*, May 30, 1861; New York Times, May 27 & 28, 1861; New York *Tribune* May 25 & 26, 1861; Randall, *Colonel Elmer Ellsworth*, 260-63. Mrs. Lincoln carried a large floral bouquet to the engine house earlier in the day but was unable to see the body because of the autopsy and embalmment. Lincoln had the body moved to the East Room of the White House for services. He wrote a letter of condolence to the parents and provided financial security for them by appointing the father to a government job.

[32] Boston *Post*, May 25, 1861.

[33] *Life of James W. Jackson*, 38-39.

[34] The bloodstained handkerchief was given to the Front Royal Confederate Museum and displayed.

[35] New York *Tribune*, May 26, 1861; Jones, "The Marshall House Incident," 7.

[36] *Life of James W. Jackson*, 38-39, 44-45. The Jackson house in McLean still exists. Jackson had three daughters, Amelia, Alice, and Caroline. The eldest was about twelve at the time of her father's death. Jackson's remains were moved to the Fairfax city cemetery sometime after 1899.

[37] Baltimore *Republican*, May 27, 1861; Boston *Daily Journal*, June 14, 1861; Jones, "The Marshall House Incident," 7; *Life of James W. Jackson*, 39-41, 45-46. Pittsburgh *Evening Chronicle*, June 19, 1861. Jackson had outstanding bills. He had

purchased $7,000 worth of furniture for the Marshall House, according to his anonymous biographer.

[38] Jones, "The Marshall House Incident," 7; *Life of James W. Jackson*, 39. Nathaniel Hawthorne visited the Marshall House in 1862 and wrote, "The memorial hunters have completely cut away the original woodwork…thus it becomes something like a metaphysical question whether the place of murder [of Ellsworth] actually exists." By early 1862 photographs of the Marshall House, Ellsworth, and Brownell were being sold. The hotel burned in February 24, 1873. A small plaque on the corner of a Holiday Inn near busy King and Pitt Streets is all that exists to remind people of what happened on this site in late May 1861.

[39] The Washington *Evening Star*, May 24, 1861; New York *Tribune*, May 25-27, 1861.

[40] Baltimore *Republican*, May 27, 1861

[41] Richmond *Enquirer*, June 4, 1861.

[42] Subscriptions were to be limited to not more than $1.

[43] Pittsburgh *Evening Chronicle*, June 19, 1861; Chicago *Tribune*, May 29 & 30, 1861

[44] Randall, *Colonel Elmer Ellsworth*, 266-74. The Ellsworth's other child, a son, died a year earlier.

[45] New York *Times*, May 27, 1861.

[46] Both Ellsworth's and Lincoln's bodies would lie in state in the East Room of the White House and would be taken by special trains to their burial sites after lying in state at New York City Hall. The number of Lincoln's funerals and viewings was far greater. It took three days to take Ellsworth's body to its grave, whereas it took two weeks to take the president's body to its place of interment.

[47] Washington *Evening Star*, May 25, 1861.

[48] Randall, *Colonel Elmer Ellsworth*, 266. Carrie would later marry Frederic E. Brett and have one son. Both her husband and son died before the son reached adulthood.

[49] Baltimore *Republican*, May 27, 1861; Randall, *Colonel Elmer Ellsworth*, 272. Ellsworth's last letter to his parents was printed in many newspapers and read aloud during at least one funeral.

[50] Glasgow, *Northern Virginia's Own*, 44-45. Union forces captured fewer than fifty of Ball's Cavalry in Alexandria. The Confederate cavalrymen had assembled on Duke Street, in front of the slave pen, where slaves were held and sold, when Union soldiers overwhelmed them. There was no exchange of fire. The Union had also taken a prisoner when they moved into Virginia from Chain Bridge.

CHAPTER II

THE VICTORY THAT GOT AWAY: THE FAILURE OF THE UNION'S TURNING MOVEMENT AT BULL RUN

While stories of Ellsworth and Jackson dominated the news, Union regiments were digging in and starting fortifications from south of Georgetown to Alexandria. "A long train of wagons, with wheelbarrows and shovels" had followed Federal troops to the Virginia shore, reported the New York *Herald*. Federals had crossed the Potomac with only two days' rations, but their objective was to stay much longer. Their immediate goal was to dig in and keep "the country within a radius of twenty-five miles of Alexandria...clear of rebels."

In the meantime, most Alexandria residents chafed under Union control and martial laws. As reflected in the writing of one of the residents, in the townspeople's eyes, Federals brought the "worst kind of despotism," under abusive foul mouths and frequently drunk and insensitive "low lifes." A great number of the residents deserted the town, while those who remained wore "an air of sullen gloom." Among the abuses heaped upon them by rowdy Zouaves was the "plundering of their gardens." The Zouaves caught a man with a Confederate flag three miles from Alexandria. They made him carry it on a pole to the Marshall House, where they trampled upon it.[1]

A reporter for the New York *Tribune* agreed that the Union soldiers' conduct was "not always generous and honorable." While intoxicated, they behaved in a way that justified Alexandrians' fear that there was "no hope of safety at the hands of the invaders." The most detested Union regiment was Ellsworth's "Pet Lambs."

According to the *Tribune,* one soldier was arrested and "charged with having ravished an Alexandria woman." Another was shot and killed by his own guard when he repeatedly refused to give the password. Zouaves were soon sent just west of Alexandria to fortify Shuter's Hill. There, they built Fort Ellsworth, the first of sixty-eight forts and batteries that would be constructed around Washington, D.C.

This was just the beginning of the influx of Federal soldiers into Alexandria. The port town would become a major Federal supply base and hospital site. As a result, even more locals would leave their hometown.

PRELUDE: THE TWO MONTHS PRIOR TO BULL RUN

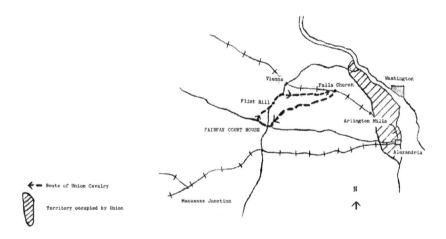

ROUTE OF UNION CAVALRY AND THE SKIRMISH AT
FAIRFAX COURT HOUSE

Union occupation of Alexandria and the nearby areas was a meager start, despite the fanfare. No battles had been fought and the penetration was just beginning. Extensive planning to further Union advances was taking place in the offices of the Union War Department in Washington. A detailed description of activity was presented in the Chicago *Tribune.* The enfeebled general-in-chief,

Winfield Scott, and his staff dressed in army and navy uniforms, worked from early morning to late at night to find solutions for "crushing the rebellion." While they worked, politicians scurried about in civilian clothing. Suffering from painful attacks of gout, Scott was often forced to place his massive frame on a "lounge drawn into the center of the large apartment, his feet resting upon pillows." by his side lay a "large light reed," which he used to point nearby to the "two large" and detailed suspended maps of Virginia and Maryland. Circles were drawn around the areas of Harpers Ferry, Richmond, and Norfolk, within which had been added numerous "minute symbols and signs" that were understood only by the military.[2] The three large circles indicated the areas targeted during the last of May for Union penetration. Virginia was vulnerable from the northwest, as well from as the north and east. Federals planned to penetrate the state from all three directions (and were also planning an invasion from the south). They hoped to menace vital rail lines, rail centers, and the city of Richmond.

The month of June would see numerous skirmishes and minor battles as Union forces moved into northwestern Virginia toward Martinsburg and probed into northern Virginia and up the peninsula from Fort Monroe. All encounters, regardless how minor, received major attention because of the newness of the war.[3] Minor clashes occurred in northern Virginia on the first day of June at Arlington Mills and Fairfax Court House and were soon forgotten. The skirmish at Fairfax Court House was a brief encounter in the middle of the night—a Federal cavalry raid that consisted of soldiers' running back and forth into the hamlet as startled and half-asleep Virginians, under Colonel Ewell, fired in the dark at the intruders.

Fairfax Court House, the county seat of Fairfax County, was officially known as Providence until 1850. This small hamlet on a modest hill was where the late James Jackson had run a hotel before moving to Alexandria. By the end of May 1861, the town had 300 or so inhabitants. It lay about midway between adversaries—the Union forces moving into northern Virginia and the main body of Confederates at Manassas, who anxiously sent patrols eastward to detect Federal movement. On the last day in May in 1861, slightly more than 200 men, consisting of two virtually unarmed Virginia cavalry companies and an infantry company, occupied the town as a Confederate outpost. This force was commanded by a bald, middle-aged former American Indian fighter, Lieutenant-Colonel Richard Stoddert Ewell. He had been born a short distance from Fairfax Court House, in Georgetown, Washington, D.C., and would rise to prominence during the war. Lieutenant-Colonel Ewell had given up his commission as a captain in the U.S. Cavalry just weeks earlier.

The most important building in the small village of Fairfax Court House was the brick courthouse, located in the center of the town, where the crossing of two roads form the configuration of a + sign. The Little River Turnpike ran east to west, and the other road, north to south. The courthouse was on a lot of several acres, south of the turnpike, but west of the intersecting road that led to Fairfax Station three miles to the south. The courthouse lot was enclosed on the northern side by a high board fence. At the southern and western end of the lot was a road, which bent around the lot, connecting the north–south road and the turnpike. To the south of the secondary road was a clover field and a lane to the Stevenson farm.

Directly northward across the pike from the courthouse, about sixty feet away, was the hotel where Colonel Ewell was staying on the night of May 31. The horses of the Prince William cavalry were in the stables behind the hotel. The sixty or so men of this company were spending the night in the Episcopal church just west of the hotel, while a like number of cavalrymen from Rappahannock were in the courthouse, with their mounts in the accompanying lot. Ninety infantrymen known as the Warrenton Rifles had just arrived in town that day and had found shelter in the Methodist church south of the courthouse. Their captain, John Quincy Marr, was quartered nearby, in a small law office on the courthouse lot. Just across the street to the east, in Joshua Gunnel's brick house, there was a prominent guest, an ex-governor of the state and a resident of Warrenton, William "Extra Billy" Smith.[4] Smith had just resigned his seat in the United States Congress and had arrived at the courthouse village late that afternoon. Before settling in for the night, Smith visited Ewell, whom he had known for many years, and his neighbors from Warrenton, who formed the infantry company he affectionately called "my boys."

After darkness fell over the town, most of the young men stationed there, despite mostly being ill-prepared for combat, fell asleep in the courthouse and churches, feeling relatively safe. Only the road to the east of the town was deemed necessary to watch; two pickets were posted there while the rest slumbered. The green

soldiers' only immediate discomfort was the oppressive humidity; it
was a close and sticky night.

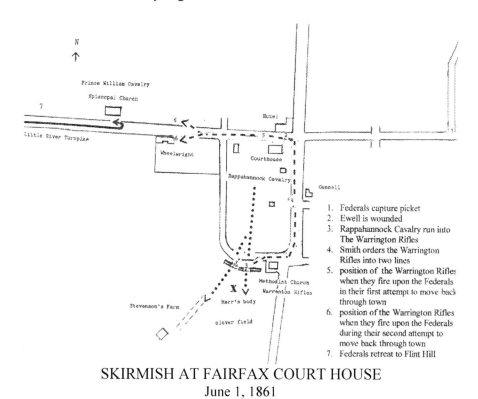

1. Federals capture picket
2. Ewell is wounded
3. Rappahannock Cavalry run into The Warrington Rifles
4. Smith orders the Warrington Rifles into two lines
5. position of the Warrington Rifles when they fire upon the Federals in their first attempt to move back through town
6. position of the Warrington Rifles when they fire upon the Federals during their second attempt to move back through town
7. Federals retreat to Flint Hill

SKIRMISH AT FAIRFAX COURT HOUSE
June 1, 1861

Suddenly, just before 3:00 A.M., the quiet of the sleeping
village was interrupted as one of the pickets, Private A. B. Francis of
the Warrenton Rifles, ran toward the center of the town and nervously
shouted, "The enemy is upon us." A Federal cavalry force of about
fifty men, under Lieutenant Charles H. Tompkins (Company B,
Second U.S. Cavalry), had been sent to reconnoiter the Fairfax Court
House area. Tompkins' force came upon the two pickets on the
turnpike a half-mile east of the courthouse.[5]

News of the arriving enemy had men confused and scurrying
about in all directions in the almost total darkness—clouds blocked all
view of the moon and stars. A few of the cavalrymen from the
Episcopal church attempted to form a line on the pike between the
hotel and the courthouse, while the other company attempted to
mount their horses in the courthouse lot.

37

Captain Marr, not knowing what to expect, hurriedly moved his ninety foot soldiers just west of the Methodist church in Stevenson's clover field. There, they formed in two lines, fifteen feet from the fence and road to their front. They waited, with muskets loaded, but without bayonets.[6]

Soon after the pickets' warning, the Federals rode west through the town, firing helter-skelter at both sides of the street and at lights being lit in the hotel. Seeing a shadowy figure emerge from the hotel, they fired at it, striking the man in the shoulder. The man, Colonel Ewell, disappeared in the darkness, but not before throwing his coat away so that if he were captured, the enemy would not know his rank.

The Prince William cavalrymen, forming in the street under the pressure of the oncoming enemy, fled westward, leaving four of their comrades in the hands of the Federals. Cavalrymen in the courthouse lot panicked and fled into Stevenson's clover field; some jumped the fence, while others ran through the gate. They emerged upon horseback upon the startled men of the Warrenton Rifles, who in the darkness believed the enemy had instantaneously leaped upon them. The riflemen fired into the horsemen, seriously wounding one of their own cavalrymen. During the confusion, half the riflemen were disorganized and separated from their company. All of the Rappahannock cavalry fled away into the darkness in a panic because of the sudden Federal attack and their vulnerability; the riders had few weapons and no ammunition.

While the Federals moved west of the village, a totally disorganized Southern force remained behind. The two cavalry companies had fled. No officer of the Warrenton Rifles could be found. Their two lieutenants were on leave, and their captain was missing. He lay dead in the clover, hidden by the darkness and the lush, waist-high grass, apparently killed by a wild shot fired by the Federals as they fled through the town.

**Sketch of Union cavalry raid and nighttime
skirmish on June 1, 1861 at Fairfax Court House.**
(Courtesy of the Library of Congress)

Startled townspeople were awakened from a deep sleep. A few of the men grabbed what weapons they could find and ran into the streets. Mrs. Gunnel, despite being bedridden after giving birth to a baby six days earlier, was curious, like other residents, about what was happening. She ordered a servant to shove her bed in front of the window in hopes that she might catch a glimpse of the action. Old Extra Billy Smith, who was sixty-four years old, fixed the tape on his Maynard rifle and went to find the Warrenton Riflemen. He found about half of them standing in the clover field and resting upon the fence.[7] Finding they had no officers, Smith, a civilian, asked the men to follow him. They agreed. Without any knowledge of tactics, the old politico started forming the men in two lines on the sidewalk along the road in front of the Methodist church and the courthouse lot.

While Smith was organizing the men, a verbal confrontation at the head of the line (northward) attracted his attention. A bareheaded bald man in his shirt sleeves, who was bleeding, imperatively said to a young man, "What, sir, do you dispute my authority?" The reply was, "I do, sir, until I know you have a right to exercise it." Interceding, Smith introduced Ewell to the Riflemen, who had only arrived the previous day and had not met their commander. Ewell had the more than forty men move between the hotel and courthouse to meet a

39

possible Federal return. When they arrived at that location, the Warrenton men were hemmed in by a high fence on both sides of the turnpike. Then the Union cavalrymen returned, but a feeble volley by the Southerners led to a Union retreat to the west of the town. Smith was left in charge as Ewell went to send a courier to bring reinforcements from the cavalry companies at Fairfax Station.

Extra Billy Smith wisely moved the riflemen to a safer place about a hundred yards forward, near the town wheelwright's lot. There, he placed his men behind the rail fences on both sides of the turnpike. Soon, the Union again reappeared, emerging from the darkness as they moved up the hill until they were about forty yards from the Episcopal church.[8] Both sides exchanged fire, but nearly three complete volleys by the Warrenton men caused the Blue horsemen to retreat again. Tompkins, the Union commander, had two horses shot out from under him during the exchange, with one falling on him and severely bruising his foot. A white horse, possibly Tompkins', lay dead with twelve bullet holes. Ewell reported that after the skirmish, the "enemy ran off ingloriously, pulling down fences and making their escape through the fields by Flint Hill" (two miles north of Fairfax Court House). During their retreat, some of the Federals rode double, with the wounded riding in front. Eyewitnesses claimed that some walked back, leading their mounts, and several of the wounded were carried back in a wagon. Their return was unimpressive. Tompkins' dragoons entered their Falls Church camp "looking as if they had been through a four week campaign." Witnesses reported: "Some had their clothes half torn off, and all were covered in dust."[9]

In all, the meager clash took less than half an hour from start to finish. The Federals, in the darkness, had foolishly rushed into a village held by an enemy of unknown size or condition, but in the process they unknowingly frightened off or disorganized three-fourths of their enemy's force. While unsuccessfully trying to return through town, Tompkins suffered his only losses: nine horses were killed, four were wounded, and three men were captured.[10] Several more men were wounded.

One Southerner, Captain Marr, was killed; two were wounded, including Ewell; and five were captured. Neither press accounts nor Union reports accurately depict what happened. The Richmond *Daily Examiner* found much to praise in its headlines: "Battle at Fairfax

Court. Glorious Repulse of the United States Dragoons—Sad Death of the Brave Captain Marr."

Tompkins incorrectly reported being fired upon first by "rebel troops from windows and housetops," "as Southern reinforcements" swelled their numbers "to upwards of 1,000 men." Union reports also tell of extensive enemy casualties, as many Rebel bodies lay on the ground.

Press accounts were as unreliable. The New York *Times* reported that the day before the skirmish there were "No Rebels at Fairfax." "They [rebels] have literally eaten up everything to be obtained at Fairfax Court-house, and were driven back in fear of starvation."[11] After the skirmish, the same paper tells of the Federals having entered Fairfax Court House "at a deliberate and slow pace." But after being fired upon from rebels in houses, they supposedly fought nobly and against seven times their numbers, "killing and wounding" forty of the rebels, while the Union force did not retreat until artillery "was brought to bear upon them."

Northern papers made Tompkins a hero. He received congratulatory letters. A man in his middle to late thirties with a brown beard and a gray sombrero, the lieutenant was gaining a romanticized reputation as an unparalleled scout. He was compared with Francis Marion of Revolutionary War fame. The New York *World* maintained, "new stories are told daily of his adventurous command, and so thoroughly are the rebels convinced of his prowess that a handbill is actually posted in Fairfax County, offering a reward of $1,500 for his head."[12] Readers of the this notice would have been well advised to listen to the Confederate cavalrymen who wrote in a letter sent from Fairfax Station to his father about the Fairfax skirmish, "I wish you not [be] alarmed by the many rumors put out."[13]

Despite the hurrahs from both sides, commanders on either side were not overjoyed with the skirmish. Confederate Brigadier-General M. L. Bonham was greatly concerned about the vulnerability and uselessness of the two cavalry companies because of their lack of weapons. He urged, "If nothing else can be had, [arm them]…with double-barreled shot guns, musketoons, or lances and pistols."

On the other side, even General Scott was displeased. Concerns about the Tompkins' impetuousness made the aged warrior conclude, "The skirmish has given considerable prestige to our regular cavalry in the eyes of our people and of the volunteer regiments, but the lieutenant acted without authority and went further than he knew he was desired or expected to go, and frustrated unintentionally, for the time, a more important movement. He has been so informed by me, verbally; and whilst in the future he will not be less gallant, he will be more circumspect." Tompkins' impulsiveness also led him to give his report of the skirmish to the New York *Tribune* prior to giving it to the appropriate military authorities. He and others were informed that it was a practice that General-in-Chief Scott did not want repeated.[14]

The morning after the skirmish, as cavalry from Fairfax Station unsuccessfully combed the area for the enemy, only thirty-nine of the ninety riflemen from Warrenton answered roll call. Early that morning, the body of their commander, Captain John Quincy Marr, was found—some say by his servant—in the tall clover several hundred yards south of the courthouse. Marr's body was reported to be lying face down, still holding his saber. Ewell immediately reported (as others would later write) that Marr had been shot through the heart. Years later, after the war, at the age of eighty-five, William Smith, who played a role in the skirmish, claimed to have examined Marr's wound and concluded that the captain had died from shock caused by "a spent round ball" that did not penetrate the body. Smith claimed, "The wound was immediately over the heart" and "had a perfect circular suffusion of blood under the skin, something larger than a silver dollar, but the skin was unbroken, and not a drop of blood was shed."[15]

Marr had been in his mid-thirties, a man of local prominence and popularity and promising military career.[16] He graduated from VMI in 1848 and was confirmed the same year as an Assistant Professor of Mathematics and Tactics at that institution. Several years later, when his father died, Marr returned to Warrenton to care for his family. There, he held numerous civic and county offices, including justice of the peace, sheriff, and mayor. After John Brown's Harpers Ferry raid, Marr formed the Warrenton Riflemen. In 1861, he was elected to the Virginia secession convention by the largest vote that had, up to that time, ever been received in Fauquier County. A family man, Marr had a wife and six children, and if local stories are true, this energetic man had a comely Cherokee mistress in Warrenton, Eliz Nickens, who also bore six of his children. He was said to have been so enamored with this beautiful woman, described as "naughty and autocratic," that it was common knowledge in Warrenton that to locate Mayor Marr when he was not in his office, you only needed to look for his carriage in front of his Indian mistress' house.[17]

Marr's death at Fairfax Court House made him a martyr for the Southern cause, although not of the same magnitude as James Jackson. Marr's death was felt intensely in northern Virginia, especially in Warrenton and the surrounding area. His body was taken on Saturday, June 1, to Warrenton, where it was greeted by a mourning populace and lowered flags. Between 6:00 and 7:00 that evening, the remains were met and escorted to Marr's mother's home by the Lee Guards and a large number of residents. The following day, more than 1,500 mourners—too many to be housed inside—stood in a green plot behind the clerk's offices. Less than two months earlier, many of the same people had stood in the same spot, at a ceremony in which Marr had accepted a flag made for the riflemen by the town's ladies. That day the captain had told the crowd he would "guard its honor" with his life. Now, on the first June Sunday of the war, as the crowd listened to a preacher's funeral tribute, aptly described in the Richmond *Times-Dispatch,* they realized they had not expected so sudden "a redemption…[of Marr's] patriotic pledge." After the funeral, they walked the short distance to the cemetery, on an undulating hill just west of town. There, at 5:00, Marr was buried in "full-dress uniform, with the honors of war."[18]

The significance of the skirmish at Fairfax Court House is not reflected in the immediate sensation it made in the press or the subsequent postwar claims of the uniqueness of the conflict. Claims varied in historical accuracy, from the "first real land fighting of the war" and "the first blood shed in the war" to "the death of the first Confederate officer." Instead, the significance of the encounter around a small country courthouse is that it is typical of what would become the war's most frequent form of combat: the skirmish. The smallest-scale form of combat, a skirmish was usually minor, both in numbers and in significance. The numerous skirmishes before and after a major battle were usually results of the probing of a location and strength of an adversary. Skirmishes at Arlington Mills and Fairfax Court House, as well as action near Vienna several weeks later, and other brief clashes in the region were among the antecedents of the forthcoming first battle at Bull Run, and would be among the thousands of similar conflicts during the war.

The clash at Fairfax Court House also revealed a lack of preparedness. Confused, inexperienced, and untrained soldiers and a lack of weapons would prove to be common characteristics of much of the combat during the first year of the war.[19] Northern and Southern participants and the press gave exaggerated estimates of a foe who outnumbered their own men, who almost always fought "valorously and with heroism," a claim that would prevail throughout the war.

Two and a half weeks after the skirmishes at Arlington Mills and Fairfax Court House, a slightly larger action occurred near Vienna.[20] The clash on June 17, 1861, resulted from contact between Confederates and 274 men of the First Ohio Volunteers, who had been sent by General Irvin McDowell to push further into Virginia. Six companies were sent by rail on the Alexandria, Loudoun, and Hampshire line. More than half were positioned to guard roads and railroad bridges between Alexandria and Vienna. The remainder were sent to Vienna, a town four miles north of Fairfax Court House. As they neared the town, they were met by Colonel Maxcy Gregg's First South Carolina Infantry (about 575 men), some cavalry, and two artillery pieces. The South Carolinians were making a reconnaissance from Fairfax Court House to the Potomac.[21]

On their way back to their camp near Fairfax Court House, at about 6:00 P.M., after having virtually completed their reconnaissance and only several miles from their camp, the Confederates heard a distant train whistle. Gregg later wrote that he marched his troops back near Vienna, "placing the two six-pounder guns on the hill, commanding the bend of the railroad," and formed the rest of his force around the guns.

The following details of what was called the action of Vienna were carried by a number of Northern papers, including the New York *Times,* the Boston *Journal,* the New York *Tribune,* and the Washington *Star.* A short distance from Vienna, an elderly Unionist ran down the railroad tracks, and before he jumped behind a clump of bushes, he motioned the Federals to turn back. His caveat failed. The Federal officers paid no attention to his story of "seven hundred rebels at Vienna" with a battery masked by bushes. The men were "having a nice time" riding in the open gondola, or platform, cars in a train that also included one passenger car and one baggage car and an engine that faced Alexandria as it backed the cars toward Vienna.[22] The only precaution was taken a mile from Vienna, when the train was slowed and an officer placed "as a lookout in the forward car." Then as the train began to "turn the curve at the deep cut, just over a quarter of a mile from the village," a rider spotted enemy cavalry on the hill ahead and said, "Boys, now we are going to have some fun!"

The Ohio men on the cars felt safe from the cavalry and were just getting their muskets ready to fire when suddenly enemy infantrymen appeared in front of them, along with artillery. "Two six-pounders opened fire," reported the Northern papers. The first shot went over their heads, but the second found its mark. Gregg later said he felt this fire would have been very destructive if the Union troops had not "made a most rapid movement from the cars into the woods." As it was, eight Federals would die and four would be wounded.

According to newspaper accounts, when the firing commenced, "the train was almost instantly stopped." The brakeman had immediately screwed the "brakes down hard" to bring the train to a halt.[23] Brigadier General Robert C. Schenck ordered Lieutenant William H. Raynor to have the "train drawn out of range." Raynor ran to inform the engineer, but he was followed by the general, who repeated his order to a railroad man who was "much excited and in evident fear." The engineer stammered out that the brakes were locked and the train was stuck.

The lieutenant frantically unloosened the brakes on the platform and the adjoined car while giving orders for the same to be done to the rest of the cars. He went back to inform the engineer that he could move, but the brakeman had uncoupled most of the cars from the engine. Schenck then ordered the engineer to move a short distance eastward, out of harm's way, and wait for the Ohioans to join him. The engineer immediately sped off "as if the devil was after him," and did not stop until arriving at Alexandria, recounted the newspapers. Schenck and his men had had no way to escape, send for reinforcements, or carry their wounded back to camp, "except laboriously and painfully in blankets." The case of surgical instruments had also been carried off, and "nothing could be done for the poor sufferers until the next morning."[24]

When fired upon, the Federals jumped to the ground. Most took immediate shelter behind the cars, where some fired in the direction of the enemy fire. There was great confusion, as some officers screamed, "lie down," while others cried, "fall in" or "retreat." Some men abandoned the shelter of the cars and ran up the bank to the protection of the woods.[25] The abandoned men "behaved admirably." A man named Mercer, "who during the attack leaned on his gun and against a tree, was scolded by his lieutenant for not falling promptly into line," responded simply by saying, "I wish I could— look at my arm." His arm was said to have been "dangling shattered at his side," but he did not complain. Mercer died the next morning from the loss of blood. A cannonball that killed another soldier had struck Mercer's musket, "bending it double and taking off his arm."

Gregg sent a troop of cavalry in pursuit, wrote the Northern papers. But the terrain and late hour of the day prevented the Federals from being overtaken. Instead, the cavalry troopers found six Union soldiers dead and another desperately wounded. "Blood was also found in the bushes" through which the Federals had fled. "One passenger car and five platform cars were taken and burned." When the news of the attack reached the Federals at "Arlington House," according to one report, "four large wagons were immediately dispatched to bring off the killed and wounded." Apparently, the wagons did not arrive on the combat site; the day after the fighting, a Vienna Unionist loaded the bodies of six Ohio soldiers into his two-horse wagon, covering the remains with bed sheets from his home, and carried the dead, despite threats and verbal abuse from other local residents, to the Union camp. This concluded the action near Vienna, which has been cited as the first time the railroad was used in warfare.

The bodies of the Union soldiers killed at Vienna were placed side by side in the camp of the First Ohio, covered with U.S. flags, and made "ready for burial." A newspaper correspondent walked toward the remains, and the attending officer "raised the folds of the flag from one." The body of a young man, no more than twenty years old, was revealed; his arm was torn off at the shoulder. It was young Mercer.[26]

The first accounts of what some referred to as a blunder tended to be greatly exaggerated. Rumors had Federals defeated in a field battle with "immense" losses and retreating back to Alexandria. The excited city responded; people who were characterized as "ugly secessionists" gathered in the streets, hoping for liberation from Union rule, and eager to revolt. When the dust settled, Union critics praised the officers' and men's bravery, but argued that the officers in command had made blunders comparable to those at Big Bethel on the peninsula, one of the early battles of the war. At Vienna, they had made a double-blunder by not sending skirmishers ahead of the cars and by not heeding the warning given by a Vienna Unionist.[27]

Federal penetration into northern Virginia prompted Confederate authorities to put more-experienced men in charge of vulnerable areas. Brigadier-General Joe Johnston had been sent to Harpers Ferry, and soon thereafter, Brigadier-General Pierre G. T. Beauregard succeeded M. L. Bonham as the commander of the Confederate forces in northern Virginia.[28] Beauregard arrived on the plains of Manassas with little fanfare, in marked contrast to his rail trip to Manassas, during which he had been accompanied by an almost-continuous ovation by crowds who had gathered at depots to see the "hero of Sumter." They saw a man of modest size, dark complexion, and striking eyes. Despite claims that he looked like the "reincarnation of one of Napoleon's Marshals," Beauregard neither wore a flashy uniform nor rode a showy steed. Once at Manassas, he quietly set about inspecting his troops.

Most found Beauregard congenial, but he was alarmed by the small size of his force—about 6,000 "effectives." As Johnston and others did when they assumed command, Beauregard asked for more men. The Federals seemed to be coming from many directions. By mid-June, Johnston had abandoned Harpers Ferry, fearing his small force would be cut off by the Union from the west and north.[29]

Beauregard, or "Old Bory," also felt threatened. While his spoken words usually won him friends, his writing was often more strident. Three days after assuming command in northern Virginia, he issued his "Beauty and Booty" proclamation. It was designed to rally, if not scare, local farmers and other male residents of Loudoun, Fairfax, and Prince William Counties into the Confederate ranks by telling them:

> A reckless and unprincipled tyrant has invaded our soil. Abraham Lincoln, regardless of all moral, legal, and constitutional restraints, had thrown his abolition hosts among you, who are murdering and imprisoning your citizens, confiscating and destroying your property, and committing other acts of violence, an outrage too shocking and revolting to humanity to be enumerated. All rules of civilized warfare are abandoned, and they proclaim by their acts, if not on their banners, that their war-cry is 'Beauty and Booty.' All that is dear to man, your honor, and that of your wives and

daughters, your fortunes, and your lives, are involved in this momentous contest.[30]

THE BULL RUN CAMPAIGN

Three months had passed since the opening shots were fired at Fort Sumter, and no major Union advance had occurred in Virginia south of Washington. The terms of three-month volunteers were expiring. Pressure mounted for a major offensive targeting the Confederate capital. "On to Richmond" was becoming the repeated demand of northern editorials. Despite the certainty of the press and politicians, the Union's high command was uncertain until late June about what should be their immediate target. For a time Harpers Ferry was the primary objective; elderly Robert Patterson slowly moved his small army across western Maryland toward that important rail stop. Talk also surfaced of having Patterson, once he controlled Harpers Ferry, cross the Potomac at Point of Rocks to Leesburg to join Brigadier General Irvin McDowell's forces in northern Virginia in an attack on Manassas. Another proposed move, favored by the War Department and General Scott, was to have McDowell meet Patterson at Leesburg before moving on the main Confederate force that was defending the vital railroad junction at Manassas. McDowell carefully responded that such a move would place green troops with their back to the Potomac River, making them vulnerable to an enemy's flanking attack. Scott dropped his Leesburg scheme, and McDowell, at the president's request, submitted a new plan of attack. The target was Manassas Junction.

A force of 35,000 would move from the outskirts of Washington over three routes toward Manassas. The intent was to brush away advanced Confederate positions at Fairfax Court House, Fairfax Station, and Sangster's Station before moving on to threaten the main Confederate force behind the stream called Bull Run, and turning the Confederates to the right, thereby cutting rail communication with the south. It was hoped the turning movement would intimidate the enemy to withdraw southward.

It was a fine plan, but implementation was another matter. To have any chance of success, McDowell argued that Patterson must engage General Joseph E. Johnston in the Shenandoah Valley to prevent the Johnston's force from moving to the aid of Beauregard's army at Manassas. Old Fuss and Feathers felt this was feasible and instructed Patterson of his vital role.[31]

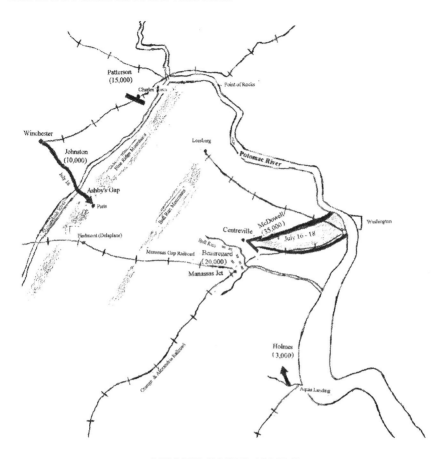

"ON TO RICHMOND"
McDowell Moves to Centreville and Johnston Joins Beauregard

McDowell and Scott were well aware of another significant problem. They knew their regiments were "exceedingly raw" and "not over steady in time." Hoping to counter this weakness, McDowell wrote, he organized his force into as "many small brigades as the number of regular colonels" would permit. Concern over the greenness of the men was expressed in a cabinet meeting, but Lincoln, feeling the pressure for action, responded that the enemy force was also inexperienced. July 8 was tentatively set for the beginning of the "on to Richmond" campaign. But the problem of preparedness would delay troop movement for another week.[32]

The Union advance would come as no surprise to Beauregard. His spy system, headed by Rose O'Neal Greenhow, informed him of the impending enemy movement. Young women rode breathlessly into Confederate camps. Some carried coded messages from Greenhow; others were individuals who believed they had had valuable information, which was not always the case. Nevertheless, they were all greeted enthusiastically and graciously by men and officers, who found it a delightful respite to hover around a young and often attractive female attempting to help.[33]

Anticipating McDowell's advance, Beauregard prepared numerous plans. They were frequently modified and were often unrealistic. His mercurial moods fluctuated between highs of great confidence and anticipated victory to lows of impending doom and railing against Davis and others of his administration for having failed to send support. He automatically assumed that the Federals would march through Centreville in an attempt to reach Manassas by crossing Bull Run at his force's strongest point, Mitchell's Ford. The stream was not over twenty to thirty feet wide and was rarely over waist-deep, but it had steep banks, forcing an enemy to cross at a fording site. Beauregard planned for his troops north of the stream to blunt the first enemy attack and then retreat to the southern bank. While the Federals were attempting to cross, other Confederates would attack the enemy's rear and flank. When informed that McDowell was about to move with 40,000 men, Beauregard became unnerved and blamed "stupid" Davis and his cohorts, who were beneath "contempt" for having caused his plight.

A few days later, Beauregard proposed to Richmond a most optimistic and grandiose scheme of grand strategy. Leaving a third of his men in the valley to contain the Federals, Johnston would join him in attacking and annihilating McDowell. Then Johnston's army, with some of Beauregard's men, would return to the valley, smash Patterson, and clear western Virginia before attacking Washington from the north, while Old Bory attacked from the south. The entire campaign was to take about two to three weeks. From mid-June into July, Beauregard proposed these and other plans; all were correctly and tactfully rejected. By mid-July, news of McDowell's approach led Beauregard to withdraw his advance brigade south of Bull Run. He telegraphed Davis of his peril and need for reinforcements. The government responded on July 17 by ordering Johnston: "Move to Manassas." The next day Beauregard was informed that Johnston was coming. He hurled the telegram on a table and bellowed, "Too late, too late. McDowell will be upon me tomorrow with his whole army and we shall have to sell our lives as dearly as possible."[34]

In the meantime, from July 16 to 18, the Federals slowly moved over three routes from their Washington and Virginia camps toward Manassas. They feared masked batteries and expected resistance, especially at Fairfax Court House. It took these citizen soldiers—dressed in a variety of uniforms, including a few who had recently joined, still in civilian clothes—two and a half days to reach Centreville, a distance of approximately twenty to twenty-five miles. Trees that had been felled by Confederate ax men required removal or detours through fields of corn and wheat. Men on the route from Alexandria to Sangster's Station were backed up for hours as thousands cautiously crossed a single log spanning a steep ravine over the narrow and fordable Accotink Creek. The men were unaccustomed to marching, and the heat and dust increased their fatigue and thirst. Thirst was exacerbated by the consumption of rations of dry hardtack and salty pork. Men fell out at every creek or well to fill canteens. Thousands stopped at every opportunity to pick blackberries. Wagons and heavy artillery impeded movement. Organization was defective and discipline, lax. Elected officers, fearful of lessening their popularity, looked the other way at improper behavior. Other officers were jeered at and ignored when they tried to stop soldiers from looting as men chased down pigs, chickens, and sheep, cleaned out a grocery store near Vienna, and set several homes ablaze near Fairfax Court House.[35]

McDowell had hoped to surprise and trap General Bonham and his brigade at Fairfax Court House. But the slow march of troops under Daniel Tyler from Vienna allowed Bonham's men, who had left meat cooking over an open fire and had abandoned other items, to beat a hasty retreat behind Bull Run. On July 18 McDowell ordered Tyler, the nearest to Centreville, to occupy that small hamlet while still planning to send other men to turn Beauregard right and hopefully cut him off from Richmond. Tyler was instructed: "Observe well the roads to Bull Run and Warrenton. Do not bring on an engagement, but keep up the impression we are moving on

51

Manassas." But Tyler, who was sixty-two, almost twenty years older than McDowell, and a graduate of West Point and distinguished veteran of the Mexican War, had a mind of his own. Encouraged by the news of fleeing Confederates behind Bull Run, he moved toward Manassas. Upon approaching Bull Run at Blackburn's Ford, he brought on a three- to four-hour clash (often called an action) with Confederates on the other side of the run on the afternoon of July 18, 1861. He lost the encounter and retreated back to Centreville.

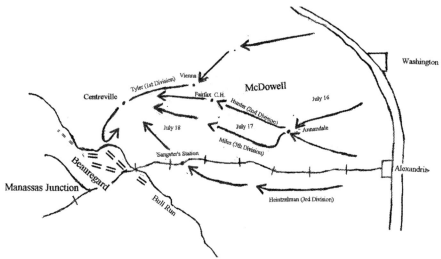

MCDOWELL MOVES TO CENTREVILLE

Bull Run flows southeast halfway between Centreville and Manassas Junction. Beauregard had placed his 20,000 men at crossing sites along eight miles of the southern bank from Union Mills northwest to Stone Bridge. Of the five fording areas in between, the two near the middle, a mile apart from each other, were Mitchell's and Blackburn's fords. They were defended by the brigades of Bonham and Longstreet and were on the most direct routes and midway between Centreville and Manassas Junction, which were about six miles apart. Tyler went to probe those areas with Colonel Israel Richardson's brigade and some cavalry as an escort. Upon reaching the spot on a ridge where the road from Centreville dipped down to Bull Run and divided, Tyler got a glimpse of the enemy. But he wanted to know more. He sent out skirmishers and had R. B. Ayres' two rifled guns (artillery with rifled barrels that can shoot farther than smooth-bore artillery) about a mile from Bull Run open fire first on the Confederate pieces on the road on his right, in front of Mitchell's Ford, and then upon the Washington artillery behind Blackburn's Ford, on the road straight ahead. This provoked little Confederate response and revealed little as Kemper's two pieces of Alexandria artillery in front of Mitchell's Ford were pulled back after firing a few shots. They joined the remaining two artillery pieces sheltered by Confederate earthworks back across the run. The Washington battery on the south side of Bull Run was also moved back out of harm's way.

The failure of the artillery to provoke the enemy into revealing their strength caused Tyler to use his infantry. Ignoring the pleas of two members of McDowell's staff, Major John C. Barnard and Captain James B. Fry, not to escalate the situation as it would violate McDowell's orders and likely bring on an engagement, Tyler sent forward men from Richardson's brigade. Five hundred men were sent toward the right in the woods in front of Mitchell's Ford, and three companies of the First Massachusetts were sent to join the skirmishers in the woods on the left of the road to Blackburn's. The latter would become the focal point of the Union attack. A frontal assault on Mitchell's would expose Federals to heavy fire while moving across the flat land in front of that ford. Whereas the terrain on the Union side of Blackburn's Ford was more favorable, it was not only wooded on the left, but higher than the flat plateau across the stream, which was occupied by Longstreet's men. Behind the Confederate position at both fords, the land gradually rose to a ridge.[36]

The gray-clad men of the First Massachusetts were led by Lieutenant-Colonel George D. Wells in their charge down the wooded incline on the Union left toward the run. Officers and men alike were anxious to get the opportunity to shoot at the enemy. Wells fought furiously, grabbing muskets from his men and firing them. Despite Wells and his men's efforts, the Bay Staters were twice beaten back. During the initial charge, a Federal lieutenant, William Smith, who was unsure if the Confederates also dressed in gray were friend or foe, stopped his men from firing and lost his life as he ran toward the Virginians in Longstreet's line, yelling for them to identify themselves.

Charles P. Poland Jr.

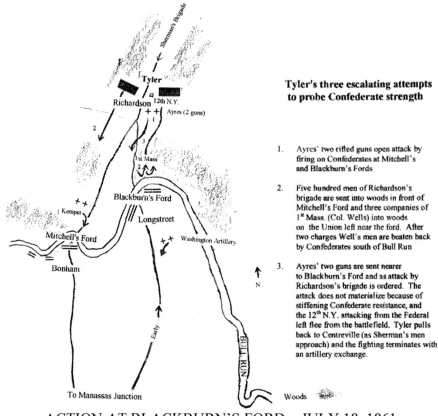

Tyler's three escalating attempts to probe Confederate strength

1. Ayres' two rifled guns open attack by firing on Confederates at Mitchell's and Blackburn's Fords

2. Five hundred men of Richardson's brigade are sent into woods in front of Mitchell's Ford and three companies of 1st Mass. (Col. Wells) into woods on the Union left near the ford. After two charges Well's men are beaten back by Confederates south of Bull Run

3. Ayres' two guns are sent nearer to Blackburn's Ford and as attack by Richardson's brigade is ordered. The attack does not materialize because of stiffening Confederate resistance, and the 12th N.Y. attacking from the Federal left flee from the battlefield. Tyler pulls back to Centreville (as Sherman's men approach) and the fighting terminates with an artillery exchange.

ACTION AT BLACKBURN'S FORD – JULY 18, 1861
(FROM CA. 1:00 P.M. TO 4:10 P.M.)

Longstreet's repulse of the Federals was not without anxious moments. Part of his line broke and started to run, as the situation was too much for the nerves of untested men. Longstreet stopped the panicking men by riding in front of them and threatening them with his saber.

The attacks of the First Massachusetts also failed to satisfy Tyler's desire to know more about the size of his opponent. So for the third time he escalated the situation. He sent Ayers' two howitzers to what proved to be a precarious position 500 yards from the ford. Acting on Richardson's suggestion, he sent the entire brigade forward, hoping for an opportunity to charge the enemy artillery. But Longstreet's intense response, aided by arriving reserves, convinced Tyler that Blackburn's Ford was heavily defended and the affair should be terminated.

Richardson, later known as "Fighting Dick," wanted to fight on. His Twelfth New York, under Colonel Ezra L. Walrath, was in the woods on the left, where the First Massachusetts had fought, in view of the run, and heavily engaged. Then one of the captains, from either fear or confusion, gave the order to retreat. Most of the New Yorkers fled. Neither Walrath nor Richardson could stop the panicky retreat. When Tyler arrived on the scene, he concluded it was hopeless and told Richardson to let them go. As Tyler pulled back to Centreville, Confederates pushed across the ford, but not far. They were caught in between enemy fire and that of Early's men arriving in their rear. The encounter concluded with three-quarters of an hour's worth of artillery duel. The artillery exchange caused men on both sides of Bull Run to duck and seek cover, including Sherman and his brigade, just arriving from Centreville. A few civilians watched from the Union position. On the other side of the run, as many as fifty Confederates lined up behind a huge tree. The action terminated with eighty-three Federal casualties (nineteen killed, thirty-eight wounded, and twenty-six missing) and seventy Confederates (fifteen killed, fifty-three wounded, and two missing).

The impact of what would later be considered a minor affair had significant consequences for both sides. It raised Confederate and lowered Federal morale. Confederate optimism soared, and Beauregard became euphoric. Scattered weapons, clothing, and corpses found in the woods from which Federals had retreated were interpreted as evidence of a victory that had demoralized the enemy. The sight of Union dead and wounded being returned to Centreville, the latter placed in pews facing each other in the small stone church, surely lowered Federal morale. McDowell would blame the rout of the Twelfth New York and Tyler's retreat for the later "defection of the 4th Pennsylvania and the 8th New York Battery on the eve of the battle of Bull Run." Doubtless the plight of gunshot victims was most unpleasant, made more difficult by the gathering of Union forces in and around the small hamlet; they drank the wells dry, creating a water shortage. McDowell was displeased to learn of Tyler's encounter, his pullback to Centreville, and his later failure to comply with his verbal order to return in front of the fords. The next day, after a written order by McDowell to Tyler, Richardson returned to the previous day's position to protect the concentrating force at Centreville. A lifelong bitterness between Tyler and McDowell would grow out of Tyler's actions at Blackburn's Ford and the battle of July 21, 1861.[37]

While Blackburn's Ford was being contested, another development was taking place that would have a paramount impact upon the forthcoming battle. McDowell was scouting the area to turn Beauregard's right, but finding the roads too narrow and crooked and the distance too great, he abandoned the idea. He returned to Centreville and sent engineers (Major Barnard and Captain Woodbury, accompanied by a troop of cavalry and Governor Sprague of Rhode Island) to find a route to turn the enemies left. This would cause a two-day delay—which would prove fatal—before launching an attack and would allow Johnston's army, taking advantage of interior lines and using rails, to arrive in time for the battle.

While McDowell worked on a new plan, his men waited for ration-carrying wagons to arrive; their three-day supply of rations had long been consumed. Men of two units were convinced they had had enough of war. Since their three months were up, they were going home. Not even the eloquence of Secretary of War Simon Cameron, who was at McDowell's Centreville headquarters, could dissuade a regiment from his home state (Fourth Pennsylvania) and the Eighth New York militia battery (who abandoned their artillery pieces) from leaving. Morale could not have improved when shocked volunteers witnessed the whipping and branding of two deserters from a battalion of regulars.

Finally, a way around the Stone Bridge was found, and at 2:00 to 2:30 in the morning of July 21, 1861, McDowell ordered his troops to move out. The plan was for some of them to fake attacks at Blackburn's Ford and the Stone Bridge to draw attention from the two divisions that were to cross Bull Run to the north and turn the enemy left. The specifics of the plan were to have Colonel Miles' Fifth Division (with Richardson's brigade at Blackburn's Ford) on the ridge from Centreville to Blackburn's Ford to act as a reserve, defend the hamlet, and make a demonstration on Blackburn's Ford with artillery. Three of the four brigades of the First Division (of Major Richardson) under Tyler were to move toward the Stone Bridge and, at daybreak, fire artillery shots. The Second and Third Divisions, (under Colonels David Hunter and Samuel P. Heintzelman) soon after crossing the rickety suspension bridge over Cub Run, were to turn north off the Warrenton Turnpike onto a secondary road in a looping movement that, at daybreak, would bring the Second Division across Bull Run at Sudley Springs and the Third Division across at a lower ford (Poplar). It was hoped that the turning movement would then force the withdrawal of the Confederate left, allowing Tyler and his fresh troops to cross Stone Bridge and join in the sweep toward Manassas Junction. It was a fine plan, but green troops and delays would hamper its implementation from the start.[38]

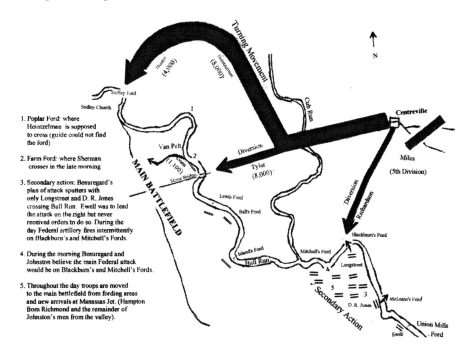

MCDOWELL'S TURNING MOVEMENT AND CONFEDERATE
RESPONSE ON JULY 21, 1861

The night of July 20, 1861, saw commanders of both sides planning to attack the other the next day. Men in both moonlight camps anxiously pondered their fate. McDowell explained his orders to the brigade commanders of his Army of Northern Virginia at 8:00 that night, while Beauregard worked until 4:00 the next morning on his. Johnston—with part of his Army of the Shenandoah including Thomas Jackson, Francis Bartow, and Bernard Bee's men—arrived during the day on July 20, after traveling sixty miles in two days from Winchester to join Beauregard's Army of the Potomac. The first half of the trip had been covered by marching, and the second, by rail. On

July 18, the men had marched into the night over the Blue Ridge through Ashby's Gap to the picturesque hamlet of Paris at the eastern base of the mountains. The next day they had taken the train at nearby Piedmont on the Manassas Gap Railroad for the second leg of the journey to Manassas Junction. The rest of Johnston's Army of the Shenandoah would arrive the next day, and adding Colonel Theophilus Holmes' brigade, which marched from Fredericksburg, and Colonel Wade Hampton's Legion, which traveled by rail from Richmond, with both arriving on July 20, the Confederates would unknowingly equal the number of Federals.

An exhausted Johnston, who had not had rest for days and who was now in command of the joining armies, was unfamiliar with the terrain and details of the situation. He feared Patterson had followed him. He met with Beauregard at his headquarters at Wilmer McLean's house, and instructed him, much to the Creole's delight, to immediately draw up a plan of attack that he hoped could be implemented before the merger of Patterson's army with McDowell's.

Considering that Beauregard had received information of the Federal concentration on his left that threatened that thinly defended area, he came up with an amazing plan. Instead of sending reinforcements to Nathan G. ("Shanks") Evans' 1,100-man brigade and two artillery pieces that defended Stone Bridge, he proposed an attack that would send the center and right of his line across Bull Run to converge on Centreville and points east. This, he confidently asserted, would lead to complete victory by noon on July 21. Johnston accepted the general plan, but he modified it, wisely, sending Bee and Jackson—as Beauregard sent Hampton's Legion—to support Evans.

The implementation of Beauregard's plan would be even more mismanaged than McDowell's. In part this was caused by confusion and the distraction of the Union's attacking first. The confusion, however, was exacerbated by Beauregard and some poor staff work. The flurry of poorly written orders modifying previous ones—often carried by disappearing civilian couriers of unknown identity—led to miscommunication. The coordinated Confederate attack that was planned never materialized. Confederates crossed over Blackburn's and McLean's fords early in the morning but proceeded no further. Throughout the day, there was sporadic Union artillery fire and the exchange of small arms fire between Bonham's men—who remained most of the day behind their works at Mitchell's—and Longstreet's.

The latter Confederates crossed a short distance beyond Blackburn's Ford, where they were surrounded by the bloated and blackened Federal dead killed on the eighteenth. (Longstreet's men did not have earthworks.) D. R. Jones' brigade crossed over McLean's Ford, but preceded no further, as they were to follow Richard Ewell's men. Ewell never received the crucial orders to cross Bull Run and open the attack on the right.

McDowell would also face difficulties implementing his plans, and since he was the one ultimately on the offense, delays would prove more costly. While Beauregard worked through the night on his offensive plans, McDowell's troops were set into motion. He had planned to lessen the distance of the movement by moving men west of Centreville the day before, but against his better judgment, McDowell conceded to the wishes of his lieutenants, who preferred to march from their camps on the morning of the battle. Tyler was to lead off; his camp was the furthest west and nearest to the Stone Bridge, only two and a half miles away. His start was so late and his advance so slow that it delayed for two to three hours the 13,000 men (with twenty artillery pieces) of Hunter and Heintzelman's division, who were to perform the turning movement. Added to this delay was the circuitous nature of the route, which was some ten miles long, rather than the anticipated six—the guides feared that the route scouted by Barnard, which led through an open field, would reveal their position, so they took the longer route. The first of Hunter's hot, thirsty, tired men splashed into the water at Sudley Springs at 9:30 A.M. instead of at the planned hour of 7:00. After resting and daring to drink from the muddied water, they proceeded past the gawking parishioners gathered on this Sunday morning at the nearby Sudley Church. The invading force, led by Burnside's brigade, headed for the Warrenton Turnpike, where the battle would commence; the enemy had discovered the turning movement.[39]

This discovery was due in part to the Confederates' good fortune, as well as to the feeble, ineffective delivery of Tyler's diversion at Stone Bridge. At 6:00 that morning, from a hill a mile east of the bridge, he opened with several shots—from a ponderous thirty-pound Parrot—at the inviting white Van Pelt house on a hill a mile and a half away. This house was assumed to be a Confederate general's headquarters. The first shot crashed through the roof of the dwelling, but this and subsequent artillery fire and several hours of skirmishing failed, as at Blackburn's Ford, to reveal enemy strength. Astutely, Evans hid his force and did not reply with his two meager artillery pieces. Instead he spread skirmishers along Bull Run to discourage enemy movement by engaging the enemy in several hours of skirmishing.

Shanks Evans' meager force was truly in a precarious position. Not only did he face an overwhelming enemy across Bull Run, but according to reports from pickets of brief exchanges with the enemy to his north and west, he was about to be turned, if not surrounded. This was confirmed by a message from Edward Porter Alexander, who was in charge of Confederate wigwagging signal stations. During the morning, eight miles away, near Union Mills, Alexander had looked through his field glasses to pick up a message from the signal station near the Van Pelt house when he saw the gleaming of metal to the north of the yard from a cannon, muskets, and bayonets. He immediately signaled Evans, "Lookout for your left, you are turned."[40] Hapless news for Evans, but McDowell's secret turning movement was now discovered. This fortuitous event, with others, would ultimately undermine McDowell's chances for victory. Evans and the Confederates were fortunate that the Union guide could not find Poplar Ford, forcing Heintzelman's division to take the longer route to Sudley's Ford, creating further delays.

Time on this day was a friend of the Confederates and an enemy of the Federals. Confederates obtained it by luck, Tyler's inaction, and especially the intrepid actions of Shanks Evans, a spirited man in every sense of the word—an orderly followed him around with a gallon of whiskey. Evans informed Philip St. George Cocke, who was a mile away at Lewis Ford, that he was sending most of his brigade westward to meet the enemy and was leaving only four small companies to check Tyler. By 9:30 A.M., Evans had 900 of his 1,100-man brigade on Matthews Hill near Sudley Road, surprisingly not on the crest, but on the southern slope. There he waited to meet the approaching enemy.

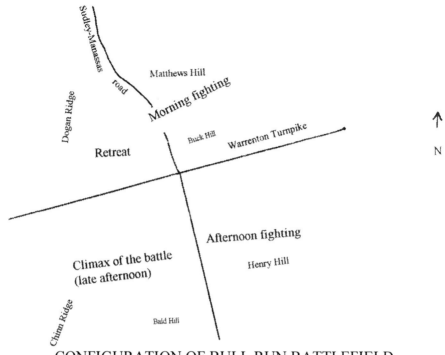

CONFIGURATION OF BULL RUN BATTLEFIELD
Momentum of the battle swirled clockwise throughout July 21, 1861 on
ridges separated by the Warrenton Turnpike and Sudley – Manassas road

The conflict there would emerge into a battle that would go
through three stages. It would first be fought on the rolling hills
separated by Sudley Road and the Warrenton Turnpike, which
crossed to form a giant + on the terrain. From 9:45 to 11:30 A.M.,
Evans and those who came to his aid at Matthews and Buck hills
would hold stubbornly until they were be forced to flee to the wooded
part of the rise across the turnpike, on Henry Hill. At the end of this
stage it would look as if the Union had won. But then a lull, though
not a stop to all fighting, occurred from noon to 2:00 P.M. This second
stage would allow the Confederates to regroup on Henry Hill. This set
up the next and third stage, which would see a Union victory slip
away into defeat. After back-and-forth combat, fresh Confederate
troops of Johnston's army would enable the Southerners to
permanently seize control of Henry Hill and outflank Federals to the
west. Shortly after 4:00, the Federals would be in retreat. Beauregard

and Johnston would win—an outcome that had earlier seemed highly unlikely.

Stage One: The "Union Victory"

For nearly two hours during the morning of July 21, 1861, the fighting centered around Matthews Hill. The first shots, ironically, were a mistaken exchange of fire between Confederates. A nervous South Carolina Company fired from a grove of trees upon the rifles of Roberdeau Wheat's battalion (which had been recruited mainly from the wharves and boweries of New Orleans) who obliged by returning fire. Their attention soon shifted to the approaching Federals, Burnside's brigade, headed by Colonel Hunter and the ubiquitous Governor Sprague. For half an hour the Second Rhode Island and Captain Reynolds' six James Rifles exchanged shots with Evans' men while more than 4,000 Federals stood idly by due to Hunter's improper positioning of troops. This was the start of a trend that would plague the Union throughout the day. Units would be sent into battle in a piecemeal fashion. After he was wounded in the neck, Hunter left Burnside in charge. Evans' men held their own for a while. Wheat boldly led his battalion in charging the Federals, coming within twenty yards of Reynolds' Rhode Island battery before being beaten back and retreating to Dogan Ridge, west of Sudley Road. There, Wheat's Louisiana Tigers fired at the enemy from behind haystacks and fought on after their major, an inviting target at six feet, four inches, and 275 pounds, was shot through the lungs and was carried from the field on a litter made out of muskets.

By 11:00 the lines extended across Matthews Hill to the rise across Sudley Road. On Dogan Ridge, Colonel Andrew Porter's brigade and Captain James B. Ricketts and Captain Charles Griffin's twelve artillery pieces were placed. Bee and Bartow had now arrived from Henry Hill to form the Confederate right.

Bee was upset at being sent to the Confederate left, fearing he would miss the anticipated battle at Mitchell's Ford. Earlier, Bee, Bartow, and their men had watched from near widow Henry's house as Evans held his own. Shots from Captain Reynolds' guns flew over their heads, close enough to cause those who had climbed apple trees for a snack to drop from the limbs like falling fruit. Soon Evans asked for help, rejecting Bee's suggestion that he pull back to Henry Hill. The arrival of Bee and Bartow on Matthews Hill enabled the Confederates to hold on longer, stopping the Federal advance for a time. Amidst the ghastly sights and sounds of battle, a Union soldier felt a stir between his legs, only to find a man firing and using these legs as a porthole.

This first stage of the battle was coming to an end. Three thousand Confederates faced vast, superior numbers that extended beyond their quarter-mile line and both Confederate flanks, mauling the Eighth Georgia on the Confederate right. The Southern artillery— Evans' two pieces (one at Buck Hill and the other near the turnpike) and Captain John Imboden's four six-pound pieces near Mrs. Henry's house—were no match for superior number (eighteen) and the range of the enemy's rifled cannons. Imboden's pieces had momentarily slight protection as they hid behind a small rise, where they were shielded from enemy shells, which plowed in front of them, making the land look as if it had been rooted by hogs. But enemy fire that killed many of the horses, as well as depleted ammunition, made Imboden's position untenable.[41] Soon Confederates gave way, fleeing diagonally across the turnpike to Henry Hill just as Wade Hampton arrived to help. His 600-man force, largely equipped at his own expense, bought valuable time. Engaging the enemy for nearly an hour, Hampton's men battled the Federals first from Robinson's Lane before advancing to the turnpike. They were driven back, but they stubbornly fired from the rail fence lining the lane before being forced to retreat to the woods near the remnants of Bee, Bartow, and Evans' brigades.

The disintegration of Confederate resistance and flight from Matthews Hill and Buck Hill made the Federals believe the battle was over and they had won. McDowell and his staff jubilantly rode among the men, waving their hats and proclaiming victory. Some of the new arrivals felt cheated that the battle had ended before they had the chance to shoot at the enemy. It was a joyous time for the beleaguered commander after the stressful days of launching his campaign— which had been complicated by his personal illness, digestive problems resulting from the consumption of canned peaches the night before the battle. He was so incapacitated that he had ridden to the battlefield in a carriage.[42]

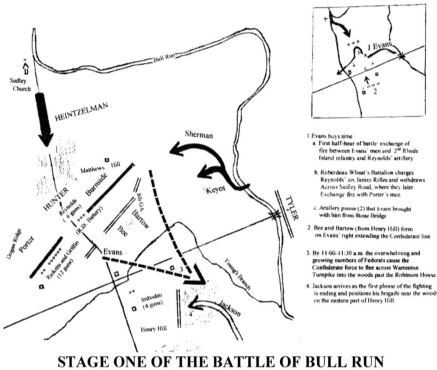

STAGE ONE OF THE BATTLE OF BULL RUN
THE "UNION VICTORY"
(ca. 9:45-11:30 a.m.)

Stage Two: The Fatal Delay

It was only the end of the battle's first stage. The Union's failure to vigorously pursue the enemy for nearly two hours allowed the dying embers of battle to reignite into a flame more intense than before. It was another costly delay for the Northerners. The Union's will to pursue had been deflated by the assumed victory, as well as by fatigue and lack of leadership. Nowhere was it more evident than in Burnside's brigade. While Southerners fled to Henry Hill, Burnside's spent brigade was pulled back into the woods along Sudley Road in order—as was later claimed—to be resupplied with ammunition. Only one regiment (Second New Hampshire) would return to the front.

The lull and delay in a coordinated Union assault from shortly before noon to 2:00 was not without gunfire. Much of the first hour of this second stage was Hampton's exchange to discourage a Union advance. This was followed by a respite from fighting, with Jackson's brigade arriving at Henry Hill, and with Johnston and Beauregard arriving soon afterwards. Then artillery fire started up again, followed by Keyes' isolated attack on the Confederate left. Hampton's fighting and the arrival of Jackson and the Confederate commanders all helped revive the Confederate resistance.

Upon learning that Bee was in trouble, Jackson, who had been ordered to support the Confederates who defended Lewis' and Ball's Fords, hurried to Henry Hill. Jackson selected a strong position, placing his 2,600-man brigade on a downslope 300 yards east of Mrs. Henry's house. There were thirteen cannons placed in front of the men, some brought by Johnston and Beauregard, who had spent most of the morning at Mitchell's Ford, thinking the battle would be fought there.[43]

Soon deadly metal was spewed from dueling artillery pieces on Henry Hill, Matthews Hill, and Dogan Ridge, as infantrymen on all three ridges lay flat upon the ground. The grass around the Confederate guns caught fire; the fire was stamped out and the grass was cut down with sabers.

Behind Jackson's prone warriors and Hampton's legion, Beauregard and Johnston were leading the reorganization of the mingled remnants of the morning fight. It was not an easy task. When they arrived, they that saw officers had stopped a further retreat but were vainly endeavoring to restore order. At first even Johnston and Beauregard's efforts were futile. Beauregard later wrote, "Every segment of line [they succeeded in] forming was again dissolved while another was being formed; more than two thousand men were shouting, each some suggestion to his neighbor, their voices mingling with the noise of the shells hurtling through the trees overhead, and all word of command drowned in confusion and uproar." Order and some confidence were eventually restored. Men claimed they wanted another crack at the enemy. Beauregard then made the unusual request that Johnston leave the field and direct troops to the battle site. At first reluctant, Johnston went to Portici (the Lewises' house), where he performed an invaluable service. He sent forth reinforcements that would be decisive in winning the day. Left in charge of the battle site, Beauregard readied his men for battle by riding among them, giving brief but dramatic speeches.[44]

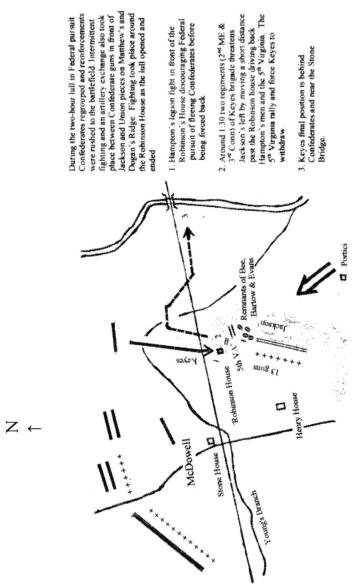

During the two-hour lull in Federal pursuit Confederates regrouped and reinforcements were rushed to the battlefield. Intermittent fighting and an artillery exchange also took place between Confederate guns in front of Jackson and Union pieces on Matthew's and Dogan's Ridge. Fighting took place around the Robinson House as the lull opened and ended.

1. Hampton's legion fight in front of the Robinson's House discouraging Federal pursuit of fleeing Confederates before being forced back.

2. Around 1:30 two regiments (2nd ME & 3rd Conn) of Keyes brigade threatens Jackson's left by moving a short distance past the Robinson house driving back Hampton's men and the 5th Virginia. The 5th Virginia rally and force Keyes to withdraw.

3. Keyes final position is behind Confederates and near the Stone Bridge.

STAGE TWO OF THE BATTLE OF BULL RUN
THE FATAL LULL
(ca. noon to 2:00 p.m.)

66

The concluding activity of the second stage was the missed opportunity of Erasmus D. Keyes to achieve what one historian describes as possibly the day's "best opportunity" for the Union to achieve "a tactical victory."[45] Earlier, during the morning fight on Matthews Hill, McDowell ordered his second-in-command, Tyler, to force a crossing at Stone Bridge. Tyler in turn sent the brigades of William T. Sherman and Keyes to cross. Unlike Heintzelman and his guide, Sherman knew where to cross. It was at Farm Ford, about a mile up from the bridge, a site he had discovered by accident. Earlier in the day this fording area had been revealed to him as he saw a Confederate horseman cross, shout insults, and make taunting gestures, then retreat across, fleeing shots from Union skirmishers.[46]

The two Union brigades crossed there. Sherman took his brigade to Matthews Hill, where the fighting was ending.[47] Shortly past noon, Keyes, accompanied by Tyler, who crossed after Sherman, were north of the turnpike opposite the home of James Robinson, a free black. They saw the enemy around and beyond the Robinson house, but did not know their size. They were also unaware of Jackson's vulnerability; he faced westward while they neared his right flank.

Tyler and Keyes saw an opportunity, nevertheless, at around 1:30 and sent two regiments to attack. The Second Maine and Third Connecticut climbed the hill south of Youngs Branch and pushed across the turnpike to the Robinson house, forcing Hampton's men and the Fifth Virginia to pull back. The Fifth Virginia rallied in woods behind a hollow southeast of the Robinson dwelling. The men fought desperately, inflicting such a intense fire from a somewhat oblique angle that Keyes felt that being subjected to it for just five minutes would have destroyed his troops. The New Englanders pulled back to the protection of the turnpike, and then moved down Henry Hill, and gradually, the entire brigade moved toward the Stone Bridge. There, Keyes remained behind the enemy for several hours, but did not attempt to menace the Confederate line.[48]

Stage Three: Confederate Victory

Around 2:00 P.M. the battle entered its most intense and decisive stage, which would last for several hours. It opened with McDowell's sending artillery to Henry Hill. Griffin and Ricketts voiced strong concerns about the lack of infantry protection. William F. Barry, chief of artillery, was also anxious about the plight of the artillery and scurried about, seeking help. Four regiments were readied with General Samuel P. Heintzelman's help, including the late Ellsworth's Fire Zouaves (Eleventh New York).[49] Griffin, who would have a dissenting dialogue with his artillery chief throughout the third stage of the battle, was adamant that Henry Hill was no place for unprotected artillery; he preferred Chinn Ridge. To Barry's repeated refrain that the Fire Zouaves would protect the artillery, Griffin vehemently insisted that they would not.

Ricketts and Griffin's batteries left Dogan Ridge and crossed the turnpike and Young's Branch, moving to Henry Hill by Sudley Road. Rickett placed his battery to the right and south of the eighty-five-year-old widow Judith Henry's house and immediately came under fire from Confederate sharpshooters in the dwelling. Ricketts responded by firing on the house, which chased away the enemy but did considerable structural damage and mortally wounded the invalid Mrs. Henry as she lay in bed.[50]

After the Confederate sharpshooters had been chased from the Henry home, Griffin placed his battery just north of the house. The thirteen Confederate and eleven Federal artillery pieces were now only 300 yards apart, negating the advantage held earlier by the longer-range Union weapons. They exchanged shots. Union fire flew over the Southerners' heads and crashed into pine trees. Jackson told his infantry to wait until the enemy got closer, preferably only fifty yards away, and the opportunity presented itself to use the bayonet. The Thirty-third Virginia, on Jackson's left, soon got their chance. The Eleventh New York (Fire Zouaves) and the First Minnesota, two of the regiments Barry had earlier arranged to protect his artillery, approached the Confederate line. Both antagonists were unsure of whom they faced, but soon Colonel Arthur C. Cummings' Thirty-third Virginians fired.[51] After a short duration, the two bloodied Yankee regiments broke and ran, leaving Rickett's battery unprotected.[52] Orders from officers—including General Heintzelman, who helped lead the Eleventh New York toward the enemy—and Rickett's pleas to save his battery had no effect. Colonel "Jeb" Stuart's voice likewise went unheeded as he first mistook the fleeing Fire Zouaves nearing Sudley Road for Confederates. Upon seeing the United States flag, the Confederate cavalry leader, Stuart, who was guarding the left (the other half of Stuart's 300 men were guarding the right) had his 150 troopers charge. Stuart's men ran through and back through the Zouaves, who got off only a few shots. The horsemen killed only a few of the Zouaves but did contribute to their disorganization.

The situation was critical for both sides. Ricketts' and Griffin's batteries were alone on Henry Hill. The Confederates had succeeding in repelling the first movement toward their left, but they needed more men. Both sides rushed men to the battle site. Their lack of coordination would later cause concerned civilians such as Governor Sprague to give orders to soldiers. Four Federal regiments, including the Fourteenth Brooklyn, were moved up Sudley Road to help protect Federal artillery. Griffin wanted to help solve the artillery's plight, so he moved two of his two pieces to a rise on the Federal extreme right, in an excellent position to enfilade the enemy's artillery. Seeing the danger, Cummings—whom Jackson had given the responsibility of watching out for their left—moved the men of the Thirty-third Virginia out of the woods, climbed over a rail fence, and moved at an angle toward the two menacing federal guns.

Two shots had been fired from Griffin's artillery pieces when he noticed the approaching Virginians and prepared to greet them with canister. He was stopped by the arrival of Major Barry, who hollered out orders to Griffin not to fire. Barry insisted that the approaching regiment in blue pants and shirts and straw hats was his support. While the two Federal officers argued, the Thirty-third charged, inflicting heavy casualties on Griffin's unprotected men and horses and seizing the two Federal pieces.[53] Of all the confusion over uniforms at Blackford's Ford and throughout the battle of July 21, 1861, nothing had as profound an impact. The Federals' missed opportunity would be labeled the turning point of the battle.[54]

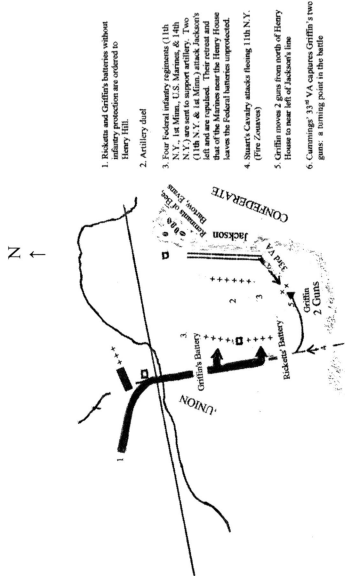

1. Ricketts and Griffin's batteries without infantry protection are ordered to Henry Hill.

2. Artillery duel

3. Four Federal infantry regiments (11th N.Y., 1st Minn, & 14th N.Y.) are sent to support artillery. Two (11th N.Y. & 1st Minn.) attack Jackson's left and are repulsed. Their retreat and that of the Marines near the Henry House leaves the Federal batteries unprotected.

4. Stuart's Cavalry attacks fleeing 11th N.Y. (Fire Zouaves)

5. Griffin moves 2 guns from north of Henry House to near left of Jackson's line

6. Cummings' 33rd VA captures Griffin's two guns: a turning point in the battle

STAGE THREE OF THE BATTLE OF BULL RUN: FIRST HOUR
(ca. 2:00 – 3:00 p.m.)

The first hour of the battle's last stage, between 2:00 and 3:00 P.M., included the movement of Federal artillery to Henry Hill, an artillery duel, a repulse of the first infantry threat to Jackson's left, and Stuart's horsemen running over those fleeing Federals. The hour ended with the capture of Griffin's two guns. It might have been during this hour that Bee made a statement about Jackson that led to the most famous sobriquet and one of the most quoted utterances of the war.

Soon after 3:00 P.M. the Thirty-third Virginia's triumph led to their disorganization as the men just milled about the two guns. They soon lost their spoils and were forced back to their original position. The Fourteenth Brooklyn, another Zouave regiment, known as the Red Stockings, recaptured Griffin's artillery. After driving away the Red Stockings, Jackson boldly took the offensive. The former VMI instructor removed his artillery from the field and had his men stand up and move toward Ricketts' battery. Screaming loudly, Jackson's men captured the battery and controlled Henry Hill.[55] For the next hour, the most intense fighting of the day would swirl around the eight captured guns (six of Ricketts' and two of Griffin's) and the Henry house, where Mrs. Henry lay dying.[56]

The momentum of the battle was shifting. The Federals made repeated attempts to gain back their artillery. Reinforcements moved from the Stone House along Sudley Road (the banks provided some protection), then turned left at Henry House Lane and the banks behind Ricketts' battery. These counterattacks were not well coordinated; only one or two regiments at a time advanced, fought until bloodied, and were forced to leave. Then another regiment or two would repeat the process. There were some temporary successes: twice the Federals regained control of the western side of Henry Hill, the house, and Rickett's battery site. Colonel William B. Franklin's Fifth and Eleventh Massachusetts were the first to accomplish this, driving back Jackson's men only in turn to be driven back by Hampton's Legion and the Fifth Virginia of Jackson's brigade.[57] Left of Hampton and the Fifth Virginia, Bartow and Bee would be mortally wounded while leading remnants of their units, as would Colonel F. J. Thomas (of Johnston's staff), while leading a makeshift battalion against remnants of Union regiments on the Federal right.[58]

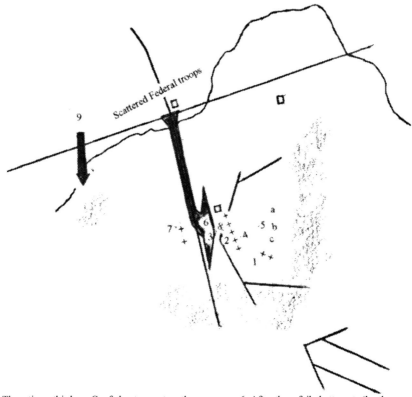

Three times this hour Confederates capture the western part of Henry Hill and twice they are beaten back.

1. The 14th N.Y. captures Griffin's two guns & unsuccessfully attack Jackson's left.

2. Jackson captures Henry Hill and Ricketts' battery.

3. Jackson is forced back by the 5th and 11th Mass.

4. Hampton's Legion and 5th VA regain control of Henry House and Ricketts' battery (for over half an hour).

5. Bartow and Bee (leading regiments of their brigades) and Thomas (leading a makeshift battalion) attack remnants of Union regiments on Federal right.
a. Bartow killed
b. Bee mortally wounded
c. F.J. Thomas killed

6. After three failed attempts (by three regiments) Sherman's fourth regiment (69th N.Y.) and a regiment from Wilcox's brigade (38th N.Y.) regain control of western part of Henry Hill for the last time.

7. They were aided by two federal guns west of Sudley road.

8. Eppa Hutton's 8th VA and the 18th VA with the assistance of Lynchburg artillery win permanent control of Henry Hill.

9. Howard moves toward Chinn Ridge.

STAGE THREE OF THE BATTLE OF BULL RUN: THE MOMENTUM SHIFTS AS CONFEDERATES WIN HENRY HILL
(CA. 3:00 to 4:00 p.m.)

The men of Hampton's Legion (positioned around the Henry house, behind fences, shrubbery, and outbuildings) and the Fifth Virginia (at Ricketts' guns) stubbornly fought the attacking Federals. Participants would tell of their plight in vivid detail: For more than half an hour these Confederates endured "deadly missiles" that fell around them "like hailstone." The shouts of the combatants, "the groans of the wounded and dying, and the explosion of shells made a pandemonium. The atmosphere was black with smoke of the battle, which raged with great violence on both sides." In this exchange, Hampton was wounded near the Henry house. Meanwhile, the Southerners stopped the advance of three of Sherman's four regiments, who were sent in one at a time amid repeated cries of "you are firing on friends." The Second Wisconsin was the first of Sherman's regiments to engage the Confederates. They had the misfortune of being shot at from behind as they left Sudley Road, and again, later, when returning to it. They were the victims of friendly fire from two other approaching regiments of Sherman's brigade who mistook their gray uniforms for the enemy. "The Highlanders" (179th New York) went in next near Ricketts' guns and fought ably before being forced back and losing their wounded colonel, James Cameron, a brother of the secretary of war. Finally, Sherman's fourth regiment (Sixty-ninth New York), a regiment from Wilcox's brigade (Thirtieth New York), and artillery (two guns) west of Sudley Road forced the Confederates back, giving the Federals control of the eastern portion of Henry Hill for the last time.[59] It was a brief possession, as Eppa Hunton's Eighth Virginia and the Eighteenth Virginia drove the Federals permanently off Henry Hill.[60]

The fortunes of combat now favored the Confederates. Between 3:00 and 4:00 P.M., 7,000 fresh troops arrived at Johnston's headquarters and were rapidly forwarded to the battle site. This would make the difference in securing a Southern victory. By 4:00 McDowell's fortunes were bleak. He was running out of fresh men. Fifteen regiments who had gone to Henry Hill between 2:00 and 4:00 P.M. had now disintegrated into a mob, with thousands milling around the Stone House. McDowell had only five regiments left, Colonel Oliver O. Howard's four and a regiment of United States Regulars. Howard's numbers had been greatly reduced by exhaustion and dehydration and were what the men called "sun struck" from the long march in the heat of the day. Some companies were left with only eight men.[61] McDowell hoped to improve his dwindling chances by sending his five remaining regiments west of Sudley Road, including sending Howard's men to Chinn Ridge to outflank the enemy on Henry Hill. Swelling numbers of Confederates, first led by Joseph B. Kershaw, then Arnold Elzey, and finally Jubal Early, blocked Howard's path. Early's line now outflanked the Federal right.[62]

The clash on Chinn's Ridge came to an end, as did the third and final stage of fighting, shortly after 4:00. Heavy Confederate fire caused Howard to order two retreats, hoping each time to reform his line, but after the second retreat his command disintegrated before they reached the turnpike. The men kept going, along with the rest of McDowell's men. McDowell and others would work desperately to rally the troops, but it was hopeless.

ROUT, PANIC, AND A DEMORALIZED NORTH

Among the fleeing men was newlywed Kady Brownell, who had marched to the battlefield beside her husband and the First Rhode Island Infantry. She wore long pants under her dress, a sash around her waist, and a sword and carried the flag. The nineteen-year-old young lady of five foot three, with dark hair and blue eyes, was wounded in the upper right thigh while retreating from the battlefield.[63]

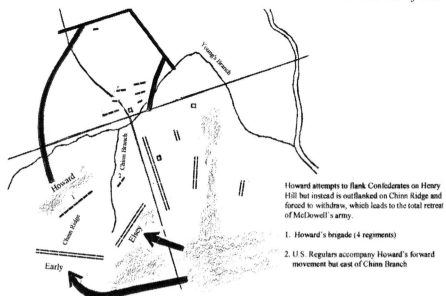

Howard attempts to flank Confederates on Henry Hill but instead is outflanked on Chinn Ridge and forced to withdraw, which leads to the total retreat of McDowell's army.

1. Howard's brigade (4 regiments)

2. U.S. Regulars accompany Howard's forward movement but east of Chinn Branch

STAGE THREE OF THE BATTLE OF BULL RUN:
CONFEDERATE VICTORY
(ca. 4:00 – 4:30 p.m.)

The rapid retreat of the Federals over the same routes they had used to arrive left the Confederates cheering but attempting only a disorderly pursuit. Stuart's small cavalry grabbed stragglers as Beauregard sent three regiments and a battery to cross the Stone Bridge to catch the fleeing enemy. The Confederates stopped at the Stone Bridge and waited for orders, allowing the fleeing mob to return to the turnpike east of Bull Run. There they were harassed by a makeshift battalion of cavalry that Johnston had sent across Lewis Ford. This renewed the alarming cries of "Black Horse Cavalry" heard earlier on the battlefield whenever horsemen appeared.[64] Belatedly, the pursuing force at the bridge moved eastward. Kemper's artillery fired upon the thousands of soldiers, dozens of civilian onlookers who never got near the battlefield, and myriad types of vehicles and wagons that jammed the turnpike and overflowed into the fields. All were hurrying toward the small Cub Run bridge. The first shot from Kemper's battery caused a wagon to turn over, blocking the bridge and causing panic for the first time during the retreat. In demoralizing terror, people ran through the creek, draft animals were cut free of their loads, and the wounded were removed from ambulances and placed on the sides of the roads. Hysteria produced an hour (6:00 to 7:00 P.M.) or so of pandemonium, as the entangled mass of people stampeded across Cub Run with some of their equipment.

While people fled to Centreville, it was critical for the Federals to keep Longstreet and Bonham at bay. The job was done by Richardson, who refused to comply with the orders of an intoxicated superior, Dixon S. Miles, to pull back to Centreville. Confederate pursuit was hindered as Ewell and Holmes' brigades were diverted by Johnston to McLean's Ford in response to reports, at 6:30 P.M., that a Federal force was attempting to cross southward toward Manassas. Beauregard, who led the counter-force, found D. R. Jones' Confederate brigade returning from a demonstration against Richardson and others on the Union left. Jones' men had been mistaken for an attacking Federal force. Soon this did not seem to matter as jubilation swept throughout the entire Confederate force; there were shouts of victory, caps thrown in the air, and officers cheering—from Beauregard on down. President Davis arrived on the scene and urged movement to Washington. But Johnston felt this would be unwise. He would later record that roads were muddied by heavy rains, and moving an exhausted army more "disorganized by victory than that of the United States by defeat," even toward the strong fortifications that covered the approach to Washington, was unfeasible.[65]

Washington became the sought-after haven for the fleeing Unionists. At midnight those on horseback and civilians in carriages arrived in the capital. All night long the president listened to stories of what had gone wrong. By morning, exhausted and begrimed soldiers started arriving with grim stories, and the city braced for the enemy's immediate attack. By noon on Tuesday, Long Bridge, across the Potomac to Washington, was blocked with wagons, and the cries of the wounded could be heard above all else.

Back at the battle site, where 18,000 men from each side had fought, was a sobering site. Four hundred eighty-one Union and 387 Confederates had lost their lives; 1,582 Northerners and 1,011 Southerners had sustained wounds, and some 1,200 Federals were missing, most of them prisoners of the Confederates.[66]

This had not been a model battle. Many would later agree with Sherman that it was one of "the best planned and worst fought" battles in history. The negatives included flawed execution of grand plans, officers' ineptitude, poor organization, confusion, delays, exhaustion of the men—with some "sun struck" and others falling victim to friendly fire—and the inappropriate habit of soldiers unaccustomed to being under fire of "firing and falling back" to reload. But these circumstances, along with intrepid fighting, bold leadership, and the rifle musket, with a range greater than the smooth-bore musket, were among the factors that made Bull Run, at that time, the largest and bloodiest battle in American history.[67]

The battlefield the night after the battle was a dismal place, wrote one of the Confederates with Jeb Stuart: "mournful sounds reached the ear from every direction—groans, sighs, prayers and curses, particularly the latter, with an occasional scream of pain from some poor fellow…. Occasionally a skulking figure could be seen passing noiselessly about the field, the vampires who infest all such places, men in search of plunder [from both friend and enemy]."[68] Suffering was intensified by a rain "that fell early the morning after the battle and continued for two days." A Southern officer who was riding over the wet field the day after the battle was moved by pitiful cries for water. He collected and filled canteens for the wounded Federals. He drew the line, however, at writing letters for the dying enemy, claiming that to do so for people who had left their friends to invade his land was "going a little too far."

The level of treatment of the unfortunates reflected unpreparedness, a shortage of surgeons, a lack of organization, and a shortage of ambulances. The wagons and conveyances that were used lacked springs, torturing the shattered bodies by bouncing them over rough roads and terrain. For a time there was also a food shortage. Physicians worked under trying circumstances. Some received praise for their efforts, not the least of whom were Federal doctors, who choose to stay with patients even at the risk of being captured.

The wounded were cared for in makeshift hospitals and aid stations, in dwellings, barns, outbuildings, and churches. Confederate wounded would eventually be taken over a wide area of Virginia, extending from Manassas Junction to Richmond and Lynchburg. But during and after the battle, prominent homes and structures like Portici and the Chinn house were used for the Confederate cause, as were the Stone House and Sudley church for the Union. The Sudley church received by far the greater number of Union wounded.

Between 200 and 300 men were brought there in wagons, from which blood trickled to the ground like melting ice, leaving a large puddle of blood near the entrance of the house of worship. Inside the church twenty-two would die while undergoing surgery.[69]

Those who witnessed the aftermath of the battle told of unforgettable sights. Surgeons left grim reminders of their work. Legs, feet, hands, and arms were thrown together, forming huge piles. "Many of the feet still retained the boot or shoe," reported one witness. Equally as gruesome, if not more so, was what greeted the eye on the battlefield. Bloated and blackened remains, covered with flies and emitting nauseous smells, were found in every conceivable position. Some were mangled, dismembered, disemboweled, or torn to pieces. Others tore up the earth in a final "death struggle," pulling up every "weed or blade of grass that was in their reach." "One poor fellow had died with his arms clasped around a small tree," wrote one witness. Another soldier "was found with his Bible opened upon his breast." Others grabbed "tightly around their muskets or such twigs or roots as were in their reach." A few were observed to have no wounds or marks. "Whether they died from sun stroke or from exhaustion or simple fright, it is impossible to say, though it was probably the first cause."

Burial took several days and was an unenviable task. One eyewitness recounted: "So intolerable was the stench arising from the dead...especially from the horse," that it compelled Southerners to suspend the burial of Federal remains. Reluctant Federal prisoners were forced to complete the tasks. The day after the battle, Confederate soldiers buried the elderly widow Judith Henry in front of her shattered house. Behind the house, in the orchard, two other Confederates buried a dear friend and a brother. There John O. Casler was digging a grave under an apple tree for his best friend, William I. Blue, when a Georgian approached and said he wanted to bury his brother. Casler was asked if he was burying his own brother. "No, but dear as a brother" was the response. Since both were without anyone else to help, the Georgian suggested, "suppose we dig the grave large enough for both, and we can help one another carry them here."

Casler replied, "All right, but I want to bury my friend next to the tree, for perhaps, his father will come after him." They "gathered up some old shingles to put over the bodies, and a piece of plank between them." Casler then carved Blue's name on the apple tree.

Less care was taken for most interments. Long trenches were dug, and bodies were thrown into gullies. Often twenty or thirty were interred together in one trench. Shallow graves were where most of the dead were buried; they were covered with dirt that soon sunk or washed away, exposing part of what the dirt had been meant to hide.[70]

The battle evoked the contradictory emotions of sadness and gladness. Both sides experienced the sorrow, but joy was reserved mainly for the victor. The South heaped praise upon her heroes. None was more deserving than Evans, and none, more underrated than Johnston. Some were heroes who had lost their lives, like Bee and Bartow. But no star shone as brightly as Beauregard's . Whatever his faults, he was inspired and unafraid in combat. During the battle he had a horse killed underneath him, and before the day was over, he had ridden three more horses, including one that had been captured from the Federals. Songs and marches were written in his honor. Babies, steamboats, racehorses, and feminine apparel were given his name.[71] But as illustrious as Beauregard's image was immediately after Manassas, his heroic status would diminish as the status of another hero, Thomas Jackson, would accelerate.

Jackson was a quiet, unpretentious, described by contemporaries as a "plain looking man," who, on the day of the battle, dressed in "a blue military coat, and wore the shoulder-straps of a colonel in the United States Army," although he was a brigadier-general. "His cap was of the old army pattern, in vogue during the Mexican War,—blue cloth, flat on top." He would emerge from the battle with not only a painful but not serious finger wound, "which he bound up in a handkerchief," but also the immortal nickname of Stonewall. The moniker came from Bee's reference to Jackson's position on Henry Hill. When, where, why, and even what Bee said is still being debated. Was his statement made in anger over Jackson's failure to support him on Matthews Hill? Was the reference to a stone wall about Jackson's men? According to a member of Bee's brigade, the statement was made simply to move, not to rally, the men to Jackson's position. Bee is said to have pointed toward the general and said, "Yonder stands Jackson like a stone wall. Let us go to his assistance." Even though the continually repeated quote of "Look! There is Jackson standing like a stone wall! Rally behind the Virginians" is not what Bee said, Jackson's sobriquet and his fame from this and other battles would be indelible.[72]

Praise was not widely given to the losing Federals, but blame was. Stunned Northerners thought the failure was caused by the inexperience of civilian soldiers and the incompetence of their officers, two hundred of whom soon sent in their resignations after the battle. Pessimism hung over the North. The press was brutally critical. The New York *Tribune* concluded, "all sense of manhood seemed to be forgotten...the sentiment of shame has gone.... All was lost to the American army even its honor."

Even General Scott was tainted by the failure, but it was General McDowell who became the scapegoat for the humiliating defeat in the eyes of Johnston and his former West Point classmate Beauregard. Charges of incompetence and drunkenness were leveled at him. But McDowell had been a victim of circumstance as well as ineptness. Patterson's failure to keep Johnston in the valley proved to be the most crucial factor in his defeat. Tyler's and Miles' actions had not helped. Many factors led to those crucial delays in the implementation of his turning movement: having inexperienced men and officers, including his own; having never before commanded a large number of men in combat; the fatigue of men who had been up since midnight before the battle; long marches; and heat. These delays allowed the Confederates to discover his movement and to respond. Good fortune had not smiled on the Federals—there were missed opportunities, such as Keyes' attack, and Griffin's artillery's flanking Jackson's left. In retrospection, McDowell's renewal of combat in the afternoon—by sending unprotected artillery to Henry Hill—looks foolish. It has been argued that he could not "deploy a proper line of battle" to "Henry Hill and regiments were sent in piecemeal." His army was "too confused" to respond properly, some said: "The most he could do was to trust to his brigadiers to deploy the men best they could." He nevertheless labored to do what he could to the bitter end. At Young's Branch, Centreville, and Fairfax Court House he tried to stop the "stream of fugitives" and later in "Arlington Heights worked to reorganize his broken army." But it was too late. There was a demand for change. Major-General George McClellan was immediately summoned to Washington to mend the military and morale of the North. Patterson and Tyler were soon mustered out.[73]

Two delays had been lethal to McDowell's efforts. The first, after the Blackburn fight, gave Johnston time to join Beauregard. The second, the midday lull in the Federals' pursuit on the day of the battle, gave the Confederates time to regroup. Joseph E. Johnston, McDowell's Confederate counterpart at Bull Run, gave a succinct and perceptive assessment of the Union general: "If tactics of the Federal had been equal to their strategy, we would have been defeated." Another writer concluded, "A curious thing about McDowell's enterprise at Bull Run is that one may fairly say that it was force ordained to failure, and yet conclude that it came within inches of success."[74]

[1] New York *Tribune,* May 26-27, and June 1, 1861; Benjamin F. Cooling III and Walton H. Owen II, *Mr. Lincoln's Forts* (Shippensburg, Pa.: White Mane, 1988), viii; Whittington, "Diary," 3-9.

[2] Chicago *Tribune*, May 30, 1861.

[3] On Lee Highway in northeastern Fairfax, near Fairfax Circle, in front of the White House Motel, stands an isolated and largely ignored gray marker. The inscription reads: "Peyton Anderson of the Rappahannock Cavalry was severely wounded 122 feet northeast of this spot [on] May 27, 1861. The first soldier of the South to shed his blood for the Confederacy." The marker was erected by the Fairfax chapter of the United Daughters of the Confederacy on May 27, 1917.

[4] *Fairfax County and the War between the States* (Vienna, Va.: Fairfax County Civil War Centennial Commission, 1961), 1; *SHSP*, vol. X, 368-69. Smith got the nickname "Extra Billy" for extra payments for the rapidly expanding mail route from Washington, D.C., to Georgia. He later served five years in the Virginia Senate and five terms in Congress. He was the governor of Virginia from 1846-49 and from January 1, 1864, to the end of the war. In his midsixties he fought in the Civil War and rose to the rank of Major-General (1863) in the Confederate army.

[5] The other picket, B. F. Florence, was captured by the Federals. Tompkins and his men had left Camp Union at Falls Church about 10:30 P.M. and came up the road that intersects with the Little River Turnpike, where the two Virginia pickets were located.

[6] None of the men had bayonets.

[7] After the war, a story circulated that Smith had gone into the fray without his boots. He had left them outside his bedroom for a servant to polish, but they hadn't been returned when the skirmish commenced.

[8] The turnpike sloped downward both east and west from the courthouse and hotel. The western slope was the more severe of the two, about a quarter-mile long. At the bottom of the latter slope was a small stream where the Federal cavalry regrouped for their second advance up the hill.

[9] Joseph A. Jeffries, "The Night Attack at Fairfax Court House," (unpublished account), Virginia Historical Society; *OR*, Ser. I, vol. 2, 59-64; *SHSP*, vol. X, 368-77; New York *Tribune*, June 2, 1861.

[10] *OR*, Ser. I, vol. 2, 59-60. The number of Union wounded is not given. Ewell wrote that he was told several Federals later died. This is not verified by Union reports. Tompkins reports having 51 men in his force; McDowell had the number at 75.

[11] In Northern papers, sketches of the skirmish based on Tompkins' reports are extremely inaccurate.

[12] *The World*, June 21, 1861.

[13] New York *Times*, May 31, June 2, 3, 4, 1861; New York *Tribune*, June 2, 1861; Richmond *Daily Enquirer*, June 3, 1861. Southern prisoners were taken to the Navy Yard. H. C. Haines, a member of the Virginia Governor Guard, arrived at Fairfax Station on June 1, 1861, after a train ride from Ashland. He was among several

Virginia cavalry companies at Fairfax Station responding to Ewell's call for reinforcements, but all arrived after the Federals had fled. Unlike the cavalry at the courthouse, each member of Haines' company was armed with a Sharps rifle, Colt pistol, and a saber. Haines and the other cavalry companies stayed at Fairfax Court House the night after the skirmish, remaining in the saddle all night in case the enemy returned. Haines wrote his father during the days immediately after the skirmish at the courthouse: "We feel perfectly safe though have to be vigilant as there are many abolitionists living in this neighborhood.... I wished you not [be] alarmed by the many rumors that are constantly put out." Haines' letter had to be carried home by a friend because by early June there was no mail service from the Fairfax Station area.

[14] Joseph A. Jeffries, "The Night Attack at Fairfax Court House;" *The Southern Magazine*, vol. 1, no. 4, September 1889; *OR*, Ser. I, vol. 1, 61-62; New York *Tribune*, June 2, 1861.

[15] *SHSP*, vol. X, 373. Rumors circulated that Marr had been mistakenly shot by his own men, but soon the common view emerged, also held by "Extra Billy" Smith, that Marr had been killed by a random Union shot.

[16] Marr was commissioned in early May 1861 as a lieutenant-colonel in the volunteer forces of Virginia. He was aware of the commission, but he never received it because it was mistakenly sent to Harpers Ferry. During the war, the document was "rescued from the letters remaining in the dead-letter office in Richmond."

[17] Eliz Nickens also supposedly bore children by other men. William Marr II, in a letter and report of his research on the Marr family sent to the Warrenton Public Library, points out that he was a "Negro, being part of that branch of the family started by John Quincy Marr" and his Indian mistress.

[18] In July 1906 the Richmond *Times-Dispatch* claimed that Memorial Day originated with Marr's funeral. A number of other towns, cities, and states also claim to have had the first memorial organization. Less valid is the untrue story published in the July 6, 1952, issue of the Richmond *Times-Dispatch* about the bullet that killed Marr. A flattened musket ball was sent to the Virginia Historical Society in 1952, along with a story claiming that it had been misshaped upon striking Marr. Marr's body servant, according to the tale, heard the bullet strike the brick walkway and saw his master die. Before daylight, the faithful servant buried Marr in a field near Fairfax Court House and planted a small cedar tree to mark the grave. When a stone marker was erected in Fairfax during the early twentieth century, the body servant pointed out Marr's grave, and several men dug up the remains. They found a flattened bullet and a "hat full of bones, with two boot heels, part of a brass belt buckle, several brass buttons." The men divided up the relics and buried the bones "beneath the monument." The only accurate part of this tale is the large stone monument to Marr erected near the front of the courthouse. It is inscribed: "This stone marks the scene of the opening conflict of the war of 1861-1865, when John Q. Marr, captain of the Warrenton Rifles, who was the first soldier killed in action, fell 800 feet South, 46 degrees West of the spot. June 1, 1861. Erected by Marr Camp, C.V., June 1, 1904." Today, what was formerly Fairfax

Court House is the center of Fairfax City. The Marr monument is little noticed by preoccupied pedestrians and motorists in a virtually continuous line of cars that often become gridlocked at rush hour. Cement and asphalt have covered up the dirt and grass around the hotel and courthouse. The courthouse was once the dominant structure in town, but is now dwarfed by additions and high-rise county office buildings. The hotel was torn down during the early 1930's. The wheelwright's place is now comprised of a parking lot, bank, and restaurant. The brick jail building remains, as do the Episcopal church and a number of other historic houses, but now they are set in a suburban rather than agrarian world. The clover field where Marr died is a parking lot.

[19] A skirmish denotes fighting on the smallest scale, involving troops other than those of the main force. When main bodies of men are engaged in fighting, the conflict is called a battle, the largest scale of combat. Second in size are engagements, which fall between a battle and a series of nebulous classification, including affairs and skirmishes. The criteria for these classifications are not spelled out. "Skirmish" implies an encounter between the skirmish lines of a small group of men, called skirmishers, in front of the main body, to protect it when it is in motion. A skirmish could be the opening stage of a larger conflict, such as a battle, when men are deployed in advance of the main force to draw the fire of the enemy to warn the larger body. A skirmish could also consist of incidental contact between detached forces a considerable distance from the main body.

[20] New York *Tribune*, June 2, 1861. Both skirmishes occurred at night on June 1, 1861. At Arlington Mills around 11:00 P.M. the Confederates fired one volley at a company of Michigan men and Company G of the Zouaves. Newspaper accounts claim that during the confusion, Michigan soldiers in the mill and Zouaves from the house fired at each other, as well as at the Virginians, who soon left. One Zouave was killed and another was wounded. Another press account tells of lawless Zouave behavior that included stealing money and terrorizing a family.

[21] The Union force under Brigadier-General Robert C. Schenck left camp for Vienna with 697 men, but he left 387 of his force to guard roads and railroad bridges between his camp and Vienna.

[22] *The World*, June 21, 1861. There were two trains that moved toward Vienna. The lead train was the one attacked. The second consisted of seven cars and was also hooked up with its engine facing east. It was nearly empty; the men had been detailed to guard duty along the track at select spots.

[23] Boston *Journal*, June 21, 1861.

[24] Washington *Star*, June 27, 1861. Lieutenant William H. Raynor was a member of Company G, First Regiment, Ohio Volunteer Militia.

[25] Boston *Journal*, June 21, 1861.

[26] Boston *Journal*, June 21, 1861; "Fairfax County and the War Between the States," 11; New York *Tribune*, June 19, 1861; *OR*, Ser. I, vol. 2, 124-30; Connie and Mayo Stuntz, *This was Vienna: Facts and Photos* (Vienna, Va.: C. P. Stuntz and M. S. Stuntz, 1987), 105-109. In an issue of *Frank Leslie's Illustrated Newspaper*, the action at Vienna incorrectly shows the Federals forming a line on an open bank of the railroad cut. The Ohio troops were disorganized and fled into the

woods. Today the combat site is in Vienna where the Northern Virginia Regional Park crosses Park Street. The railroad went out of business during the 1960's, and the tracks were torn up. The former rail right-of-way became a trail for hikers and bicyclists.

[27] *The World*, June 21, 1861.

[28] Long, *Civil War Day by Day*, 81. The Southern force and military district in northern Virginia were known by several names: Department of Alexandria, the Potomac Department, and the Army of the Potomac. Beauregard took command on June 2, 1861.

[29] John E. Cooke, *Wearing of the Gray* (Bloomington, Ind.: Indiana University, 1959), 72-77. Freeman, *Lee's Lieutenants*, vol. I, 6-7; T. Harry Williams, *P.G.T. Beauregard: Napoleon in Gray* (Baton Rouge, La.: Louisiana State University, 1965), 21. Johnson found Lew Wallace's raid into Romney on June 13 ominous, and he feared that McClellan's troops in western Virginia or Robert Patterson's force from the north could menace his own. After burning the railroad bridge at the ferry, he pulled a short distance north of Charles Town. In the meantime, Federals moved to the Edward's Ferry area in what was known as the Rockville Expedition. By mid-June, Colonel Charles P. Stone occupied two ferry crossings (Edward's and Conrad's), protecting the banks of the Potomac north and west of Washington.

[30] *OR*, Ser. I, vol. 2, 907.

[31] Ibid., Ser. I, vol. 2, 720, 721.

[32] R.M. Johnston, *Bull Run: Its Strategy and Tactics* (Boston: Houghton Mifflin, 1913), 29-89; *OR*, Ser. I, vol. 2, 720, 721. Sending reinforcements to Patterson "by drawing off wagons" was one of the factors in the delay.

[33] One of Greenhow's coded messages was concealed in the hair of beautiful Bettie Duval, who carried it to General M. L. Bonham at Fairfax Court House. It stated McDowell would advance on July 16.

[34] New Orleans *Picayune*, March 1, 1893; Williams, *Beauregard*, 69-77.

[35] William C. Davis, *Battle At Bull Run: A History of the First Major Campaign of the Civil War* (Baton Rouge, La.: Louisiana State University, 1981), 90-99.

[36] Except for the fording areas, the northern bank of Bull Run at Blacksburn's Ford was ten to fifteen feet above the water.

[37] James B. Fry, *McDowell and Tyler in the Campaign of Bull Run 1861* (New York: D. Van Nostrand, 1884), 20-21; John Hennessy, *The First Battle of Manassas* (Lynchburg, Va.: H.E. Howard, 1989), 17-23; Johnston, *Bull Run*, 131-36; James Longstreet, *From Manassas to Appomattox* (Philadelphia: J.B. Lippincott, 1896), 38-40; *OR*, Ser. I, vol. 2, 306, 312-321. Tyler failed to comply with the original order due to either a misunderstanding or his obstinacy.

[38] *OR*, Ser. I, vol. 2, 317.

[39] Both sides were concerned with possible enemy reinforcements: the Federals about Johnston and the Confederates about Patterson. Sounds of the moving trains from Manassas Junction prior to the battle and clouds of dust by Southern soldiers moving to Henry Hill were construed as evidence of Johnston's arrival. Beauregard had some anxious moments late in the battle when he at first feared that the approaching men of Early's brigade were the arrival on the field of Patterson.

[40] Alexander also sent a note to Beauregard about what he had seen.

[41] One of Imboden's last acts before withdrawing was to fire on Federals arriving at the Stone House (at the intersection of Sudley Road and the turnpike), forcing the Twenty-seventh New York to move left. Here another incident of confusion over uniforms and identity occurred. Before firing, Colonel Henry Warner Slocum attempted to get Hampton's gray-clad men to identify themselves (instead he saw the Confederate flag.) As Imboden's battered battery was forced from the field, he vented his frustration over being left too long in an exposed position. With Imboden's withdrawal Hampton's left was exposed.

[42] McDowell had a prodigious appetite and is known to have eaten a whole watermelon after a large meal.

[43] While at Mitchell's Ford, Johnston became increasingly concerned as the sound of battle on his left increased. Finally, around 11:30, he yelled that he was going there. Beauregard soon followed him

[44] *B & L*, vol. I, 210; William M. Owen, *In Camp and Battle with the Washington Artillery of New Orleans* (Boston: Ticknor & Company, 1885), 38.

[45] Hennessy, *The First Battle of Manassas*, 74-77.

[46] Roberdeau Wheat has traditionally been considered the rider, but it has been argued that the rider could have been a Confederate cavalryman from William Terry's squad.

[47] Tyler left Robert C. Schenck and his brigade back at the Stone Bridge. Keyes passed behind the Van Pelt house, crossing Young's Branch, brushing away Confederate cavalry, and then ascending to the high ground across from the Robinson house.

[48] Charles L. Dufour, *Gentle Tiger*, (Baton Rouge, La.: Louisiana State University, 1957), 134-35; Hennessy, *The First Battle of Manassas*, 64-67; *O.R.*, Ser. I, vol. 2, 353, 369; Williams, *Beauregard*, 85. Once again confusion existed over identification of the troops as Keyes—when first approaching the gray-clad men around the Robinson house—was unsure if they were friend or foe.

[49] The other regiments were the Fourteenth New York, U.S. Marine Battalion, and the First Minnesota.

[50] Several members of her family and a young black lady who cared for the elderly women were caught by surprise when the battle started in the morning; they tried to escape to a neighbor's house by carrying Judith out of the house on a mattress. At Mrs. Henry's pleading, they returned to the house as Federals crossed the turnpike and the firing increased.

[51] Heintzelman contends that Cummings' men wore civilian clothing.

[52] The marines behind the battery also fled.

[53] Hennessy, *The First Battle of Manassas*, 79-86; *Joint Committee on the Conduct of the War*, vol. II, 168-73; *OR*, Ser. I, vol. 2, 345, 347-48; Williams, *Beauregard*, 84-85.

[54] The three remaining pieces of Griffin's battery north of Henry House had been removed by the Federals

[55] Jackson was joined by other units. On his left was the Sixth North Carolina, who fell back from the fire of Federals in the woods on their left.

[56] Old Bory was busily gathering men to send forward, giving them words of encouragement, including, "Give them the bayonet."

[57] Bartow, Bee, and Johnston were fighting remnants of the First Michigan, Eleventh New York, and Fourteenth Brooklyn.

[58] Hennessy, *The First Battle of Manassas*, 98-104; *Joint Committee of the Conduct of the War*, vol. II, 214-416; *OR*, Ser. I, vol. 2, 369-70, 567; John N. Opie, *A Rebel Cavalryman with Lee, Stuart and Jackson* (Chicago: W.B. Conkey, 1899), 32. Sherman first sent the Thirteenth New York near Imobeden's morning position, followed by the Second Wisconsin, who had the misfortune of being fired on by the Sixty-ninth and Seventy-ninth New York. The third regiment was the Seventy-ninth New York.

[59] The Eighth and Eighteenth Virginia came from Cocke's brigade and were supported by the recently arrived Lynchburg Artillery. The Thirteenth, Thirty-eighth, and Sixty-ninth New York fled down Henry Hill toward the Stone House without putting up a fight.

[60] The minimum size of a company was sixty-four privates; maximum, eighty-two privates. The maximum number of officers and men was 101.

[61] E. Kirby Smith brigade had not arrived in time from the valley so he commanded Elzey's brigade. Smith was wounded so the brigade reverted back to Elzey.

[62] Kady C. Brownell, Invalid Claim for Pension, July 7, 1884, National Archives; Sylvia G. L. Dannett, *She Rode with the Generals* (New York: T. Nelson, 1960), 64-78; Mary E. Massey, *Bonnet Brigades* (New York: Knopf, 1966), 69-70; Frank Moore, *Women of the War* (Chicago: R. C. Treat, 1866), 55-57; Agatha Young, *The Women and the Crisis* (New York: McDowell, Obolensky, 1959), 118-125. Brownell did not fight, but came under fire. She had participated in marksmanship drills before the battle and was designated "regimental daughter" by General Burnside. Several other women also claimed to have been on the battlefield. Among them was Sara Emma Edmunds (S. Emma E. Edmonds [pseudonym]) in her book *Nurse and Spy in the Union Army* (Philadelphia: W. S. Williams, 1865), 33-34. She later acknowledged exaggerating her activities. It was also difficult to verify the claim that Anna Etheridge, of Michigan, accompanied her husband to Blackford's Ford.

[63] The force Beauregard sent to Stone Bridge was Joseph B. Kershaw's Second South Carolina, and E. B. C. Cash's Eighth South Carolina, and Kemper's battery. The battalion of cavalry was sent by Johnston across Lewis Ford was under R. C. W. Radford.

[64] *B & L*, I, 252; Johnston, *Bull Run*, 233-44; Hennessy, *The First Battle of Manassas*, 115-23; *Joint Committee on the Conduct of the War*, vol. II, 216-17.

[65] McDowell lost twenty-seven artillery pieces.

[66] The Federals frequently named their battles after prominent geographical features; thus, the fighting on July 21, 1861, was called the Battle of Bull Run. Confederates liked to use the name of the nearest village, town, or city, so they referred to this fight as the Battle of Manassas.

[67] Blackford, *War Years with Jeb Stuart*, 42. Most of the Confederate wounded had been removed from the field.

[68] The overflow of wounded at Sudley Church were placed in nearby buildings and under trees. In addition to amputations, the primary treatment was the application of "water dressing." Mortally wounded Colonel John S. Slocum (Second Rhode Island) was first treated at the Stone House, then carried on a door to an ambulance and taken to Sudley Church. The Federal wounded at Sudley and elsewhere primarily suffered from wounds inflicted by the round ball fired from Confederate muskets. Conversely, the Confederates suffered from conically shaped so-called minnie ball from Federal rifle-muskets. Union dead were also buried near Sudley Church.

[69] Atlanta *Southern Confederacy*, August 17, 1861; Joseph K. Barnes, *The Medical and Surgical History of the War of Rebellion* (Washington: Government Printing Office, 1861-1865), pt. I, appendix 1-10; John O. Casler, *Four Years in the Stonewall Brigade* (Gerard, Kans.: Appeal, 1906), 30-33; Horace H. Cunningham, *Field Medical Services at the Battles of Manassas* (Athens, Ga.: University of Georgia, 1968), 15-37; Opie, *A Rebel Cavalryman*, 38-41. Letter from Daniel McCook, August 10, 1861; Paper of the McCook Family; Box 1, General Correspondence 1838-1875, Folder 1860-1861, Library of Congress.

[70] Williams, *Beauregard*, 91-92.

[71] Owen, *In Camp and Battle*, 41.

[72] Freeman, *Lee's Lieutenants*, vol. I, 733-34; Hennessy, *The First Battle of Manassas*, 152, and his unpublished manuscript "Jackson's Stone Wall: Fact or Fiction"; James I. Robertson Jr., *Stonewall Jackson*, 835-36; *SHSP*, vol. 19, 166.

[73] Both received new commissions in 1862.

[74] Joseph E. Johnston, *Narrative of Military Operations* (New York: D. Appleton, 1874), 57; R.M. Johnston, *Bull Run*, 269, 273-75.

CHAPTER III

THE PICKET WAR: WATCHING, WAITING, PROBING, AND POSTURING

For troops along the Potomac and in northern Virginia, the second half of 1861 was a time of military posturing and probing: picket war. Yanks and Rebs watched each other across the Potomac and exchanged sporadic shots. Confederates in northern Virginia moved their advance positions a dozen or so miles nearer to Washington for a stay of several months before pulling back to their original positions. Each side talked about major advances, but instead settled for numerous reconnaissances that led to frequent skirmishes and two small battles at Ball's Bluff and Dranesville. The probing activities were supplemented with military reviews—a safer way to flex military muscle.

Cautious military leadership and the continuing demands of army building limited military activity and overrode the ceaseless demands by the press, politicians, and some military leaders for more vigorous action. Doubts about Federal forces around Washington after the first major battle of the war plagued the new Union commander, George McClellan. Threats of mutinies, insubordination, and lack of military discipline and efficiency made him wary of taking on a foe who, he believed, greatly outnumbered his own forces. McClellan's counterpart, Joe Johnston, likewise hesitated to commit his Confederates to a major offensive.

PLANS, MUTINY, AND REORGANIZATION

The major proponent of vigorous Confederate offensive action was Beauregard. Since the Battle of Manassas he had been yearning for offensive action that would allow him to liberate Maryland and occupy Washington. [1]

He was annoyed by inaction, by not being appointed to head the northern Virginia forces, by the rejection of his proposals by the Richmond authorities, and by feuding with the president and secretary of war. Beauregard would later gladly transfer to the western theater.

The exception to Beauregard's rocky dealings with his superiors was his relationship with the cautious Johnston. Both men liked each other on a personal level, and Johnston often let Beauregard have his way. Early in August he reluctantly succumbed to Beauregard's persuading to undertake a forward movement. The Confederates had remained along the Bull Run line and occupied Centreville. Beauregard now moved his brigades to Fairfax Court House and other advanced positions. His advanced contingent went to heights near the southern banks of the Potomac, where they could see the gleaming white but unfinished dome of the Federal Capitol. Beauregard, the "Creole in Gray," wanted to harass the Federals and take offensive action or at least lure the enemy into battle on a site favorable to him. Johnston feared Beauregard had moved too close to the enemy, and he wanted to pull back. Beauregard talked Johnston into letting him stay, but when he proposed that all the Confederate forces be moved forward to Fairfax Court House to launch an offensive against the enemy, Johnston vetoed the idea. The army lacked the manpower, he said, to take the offensive action so near to enemy lines.

Still undaunted, Beauregard proposed a new and more ambitious plan. They would ask the government for 40,000 to 60,000 additional soldiers. This would enable Johnston and Beauregard to cross the Potomac into Maryland behind Washington, giving the Federals no choice but to fight them in the open. Johnston, convinced by Beauregard that the longer they waited the stronger the Federals would become, wrote to the Confederate President, Jefferson Davis, requesting that either the president or the secretary of war come to

Fairfax Court House to discuss the matter. The president arrived on September 30, stayed for two days, reviewed the Confederate forces, and on or about October 1 discussed the matter of offensive action with Generals Johnston, Beauregard, and a close friend of both, Major-General G. W. Smith. Davis told them that the additional forces could not be raised and armed, and he could not pull troops from other parts of the Confederacy. Instead Davis proposed sending small forces to make surprised and limited attacks on the enemy. This was not enthusiastically received by the generals, and the matter was dropped. So ended the "Council of War" and the movement for offensive action. The meeting was the disappointing culmination of Beauregard's work for offensive action. Disgusted by the results, Beauregard asked to be transferred to New Orleans, but Davis said he was too valuable in Virginia. Old Bory also found little to cheer about in mid-October, when Johnston pulled back to the Centreville line.[2]

The new commander of the Union Army of the Potomac, George McClellan, fresh from his western Virginia triumphs, grappled with the enormous task of reorganizing a defeated army on what his biographers have called the European model while first making sure that his army and the capital were secure from enemy attack. Countless hours of overworking and delaying or forgoing meals took a toll on his health. He suffered from the additional self-imposed stress that came from assuming that he alone would have to save the Union. Key government officials were considered impediments to his efforts. Lincoln—whom McClellan privately called the "original gorilla"—invited him to cabinet meetings, which bored McClellan and wasted his time. In letters to his wife, he referred to the high-ranking government officials in attendance at these meetings as "some of the greatest geese...I have ever seen," men who would try the "patience of Job." He did not appreciate the president's informal, unexpected visits to headquarters. According to McClellan, Lincoln had no particular point to make or topics to discuss, although he did respond to any subject that arose with pertinent and amusing anecdotes.

Despite McClellan's sense of annoyance, the relationship between the commander and the president was friendly in the early stages.[3] This belied the fact that McClellan confused the president's informal camp visits and chats at headquarters with weakness and ineptitude. He was unappreciative or unaware that the president's visits were his way of seeking information and reassurance about military efforts to save the Union. But McClellan felt hindered not only by an incompetent president and the head of a government in crisis, but also by Scott, his immediate superior. He considered Scott a frustrating impediment to the reorganization of the army, and believed the old general had failed to realize the dangers of an imminent Confederate attack. On August 6, McClellan had a long talk with Secretary of State Seward about the hindrance of Scott, stating, "How does he [Lincoln] think that I can save the country when clogged by General Scott?" McClellan added, "I don't know whether Scott is a dotard or a traitor! I can't tell which."[4]

McClellan's proclivity toward secrecy about his plans and lack of confidence in the government was no doubt fueled in part by the retention of many southern sympathizers in the government's departments and Federal camps. The latter problem was shown in an October New York *Tribune* headline: "Traitors in Camp." The paper claimed that several officers "prominent in the volunteer service are suspected of giving information of our movements to the enemy." The article continued, "A New York Colonel, now under arrest for insubordination, is one of the number."[5] The House of Representatives was so concerned about disloyalty in the government that it appointed a Select Committee on Loyalty of Government Clerks. It was chaired by a belligerent Wisconsin Republican, John F. Potter.

Potter's group, which was referred to in the press as "The Treason Investigating Committee," became an agency for receiving secret accusations, every whisper and bit of gossip about disloyalty, well founded or not. Government offices clerks feared for their jobs, spied, and tattled on others. Hearing 550 accusations kept Potter's committee meeting every day from July 8 through October 9. Five hundred witnesses were examined—many of them more than once. Their condensed answers produced over 500 pages of testimony. The committee's first report gave the names of 231 government workers "against whom evidence of treason or disloyalty was present." A second report contained the names of 235 more disloyals. The publication stated the names of witnesses and a summary of charges indicating unfaithfulness. A number of the "talebearers" hurried out of town to avoid facing those they had testified against; one witness was beaten near the Capitol.

The House and its committee created a commotion, but Southern sympathizers were treated leniently. Many identified by Potter's committee denied the accusations—some of which no doubt, were untrue—and remained in their positions. The War Department mail bag, which hung in the hall, was used freely by Confederate sympathizers to send information to Richmond.[6] Such circumstances did not create confidence in the government.

McClellan's administrative acumen was constantly challenged by the flow of regiments arriving by rail. With the new arrivals came their idealized vision of army life. Their view of military service did not include discipline or obedience; officers and their men clashed. When one private refused to perform his duty, his officer summarily shot him. A Private Lanahan of the Forty-sixth Pennsylvania killed his major, a man named Lewis, because of a dispute. Lanahan was tried, found guilty, and shot.[7]

A less-grave symptom of the lack of uniformity was the matter of military clothing. One Washington correspondent noted on October 1, "I have not seen a single regiment, company, platoon, or squad, uniformly and fully dressed."

The press, along with politicians, was demanding offensive action and redemption from the earlier defeat at Bull Run. Papers chided the government and military officials and argued with each other over the appropriate military action. An editorial feud between two New York papers, the *Tribune* and the *Times,* was such a dispute. The *Tribune* said that the editor of the *Times,* "made itself rather ridiculous by knowing so much more than Gen. Scott or anybody else about the details of military strategy, and pointing out the precise path over which the advance of the army should take place." The *Tribune* retaliated by printing, "The New York *Times* is a good deal bothered with a foolish menace or prediction once more through its editorial columns that President Lincoln would be superseded if he did not show more vigor in prosecuting the war."[8]

All these factors were enormous pressures for Lincoln, McClellan, or anyone to endure. First and foremost, McClellan had to shape up the army to make sure it and Washington were secure from enemy attacks. He approved plans for the construction of forty-eight forts to defend the Union's capital city.[9] Confidence increased and order would improve soon when McClellan assumed command. But serious problems remained. There was still a lack of discipline, and men pursued the vices of "drinking and whoring," plundering, and threatening to mutiny. Some observed that if those in uniform pursued the enemy with the same vigor and single-mindedness as they did prostitutes, liquor, and plundering, it would be a short war. Instead the men were preoccupied with sex, hard drink, and taking anything not nailed down—and often, nails did not stop them. As soon as they received their wages, many men exchanged their money for liquor. The result was, according to the New York *Tribune,* "scenes of disgraceful drunkenness along the roads leading from Arlington to Alexandria."[10]

Under McClellan's direction, sixty-two noncommissioned officers and privates of the Second Maine Volunteers were considered to have displayed "insubordination, if not open mutiny," and were arrested and shipped off to the Dry Tortugas. There they were to perform fatigue duty until they proved themselves "worthy to bear arms." The offenders had audaciously, defiantly—and in the presence of their regiment—refused to "do any further duty," claiming that their "term of service had expired." The same day as he ordered this arrest, August 14, McClellan dealt with a potentially graver problem. The brigade commander of the 179th New York Volunteers reported that the regiment was "in a state of open mutiny." McClellan ordered the Provost Marshal, General Andrew Porter, to take a battery of artillery, two cavalry companies, and as many infantry companies as needed to the troubled camp. There he was to isolate the troublemakers by ordering those willing to obey orders to leave camp. Porter was to order the remaining men to lay down their arms and be placed under a strong guard. The "ringleaders" were to be placed in double irons. The provost marshal was authorized to use force, if necessary, to carry out McClellan's orders.

Apparently, the men of the 179th New York mended their ways. On August 20, less than a week after McClellan had to deal with the Maine and New York troops, he notified the provost marshal to be ready to move with artillery, cavalry, and infantry at a moment's notice to put "down a mutiny in Colonel Baker's California Regiment." Porter was told, "Should any portion of that regiment mutiny (and there is now some reason to suppose that they will) use the necessary force to quell it." McClellan continued: "[if] they refuse to obey, you are authorized to fire on them."[11] McClellan prevailed. There was no widespread mutiny, and order was restored.

A masterful organizer, McClellan did an exemplary job of whipping what some have called a mob into a well-organized and well-supplied army while gaining the respect and devotion of his men. Incompetent officers also needed to be weeded out. By the end of September, many volunteer officers were summoned to appear before the Board of Examiners, organized on September 26. The *Tribune* reported, "The stampede of the incapable has begun. Two colonels and twenty-five of the commissioned officers in General McCall's Division, and several from other divisions have resigned in anticipation of a call before the dreaded Board. It is believed that many will be discharged for incompetency."[12]

McClellan responded to renewed cries by the press and politicians for action against the enemy with caution. His carefulness was spawned not only from his mindful nature, but also from unsettling reports from the new head of the secret service, Allen Pinkerton, (alias E. J. Allen). Pinkerton reported—inaccurately—that the Federals were facing an enemy twice their numbers and that the enemy was poised to attack at any moment.[13] Not wishing to be hurried into action, after a cabinet meeting he was obliged to attend and which bored him, McClellan said to Lincoln, "I intend to be careful, and do as well as possible. Don't let them hurry me is all I ask." The president assured McClellan he would be given his way.[14]

SUBSTITUTES FOR BATTLE

McClellan's cautious approach included sending forces that varied in size from just one company to whole regiments and brigades against advanced enemy positions to engage in limited skirmishing. He hoped this would reverse some of the stigma of Bull Run and lessen the cries of "On to Richmond." Where the troops were not divided by water, they probed the enemy with reconnaissance, resulting in an occasional skirmish. Where they were separated by the water, the pickets who were scattered from Great Falls to Harpers Ferry frequently fired at each other, and occasional artillery fire was exchanged near crossing points. Islands in the middle of the Potomac were often occupied in an attempt to gain a tactical advantage, while the high command of both sides debated among themselves what was the proper level of aggressiveness.

From August through December, Federal sallies and scouting took place, and, combined with the Confederates' caution under General Johnston, meant that there was limited combat in northern Virginia and along the banks of the Potomac. Two and a half dozen clashes took place during that time. All were skirmishes, except for one action and two small battles. The probing that escalated into the largest confrontations of the period, at Ball's Bluff, on October 21, and at Dranesville, on December 20, would receive extensive press coverage. Ball's Bluff would have repercussions far greater than usual for a conflict so small.[15]

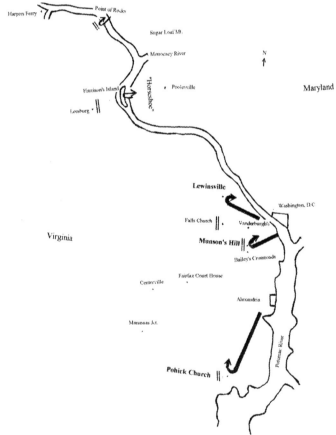

MAJOR AREAS OF THE PICKET WAR AFTER BULL RUN:
UNION PROBING OF ADVANCED CONFEDERATE POSITIONS

POHICK CHURCH, LEWINSVILLE AND MUNSON'S HILL

Although Union forces kept a vigilant watch, and numerous minor exchanges took place along the seventy- to eighty-mile line stretching from the Occoquan River and Pohick Church to Harpers Ferry, the primary concern after Bull Run was in select areas on the Potomac and in northern Virginia. Federal reconnaissance on the Potomac focused on the area the Union called the horseshoe, a large bend in the river near Edward's and Conrad's Ferries and Harrison Island. In northern Virginia to the west and south of Alexandria and Washington, Lewinsville, Bailey's Crossroads, and Pohick Church were the focal points of Union probes. Lewinsville's appeal lay in five roads that intersected and connected two of the three major turnpikes in northern Virginia.

James Longstreet's brigade, with its one artillery battery, and the cavalry under Jeb Stuart protected the line from Falls Church to Munson's Hill and Mason's Hill. To compensate for the shortage of artillery pieces, Confederates formed what they called "stove pipe batteries." Men mounted stovepipes of varying caliber onto wagon wheels. Like the logs that formed "Quaker guns," they looked formidable—from a distance.

Longstreet's position, as he stated, was "provokingly near Washington," but he had specific orders not to advance, even to Alexandria. Longstreet recounted:

> We had frequent little brushes with enemy parties pushed out to reconnoiter, but nevertheless we were neither so busy nor so hostile as to prevent the reception of a cordial invitation to a dinner-party on the other side, to be given to me at the headquarters of General Richardson. He was disappointed when I refused to accept this amenity, and advised him to be more careful lest the politicians should have him arrested for giving aid and comfort to the enemy. He was a singularly devoted friend and admirer before the war and had not ceased to be conscious of old-time ties.[16]

Confederates also kept small forces in the area of Pohick Church, about ten miles south of Alexandria. It was of special interest to the Confederates because Old Ox Road and Pohick Road ran northeast to Centreville and Fairfax Court House. These byways could be used by the Federals to flank or turn their advanced forces. The Federals had no desire to attempt such a move; their reconnaissance to the area had proved embarrassing. It had become far too common that military orders to probe sites did not always go according to plan.

Although McClellan had suppressed the threats of mutiny by the end of August, it took much longer to achieve efficiency and discipline. During the summer and fall, all Union forays from Alexandria to Pohick Church failed to capture their targeted enemy. A frustrated General Slocum lamented after a failed mission in which 300 infantrymen failed to follow his orders or capture fifty of the enemy: "More annoying and disgraceful to my command is the fact that instead of being marched back to camp in good order, a large part of the command was disbanded beyond our line of pickets, and as might have been anticipated from such a proceeding, this force sent to operate against the troops of the enemy was converted into a band of marauders, who plundered alike friend and foe."[17] At times Federal troops who were scattered on roads on reconnaissance missions were a far greater threat to themselves and civilians than to the enemy.

Later, Federals returned to the Pohick Church area to quell Confederate firing on Union pickets, supposedly by 400 enemy cavalrymen and a couple of infantry regiments. General S. P. Heintzelman was authorized to take two brigades, artillery, and two companies of the Lincoln cavalry to remove the enemy. After they could not find their opponents, the command was ordered back to camp. Longstreet wrote that three wayward soldiers, two of whom were wounded by people they robbed, returned with "plunder strapped on their horses consisting of a side saddle, bedclothes," and other items. Returning infantry regiments were often not models of proper behavior. A captain on the way back to camp "found the whole road scattered with soldiers from different regiments hollering and shooting." Musket balls came over "the heads of his men, and reached their own camp," where one horse of his company was wounded.[18]

Federal probes at Lewinsville engaged the enemy on occasion, but overall they were no more successful than in the Pohick area. On September 12, Brigadier-General William F. Smith sent a 2,000-man reconnaissance force from Chain Bridge to Lewinsville, resulting in fairly intense artillery exchange. Jeb Stuart led the Confederate force; his actions against the Union movement were intrepid and effective.

From his headquarters at Munson Hill, Stuart moved his force of fewer than 500 men toward Lewinsville. Before arriving there, he learned from his cavalry pickets that the enemy was already at that site in large force.[19] Stuart made sure he had a way of retreating, and, using the woods surrounding the town as a screen, he sent out about 100 skirmishers while his artillery surprised "a cluster of the enemy a quarter of a mile away sending the enemy in full retreat," claimed the Charleston *Daily Courier.*

According to Stuart, the Federals rallied a mile and a half away, where their artillery fired "round after round" at a position "up the road where they supposed Confederate columns would be pursuing them." Hidden by the woods, Stuart's small force of infantry and artillery did not openly reveal itself during most of the conflict. They moved from one location to another to give the illusion both of firing from many directions and of a much larger force. One of the participants recorded that some of the Confederates were "yelling like so many devils, firing as they ran, each trying to get ahead of the rest," did charge a portion of the enemy infantry who occupied a house and adjacent fields 1,000 yards away. Some of the Yankees scattered, but another group appeared on the left in an attempt to flank the Confederate infantrymen. A howitzer of the Washington artillery was sent to support the Southerners, and after several shots, the new group of Northerners disappeared. The Confederates entered a house and captured a Union officer and four privates. They paroled a parson and freed four frightened ladies hiding in the basement. The Charleston *Daily Courier* reported that one of the prisoners was asked, "What was the general impression in the Northern Army concerning our forces here?" He replied, "Well, we know you've got ninety thousand right around here; as to how many elsewhere, we have no idea."[20]

The contest was dominated by artillery. By using the elements of surprise and partial concealment, Stuart's four guns got the upper hand over eight Federal pieces. A hundred shots from Southern guns plowed up the road that Federals occupied, leaving it littered "thick with fragments of shell, and strewn with canteens, haversacks and a few muskets and two Union dead," according to the *Daily Courier.*[21]

Both sides claimed victory in the nonconclusive exchange of fire. Both bragged how well their men had behaved under fire. A Southern officer at the scene called the event "one of the most successful and creditable achievements which has thus been recorded during the present war." The reaction to Federal troops standing their ground—and not running—under fire was one of jubilation. Colonel Isaac I. Stevens, who would later die in the battle of Chantilly, called the operations of September 11 "a beautiful specimen of a reconnaissance in presence of the enemy." McClellan reported to Winfield Scott that the men "behaved most admirably under fire." "We shall have no more Bull Run affairs," he assured Scott. McClellan was especially pleased that his men had not panicked and run. He was pleased with the Seventy-ninth New York, who, less than a month earlier, had been thought of as mutinous. As these men returned to camp, they saw their commanding general waiting to greet them. He was cheered by the men, and then he visited the wounded, telling one of the mortally injured, "I was mistaken in you, you are brave men." As a reward for their good behavior under fire, McClellan returned their regiment's flag.[22]

On the other side, Joe Johnston sent congratulatory orders to his men for having turned back the enemy. Colonel Jeb Stuart was singled out for boldness and skill; Johnston recommended creating a cavalry brigade and "putting Stuart at its head." Brigadier General James Longstreet, Stuart's immediate commander, who was camped at Falls Church, felt Stuart had "fairly won his claim to brigadier," and recommended such a promotion.[23]

The extensive adulation belied the fact that except for limited infantry fire and the more extensive two-hour artillery exchange from batteries often 2,800 yards apart, much of what had been done—especially by the Federals—was military posturing. Most of the artillery shells sailed over the heads of their targets. Confederates had defective fuses, unreliable case shot, and shells that failed to explode. Casualties were light. Two Federals were killed, three were wounded, and four were captured. Not one Confederate was hurt, and not one of their horses received a scratch. The action in the overall picture of the war was, as Union Lieutenant Colonel Isaac J. Wistar labeled it, a "trifling movement." Captain Charles Griffin, who commanded a Union battery on a high ridge of ground, received the hottest enemy fire, becoming, said Wistar, "[so crowded with] infantry colonels and field officers anxious to get under fire for the first time, that they had to be requested to move away."

The Federals' effort was not without reward; during the action, Federal pickets brought in a small New York newsboy, still carrying his bundle of Northern newspapers, was brought in by Federal pickets. The lad of not more than twelve years explained that for many days he had "been alternately peddling through both armies without molestation from either."[24]

After Lewinsville, nervous Washingtonians who believed they were under attack breathed a temporary sigh of relief. During the skirmish, Federal troops were practicing at Fort Runyon, and at the Navy Yard, they were giving a salute to Pennsylvania Governor Andrew Curtin. This made it seem as if the city was surrounded and under attack. Those practicing artillery firing and saluting were telegraphed to stop once authorities learned of the skirmish.

The Federals also paid attention to the Confederates who were dug in at Munson's Hill, seven miles southeast of Lewinsville and only six miles from the Union Capitol. From its unfinished dome, the Confederate earthworks and flag could be seen. The imposing and beautiful view was a magnet for visitors. Apparently whoever wished to do so could ascend to the unfinished dome; a reporter for the Baltimore *Sun* went to take a look twice in one September week. He observed encampments across the river that had been "materially augmented during the past week as well as on a clear day Munson's Hill was in full range of the naked eye." Within two miles of Munson's Hill were Union encampments, and beyond the farthest one rose "dense columns of dark blue smoke, caused from the burning of brush and underwood." A good number of people standing on top of the Capitol thought this smoke indicated battle, but they heard no sounds of cannon or musketry.

An old soldier who had been in battle set the onlookers straight. This was no fight, he informed them, as the smoke from gunpowder rising over a battlefield "was a paler cast; almost white." The onlookers, along with many other Washingtonians, believed that a "decisive conflict" was not "many days distant." Another commentator contended, "Panic making seems to be a favorite vocation, and the most preposterous reports are readily believed and circulated."[25]

Southern troop movement to Munson's Hill had created trepidation among the inhabitants of Washington. News on August 20, 1861, that 15,000 Confederates were advancing from Fairfax Court House convinced both military and civilian inhabitants that the city was in danger of imminent attack. Families by the hundreds fled from the city. Military guards were doubled, weapons were checked, and soldiers were ordered to sleep in their clothes with their muskets by their sides.

Washingtonians thought that something needed to be done to get rid of the enemy that was so near at Munson's Hill. A New York *Tribune* correspondent complained:

> Everybody reads about it and everybody talks about it; and just because everybody is in doubt as to its exact position and importance, it is invested with a greater interest than it had really any right to claim. Few people, even in Washington, knew where Munson's Hill is and since the granting of passes has become so exceptional, the curious public is forced to remain still anxious and doubting...It is certainly the choicest conversational subject now afloat. So constantly does it occupy the public attention, that there is talk in an enterprising restaurant of fabricating a novel and dulcet compound, both cheering and inebriating, which shall receive no other title than 'Munson's.[26]

For soldiers in the eastern corridor in 1861, these were days of what one observer called "great anxious waiting and listening for the roar of the long expected battle." The Union soldier saw Beauregard's advance as a move to cross the Potomac into Maryland. Confederate reconnaissance toward Chain Bridge, and firing of Confederate artillery from Munson's Hill caused Washingtonians to believe that the Southerners were attacking their city.

Federals continued to probe the Munson's Hill area by air and land in an attempt to determine if the big enemy attack was near. Endeavoring to find out what the Confederates were doing, Professor Lowe, who was two and a half miles away at Ball's Crossroads, ascended in his balloon. It was attached to a 1,000-foot rope that ran through a pulley fastened to a tree, with a reported "down pulling power of thirty men." A guard of riflemen scouted the woods while the balloon ascended. Before he was fired upon by T. L. Rosser's four guns and immediately drawn down, Lowe claimed to have observed several guns in place and about 1,000 of the enemy working on entrenchments.[27]

By the end of August the Union sent about 300 infantry, twenty cavalry and some artillery to Bailey's Crossroads, just a mile south of the Confederates under Colonel Jeb Stuart, who were dug in at Munson's Hill on the Leesburg and Alexandria turnpike. This touched off days of skirmishing. Occasionally men were shot, and some were killed—one was accidentally shot by his own comrade. A half-dozen or so casualties were suffered before both sides withdrew to their former positions. The Confederate skirmishers went back to Munson's Hill, and the Federals headed several miles east to Arlington Mills.

The heaviest skirmishing was from August 28 to September 2 and was fought in corn fields, thickets of pines, behind and along fences, and roads usually separated by an open field. The exchange of gunfire often started in the morning and frequently lasted after dark; in one incident, gunfire continued as late as 10:00 P.M.[28] Those hidden by trees and underbrush had limited visibility, and on windy days, the rustling of leaves and brush kept the men nervous and fatigued, as they watched to make sure that what they heard was not the enemy. At night both sides' pickets were pulled back. Mosquitoes then replaced soldiers as the enemy and attacked with vigor, preventing and interrupting the sleep of weary men already beset by grime and dirt and soaked to the skin by summer rains. When Union pickets were not on duty during the day, the few structures at Bailey's Crossroads, a church and three or four nearby houses, provided sanctuary for the pickets. The cemetery behind the house of worship was a relatively safe staging area. Inside the church the walls were covered with graffiti. Interspersed among ludicrous sketches of the Confederate president and other prominent Southerners were many names of men and regiments—they were scrawled there by Federals before Bull Run.[29]

General McClellan
at Munson's Hill.

Union occupy Munson's Hill.
(Courtesy of the Library of Congress)

Sporadic shots back and forth between the combatants did create a sense of danger in spite of some soldiers' attempts to make a game out of it. The picket lines near Munson's Hill were 400 to 500 yards apart. An account of the action was described in the New York *Tribune*. Firing was desultory, with each combatant lying in wait for "his peculiar mark" to show up. Pickets could occasionally be seen pushing aside the corn, which concealed them, or "peeping from behind some temporary barricade" that they had "thrown together for protection."[30] They frequently exchanged epithets, with each daring the other to reveal himself so they could aim properly. Confederates nearby Union camps listened to the roll call and shouted, "Here!" to each name called. At times behavior was reckless. A Union soldier who got up on a post and began clowning by dancing, shaking his fists, and mocking the Confederates, soon became the recipient of a bullet from a Reb sharpshooter. A favorite trick of the Southerners was to mount a section of stovepipe on two wheels, roll the contraption into the middle of the road, point it at the enemy and go through the motions of getting ready to fire. It never failed to scatter the Federals who believed they were about to come under artillery fire.[31]

While the picket war was being fought at Munson's Hill, minor clashes took place in other areas of northern Virginia. Federal probes and skirmishing caused Confederates to counter by sending night patrols ranging miles from Munson's Hill in search of enemy picket lines. Contact with the Federals near Chain Bridge resulted in the death of Captain Lingenfelter of Colonel Baker's Seventy-first Pennsylvania. This and other raids prompted the no-nonsense General William F. Smith to send two divisions southward from the region of Chain Bridge toward Munson's Hill to put an end to the harassment. This resulted in an encounter, called an "affair," that occurred about three miles north of Munson's Hill near the Vanderburgh house early in the morning on Saturday, September 28. To the Union's despair, all of the combatants were Federals.

Things did not go well for the Federals from the start. One regiment failed to receive its orders, and the men were asleep when General Smith arrived to move them out. The lead regiment, the Seventy-first Pennsylvania under Lieutenant-Colonel Isaac J. Wistar, upon moving toward Munson's Hill, arrived where a thick wood hugged the shoulders of the narrow road. There Wistar told them that from this point on they would see only the enemy. Suddenly flames from rifle fire pierced the darkness from the left woods. Wistar's men had collided with a skirmish line of Porter's division. Porter's men fired back from the woods, thinking Wistar's men were the enemy. Wistar, ahead of his regiment and having just moments before identified some of Porter's pickets, galloped up and down the road in a vain attempt to stop the firing between the two lines, which were full of excited individuals shouting and firing on each other at close range. Wistar's valuable horse was hit and became nearly unmanageable. After two seemingly interminable minutes, the firing stopped as the invisible party in the woods apparently left. While Wistar was reassuring his men and was sending the killed and wounded to the rear, the party in the woods returned to throw a volley of at least forty shots from only six yards away into the men near the rear of Wistar's first battalion. As stated in officers' official reports and in newspapers, this produced "a panic among the artillery horses, who turned and dashed off to the rear, breaking loose from the guns, and producing great confusion" in the second battalion as the horses rushed "over them at full speed." A number of the horses shot; others ran from the road and were later caught. In the meantime, Porter's skirmishers had fled through the woods.

Friendly fire had killed at least four and wounded fourteen of Wistar's men, two of whom were seriously injured by the gun carriages and trampled by cavalry horses. It was a repeat of a similar mistake made months earlier during the Federal movement toward Big Bethel. Newspaper accounts excited the North by telling of the ineptness of the venture and condemning everyone from the general-in-chief down, "except for the real culprit who was never discovered." Many felt as Wistar did; he found it "hard to imagine the muddled condition of the officer's mind who…ambushed his command against the head of a column coming from the direction of his own rear.... Though the officer in charge of the strange skirmishers was undoubtedly next to an idiot, the person originally responsible was probably some inexperienced staff officer." Surprisingly, there was no public investigation. Wistar found one redeeming point in his regiment's behavior. For inexperienced men under fire at night at close range, he said, "it was a supreme test of their brief experience of discipline to refrain as well as they did from using the arms in their hands, for certainly not over one shot was fired for ten that they received."[32]

ALONG THE BANKS OF THE POTOMAC

Both sides were gripped with the fear that the enemy would cross the Potomac River, so both Blue and Gray guarded the river banks. This guarding intensified after the battle of Bull Run. Long before Bull Run, on June 9, 1861, a committee on behalf of concerned citizens of Loudoun County, Virginia, penned a petition. They wrote to their protector, Colonel Eppa Hunton, that the troops he had were "totally inadequate" to protect them. They pointed out the unique geographical and economic position of Loudoun: bordering the Potomac River for thirty-five miles, upon which there were "not less than thirteen fords and ferries." [33]The county lay thirty miles from Washington, and Federals could reach it by the Chesapeake and Ohio Canal, which ran parallel to the Potomac River, and by the B&O Railroad at Point of Rocks. "We are a large wheat and corn growing county," stated the petitioners, "with not less than twenty thousand cattle now grazed, a large portion of which are fat and ready for market, and at least one thousand of these are upon the flats of the river." In addition, there were dairy cows, hogs, sheep, and "a very important item…a large stock of the finest horses suited to cavalry and artillery service." Federals would also be eager to advance to protect the large Union population in the northwestern part of the county. The petition would prove to be a prophetic document; Loudoun County would become a microcosm of the Civil War as well as a thoroughfare of blue and gray armies on their way to or from Antietam, Gettysburg, and Early's raid on Washington.

Eppa Hunton forwarded the Loudouners' concerns to Richmond. At the behest of Robert E. Lee and at the threat of arriving enemy troops across the Potomac, the bridges into Loudoun County for the Loudoun and Hampshire railroad were destroyed, and the turnpike bridges over Goose Creek and the Potomac at Point of Rocks were burned. A feeble, unsuccessful attempt was made to destroy part of the C&O Canal.[34]

While Loudouners were pleading for more troops to protect them, elderly Winfield Scott ordered Charles P. Stone, then a colonel, to seize and hold Edward's Ferry and, if prudent, to seize Leesburg.[35] Stone was given discretionary power to do what he deemed best, with the general-in-chief's instructions to be cautious. Stone took the District of Columbia Volunteers and three other regiments, Ninth New York, First New Hampshire, and First Pennsylvania; some cavalry; and a section of Griffin's battery. They headed west toward the Potomac in what was called the Rockville Expedition.

After leaving some contingents to watch crossing points at Great Falls and Seneca Mills, Stone arrived at Poolesville on June 15 and found a small group of enemy across the river at Edward's Ferry and other sites along the Potomac. Stone thought he could take Leesburg with limited risk, but he thought it was of little military value. He wanted to protect Unionist citizens of the county, but he felt he lacked the manpower. He worried about being unable to protect the canal and the B&O Railroad and to defend the long stretch of the Potomac from Great Falls to Harpers Ferry. Stone asked for more men so he could extend his forces beyond Point of Rocks. He feared the enemy would cross above him near the Monocacy River, trapping him in the horseshoe formed by the Potomac's meandering.

What occurred—with the exception of Ball's Bluff—was sporadic musket and artillery fire across the river, occasionally escalating into so-called incidental skirmishes. High-command priorities as July 4 neared did not include the Potomac along the Loudoun border; rather, top priority was placed on General Patterson's southward movement to Martinsburg on his way to counter a Confederate army in the Winchester area. Stone was sent to join Patterson's column, leaving only the District of Columbia militia to guard select points east of Harpers Ferry.[36]

Bull Run intensified both armies' interest in defenses along the Potomac. Confederates were now well aware of their vulnerability to enemy invasion of Loudoun, which could menace their army thirty-five miles away in the Centreville and Manassas area. So General Beauregard sent a brigade (the Seventh Brigade) to Leesburg in mid-August. The commander was a skinny-legged colonel nicknamed Shanks, and a hero of the battle of Manassas, Nathan Evans. From his Leesburg headquarters, Evans established a line of pickets along the Potomac and continued the fortifications that had been started by the local militia. His adversary across the river, now General Stone (who had headquarters at Poolesville and headed a division of three brigades called the Corps of Observation), did similar work.

The first large battle of the Civil War also greatly heightened the Federals' fear of an attack on Washington. McClellan sent two divisions, under George A. McCall and William F. Smith, into northern Virginia to protect the southern approaches; two more divisions and one regiment were to protect the northern banks of the Potomac from Great Falls to Harpers Ferry.[37]

The location of the enemies, across the river from each other, would magnify the importance of the land and water that lay between them. The Potomac was divided in many places by large islands, like enormous whales crowding the river, especially from near Leesburg to Point of Rocks. These islands became targets of contending forces.

Stone's job, while establishing military discipline, was to keep a watch on the enemy at Leesburg and to guard along the river where it formed a giant arc. The latter is a large horseshoe bend in the river with Poolesville, at that time a town of about 200 residents, at the center. Evans was at Leesburg, approximately eight miles from Poolesville and about three miles from the western bank of the river. In between these two towns and dividing the river was Harrison's Island, which faced a seventy- to 100-foot bluff on the Virginia shore. Below the over-two-mile-long island was Edward's Ferry, near the mouth of Goose Creek. A little above the northern end, five miles away, was another crossing point, Conrad's Ferry. Roads on both sides of the river approached each ferry.[38] Parallel and near the eastern banks of the river ran the Chesapeake and Ohio Canal, which was used to bring men and supplies to Edward's Ferry on the Maryland shore.[39] Towering above the Federals to the northeast was Sugarloaf Mountain, from whose top the Union signal fires conveyed the enemy's movements.

Life for uniformed troops on both sides of the river was dominated by watching the enemy and training in the fundamentals of soldiering. Since enemy watching was the more immediate concern, the Federals assigned two and later three companies to five- to ten-day shifts of picket duty. Pickets were stationed on the slopes between the Potomac and the canal, which was somewhat higher and fifty to 100 feet away from the river. Companies who were assigned to picket duty were spread out in thirty- to forty-man groups over three miles.[40] Like their counterparts across the river, they used no tents. Tents were too easy for the enemy to spot. Instead, makeshift huts that were constructed with poles, brush, and weeds provided protection from the sun, but not from rain. Lights and fires after dark were also prohibited. These were advantages to soldiers because there were no drills, and those not on duty patrolling the river banks could lounge about in their huts. Falling asleep while at their post was another matter. In September three Federals were disciplined for such lapses. One man, found asleep on duty for a second time, deserted, fearing that he would be shot.[41]

Most pickets practiced vigilance. So did Charles Stone, who put in unexpected appearances, day or night, to check on his men. One evening while the general was making his own reconnaissance in a boat on the canal, he was challenged by one of his pickets. Stone gave the countersign and continued to row away when the sentry shouted, "God damn you! I'll blow your damn head off, as I would anybody's who rows about the canal at such an untimely hour, disturbing quiet folks!" The sentry was shocked upon discovering the identity of the intruder.[42]

August and September witnessed almost-continual firing across the river between the pickets, but rarely was anyone hurt. In part this was due to the nature of some if the Federal weapons. Men of the Fifteenth Massachusetts complained about their old smooth-bore muskets that had been altered from "flint to percussion lock." These could not harm the enemy—the Massachusetts men could rarely fire a ball across the river, while the Confederates "could shoot effectively across the river and three hundred yards and beyond." An angry soldier wrote his hometown newspaper in Massachusetts, "With these miserable weapons we are expected to victoriously contend with an army that have arms of more than three times [the] range of our own."

There were lighter moments. Two soldiers in a Massachusetts regiment recorded how it was common for Confederate and Union soldiers stationed on the banks in Loudoun and Maryland to talk to each other across the river. They taunted and joked with each other. Early in October, according to the soldiers, Southern picket thumbed his nose and shouted across the river to his counterpart, "When are you going to Richmond?" Back came the reply, "The day before you go into Washington." After a while they were familiar with each other. A number of the pickets agreed not to fire upon each other "and were of the opinion that the shooting of pickets [was] all foolishness." It became fairly common for pickets to meet in the middle of the river, shake hands, drink to each other's health, exchange newspapers, and occasionally, as a fellow from Mississippi did, row across the river to have dinner with the Yankees.[43] Even Stone seemed to condone restraint in firing. He reported that the "Virginia picket men said they did not wish to fight, but 'wanted to go home.'" A few days later he wrote that the "Virginia guards at the ferries seem to have been replaced by South Carolina troops, who recommend the unsoldier-like practice of firing at pickets across the river."[44]

POSTURING

In addition to attempts to look formidable to the enemy, probing, and occasional clashes of the "picket war," an occasional review took place. Such an event was a cavalry and artillery review near the Capitol building on a chilly and damp October 8, 1861. A large crowd of civilians from all walks of life walked, and others rode in carriages to view the procession. At 12:30, which was nearly time for the review to start, McClellan arrived with his staff, a party of forty. The general-in-chief was welcomed by a salute of thirteen guns. Shortly thereafter, the president and his wife arrived in a carriage on their way into the center of the viewing area—without any fanfare or salutes.

For an hour, eager onlookers viewed the procession of the artillery corps, consisting of eighteen batteries commanded by General William Birney. The artillery passed first, pulled by six to eight horses. As each battery passed, trumpets sounded. Then came the cavalry, 5,500, commanded by General George Stoneman. They were led by a mounted band. After each cavalry regiment passed by the onlookers near the Capitol, new "bodies of trumpeters and bands appeared." In many of the squadrons, all of the horses were of "one color, which will be universally the case"—reported one writer—as soon as General Stoneman can arrange it. (This plan was soon abandoned.) Most of the cavalrymen were volunteers and, according to a correspondent viewing the ceremony, were "not yet up to army standard." Nevertheless, it was esteemed as "the largest review of this kind ever witnessed in America."

McClellan's Grand Military Review

November 20, 1861 at Bailey's Cross Roads, Virginia. At that time it was the largest military review to be held in the western hemisphere.
(Courtesy of the Library of Congress)

Review of Federal troops

(Garibaldi Guard) on July 4, 1861 by President Lincoln (standing) and General Scott (sitting). (Courtesy of the Library of Congress)

After the review, the artillery and horses retraveled various streets of Washington to their camps. According to newspaper accounts, as the Campbell Artillery was passing the White House, "the ammunition box of one of the gun carriages, containing shell and solid shot exploded with a noise like a cannon. The three artillerymen sitting on the lid of the box were violently lifted several feet high and were slightly scorched before falling into the street considerably bruised. They were at once placed in ambulances and sent to the hospital." Luckily for the men, the "explosive force was principally toward the back of the box, that section being broken into charred fragments, while the lid on which the men were seated escaped fracture." A reporter speculated that it was "doubtless owing to these circumstances that they were not seriously injured."[45]

---

1 Williams, *Beauregard*, 96.

2 Williams, *Beauregard*, 99-101; *OR*, Ser. I, vol. 5, 884-87. This was a triangular position: Centreville formed the apex; the two sides were troops at Union Mills Ford and the Stone Bridge.

3 Warren W. Hassler, *General George B. McClellan* (Baton Rouge, La.: Louisiana State University, 1957), 33-34; Stephen W. Sears, *The Civil War Papers of George B. McClellan* (New York: Ticknor & Fields, 1989), 135.

4 H. J. Eckenrode and Bryan Conrad, *George B. McClellan* (Chapel Hill, N.C.: University of North Carolina, 1941), 28-30; Sears, *George B. McClellan*, 120. Scott was forced into retirement in December 1861 and his successor as general-in-chief was McClellan, who had worked behind the scenes to get the old general out of the way.

5 New York *Tribune*, October 21, 1861.

6 Leech, *Reveille in Washington*, 144-45; New York *Tribune*, October 10 and 14, 1861.

7 New York *Tribune*, September 27, 1861.

8 Ibid., September 29, 1861.

9 Cooling, *Symbol, Sword, & Shield,* 66. At about the time of Ball's Bluff, the War Department announced a decision that was well received by Federal soldiers: "Hereafter laborers will be employed in the erection of fortifications, and soldiers will not be assigned to that duty." See the New York *Tribune*, October 21, 1861.

10 Stephen W. Sears, ed., *For Country, Cause and Leader: The Civil War Journal of Charles B. Haydon* (New York: Ticknor & Fields, 1993), vol. X, 63, 65, 99. Haydon contended the sick list was greatly expanded as a result of contact with prostitutes in downtown Washington.

11 *OR*, Ser. I, vol. 5, 561-62, 574-75.

12 New York *Tribune*, September 27, 1861.

13 *OR*, Ser. I, vol. 5, 193-97. Another crisis facing Washington was the fear that the Maryland legislature would pass an act of secession imperiling the security of the city. Orders went out during September to arrest any or all of the legislature members to prevent this from occurring. Lincoln kept a watchful eye on the state and suspended the privilege of the writ of habeas corpus there as the military arrested nineteenth prosecessionist legislators. The Unionists, who outnumbered the secessionists, won the day in Maryland with the assistance of the Federal military.

14 Hassler, *McClellan*, 34.

15 Clashes also took place on the Potomac River south of Washington at Budd's Ferry, Maryland.

16 Longstreet, *From Manassas to Appomattox,* 59-60.

17 Ibid., 236-37.

18 Ibid., 414-20, 949.

19 Stuart had the Thirteenth Virginia Volunteers (350 men), a section of Rosser's Battery, Washington Artillery, and a detachment of cavalry.

20 Charleston *Daily Courier*, September 24, 1861.

[21] Charleston *Daily Courier*, September 24, 1861; *OR*, Ser. I, vol. 5, 183-84.

[22] New York *Tribune*, September 12, 1861; *OR*, Ser. I, vol. 5, 167-68, 171.

[23] *OR*, Ser. I, vol. 5, 167-84.

[24] Wister, *Autobiography*, 359. Wister felt the incident of the newspaper clearly showed the need to overhaul picket duty of some of the regiments.

[25] New York *Tribune*, September 12, 1861.

[26] Baltimore *Sun*, September 30, 1861.

[27] New York *Tribune*, August 24, 1861.

[28] Sears, ed., *For Country, Cause and Leader*, 74.

[29] Richmond *Whig*, September 13, 1861. Confederates built earthworks about seven miles from Chain Bridge, Munson's Hill and elsewhere. The earthworks at Munson's Hill were built with slave labor and extended about 150 yards to the right of Leesburg Turnpike.

[30] Owen, *In Camp and Battle*, 55-56; New York *Tribune*, August 31, 1861. General Beauregard's son, Rene, pitched a tent in the camp of the Washington Artillery of New Orleans in northern Virginia. "He came to prefer himself in artillery."

[31] *OR*, Ser. I, vol. 5, 119-22. Pickets and companies from the Second and Third Michigan and the Third New York infantry engaged Confederates in the August 28 and September 2 confrontation.

[32] The New York Weekly *Journal of Commerce*, October 3, 1861; "Sears, ed., *For Country, Cause and Leader*, 80-81.

[33] Charleston *Daily Courier*, September 23, 1861.

[34] Edgar Warfield, *Manassas to Appomattox: The Civil War Memories of Pvt. Edgar Warfields, Seventeenth Virginia Infantry* (McLean, Va.: EPM Publications, 1996), 59-60.

[35] *OR*, Ser. I, vol. 5, 217-20; Isaac Jones Wistar, *Autobiography of Isaac Jones Wistar* (Philadelphia: Wistar Institute of Anatomy and Biology, 1937), 359-62 (Hereafter cited as Wistar, *Autobiography*).

[36] *OR*, Ser. I, vol. 2, 915-16.

[37] Ibid., 915-17. Confederate attempts to destroy the canal at Edward's Ferry prior to Stone's arrival were aborted when the lock-keeper drew off water. The draining of that section of the canal satisfied the small Southern force, which returned to the Virginia shore of the Potomac, leaving the embankments unharmed and the canal intact.

[38] On August 2, 1861, Stone, Sherman, Porter, Hooker, Lander, Baker, and three others were appointed to the rank of brigadier-general. Edward D. Baker, on August 6, 1861, in his last speech in the Senate, declined the appointment to prevent having to resign his U.S. Senate seat as required by law.

[39] *OR,* Ser. I, vol. 2.

[40] Nathaniel Bank's division covered the Potomac shores from Great Falls to Edward's Ferry, Stone's division from Edward's Ferry to Noland's Ferry, and John W. Geary's regiment of Bank's division from Point of Rocks to Harpers Ferry. In early September Stone's division consisted of only five regiments, two artillery batteries, and a troop of cavalry. By mid-October his "Corps of Observation" had swelled to more than twice the number of infantry regiments, twelve in three

brigades; three artillery batteries, and six cavalry companies.

[41] The road on the Virginia shore to Edward's Ferry is used today except for a mile and a half from the river bank. Conrad's Ferry is now White's Ferry and is extensively used by commuter traffic.

[42] George A. Bruce, *Twentieth Regiment of Massachusetts Volunteer Infantry* (Boston: Mifflin, 1906), 17; Andrew E. Ford, *The Story of the Fifteenth Regiment Massachusetts Volunteer Infantry in the Civil War* (Clinton, Mass.: W.J. Coulter, 1898), 54-55. A storehouse, some stores and other buildings were erected. Supplies arrived by the canal.

[43] Guard duty at Edward's Ferry was the heaviest. Four companies of the Fifteenth Massachusetts were marched two miles from camp to Edward's Ferry where after crossing the canal they went another four miles up the towpath to support the "picket guard."

[44] Ford, *Fifteenth Massachusetts*, 55-57, 59, 115, 117; Bruce, *Twentieth Massachusetts*, 18; *Democratic Mirror*, August 8, 1861.

[45] Baltimore *Sun*, October 9, 1861; New York *Tribune*, October 9, 1861.

CHAPTER IV

A STRANGE PLACE FOR A BATTLE: BALL'S BLUFF AND THE AFTERMATH

Northern morale had not recovered from the defeat at Bull Run when another disaster rocked the psyche of Union supporters. The event occurred in the fall of 1861 near Leesburg and Ball's Bluff, which overlooked the Potomac. It was an unlikely site for a battle, so the Confederates left it unguarded. The Union high command had neither planned nor sought a battle at the northern Virginia bluff. The Battle of Ball's Bluff, also called the Battle of Leesburg, resulted from misunderstanding, the Union reaction to a limited Confederate withdrawal, and an overzealous Union colonel who was a close friend of the president. Encouraged by the Southerners' withdrawal from the advanced position in northern Virginia back to their main Centreville line, the Union launched another series of probing actions. Those to Munson's Hill, Accotink Creek, Lewinsville, and Dranesville were uneventful, but an attempt to intimidate the enemy into evacuating Leesburg resulted in the second-most-consequential battle of 1861.

PRECURSOR TO COMBAT: BEAUREGUARD'S WITHDRAWAL ENCOURAGES UNION ADVANCE

Johnston had always felt uneasy about Beauregard's advance position in northern Virginia, at Munson's Hill and elsewhere. This concern was compounded by what he considered disadvantageous topography, as well as reports of McClellan's increasing strength. Johnston believed that "the semicircular course of the Potomac, and roads converging from different points on it to our position, made it easy for the Federal army to turn either of our flanks without exposing its own communications." As the enemy became stronger, "the position of ours," he wrote, "of course, became more hazardous." Advanced positions such as Munson's Hill were abandoned in late September, so by October 19, Confederate forces were "drawn back to Centreville—a position much stronger in front, as well as less easily and safely turned." Major-General Earl Van Doren's and Longstreet's divisions defended the area between Union Mills and Centreville, while G. W. Smith's men occupied Centreville. Jackson's force was posted to the rear of that village and constituted the reserve, while Evans' small force continued to guard the frontiers of the Potomac to the north.

The Centreville forces did their best to make up for their weaknesses. Engineers were ordered to fortify the summit of Centreville so several thousand men could defend it and the rest of the army would be free to maneuver about as needed. To make up for a shortage of artillery, Johnston recounted, "rough wooden imitations [Quaker guns] were made and kept near the embrasures, so as to be ready for exhibition. To conceal the absence of carriages the embrasures were covered with sheds of bushes."[1]

Johnston's pullback from the Munson's Hill line in late September puzzled many a Unionist. Was the move an unconditional falling back of Confederates to their former position, or was it, as one Northern paper contended, "a cover to some impervious attack upon another and more remote position" of Federal lines? Many speculated it was the latter but confided they would not be "fooled twice" or be "tricked into a position to be annihilated." Others argued to the contrary, pointing out, "[The] circumstances of this rebel retirement are wholly different from those of the retreat before McDowell's army. Then the enemy showed only in small bodies, and at first sight of our advancing column made off with symptoms of great terror" and "undignified haste." Now they had voluntarily relinquished a position that they had seemed to treat as formidable.

Upon arriving at Munson's Hill, the Federals were unimpressed by the unfinished works. All onlookers were laughing, said one reporter. "The utter absurdity of the works as a means of defense, their smallness, meanness, insignificance touched everybody's sense of the ludicrous," he wrote. "The inclosure comprises about four acres, around which earth is roughly thrown up to a height of four feet." There was "no ditch, no glacis—nothing in fact to give it the character of a fortification of any kind." "It is not even regular in form, but coils loosely and waveringly about the ground, as a huge snake might unfold it…. There are no embrasures for guns but upon two of its projections are mounted—What! Guns? No indeed, but old logs with a barb point to represent a formidable armament [Quaker guns]." The scornful reporter noted that a number of shanties, a considerable quantity of straw, and a "few forgotten rations lay about." Plus the "usual offensive odors of a Rebel Virginia camp were heightened in this case by the stench from a dead and decaying horse, which the Rebels apparently had not energy enough to remove, but left to rot among them."

Across the road 600 yards to the rear of Munson's Hill and on the other side of Leesburg Turnpike, the Federals found another former Confederate work. They found it "somewhat more imposing than the mud-mound on Munson's Hill, having embrasures, and something like a ditch." They assumed it was built as "a place of refuge in case Munson's Hill" was stormed and taken. Even this structure was deemed evidence of the "hapless and toil-evading Virginia spirit." "Only three sides were completed and those were composed of barrels and hogsheads filled" with loose dirt. The bitter critic went on to say, "I am astonished that the Rebels were not ashamed to leave so slip-shod and contemptible a work behind them. They might at least have spared themselves ridicule by destroying it."

Destruction was left to the Federals. They burned Confederate huts on Munson's Hill, and also indiscriminately burned $30,000 to $40,000 worth of property, mainly untenanted houses and their contents, belonging to both Union and Confederate supporters. Even the reporter who belittled the Rebels and Munson's Hill fortifications believed that these "wanton acts" should be investigated by military authorities.[2]

Munson's Hill, which had previously evoked fear, was now the object of derision. Its evacuation, as well as the advance of the Union line (which had moved forward four miles to the formerly Confederate position occupying the line of hills south of the Potomac River from Great Falls to beyond Little River Turnpike), made daily headlines in the major papers in the North. "Another Advance of Our Pickets," "Further Withdrawal of the Enemy," "Evacuation of Munson's Hill," "Occupation of Lewinsville," and "Occupation of Falls Church" are just a few of the bold headlines splashed across major papers such as the New York *Tribune* in late September and early October.[3]

Federal troops in enemy territory continued to have little respect or concern for local property. The little Lewinsville Presbyterian church—with only a dozen and a half members, the majority of whom had voted against secession—was taken as a stable for Federal horses. Windows were smashed and several walls were knocked out to accommodate the animals. Orders were given to burn the former house of worship if Federal troops were forced to withdraw.

Northerners were starving for some military success. They claimed it in the most modest circumstances, as evidenced by the clamor over the Federal soldiers' failure to panic and run at Lewinsville. Unionists now saw the enemy's evacuation of Munson's Hill, Upton's Hill, and Mason's Hill as a turning point. "Three or four miles beyond our former lines do not appear to count much in a march which is to be measured by such vaster figures; but still it is an advance—the first for many weeks, the first under the new order of affairs," wrote a jubilant reporter. He continued by calling the small Federal advance a portent of greater success. A "new orders of affairs," or shift from the defensive, was declared: "our attitude is openly changed to offensive. The first step is taken, and with an army like ours, that must mean that there is to be no retrogression."[4] Editorials in Northern papers were confident the war had turned in their favor.

The advancement of Federal troops, however, was cautious, like feelers testing to make sure the enemy was gone. Reconnaissances were made to the south on Telegraph Road toward Occoquan as far as Accotink Creek; from Alexandria through Annandale to Fairfax Court House; from Chain Bridge to Dranesville; and across the Potomac near Leesburg to verify the evacuation and to hasten the retreat of any remaining foe. Only one reconnaissance would lead to a serious confrontation—this would reverse the mood of optimism to one of gloom.

The forward Federal movement in northern Virginia was accompanied by an interrogation of civilians, as the officers hoped to obtain valuable information about the enemy. Pumping the inhabitants for information revealed little of value. Near Fairfax the Union forces found deserted Confederate wigwam huts. While the Northerners examined the abandoned site, an aged couple "tottered forth in great terror while" making derogatory gestures. Once assured of their safety, the couple grew gregarious and informative about the Confederate retreat. They claimed the retreat had been without ceremony and had taken place after Confederates had finished "abstracting one turkey and an assortment of chickens from the aviary of the aged couple," as reported in the New York *Tribune.* After entering the town of Fairfax Court House, the Federals were "met by a collection of chameleon-conscience citizens," who were emerging from Cayle's Tavern. They professed to have "Unionists sentiments...deposited in their hearts" and were anxious to know the size of the Union force. Answers to their questions were in double-talk and did not reveal the size of the reconnaissance or their intent. The disgruntled locals retreated back to their tavern.[5]

CONFRONTATION NEAR LEESBURG

The reconnaissance near Leesburg was more difficult than the others. It required crossing the Potomac and moving up a steep path to the side of a 100-foot bluff. Confederates deemed the site unnecessary to guard; no one would cross there. The bluff stood between two giant ravines and towered over the Potomac at heights of seventy to 100 feet for nearly a fifth of a mile. The cliff rose almost vertically, with jagged rocks protruding from the center of the face, and elsewhere, bushes, trees, and other forms of vegetation were clinging to the side of the precipice. Below was a narrow beach, slanting toward the river and covered with trees and fallen rocks. The beach varied in width from nearly fifty yards—at the mouth of the ravines and narrows—to only about fifteen yards—midway between them. The opposite bank, of Harrison's Island, was also covered with trees; most sections of the bank sloped gradually to the water, affording boating. However, the banks fifty to sixty yards away on the Virginia shore had steeper inclines, with often-abrupt six-foot drops to the water. One of the exceptions was a gradual slope near the center face of the cliff. Any surprise crossing to this bank would have to reach this spot, then traverse several hundred yards along the muddy base to a large ravine on the left side of the cliff. There on the northern bank of the ravine was a path used by cows, who grazed the approximately eight-acre clearing and drank from the river below. This narrow, often steep path was the only way directly to the top of the bluff.

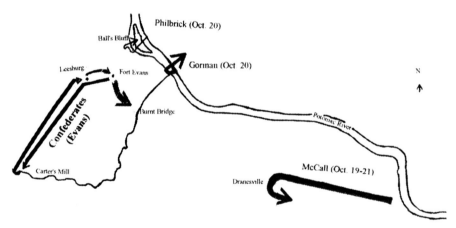

THE PRECURSOR TO BALL'S BLUFF
UNION PROBING OF CONFEDERATE POSITION AT LEESBURG ON
OCTOBER 19-20, 1861

Ball's Bluff was one of the sites used in McClellan's attempt to intimidate the enemy into leaving Leesburg. Evans obliged, fearing he would be cut off from the main Confederate army. Upon hearing (on October 16) false rumors of a battle at Fairfax Court House, he got his men up at 3:00 A.M., fed them cold water and bread, then pulled back southward to a strong position on Goose Creek at Carter's Mill on the palatial Oatlands estate. A concerned Beauregard, not wanting to give the enemy easy access to the Leesburg area, had Colonel Nathan "Shanks" Evans return to Fort Evans on October 20. Soon the colonel moved his entire brigade to the east on the formidable west bank of Goose Creek at Burnt Bridge. There he could block any movement up the turnpike by the newly arrived Federal force at Dranesville under General George McCall. Believing McCall was approaching and only a couple of miles away, the skinny-legged Southern colonel gave a short but emotional speech, telling his men that if they died there, he would die with them.[6]

The enemy didn't come. It was only a feint; McCall's force was scouting the Dranesville area. Federals would soon try other movements in addition to McCall's in an attempt to bluff the Rebs out of Leesburg. A seemingly innocuous order from McClellan to Stone on October 20 set off these movements. General Stone had been informed that General McCall's brigade had occupied Dranesville twenty miles east of Leesburg the previous day and was sending out "heavy reconnaissance...in all directions." Stone was told, "keep a good lookout upon Leesburg" to see if McCall's movement would drive away the enemy. "Perhaps a slight demonstration on your part would have the effect to move them," suggested McClellan. This touched off a chain of events that would end in battle at the bluff.

Upon receiving this order, Stone immediately set about gathering his troops at or near Edward's Ferry and Harrison's Island. He feigned a crossing at Edward's Ferry, sent four companies of Colonel Charles Devens' Fifteenth Massachusetts regiment to join a company on picket duty at Harrison's Island, and that night, under cover of darkness, sent a small scouting party toward Leesburg.[7]

The feint at Edward's Ferry, where Stone had placed General Willis A. Gorman in charge, consisted of a battery firing shells across the river into a wood, scaring away the Confederates who had been guarding that area. Two regiments, the Eighty-second New York and the First Minnesota, crossed to the Virginia banks—only to be returned at dusk to the Maryland shore. This completed the "slight demonstration," but it had little effect on Shanks Evans, who remained at Burnt Bridge.

After Gorman faked a crossing at Edward's Ferry during the day, that night Stone complied with the second part of McClellan's order to "keep a good lookout upon Leesburg." A party of twenty men, under Captain Chase Philbrick, left Harrison's Island. They crossed to the base of the bluff and climbed up the winding path. Philbrick and a couple of men had climbed to the crest of the bluff a few days earlier and found that this portion of the river was not picketed.[8] Now they went further to the edge of the woods that covered most of the land back to the bluff. The woods were a mile inland on a ridge that ran parallel to the river for about a mile and about sixty feet higher than the crest of the bluff. From the edge of the woods, looking in the direction of Leesburg, the captain and his men from Company H of the Fifteenth Massachusetts believed they saw thirty tents of a small unguarded Confederate camp about 140 yards away. Elated upon hearing this, Stone was anxious to make the enemy pay for their error. He ordered two small forces to cross to the Virginia shore: one beyond Ball's Bluff to the "unguarded camp," and the other to Edward's Ferry to divert attention from the first force.

Around midnight, Devens began the mission to destroy the unguarded enemy camp. As quietly as possible, he crossed five companies of his Fifteenth Massachusetts regiment from Harrison's Island, where the men had been lying on some corn stalks they found on the island. It was slow going. There were only three small rowboats with a combined capacity of about thirty. It was 4:00 A.M. before all of Devens' 300 men were on the Virginia banks.[9] The slowness of this crossing foreshadowed a fatal flaw. At dawn, Major Paul J. Revere of the Twentieth Massachusetts supervised taking a flatboat from the Maryland shore around Harrison's Island to its western bank to aid in the crossing. The flatboat and the few additional small rowboats still failed to provide adequate passage.[10]

Once across, Devens' men followed Philbrick's route to the top of the bluff into an open field. Devens halted there until daybreak. During the wait, he was joined by a 100-man company from the Twentieth Massachusetts, under Colonel William R. Lee; the company had been sent as cover for Devens in case of contact with a formidable enemy. Like Devens' men, Lee's found the bank slippery and had trouble standing as they moved single file up the path on the side of the bluff.

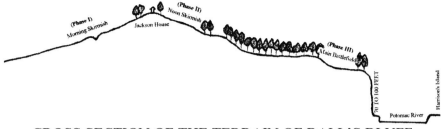

CROSS SECTION OF THE TERRAIN OF BALL'S BLUFF

At daybreak, Lee's scouts scoured the area, and Devens moved a mile inland. His men continued along the path through the eight to ten acres of open field—trapezoidal in shape—that would be the center of the battleground later that day. After moving along the path and through woods, Devens arrived at open ground facing Leesburg. He was near the spot where the enemy was supposed to be camped. No one was there. A puzzled Devens asked Philbrick, "Are we not mistaken?" Philbrick insisted he was not. As Devens moved gradually closer to a row of trees where the row of tents were believed to be, he concluded that Philbrick and his scouts had been deceived by moonlight filtering through a line of trees growing on the brow of a slope, giving the illusion of tents. It was a mistake easily made. In the uncertainty of the first light of morning, there did seem to be a row of tents.[11]

Finding no enemy there, Devens concealed his force in the woods and rode with Philbrick and several scouts along the slope toward Leesburg for no more than an eighth of a mile. They stopped frequently along the way to reconnoiter the town and country. Devens saw only four enemy tents. About 6:30 A.M. he confidently returned to his men in the woods, where he remained, believing he was undetected and no sizeable foe was in the area. He sent a report of his findings to General Stone and asked for orders.

As Devens was carrying out his reconnaissance, General Gorman was carrying out his diversionary action, which was designed to reconnoiter the Edwards Ferry road toward Leesburg and the area to Goose Creek. Two infantry companies (First Minnesota Volunteers) and thirty-one cavalry (of the Van Alen Cavalry) crossed the Potomac at 6:00 in the morning under the cover of artillery (Ricketts' battery) fire from Maryland. When the Union cavalry neared the position of the hidden Confederate battery, two miles from

125

the ferry, they were suddenly fired upon by a Mississippi regiment returning from Burnt Bridge. The Federal horsemen returned fire with their pistols before beating a hasty retreat. The rest of the day the Federal force—which by 11:00 A.M. had grown to 1,500—waited on the Virginia side of Edward's Ferry, intimidated into inaction for fear of fire from Confederate artillery from the battery on the ferry road.[12]

While Devens waited in the woods for orders from Stone, early morning contact with enemy pickets touched off the first of three phases of fighting around and on Ball's Bluff. Each phase involved more men, was more intensely contested, and was fought nearer the bluff: The first occurred at 7:00 A.M. between 150 men in front of a ridge. The Jackson house sat on top of this ridge, one mile from the bluff. The second clash happened around noon between approximately 1,300 men in back of the Jackson house, on the other (eastern) side of the ridge, about three-quarters of a mile from the bluff. The third and main battle was between 3,400 men and involved a series of Confederate attacks on Union forces. These attacks took place in front of the bluff from 3:00 to 6:00 P.M. and drove the Union forces from the precipice to the base and river below.

Evans' response to each phase was to shift the bulk of his brigade to where he believed the main enemy attack would occur. Good fortune smiled on him on October 20 with the capture of one of General McCall's couriers, who had papers revealing the position and intent of the enemy near Dranesville: to reconnoiter that area, not to attack Leesburg. With this knowledge, on the morning of October 21, Evans was able to shift the bulk of his brigade to Edward's Ferry— where he believed the main Federal attack would take place—and later in the day, to move the brigade to the battle site at the bluff.[13]

Phase One: The Morning Skirmish

Phase one of the fighting started when members of Captain W. L. Duff's Company K of the Seventeenth Mississippi Infantry, who were on picket duty at Smart's Mill and above the bluff, fired on one of Lee's small Union scouting parties.[14] Duff immediately started pulling back toward Leesburg to prevent being cut off from the main Confederate force.[15] While moving toward Leesburg, Duff saw what he called a "large force" of enemy 150 yards away in the yard of the Jackson house. The yard was near a road on a hilltop where the Mississippians were headed. Duff immediately filed 300 yards to the right, toward the base of the hill, to get between the Federals and Leesburg. At the same time, he drew part of the enemy away from their reserve near the woods.

The movement—into a cornfield—thwarted Devens' plan to trap the Mississippians. He had planned for Philbrick's company to attack from the front while another company moved to the right to cut off Duff and prevent his retreat toward Conrad's Ferry. Philbrick, whose company was armed with old smooth-bore flint-lock muskets that had been altered to percussion muskets, was obliged to move closer to the enemy for his company's outdated weapons to be effective.

Seeing the Federals advance toward his forty-man force, Duff took refuge in a hollow or ditch in the cornfield. There he repeated—six times—the order for the Federals to halt. Each time Philbrick's men were alleged to have responded that they were "friends." When the Federals got within sixty yards, Duff's men fired. What happened in the hot skirmish for the next twenty or so minutes is unclear, but it resulted in a dozen casualties.[16] Duff claimed his company had been victorious. He reported that he had broken Philbrick's line, forcing the Federals to retreat until they rallied after receiving reinforcements. Then, after a twenty-minute stand, the Federals supposedly fled in confusion into the woods. Duff felt vulnerable to any enemy movement to his right, so he pulled back another 300 yards to Big Springs, on the main road to Leesburg. When he learned there were Confederates near Leesburg, he resumed his former position.

Devens claimed that Philbrick's men drove the Confederates from the hollow or ditch to behind the shocks of corn that dotted the cornfield. In the meantime, Devens learned enemy cavalry was "reported to be on his left," so he called for another company to assist in the attack. Then Devens ordered Philbrick back into the woods, ending the skirmish. After waiting there for half an hour, until about 8:00 A.M., Devens pulled his entire force back to the bluff. Colonel Lee reported that he and his men saw the Fifteenth Massachusetts march back on the cart path "in excellent order, coming by flank column, in double files." But Charles Devens was not a happy warrior. Lee—who had some idea of what had passed, from

127

information obtained earlier from wounded men and those who had assisted them—moved a short distance to greet Devens and asked him what had happened. Colonel Devens did not say much. He seemed to Lee, "very much vexed; in fact, he seemed angry at the result of the operation." Finally Lee told him, "If you are going to stay here, Colonel, you had better form your line of battle across the road, instead of leaving your battalion in column and halted in the road." Devens made no reply. Lee waited to see if Devens would retire across the river. Devens remained only for a brief time. After scouting the woods and finding no enemy, he returned to his former position, to the rear of the Jackson house.[17]

The approaching cavalry that caused Devens to call off his early morning skirmish with Duff consisted of three companies of cavalry that had been sent by Evans, along with four infantry companies. All were under the command of Lieutenant-Colonel W. H. Jenifer, who was to relieve Duff and to counter any enemy attacks near the bluff.[18] Several hours later, around 10:00 that morning, Evans sent Colonel Eppa Hunton and the 375 men of his Eight Virginia infantry at Burnt Bridge to reinforce Jenifer; Evans was "convinced," as he would later attest, that "the main attack would be at Ball's Bluff."[19]

Evans was doing his best to get every man available to repel what he called the "invaders." He sent a courier into Leesburg to mobilize the militia, but only Commander R. L. Wright and a few men responded. Most were rumored to have stayed, cowardly, in the town's bars.

The Union increased its numbers at the bluff throughout the day, although slowly, because of the limited number of vessels, lack of supervision, and need for the troops to cross the river twice. Troops had to cross the canal before they reached the river; many had to pass under the canal through a culvert that was partially filled with water. (Not until the night after the battle was a canal boat slung across the channel to aid in crossing.) Once by the canal, troops crossed from the Maryland bank on the Potomac to Harrison's Island, then from the island to the shore at the base of the bluff.

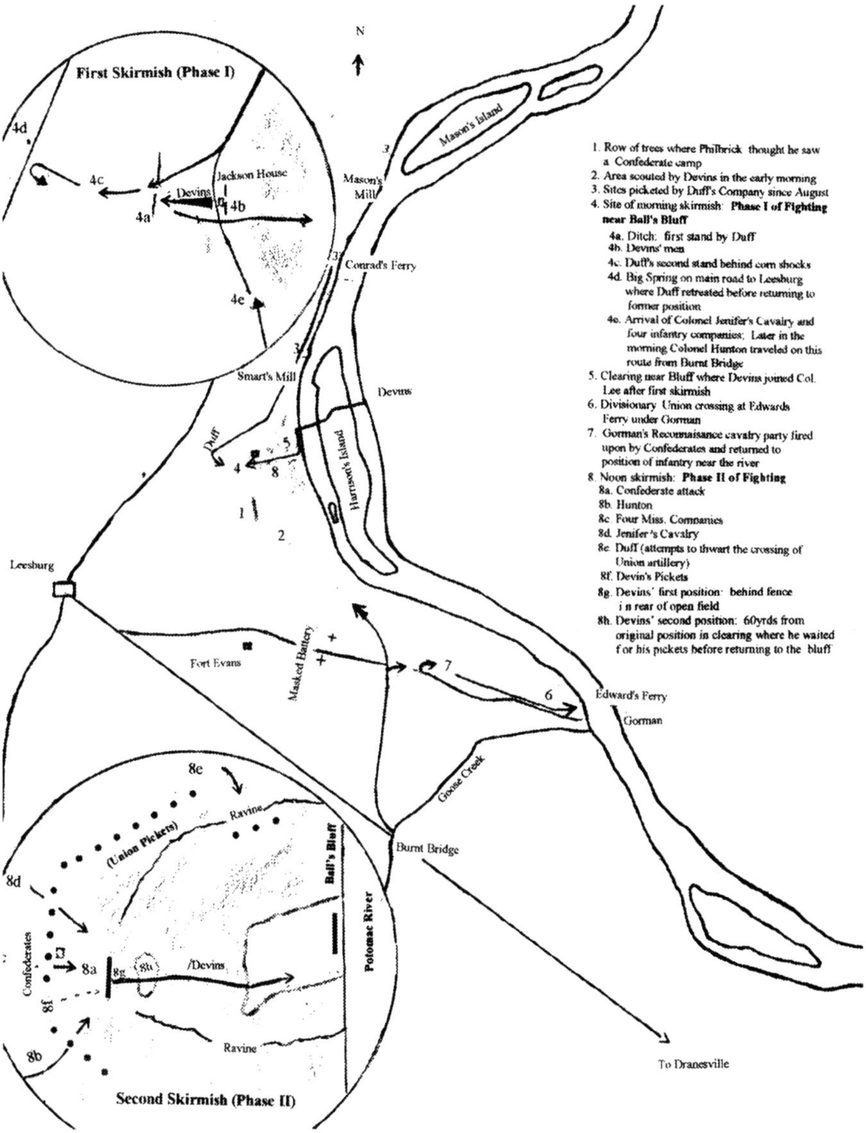

The map legend reads:

1. Row of trees where Philbrick thought he saw a Confederate camp
2. Area scouted by Devins in the early morning
3. Sites picketed by Duff's Company since August
4. Site of morning skirmish: **Phase I of Fighting near Ball's Bluff**
   4a. Ditch: first stand by Duff
   4b. Devins' men
   4c. Duff's second stand behind corn shocks
   4d. Big Spring on main road to Leesburg where Duff retreated before returning to former position
   4e. Arrival of Colonel Jenifer's Cavalry and four infantry companies; Later in the morning Colonel Hunton traveled on this route from Burnt Bridge
5. Clearing near Bluff where Devins joined Col. Lee after first skirmish
6. Divisionary Union crossing at Edwards Ferry under Gorman
7. Gorman's Reconnaisance cavalry party fired upon by Confederates and returned to position of infantry near the river
8. Noon skirmish: **Phase II of Fighting**
   8a. Confederate attack
   8b. Hunton
   8c. Four Miss. Companies
   8d. Jenifer's Cavalry
   8e. Duff (attempts to thwart the crossing of Union artillery)
   8f. Devin's Pickets
   8g. Devins' first position: behind fence in rear of open field
   8h. Devins' second position: 60yrds from original position in clearing where he waited for his pickets before returning to the bluff

MILITARY ACTIVITY ON THE MORNING TO EARLY AFTERNOON OF OCTOBER 21, 1861

The river's uncooperative current also impeded the process; it carried the vessels downstream. On return trips, inexperienced men awkwardly poled or rowed the boats upstream, so the path of the original crossing and return trip was in the shape of an X. Though the optimistic projection was for 1,000 men to cross each hour, the crossing rate was a mere trickle. Several hours after his early morning request for orders, a nervous Devens, fearing he was about to be overwhelmed by an increasing Confederate force received instructions from Stone. Help was on the way. Stone told Devens to remain where he was and wait for reinforcements. Lieutenant-Colonel George H. Ward and the remainder of the Fifteenth Massachusetts were to cross Harrison's Island to Smart's Mill (also Stuart's Mill) about a mile north of Devens. There the river could be forded and Ward could cover any Union withdrawal, if necessary. Ten cavalrymen were also ordered to cross the river and report to Devens to reconnoiter the area.

These orders would not be carried out, and the consequences would contribute mightily to the afternoon's disaster for the Union. Upon receiving news that help was on the way, Devens sent his messenger, the quartermaster, back to Stone, this time to inform him that the enemy had discovered his position and an early morning skirmish had occurred. By 10:00 that morning the messenger returned with news that Colonel Edward Baker was on the way with his First California regiment, and he would take command.[20] Before returning to Devens with this message, the courier ran into Ward on Harrison's Island on his way to Smart's Mill. The excited messenger greatly exaggerated Devens' situation; he claimed it dire and that Ward's help was needed. Smart's Mill was not secured, as Ward's men waited for boats to cross to the bluff. Inexplicably, the ten cavalrymen who crossed over to the bluff after their leader had a brief conversation with Colonel Lee, went back without reporting to Devens—who anxiously awaited them.

Colonel Eppa Hunton, anxious for combat, joined Jenifer's forces around noon and assumed command (though Jenifer's report after the battle incorrectly stated that he had remained in charge at the battle site all day).[21] Hunton, who suffered from a painful, chronic infection called fistula, which would plague him throughout the war despite several operations, left his sick bed to lead his men in combat.

Phase Two: The Noon Skirmish

Shortly after Hunton joined Jenifer, the second phase of fighting began. It took place behind the Jackson house in a cleared field that ran downhill for almost a quarter of a mile to the woods. "This space," described a soldier, "was bounded by woods on the left and partly so on the right." At the bottom of the sloping clearing were most of Devens' 650 men. Most were on a slight rise, several hundred yards long, between two ravines, which dropped thirty to fifty feet.[22]

Devens was extremely anxious about what he deemed to be his precarious position, nearly a mile away from help and facing a large foe poised to overwhelm his isolated regiment. Help had not arrived. He waited nervously and once or twice sent back to the river to, in his words, "ascertain whether re-enforcement would come, and what he was to do," but he "got no order or message." While he waited, he kept a sharp eye on the enemy by placing three companies of skirmishers one-quarter mile up from his main force, at the top of the slope. The men stood five paces apart and formed their line to the left and the right in front of the rest of Devens' force in the woods.

The men of the Fifteenth Massachusetts waited impatiently for action in the woods until ordered to rest; then they sat on the ground and attempted to relax. According to the historian of the Fifteenth Massachusetts, one soldier "refreshed the inner man with a salt beef and hard-bread, and the outer man with a short nap." At about noon the colonel was told that the enemy was gathering for an attack. Assuming he faced a force of thousands instead of a force about the same as his own, he feared for his skirmishers, who were a quarter-mile in his front and vulnerable to enemy cavalry who might be behind them into the sloping open field. At 12:30 P.M. the Confederate attack began. Jenifer's cavalry—from the left side of the Confederate line—hit the Federal skirmishers as Hunton's Eighth Virginia infantry struck from the woods to their right of the open field. The center of the Confederate line was formed by four companies of infantry from Mississippi regiments that were with Jenifer.

Duff, commanding another Mississippi company, was sent to the Confederate extreme left, where he threw twenty skirmishers forward to the river near Smart's Mill. From there they saw downstream, 500 to 600 yards away, Federals crossing the river with artillery. When informed of this, Jenifer sent the rest of Duff's men and a dismounted cavalry company to stop the crossing. Union skirmishers, a deep ravine, and dense thickets prevented Duff's penetration and resulted only in a half-hour exchange of musket fire as the enemy pieces crossed the river unimpeded. In the meantime, Devens posted his men behind a fence in the rear of an open field near some woods. There a heated but brief period of fighting took place.

After ten to fifteen minutes Devens broke off the engagement, pulling his men further back. Fearing the enemy infantry on his left—the Eighth Virginia—might flank and cut him off from the bluff. He withdrew sixty yards to an open space in the woods, reformed his line, and made plans to fall further back to safety. He waited for half an hour or more for his skirmishers to join him.[23]

The Union skirmishers, especially those in the center and left, suffered the most.[24] Some of the wounded were carried back, but a number did not make it to the main line. The scene is vividly described by Andrew E. Ford in his book about the regiment. A nineteen-year-old Massachusetts carpenter, George B. Simonds, was among those who ran for safety when the enemy cavalry dashed upon them. After going only twenty or thirty yards, "balls were whistling on all sides," and he felt a "peculiar sensation in his right thigh." He knew he was hit and "carrying an ounce of lead besides the forty" in his "cartridge box." In a minute or two his shoe was full of blood and his pants were saturated with the same. He ran past two soon-to-be-captured wounded comrades, who sought momentary protection behind a corn stock. Simonds ran on, only stopping briefly behind a little house near the woods to catch his breath. There two more friends hid. One was wounded in the wrist. The other went to the corner of the small structure and fired. "There," the shooter shouted, "I've fixed him; I saw him fall." Simonds then ran to safety.[25] The second phase of the day's combat was over. Like the first phase, fought on the other side of the slope, it was brief—and was only a preface of things to come.

Back at the bluff, around 2:00 P.M., Lee heard a voice behind him asking for Colonel Lee and Major Revere. Then someone, apparently pointing to Lee, responded, "There he stands." Lee turned around, and saw "a military officer on horseback present himself, and bow very politely and said: 'I congratulate you upon the prospect of a battle.'" Lee recognized Colonel Baker, whom he had met briefly at Poolesville. Lee bowed and said; "I suppose you assume command." Baker said that would be the case.[26]

Phase Three: The Afternoon Battle and Disaster at the Bluff

At 2:15 P.M., a relieved Devens joined the Union forces near the bluff. There, for the first time that day, he saw and heard from Colonel Baker, who had also recently arrived at the bluff. Baker greeted the commander of the Fifteenth Massachusetts: "Colonel Devens, I congratulate you upon the splendid manner in which your regiment has behaved this morning. I think we better form the line of fire, and prepare to receive them here, and you shall have the right of the line."[27]

Stone had faith in Ned Baker, the man finally at the bluff. After all, the fifty-year-old English-born colonel was a close friend of the president, a veteran of the Mexican War, credited with playing a major role in keeping California in the Union, and one of the most eloquent and prominent politicos in the country. When the war started, Baker had been offered a brigadier-general's commission, but he rejected the appointment because the law would require him to vacate his U.S. Senate seat representing Oregon. Instead he accepted a colonelcy. Shortly before Ball's Bluff he had been offered an appointment as major-general, but he had not responded to this proposal.[28]

It is not surprising that Stone gave Baker the responsibility for probing the area of the bluff. Stone had met with Baker on the morning of the battle at Edward's Ferry, where Stone would remain throughout the day. The general wrote that he stood on a high point where he "could see much of the area of his planned military action for the day." He had a map spread before him. He told Baker "about the boats" and the position of batteries between Edward's Ferry and Ball's Bluff and showed him on the map "the lines the enemy used for communication, as near as they knew them." Stone told Baker, "go up and take the entire command, entire control of the right," which was four miles from where they stood. Once Baker had viewed the ground, he was to decide if he wanted to stay and bring across additional men or retire from Virginia. He was cautioned, according to Stone, that "no advances" were to be made "unless the enemy were in inferior force and under no circumstance" was he "to pass beyond Leesburg."

Baker responded: "Then I am to have the entire command?"

"Yes," answered Stone.

"Please put that in writing" Baker requested. Stone took out his pencil, bent down on his knee, and wrote on a jagged-edged piece of paper that Baker was to take command at the bluff and was to use his discretion in deciding whether to retire or advance troops to that site.[29] After reading the order, Baker rolled and inserted the page into the interior band of his hat, a practice not unlike that of his friend Lincoln. Sometime between 8:00 and 8:30 A.M., the colonel mounted his horse and rode down the towpath toward Harrison's Island. Stone was optimistic. The Confederates had been pulling back in northern Virginia. Perhaps Baker would convince them to do the same at Leesburg.

Why would it take Baker so long to arrive at the bluff? Apparently he spent the time doing what he felt was necessary to prepare for combat. Baker seemed determined to fight a battle. He had an impetuous streak that may in part explain his actions. He was quick to take a gamble and jump into the thick of things, from playing a game of cards—a game he dearly loved—to engaging in effective, impromptu political responses throughout his career (in the Illinois legislature, then in the U.S. Senate, where he defended his friend the president). Nor was he wanting in courage. When a lower-ranking officer was unable to stop a fight among his troops during the Mexican War, Baker plunged into the fray to stop it. It almost cost him his life; a disgruntled brawler shot him.

After assuming command at the bluff, Baker's primary concern early in the morning until midafternoon was to get men to cross to the bluff, at the exclusion of all else. He was so preoccupied with the crossing that he ignored Devens and failed to secure the crossing at Smart's Mill, which was so vital to his safety. According to Stone, he also failed to cross in order to examine the field at the bluff personally "until he had ordered over his force and passed over a considerable portion of it." Instead, he busied himself for more than an hour with supervising the lifting of a boat from the canal—a task that could have been delegated to someone of lesser responsibility. Additional time was lost when he engaged in unsuccessful attempts to stretch a rope from the Maryland side to Harrison's Island. (This was later successfully done.) Baker was too busy to keep in contact with Stone, despite having been told early that morning to keep closely in touch. Stone did not receive a message from Baker until 2:15 P.M. The message stated that Baker had decided to cross and was "increasing his means of transportation by a large boat lifted from the canal." The general cautioned the colonel that he "believed 4,000 troops would be opposed to him," and, "there was still time to retire." A confident and optimistic Baker is to have responded, "I shall not retire."[30]

Soon after his arrival on the bluff, the senator-colonel, still unfamiliar with the terrain, hastily formed his line around the position of Lee's men. The men of the Twentieth Massachusetts, numbering over 300 as a result of the midday arrival of 200 men under Major Paul Revere (the namesake of his famous grandfather), were in a clearing with their backs to the bluff. To their left were one Tammany Company and most of the First California regiment. And to the right in the woods and perpendicular to the men in the line along the bluff were two California companies and the Fifteenth Massachusetts. On their extreme right, there were skirmishers from the Twentieth Massachusetts. The Union line formed an L, a fishhook, or what Colonel Lee called a "crotchet thrown forward." Regardless of the name of the configuration, it was defective in battle. If the Twentieth Massachusetts advanced 100 yards in open field to slight rise, the flank of Devens' Fifteenth Massachusetts and California companies could not fire without enfilading them.[31]

Baker's line was augmented by three artillery pieces that earlier had been dragged over what were described by those present as "miry clay banks," poled across the river in a scow, and carried up the steep path to the bluff. This was accomplished only after great "exertion and labor" and help from the infantry. Once on top of the bluff, they were placed in the open field in front of Baker's men in the clearing. The two twelve-pound mountain howitzers were placed on the right, on a rise in front of the men of the Twentieth Massachusetts, approximately forty to fifty yards from the bluff. Shortly before the main battle began, the third piece, a twelve-pound James Rifle (under Lieutenant Bramhall of the Sixth New York battery), arrived and was positioned near the path.[32]

Baker's faulty line formation was not his greatest tactical error. Surrounding the open fields were heavy woods, with two steep ravines running through the woods, ravines that almost circled the clearing and encased Baker's line. Along the ravine near to the Union left ran the narrow serpentine cow path used by Federals to reach the top of the bluff. Beyond the ravine to the left, and in front of the center of Baker's line, was high ground, which commanded much of the open field, Baker's left, and his narrow escape path to the bank of the river. Yet his line was the weakest on the left and opposite this high ground.

Shortly before the battle started, Colonel Milton Cogswell of the Forty-second New York infantry emphatically pointed out this deficiency to Baker. Cogswell had crossed from Maryland to Virginia early in the afternoon. When he arrived at the landing opposite Harrison's Island, he "found the greatest confusion existed. No one seemed in charge." The scene from Harrison's Island to Virginia was one of "still greater confusion." He had to have been concerned when he arrived at the bluff and was welcomed by an upbeat Baker, who seemed "very confident of a successful day." Baker asked Cogswell to examine his line of battle. When the two men had passed along the whole front, Baker asked Cogswell his opinion of the disposition of troops." The Tammany colonel would later write, "frankly...I deemed them very defective, as the wooded hills beyond the ravine [on the left] commanded the whole so perfectly, should they be occupied by the enemy he would be destroyed, and I advised an immediate advance of the whole force to occupy the hills" before the enemy did.[33] Instead of pushing his battle line a quarter-mile or so forward, Baker ignored Cogswell's prophetic advice. Instead he left his line as it was and ordered Cogswell to take charge of the artillery.

Evans, in the meantime, was correctly gauging the Federal intent. Barksdale's Thirteenth Mississippi was left on Edward's Ferry Road to hold or check the enemy there as Evans rushed the two other Mississippi regiments, the Seventeenth and Eighteenth, toward the bluff. Similar Federal efforts to rush additional men to the bluff were less successful.[34]

When the battle started, twenty-six Union companies and three artillery pieces were on the bluff. They were later hindered by too few boats, which were slowed by the return of wounded and dead to Harrison's Island, so only four more companies of the Tammany regiment could cross during the three-hour battle. More of this regiment's companies waited but never crossed. The Nineteenth Massachusetts got to the island, but no farther, while the Sixty-ninth and the 106th Pennsylvania waited helplessly at the canal on the Maryland shore and listened to the sounds of battle.[35] About twenty minutes after Cogswell had pointed out to Baker the critical nature of occupying the high ground to his left, it started being occupied by enemy skirmishers. It was now 3:00 P.M., and the day's most intense fighting was starting.

The details of what happened for approximately the next three hours, until the Federals were shoved from the bluff, are not altogether clear. Union and Confederate accounts differ, which is not unusual, but so do those on the same side, and to a greater extent than usual. Even accounts by the same individual may substantially differ, from official reports given immediately after the battle to testimony given months later before the Joint Committee on the Conduct of the War to memoirs written years after the war.

In part, the difference between individuals' accounts stems from their having different vantage points on the field. Some Federals contended that the battle opened on their right and spread to the left. Another stated that it started on the Union left and spread throughout the lines. Assessments of the use of the three Federal artillery pieces range: one source believed the artillery were fired less than a dozen times early in battle and were totally ineffective; another held that at least one of the pieces was effective; yet another source claims that a twelve-pound rifle gun helped keep the enemy at bay until late in the contest.

It is also unclear whether horses were used to place the pieces on the field. The number of supposed Confederate charges varies from a few to as many as nine. Had a deceptive Confederate officer, Charles Wildman, tricked Union soldiers late in the battle to follow him into a deadly Southern volley? Or was it a Union officer, Colonel Cogswell, attempting to save his force by trying to fight though the Confederate line and to escape to Edward's Ferry? Descriptions of the collapse of the Union line vary from one of panic and bedlam to one of relative calm and orderly retreat to a beleaguered position at the base of the bluff. The greatest controversy of all emerged over who was to blame for the Union disaster. Was it Baker's tactical blunders, or had Stone ordered him and hundreds of Union men into a murderous trap?

An overall picture, however, does emerge from contemporary accounts. After the battle started, two Confederate regiments reinforced their side, but because of the slowness in crossing the river, less than one regiment joined the Union line; this brought both sides to about 1,700 combatants. As the battle progressed, Confederates formed a semicircle around the Union, seizing the high ground on the Federal left and cutting off their means of escape from the top of the bluff. Throughout the late afternoon, the Southerners made unsuccessful charges, including an attempt to capture the Federal artillery. The Union lines held until after the death of the commander, Colonel Baker, between 4:30 and 5:00 P.M. Realizing they were trapped, Colonel Cogswell (who succeeded Baker in command) attempted to break through the Confederate line on his left. This failed. The Southerners converged on the Blue line on the bluff and forced its members to retreat from the heights, in panic, to a narrow beach below. There they were trapped, and many were captured; there were not enough boats for them to escape across the Potomac. Some threw their weapons in the river and tried to swim across, with many drowning or being shot by Confederate fire from the bluff. What had started as a probing action ended in a Union disaster.

Baker might have had some doubts about his line of battle. Colonels Lee, Wistar, and Cogswell all claimed he requested each of them to review the line with him, then asked for their opinions. Wistar, during his review, claimed no enemy was in sight, but some had climbed trees, and "a slight spitting fire" came from treetops. The fire was aimed at officers, including Baker, Cogswell, and Wistar. The officers and men of the line were all lying down, by Colonel Baker's order "to avoid this fire." Only Cogswell had expressed any opinion about the men's disposition. Wistar's only response was a request to extend the skirmishers of his regiment on the left.

Baker responded, "I throw the entire responsibility of the left wing upon you." "I throw it upon you, Do as you like." Baker soon returned after examining the other parts of his line. He pulled a dispatch out of his waistcoat pocket, and read Stone's dispatch that stated, "four thousand enemy are marching from Leesburg to attack you."

Wistar, thinking about the time it must have taken this dispatch to have passed through to them, remarked, "We are greatly outnumbered in front."

"Yes," said Baker, "that is a bad condition of things." Baker then left, apparently to read the order to the other colonels, and Wistar prepared to send out his skirmishers. As they were about to leave, Baker returned, along with Colonel Cogswell. Baker then said, "Colonel Wistar, I want you to send out two of your best skirmishers companies to the front and feel the enemy's positions."

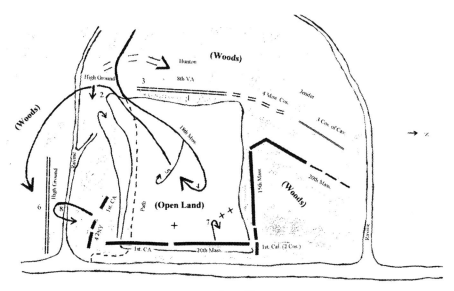

1. Confederates' first fire was scattered and came from treetops around the field
2. Clash between two companies of 1st CA and Hunton's 8th VA opens the battle
3. Shortly after 3:00 p.m. Hunton shifts his regiment to the left upon the arrival of 18th Miss.
4. 18th Miss. attempts to silence the two howitzers
5. One Miss. Co. is sent to right to counter Federal skirmishers firing on them from the woods
6. Unsuccessful in their attack on the howitzers 18th Miss withdraws to high ground on the other side of the ravine, threatening the Union left
7. Small ridge where the 20th Mass. repeatedly moved forward and back to reload (Where H. Oliver Wendell Holmes was wounded)
8. Three Federal Cos. (two 42d N.Y. and one 1st. CA.) fail to drive the 18th Miss. from high ground across the left ravine

BATTLE OF BALL'S BLUFF
THE FIRST HOUR (3:00 – 4:00 P.M.)
OCTOBER 21, 1861

Charles P. Poland Jr.

A less-than-pleased Wistar responded, "The enemy cannot be less than 5,000 men, and probably 7,000 in front and around this field; and to send out two companies of skirmishers will be to sacrifice them."

Baker replied, "I cannot help it; I must know what is there."

"Well," said Wistar, turning to Captain Markoe of the company about to be sent forward, "You hear what my orders are; do you understand them?"

"Yes sir," was the reply.

"Don't go off in a hurry," Wistar instructed. "Do you understand thoroughly what to do?"

"Yes, I do," replied the captain to his lieutenant-colonel. Markoe's company, one Wistar deemed to be excellent and trustworthy, went forward. To provide support, another company followed, led by Wistar himself, who felt there was "nothing particularly for me to do with the bulk of my regiment." The second company was reluctant to advance, but Wistar finally got them going.

Both companies moved through the woods on the left of the open field toward the high ground in the woods several hundred yards before them. Before reaching the high ground, the Eighth Virginia "arose up from the ground about thirty yards away and ran at Markoe's company" with their bayonet and without firing a shot. Markoe's men fired and took refuge behind trees, as Wistar and the second company—thirty yards to the rear—ran forward to provide support. Markoe's men first volley momentarily checked the Virginians' advance. According to Wistar, some "broke and ran away." The rest fell to the ground and fired, "laying down" or from behind trees. This firing touched off the battle, according to Wistar. Confederates assumed the Federals were attacking their right flank in force "and immediately threw a heavy volley" upon the main body of Federals, who returned it. Wistar immediately left Captain Markoe in charge of the two companies who were heavily engaged with the Eighth Virginia and hurried back toward the bluff to take command of his regiment.

Captain Markoe's two companies, greatly outnumbered, held his position for fifteen minutes, "during which time they lost all their officers" and two-thirds of their men, reported Wistar. Markoe was wounded and taken prisoner, along with some of his men. Wistar wrote that the remainder of Markoe's men fell back under the leadership of the only unwounded sergeant, bringing with them a lieutenant and fourteen men of the Eighteenth Virginia, who would prove to be the only Confederate prisoners of the day. The remnants of the two decimated Federal companies were put in the woods as skirmishers "to cover the open place there," and to prevent the Union forces from being flanked. Baker moved up his reserves, extending the Union left in the area of the skirmishers.[36]

Details of what occurred were given by Union officers in their battle reports and were later given to the congressional committee investigating the battle. Farther to the right in the clearing, the Twentieth Massachusetts was receiving the first volley there. The first shots sailed "rather high, for the aim of the rebels was diverted from the Massachusetts men" to the bright red lining "of their gray overcoats, which had been hung in the trees near the edge of the bluff."[37] This aim soon changed, as balls fell upon the Federals like hail, landing low—within one to four feet from the ground. It was a new sensation for the men of the Twentieth, many of whom were Harvard men. Men began to drop, but most were already lying down. If they "lifted a foot or head it was struck." One poor fellow was "struck on the hip while lying flat, and rose to go to the rear when another [ball] struck him on the head, knocking him over." Some were shot in their back and feet as they "lay upon their faces on the ground."[38] Captain William F. Bartlett became convinced he was going to be hit, whether prone or standing. He stood up and walked among his men, stepping over them, and was surprised by his calmness. He kidded several men, one for not being hit and another for getting his coat dirty. Under the heavy fire, the men of the companies "wilted away," but without panic.[39]

On the Confederate side, Hunton repeatedly asked Shanks Evans for help. Hunton felt uneasy, despite the Eighth Virginia's success in repelling the two enemy companies who had probed his right and in inflicting heavy fire in a charge upon the Twentieth Massachusetts further to his left. These victories and the midday charge had expended most of each soldier's forty cartridges. Hunton was convinced that his Eighth Virginia, three companies of Mississippians, and three cavalry companies were insufficient to meet what he was sure was a reinforced enemy. Before opening the main battle, he sent a local farmer, who was a volunteer guide and courier, E. V. "Lige" White, to General Evans to ask for reinforcements. "Tell

Hunton to fight on," was Evans' response, as the opening of the third stage of the day's combat had by then begun. Hunton soon ran low on ammunition and sent Major Norborne Berkeley, one of four brothers in the Eighth Virginia, to Evans for a supply at least twice. None came. At 3:30 he again sent Lige White, who later recalled the time Hunton had him tell Evans "that unless he was reinforced and supplied with ammunition," he would lose his position.

The feisty Evans, who, rumor claimed, had been drinking to the point of intoxication, responded, "Tell Hunton to hold the ground till every damn man falls." Hunton ordered his regiment to withdraw fifteen or twenty paces back into the woods for protection. Somehow confusion broke out, and some believed it was an order to retreat. Almost a fourth of Hunton's regiment, along with Lieutenant-Colonel Charles B. Tibbs, pulled back 400 to 500 yards from the line of battle. White, who was returning with orders from Evans, asked Tibbs what was the matter and if the Eighth Virginia "was whipped." Tibbs replied that he didn't know, but he understood Hunton had ordered a retreat. White galloped to Hunton, giving him Evans' message and telling him that the Seventeenth and Eighteenth Mississippi were being sent as reinforcements and what Tibbs had said to him. Hunton immediately sent White, who brought the men back to the line of battle—except for a few, who had seen enough combat. They returned to their nearby homes.

Another Confederate concern was the three Federal artillery pieces that sat in the open space in front of the Union line. It was a focal point of Southern fire early in the battle. It is unclear how the artillery reached this position. Some claimed that horses pulled the weapons onto the battlefield; others insisted men drew the artillery into the open field. Colonel William R. Lee of the Twentieth Massachusetts, who was on the battle site throughout the day, testified before the Joint Committee on the Conduct of the War; he described horses pulling the artillery pieces to the battle field and then being hit by gunfire.

"I will not...say how many horses were shot," testified Lee, "but the two leading horses were badly hurt—the head of one of them was very nearly shot away, and the rider, if my impression serves me right—and he was the only rider for the six horses—was shot out of his saddle ...just as the horses were turning for the purpose of unlimbering, the gunners were shot down. The horses became frantic;

the leading horses broke the traces, and they all rushed down the hill, dragging the limbers after them. They rushed through my line, disturbing it somewhat of course, and passed to the rear a short distance, the limber with horses attached."

Lee further contended that after a few discharges had been made, "the man with the friction primers was wounded and carried to the rear with the primers in his pocket; but one of the men happened to have some in his pocket," so firing continued.[40]

Resolution of the conflicting accounts is not provided in the report of Colonel Cogswell, the man who brought over the artillery and horses to Virginia, (who was sent by Baker to oversee the pieces as the battle opened). Cogswell directed the first fire of the artillery upon skirmishers of the Eighth Virginia who had occupied the high ground. The colonel had warned Baker twenty minutes before of the need to seize those heights. Cogswell soon believed the artillery fire was "ineffectual as the enemy was under cover of trees, shooting down the artillerists at easy musket range." After a short period, Lieutenant Bramhall and "nearly all the artillerymen had been shot down and the pieces were worked for a time by Colonel Baker" and other officers.[41]

The two howitzers did inflict casualties on the Eighth Virginia—casualties far greater than the Federals imagined. From the surgeon's report, it seems that "tree bursts" sent flying some pieces of wood that had first provided protection but then wounded and maimed.[42]

Certainly the first order of business for the Eighteenth Mississippi was to charge across the open field in an attempt to capture the two howitzers. Colonel E. R. Burt arrived at the battle site via the cow path behind Hunton, probably shortly after 3:00 P.M. Burt led his Mississippians to the right of Hunton's Virginians (who shifted some to the left) and then diagonally across the open field toward the enemy artillery.[43] Colonel Burt led his men from on horseback and soon fell to the ground, mortally wounded, just after the start of the charge.[44]

The lieutenant-colonel, Thomas M. Griffin, took charge and soon had to divide his force, sending a company to counter the heavy fire of Baker's skirmishers, who were in the woods and in front of a deep ravine on the Confederate right. The rest of the Southern line advanced to within a short distance of the enemy guns, where several heavy Union volleys forced the Mississippians from the open field. The men of the Eighteenth Mississippi then crossed the deep ravine on the Union left to the high ground. There they threatened the Union left and any movement up the cow path.[45]

A Bay Stater on the front stated that during this attack, one member of the Twentieth Massachusetts took dead aim at a mounted enemy officer on a white horse and "undertook to pull the trigger and found to his surprise that he had already lost half the forefinger of his right hand by a rebel bullet without knowing it."[46] Lieutenant Oliver Wendell Holmes Jr. was among the casualties in the Twentieth Massachusetts' repelling of this attack. The future Supreme Court justice, who would later be known as the Great Dissenter, was struck twice while encouraging his company forward. He was first hit by a spent ball that struck him in the stomach, knocking the wind out of him. He crawled a short distance behind the line on his hands and knees as his colonel, Lee, told him that leaving the line was the proper thing to do. But after being helped to his feet by a sergeant, he realized he had only suffered a severe bruise. Not wishing to be left out of the action, he returned to the front of the line. There he waved his sword and shouted for the Massachusetts men to follow him. Suddenly he fell near his colonel's feet. A shot had entered his left side and exited out of his right breast, where the spent bullet was found in his clothing. Holmes was dazed and faint. While he was carried from the field, he hoped he had been hit only once so his chance of surviving would be greater.[47]

While Holmes was being carried to the rear, the Twentieth Massachusetts moved forward a short distance to just beyond a small ridge that ran 100 feet or so in front of the bluff. Despite Lee's objections to Baker's order to fire by files (a difficult order for green troops to execute), the order was given for the men on the right to commence firing. But all of the men brought down their rifles and discharged their weapons very quickly, as the whole line delivered their fire almost at once. In the meantime, as Colonel William Lee later reported, the Confederates were "delivering their fire by companies, so that their fire was continuous." Once Lee's men fired, they fell back about ten feet to the descending side of the slight rise. There they reloaded and were ordered forward to fire again. This continued for some time. Two companies on Lee's right—from the California regiment, according to Lee—did not move forward and remained lying on the ground. Baker finally asked why they were not in action. Lee said he could not get them to move. Baker then went among them and, according to Colonel Lee, "was very energetic in his effort to get them into action," but he failed. "They rose only once to deliver their fire." Meanwhile, the men of the Twentieth went forward obliquely to avoid the artillery in front of them. The California companies would have fired "into them had not Major Revere and Lee's adjutant" gone "among them and beat down their pieces." Most Federals did their duty, but an occasional group of eight or so men looking for an opportunity to escape harm's way leaped forward and hurriedly ushered a wounded comrade from the field.

While the men of the Twentieth Massachusetts were in the open suffering the greatest of Union causalities, they broke only once, according to Colonel Lee, "and seemed to be very much disturbed by the example of a company on their right" which had broken in a panic. By efforts of officers headed by Major Revere, the line of the Twentieth Massachusetts was reformed and "fought with steadiness." Lee was obliged to move forward two of his companies, who had been held in reserve, to take the "place of companies in the front decimated or broken up by fire." Their resources were exhausted; enemy bodies were searched for ammunition. In the meantime, the Fifteenth Massachusetts, in the woods to the right and ahead of Lee's men, maintained its line with "great steadiness." The right wing delivered its fire at the enemy, with the left wing of the "crotchet not being able to fire, for being on lower ground" and in such a position, they would have fired into Lee's regiment.

Things were becoming more ominous for the Federals as the battle continued into the second hour. A great cloud of smoke hung over the battlefield. The artillery had no canisters, only shells, and all the artillerymen had been killed or wounded or had left. Baker and other officers briefly assisted in firing the rifle gun. They had other duties, and soon there was only one man left at the gun. He went "bleeding" to Lee and said, "I have done all I could."

Lee told him, "Yes, you have been a brave man." Then the man went bleeding to the rear, and the gun was left unattended.[48]

The Union left now came under the heaviest attack as the enemy's semicircling of the Union line was being completed. The Eighteenth Mississippi, after attempting to capture the enemy artillery pieces, occupied the extreme Confederate right, across the deep ravine, on high ground that extended to the river. The gap between them and the Eighth Virginia was soon filled by the arrival of the Seventeenth Mississippi, occupying the high ground that Cogswell had advised Baker to take just before the battle.

Occasionally Southerners would show "themselves by coming out of the woods in squads," wrote the regiment's historian, George A. Bruce. "Several old gentlemen in citizen dress were seen among the rebels. They were richly dressed in dark suits, white or buff vest. Some of them were seen to fall."[49]

The bulk of the California regiment had been recently joined by members of the Tammany regiment and was attempting to hold the left. Their leader, Wistar, would be wounded three times. First he was struck in the jaw by a bullet or small stone, which inflicted what Wistar called "severe pain and the loss of blood which matted his beard and dripped down in front presenting a ferocious sight." Later he suffered a flesh wound in the thigh near the spot of an old arrow wound he had suffered years before in an Indian war. The blood from this wound filled his boot, requiring him to cut a hole in it to drain the blood. As the sun was setting and the Union position was becoming more desperate, Wistar's right elbow was shattered, causing him to drop his sword. Confused and momentarily losing his sight, he tried to find his sword. He gathered it up along with a handful of bloody grass, and, as he stood up, Baker put his hand on Wistar's shoulder and said, "What, Wistar, hit again?"

Wistar replied, "Yes, and I am afraid badly this time." Then he asked his friend to sheath his sword. Baker did this, then sent a man to help Wistar return to the island.

After the wounding of Wistar, Cogswell saw the men of the Eighteenth Mississippi—on the high ground across the ravine—as a threat to the Union left. He sent three companies, one California and two Tammany (the Forty-second New York, who had just arrived on the battlefield), to drive the Confederates from the high ground across the ravine. The three companies valiantly charged, driving the enemy back fifty yards, but they were unable to dislodge the Mississippians from the high ground. Things now started looking bleak for the Federals. They were trapped on their left. Jenifer's cavalry had forced their way near the river on the Union right, completing the envelopment of the embattled Federals. Making a last-ditch effort for help, Baker ordered quartermaster Captain Francis Young to get reinforcements and to inform Stone of the desperate situation. Young was unable to carry the message to Stone. He climbed down the bluff and saw no boats. He returned to the top and found Baker dead.

Baker had been an inviting target. He walked back and forth in front of his men, along the width of the open field, with a hand struck in the front of his frock coat and the other gripping his showy gold presentation sword. Earlier he had told Wistar, "the bullets seem to be seeking you, but avoid me." He is said to have claimed, "The officer who dies with his men will never be harshly judged." He rejected many pleas to take cover, including one from an officer, but Baker told him to care for his company. "I will look after myself," declared the colonel.

Despite their plight, observed the wounded Colonel Wistar, the men almost found amusement in the repeated enemy action of terrible yells followed by their pouring "a shower of bullets everywhere over the field." They "did not seem to take any aim at all." Several times officers in blue joked that the enemy did not seem to hit anybody. "They would shoot into the trees, and the limbs would fall and the bullets would go clear across the river" to the island. "I do not think one was hit in a hundred bullets," surmised Captain Young.[50]

Around 4:30 to 5:00 P.M. Baker, was standing near the left woods, watching an enemy mounted officer ride into the open field and get shot. Baker turned about and said, "See, he falls," and immediately, Baker fell. He was instantly killed by at least four balls from what was believed to be an enemy cavalry revolver. Each ball was probably fatal; one hit his temple, piercing his brain and leaving a ghastly wound. Baker's killer seems to have run from the nearby woods, along with several others, near enough to his target to empty his revolver and riddle the colonel's body.

Captain Casper Crowinshield of the Twentieth Massachusetts, who stood nearby, was covered with Baker's blood. An attempt was made to steal the slain officer's sword, if not his body. The assailant, some claim, crawled to the colonel's body to steal his sword. But Captain Beiral and ten of his men rushed up and shot the Confederate through the head and rescued Baker's body. The corpse was then carried down the cow path and taken to Harrison's Island.[51] Regardless of the specifics, Baker was dead. The news of his death and the sight of his bullet-ridden body—still oozing blood, with clothes drenched with gore, his hat covering the shattered face, his sword laid on top of the body, as his hands dangled limply toward the ground—shocked and demoralized those on the bluff as well as those on the island who were waiting to cross.[52] His death also led to some confusion as to who was in command.

Colonel Edward D. Baker
A confidant of President Lincoln and prominent politico. His popularity and death at Ball's Bluff on October 21, 1861 elevated his status to that of a martyred hero and masked his failures as the commander of the Union forces in the battle. (Courtesy of the Library of Congress)

Lee, thinking he had seniority, believed that all was lost and ordered a retreat. Before this could be carried out, it was discovered that Colonel Cogswell was the senior officer. He immediately ordered the men to cut their way through the enemy line on their left and escape to Edward's Ferry, nearly four miles away. As enemy fire coincidentally slackened on the center of the Union line, men from the right, Devens' Fifteenth Massachusetts, were moved to the left of the original line. Smoke continued to fill the air. The ground was covered with blood, eyewitnesses report, and "the noise was deafening." Reports state: "Men were lying under foot and here there was a horse struggling in death. Coats and guns were strewn over the ground in all directions."

As Devens moved behind the Twentieth Massachusetts, he noticed that they had suffered more severely than his regiment. The troops there were "not in so good order" and seemed "almost broken." Once on the Union left, Devens' men were joined by the recent arrival of five Tammany companies. Their crossing had been slow and tedious. Not only could the boats carry just one company across at a time, but they were further slowed on their return by being swamped and laden with wounded and dead from the battlefield.

Cogswell's attempt to save his force by moving it through the Confederates on his left ended disastrously. Traditional accounts contend that the movement started badly, with part of the Union force being duped by a Confederate officer who led them into Southern fire. The story goes that the Massachusetts and Tammany men were forming to attack when a Confederate Lieutenant, Charles B. Wildman, appeared on horseback in front of the Tammany men, took off his hat, and waved the Yankees toward him. Eppa Hunton later wrote that Wildman was in an inebriated state and had mistaken Federals for Confederates. On the other side, Devens claimed, "Someone appeared on horseback in front of the Tammany regiment—a rider on a gray horse. I do not know who he was. He took off his hat and waved it in front of the regiment [to signal them to follow him]."[53]

The mystery man urging the Federals forward was in all probability not the Confederate Wildman, but Colonel Cogswell. When the Tammany men rushed forward toward the enemy in the woods, the Fifteenth Massachusetts lowered their muskets as if to make a bayonet charge and moved forward. Before they had gone ten paces, Colonel Devens, who—on the smoky battlefield—apparently mistook Cogswell for an enemy officer attempting to lure the men into a deadly trap, ran in front of his regiment, shouting, "For God's sake, men, stand where you are." The other officers repeated the colonel's command, and the men stopped. This explains what puzzled Cogswell long after the battle. A year after Ball's Bluff, when he was released by the Confederates who captured him at the end of the battle, Cogswell pinned a belated and little-noticed report. In it he stated, "I ordered an advance of the whole force on the right of the enemy line. I was followed by the remnants of my two companies [Tammany] and a portion of the California regiment, but for some reason unknown to me, was not joined by either the Fifteenth or Twentieth Massachusetts Regiments."

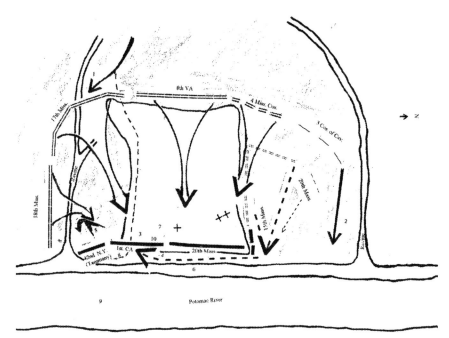

1. Arrival of the 17th Miss about 4:00 p.m. between 8th VA and 18th Miss
2. Two Cos. of Jenifer's Cavalry move toward the river, completing the encirclement of the Union line
3. Site of the death of Col Baker
4. Cogswell pulls the 15th Mass. To the left
5. An attempt to break through to Edwards Ferry fails and the Union line collapses as men flee the bluff
6. Federals trapped at the base of bluff (6:00 to (9:00 p.m.)

7. In an attempt to protect the men on the river bank, Capt. Wm. Bartlett with 80 men of the 20th Mass. reascend to the top of the bluff and is driven away by the 8th VA (Site where Clinton Hatcher is killed.)
8. To stop enemy fire from the bluff, two recently arrived Tammany Cos. Unsuccessfully attempt to reach the top of the bluff as Coswell and a dozen men attack enemy on the left ravine and are captured
9. Union soldiers attempt to swim to Harrison's Island, but many are shot and drown
10. Present cemetery site

BATTLE OF BALL'S BLUFF:
THE ENVELOPMENT OF THE FEDERALS ON THE BLUFF
AND DISASTER (4:00 TO 6:00 P.M.) OCTOBER 21, 1861

Cogswell records that the small number who followed him ran into "a most terrific fire." Reeling backward in confusion, they broke Devens' line. It was rapidly reestablished, but not as well as before. After several exchanges of volleys, the situation became hopeless. The Confederates were surrounding the Federals. The withdrawal of Devens' force from the right left only the skirmishers of the Twentieth Massachusetts to combat Jenifer's forces, as Hunton's men pressed forward from the center across the open field toward the bluff. Reluctantly, Cogswell soon gave the order to retreat.[54]

Twice Tammany men charged on the enemy, impetuously and with great effort, after the order to retreat. They too were swept from the bluff. One soldier later testified to the congressional committee that the advancing and firing by the Seventeenth Mississippi formed a crescent line that enabled them to strike "with a raking fire to cut down any advancing enemy. Suddenly, above the roar of musketry, was heard the command of Colonel Featherston, their commander: "Charge, Mississippians, Charge! Drive them into the Potomac or into eternity." As the enemy came in on the Union left, delivering heavy volleys, Federals fled, abandoning what protection they had behind the trees. The three silent artillery pieces were abandoned. Major Revere was slightly wounded while unsuccessfully trying to have the two howitzers pushed into the river, only to have Hunton's men—charging with bayonets as their ammunition was exhausted—capture the two pieces. A soldier near the elderly Colonel Lee recorded that Lee, "protected for a time by a horse that had been wounded and had fallen to his knees, now sat under a tree swearing he would rather be taken prisoner than take another step."

On the bluff, panic set in. The Confederates had enveloped the Union force by cutting off their escape routes to the left and the right. In desperation, Federals fled down the narrow path to the riverbank below. A few might have been shoved or jumped over the bluff.

For the Union, all was lost. Exhausted men, many of those who had been on the field all day, fled below the bluff. It was "an awful spectacle!" wrote a shocked Confederate eyewitness years after the war. "A kind of shiver ran through the huddled mass upon the brow of the cliff; it gave way, rushed a few steps, then in one wild, panic stricken herd, rolled, leaped, tumbled over the precipice! The descent is nearly perpendicular, with a water laved base. Screams of pain and terror filled the air. Men seemed suddenly bereft of reason…[and leaped] over the bluff with muskets still in their clutch, threw themselves into the river without divesting themselves of their heavy accouterments—hence went to the bottom like lead. Others sprang down upon the heads and bayonets of those below. A gray-haired private of the First California was found with his head mashed between two rocks by the heavy boots of a ponderous Tammany man, who had broken his neck by the fall! The side of the bluff was worn smooth by the number sliding down." The few boats loaded with wounded were swamped with what the eyewitness called a "torrent of terror-stricken fugitives" who "rolled down the bluff upon them." "Boats were instantly submerged, and their cargoes of helpless [wounded]…were swept away to unknown graves! The whole surface of the river seemed filled with heads, struggling, screaming, fighting, dying! Man clutched at man, and the strong, who might have escaped, were dragged down by the weaker. Voices that strove to shout for help were stifled by the turbid, sullen waters of the swollen river and died away in gurgles. Men grabbed one another in a frantic effort to keep from drowning." Captain Otter (who was named appropriately for a swimmer) of the First California was found "dead a few days later with two men of his company clutching his neckband." Another officer "was found with $126 in gold in his pocket,"—"it had cost him his life."[55]

A similar scene was described by a Federal officer, Captain Young, a member of Baker's staff who had helped take his colonel's body to the island. From there he looked back "to the Virginia shore," where he "saw such a spectacle as no tongue can describe." The rout was at its worst, according to a Union eyewitness: "Our entire forces were retreating, tumbling, rolling, leaping down the steep banks; the enemy following them, murdering and taking prisoners. Muskets, coats, and everything were thrown aside, and all were desperately [attempting to escape]." "Hundreds plunged into the rapid current, and shrieks of the drowning added to the horror of sounds and sight. All was confusion, terror and dismay. Many not drowned were shot when about to reach the island."

Even when accounting for any exaggeration that might have occurred in these accounts, the overall view is correct. It was a horrible and terrible scene. Contrasting with the scene of panic were some heroic yet futile attempts to alleviate the plight at the bluff. Such was an attempt made by Captain William F. Bartlett of the Twentieth

152

Massachusetts, who called on his men for one last rally. About eighty men from his regiment responded and again ascended to the open field at the top of the bluff. There they came upon two companies of the Eighth Virginia who were just emerging from the woods. In front was the Virginians' flag bearer, a lanky twenty-two-year-old sergeant, T. Clinton Hatcher, who had put aside the pacifist beliefs of his Quaker religion to defend his homeland. "Both sides were so surprised," Bartlett wrote, "at seeing each other—they at seeing us coming up with a handful of men, we at seeing these two new companies drawn up in perfect order,—that *each side forgot* to fire. And we stood looking at each other (not a gun being fired) for some twenty seconds, and then they let fly their volley at the same time we did."

The Federals were driven back, amid sheets of bullets. At first several men refused to follow the order to retreat. The six-foot-five Hatcher, the Eighth Virginia flag bearer, was killed, the victim of a bullet wound in his chest. Only the previous March Hatcher, while a student at Columbia College in Washington, had attended Lincoln's inaugural reception at the White House. Upon seeing the tall youth, Mr. Lincoln is said have called to him: "Stranger! I never allow anyone taller than myself to pass me unchallenged, I acknowledge myself beaten."[56]

In the meantime Cogswell was among those who left the bluff and descended to the riverbank. He found the scene disheartening. It was around 6:00 P.M., and his whole force was trapped below the bluff in "a state of great disorder." The enemy was firing down upon them from the bluff and the ravine on their left. Cogswell told Devens, "We shall all be destroyed here. We must do something to retard them."

Devens asked, "What shall we do?" Cogswell had Devens' men fire desperately up toward the crest of the bluff, which was thick with the enemy. But, said Devens, "it was hopeless." Devens claimed if he had been fighting "with Englishmen or Frenchmen," he would have surrendered, but he could not surrender to men attempting to destroy the Union.[57] After Devens' men fired ineffectively up at the enemy once or twice, they were told to throw their muskets into the river. Devens ordered: "every man may now take care of himself."

The only glimmer of hope was the arrival of two Tammany companies commanded by Captains Michael Garrity and Timothy

O'Meara. They were immediately ordered up the bluff to serve as skirmishers to cover passage to the island while Cogswell and a dozen men attempted to "check the heavy fire" of the enemy from the nearby ravine. This was also futile. Cogswell and his small band were "almost immediately surrounded and captured," and the two New York companies were repulsed, leaving Captain Garrity dead. O'Meara swam frantically to the island for help. There he implored Colonel Hines, who was then in command of the island, for the use of a boat to rescue his men. Failing, O'Meara dutifully and selflessly returned to the dark, foreboding Virginia banks. Later that night, at about 8:00—some say 11:00—he and 324 others were captured at the base of the bluff, the victims of a party of fifty Confederates guided by Lige White who had hunted over the area.[58]

Earlier desperate men had seen the few vessels—their only escape—disappearing. Just as the scow, loaded with wounded, was pushed off, a sudden rush of men fleeing from the bluff ran onto the flatboat. The boat was dangerously overloaded and was the target of enemy fire from the bluff, which felled several men pushing the poles. The vessel made it only to the middle of the river. There it suddenly rolled over, dumping everyone, the unhurt as well as the wounded, into the three- to five-mile-an-hour current. As the upside-down scow floated out of sight, men frantically grabbed each other in futile attempts to delay drowning. The three smaller vessels had also disappeared. A metal lifeboat sank after it was riddled with bullets.

Within half an hour of when the boats left, "not a single boat of any description was within reach." Some nonswimmers were accompanied by friends who would not abandon them, searched for relief on the banks above the bluff. One group, Colonel Lee, Major Revere, his brother—the only physician on the battlefield that day—and several others searched upstream for a crossing. They attempted to make a raft out of fence rails and their sword belts, but it sank almost immediately. They continued up to Smart's Mill, opposite the upper end of Harrison's Island, where they considered fording, "but the water was so high and Colonel Lee was so exhausted" (earlier they had had to assist him down the bluff) that they did not dare attempt it. On member of Lee's party recalled that a "colored man, in consideration of their only ten-dollar gold piece" showed them a boat, which they pulled out of the mill stream. It was full of water, the firing was close, and they believed they did not have enough time to repair it, so they continued on only, to be captured by the enemy cavalry.[59]

Those who could swim were urged by their officers to try to escape. Most threw their weapons and equipment in the river and stripped down to their underwear. Some took everything off and plunged nude into the river. Those with smooth-bored muskets gladly heaved them in the water; those with the more accurate rifle-muskets were more reluctant. Some swam across with them on their backs. To save his weapon, a nonswimmer spent two nights ten miles up from the bluff, eluding capture, before finally calling to a Federal picket across the river, who went over and brought the man and his rifle-musket back.[60]

A lieutenant attempted to save his sword, boots, pistol, and belt by placing them on a small board. He made slow progress swimming with one hand, so he soon had to let go of the board that carried his treasured possessions. Like many of his comrades, he was exhausted from spending all day on the battlefield, and swimming in chilling water with his clothes on and pockets full made his task more difficult. Every struggling effort pushed his head under water. It suddenly "flashed upon him" that he was going to drown. He continued to swallow water until he sank unconsciously beneath the river's surface. The current carried him onto a small island, where he gained semiconsciousness and took feeble steps up the muddy bank, where he collapsed. Fortunately for him, soon Colonel Devens and his party, who were clinging to a log, landed where the soldier lay. They carried him with them as they waded the shallow water between the small island and nearby Harrison's Island.[61]

The muscular Captain Caspar Crowinshield of the Twentieth Massachusetts swam across the river, saving his sword and carrying his watch in his mouth. Totally exhausted, he fell asleep under a haystack on the island. Upon waking, he crossed over into Maryland, but he forgot the watch he had taken such great pains to save.

A captain and a lieutenant of German descent attempted to swim across with their clothes, shoes, equipment, and their even pistols. They were doing fine until one of them shouted in German that he had been shot. Soon both disappeared. Almost two weeks later, one of the bodies was found twenty miles downstream. Other pitiful pleas or cries for help could be heard from heads barely above the water, the victims of fatigue, the lead hail from enemy muskets, and limited swimming skills.

Some were lucky; others were not. Among the fortunate survivors was Lieutenant Church Howe, the quartermaster of the Fifteenth Massachusetts. He had sundry duties that day. Several times that morning, Devens had sent him to see if Baker had arrived on the bluff. Since Howe had a field glass, as the battle was opening, Baker ordered him to look for enemy cavalry and to direct Lieutenant French to "throw shells among them." Howe received four shots while standing near two Federal pieces during an enemy charge. One shot went through his cap, one struck his belt, and two hit his sword, leaving only dents. His miraculous escape from injury later enabled him to help carry Baker's body from the bluff. He was also able to cross the river in an attempt to resupply dwindling ammunition from the 40,000 rounds on the other side of the river. Before Howe could return to Virginia, his comrades had been shoved from the bluff.[62]

Others were less fortunate. Seventeen-year-old John "Willie" Grout of the Fifteenth Massachusetts started to swim the river with his companions, but before he could reach the island, he was struck by enemy fire. His body was not found until November 5. It was sent to his family in Worcester to be laid to rest. Henry S. Washburn wrote "The Vacant Chair" in his memory; it became a well-known song that touched all who had lost family and friends in the war.[63]

For the pitiful horde stranded on the Virginia shore, Harrison's Island was the immediately sought-after haven. Once men reached the island, they found it no haven. One Union soldier observed that wounded men were crowded "together in and about the two farm houses" that were used as makeshift hospitals. As darkness fell, no light was provided. The surgeon, running about, found "two inches of candle in an old battle, by the light of which Lieutenant-Colonel Ward's limb was amputated."[64]

The wounded Holmes was there, occasionally touching the bottle of laudanum in his pocket, which he had carried into battle for just such an emergency. What he witnessed was not reassuring: the sickening sight of an amputated arm on top of a blanket in a pool of blood. Two men were standing near the entrance, one a surgeon, who held the other man's finger, cutting it off as the man grimaced. Holmes was plagued with wondering if he would die and whether he would go to heaven or hell. Concerned friends visited him, and in his light-headed state, Holmes expressed uncertainties about his fate—laced with profanity. A horrified friend tried to stop these utterances for fear that they would ensure his wounded friend's damnation.

Later that night, Holmes was taken to Poolesville on a rough ride on a broken two-wheel ambulance with an inept driver and a balky horse. In Poolesville he was placed in a bed next to a wounded comrade, who presented a "ghastly spectacle," Holmes wrote, with two black holes that were all that was left of his eyes, and with whiskers and beard matted with blood still running from his mouth, which presented a "most horrible stench." A male nurse, who charged Holmes for his services, plugged the wounds with lint and tightly bandaged him, making the future jurist physically uncomfortable but mentally reassured that he would survive.[65]

Confederate hospitals were set up in churches in Leesburg, while the Union dead and wounded were placed in an old house on Harrison's Island and were ferried to the Maryland shore during the night. From there they were taken by canal boat to Edward's Ferry, where the injured were sent to various regimental hospitals. The dead had been placed on stretchers and on shutters and doors taken from the island, which were placed on the porch of a building at Edward's Ferry with the other bodies. The troops that were gathering to be sent to Virginia passed by these corpses, often expressing sorrow. One curious soldier lifted the rubber blanket of the wounded soldier he believed to be a corpse and was astonished to see the "dead man open his eyes and look around to see where he was."[66]

The route to Poolesville the night after the battle was a somber one. The moon was behind a cloud, but it still provided illumination. Picket huts, resembling dog kennels, near the river could be seen from a distance, as could the "shivering crowds standing in gloomy groups in deep mud and vehicles of various description carrying the wounded with bloodstained bandages along with the dead to Poolesville." After the vehicles came men in groups of "twos, threes and squads." Some were fully clothed and accoutred, but the majority lacked "most of their garments and arms [weapons]." Not half had caps or weapons. Many walked with the assistance of others. Nearly all were "drenched or dripping with the water of the Potomac," but they all trudged toward Poolesville in silence and gloom. After midnight, rain began to fall on the demoralized crowd, adding to the "squalidness of the scene" and making bad roads even worse.

IMMEDIATE CONSEQUENCES OF THE BATTLE

As light appeared the morning after the battle, on Harrison's Island, sights of the Union's disaster were illuminated. A man who observed the scene on the island the day after the battle, described the details: The farmhouse, flanked by the traditional outbuildings, had been used by the surgeons. The largest room was on the first floor and was "completely covered with blood, and in one corner feet, hands, and arms were [piled] like pig's feet in a butcher's shop, while in a shabby structure attached to the house" lay the bodies of those who had died. All were naked, their clothing taken by shivering and partially nude men who had fled from the bluff. Outside the house in one corner of the yard under a large chestnut tree, men were digging a trench to bury the dead in the rain.

Nearby were long ricks of straw and hay under which men, horses, cannons, and provisions were crowded together. Some men sought refuge inside the unfinished stone barn, which was surrounded by an extremely high hedge. It was an unusual structure: the center was an octagon with a fifty-foot diameter, and attached to it were two wings, one facing south, and the other, east. Inside the two wings were men of the Nineteenth Massachusetts (who had been assigned to cover the retreat), eating raw pork and hard bread. While they ate breakfast, their colonel, Edward W. Hicks, moved past the more than twenty rifle pits they had constructed earlier to defend the island. He walked to the western edge of the island to talk with the enemy about returning the Union dead and wounded. There the colonel and about twenty men stood on one bank, talking to Confederate pickets on the other. Behind the latter could be seen, Hicks and his men spotted about twenty Union soldiers lying on the ground. A dozen or so Confederates repeatedly hollered to the Union to send for their dead and wounded. The Federals replied they would gladly do so if the lone boat on the Virginia side was sent to them, as they had no vessels. Then two Confederates picked up one of the wounded, but before placing him in the boat, they laid down the Federal soldier, ransacked his pockets, and cut off his buttons. Finally a Union soldier swam over and retrieved the boat.[67]

On the Virginia side of the river, there was also an atmosphere of concern and hustle during the day and the night after the battle. Civilians had gathered during the day to try to watch the battle. At day's end, concerned fathers and friends surveyed the battlefield for loved ones, and on several occasions, they failed to recognize the begrimed and smoke-covered faces of a son or friend standing in front of them. Federal prisoners were taken to Leesburg and were viewed by curious local residents. Colonel Lee and the men with him who were captured near Smart's Mill were taken to a tavern, where Colonel Evans offered to parole them if all would "agree not to serve again during the war." No one accepted, and a short argument erupted. Offended by the offer, they castigated Evans. Colonel Cogswell, who had known Evans before the war, said, "Shanks, you ought not to offer this to gentlemen."

Another added, "You are no gentleman yourself to offer this."

Finally, an exhausted Evans blurted, "Then you get out of this."

Later the Union officers and other prisoners were fed. At midnight guards and their captives started on foot to Manassas in a downpour. A lumber wagon was provided for the few who could not walk. Prisoners wearily sloughed through the mud during the night and into the next morning, when they were greeted by women who came out of their homes and shouted, "Kill the damn Yankees."

They finally reached the Bull Run battlefield and were temporarily halted at the Stone House, which had served as a hospital earlier that summer. There they were fed, before being sent by rail to Richmond prisons, where they were confined until they would later be released in a prisoner exchange. Before leaving the battlefield, the prisoners witnessed one embittered Rebel guard pull a fence rail from a fence and pry up the grisly remains of a Union soldier. Once in Richmond, Colonel Lee and Major Revere would face the most unnerving incarceration. They were among those who would be selected as hostages to receive the same treatment the Union authorities gave a captured Confederate crew accused of piracy. Fortunately for all, the crisis would abate without executions.[68]

The day after the battle was filled with burial of the dead, care for the wounded, and an anticlimactic skirmish at Edward's Ferry. Under a flag of truce, ten Federals and their captain crossed the river to the battlefield to bury the Union dead. They labored at their task until dark, finding two dead wearing only shirts; others had jackets missing, and almost all had had the contents of their pockets removed. The dead were buried in their remaining clothing and were placed in the graves on their sides, with usually two, three, or four lying side by side—except in one trench, where eleven corpses were placed. The dead faces were covered with leaves and several feet of dirt and a small rock at head and foot of each grave.[69]

The skirmish at Edward's Ferry the day after the battle was the result of defensive actions taken by a shocked McClellan. Ironically, Stone and McClellan had been optimistic throughout much of the day of the battle, remaining ignorant of the impending disaster. Stone had been confident that Baker could handle the situation. Stone did not hear from him until 1:30 P.M. and was not told that McCall had left Dranesville that morning and returned to his camp near Prospect Hill. McClellan had telegraphed Stone several times during the day to take Leesburg and to call on General Banks for help. McClellan was alarmed by the news of Baker's death and the rout of his men.

Fearing another disaster at Edward's Ferry, on the day of the battle, he immediately ordered Gorman's men (2,250) across the river to stay on the Virginia shore. They were to entrench until help arrived to ensure a safe recrossing of the Potomac. The following day Banks arrived with his division, assumed command, and sent more men to Virginia, bringing the total there to 4,400.

That afternoon, October 22, a brief skirmish ensued, as Confederates became concerned about the Federal buildup. Colonel Barksdale and his Thirteenth Mississippians were sent to reconnoiter and, if feasible, to attack the enemy. After driving the Federal pickets behind their earthworks, a brief exchange took place, during which Union General Frederick Lander was wounded. The Confederates soon pulled back. The following day Federal entrenchments continued. Despite high winds that had plagued the crossing, the Federals returned to Maryland from 9:00 P.M. on October 23 to 5:00 the next morning.[70] This ended the military operations of Ball's Bluff—but not the repercussions. No battle of similar size would touch off such a controversy in the North.

AFTERMATH: RECRIMINATIONS AND A PROMISING CAREER RUINED

The casualty statistics of the battle attest to its tragedy. Although both combatants were similar in strength, about 1,700 each, Union losses of 921 numbered about half (49 killed, 158 wounded, and 713 captured or missing) their total force engaged. Confederate losses were much lighter, 149 (33 killed, 115 wounded, and 1 missing.)[71] The key ingredients that produced disaster were confusion about and failed execution of orders, lack of communication, insufficient vessels for crossing the Potomac, an ambitious politician-colonel itching for combat, and the improper placement of his men (with their backs to a steep bluff).

The Federal loss had not denied the Union control of strategic territory, but it severely damaged morale in the North. The loss also exacerbated the perplexing problem the Washington government faced: how to gain and keep the support and confidence of the Union citizenry for a war that was six months old and still without a major victory in the eastern theater.[72]

Fearing repercussions of the disastrous defeat, the government blocked the release of battle details. After all, McClellan had promised no more Bull Runs. Under the pretense of protecting top-secret information connected with foreign diplomacy and the New York stock market, the State Department ordered the telegraph office to withhold all dispatches dealing with Ball's Bluff, except those written and approved by the government. For nearly a week, government censorship prevented the press from presenting accurate accounts of the battle. The day after Ball's Bluff, reporters flocked to McClellan's office in search of information. There they saw a grief-stricken president who had just learned of the death of his friend Baker. Teary-eyed, head bowed, Lincoln stumbled as he left the office. Newspaper men jumped forward to offer help, but the bereaved leader regained his balance. A few moments later the general appeared. He announced that a Union force had crossed the Potomac and Baker was reported to have been killed. McClellan concluded, "That is about all I can give you."[73]

The correspondent for the New York *World,* Edmund C. Stedman, wanted more. Once he learned of the battle he hurried to the scene. Angered by the disaster, he frantically rode back to get the news in print. He persevered through an attack of camp fever by holding a wet cloth to his feverish brow as he wrote perhaps the best newspaper account of the battle. But the government delayed publishing his account of the battle for a week.

The delay in releasing information only fueled speculation, and Ball's Bluff continued to be a controversial subject for months. Ugly tales surfaced that Baker and his men had been sacrificed by the disloyal Stone. Baker's defenders published an erroneous statement— they claimed that on receiving Stone's order to the cross the river, Baker said: "I'll do it, but it is my death warrant."[74]

"Who was responsible for all this slaughter," asked the New York *Tribune*? Details of the battle gradually reached the country, and the most repugnant news was of finding bodies of Union soldiers weeks after the battle at Chain Bridge, the wharves along Washington, and beyond. One was virtually naked, another carried a New Testament, a looking glass, and a lock of the deceased's hair. All of this somehow seemed more senseless and more unacceptable than the usual tragic death harvests of combat. Even residents of Virginia swore they would no longer eat fish taken from the Potomac.[75]

The North would formally mourn Baker's loss into the new year. The Lincolns had wanted their dear friend's body placed in the East Room, but redecoration of the White House prevented this. Instead Baker was placed in the home of another friend, Colonel J. W. Webb, for viewing prior to being temporarily interred in Congressional Cemetery. The ceremony included hundreds of mourners, including the president. Baker's family, along with others, insisted he should be buried on the Pacific coast. In preparation for such a lengthy move, the body was taken from Congressional Cemetery and embalmed, a difficult task that required the mortician to work for two days on the bullet-riddled corpse. Thousands passed by Baker's bronze casket in Philadelphia and New York City before it was placed on a ship bound for the west coast via the isthmus of Panama.

The body arrived in San Francisco on December 6, 1861. It was received by a delegation from California and Oregon and a city draped in black mourning cloth. Five days later funeral services were held. An overflow crowd of people shoved one another to see the large catafalque covered with black velvet. At each corner of the stand stood a broken Corinthian column, symbolizing, as in ancient Greece and Rome, the death of a statesman. The final rites took place at Lone Mountain Cemetery, a disappointment to the Oregonians who had wanted their senator buried in their state. Back east on the day Baker was buried, the Senate held a memorial service with the president in attendance and eulogized their former member. The House did the same on January 22, 1862.[76] The papers adequately covered these ceremonies, but coverage was far less extensive than it had been after Ellsworth's death. The events of the intervening months between the two deaths had made the death of a soldier, even a prominent one, less newsworthy.

While Baker was mourned in the North as a martyr, the opposite was true in the South. A week after the battle a Leesburg man wrote to the Richmond *Dispatch*:

Shall I? Can I have sympathy for any man who invades my home, and strives to lay waste the loveliest portion of God's creation, destroy my property, murder my wife and children? And shall I go further and respect the 'beauty and booty' principles of those invaders? But my heart sickens at the thought. No, I have no sympathy for such, and I thank God I have none. General Baker was the tool of a vile despot to carry out the subjugation—Oh? Annihilation—of a people that never threatened him.[77]

During the months Baker was mourned and eulogized by Northerners as a martyred hero, Stone continued to be vilified as a traitor. By December Baker's congressional colleagues entered the fray over who was responsible for Ball's Bluff. They launched a protracted investigation through the newly created Joint Committee on the Conduct of the War. They heard forty witnesses who gave over 250 pages of testimony, and most placed the blame on Stone. Witnesses were repeatedly asked if they knew any reason why the men on the bluff could not have been saved if help had been sent from Edward's Ferry. Ignoring the fact that enemy artillery would have made such a move dangerous, most witnesses replied by answering no. They added the men had no confidence in Stone, who they claimed communicated with and befriended the enemy. They recounted rumors that Stone had secretly met with enemy officers, passes were issued to secessionists, sealed letters and unopened packages passed through the line, and much more. Even Stone's order to Devens the day before the battle—that the latter should use "great care…to prevent any unnecessary injury of private property, and any officer or soldier straggling from the command for curiosity or plunder will be instantly shot"—was deemed to be a manifestation of sympathy and concern for the enemy.[78]

Any testimony favorable to Stone, even from Baker's good friend and colleague Isaac Wistar, had little, if any, impact on the committee and other Stone critics. Stone's proven loyalty in preparing Washington's defenses during the early days of the war was seemingly forgotten. Evidence was kept secret; Stone was not allowed to know the charges against him or the names of witnesses. His persistent demands for a military court of inquiry were rejected. He was arrested and illegally detained for 189 days and was finally released by an act of Congress. His military career never recovered. Relegated to relatively minor military assignments and viewed constantly with suspicion, he resigned from the army.[79]

Stone was swallowed up in the contest over how the war was to be fought. He became the scapegoat for the Ball's Bluff disaster because of his politics (a conservative Democrat from Massachusetts) and his practice of returning fugitive slaves to their owners. The latter infuriated Massachusetts soldiers who had strong anti-slavery feelings, as well as their governor and Senator Charles Sumner, who had denounced Stone on the Senate floor before the battle. Stone had retaliated by attempting to draw Sumner into a duel, which the wily politico avoided.

Long before Ball's Bluff, Stone had many powerful enemies. But he was not the primary target of the Republicans, who wanted a more vigorous prosecution of the war. It was Stone's boss, McClellan, also a conservative Democrat, who also felt it was not his duty to attack the institution of slavery. McClellan first defended Stone, but then backed away once he realized he was the main target. Early in 1862 he forwarded to Secretary of War Stanton the latest rumors gleamed by Pinkerton. A less-than-reputable recent Leesburg refugee claimed that Confederate officers held General Stone in high regard. Stanton, who felt there was no place for conservative generals in the Union Army, used this "evidence" to order McClellan to immediately arrest Stone.[80]

It was out of the question for Baker to receive blame. Neither Lincoln—who tolerated no criticism of his friend—nor members of

Congress were about to recognize the major role Baker played in the Ball's Bluff disaster. The doting Congressmen had heaped more than eighty pages of eulogies on their charismatic fallen comrade, who had provided indelible memories of striding into the Senate chamber adorned in his colonel's uniform and dramatically and eloquently calling for an unfettered defense of the Union. Stone would find no help in the president. He was distracted at first by the serious illness of one of his children. Firmly believing the salvation of the Union was so paramount that even the rights of the individual must be subverted when they collided with the war effort, Lincoln let Stanton and the Committee on the Conduct of the War have their way.[81] He argued it was probably unfair to Stone, but it was not in the best interest of the country to withdraw on-duty officers for a trial, and he promised Stone would soon have his day in court. In February 1864, after almost three years of struggling unsuccessfully to clear his name, Stone made one last appeal to Lincoln for justice. In April the president started a letter addressing this request in which he stated he did not believe the evidence conclusively proved Stone's guilt. Apparently the latter was never completed or mailed. A frustrated Stone resigned from the army on September 13, 1864.[82]

Following the Ball's Bluff setback, McClellan's army once again relapsed into watchful waiting. Yankee pickets posted along the river ventured no farther than Harrison's Island. During the late fall, pickets had to climb the trees that lined the island to avoid the flooding waters that swept over the island. Northern newspaper correspondents criticized McClellan and the Union inactivity. The press fumed about the inaction against the Confederate blockade of the lower Potomac River, which led to the use of drays to transport needed items from Baltimore. McClellan in turn became more critical of the press.

The continuous military information about McClellan's army being published in newspapers included a large map of the location of his lines and numbers of men outside Washington angered him. He protested to the Secretary of War the publishing the position of his army was treason. One month after Ball's Bluff, on November 20, 1861, in an attempt to lessen criticism and to show off his army, McClellan staged the largest military review that had ever been seen in North America. He selected a site recently held by the enemy, Munson Hill. Sixty-five thousand men spread over 200 acres presented a pageantry that involved the president and his cabinet heading a military cortege "riding down the long lines [of] troops to the rattle of drums, the flourish of trumpets, and the loud huzzas of the whole army." The pressure for McClellan to act did not lessen.

Editors of Southern papers even decried his failure to attack. Their editorials ridiculed the Yankee inactivity, proclaiming: they "will not come, but linger about Fairfax, foraging and plundering, tearing down houses, and felling timber with 'a thousand axe men engaged.' Hay, oats, straw, lumber, wagons, cattle, horses, hogs—yea even 'dogs' are fast disappearing; and when these thieves are satisfied with wasting and devastation there will be very little left to tell the stranger where Fairfax once stood."[83]

[1] Johnston, *Narrative of Military Operations*, 77-78.

[2] New York *Tribune*, October 1, 1861.

[3] Ibid., October 11, 1861. General Smith's division moved from near Chain Bridge to Lewinsville and Falls Church as General George A. McCall's division crossed Chain Bridge to support the advance.

[4] New York *Tribune*, October 8, 1861.

[5] Ibid., October 21, 1861.

[6] Eppa Hunton, *Autobiography of Eppa Hunton* (Richmond, Va.: William Byrd, 1933), 46; Robert A. Moore, *A Life for the Confederacy* (Jackson, Tenn.: McCowat-Mercer, 1959), 67-69; *OR*, Ser. I, vol. 5, 347. Burnt Bridge was three miles upstream from where it empties into the Potomac River across from Edward's Ferry.

[7] *OR* , Ser. I, vol. 5, 290-91.

[8] *Report of the Joint Committee on the Conduct of the War in Three Parts* (Washington, D.C.: Government Printing Office, 1863), pt. II, 401.

[9] They were carried to the Virginia shore in three boats: one "whale boat" that could carry sixteen, and two small boats, which held five and four respectively.

[10] *OR*, Ser. I, vol. 5, 295-96, 304, 310; *Report of Joint Committee on Conduct of the War*, 404. Stone felt the available vessels were sufficient.

[11] Recent writers have maintained that haystacks were mistaken for tents. This is unlikely because hay is not harvested in October. By October 20, small hay ricks in the field would have been moved into barns or placed in larger ricks.

[12] Kim Bernard Holien, *Battle at Ball's Bluff* (Orange, Va.: Moss, 1985), 27; *OR*, Ser. I, vol. 5, 308-309; *Report of Joint Committee on Conduct of the War*, 290-291. By nightfall the Union had 1,513 infantry, cavalry, and artillery (early in the morning two twelve-pound howitzers were sent over) on the Virginia side of Edward's Ferry.

[13] *OR*, Ser. I, vol. 5, 349.

[14] Francis W. Palfrey, *Memoir of William Francis Bartlett* (Boston: Houghton, Osgood & Co., 1878), 16, 20-21.

[15] *OR*, Ser. I, vol. 5, 363.

[16] Philbrick had one killed, nine wounded, and two captured while the Confederates—protected by a ditch—had only one wounded.

[17] *OR*, Ser. I, vol. 5, 309, 363-364. *Report of the Joint Committee on the Conduct of the War*, 406, 476-77.

[18] *OR*, Ser. I, vol. 5, 349, 361.

[19] Jenifer had made a request to Evans before 10:00 A.M. for reinforcements.

[20] The First California, later known as the Seventy-first Pennsylvania regiment, and the others from the Quaker State who formed Baker's brigade, had unique origins. They were originally called California regiments but soon became known as the Philadelphia Brigade. Citizens of the Pacific coast who were in Washington, D.C., in May 1861 decided that California ought to be represented in the Union army in the east. They urged Edward D. Baker, who had practiced law, was active in

California politics, and was now was a senator of the new state of Oregon, to "form a regiment in the east to be credited to California." The president, Baker's friend, approved, and the secretary of war instructed the senator to form in New York City the California Regiment, also called the First California. The eloquent Baker had planned to raise the regiment from the men of the city of New York, but his friend and former law associate in California, Isaac J. Wistar, was from Philadelphia and convinced him to raise men from the Quaker City. Nine companies came from Philadelphia and one from New York City. The men were mustered into service in New York for three years as part of the regular army. They were clad in gray uniforms confiscated in New York and shipped to Fort Monroe.

[21] Evans later strongly rebuked Jenifer for his claim of remaining in charge after Hunton joined him. Jenifer's report after the battle contends that he was in charge throughout the battle, and his description of the combat often greatly differs from those of others at the scene.

[22] Ford, *The Fifteenth Regiment*, 78; *Report of the Joint Committee on the Conduct of the War*, 407. The actual number of Fifteenth Massachusetts men present at the time was 625 men and 28 officers. This number is based on a roll call taken at the site between 10:00 and 11:00 A.M., shortly prior to the skirmish during phase two.

[23] *OR*, Ser. I, vol. 5, 310, 364, 366-67, 369-70; *Report of the Joint Committee on the Conduct of the War*, 407. It took thirty minutes to an hour to pull back all the skirmishers because Company C was a considerable distance away on the right, towards Edward's Ferry Road and Smart's Mill.

[24] The number of casualties in this skirmish (phase two) is not known, so they are included with those of the main battle.

[25] Ford, *The Story of the Fifteenth Regiment*, 79-80; William R. Hamilton, ed., "Ball's Bluff: From the Diary of Major L. H. D. Crane...," *The United Service* (January 1897), 13.

[26] *Report of the Joint Committee on the Conduct of the War*, 477-78. Shortly after noon Lee had started toward Harrison's Island to explain to Baker the conditions and the nature of the terrain he had reconnoitered, when he heard heavy firing (Devens' second skirmish). Lee stayed on the bluff to cover Devens.

[27] *Report of the Joint Committee on the Conduct of the War*, 406.

[28] If he had accepted this proposal, he would have outranked Charles Stone, a brigadier-general.

[29] *Report of the Joint Committee on the Conduct of the War*, 275. Baker probably wanted to have something in writing to show the other colonels that he was in command.

[30] *OR*, Ser. I, vol. 5, 301. It was Stone's opinion that Baker was anxious for combat and that the bloodstained order to the contrary that was found on Baker's body had been altered.

[31] Divine, *Loudoun County and the Civil War*, 27; Holien, *Battle at Ball's Bluff*, 53; *Report of the Joint Committee on the Conduct of the War*, 478-79.

[32] Battery R of the First Rhode Island Light Artillery was commanded by Lieutenant French. These would be the only artillery pieces used in the battle at the bluff. They were dismantled, taken across the river, and reassembled upon reaching Ball's

Bluff.

[33] Captain Francis G. Young, Baker's quartermaster and supporter, testified at the Committee of the Conduct of the War that Cogswell said nothing when Baker asked him about the troops' position.

[34] Evans ordered Colonel Erasmus R. Burt's Eighteenth Mississippi Regiment to the bluff at approximately 2:30 P.M., giving the same order half an hour later to Colonel Winfield Scott Featherton's Seventeenth Mississippi.

[35] Divine, *Loudoun County and the Civil War*, 26; *OR*, Ser. I, vol. 5, 324, 349.

[36] *Report of the Joint Committee on the Conduct of the War*, 309; Wistar, *Autobiography*, 365.

[37] Bruce, *The Twentieth Regiment of Massachusetts Volunteer Infantry*, 48-49.

[38] *Report of the Joint Committee on the Conduct of the War*, 321

[39] Palfrey, *Memoir of William Francis Bartlett*, 23-24. Bartlett said an old German soldier who had seen many a battle told him he had never seen such concentrated fire before.

[40] *Report of the Joint Committee on the Conduct of the War*, 479-80; *OR*, Ser. I, vol. 5, 327-28.

[41] *OR*, Ser. I, vol. 5, 321. Other Union officers later testified the artillery was ineffective and fired only half a dozen to a dozen times at an enemy they could not see.

[42] Divine, *Eighth Virginia Infantry*, 5-6.

[43] Evans orders Colonel E. R. Burt at 2:30 P.M. to move the Eighteenth Mississippi from Edward's Ferry Road area to reinforce Hunton at the bluff.

[44] All the Union officers were now dismounted, their horses tied to trees on their left.

[45] Divine writes (*Loudoun County and the Civil War*, 29) that Cogswell, seeing this threat to the left, sent three companies (two Tammany Companies and one California) across the ravine to dislodge the enemy but was forced back.

[46] Bruce, *Twentieth Regiment*, 47.

[47] Mark DeWolfe Howe, ed., *Touched with Fire: Civil War Letters and Diary of Oliver Wendell Holmes, Jr.* (Cambridge, Mass.: Harvard University, 1946), 13-14. Holmes was later told by a friend that he was wounded at 4:30. It was more likely earlier, as Holmes said he had gone down very early in the battle.

[48] *Report of the Joint Committee on the Conduct of the War*, 479-80.

[49] Ford, *The Story of the Fifteenth Regiment*, 86-87.

[50] William F. Howard, *The Battle of Ball's Bluff: "The Leesburg Affair," October 21, 1861* (Lynchburg, Va.: H.E. Howard, 1994), 40; *OR*, Ser. I, vol. 5, 323; Wistar, *Autobiography*, 370-371.

[51] *Report of the Joint Committee on the Conduct of the War*, 321-322; Wistar, *Autobiography*, 370.

[52] A few accounts contend that Baker was shot by an enemy sniper in a tree; another claims he was shot by a cavalry officer who rode up and emptied his revolver; and others have several Confederates running out of the woods near Baker and a red-headed private firing the fatal shots. Hand-to-hand combat occurred, some claim, around Baker's body. Byron Farwell, *Ball's Bluff: A Small Battle and Its Long*

Shadow (McLean, Va.:EFM Publication, 1990). Howard, *The Battle of Ball's Bluff*, 46; *OR,* vol. 5, 320; *Shotwell Papers*, 117.

[53] *Report of the Joint Committee on the Conduct of the War*, 409, 410.

[54] Farwell, *Ball's Bluff*, 49-50; *OR*, Ser. I, vol. 5, 311, 322. *Report on the Joint Committee on the Conduct of the War*, 401; Howard, *The Battle of Ball's Bluff*, 52; Palfrey, ed., *Memoir of William Francis Barlett*, 25.

[55] J. G. De Roulhac Hamilton, ed., *The Papers of Randolph Abbott Shotwell* (Raleigh, N.C.: North Carolina Historical Commission, 1929) vol. 1, 118-19. Shotwell was a lad of seventeen with the Eighth Virginia at the time of the battle.

[56] Howard, *The Battle of Ball's Bluff*, 55; Palfrey, ed., *Memoir of William Francis Bartlett*, 25-26; Poland, *From Frontier to Suburbia*, 180; *OR*, Ser. I, vol. 5, 319-20. Long after the war, when veterans of the Twentieth Massachusetts revisited the battlefield and learned of Hatcher's actions, they donated a granite monument, which still stands marking where the tall flag-bearer fell.

[57] *Report on the Joint Committee on the Conduct of the War*, 411.

[58] Divine, *Eighth Virginia Infantry*, 6; Howard, The Battle of Ball's Bluff, 58-59; *Report on the Joint Committee on the Conduct of the War*, 481; *OR*, Ser. I, vol. 5, 322-25; E.V. White, *History of the Battle of Ball's Bluff* (Leesburg, Va.: "The Washington" Print, 1902), 16-20. After the Confederate force was pulled back to Leesburg, only two companies were left near the bluff with a dozen pickets under Lieutenant Charles Berkeley of the Eighth Virginia. Fearing Federals were still trying to cross to the island, Berkeley sent back to Hunton for volunteers to capture the beleaguered enemy. White's voluntary role in this and throughout the day (including guiding the Eighteenth Mississippi to high ground across from the left ravine, which trapped the Federals and shut the door to their escape to Edward's Ferry) made him one of the heroes of Ball's Bluff. At that time he was a corporal on leave from Ashby's cavalry, but would rise to command the Comanches (Thirty-fifth Battalion, Virginia cavalry) and by the end of the war would command the Laurel Brigade.

[59] Bruce, *The Twentieth Massachusetts*, 53-54.

[60] *Report on the Joint Committee Conduct of the War*, 411.

[61] Ford, *The Story of the Fifteenth Regiment*, 92.

[62] *Report on the Joint Committee on the Conduct of the War*, 376-7.

[63] Howard, *The Battle of Ball's Bluff*, 94-95.

[64] More candles were later found in a closet.

[65] Mark D. Howe, ed., *Touched with Fire*, 24-20.

[66] Bruce, *Twentieth Massachusetts*, 61-62.

[67] "Ball's Bluff," *The United Services*, January 1897, 12-16.

[68] Bruce, *Twentieth Massachusetts*, 65-67; Ford, *Fifteenth Massachusetts*, 108-10; Randall and Donald, *Civil War and Reconstruction*, 448-49.

[69] Ford, *Fifteenth Massachusetts*, 95-96. After the war the fifty-four Union bodies, all unknown except for Captain James Allen, were reinterred on the battlefield behind a stone wall and marked by a semicircle of twenty-seven white markers.

[70] *Joint Committee on the Conduct of the War*, 255-56; *OR*, Ser. I, vol. 5, 32-33, 334, 355; Sears, *The Civil War Papers of George B. McClellan*, 109.

[71] OR, Ser. I, vol. 5, 308, 353; Poland, *Frontier to Suburbia,* 201.

[72] Poland, *Frontier to Suburbia*, 201. Across the Potomac, Confederate papers stressed the inevitability of the Federal disaster at the bluff. Three thousand newspapers, Union and Confederate, extensively covered Ball's Bluff in their often-jaundiced accounts. Southerners rejoiced over "The Grand Fight Near Leesburg." Local residents, despite some fears that "Yankees" might still threaten Leesburg, visited the battlefield immediately after the fighting and carried off much of the Confederate spoils of war. This sparked Evans to issue a proclamation requiring local citizens to return to him enemy arms.

[73] Generals frequently tried to obtain favorable press coverage. Shortly after Ball's Bluff, Stedman accepted $15 as a token of General Charles T. James' appreciation of a favorable article on his career.

[74] Stone would later argue that his order to Baker had been modified by "friendly hands."

[75] J. Cutler Andrews, *The North Reports The Civil War* (Pittsburgh, Pa.: University of Pittsburgh, 1955), 155; Leech, *Reveille in Washington*, 116; New York *Tribune*, October 25, 28 & 29, 1861.

[76] Blair and Tarshia, *Lincoln's Constant Ally*, 157-67.

[77] Richmond *Dispatch*, October 30, 1861.

[78] *OR*, Ser. I, vol. 5, 330

[79] Later Charles Stone became chief of staff to the Khedive of Egypt.

[80] The Joint Committee on the Conduct of the War reached no final conclusions, but reported their finding to the concurring newly appointed Secretary of War, Edwin Stanton.

[81] Basler, *The Collected Works of Abraham Lincoln*, vol. V, 201, 204-5 and vol. VII, 285-86; Howard, *The Battle of Ball's Bluff*, 70-73; J. G. Randall, *Lincoln: The President* (New York: Dodd, Mead, 1945), 63-64; Sears, *George B. McClellan*, 144-45; Benjamin P. Thomas and Harold Hyman, *Stanton: The Life and Time of Lincoln's Secretary of War* (New York: Knopf, 1962), 261-62. After the war Charles Stone served with distinction for thirteen years as chief of staff of the Army of the Khidive of Egypt. Later he engineered the foundation of the Statue of Liberty. He died in New York City on January 24, 1887, and was interred at West Point.

[82] Andrews, *The North Reports the Civil War,* 155; *Harper's Weekly,* December 7, 1861; Memphis *Daily Appeal,* December 1861; Sears, ed., *The Civil War Papers of George B. McClellan,* 137.

[83] Memphis *Daily Appeal*, December 1861.

CHAPTER V

THE UNION FINALLY WINS: THE DRANESVILLE ENGAGEMENT

After Ball's Bluff each side continued its vigilant watch for surprise moves from the enemy. The almost-daily skirmishes in northern Virginia between reconnoitering cavalry were manifestations of that vigilance.

THE DEBATABLE LAND

The territory between the contending forces in northern Virginia continued to be, as described by the Reverend William S. Hammond, a resident of Dranesville, during the Civil War, "debatable ground—a region where terrifying rumors and dire alarms were continually afloat." The boiling cauldron of the most improbable rumors was additionally fueled by the division of political loyalty among the citizens "whose homes stood between the lines of the opposing army." A few were diehard Unionists, while the "greater majority were heart and soul with the Confederacy."

Protecting the Federal right on their outer line was the division of Pennsylvania Reserves under Brigadier-General George A. McCall, a West Pointer and veteran of the Mexican War. His division was at Camp Pierpoint, at Langley, on the Georgetown Turnpike, several miles in advance of Chain Bridge (three miles from Washington). The division consisted of three brigades under Brigadier-Generals J. F. Reynolds, George G. Meade, and E. O. C. Ord.[1]

As cold weather gripped the region, military activity in the debatable territory was motivated by the need for forage (corn and hay). McCall sent men to scour the vicinity to his west for corn and hay. A favorite area was Dranesville, where he sent men and wagons to take forage from John Grunnell's farm and from those McCall dubbed "rank secessionists."

Dranesville had a bad reputation in the eyes of the Federals; they saw it as a hotbed of secession and home of "bad men" and "murderers" of Union pickets. The village women were considered evil. Members of the First Pennsylvania Infantry Reserves attested to this belief, recorded by a soldier: "'Only for the soldiers, none for the officers,' were the words that met [a sergeant]…as he took a cup of water out of a bucket at a yard gate in the neat village of Dranesville while the…[Pennsylvania] Reserve were passing through on a reconnaissance in the fall of 1861." An aged lady and two young girls stood by "granting" the vessel of water, and one of the girls had "uttered the words" quoted above. The sergeant had been about to drink from the well-filled cup when General Reynolds rode up to the gate and requested some water. The sergeant promptly handed the cup, still untouched, to the general, who drank the water, expressed his thanks, and rode away. Deprived of his drink, "the sergeant now turned to get another cup for himself, but was met by a blunt refusal from one of the girls, who said, 'You gave your cup of water to that officer, and you cannot have any more.'" His reply was "I'll give my Brigade commander a cup of water every time, even if it deprives me of a drink at the hands of a she rebel." As he finished "his direct language she turned quickly and spit in his face not once but twice." The sergeant turned and walked away, "but took along the bucket of water."[2]

Dranesville, which sat about twenty miles from Washington and fourteen from Leesburg, was unique from other hamlets in the surrounding region because of the half-dozen taverns and inns lining the roadways. Much of the small town lay along the Leesburg Turnpike, which sloped westward and overlooked Sugarland Run (two miles away) and what the Reverend Hammond called the "rolling, open country of farm and woodland" beyond. The eastern edge of the village sat on the commanding Dranes Hill, near the intersection of the turnpike to Georgetown and the one to Leesburg and Alexandria. The two eastern cities were earlier destinations for wagon and drover traffic, making Dranesville an important stopover.

The wagons and drivers that had previously crowded the turnpikes had been replaced by traveling military men.[3] In a matter of a couple of weeks in late November and early December, the Federals had carried off virtually the entire white adult male population of Dranesville and had placed them, as political prisoners, in the Old Capitol Prison. These and other local "gentlemen" of the Dranesville community were arrested on charges that during the month of August 1861 they had committed—according to military authorities— "sacrilegious acts...of fiendish barbarity...scarcely paralleled in the civilized world." According to Hammond, Union soldiers on Lowe's Island were "shot down by these men in ambush, their pockets rifled of precious mementoes, their bodies stripped to furnish clothing for the negro slaves, and left unburied to be eaten up by hogs, while the money taken from them was made to contribute intoxicated madness to their bitter hate of the Union" and to the "bestial joy over their brutal accomplishment of savage barbarity." The Dranesville "gang" was also charged with taking a letter from the wife of one of the Federal soldiers and insensitively and mockingly reading it in public as well as showing "relics" of the "murdered" men to others.[4]

Union refugees from Dranesville swore to Federal authorities that the 275-pound Dr. William Day had "cut off a Union soldier's head and stuck it upon a pole in front of his house." The doctor was also accused of stealing "Yankee corpses from the Manassas battlefield" and putting "the skulls of two Yankee soldiers in the two wooden balls that topped his front gate posts."

The authorities lacked irrefutable evidence to substantiate the charges against the Dranesville men, who were subsequently released. It is more likely that some or all of the accused had participated in the Dranesville "home guard" in the skirmish with Union pickets on Lowe's Island. The details of this incident are at best nebulous. Testimony regarding the details of the event may have been fabricated by the fugitive slaves to remain behind Union lines and by Union supporters, bitter and resentful of expulsion from their Dranesville homes by the accused. The extraordinary accusations made against

Dr. William Day by neighbors are examples of recrimination through unreliable and deceptive testimony.[5] Nevertheless, the nine men who were charged with murder and robbery spent five to eight anxious months as political prisoners in the Old Capitol Prison in Washington, D.C.

AN ATTACK TO SAVE WAGONS

Just over three weeks after the arrest of most of the so-called bad men of Dranesville, by chance 2,500 men under Jeb Stuart and a slightly larger force under General Ord met in a clash on the afternoon of December 20, 1861; it was known as the action at Dranesville.[6]

Winter's winds, freezing temperatures, and snow prompted the forces at Centreville to send all the wagons they could spare (about 200) to Dranesville and lower Loudoun County to obtain hay to help sustain Confederate horses through the winter. The audacious Stuart was sent with a force of four regiments of infantry, 150 cavalrymen, and a battery of four pieces of artillery to cover and protect the forage expedition. Stuart sent his cavalry in advance to take possession of the two turnpikes to the east of the town of Dranesville in hope of preventing any information from enlightening the Union about the Confederate activity.[7] But Union General George A. McCall was already aware of Confederate activity around Dranesville. Confederate cavalry had previously been sited at Difficult Run and four miles from Camp Pierpont. Feeling his force was vulnerable to attack by what he believed was a larger enemy force, McCall took preventive action. He sent Ord from his camp at Langley, Virginia, over the Georgetown Turnpike to clear Dranesville of any Confederates and to obtain forage at Gunnel's or what McCall called "some other rank secessionists."[8]

Most of Ord's men had never been in combat and were anxious to fight. Among the Pennsylvanians who made up his force were the Bucktails, or the Pennsylvania Reserve Rifles, recruited among the lumbermen of the Quaker State. They brought with them their own rifles and had a reputation for excellence in marksmanship.

They earned their nickname from killing a buck (male deer) and adorning their hats with its tail as a symbol of crack marksmanship. No unit was more anxious for combat than the Bucktails, and no individual more so than their commander, Lieutenant-Colonel Thomas L. Kane, who got out of his sickbed to lead his regiment. Two days before the Dranesville fight, according to authors of the history of the Bucktails, Kane was "lying ill in Washington." Fearful that a military operation would occur without him, Kane "had extracted promises from a friend and his surgeon to advise him should marching orders be received." Upon receiving notice of the impending movement, the adamant colonel "insisted on being moved." Wrapped in blankets, he was carried to an ambulance and transported to his tent at Camp Pierpoint in Langley, Virginia. The following morning, "to the surprise" of the Bucktails, Kane was on horseback, leading them toward Dranesville.[9]

Meanwhile, Stuart had started from his camp at Centreville with four days' rations. He left at daylight on a frosty morning and was approaching Dranesville from the south over Ridge Road when he received word from his cavalry that the enemy had already occupied the area at the juncture of the two turnpikes just east of the town. He galloped forward at once to see for himself. Sure enough, the enemy was in possession of roads on the ridge just east of Dranesville. In his official report, Stuart stated he could "hear distinctly artillery carriages raddling" up the Georgetown pike near the intersection and saw the "cannons mounted on limber boxes moving toward Dranesville." Jeb's heart beat faster. He now knew the enemy's infantry was already there and suspected, incorrectly, that the Federals were either marching upon Leesburg or had learned though a spy of his intended forage expedition and were pursuing it. "In either case," he thought, all of the wagons of Confederates in northern Virginia would be easy prey for the enemy. The bold cavalry leader thought at once that the only way to save the wagons "was to make a vigorous attack upon" the enemy's "rear and left flank." He ordered the infantry to hurry forward and sent a detachment of his cavalry under Captain A. L. Pitzer to "gain the roads toward Leesburg, order the wagons immediately back to camp, and stay between them and the enemy." Soon drivers were shouting and slapping the reins on horses who were running as fast as they could while pulling bouncing wagons over bumpy roads in lower Loudoun and northwestern

Fairfax counties. Later that day, all would reach Centreville safely, thanks to the frantic, skillful, and sometimes reckless driving of men who feared they were about to be captured.

While Stuart was preparing to make a preemptive strike, Ord, expecting the main threat to come from the west, was rushing his force along the Leesburg Turnpike to the west of the town. On Church Hill, which commanded the area, he placed the four artillery pieces of Easton's battery (two twelve-pound smoothbores and two twenty-four-pound howitzers). To protect his flanks, he sent two companies of skirmishers in the "dense pines" on Ridge Road about 800 yards from the intersection. Stuart's infantry approached, three-fourths of a mile farther south.[10]

At 2:30 P.M. Stuart sent forth several companies, who cleared the woods of enemy pickets.[11] Soon afterward, Captain A. S. Cutt's four pieces of the "Sumter Flying Artillery" (a sixteen-pound Parrott and three twenty-four-pound howitzers) were rushed forward, stopping at a dip in the road a hundred yards or fewer from cleared land on both sides of the road, to the front of the troops. Cutt's position on the country road, an eyewitness later wrote, was "walled in by a thick pine grove." "The road was so narrow and the forest so thick there was no room to work but three guns."[12]

While Cutt's battery opened fire, Stuart fanned his infantry out into the woods on both sides of the road to attack. Garland's Eleventh Virginia went to the right and a short distance ahead of Cutt's artillery, while the Sixth South Carolina Volunteers, under Lieutenant-Colonel Secrest, moved left. Colonel J. H. Forney's Tenth Alabama soon arrived, taking Garland's position as the latter "moved by the flank farther to the right," attested Stuart. Colonel Thomas H. Taylor's First Kentucky, "intended as a reserve, was ordered to take a position on the far left of Ridge Road," left of the Sixth South Carolina. The Sixth South Carolina and First Kentucky tried to move through a dense pine thicket, but their vision was obscured, and they mistook the other for the enemy. The First Kentucky, without orders, fired upon the Sixth South Carolina, reportedly killing five men.[13]

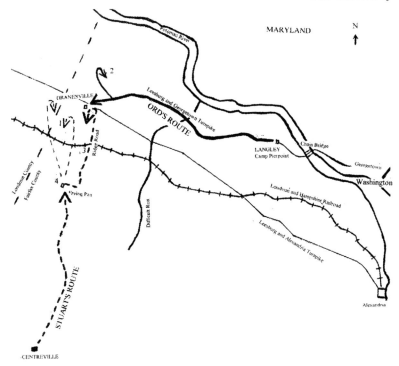

TROOP MOVEMENT THAT LED TO THE ACCIDENTAL CLASH AT DRANESVILLE DECEMBER 20, 1861

1. Confederate wagons searching for forage
2. Union foraging party
3. Stuart's defensive position behind railroad after the engagement
4. Stuart's force spends the night after the engagement

While the Confederates approached along Ridge Road, Ord had to move troops eastward. Their original movement toward Dranesville had left them too far west. Colonel Thomas Kane of the First Pennsylvania Reserve Rifles was the first to move back. When he saw a Confederate flag—and the enemy—appear, in view from the edge of the woods on the Union left, Kane knew at once how important it was to take hold of the hill on which a brick house (the Thorton house) stood. It was just right of the intersection of Ridge Road and the Leesburg-Georgetown Turnpike, behind and just to the right of where Ord would later place most of his artillery. The Thorton house was well known to Kane, as General McCall had used it as his headquarters when Ball's Bluff was being fought. Upon seeing the enemy coming out of the woods in what looked like an attempt to flank the Federals, Kane was determined to reach the house and hill before the enemy. He positioned twenty men under Lieutenant Rice at the brick house. Kane positioned the rest around it as the enemy's artillery opened fire. The action was described by newspaper accounts in the *Rebellion Record,* which states that sharpshooters broke out and fired from the windows and doors as an elderly "negro and two children" nervously hid in the cellar. Enemy fire was now directed at the house. It was "shattered and pierced, the roof being broken and some of the walls gave way." But the brick structure still provided valuable shelter.[14]

As the Bucktails were busily firing from the two-story structure, a regimental surgeon was examining the house in preparation for using it as a field hospital. Dr. S. D. Freeman gazed into an upstairs room. He was astonished to find a private, E. W. Seamons, alone in the room during the critical time. He was not firing at the enemy, but calmly and vainly grooming himself, bent almost double to look into a small mirror, and oiling his hair with the contents of an item he had found while rummaging through a dresser in the room.[15]

Outside the Thorton house were anxious Bucktails, forced to lie on the ground to avoid becoming inviting targets. They would rise, fire, and then drop to the ground to reload. Confederate muskets and cannons hammered at them for twenty minutes, until three of Easton's guns were placed on the rise about forty yards behind them and a little to their left. The Bucktails breathed a little easier and cheered at each discharge, throwing their caps in the air from their prone positions. They would suffer the greatest loss of any Union regiment that day, most of their casualties being from the first fire of the Confederate artillery. The "Bucktail Brass Band," as they referred to Easton's battery, had brought them "good backing and a chance for a fair fight," according to a member of the Bucktails.[16] The Philadelphia *Press* recorded that soon the Bucktails rose and moved "off obliquely to the right into the large chestnuts and tall timber [that] stretched toward the pine forest" that protected the Carolinians. From their new position, the Bucktails fired at the Confederates' white haversacks, which made inviting targets, as they were the easiest seen when their owners moved or changed position.[17]

The tide of the battle was shifting. The Sixth South Carolina and the Tenth Alabama were sent forward toward the Thorton house in an attempt to stop the devastating fire of the Federal artillery just north of the structure. The artillery fire was wrecking Cutt's battery. In hopes of silencing the Federal guns, the two Confederate regiments entered open fields. This brought them under fire from the Bucktails around the Thorton house, especially from their sharpshooters, who poured fire from every door and window. Along with shots from the Union battery and additional Union infantry, the two Confederate regiments were forced back into the woods, having suffered two-thirds of the Confederate losses in the engagement.

The battle was being fought a short distance east of Dranesville. General Ord had redeployed his Union force around the Leesburg and Alexandria turnpike, facing the Confederates to the south in the woods. Bisecting the center of the Confederate line was Ridge Road, running north to south. It formed the center of a giant capital I, connecting the two combatants, who formed the ends of this configuration. Both sides placed their artillery in the center looking up and down Ridge Road and facing each other from 500 yards away. Three Federal pieces were placed on a rise just north, where the road to the south, Ridge Road, joined the turnpike; they were in an excellent position to rake this road. A fourth Union piece was later placed on the Union left in an open field to enfilade the same road. (This piece had little impact upon the battle.) The straightness of the road in front and behind Cutt's troops made them a primary target of enemy artillery. Federal guns raked the road with shell and round shot where the exposed position of Cutt's pieces, limbers, and caissons meant they "were necessarily crowded," as James A. Folson recorded in *Heroes and Martyrs of Georgia.* "There was no outlet" to the "right or left for a mile back by which the battery" could change its position. It would suffer greatly.

In one hour, Folson states, the Sumter artillery battery "suffered a loss of one caisson blown up, another demolished, a limber shot down, twenty horses killed, six men killed and fifteen wounded out of forty cannoneers and drivers of the guns." Damage came early in the battle. The third Union shell struck one of the Georgian caissons, setting off a great explosion that decapitated three cannoneers. The three blackened and headless Confederate corpses were all too graphic evidence that Cutt's position on Ridge Road was the most dangerous spot on the battlefield.[18]

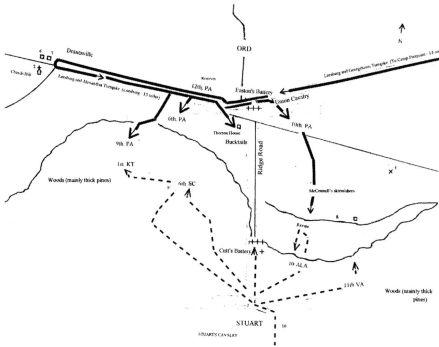

ENGAGEMENT AT DRANESVILLE (DECEMBER 20, 1861)
THE "I" CONFIGURATION OF THE BATTLEFIELD

1. Where Federal skirmishers first clash with Confederates
2. Original position of Easton's Battery
3. Position of three of Easton's guns during the engagement
4. Position of Easton's fourth gun
5. Cutt's three guns that saw action
6. Dr. William B. Day's Home
7. Dr. John T. Day's home
8. Captain Thomas McConnell's skirmishers advance to the ravine
9. 1st KT fires upon 6th SC
10. End of Ord's pursuit

Five hundred yards away, Easton's battery, manned by thirty-six men, fired nearly 200 shells. Unlike the Confederate artillery, Union caissons and limbers were relatively protected from hostile fire. The artillerymen and their horses survived unscathed.[19] Stuart's infantrymen, unlike his artillery, were no easy targets.

Early in the contest, "having nothing to indicate the position of the enemy" infantry but the smoke of their guns, Easton guessed at their position and fired into the woods in the direction of the smoke from their muskets. To further counter the approaching enemy infantry, Ord sent regiments down both sides of the Bucktails and down Ridge Road. To the west he sent the Ninth and Sixth Pennsylvania, keeping the Twelfth Pennsylvania as reserves (behind and north of the Leesburg Turnpike). The Tenth Pennsylvania had the task of countering the enemy coming out of the woods east of the Ridge Road (in what Ord feared was an attempt to flank him from the left and silence Easton's guns).[20]

The fighting to the west of Ridge Road was more restricted and confused than it was to the east; one was in the woods, and the other, in an open field. Colonel C. Ferger Jackson's Ninth Pennsylvania on Ord's extreme right, the only Federal force totally in the wooded front, mistook the First Kentucky for Federals. Jackson was told by an officer that the troops opposite them were the Bucktails. According to the New York *Herald,* another officer assured his colonel "in the most emphatic manner they were rebels." "The order to fire was then given and promptly obeyed," held the *Herald.* But Jackson found his men still believed they were firing upon fellow Pennsylvanians, "which caused considerable confusion in the ranks, which was overcome to a great extent with some difficulty." Jackson later learned "that the impression the Bucktails were forming in front was strengthened" when one of the enemy called out, "Don't fire on us." One member of the Ninth Pennsylvania Reserves is said to have imprudently asked, "Are you Bucktails?" The response was, "Yes, we are the Bucktails; don't fire"—then the Kentucky regiment fired a volley into the Ninth Pennsylvania Reserves.[21]

On the Federal left the Tenth Pennsylvania Reserves, many of whom were college men recruited from western Pennsylvania, under Colonel J. S. McCalmont, had moved from the west around the back of the Federal artillery. They were placed in a new position among a growth of cedar trees in between the turnpikes to Georgetown and Alexandria and to Easton's left.[22] To determine the enemy's intent and possibly pick off their gunners, a platoon of skirmishers under Captain Thomas McConnell was ordered to move through the open field east of Ridge Road to the outer edge of the woodlands south of the turnpike.[23]

When McConnell's platoon, half of Company B, was marching in the open field toward the woods near the enemy battery, they noticed that one enemy gun was retiring and the others had already been pulled back out of the skirmisher's sight. At the same time they saw Confederates coming out of the woods in front of them. This put McConnell's platoon in a position of seeking cover by falling back or secreting themselves in gullies in front of them. McConnell chose the latter option, running his men ten to fifteen paces for the protection of the eroded depressions. As they flopped into the ravine, their numbers were increased, as a sergeant of the pioneers, who had earlier removed the fences for the movement of the Tenth, brought his men and joined the skirmishers in the gullies. From this strong position they fired into the enemy, the Tenth Alabama, creating some confusion in their ranks. After a second volley by McConnell's men, the Alabamians retreated into the woods that they had just left behind. A few Confederate adventurers later came out of the woods, but for some minutes there were no Confederate attacks. But the men of the Tenth Alabama would soon rally—in considerable numbers, they engaged the Union skirmishers for the remainder of the battle. Confederate lead fell thick around the Federals in the gullies, but it failed to inflict any injury. The ravine played a primary role, along with good fortune, in saving McConnell's men from wounds.

The two-hour contest was ending. With Stuart's wagons now safe, and convinced he was about to be overwhelmed by a reinforced enemy, the brigadier general left. And when he pulled the Alabamians back, along with the rest of his force, McConnell moved his own small force, his men, and the pioneers, a distance down the turnpike to Alexandria and remained there until satisfied that the enemy had retreated and was not moving east to flank and attack Easton's guns.[24]

According to the Philadelphia *Inquirer,* General J. F. Reynolds, who had been sent by McCall to Difficult Run with the First Brigade, came forward "on a double quick, but was not in time to take part" in the battle "except to see the retreat and hear the parting salutes."[25]

While Reynolds was approaching the battlefield and Ord was superintending the attack on the fleeing Rebels, at the head of the charge was Colonel Kane and his Bucktails. No less eager was the

Ninth Pennsylvania, led by Colonel Jackson. While this column was surging forward, General Ord was "doing his utmost to urge on the near regiments," stated the New York *Tribune*. Ord rushed the cheering Twelfth Pennsylvania Reserves, led by Colonel Taggart, who in the excitement is reported to have thrown away his scabbard and led his men "with his saber in one hand and his pistol in the other."

But no one was more conspicuous than Kane. Shortly before he formed the Bucktails in line for the last charge, he "was struck in the face by a ball that pierced his upper jaw" and broke off a tooth.[26] In spite of the pain, the bleeding, and the difficulty in speaking, Kane stopped only momentarily to apply a white handkerchief as a makeshift bandage, then continued forward. As McConnell and Jackson cheered their own men, Kane led his men out of the woods, past Southern dead and wounded, into the open space of Ridge Road. When Kane's men were about a quarter-mile beyond the former position of the Confederate artillery, Ord ordered them to halt. Kane wanted to go further and his men cheered the idea. But it was not to be.[27]

After only a half-mile pursuit, the Union force stopped. McCall was now on the scene and was afraid of running into heavy Confederate reinforcements that might have been sent forward from Centreville.[28] Before returning, the Federals gathered up items left behind by the Confederates, including much clothing and Richmond newspapers found in the pockets of the Confederate dead. Mississippi and Springfield muskets were gathered. In the woods near where Cutt's battery had been were shells and balls that had been piled up by the good order.

The greatest booty was the knapsacks, haversacks, blankets, and overcoats temporarily discarded by the South Carolinians as they went into battle. Their path of withdrawal went a different way. The Union soldiers who captured the items stated that "all the garments [were] cotton, of a dark brown color, as though dyed by tobacco juice."

A Union private found in an abandoned overcoat $50 in treasury notes and $20 in Georgia notes. Many of his comrades discovered money, watches, letters, and papers. Federals piled up their finds. In one pile were over 100 guns and "all kinds of clothing." The Pennsylvanians carried "away as much as they could carry," with almost everyone having something for a trophy. Two Confederate caissons were left on the field because Ord's men did not have the horses to bring them in. They cut up the caissons with axes. The boxes from the caissons, however, were brought back to camp by Captain Easton. In one, claimed Northern papers, was "a well-cooked turkey evidently prepared for an officer's dinner."[29]

Eight Confederate prisoners had been taken, including local resident John W. Farr, who was accused of shooting Union pickets, and Private William Nelson of the First Kentucky Volunteers, who was a nephew of Sam Black, a colonel of a Pennsylvania regiment in General Porter's division. The final brief Federal charge southward on Ridge Road led to the capture of two Kentuckians by a contraband who had become the body servant of Colonel Jackson. One of the prisoners stated that he "wouldn't care a —— if he had not been caught by a nigger." A drummer of the Ninth Pennsylvania said he "took two prisoners, having no other weapon than a club."[30]

The remainder of the cleanup was not enjoyable. Union men gathered up their own dead and wounded and the wounded of the enemy. Leaving the Confederate dead, many Union soldiers passed disturbing sights of a body cut in half and charred and blackened headless bodies—the remains of several of Cutt's men who were killed by exploding ammunition ignited by a Federal shell. The passing soldiers found, according to the New York *Herald,* "one rebel soldier, who was unhurt" standing by the side of his dying brother. He said he would not "leave his brother till he was dead." One of the Federals recalled that another dying Confederate asked him "to take a pack of cards from his pocket, as he did not wish to die with them in his possession." One asked for whiskey, another for water, and others for surgeons, ministers, Bibles, and to be treated well.[31]

Among the dead were two Confederates wearing U.S. Army overcoats. Another, stated a Union soldier present at the scene, was "an old man with long silvery hair, a private in the South Carolina regiment. His hands were soft and fair, and he appeared to have lived the life of a gentleman." He was private James McKeever. Like a number of wealthy Southerners, he had apparently felt it was more noble to fight as a private than as an officer.[32] Also touching was the plight of a wounded officer of the Sixth South Carolina Volunteers who was taken to the porch of the Thorton House. There, one of the

Union soldiers held the dying man's head, grasped his hand, and prayed for him.

That night at 9:00, tired and cold, the men of Ord's brigade returned to Camp Pierpoint. They were met by thousands of cheering comrades, who proclaimed, "This had been a glorious day for the Pennsylvanians." Giddy with triumph, Ord's men told how they had "utterly routed and destroyed the enemy." Since 6:00 A.M. they had marched twenty-four miles and fought an engagement. They brought with them loads of hay and at least five wagons of corn gathered up while the fighting was going on. After the battle, men walked the twelve miles back to camp carrying wounded Union soldiers on stretchers; the ambulances for McCall's division lay, empty, in Washington.[33]

Stuart's men's journey back to Centreville was more difficult. First they slowly pulled back to the protection of the Alexandria, Loudoun, and Hampshire railroad four miles to the south. There, a stand could be made. When that proved unnecessary, they gathered up the blankets and knapsacks they had left there on their way to the battlefield and proceeded with some of their wounded to Frying Pan Church.

Early on the morning after the battle with two fresh regiments sent to him from Centreville (the Ninth Georgia and the Eighteenth Virginia), along with a detachment of cavalry, Stuart moved back to Dranesville. He had learned the enemy had evacuated the town but had left some of the Confederate wounded there. He returned to recover his wounded and tend to the dead.[34]

Stuart now had any wounded men who could be moved placed in ambulances and wagons while mothers and daughters of the town rushed forward, bringing bedclothes and soup and other delicacies for the wounded they had been caring for.[35] Once the wounded were loaded, the members of the Eighteenth Virginia and a friend decided to go over the battleground. They saw where the detail of men sent to collect the dead had placed the lifeless forms along the road.

Having put all their dead in wagons by 4:00 that afternoon, Stuart and his men started back toward Centreville, twenty miles away. As darkness descended upon them, the colonel of the Eighteenth Virginia stopped and let his regiment vote on whether or not they were willing to continue the long march to Centreville. The reply was a resounding yes. Soon, some of the poor fellows lamented having sore feet from traveling on hard frozen ground. One or two were lucky to get a ride on the back of a horse; others had to stop and return to Centreville the following morning as no order or regularity of marching could be maintained. Each moved along the best he could, suffering from the cold, walking over forty miles in little over twenty-four hours on half rations. The first to arrive was a captain of the Eighteenth Virginia and several of his men. How glad they were to be there, drinking hot coffee and warming their cold feet in front of warm fires before retiring for the night.[36]

Almost two days after the battle, the frozen corpses arrived in Centreville. The weather had turned extremely cold. The bodies were described by an eyewitness: "in the posture in which the agonies of death were endured; some lay doubled up, others with their rigid fingers clutched in their clothing or around their accouterments." The following day they were buried.[37]

A GRAND AND SIGNAL UNION VICTORY

Both commanders who fought at Dranesville claimed great victories. In reality it had been a modest but bloody chance encounter. There was no grand maneuvering of troops, in part because the terrain forbade it. Stuart attacked from the south of the Leesburg and Alexandria Turnpike, and the Union, after some confusion, fought back successfully. After two hours of combat, Stuart was discouraged by the stubborn Union resistance and the news of their reinforcements. He slowly disengaged and pulled back. Misconceptions—along with ego and career concerns—made Ord and Stuart recount the events in ways favorable to them. Ord had misinterpreted Stuart's movement as stealing a march on him, and he claimed that he had not only prevented this but had also routed the enemy. Stuart incorrectly assumed that Ord was moving toward the Southern wagons or to Leesburg. In an attempt to prevent this, Stuart attacked. In Stuart's words, he and his men had saved "the greater part of the available transportation" of their army, and, he claimed, had "inflicted upon the enemy a loss severer than our own, rendering him unequal to the task of pursuit, retired in perfect order and bringing with us nearly all our wounded, we may rightly call it a glorious success." In reality it was Stuart's first major setback. His 194 casualties were almost three times that of the Federals' sixty-eight.[38]

Lieutenant-Colonel Thomas L. Kane
A competent commander of the 1st Pennsylvania Reserve Rifles ("Bucktails"), Kane left his sick bed to fight at Dranesville on December 20, 1861. (Courtesy of the Library of Congress)

Celebration in the North was extensive. Political rivals from Pennsylvania, Secretary of War Cameron, and the popular Pennsylvania Governor Andrew G. Curtin tried to outdo each other in heaping praise on their state's warriors through congratulatory letters and visits to their camps.

General Ord was the man of the hour, the nation's new hero. The saga of his exploits included the tale that he had "whipped all the Rebels he could find" without going too far out of his way, as he had orders not to bring on an engagement; otherwise, they claimed, Ord would have chased them further.

Of the Pennsylvania heroes, none received greater praise than Colonel Kane. The day after Christmas, a Philadelphia reporter visited Kane, who was called "the Fighting Colonel." The reporter wrote that Kane was alone in his tent, "reclining on a buffalo robe, with a mess of papers at his side." The reporter had seen him before the battle "full of life and health, and vigor," but his wound in the cheek had taken its toll. The colonel was pale from the loss of blood, his right eye was swollen, and "a plain black patch" extended along the check, said the reporter. He still performed his regimental duties, despite friendly pleas to convalesce until he was completely "restored to health." Kane was now a Northern hero known for his total commitment to the Union.[39]

The Federal glow of victory continued through Christmas into the new year. Compliments flowed freely from official reports, the Northern press, and the Secretary of War to Congress and the Committee on the Conduct of the War.

None surpassed the hyperbolic exaltation of the Northern press. "Heroic Courage of Union Troops," "Gallant Charge on Rebels in Ambush," "Total Rout of Rebels," and "One Hundred and Sixty Dead Rebels Buried" were headlines splashed across Northern papers. They argued that Dranesville was "a most grand and signal victory." It signaled a shift in the war in favor of the Union and erased the disaster at Bull Run and the sting of the fiasco at Ball's Bluff. Readers were also informed, "The victory on the part of our troops [Federal] is considered more brilliant as they had never before been in any action." The Pennsylvania *Press,* starving for victory, wrote, "There may be greater encounters, and battles more terrible and fearfully contested, but none there can be in which the victory is more decided and undeniable."[40]

High praise indeed was heaped on the blue-clad warriors for their "noble" efforts at Dranesville. Whispers that all was not right, however, circulated among officers of the Union army; rumor had it that the voluntary soldiers' actions were far from exemplary. Philip Kearny, the commander of a New Jersey brigade camped at the Episcopal Seminary near Alexandria, confidentially wrote to a friend that the truth was suppressed and "every high officer *distrusts* (and with reason) our volunteer troops." Kearny wrote, "I dare not quote you the high names, as it would betray information which, even among ourselves, we convey by innuendoes rather than by words. And [although] the affair at Dranesville (this is highly confidential)," he continued, was "a brilliant victory by Gen'l Ord," his "maneuvers with the Artillery, himself sighting" the pieces, were, according to Kearny, "another signal proof of the cowardice of our troops." He wrote of the troops, "They refused to fight; officers ran. Painful as is the conclusion, out northern men are cowards. They were not so when they left home but they have become so by their long contact with their *debased,* worthless, pusillanimous, negligent officers." The immediate future did not look bright, said Kearny. "When we move the whole line, you may expect some painful *catastrophe.* It must be so."[41]

General George Gordon Meade agreed with Kearny's assessment. The day after the battle, Meade asked General Ord "how the men behaved" at Dranesville. Ord's reply, according to Meade, was that the men had done "better than he expected…but not as well as they ought…there was much shirking and running away on the part of both officers and men." Ord had persuaded two regiments, Kane's Bucktails and the Ninth Pennsylvania, to hold their ground and "finally to charge." "One regiment," Ord complained, he "could do nothing with." Meade predicted that these cowardly acts would be overshadowed by the "fact that the enemy were routed, leaving killed, wounded, baggage…on the ground." Dranesville would—continued Meade—"always be held up to show how gallantly the volunteers can behave, and the world will never know that it was the judicious posting and serving of the battery by Ord (himself, an artillery officer) which demoralized and threw fear into the enemy, and prepared them to run the moment our people showed a bold front, which it required all Ord's effort and some time to get them to do."[42]

There were also Southern critics of their leadership. They exaggerated—as did the Federals—the size and losses of the enemy, insisted their opponents had been informed of their prebattle movements, and waited in ambush, but a degree of realism was expressed by several Southern soldiers. One such realistic Confederate participant at Dranesville wrote to the Richmond *Dispatch* shortly after the conflict that Dranesville was a bloody "affair...that will probably be magnified by the enemy as a real battle." The men with Shanks Evans' force at Leesburg were shocked by what they had heard about Dranesville. One took Stuart to task, concluding that the general had learned a valuable lesson: not to be caught "napping." This Confederate critic wrote, "our boys fought well," and, "hopefully the little affair should teach our generals not to despise the enemy as supremely as some do...although our men are willing to 'do or die' when called upon. I cannot see that any general should lose fifty or sixty men, simply from his own carelessness in not providing against a surprise."[43]

Southern newspaper readers easily got the impression that Dranesville was a defeat. The Charleston *Mercury,* which gradually received information from northern Virginia, came close to the truth. The *Mercury* assessed the event as a "heavy skirmish which occurred near Dranesville on Friday in which a portion of our army suffered a check."[44] A few days after the engagement, the Richmond *Examiner* concluded from trickled-in accounts, "The impression is, that we suffered no inconsiderable disaster. If so we will have received another lesson to check our immediate confidence, and to teach us the necessity of real earnestness and renewed exertion in the contest before us."[45]

Time soon erased the impact of Dranesville. Despite the trauma suffered by those who were wounded and killed there and the sadness of their loved ones, larger and more terrible battles rapidly superseded the nation's memories of that December engagement. It has become a virtually forgotten sideshow of the war.

[1] William S. Hammond, "The Battle of Dranesville," *SHSP*, (Richmond, 1907), vol. 35, 71-72. The first brigade was under Reynolds, the second, Meade, and the third, Ord.

[2] Henry N. Minnigh, *History of Company K, First (Inft.) Pennsylvania Reserves* (Duncansville, Pa.: Homeprint, 1891), 29-30.

[3] Hammond, "The Battle of Dranesville," 69-70; Charles Preston Poland Jr., *Dunbarton, Dranesville, Virginia* (Fairfax, Va.: Fairfax County Office of Comprehensive Planning, 1974), 17-21. During the antebellum era it was commonplace for forty to fifty wagons, pulled by four to six horses, to daily traverse the small town on their way to Georgetown.

[4] *OR*, Ser. II, vol. 2, 1285-1286, 1289.

[5] Ibid., 44-45.

[6] Ibid., 35. There were a half-dozen clashes between Union and Confederates at Dranesville from 1861 to 1865. The one on December 20, 1861, was the largest. The rest were skirmishes.

[7] Ibid., Ser. I, vol. 5, 490. Stuart had plans "to take a position with two regiments and a section of artillery on each turnpike" just east of Dranesville, "and close enough to the intersection to form a continuous line to hold against almost all odds."

[8] *OR*, Ser. I, vol. 5, 474; O. R. Howard Thomson and William H. Rauch, *History of the "Bucktails,"* (Philadelphia: Electric, 1906), 74.

[9] Thomson and Rauch, *History of the "Bucktails,"* 73-74. Kane took command of the Bucktails when the regimental commander, Colonel Charles J. Biddle of Philadelphia, who had been elected to Congress, resigned on November 25, 1861.

[10] Ibid., 491. The Union skirmishers were a company of the Pittsburgh Rifles and Company F of the Bucktails.

[11] Colonel Samuel Garland Jr. (who, within the year, would lose his life at Fox's Gap in the Antietam campaign) was ordered by Stuart to deploy two companies of his Eleventh Virginia made up of men from Lynchburg, to each side of Ridge Road to rid the pines of enemy pickets. One company lost its direction and veered too far to the right, forcing Garland to replace it. Probably sometime during the early movement Private John Henry of the Eleventh was killed by accident.

[12] James A. Folsom, *Heroes and Martyrs of Georgia* (Macon, Ga.: Burke, Boykin & Co., 1864), 111.

[13] *OR,* Ser. I, vol. 5, 491-92.

[14] *Rebellion Record*, III, 499. The Thorton house faced east. It was about 50 yards from Ridge Road and about the same distance from the turnpike.

[15] Edwin A. Glover, *Bucktailed Wildcats* (New York: T. Yoseloff, 1960), 63.

[16] Samuel P. Bates, *Record of Pennsylvania Volunteers for Three Months Service* (Harrisburg, Pa.), 910; Mark M. Boatner III, *The Civil War Dictionary* (New York: D. McKay, 1949), 636-37; *OR*, Ser. I, vol. 5, 475. The First Pennsylvania Rifles, or Bucktails, were also known as the Thirteenth Pennsylvania Reserves.

[17] Philadelphia *Press*, December 27, 1861.

[18] Folsom, *Heroes and Martyrs of Georgia*, 111; Glover, *Bucktailed Wildcats*, 63; Poland, *Dunbarton*, 37. Shortly after the third Federal artillery shot, Ord ordered

Easton's capsized gun—turned over hastily—pulled to the west of the town to a position on the far Union left. From this position the Federals could enfilade Ridge Road.

[19] Philadelphia *Inquirer*, December 23, 1861.

[20] *OR*, Ser. I, vol. 5, 489.

[21] *Chronicle & Sentinel* (Augusta, Ga.), December 27, 1861; New York *Herald*, December 23, 1861; *OR*, Ser. I, vol. 5, 483. Southern newspapers presented a different and reverse scenario of this episode. They have the Union firing first into the Kentucky regiment.

[22] Two companies were recruited from Jefferson and Allegheny Colleges. Other companies were made up of men of comparable literacy, with teachers and students serving together in ranks.

[23] OR, Ser. I, vol. 5, 484-86. McConnell was "to keep a good lookout" so they "were not flanked on the left."

[24] Ibid., 485-86. After waiting a while on the turnpike, McConnell marched his force back and joined the main force.

[25] Philadelphia *Inquirer*, December 23, 1861. Reynolds apparently was on the Alexandria–Leesburg turnpike where it crosses Difficult Run. General McClellan started for Dranesville but turned back when informed the fighting had ended.

[26] The New York *Daily Tribune*, December 23, 1861, reported that Kane was struck by buckshot.

[27] Bates, *Record of Pennsylvania Volunteers*, 910; Moore, *Rebellion Record*, vol. III, 502; Philadelphia *Press*, December 27, 1861; Thomson and Rauch, *History of the Bucktails*, 77; E.M. Woodward, *History of the Third Pennsylvania Reserve* (Trenton, N.J.: MacCrellish & Quigley, 1883), 54-55.

[28] *OR*, Ser. I, vol. 5, 472.

[29] Philadelphia *Inquirer*, December 23, 1861; New York *Daily Tribune*, December 23, 1861.

[30] New York *Herald*, December 23, 1861; Pittsburgh *Daily Post*, December 31, 1861.

[31] New York *Tribune*, December 27, 1861.

[32] William H. Morgan, *Personal Reminiscences of the War 1861-1865* (Lynchburg, Va., 1911), 93-94; Philadelphia *Press*, December 27, 1861.

[33] Philadelphia *Inquirer*, December 23, 1861; *OR*, Ser. I, vol. 5, 480. The seven Federal dead were taken to Camp Pierpont, placed in a row on separate tiers, and viewed by nearly every soldier of the division.

[34] One regiment, the Sixth South Carolina, reached the railroad from a different direction from their approach to the battlefield and had to leave their blankets and knapsacks. This bothered Stuart; he feared the enemy would infer that he had left in precipitous flight.

[35] Federals left the Confederate wounded at Dranesville. Stuart took eight back to Centreville.

[36] *Rebellion Record*, III, 502-503.

[37] *OR*, Ser. I, vol. 5, 491-93; Poland, *Dunbarton*, 37-38; Wise, *History of the Seventeenth Virginia Infantry,* 50-51.

[38] *OR*, Ser. I, vol. 5, 489, 494. The greater Confederate losses were largely caused by their taking the offensive. Stuart had 43 killed, 143 wounded, and 8 missing. By comparison, Ord only had 7 killed and 6 wounded, and of these, Kane's Bucktails suffered forty percent of the Federal losses, with 3 killed and 24 wounded.

[39] The night after the battle, Kane sent a note by courier to Stuart. It praised the "gallant conduct of the officer who rode the gray horse." The rider was Mississippian Major C. L. Jackson, a staff officer of General Sam Jones' brigade. Jackson happened to have been passing through Dranesville on his way back to Centreville camp and plunged into the fight.

[40] Moore, *Rebellion Records*, vol. III, 500; Philadelphia *Inquiry*, December 23, 27 & 31, 1861; New York *Sun*, December 23, 1861; Woodward, *Our Campaign*, 76.

[41] Philip Kearny, Letter to Cortlandt Parker, January 13, 1862. "The Papers of Philip Kearny," MSS 19, 610, Microfilm, Library of Congress.

[42] George Gordon Meade, *The Life and Letters of George Gordon Meade* (New York: Charles Scribner's Sons, 1913), vol. I, 237-38. Ord also told Meade that if the men "had charged when he first ordered them," he would have captured the enemy battery and "lots of prisoners."

[43] Memphis *Daily Appeal*, January 3, 1862.

[44] Charleston *Mercury*, December 23, 1861.

[45] *Daily* (Richmond) *Examiner*, December 23, 1861.

PART II

THE SOUTHERN INVASION CORRIDOR

CHAPTER VI

"DEATH TO TRAITORS": THE BATTLE OF BIG BETHEL

The end of May and early June of 1861 saw reports of nascent military action being splashed across the papers in bold headlines that claimed earthshaking military achievements. These included the Union occupation of Alexandria, subsequent forays into Fairfax Court House and Vienna, followed by a Federal movement in northwestern Virginia that surprised and chased a small ragtag Confederate force out of Philippi. A week later in southeastern Virginia, a less-successful Union force attacked fortified Southerners southeast of Richmond, at Big Bethel. Union forces on the tip of the peninsula were under the command of Benjamin F. Butler, a political general who would become a symbol of Northern villainy in the eyes of Southerners.[1]

The clash on June 10, despite being called the "first real land battle of the war," was a small fight by later standards. Its significance derived from its newness in the war and its location—on one of the four Union invasion routes of Virginia, the peninsula between the James and the York Rivers. It was the Union's shortest land route to Richmond, a movement that could be launched from the Federal base at Fort Monroe on the peninsula tip. Across the water to the south was Norfolk, which lay in Southern hands after an earlier Federal evacuation.[2]

Charles P. Poland Jr.

FEARS FOR THE SECURITY OF RICHMOND

Federal evacuation of Norfolk in late April did not allay fears over the security of Richmond. The Union position at Fort Monroe was a menacing one. This large base could supply a land movement toward Richmond, while the flanking and broad waters of the James and the York provided avenues for even more rapid assaults by the Union navy. Rumors since the last of April told of approaching Federal ships or impending invasions. Such rhetoric kept Richmond in a constant state of alarm. On a bright Sunday, April 21, Richmond was thrown into turmoil as a rumor swept through the city of an impending shelling by the USS *Pawnee,* which was believed to be steaming up the James. J. C. DeLeon's *Four Years in Rebel Capitals* describes the scene in Richmond, telling of the alarm bell in the square, which "pealed out with" a frightening "chime." Church congregations refused to wait to be dismissed. Instead they fled en masse from their places of worship and looked skyward for "rockets." Men of all ages, attired in their Sunday best, hurried through the streets with "rusty muskets as the fairer sex gathered on street corners" to inquire of any news and to repeat "every fear-invented tale." Men were seen "with hand-baskets loaded with rock, to dam the River!" After six hours of panic, people realized it was a false alarm. This episode, referred to as Pawnee Sunday, had frightened Virginians into an awareness of the "utter defenselessness of Richmond."[3] Letters were written to President Davis in Montgomery, warning him of the impending danger and pleading for him to do something. Any exchange of fire between Federal ships and Virginia batteries along the shores of Virginia's eastern waterways was considered ominous.[4]

Union land movement on the peninsula was considered no less threatening. Even minor movements were seen as possible precursors for larger assaults. In late May, soon after Butler's arrival and the arrivals of additional Federal forces, Union troops were sent from Fort Monroe by water. They took—unopposed—Newport News, eight miles away. The Union now had control over the southern tip of the peninsula and had a much larger staging area for future military operations. Virginia troops pulled back after a fairly benign Federal reconnoitering of Hampton on May 23.[5]

Civilians demanded a better defense for Richmond and the vicinity. Responding to this demand, authorities sent Colonel John B. Magruder of the Provisional Army of Virginia to Yorktown to command the Department of the Peninsula. Additional troops accompanied the flamboyant Magruder, including the well-trained First Regiment of North Carolina Volunteers, under Colonel D. H. Hill.[6]

Who was the man sent to protect the peninsula? Magruder, nicknamed "Prince John" for his handsome appearance, was a professional soldier in his fifties, a graduate of West Point, and a veteran of the Mexican War. Despite his slight lisp, he enjoying talking and writing endlessly to his superiors. Coupled with his impatience, zeal, and brashness was a flair for the dramatic. These were characteristics of a personality not easily ignored. His propensity for brashness surfaced at the start of the war, when he boldly stated to unimpressed Virginia authorities in April of 1861, "Give me 5,000 men and if I don't take Washington, you may take not only my sword but my life!"[7]

The officer under Magruder, Daniel Harvey Hill, who was in command of the post at Yorktown, was unimpressed with the colonel's theatricality. Like "Prince John," Harvey Hill had a West Point education and had fought in the Mexican War. After the war he taught at several colleges and penned two religious tracts and an algebra textbook. In the book, his rabid anti-Northern feelings and his support of the South were displayed in algebraic problems that ridiculed Northerners.

Hill was a man of deep religious conviction whose faith seemed to at least equal that of his brother-in-law Stonewall Jackson. Hill had been a fiery combatant in the Mexican War and displayed strong opinions and an iron will. He was outraged when a general harshly chastised him for not properly obeying orders. Hill's reaction was immediate. He drew his saber, waved it in the startled general's face, and forbade him to use such offensive language again. D. H. Hill's individualism continued to be displayed throughout the Civil War in friction with Robert E. Lee and in refusing to approve a soldier's transfer from the infantry to the band. He signed the papers in a manner that also revealed his dry sense of humor: "Respectfully forwarded, disapproved. Shooters are needed more than tooters." Prior to the battle of Big Bethel, Hill muted his low opinions of

Magruder, expressing them only in private correspondence to his wife. Hill told her Magruder was always intoxicated and gave "foolish" and "absurd orders" that the men would soon refuse to obey. Outwardly there was no conflict between the colonels.[8]

Between the end of May and early June, Hill's First North Carolina Volunteers were busy drilling and entrenching at Yorktown. Walter Clark, historian of North Carolina's regiments, states, "While engaged in the latter" they found it interesting "to trace the outline of Cornwallis' works erected in defense against their forefathers four score years before." "Sometimes their spades and picks would renew, sometimes demolish, those ancient war marks, and occasionally they would unearth a souvenir of battle."[9]

Others found their Yorktown camp dreary. Melancholy and gloom settled over the North Carolinians' camp. Soon after their arrival at Yorktown, they heard of the sad fate of a young comrade, Julius Sadler. Shortly after leaving Richmond by rail, Sadler, presumably asleep, fell from the platform car and was instantly killed. His comrades found solace in religion and an anticipation of victory in an impending battle. One Carolinian wrote home that their leader, Hill, was "a model Christian soldier," and, "There are many servants of God in our camp. Can such a regiment be conquered? Never!"

Among the companies of the First North Carolina, which would later be known as the Bethel Regiment, was a company of youths all under the age of twenty-one—they were known as the Boy Company. An optimistic performance was predicted for them as well; others predicted, "On the day of battle this gallant little band will do its duty."[10]

On June 6, Magruder sent Hill and his regiment south. Hill was accompanied by four artillery pieces under Major George W. Randolph, the grandson of Thomas Jefferson. Their destination was Big Bethel. The thirteen-mile trip, despite passing over level sandy roads, was not an easy one. The North Carolinians had loaded themselves down with knapsacks, haversacks, canteens, loaded cartridge boxes, Bibles, tin cups, and extra pairs of shoes. They had not yet learned the lessons of marching.

The tired men marched to Big Bethel, which was eight miles from the Federal camps at Hampton and Newport News, reaching their destination after dark. On the west side of the road was a large unpainted and somewhat dilapidated wooden church surrounded by a grove of trees. Around the lone structure, amidst a drizzling rain, the regiment had its first experience at bivouacking without tents and with cooking with ramrods. Inside the church, they found annoying inscriptions such as "Death to Traitors!" and "Down with Rebels." Union soldiers (who had signed their names to the threats) had left the inscriptions during an incursion in the area a couple of weeks earlier.

To the Southerners, such inscriptions were evidence of the kind of foe they faced. They not only defiled their houses of worship, but also pillaged the homes of civilians. Even their Union commander, General Benjamin Butler, lamented, "volunteer troops seem to have adopted the theory that all property of the inhabitants was subject to plunder." This certainly did not make Butler's task any easier. A sharp-tongued, physically unattractive Massachusetts Democrat, and a skillful—if not unscrupulous—criminal lawyer and opportunist who attracted arguments, Butler had an unshakable belief in his ability, which he considered extraordinary in political and military matters. He was extremely displeased about being transferred from command of the Department of Annapolis to the Department of Virginia at Fort Monroe—so much so that he bitterly complained to the secretary of war and went to see Lincoln, who skillfully persuaded the irascible general to keep his new assignment.

Butler was not happy about being the commander of the Department of Virginia, which included sixty miles around the headquarters at Fort Monroe (usually referred to as Fortress Monroe), and he intentionally sparked a protest by the soldiers who were arriving at Fort Monroe by telling them that the commanding general, Scott, was thinking of encamping them in the graveyard of the fort where soldiers and others had been buried for half a century. Butler was also displeased by the lack of preparedness. He claimed that the "only four-footed animal" he found there, besides the cats, was a "small mule which dragged a sling cart, into which was regularly emptied "sewage to be carried to the seashore and dumped." Butler described the fort itself as one of the "strongest and best in the United States, and certainly the largest," and one of the few spots in Virginia that Confederates would not at some time control. Butler's headquarters was a "bastion fort" with "a water battery casemated on its sea front, and some guns mounted *en barbette.*" He found the ramps and ramparts in good condition and felt that the only weak point in construction was its magazines, which were well protected from the sea front, but would be vulnerable to artillery fire from the land to the north.[11]

Butler's new headquarters had a long history. The site on Old Point Comfort was a narrow sand spit on the very tip of the peninsula between the York and James Rivers. The largest part of Old Point Comfort was cut off from the mainland by an inlet called Mill Creek. To the east of Point Comfort lay the Chesapeake Bay, and to the south, Hampton Roads. (The name Old Point Comfort derived from the first settlers who briefly stopped there on their way to Jamestown in the spring of 1607.[12]) Construction of the fort started during James Monroe's presidency (hence its name), but was not completely finished when the Civil War started.[13] The fort covered about sixty-three acres, had seven fronts and was surrounded by an eight-foot-deep moat that varied in width from sixty to 150 feet. The works were designed to have 380 guns with a peacetime garrison of 600 men, and in war, slightly more than 2,600.[14]

Butler found the moat "partially filled in a curious manner." The local water was filled "with the finest possible oysters, and they were extremely cheap," wrote Butler. The men in the fort, especially officers, were quartered mainly in the casemates built into the walls of the fort under the ramparts and, he added, "had embrasures pierced in the outside walls for guns." These openings overlooked the moat and also served as windows for the casemates when the guns were withdrawn. Through these narrow windows, oyster shells were "easily tossed onto the moat, and as the larger shells had small oysters attached to them, there was quite an oyster bank in the bottom of the moat and one which filled it up considerably."[15]

The general had the moat cleared and the water kept at his desired depth; he also made other improvements. Cynics said that some things could not be done—such as laying track over soft sand from the wharves into the fort to carry a twenty-six-ton cannon—but they were proved wrong. A solution also had to be found to the most pressing necessity: providing water for those garrisoned inside the fort. There were no wells or springs in the fort or on the land on which it sat. The only water supply for the fort was rainwater "caught on the ramparts which drained into cisterns," Butler reported. This supply had been inadequate for 400 men in the garrison, and now Butler had many times that number. Attempts to provide an adequate water supply failed. Water from springs on the other side of Mill

Creek was inadequate, and an artesian well dug in the fort was unfinished, so Butler was forced to import water from Baltimore for what was considered the high cost of $0.02 per gallon. This supply was meager and fell far short of the fort's need for 700 gallons of water per day.[16]

Finally, an ingenious method temporarily solved the water problem. A plant was erected, said Butler, to "distill seawater taken from the moat, by converting it into steam and allowing the steam to condense." By this means they supplied the fort with water "at the expense of a pound of coal for a pint of water."[17]

Benjamin Butler also devoted his attention soon after his arrival at Fort Monroe to strengthening his position on the tip of the peninsula. He fortified a bluff five miles away from Fort Monroe, on the point known as Newport News. He would place heavy artillery pieces at his new works, named Camp Butler, which would protect the tip of the peninsula and the James River and would provide a place for Union ships to anchor and menace the enemy across the water at Norfolk.

Butler became inexorably involved in controversies, not the least of which was his policy of not returning the fugitive slaves who, he claimed, "flocked" into his camps. He proclaimed them "contraband," gave them food and clothing, and, as he said, put the "able-bodied to work."[18] Butler not only coined the phrase "contraband of war," which would be used for the rest of the war, but had also started a practice known as the First Confiscation Act, which Lincoln signed into law on August 6, 1861. It authorized the seizure of all property, slaves included, that was used in military work by the Confederates. This act was applied to only a few slaves and was, like Butler's action, only the earliest stage of an intensifying heated policy debate in the North over the issue of emancipation.[19]

As a general rule, fugitive slaves spoke kindly of the late masters whom (in most instances) they had fled. They ran off because they feared being sold or forced to work in Confederate entrenchments until a battle started. There was a prevalent fear, although unfounded, of being placed on the front line.[20]

Somewhat more pleasing to local residents than Butler's contraband policy was his order prohibiting Federal soldiers from plundering civilian property. Those accused of such "outrages," said Butler, who condemned them as "very grave," would be court-martialed. But Butler's threat had little effect upon Federal troops. Union foraging parties liberally helped themselves to civilian property. At times vandalism was rampant—a situation expanded upon by the New York *Times*: "A number of the Troy regiment, who were in Hampton, got drunk. They went in the private houses, breaking furniture, destroying pictures, looking glasses, etc., and in short kicking up a general row, and ending in a fight among themselves, in which pistols were used."[21] Butler's orders tried to reassure local residents: "we are here in no war against you, your liberty, your property, or even your local customs," but he failed to assuage the civilians' fears.[22] The wealthier and more refined local residents feared for their well-being and fled the region for miles around Hampton. Union scouting parties found the area depopulated, and often, only slaves had been left in charge of farms with large fields of excellent wheat and corn and fine livestock grazing the pastureland.

In the meantime, Colonel Hill's men were frantically digging in at Big Bethel, fearing a Federal attack. Having at first only twenty-five spades, six axes, and three picks for the regiment, the men worked throughout the day and night of June 7 and all day on June 8.[23] By the end of the second day, their vigorous efforts had produced the outline of an enclosed fortified camp that straddled the road from Yorktown to Hampton. Hill had selected this spot because it afforded the best defensive position. The camp stood on high ground just north of the west branch of the Back River and commanded the bridge across it to the south. The branch of the Back River meandered northwest of the old church, and nearby marshes offered protection. Woods surrounded the main fortification, except for an open field north of the stream where the eastern portion of the earthworks was being dug. South of the creek, past the woods and marshes, were large open fields. These worried Hill. He did not have the manpower to occupy more than one of the two commanding eminences there. A site west of the road to Hampton was selected for locating a Southern battery; one of Randolph's howitzers would assist in blocking the enemy's approach to the bridge through the open field on that side of the road. When Magruder arrived shortly before the battle, he made only slight adjustments in the entrenchments and the disposition of the 1,400 Confederate troops. These consisted of Hill's well-trained regiment, about 600 Virginians that included infantry, Randolph's artillery, and three companies of Virginia cavalry.[24]

A BLUNDER: FEDERALS FIRE ON FEDERALS

Rumors of approaching marauding parties of the enemy—with one supposedly near Big Bethel—led Colonel Hill, on June 8, to send two detachments, each with an artillery piece, to drive away the unwanted intruders found pillaging local citizens' properties. The missions were successful. The Federal parties were driven back across the New Market Bridge over the southern branch of the Back River and in sight of Union flags at Hampton. The boldness of the Confederate action, so near to a Federal camp, prodded Butler to take action that culminated in the Battle of Big Bethel.[25]

Events leading to what most Richmond papers called the first land battle of the war involved, to varying degrees, a twenty-one-mile strip of land from the key Confederate base at Yorktown southward to the main Union bases at Hampton and Newport News. The outline of this portion of the lower peninsula roughly resembled the head of a dinosaur leaning backward. At the top of the pointed head (the bottom of the peninsula) were Fort Monroe, Hampton, and Newport News. Roads from these Union bases to Big Bethel crossed two branches running easterly and forming a giant tongue of land that ended abruptly where the two tributaries met to form the Back River. The outline of this river formed the configuration of the slightly opened mouth of the dinosaur. Big Bethel was located just north of the northern branch of the Back River, at the base of the mythical tongue. A dozen or so miles north of Big Bethel was Yorktown, west of a disfigured hand created by the outline of Back Bay and the Poquosin River.

Benjamin Butler's plan was to remove the annoying Rebels who harassed his bases by destroying what he believed were their key southern outposts at the sites of two churches, a small African-American church called Little Bethel and a much larger house of worship at Big Bethel.[26] This was to be a limited attack, a

207

continuation of the recent sparring and bridge burning of the two contending forces. At this time, no attack was to be made on Yorktown that would threaten Richmond. Federal knowledge about the Confederates at Big Bethel was more accurate than their knowledge of Little Bethel, an outpost abandoned by the Southern cavalry several days before the Federals arrived there. Much of what the Union knew about the Confederates at Big Bethel was obtained from a contraband, George Scott. He had run away from his owner and was working for the Federals at Fort Monroe. Scott knew the region, and according to the New York *Times,* he could "smell a rebel furderer dan he kin a skunk." Armed with a pistol, Scott was sent to see what he could find out about the enemy. Eluding the Confederate pickets, he found and later told Union authorities about "a battery at Big Bethel."[27]

Tactics to achieve the limited Union objective were anything but simple. Butler expected his untested warriors to move in the dark from two separate bases, leaving at different intervals so a part of the troops would merge at a juncture in the road at dawn. From there they were to surprise the enemy, believed to be at Little Bethel, and would drive them into the remainder of the Federal force, which had previously moved north of the small church via a byway through the woods. Then, if the general in charge, Ebenezer Pierce (a general in the Massachusetts militia), so wished, he could attack and capture Big Bethel (also referred to by the Union as Great Bethel). The overall pattern of the Federal movement would be that of an inverted Y. The difficulty of executing, with green troops, a march and juncture that required parade timing, plus the difficulty of having separate Union units communicating with each other in the dark made Butler's plan—though it might have looked great on paper—a blueprint for failure.

Preparations included boats for crossing Hampton Creek, since the bridge over the creek had been burned. The New York *Times* reported that all day the Sunday before the infantry left for the Bethels, in the water near Fort Monroe, men practiced "the management of eight to ten row boats, each carrying twenty-four oars and capable of transporting 130 men each, besides the rowers." When evening approached, each oar-lock was "carefully muffled and each vessel manned by a coxswain and twenty-six rowers from the Naval Brigade." Hidden by the darkness of night, the scows glided away from Fort Hamilton at 1:00 A.M. on June 10. The Fifth New York Zouaves, nicknamed the "Red Devils," under Colonel Abram Duryea, were aboard. Their destination was three miles away at Hampton Creek. From there the infantrymen would march "four abreast" through western Hampton on their way to Little Bethel.

When the soldiers moved through Hampton, they found a beautiful village, full of trees and pleasant dwellings, which once housed 1,200 residents. The home of President Tyler was here, next to the placid stream that divided the village. The village was now inhabited almost entirely by runaway slaves, as whites had abandoned their homes weeks earlier. The dwellings were, according to the *Times,* "literally thronged with negroes who looked on" in the darkness in "terrified astonishment at the number of armed men tramping the streets." They whispered, "The secessionists is come," for they feared it was another nighttime incursion into the town to capture runaways and take them to Norfolk to work upon batteries. The townspeople rejoiced when they discovered the troops were not Southerners, but "Unioners," as they referred to them. As the Federals passed, contrabands raised their hats in "profound respect," and "the females bowed obsequiously."[28]

One hour after the departure of the Red Devils, General Pierce left Hampton with Colonel Frederick Townsend's Third New York, made up of men from Troy, New York.[29] At about the same time the Troy regiment left Hampton, a similar-size force left Newport News; it was made up of detachments of the First Vermont and Fourth Massachusetts under Lieutenant-Colonel Peter T. Washburn, with two field pieces, under Lieutenant John T. Greble. Washburn was ordered to make a late-night or early-dawn attack on Little Bethel. Support would be provided by Colonel John E. Bendix's Seventh New York, who also left Newport News, and the gray-clad men of Townsend's regiment from Hampton.[30] These two regiments were to merge at the crossroads midway between the New Market bridge over the southern branch of Back River and Little Bethel.[31]

To prevent Union troops from firing at each other during the foray in the dark, Butler directed that any attacking regiment must first shout the watchword: Boston. To further help the men identify each other, the men of Townsend's regiment wore a white rag or patch or something white or nearly white on their left arms. Such precautions would fail to prevent confusion or the fiasco of their

Union soldiers mistakenly firing on each other in what Butler called a "strange fatuity" and an "almost criminal blunder."

While the most advanced of the Federals were moving toward Little Bethel, the Red Devils circled north of the small church as Washburn's men were moving to it from the south. The remaining Union forces further to the south, between the fork in the road and New Market bridge, fired on each other. At about 6:00 A.M. Bendix's troops (from Newport News), near the crossroads, had noticed a force (Federals from Fort Monroe area) 100 yards to the south, approaching them over a narrow road surrounded by thick woods. Thinking this force was a Confederate one, Bendix's men, a German regiment, had fired, first with muskets and then a field piece.

Pierce and his staff, riding in front of Townsend's Albany men, were shocked. Only moments before they had seen Bendix's men coming out of the woods and wheeling a six-pounder to the middle of the road and assumed, correctly, that they were Federals. All in Pierce's column now believed Confederates were ambushing them. According to Butler's official report, the first company of Townsend's regiment became "panic stricken, and hastily sought shelter in the adjacent woods, and opened a blind and reckless fire intended" for the enemy, but "only dangerous to their own artillerists," who were in the road a short distance in front of them. Confusion prevailed throughout the line as Townsend's men "yelled and fired in all directions." While a fairly steady fire came from the assumed enemy, about twenty of Townsend's men, believing they had been led into a trap, were "seen creeping on their stomachs through a ditch—having left the ranks without firing a gun." They were later placed in a guardhouse.[32] Pierce and Townsend, amidst heavy fire, shouted at their men and somehow were able to reassemble most of them in the road. The sound of firing weapons caused all Federal forces, including Duryea's Zouaves and Washburn's men, to immediately reverse their direction and head southward.

Two doctors in the German regiment were so frightened by this encounter that they fled back to their Union camp, under the guide of looking for bandages.[33] Others also fled back to Hampton in confusion, among them forty men from Colonel Townsend's regiment. The New York *Tribune* reported they were arrested for desertion, with their "arms taken from them and stacked by the roadside." Among the deserters was the entire band. All of the deserters brought the "wildest excitement and news" of the battles back to Colonel Allen and the men of the First New York. "If accounts were to be believed, the secessionists at Hampton had assembled in enormous force, and were hewing Colonel Townsend's regiment to pieces."[34] Allen's regiment responded by moving rapidly northward to help Colonel Townsend's distressed regiment.[35]

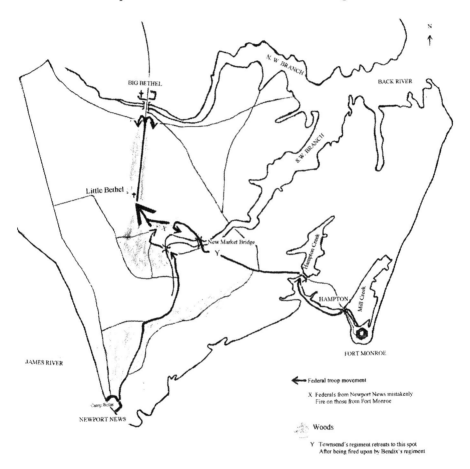

FEDERAL TROOP MOVEMENT TO BIG BETHEL
(JUNE 10, 1861)

In the meantime, General Pierce, who wore no military uniform at all but "had a military cap and civilian coat marked with shoulder straps," pulled his beleaguered force a mile and a half back until they were south of the New Market Bridge. There they waited on high ground for a renewed attack. Their attackers moved southward in pursuit, but were soon horrified to find that they had made a tragic error. Bendix's men had fired on the man in charge of leading the expedition, General Pierce, and his staff, as well as Colonel Townsend's regiment. They were responsible for firing artillery plus nine rounds with their muskets during the fifteen-minute exchange that led to the wounding of twenty-one Union soldiers, two mortally.

Disregarding the advice of several of his colonels that they should turn back now that the element of surprise was gone, General Pierce moved toward Big Bethel. He also sent a request for reinforcements to General Butler back at Fort Monroe. As the Federals moved forward, the Zouaves, in accordance with Butler's orders, burned the small church at Little Bethel and secessionists' homes.

At 3:00 that same morning, the Confederates at Big Bethel were awakened to advance upon the enemy. They had marched three and a half miles when an elderly lady informed them that their adversary, in large numbers, was only a few hundred yards away. The Southerners hastened back to Big Bethel to their earthworks that formed a broken outline similar to that of a lowercase printed g. The main purpose of this defensive formation was to prevent the enemy from crossing over a bridge on the road to Yorktown. The top, or head, of the g was vertically intersected by two roads and separated from the bottom of the tail by the northwest branch of the Back River. Most of Hill's North Carolinians found security in the top of the g, the earthworks north of the branch. Several hundred Confederates were positioned in the more tenuous position at the bottom, or tail, of the configuration. These men were located in an open field south of the branch and west of the road to Hampton. Men were positioned here to protect the howitzer in this field. Some were put behind an old mill dam, others were in the works with the howitzer, and still others were placed westward in the field on a hill without earthworks and near a thirty-foot-deep ravine running northward into the branch. Soldiers next to the ravine, under Colonel William Stuart, worked hurriedly to dig a modest entrenchment, as the Yankees were only several miles away and were marching ever closer. Southern horses were also pulled back north of the branch—with some difficulty, as the horses of Nottoway's cavalry got mired down in the marshes. Most of the land immediately in front of the southern bank of the branch was also swampy and covered with trees.[36]

Less than a mile south of the branch, the Union force halted. Pierce was informed of a reconnaissance made by Captains Judson Kilpatrick and Charles G. Bartlett. Around 8:00 A.M. Captain Kilpatrick, a future Union cavalry leader, exchanged fire with the Confederate scouts and videttes. This announced the Federals' arrival. The Richmond *Dispatch* stated that the Southern "cannoneers and infantry in the line of fortifications were notified and stood ready, ammunition in hand." Colonel Stewart's men were ordered in the fort and were "compelled to kneel in order to escape observation, it being the Confederate plan to let the enemy advance into the middle of the open field and then open fire."[37]

Magruder busily checked the position of his men, and with his theatrical flair, he spouted spirited and succinct remarks to each company. To one he concluded with the words used by a Baptist minister, the Reverend Adams, who had preached to the troops in Bethel Church the previous night, saying, "God is with us, and victory is sure." To another company, he quoted Garibaldi, "God never made a more beautiful day for his men to die in defense of their country." To the men from Hampton, he proclaimed that they had the strongest incentive of all: "they had deep and grievous wrongs of their own to avenge."[38]

While the Confederates waited, at times yelling, Kilpatrick reported to his leaders that his reconnaissance, plus information received from a "negro" and a woman in a nearby farmhouse, made him believe that Rebels had 3,000 to 5,000 men behind earthworks and masked batteries with thirty artillery pieces.[39]

Both sides had difficulty getting a clear view of the other. Confederates hid behind their works, which, to the Union, looked like a large fort, thirteen feet high. The shade of the woods obscured the Federals' position on their right. Two small buildings, on their left and in front of them, also hid the Federals. What Magruder's men, including Major Randolph—in charge of the main Confederate battery, north of the branch and left of the road—could see protruding in the air a half-mile away in a line were glittering bayonets and the star-spangled banner.

What followed was four and a half hours of intermittent fighting, from 9:00 A.M. to 1:30 P.M. Artillery fire was also sporadic.

At three-minute intervals a shot belched forth from one of the five Southern pieces.[40] East and west of the road to Big Bethel church, Confederate musket fire and Southern artillery foiled Union attempts to advance northward. After failing to successfully move forward, and convinced they faced an enemy of 3,000 to 5,000 men—a force at least equal, if not greater than, their own—the Federals would retreat to their camps on the southern tip of the peninsula in the afternoon.

The battle opened around 9:00 A.M., when the future Confederate Secretary of War Major George W. Randolph, commanding the Howitzer Battalion, aimed a Parrott gun at the gleaming enemy bayonets and fired. The shot struck in front of the Federal column and ricocheted into it, killing a soldier standing next to Colonel Bendix. Other projectiles flew over their heads and smashed into the trees. "Well, we could have stood that," said one soldier later to Butler, "but General, they fired 'rotten balls.'" "You mean shells, I suppose?" Butler asked. "Well, yes," replied the soldier, "that is what they told me afterwards they were; but they would strike a tree and burst, and the pieces would drop around among us. I guess if they had been regular balls the men would have stood it, but they broke and scattered to the woods."[41]

Confusion broke out in the Seventh New York as Bendix tried his best to get his men, who sought protection in the woods east of the road, into some semblance of order. At first at every boom of the cannon, recalled a soldier from New York who was at the scene, men "would drop on their faces and rise instantly," but the shots came so fast that "many felt it was useless and stopped." Some believed their fate was predestined. If they were to be hit, they would be, regardless of whether they stood or lay down. Men of other units dropped to the ground to dodge artillery shots. According to a Union soldier, a lieutenant was "slightly wounded by a bayonet of one of his own men," when he accidentally fell against it while dodging a cannonball. As enemy shots crashed around them, men talked to each other as if they were in the safety of their camp, with two of the fellows even engaging in a heated argument.

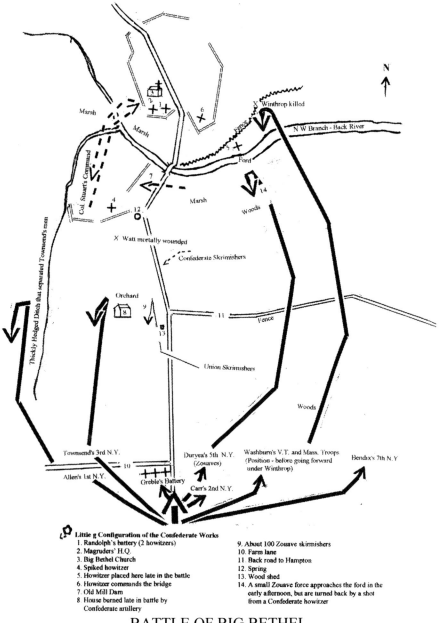

N

Marsh

Winthrop killed

N W Branch - Back River

Marsh

Col. Stuart's Command

Ford

Marsh

Woods

Thickly Hedged Ditch that separated Townsend's men

Watt mortally wounded

Confederate Skirmishers

Orchard

Fence

Union Skirmishers

Woods

Townsend's 3rd N.Y.

Duryea's 5th N.Y. (Zouaves)

Washburn's V.T. and Mass. Troops (Position - before going forward under Winthrop)

Bendix's 7th N.Y

Allen's 1st N.Y.

Greble's Battery

Carr's 2nd N.Y.

Little g Configuration of the Confederate Works
1. Randolph's battery (2 howitzers)
2. Magruders' H.Q.
3. Big Bethel Church
4. Spiked howitzer
5. Howitzer placed here late in the battle
6. Howitzer commands the bridge
7. Old Mill Dam
8. House burned late in battle by Confederate artillery

9. About 100 Zouave skirmishers
10. Farm lane
11. Back road to Hampton
12. Spring
13. Wood shed
14. A small Zouave force approaches the ford in the early afternoon, but are turned back by a shot from a Confederate howitzer

BATTLE OF BIG BETHEL
June 10, 1861

Across the road, behind a farm lane that merged perpendicularly into the main road was Greble's battery of two howitzers and a brass six-pounder manned by eleven men. They hastily returned the Confederate artillery fire, but with scattered and ineffective shots. Meanwhile, Pierce moved his force forward to the right and the left of the Hampton road. Into the woods on the right went Duryea's Fifth New York (Zouaves), Washburn's Vermont and Massachusetts troops, and Bendix's Seventh New York. To the left, joining Greble's battery, were Townsend's Third New York, followed by Allen's First New York. From these positions attacks would later be launched on the Confederate left and right.

ATTACK ON THE CONFEDERATE RIGHT

The first movement forward was by skirmishers sent forth to probe the Confederates' strength, especially in the ominous earthworks south of the Northwest Branch of the Back River. Those who stayed east of the road crawled near a fence on the outskirts of the woods, only to soon be forced back into the woods for shelter. Others, including some of the Zouaves from the Fifth New York (Red Devils), crossed the road on their left into a plowed field (some say a cornfield) in front of the advanced Confederate works. There two companies of skirmishers, one led by General Butler's nephew, Captain John G. Butler, and the Red Devils, led by Captain Kilpatrick, found heavy enemy fire. After firing one round, stated the Richmond *Dispatch,* "The skirmishers retreated fifteen yards and threw themselves upon the ground, loading and firing as rapidly as possible. They had nothing to cover them but a slight orchard tree here and there, a wood shed, and a house with a picket fence." These provided but slight protection, as one of the Southern artillery shots went through the farmhouse, then through one of the Zouaves— leaving what the *Dispatch* called a "hole in the man was about the size of a common water bucket"—and cut down a tree.[42]

Finally, around noon, the New York Troy regiment (Third New York), led by Colonel Townsend, came forward to the position of the skirmishers. Townsend sat unflinching upon his horse at the head of his men. They saw the unsettling scenes of dead and dying Red Devils and passed an arm and a head torn to pieces by enemy artillery fire. Ordered to attack the enemy works, they got only 500 feet from the Confederates' forward-most battery. Exposed to awful fire, they were ordered to lay their faces down on the hot sand. Shells tore up the ground around them and threw sand in their eyes. The Troy men stayed there and fired for about twenty minutes before Townsend pulled them back; he feared they were being flanked.[43]

Townsend's attack sparked great concern within the Confederate lines. Their concern was heightened by the accidental breaking of a priming wire in the vent of the howitzer in the advanced works, which rendered useless their only artillery piece at that location. The spiked piece was rolled over a hill to prevent it from falling into Union hands. The works were evacuated, as Lieutenant Colonel William D. Stuart pulled back his 200 men (Third Virginia) through the swamp and over the branch to a hill near the church. Stuart's men had pulled back not only because he believed 1,500 enemy soldiers were moving on his front, but because some of them were moving northward to his right, west of the ravine—lined by thick hedges—and were about to flank his position.

Magruder, wanting to re-occupy the abandoned area, sent another howitzer back to the abandoned works, with the North Carolinians who were positioned in the swamp east of the road, and those to the west near an old mill dam, as well as Colonel Stuart's men. Both Magruder and Hill felt this counter-move saved the day. Ironically, Townsend had pulled his men back not solely because of new Confederate resistance and reoccupation of the work, but also because he mistook a company of his regiment that had separated from the rest (by going west of the hedged ditch) as the enemy. Townsend had been unaware of their separation, only "seeing among the breaks in the hedges, the glistening of bayonets in the adjoining field." He immediately concluded that the enemy was outflanking him, so he pulled his regiment back to their original position. There he wanted to repel any enemy advance. Now in front of the Troy men were the original skirmishers, who stayed forward, still using the orchard, house, outbuilding, and fence paling as protection, all the while damning Pierce for their plight.

At another place on the field a soldier was sitting exposed to the fire and cradling the head of a wounded friend who had been shot through the lung by a rifle ball. Readers of the New York *World* would read about how the wounded man's face was distorted with pain. Blood "welled out from the wounds and the death sweat stood upon his forehead as he was breathing his last" and uttering parting words to the friend who attempted to soothe him. A moment later his friend was struck. Then "a rush forward by the rear ranks" soon concealed both of the unfortunates from sight. As soldiers moved forward, there lay in the dust, unnoticed, a comrade who had lost a hand. Earlier, claimed the *World,* he had "a minnie ball pass through his wrist, leaving the right hand hanging loosely by one or two tendons and pieces of skin." A fellow soldier who next to him took a knife from his pocket and completed the amputation; he would later be praised for his commendable presence of mind.[44]

ATTACK ON THE CONFEDERATE LEFT

While Townsend was threatening the Confederate right, skirmishers of the Fifth New York, on the east, were attempting to turn the Confederate left. Captain Judson Kilpatrick led the Zouave skirmishers who had earlier cheered the first Confederate shots through the woods on the left. When they arrived at the edge of the woods, enemy fire hit them, with telling effect. Men were falling one after another, wrote an eyewitness, and Lieutenant-Colonel Gouverneur K. Warren, "riding a white mule and waving a croquet stick," started leading the men eastward toward the ford. Confederate skirmishers, east of the Hampton road, soon reported that Zouaves were moving eastward to cross the ford three-fourths of a mile east of the main road, in an attempt to turn the Confederate left. Confederates had earlier obstructed the ford by felling trees, but the platoon guarding it was not sufficient to fend off the Federals.

Magruder ordered a company under Captain W. H. Werth, with a howitzer, to the ford to reinforce the small force of forty men positioned there earlier. As he moved toward the ford, Werth could see Zouaves advancing down the opposite bank of the stream. He at once moved rapidly over the distance of more than a mile in about nine minutes, arriving before the Zouaves. Werth tore down the fence on both sides of the creek. His men cleared away the undergrowth and lay down timber to obstruct the ford and make the fire from the naval howitzer more effective if the enemy tried to cross. When the Zouaves arrived at the branch, one shot from the howitzer scared them off. But they had not given up. Zouaves back along the wood line, in front of the open field between the trees along the branch, continued to fight and to sustain casualties. Grape shot ripped off part of the rectangle on Colonel Duryea's left shoulder, went through Captain Judson Kilpatrick's leg, and killed a soldier behind them. After several hours in front of the woods, the exhausted Zouaves, at their colonel's request, were pulled back, and reinforcements were sent to take their place.

Major Theodore Winthrop
A descendant of John Winthrop and acting secretary to General Benjamin Butler, Winthrop refused to go on furlough in order to fight at Big Bethel. Like Greble, his display of valor while seeking glory cost him his life.
(Courtesy of the Library of Congress)

A few minutes before noon one last attempt was made to penetrate the Confederate position. The man who would lead the charge was Major Theodore Winthrop, General Butler's acting military secretary. Winthrop was exhausted from the heat and the lack of sleep, food, and water. Before being ordered to move toward the works, Winthrop and others stuck their heads out of the underbrush, and instantly a shower of balls rained upon them, forcing them to draw back into the woods. Winthrop sat behind a tree, remarking that if he could only sleep for five minutes he would be fine. He said that he was "going to see the inside of that entrenchment before he went back to the fortress."[45] Soon Colonel Washburn ordered him forward with a detachment of Vermont and Massachusetts troops, numbering about 200. They crossed the branch, eight feet wide and waist deep, to the left of the Confederate works. Winthrop's men had been able to cross the creek uncontested because of a ruse. The major deceived the Southerners by using the North Carolinians' distinctive badge of a white band around their caps and repeatedly shouting, "Don't fire!" Once across the creek, believing they could take the Rebel works by entering with a sudden rush, the Yankees began to cheer lustily.

Two companies of Hill's regiment dispelled the Federals' illusion of taking the fort calmly and accurately firing on the approaching enemy.[46] The Carolinians seemed to Hill to "all be in high glee" and "seemed to enjoy" shooting at Yankees "as much as boys do rabbit-shooting." Most waited for permission to fire and repeatedly declared, "I think I can bring him down," and asked, "May I fire?" While the Confederates fired, Captain Winthrop, who had reached a fence and leaped onto a log, was waving his saber and shouting, "come on boys, one charge and the day is ours." These words were his last, for a Carolina musket ended his life by sending a bullet into his heart. The Federals rapidly retreated. A Carolinian ran forward and took Winthrop's saber, one borrowed from his friend, Colonel David W. Wardrop of Massachusetts, as a trophy. Furlough papers were found on Winthrop's body, but he had not wanted to miss the action and had volunteered to accompany the Federal forces.[47]

Winthrop's gallant action was an unsuccessful attempt to rally his fleeing men. Colonel Hill claimed Winthrop was the only one of the enemy who had exhibited even an approximation of courage during the whole day. The men Winthrop was trying to rally had been fired upon for twenty minutes and were called back. Continued attack would be futile.

THE BATTLE ENDS

No further Union charges were made. But on the Union left, Federals still harassed the Southerners by firing from the house and from behind the outhouses and fence palings. These structures also hid the three six-pounders 250 yards behind them. During the encounter, these and several other Union pieces (six- and twelve-pounders) had fired shot, shell, spherical case, and canister. But the only Confederate injury was the loss of one mule. A frightened Union prisoner, whose captor tied him to a tree behind the church to prevent his escape, was in the line of fire. The frightened look on his face when he was exposed to enemy fire revealed his fear of becoming a casualty.

At the behest of Colonel Hill, four volunteers were obtained to burn the house that protected enemy sharpshooters and artillery. The volunteers were given matches and a hatchet, and they scrambled over the breastworks and ran for the targeted house. Soon Federals fired at them, not from the house, but from across the main road to their left. The four men, from Company A of the First North Carolina, instantly fell to the ground to escape the shots. As they hugged the ground, Private John H. Thorpe could see a shot comrade lying less than four feet away. He was a short, stout private, Henry L. Wyatt, lying limp on his back, with, recalled a soldier, "his arms extended, one knee up and a clot of blood on his forehead as large as a man's fist." The three surviving volunteers were ordered back to the safety of the Confederate works.

Soon after the three surviving volunteers had been ordered back to their works, the skillful Randolph, who was north of the branch, fired upon the house with shell to set it on fire. The enemy battery—which was south of the structure, hidden from Confederate view—incorrectly assumed they were being fired on and immediately returned Randolph's fire with solid shot. This disclosed Greble's position. Randolph fired at the house and the Federal battery at the same time as an intense thirst made Federals, who were short on water, drink from polluted buckets used for rinsing artillery sponges.

Private Henry L. Wyatt
A member of the 1st North Carolina Infantry (later known as the "Big Bethel Regiment"), Wyatt was the only Confederate fatality at Big Bethel.
(Courtesy of the Library of Congress)

Pierce now ordered everyone to leave, but Greble refused to pull back until the very last. His mild looks—some called him effeminate—belied the fact that he was intrepid under fire. His artillerymen had fallen one by one and been carried away, their places filled by others. At each discharge from the battery, only Greble remained on his feet; the rest fell behind their artillery pieces for protection, rising only momentarily to reload and fire. When Lieutenant Butler pleaded with him to at least do what the rest were doing and "dodge," he replied, "I never dodge." He personally sighted each of the three guns in his battery and looked eagerly through field glasses to examine the results.[48]

Lieutenant John T. Greble

The son of a wealthy Philadelphia businessman, graduate of West Point and veteran of fighting the Seminoles, competently commanded two artillery pieces on the Union left, but his intrepidness and reluctance to withdraw cost him his life as the battle ended. (Courtesy of the Library of Congress)

Greble was running low on ammunition and was preparing to leave, according to the New York *Times,* when "a cannon ball struck his head, shattering the back part of it to atoms, and killing him instantly." "The blow left his face unmarked...Confusion followed and a disposition was shown to desert the guns, when a band of men rushed back" under Colonel Warren and "placed the bleeding corpse on the carriage, and bore off the piece" toward Hampton.

The trip back from Big Bethel was a difficult one for the Federals. They were pursued by 100 Confederate dragoons, but they suffered more from fatigue.[49] Retreating in the heat of the day, exhausted, the men threw away hundreds of overcoats, haversacks, and canteens. A Southern lady living near the road critically watched the retreating soldiers, claiming, "the affrightened creatures left the scene of their exploits in the wildest confusion. Some were crying with pain, others screaming with terror, and still others yelling like demons, in the hope probably of frightening back all pursuers."[50] Bringing the wounded back was a solemn sight. Some were carried on the backs of comrades, "some on litters, some on carts, and six on gun carriages." Finally, the exhausted and foot-sore men of Pierce's force returned to camp. They had been on their feet from 11:00 P.M. Sunday to 5:00 P.M. Monday.

It was a much happier scene for the Southerners. Men felt that their hours of toiling to construct earthworks had saved the day. D. H. Hill wrote that the North Carolinians "shook hands affectionately with their spades, calling then 'clever fellows and good friends.'" One concluded, "Had we not had God on our side we must have been whipped." Gratitude was also given to an elderly lady. Officers of Hill's North Carolina regiment were deeply appreciative because she had warned them of the approaching Federals. Out of their own pockets they raised $225 and gave it to her.[51]

Many Confederates surveyed the battlefield; the sights that met their eyes were said to be sickening. One later descried what he saw: the ground "was strewn with broken muskets, haversacks, canteens, artillery equipment and fragments of the dead and wounded." Some Union "dead bodies were burned" in the house fired by Southern shell. Around it the Southerners saw bodies "mangled in the most frightening manner by Confederate shells," orchard trees scarred by battle, and a gum tree struck sixty times by musket fire three to thirty feet off the ground. A little further on they came upon a spot "where the Federals had carried their wounded who had since died." A number of the bodies were "piled one upon another." To one Southerner it looked "as if in the retreat the enemy had dumped them from a cart." Here the bright and "gay looking uniforms of the New York Zouaves contrasted greatly with the paled, fixed faces of their owners." Catching the eye of the battlefield visitors were the remains of a "boyish, delicate-looking fellow lying in the mud, with a bullet hole through his breast. His hand was pressed on the wound from which his blood had poured and the other was clinched in the grass that grew near him. Lying on the ground was a Testament, which had fallen from his pocket, dabbed with blood." One Southerner opened it and read the inscription: "Presented to the Defenders of their Country, by the New York Bible Society." As ghastly as these sights were, the Confederates were curious about their enemy, so they closely examined the dead, their wounds, and clothing and the personal effects in their haversacks. One curious explorer of the battlefield found uniforms on the bodies that "very different"—many of them "like those of the Virginia soldiery." They opened and read letters asking if they liked the Southern farms, and if the "Southern barbarians had been whipped out yet."[52]

Later that afternoon, the Southerners buried the Union dead who were left on the field, including the body of Major Winthrop, which was placed near their works. They kept his gold watch, sword, and eighty dollars in gold.[53] That night Magruder pulled his entire force, except for the cavalry left at Big Bethel, back to Yorktown.

The battle had lasted for four and a half hours, approximately from 9:00 A.M. to 1:30 P.M. Randolph's artillery fired ninety-eight times, at a somewhat leisurely pace, averaging a shot every three minutes and suspending fire when the enemy was out of range. Despite praise for the artillery, the action of that day revealed serious defects in Southern ammunition and equipment. A somewhat frustrated Randolph found that shells for the Parrott gun had precut wooden fuses that could not be removed. Their limbers were too small, were pulled by only two horses, and could carry only two men.[54]

More positive were the Confederate fortification efforts. Their earthworks proved to be crucial in overcoming the 4,000 Union soldiers with only 1,400 men (only 1,200 of whom were engaged)—a four-to-one disadvantage in manpower.[55] Magruder's men had won a relatively easy victory, suffering only one fatality and seven wounded, compared to the Union losses: eighteen deaths, fifty-three wounded, and five missing.[56]

News of the victory slowly spread throughout the South. Families in North Carolina failed to learn the particulars for a week or more, until someone claiming to have been present returned by train to give the particulars to the local paper.[57] An elated South received the jubilant news of the victory of Big Bethel. The Richmond *Dispatch* put out an extra edition with these headlines: "Battle at Bethel Church," "The Enemy Routed," "Gallant Conduct of Our Troops," "Large Number of Yankees Killed," and "Panic and Flight." The same paper called it "one of the most extraordinary victories in the annals of war." The number of Northerners killed and wounded was reported to be at least 1,000.[58] The Petersburg *Express* introduced their tale of the battle with the headline "A Battle at Last."

To many Southerners, these reports were evidence of the military might of the South and evidence that God was on her side. Colonel D. H. Hill concluded his official report by penning, "Let us devoutly thank the living God for this wonderful interposition in our favor, evince our gratitude by the exemplariness of our lives."[59] "Two hundred of the enemy killed," the *Dispatch* incorrectly reported, "and on our side but one life lost. Does not the hand of God seem manifest in this thing...[in which] the courage and conduct of the noble sons of the South engaged in the battle are beyond all praise?" The *Dispatch* continued in praise its of Southern soldiers, "They have crowned the name of their country with imperishable luster and made their own names immortal." The Richmond *Whig* added, "Their dashing bearing, in the face of four times their number, will inspire a spirit of emulation among all our forces, and lead to the rout of the invaders whenever they show themselves."[60] Proudly, residents displayed trophies of the battle in Richmond store windows.[61] Among the praise, Magruder's fear—that the Union would return to Big Bethel—went unnoticed, but he evacuated for Yorktown.[62]

HEROES, MARTYRS, AND LOSERS

A jubilant South proclaimed all their participants of the battle—which some would call the first land battle of the war—heroes. At the top of the list was "Prince John" Magruder, followed by D. H. Hill. Both were soon rewarded with promotions to brigadier-general. Major George W. Randolph, the grandson of Thomas

Jefferson, was also praised, with some justification; there was said to be "no superior as an artillerist in any country." After the battle, the First North Carolina Infantry proudly became known as the Big Bethel Regiment.[63]

The South's martyr in the battle was her only fatality, Henry L. Wyatt, later called "the first Confederate soldier slain in battle."[64] After the battle, Wyatt was taken off the field by his comrades and carried to Yorktown, where he died, never having regained consciousness. The following day the nineteen-year-old's body was taken to Richmond, where he had once lived, and was buried with military honors in Hollywood Cemetery.[65]

Coupled with the praise of dauntless warriors was the recognition of occasional acts of compassion and understanding toward the enemy. Despite the continual publication of incidents of enemy outrages, some felt that the war could be fought with civility. At Yorktown, under a flag of truce, Magruder had met with a Federal party seeking the body of Winthrop. Magruder granted removal of the remains and shook hands with the departing Federal officer, telling him, "we part as friends, but on the field of battle we meet as enemies."[66] Benjamin Butler was impressed. He wrote to Winfield Scott, "I am happy to add that upon sending a message to Yorktown I found that the courtesies of civilized warfare have been and are intended to be extended to us by the enemies of the country now in arms which in this department at all times shall be fully reciprocated."[67]

Winthrop's brother, who accompanied the Federal party to the Confederate lines, also had praise for the enemy. He saw a Southern honor guard, made up of the Charles City cavalry, and a detachment of artillerymen solemnly and respectfully escort the disinterred body toward him. A moved and heartbroken brother, who brought "a metallic coffin to receive the moldering form," with a bowed head, said in choking tones, overcome with emotion, "I did not expect this. Will this simple incident find its way into a northern paper? I doubt it."[68]

A few Union officers, such as Townsend, received praise for their work at Big Bethel, but the highest adoration went to the two slain officers, Major Theodore Winthrop and Lieutenant John Greble. They were the Union counterparts of the Southern martyr, Henry Wyatt. Saddened soldiers at Fort Monroe and other nearby camps mourned the deaths of Winthrop and Greble. The grief displayed there soon spread northward like a chilling wind. Details of what was considered their heroic deaths and sorrowful funerals were printed in the Northern newspapers. Civilians read the moving account of Greble's body being placed on ice upon its arrival at Fort Monroe and of the imposing funeral held for the lieutenant in the fort's chapel before his remains were sent to Philadelphia. The day after Big Bethel, Union officers at Fort Monroe adopted resolutions honoring Greble for his coolness and bravery in combat; as a mark of respect to his memory, they would wear mourning badges for thirty days. They lauded his heroic demise, saying that a "death so glorious, can but tend to lighten the burden of grief for all."[69]

Winthrop's disinterred remains were also given a respectful ceremony at Fort Monroe before they were sent north for a hero's burial, accompanied by impressive military and civilian processions. Services were held in the large New York City National Guard Armory, a place he had marched from just a couple of months earlier on his way to war. His body was interred at New Haven, Connecticut, on June 20. A graveside eulogy was given by Professor Noah Porter, who pointed out: "our deceased friend...was descendant in the direct line of the first John Winthrop, who in 1630" came from England with immigrants to America. "Although his life was cut short, "he had not lived in vain. "He has given his life for his country in the field, and his example to those who are to follow, by dying as a soldier should. 'The paths of glory lead but to the grave.'"[70] So ended a eulogy of which Winthrop would have highly approved.

Had Winthrop's life ended the way he wanted? One would think not, but an unpublished poem he had written reveals his romantic view of combat and his desire for martyrdom:

> Let me not waste in skirmishes my power,
> In petty struggles. Rather, in hour
> Of deadly conflict may I nobly die,
> In my first battle perish gloriously.[71]

This statement was not the manifestation of a tormented mind seeking release from an unbearable life. Winthrop seemed to jubilantly enjoy life. His poem expresses a fantasy fueled by a romanticized perception of a war that offered opportunities for heroic deeds and sacrifice, which would set one apart from most of mortal mankind and earn wide respect and fame as a hero.[72]

While New Yorkers lamented the loss of Winthrop, Pennsylvanians mourned for Greble. They read with sadness excerpts from letters Greble had written at Camp Butler at Newport News on June 9, the day before his death. He wrote to a friend, "as far as I can see, there is not much damage to be incurred in this campaign. At present, both sides seem better inclined to talking than fighting." Later that day he found he was going into combat. Just before marching off, and less sure of his fate, he hurriedly wrote on a piece of paper, in pencil, to his wife:

> May God bless you, my darling, and grant you a happy and peaceful life. May the good Father protect you and me, and grant that we may long live happily together. God, give me strength, wisdom and courage. If I die, let me die as a brave and honorable man; let no stain of dishonor hang over me or you.[73]

Edwin Greble, father of the lieutenant and a wealthy proprietor of an extensive marble works in Philadelphia, received a special dispatch at 3:00 P.M. on June 11 that told him of his son's death. The palatial Nineteenth Street house and the nearby factory were immediately closed. A special correspondent was soon sent to the house. He wrote that he rang the doorbell and was ushered through a wide hall to a "dark, melancholy parlor." Standing in the doorway he could hear "smothered voices of sobbing" coming from occupants on every side of the room. In a few minutes, a member of the family gave the newspaperman some details about the slain lieutenant's life. He was told that Lieutenant John T. Greble had died at the age of twenty-seven, leaving a widow and two infant children. An 1854 graduate of West Point, he had spent several years fighting the Seminoles, and before going to Fort Monroe, served in a teaching capacity at West Point.

While gloom overwhelmed his home and city, Greble's father went to Fort Monroe to accompany his eldest son's body to Philadelphia. Anger, fueled by grief, exhaustion, and the frustration that his great wealth was useless in this situation made him say that from the accounts given of his son's death, he was "satisfied" that his son died because of "gross cowardice and mismanagement on the part of leading officers of the expedition." According to the New York *Herald,* Greble's father believed "the loss of his boy was a deliberate murder for which certain officers at Fortress Monroe should be held to a stern account."

Upon arriving at Philadelphia, the body was taken to the home of Edwin Greble. The coffin was removed from the pine box that had encased it was and placed in the reception room. Soon viewers arrived but were dismayed at what they saw. The coffin had been "hermetically sealed and a pane of glass set in the lid to disclose the face," they recalled. Those who saw it could not forget. They said that the face was "already partially decomposed, with marks of corruption in the cheeks and even the eyes." Others refused to look, scared off when told of the "distortion and decomposition." Viewers said that the family could only wait "at their shrouded dwelling, and count the slow march" of time "until the hearse and procession came to the door to bear the body away."

At 1:20 P.M. on the day of Greble's funeral, the procession started toward historic Independence Hall. The New York *Herald* described the events: Crowds had been assembling there before 1:00 as a "double file of police officers guarded the doorway and pavement." The American flag that President Lincoln had raised on the previous February 22, in honor of the birthday of the first president, was at half-mast. "All the balconies, windows and roof tops" for long distances above and below the grand hall, were "thronged with family groups and parties of strangers, many of whom bore in their hands and about their bodies the Stars and Stripes, crape and variously mottoed." The city had virtually shut down for grieving.

Inside the main hall stood sentries from an army regiment, reported the *Herald.* Civilians and military men—many from New York regiments "absent from their stations upon furlough"—closely packed the hall. Above the crowds, there hung portraits of storied men, Clay, Penn, Lafayette, and Jackson, which seem to look down upon a long narrow bier covered with black velvet that had previously received the bodies of notables such as John Quincy Adams. "The old bell that proclaimed liberty throughout the land" towered above the dead, "with a plumed eagle brooding above it." Down below, the rusty furniture that had been used by luminaries of an earlier era "studded the plain room on all sides." Several young women adjusted the draperies and placed flowers on the coffin.

At the top of the coffin sat a picture of Greble; his sword, wrapped in a flag, lay lengthwise on the coffin lid; and "over the sword lay his hat—a black Kossouth, with an ostrich feather in the band." Below the sword rested two wreathes of flowers and between them white roses whose sweet aroma filled the room. Two lengthy white ribbons hung gracefully below the flowers on which was inscribed "Purity—Purity." These funeral arrangements hid the glass pane that revealed the decomposing and disfigured head. Standing guard over the remains were four soldiers, "with bayonets at shoulder arms," pacing "up and down beside the bier," as several reporters, councilmen, and "privileged citizens stood in the background."

Until 3:00, people poured into the front and out of the back of the building to see the casket, a scene that would be repeated four years later, when many of the same people would return to view the remains of their slain president, Abraham Lincoln. Seven thousand eight hundred people filed by: men, women and children "of all degrees and characters." Many placed tributes upon the bier. Several small girls dressed in white approached and threw flowers upon the flags, "at the same time kneeling and kissing the picture of the deceased." Scores of the mourners "broke into loud laments at passing the coffin." Many elderly persons who had cared for and watched the deceased from childhood "silently wiped away tears from their eyes and gave vent to pathetic exclamations." One was overheard to say, "Poor Johnny! I knew he would die young, for he was always brave." Brownell, the so-called avenger of Ellsworth, also visited the hall to pay his respects. Wherever he went, a crowd followed him.[74] The funeral service in the afternoon at Independence Hall was followed by another slow procession to Woodland Cemetery. There, reported the New York *Herald,* a company fired "thirty-four guns over the grave," the minister read the funeral service, and "the immense concourse, walking in line about the grave, looked silently upon the coffin lid" and then went away.[75]

In sharp contrast to the adulation bestowed upon to Winthrop and Greble was the condemnation heaped on their commanders. Northerners found little to praise in the leadership of the top commanders involved in the conflict they called Great Bethel. Some papers condemned Butler; others praised him. The defeat, however, nearly cost him the Senate's confirmation of his appointment as major general.[76]

231

Everyone blamed poor Ebenezer Pierce for the Union defeat.[77] Almost immediately after the battle ended, the militia general was villainized. He was condemned for his incompetent handling of his force, or, as one writer put it, "[Pierce] is execrated by everyone for his total want of efficiency." Others condemned him as unfit to command and guilty of great blunders that caused the disaster of Big Bethel.[78]

Back in the Union camps, the men felt a sense of shame over their defeat, but it was their unanimous opinion that Pierce was to blame for their loss at Big Bethel. They wrote to newspapers, stating that during the battle, there had been no coordinated Union effort and fighting had been sporadic. At times in the woods on the Union right, each soldier had become his own officer. Bendix's adjutant complained that there was confusion over who was in command, and that valuable time was wasted in futilely attempting to find Pierce— who failed to provide leadership, and instead left matters up to the discretion of the regimental commanders. According to the New York *Herald,* both the private and officer believed that if a "more experienced commander" had "undertaken the expedition the stars and stripes would" be "floating over the batteries of Great Bethel, and another great step" would have been accomplished toward "ending this horrid war." One soldier assessed Pierce's leadership in the following way: "The General who had command of our brigade knew no more about his business than a child, and his incompetency caused us to suffer the way we did without gaining one single point."[79]

A private's comments were even more searing, dubbing Pierce's name a "synonym for imbecility."[80] Rumors were bandied about that Pierce would be court-martialed or forced to resign. Others proclaimed that if Pierce "should ever attempt to lead the same command into action, he will fall by the hands of his own men."[81]

Two days after Big Bethel, Pierce responded to the increasing criticism by writing to the editor of the Boston *Journal* "to correct the erroneous reports" created by his "enemies." He argued, "I gave my orders properly...under the circumstances the battle could not have been managed better." Furthermore, he wrote, "General Butler has not intimated to me as yet he blames me at all."

This is in contrast to an exonerative account published by one newspaper—an account of a private scene that was unpleasant for all present. This story claims that "General Butler was perfectly enraged against" Pierce, and when the latter was brought before Butler, "he cursed him, called him a fool and a coward, told him he had failed in the performance of his duty, declaring that he had no confidence in him, and that he would not hereafter trust him, no matter how small or unimportant the affair."[82]

Butler would soon publicly acknowledge Pierce's shortcoming, though in far more restrained language than he had used in the private meeting. He condemned the Union errors, such as twice mistaking each other for the enemy and failing to follow his order to charge the enemy's works at Big Bethel with fixed bayonets. Had Pierce obeyed the order to charge, then, in Butler's view, there would have been an almost certain Union victory. The legal training and the political nature of the cross-eyed Union commander led him to play down the loss and try to put a positive spin on the event. Two days after the battle and before receiving the official reports of his officers, Butler arrived in Washington to control the damage by delivering, in person, his official report of the battle to General Scott, who disliked him.[83] In his first official report to Scott, Butler concluded: "I think, in the unfortunate combination of circumstances and the result which we experienced, we have gained far more than we have lost. Our troops have learned to have confidence in themselves under fire."[84]

The real impact of Big Bethel was the short-term influence upon Northern and Southern morale. It heightened the South's enthusiasm for the war, while dampening Northern morale in part, and at least evoking criticism of Union military leadership. There was quite a difference in attitude between the Richmond *Dispatch,* which called Big Bethel "one of the most extraordinary victories in the annals of war" and the lament by the New York *Tribune.* The *Tribune* editor pessimistically stated that Lincoln would be well advised to make peace with the Confederates immediately if he was unwittingly going to send generals into Virginia who were not "up to their work."[85]

The press and public attention that were accorded to Big Bethel, because of the newness of the war, were as extensive as the attention given to later major bloodbaths. But time has relegated Big Bethel to minor importance. Interest in both the battle and the battle site has all but disappeared. Today most of the site is beneath the waters of the Big Bethel Reservoir and inside Langley Air Force

Base. A couple of monuments and a small cemetery are all that remains.[86]

The Federal attack on Big Bethel was the last offensive move by the Union on the peninsula in 1861. Everyday life continued on the peninsula in a very similar manner to that before the battle. Both sides continued to dig in and plead for additional troops. Magruder and Hill were convinced the Federals were spoiling to avenge their loss at Big Bethel and kept a vigilant eye on them through reconnaissances; these reconnaissances led to an occasional skirmish and the most dramatic event after Big Bethel, the Confederates' torching of Hampton. This burning was related to repercussions from the Union defeat at Bull Run. Fearing for the security of Washington and having apprehensions that Southern sympathizers might again rise up in Baltimore, General Scott ordered four regiments, 4,000 of Butler's best men on the peninsula, to Baltimore.[87]

Ben Butler was concerned about his weakened position and evacuated Hampton, creating a crisis for hundreds of contrabands who had made this town their new home. One *Tribune* correspondent listed the number of contrabands as 2,000. Some blacks remained after the Federals' evacuation, but their conditions worsened, with scant supply of food and no employment. More than 800 others traveled to Fort Monroe. Most were housed in tents inside the fort, but women who did not work for the families of officers or have other employment were housed in buildings outside the fort, along with the children and those who were deemed unfit to work.[88]

General Magruder, inspired by the Southern victory at Manassas, ordered expeditions to Hampton and Newport News to take advantage of any opportunities that might arise.[89] The Confederates were unable to draw the enemy from their works at Newport News, but they discovered Hampton had been abandoned. Aware of the approaching enemy, Butler had the planking removed from the thirty-foot bridge spanning the Hampton Creek. Soon the Confederates attempted to burn that structure, touching off an inconsequential thirty-minute skirmish. This was followed by 3,500 Confederates devoting their attention to torching the town.

The idea of runaway slaves' living in white Southerners' former homes did not sit well with Magruder's men, especially those from the Hampton area. Their resentment was exacerbated by the discovery of an August 5, 1861, issue of the New York *Tribune*, which the Federals had left behind.[90] In it was printed a letter from Butler to the Union Secretary of War that convinced the Confederates that Butler was fortifying and planned to continue to use Hampton as a haven for runaways.

After notifying the few remaining citizens to leave and removing the sick and infirm to nearby friends' houses, buildings were set on fire. By midnight Hampton was in flames. The Confederates, who had arrived at Hampton at 11:00 P.M. on August 6, left at sunrise the next day because it was not prudent to remain in range of Butler's guns. However, the Union general offered no resistance to Hampton's burning, claiming, "It would have been easy to dislodge" the Confederates from the town with, he claimed, "a few shells from the fortress, but I did not choose to allow an opportunity to fasten upon the Federal troops any portion in this heathenish outrage." He denounced the enemy for destroying the town after giving the inhabitants only fifteen minutes to evacuate their homes. Butler proclaimed, "A more wanton and unnecessary act than the burning as it seems to me, could not have been committed."[91]

A sort of status quo set in after the destruction of Hampton. Both sides watched, probed, and castigated the other for vandalizing civilian property. Butler attempted, unsuccessfully, to stem the continued Union destruction of civilian property. Other administrative problems continued to plague him, such as the increasing number of civilian visitors from the North, contrabands, sick and intoxicated officers and men, and Pierce's annoying and ceaseless demands for restitution. Before the year ended, Butler was superceded as the commander on the peninsula.[92]

By the year's end, the Union efforts on the peninsula—the Southern invasion corridor—had yielded little. Fort Monroe remained in Union hands, fortifications of Newport News had taken place, the small battle of Big Bethel and lesser conflicts had been fought, but none significantly changed the parameters of contested territory.[93] No serious threat would be made upon Richmond via the peninsula until McClellan arrived there in the spring of 1862. The land between Hampton and Big Bethel, however, saw a tremendous transformation. It bore the scars of war. Farms had been abandoned, and homes, burned and destroyed. These were the hallmarks of a region that saw little military gain while being reduced to a no-man's-land.

[1] Quarles, *Lincoln and the Negro*, 69. Butler protested to Secretary of War Simon Cameron about being moved from Annapolis to Fort Monroe and asked for an interview with Lincoln to discuss the matter. On May 22 Butler arrived to take command at Fort Monroe. Three days later he was involved in a controversy when he refused to return three slaves to the owner. The slaves had rowed to the Union lines, where Butler put them to work. When the owner arrived to collect the slaves, Butler refused to let him have them, maintaining they were "contraband of war."

[2] On April 20, 1861, the Federals evacuated Gosport Naval Yard, near Norfolk, after setting fire to several abandoned vessels. Among them was the U.S.S. *Merrimack,* later refloated by Southerners as the C.S.S. *Virginia.*

[3] T. C. DeLeon, *Four Years in Rebel Capitals* (Mobile, Ala.: Gossip, 1892), 103-4; Hotchkiss, *Virginia*, vol. III, 126. The *Pawnee's* reconnaissance up the James on April 21, 1861, triggered the excitement in Richmond. During the alarm, troops were rushed "down to Chaffin's Bluff, where the river is quite narrow."

[4] Walter Clark, ed., *Histories of the Several Regiments and Battalions from North Carolina in the Great War 1861-'65* (Raleigh, N.C.: E.M. Uzzell, 1901), vol. I, 80-81 (hereafter cited as *N.C. Regiments*); Hotchkiss, *Virginia*, 125-31; Long, *The Civil War Day by Day*, 63, 79, 82. For example, Federal ships fired upon Virginia batteries on May 31 at Aquia Creek and on June 5 at Pig Point, on the James River.

[5] Major J. B. Cary of the Virginia artillery was in command of Hampton. He arranged for the bridges in the area to be fired when the enemy appeared. When told by Federals they were reconnoitering the area and would not harm anyone unless attacked, both sides joined in extinguishing the fires at the bridges. After this joint venture, the Virginians soon withdrew.

[6] Magruder was given the peninsula assignment on May 21. He and additional troops traveled by rail from Richmond to West Point, on the James. From there they went by steamboat to Yorktown.

[7] Freeman, *Lee's Lieutenants*, vol. I, xxxiv. For the details of Magruder's proposal to take Washington, see pages 15-16.

[8] Edward Porter Alexandria, *Military Memoirs of a Confederate* (New York: C. Scribner's Sons, 1907), 367; Hal Bridges, *Lee's Maverick General: Daniel Harvey Hill* (New York: McGraw-Hill, 1961), 17, 20-22, 26.

[9] Clark, *N.C. Regiments*, 81-82.

[10] Charlotte, *The Western Democrat*, June 4, 1861.

[11] Benjamin F. Butler, *Butler's Book* (Boston: A.M. Thayer, 1892), 243-45; Richard P. Weinert Jr. and Robert Arthur, *Defender of the Chesapeake: The Story of Fort Monroe* (Shippensburg, Pa.: White Mane, 1989), 98-99.

[12] Weinert and Arthur, *Defender of the Chesapeake*, 2-3. The first settlers name it "Cape Comfort," but soon the word "Cape" was replaced with "Point" and later added the word "Old."

[13] Cholera broke out among the workers and stopped work for a time in the 1830's. The fort was designed by General Simmon Bernard.

[14] Weinert and Arthur, *Defender of the Chesapeake*, 24, 31-32, 72-75. The number of guns was increased to 412, but many of them were never mounted.

[15] Butler, *Butler's Book*, 248-249.

[16] An artesian well was started long before the Civil War and was never finished. Butler had another one started, but he was transferred elsewhere before it was completed. His local water supply for Fort Monroe was reduced by a regiment encamped on the other side of Mill Creek that dug wells there.

[17] Butler, *Butler's Book*, 249, 252.

[18] *OR*, Ser. I, vol. 2, 53-54; Sandburg, *Lincoln*, vol. 1, 278.

[19] New York *Tribune*, August 10, 1861.

[20] Butler, *Butler's Book*, 258-263. Butler found dealing with contrabands "was becoming onerous, so he appointed a commissioner of Negro Affairs" to free him from the burden.

[21] New York *Times*, June 16, 1861.

[22] *American and Commercial Advertiser*, June 1, 1861.

[23] On Sunday, June 9, Hill received "a fresh supply of tools," allowing him to put more men to work. "When not engaged in religious duties, the men worked vigorously on the entrenchments."

[24] Clark, *N.C. Regiments*, 89. The Confederate forces at Big Bethel were Hill's First North Carolina Regiment (800 men); three companies of the Third Virginia (208 men) under Lieutenant Colonel William Stuart; three companies of soldiers, about 150, under Major E. B. Montague; about 150 men in Randolph's battalion of Virginia artillery; and approximately 100 Virginia cavalry.

[25] Clark, 85; New York *Herald*, June 12, 1861; *OR*, Ser. I, vol. 2, 77-78. General Butler sought assistance for reconnoitering; he contacted the balloonist John La Mountain, directing him to Fort Monroe with his balloons and apparatus.

[26] Butler, *Butler's Book*, 268. Both religious structures at the Bethels, since they were being used by the enemy, were targeted by Butler to be burned, if wooden, or leveled by the artillery, if masonry.

[27] New York *Times*, June 13, 1861; *OR*, Ser. I, vol. 2, 83.

[28] The greater part of the settlement was on the western side of Hampton Creek.

[29] All the Federal troops carried rations for one day. Two hundred of these bright-uniformed men had been selected to carry rifle-muskets instead of smooth-bore muskets to increase their firepower.

[30] New York *World*, June 14, 1861. Along with Townsend's regiment of 650 men was a detachment of the Second New York Infantry and two mountain howitzers.

[31] Bendix was minus 150 of his Seventh New York men; they were with Washburn's advance force.

[32] *OR*, Ser. I, vol. 2, 78-83.

[33] Boston *Daily Journal*, June 14, 1861.

[34] New York *Tribune*, June 16 & 17, 1861.

[35] New York *World*, June 14, 1861.

[36] Richmond *Dispatch*, June 11, 1861; *OR*, Ser. I, vol. 2, 97-102. A company of Hill's was stationed at the dam, and others were in the works with the howitzer. A Virginia battalion under Major E. B. Montague was further west, next to the ravine. His men dug their entrenchments during the hour before the Union forces arrived.

[37] Richmond *Dispatch*, June 13, 1861.

[38] *Daily True Delta*, June 23, 1861

[39] Captain Kilpatrick of the Fifth New York Infantry and a Captain Bartlett carried out their reconnaissance. At approximately 8:00 A.M. on June 10, 1861, they drove away the advanced Confederate pickets.

[40] The Confederates fired eighty to ninety artillery shells.

[41] Butler, *Butler's Book*, 271-71.

[42] Richmond *Dispatch*, June 17, 1861.

[43] New York *Tribune*, June 16, 17, 1861; Richmond *Dispatch*, June 19, 1861.

[44] New York *World*, June 14, 1861.

[45] New York *Tribune*, June 16, 1861. Most Confederate accounts claim Winthrop was shot in the heart. An account in the New York *Tribune* states he was shot in the side.

[46] *OR*, Ser. I, vol. 2, 97. Magruder sent portions of Companies G, H, and C to join Company B and part of C, also from Hill's regiment, in defending the southeastern part of the works.

[47] Butler, *Private and Official Correspondence*, vol. I, 137; Washington Chronicle, June 30, 1861; Richmond *Dispatch*, June 13, 1861. Many accounts have Winthrop standing on the fence when he was shot. Because the saber Winthrop carried had Colonel Wardrop's name inscribed on it, Confederates assumed they had Wardrop's body.

[48] New York *Times*, June 14, 1861; New York *Tribune*, June 16, 1861. Some of the accounts contended Greble had just finished spiking one of his artillery pieces when he was killed.

[49] Pierce had the regiments of Allen and Carr cover and protect the Federal rear during the retreat.

[50] *Daily True Delta*, June 23, 1861.

[51] Clark, *N.C. Regiments*, 87; Pittsburgh *Evening Chronicle*, June 19, 1861.

[52] Greensborough (N.C.) *Patriot*, June 21, 1861.

[53] Richmond *Dispatch*, June 17, 1861.

[54] *OR*, Ser. I, vol. 2, 91, 94-99, 100-101; Richmond *Dispatch*, June 13 & 17, 1861. Magruder contended the battle lasted two and a half hours, from 10:00 A.M. to 12:30, but Hill and Randolph maintained it lasted from 9:00 A.M. to 1:30 P.M.

[55] D. Hill said that of the 800 men in his regiment, fewer than 400 pulled a trigger. Of the 4,000 Federals, only about 2,500 were actively engaged.

[56] *OR*, Ser. I, vol. 2, 82. The breakdown of Union casualties follows: staff, 1 killed (Winthrop); Fourth Massachusetts, 1 killed; First New York, 1 killed; Second New York, 2 killed, 1 wounded; Third New York, 2 killed, 27 wounded or missing; Fifth New York, 6 killed, 13 wounded; Seventh New York, 3 killed, 7 wounded, 2 missing; First Vermont, 2 killed, 3 wounded, 1 missing; Second U.S. Artillery, 1 killed (Greble).

[57] Weekly Raleigh (N.C.) *Register*, June 19, 1861.

[58] Richmond *Dispatch*, June 12, 1861.

[59] *OR*, Ser. I, vol. 2, 97.

[60] Clark, *N.C. Regiments*, 103-104.

[61] Magruder later reoccupied Big Bethel.

[62] Richmond *Dispatch*, June 19 & 22, 1861.

[63] This regiment was also proud of its body servants. One fired at the enemy and another held horses during the hottest of the action.

[64] Clark, *N.C. Regiments,* 100-110.

[65] Mary H. Mitchell, *Hollywood Cemetery: The History of A Southern Shrine* (Richmond, Va.: Virginia State Library, 1985), 47-48.

[66] Richmond *Dispatch,* June 24, 1861.

[67] *OR,* Ser. I, vol. 2, 82.

[68] New York *Tribune,* June 16, 1861; Richmond *Dispatch,* June 19 & 26, 1861. It seems that earlier Winthrop's spurs, cap, notebook, and watch were handed over to the Federals before his body. When his body arrived at Fort Monroe, a funeral was held, attended by General Butler and other officers.

[69] New York *Tribune,* June 16, 1861. Copies of the resolution were sent to Greble's family and New York and Philadelphia papers for publication.

[70] Boston *Daily Evening Transcript,* June 24, 1861.

[71] Theodore Winthrop, *Life In The Open Air, and Other Papers* (Boston: Ticknor & Fields, 1866) Front page.

[72] The story of Winthrop's heroic death was later challenged by the ex-colonel of First New York Volunteers, William Allen. He said the Winthrop story was a "sheer fabrication...all nonsense." Allen's account is refuted by eyewitness accounts. Allen was on the other side of the battlefield and saw little or nothing of Winthrop's activities. Angered by court-martial proceedings brought against him by Butler in the summer of 1861, and annoyed that a person without a command could get such praise, seemed to make Allen's attempt to "correct the record" one of sour grapes.

[73] Washington *Chronicle,* June 30, 1861.

[74] Brownell had been staying in Philadelphia for a while and helped fight a fire a few days later.

[75] New York *Herald,* June 15, 1861.

[76] Butler, *Butler's Book,* 275-76. The senior senator from Butler's home state of Massachusetts voted against his confirmation because of the general's differences with Governor Andrew on slavery. Colonel Edward Baker was critical in turning the tide in Butler's favor; Baker had been detailed to join Butler at Fort Monroe and happened to be in his senate seat. He used his eloquence for Benjamin's confirmation.

[77] New York *Herald,* June 13, 1861. Ebenezer W. Pierce, a man in his mid-forties, was appointed by Governor Andrews of Massachusetts to be brigadier-general of the Massachusetts militia; he was to fill the vacancy caused by Benjamin Butler's promotion to major-general of the U.S. Army. Pierce's home was Roxbury, Massachusetts.

[78] Boston *Daily Evening Transcript,* June 14, 1861; New York *Times,* June 14, 1861; New York *Tribune,* June 16, 1861.

[79] New York *Herald,* June 13, 1861

[80] Boston *Daily Journal,* June 18, 1861.

[81] New York *Herald,* June 13, 14, 17, 1861. A correspondent of this paper concluded, "It is the general impression he [Pierce] is not a coward, but utterly unfit for his position."

[82] Boston *Daily Evening Transcript*, June 14, 1861.

[83] *OR*, Ser. I, vol. 2, 79-82. In his first report Butler called the firing upon Townsend's men on the early morning of June 10 an "almost criminal blunder."

[84] Clark, *N.C. Regiments,* 102; Richmond *Dispatch*, June 13, 1861.

[85] One of the monuments is the site where Wyatt was shot.

[86] New York *Times*, August 3, 1861. When troops were removed from the Peninsula to Baltimore after Bull Run, Butler gave permission to officers of the regiment to take their contraband servants with them. These servants were paid and "acted voluntarily on engaging their own services." The officers agreed to return the contraband or "pay their value to the government on demand."

[87] New York *Tribune*, August 9, 1861.

[88] Ibid., August 3 and 5, 1861.

[89] The first expedition was terminated when Southerners saw a large balloon near Hampton, sent up by the Federals.

[90] Richmond *Whig*, August 14, 1861.

[91] *OR*, Ser. I, vol. 4, 569-73. Magruder contended Butler had already burned part of the town prior to the Confederates. Butler claimed Federals did less $100 damage during their entire stay at Hampton.

[92] On August 18, 1861, seventy-seven-year-old General Ellis Wool superseded Butler as the department commander on the Peninsula.

[93] Minor clashes occurred in Hampton Roads between Union ships and Confederate batteries on the shores to the south. May 18–19, 1861, saw Union ships engage a Southern battery on Sewell's Point. Federal ships also shelled Confederate batteries on Pig Point on June 5.

PART III

THE WESTERN INVASION CORRIDOR

CHAPTER VII

"YOUNG NAPOLEON," RICH MOUNTAIN, AND CHEAT MOUNTAIN

The South's cheering over Big Bethel muted, for a time, ominous events in western Virginia. Union forces from Ohio had moved into western Virginia, seizing control of the rail lines in the North. Others would later cross the Ohio River into the Kanawha Valley. By the end of July 1861, Federals were in control of Virginia west of the Allegheny Mountains.

The Alleghenies, in addition to separating the eastern and western theaters of the war, also cut diagonally across the Old Dominion, separating the two Virginias. Most of the state's one million whites and almost all of the half-million slaves lived east of the Alleghenies in what would become present-day Virginia. In 1861 this region was a critical part of the Confederacy. The trans-Allegheny region comprised about one-third of the state's territory and would make up most of what would become West Virginia. This unique separation of control was spawned by economic differences, and by geographical features. Much of what would become West Virginia had an economy that was more closely tied to that of the Ohio Valley and the North rather than to the neighbors to the east and south. This led to strong Unionist sentiment in western Virginia (twice that for the Confederacy) and difficulties for Confederate recruitment.

The Alleghenies not only divided Virginia but also served as a barrier against Union penetration into the Shenandoah Valley. As the war progressed, Union forays across the gaps in the mountains and movements up and down the seams created by the narrow valleys between the numerous mountain ridges in the Allegheny chain would increasingly threaten eastern Virginia's breadbasket, the Shenandoah Valley, also known as the Great Valley.

The Ohio Volunteers moved into western Virginia in late May 1861 and were joined by Unionist recruits from the western regions of the Old Dominion.[1]

Among the Yankee invaders who crossed the Ohio River were two future presidents, Rutherford Hayes and James Garfield. They had been joined by men who poured into makeshift destination centers near Columbus (Camp Chase), Cleveland (Camp Taylor), and Cincinnati (Camps Harrison and Dennison). These new citizen-soldiers moved toward their destinations amid great public clamor, similar to scenes repeated throughout the country. Relatives, friends, and sweethearts crowded depots to see their soldiers off. To do this, they pushed, elbowed and stomped about irrespective of the next person's toes. Trousers and coats were torn. A reporter wrote that hoops were crushed "like egg shells." "Young women became so enthralled with the widespread kissing many stayed on rail cars as they left depots."[2]

The festiveness continued as regiments reached their camp. They were frequently visited by friends and relatives toting baskets overflowing with food and drink. When the novelty of camp life and delectables abated, the nascent warriors improvised solutions. To counter boredom, they played baseball, fenced, boxed, held dances, and danced with one another. They also held readings, recitations, and plays. When dissatisfied with bland camp fare, they made nightly raids on nearby farms, depleting their chickens and occasionally receiving a blast from a farmer's shotgun. Finally officers had to watch the woods of the camps to prevent soldiers' stealing from farms.[3]

"YOUNG NAPOLEON"

The man in charge of the troops west of the Ohio River was George McClellan. His successes in western Virginia, as well as his physical appearance, would cause some to refer to him as Young Napoleon. He had known and expected success, no doubt in part because of the nurturing of his family, who belonged to the Philadelphia social elite. Well schooled as a child, McClellan had no difficulties with academic work, graduating second in his West Point class.

While at the academy, his amicable manner led to many friendships, especially with Southerners, many of who would later fight against him in the war. Like other cadets at West Point, he was trained primarily as an engineer and only secondarily as a military commander. He distinguished himself in the Mexican war, but in the late 1850's, while holding the rank of captain, he left the military to enter the business world. He was equally successful there, rising to the vice-presidency of the Illinois Central Railroad. A year before the war, at age thirty-three, McClellan was also victorious in romance. He married the highly desirable and sought-after Ellen Marcy, who had received at least nine marriage proposals before the age of twenty-one. Their union occurred after a lengthy and persistent courtship that enabled McClellan to win out over a host of suitors, including a West Point friend, Ambrose Powell (A. P.) Hill.

When the war started, three states (Ohio, Pennsylvania, and New York) sought McClellan to command their troops. The governor of Ohio, William Dennison, was the most persistent and convincing, so on April 23, 1861, McClellan became a major-general of the Ohio Volunteers. This was a sizable leap forward for the former captain of the regulars.[4]

Eagerly and with a sense of urgency, McClellan delved into his new job. He diligently sought weapons for his men and set up a training center and a school of instruction for volunteer officers. His task was a challenge for even his organizational skills. He found the Ohio State Arsenal contained nothing of practical value—only some boxes of rusted muskets, several unusable six-pounders, and a pile of moldy harness. McClellan's charm and capacity for hard work

245

impressed those around him. To those who saw him confidently moving about overseeing, activities on his large reddish-brown mount, Dan Webster, he looked like a general upon whom the North could rely to help bring important military successes. Befitting a man of such promise, on May 3, 1861, he was put in charge of the Department of Ohio and less than two weeks later was made major-general of the regular army. Only old Winfield Scott outranked him.[5]

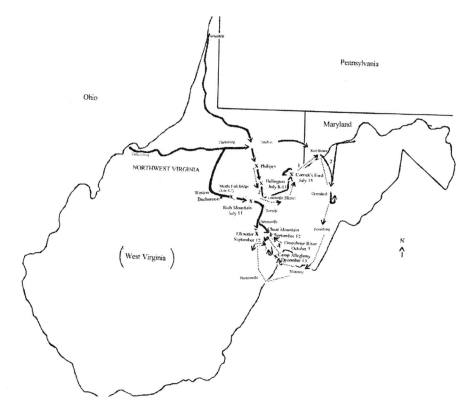

UNION PENETRATION IN NORTHWEST VIRGINIA, 1861

1. Garnett's retreat
2. Union pursuit after Rich Mountain
3. Lee's Cheat Mountain campaign, only Confederate offensive in N.W.VA, 1861

At first the young general praised the elderly general-in-chief, proclaiming to have the utmost confidence in him and patterning his operations in western Virginia after Scott's Mexican War campaign. This soon changed. Annoyed by what he considered Scott's slowness in sending weapons, and by his failure to send McClellan the officers he had requested, McClellan became critical of his superior and of the Lincoln administration.[6]

McClellan, nevertheless, sent Scott strategic plans to end the rebellion. Ohio was viewed as pivotal to his plan, which called for strengthening the Union defense along the Ohio River and launching an invasion from that area into the South. This could be done by one of two strategic moves. One was to move southward, west of the Appalachians, into Alabama; the other option was to go through western Virginia along the Kanawha River valley to Staunton in the Valley of Virginia, and from there, to Richmond. McClellan's plan, perhaps the first attempt to map an overall strategy for fighting the war, was rejected by Scott, who thought it was too hastily conceived and would create a logistical nightmare. Instead Scott favored his own plan of blocking Southern coastal ports and gaining control of the Mississippi River—the Anaconda plan.

It was not McClellan's or Scott's grand scheme to end the war, but the security of the Baltimore and Ohio Railroad, that caused the first Federal invasion into western Virginia. In 1857 the Baltimore and Ohio Railroad and a spur line had reached the Ohio River at two places, Wheeling and Parkersburg, connecting with rail lines west of the river and forming a vital rail link between the Midwest and the East. The B&O route traversed some of the most formidable and remote terrain in the East, and the construction of the railroad was considered, at that time, a phenomenal engineering achievement. The B&O would play an important logistical role in the war; its rails would carry men and supplies to both the eastern and western theaters. It would be the cause of numerous raids, skirmishes, and battles, as Southerners attempted to cut this rail link used by the Federals. The security of the railroad forced Federals, throughout the war, to keep thousands of Union troops along the line.

247

THE CONTEST FOR GRAFTON

Southerners targeted Grafton as the place to launch their disruption of rail traffic in northwestern Virginia. This small town on the western edge of the Allegheny Mountains was the juncture of the B&O line from Wheeling and the spur line known as the Northwestern Virginia Railroad from Parkersburg.[7]

Robert E. Lee, as the commander of Virginia's military forces, attempted to encourage units in northwestern Virginia to be formed at Grafton. Southern sympathizers in the region were a minority, and their recruitment was meager. When Colonel George A. Porterfield of Jefferson County, Virginia, arrived at Grafton on May 16 to assume command of the Southern forces, he found not one Southern soldier.[8] Instead he found a strong Unionist town professing to know nothing of the whereabouts of his troops and one of her leading citizens, George R. Latham, ominously threatening to hang all sympathizers of the Southern cause. Porterfield found his "army" at the small hamlet of Fetterman, two miles north of Grafton on the B&O line. Accounts differ as to what he found. Some say he found three or four poorly armed men without uniforms; others contend there were a couple of militia companies. In any event, it was an inadequate force, which caused Porterfield to ask Virginia authorities for more men and equipment.

Porterfield spent much of his first week recruiting in nearby towns. During this time he was informed that the Unionist leader of the Grafton Home Guard, Captain George Latham, was at Wheeling on military matters. Thinking this a golden opportunity to seize Grafton, Porterfield sent three companies, totaling about 130 men, to capture the town. The result was a minor incident revealing the intense emotionalism and division of loyalties in northwestern Virginia. As the Southern force, led by the Letcher Guards under Captain John Robinson, arrived in Grafton, they were met by town residents, who shouted verbal abuse and attempted to block the Southern force by holding a large U. S. flag across the street. Robinson jumped the flag, but his horse's feet struck it, forcing one of its holders to let go. The Southerners proceeded.

248

Robinson noticed another U.S. flag hanging over Latham's office and recruiting center. He ordered two men to take it down, damning the emblem and referring to it as a rag. A young man on the porch of a nearby hotel was so infuriated by what he considered an insult to his flag that he hurled a chair at Robinson, knocking the captain unceremoniously off his horse. Robinson got up to retaliate when he noticed Latham's armed men formidably located on rooftops and in windows and doorways. After remaining in town for an hour, Robinson and the Southern force left with their mission of capturing the town unaccomplished. Three Confederates from the Letcher Guards, however, remained not far away to guard Fetterman Crossing, located between Grafton and Fetterman, where the Northwestern Turnpike and B&O Railroad intersected.

Trouble started later that evening, May 22, 1861, when two men of the Grafton Home Guards attempted to travel over Fetterman Crossing. An argument ensued between Private Thornbury Bailey Brown of the Grafton Home Guard and Private Daniel W. Knight of the Letcher Guards. Brown, perhaps emboldened by a few drinks, was indignant when told he could not cross—especially by Knight, a person he had captured before the war and had turned over to the sheriff for shooting a neighbor's cow.[9] As the confrontation escalated, Brown drew his pistol and shot a lobe from Knight's ear. Knight then fired his flintlock musket. Three slugs hit Brown's chest in an irregular pattern near his heart. Brown fell to his hands and knees, telling his companion, Lieutenant Daniel Wilson (also of the Grafton Home Guard), who was preparing to flee, to wait briefly as he believed he could make it. Brown then collapsed and died. His was the first combat death in western Virginia.[10]

Residents of Grafton were greatly agitated and angered by the news of Private Brown's death. The night of May 23, at about 2:00 A.M., a number of the men marched to the bridge near where Brown was shot, planning to cross and then attack the Southerners. But as they neared the bridge, they reconsidered their plan. Realizing that their enemy had three times their numbers, the Grafton men returned to town.

Southerners had taken Brown's body back to their camp at Fetterman. A request for its return was first refused by Porterfield. Latham then started with his Grafton militia company to retrieve Brown's remains by force. When the men were halfway to Fetterman,

249

they met several of Porterfield's men bringing the body toward Grafton on a railroad handcar.

The bloodstained body was placed in the wide halls of the Grafton Hotel for viewing, then laid to rest in the Fleming graveyard, south of Grafton. There it remained until the early twentieth century, when it was re-interred in the Grafton National Cemetery.

Two days after Brown's death, Latham's militia company left Grafton for Wheeling to be officially mustered into the Federal army. The eighty-man force had to travel twelve or more miles out of their way to avoid Porterfield's men, who were stopping and searching all train traffic within a dozen miles north of Grafton. Latham's men flagged down a train at Valley Falls with a lantern borrowed from an elderly lady, they traveled the rest of the way to Wheeling by rail. With the Union militia gone, Porterfield occupied Grafton. While there he received a dispatch from Governor Letcher suggesting he go by rail to Wheeling and cut the telegraph lines and seize weapons to arm Unionists. Virginia Governor Letcher was emphatic that if a Federal force from Ohio or Pennsylvania attempted to enter northwestern Virginia by rail, they must be prevented by whatever measures Porterfield could take, including the destruction of railroads and bridges. Any move by Porterfield—with his ill-equipped and ill-trained force—to confront the superior force of Colonel Benjamin F. Kelly at Wheeling was out of the question. Porterfield could, however, destroy the railroad bridges if the need arose. Convinced that the rumor of Union troops advancing to flank him was true, Porterfield dispatched men in Grafton northward and westward to burn bridges on the Baltimore and Ohio and Northwestern Virginia Railroads.[11] News of this activity prompted McClellan, as ordered by Scott, to send Union soldiers across the Ohio River at Wheeling and Parkersburg; the soldiers were to proceed by rail to Grafton to protect Unionists and the vital rail link between the East and the Midwest.[12]

McClellan attempted to smooth the way for his invasion by issuing a proclamation on May 26, 1861, to the "Union Men of Western Virginia": "Armed traitors have in vain endeavored to deter you from expressing your loyalty at the polls...They now seek to inaugurate a reign of terror...They are destroying the property of citizens of your State, and ruining your magnificent railroad." The U.S. government, he continued, "cannot close its ears to the demand you have made for assistance. I have ordered troops to cross the Ohio

River. They come as your friends and brothers—as enemies only to armed rebels who are preying upon you. Your homes, your families, and your property are safe under our protection. All your rights shall be religiously respected, not withstanding all that has been said by the traitor to induce you to believe that our advent among you will be signalized by interference with your slaves. Understand one thing clearly. Not only will we abstain from all such interference, but we will on the contrary, with an iron hand, crush any attempt at insurrection on their part." This was certainly a sharp contrast to Butler's policy toward slaves and even went beyond Lincoln's hands-off policy. Otherwise, the proclamation was similar to numerous others issued by commanders on both sides. All called for men to "fly to arms and cast off their oppressors or subdue the traitors."[13]

McClellan's proclamation was an attempt to counter secessionist voices and the fear of Southern sympathizers. Pockets of secessionists in western Virginia had long been vociferous in denouncing those they called, as reported in papers, "Union-shrieking knaves and traitors," for caring "nothing about the rights and honor of the State." One such secessionist place was Philippi. The editor of the *Jeffersonian* believed Unionists were betraying the state and claimed that those "Union-shrieking Tories" in the state secession convention were "divided into classes—demagogues and fools." He continued, "The Satanic ingenuity of those cold-blooded politicians…will be instrumental in opening the eye of the people to their degradation and shame."

THE PHILIPPI "RACES"

Despite his proclamation, McClellan believed he was secretly sending Unions soldiers to trap Porterfield's force. But Porterfield's friends in the telegraph office at Grafton immediately alerted him of Federal movement. The Confederate colonel had no choice but to pull back to Philippi, fifteen miles south of Grafton. His motley force of fewer than 600 was still ill-equipped and ill-trained and lacked provisions and ammunition, especially percussion caps. The caps that had been sent to them were meant for shotguns and were too small for muskets.

Charles P. Poland Jr.

On May 28, Porterfield pulled his men out of Grafton. As they left, the townspeople were delighted to see them go and verbally harassed Porterfield's men with taunts such as, "Why are you leaving in such a hurry? Why not stay longer, McClellan will only put you in jail."[14]

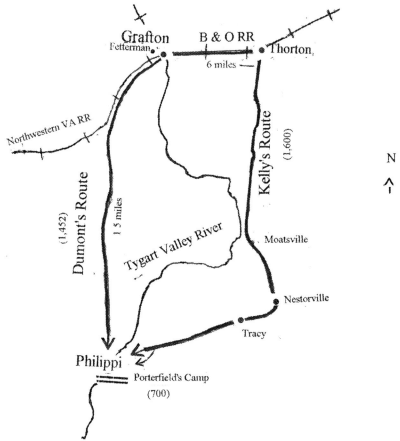

UNION ATTEMPT TO TRAP PORTERFIELD AT PHILIPPI
JUNE 2 & 3, 1861

Fear seized many people in western Virginia when they heard Federal soldiers were approaching. Rumors spread that "a terrible example was to be made of them," as a vast force of "sixty thousand Union troops had been scattered along the Baltimore and Ohio Railroad with orders to sweep southward and destroy all property of Southern sympathizers, and drive the people from their homes."

Families congregated together, expecting to meet "death from the advancing Federals, while the men, with what guns they had, stood ready to fight for their families till death."[15]

Porterfield at first hoped his stay at Philippi would be brief. As soon as he organized and properly equipped his force, he planned to return to Grafton and to keep interrupting the rail lines there. Frustration, however, continued to plague him. Despite his pleas for more recruits, recruits and additional equipment and ammunition were sent to him in trickles. Porterfield's plight was characterized by the Upshur Greys, who joined the colonel's force as they were withdrawing to Philippi. They had no arms or knowledge of military drill. But their eighteen-year-old captain, John C. Higginbottom, proudly and enthusiastically told Porterfield that they had tents. Upon arriving in Philippi—a picturesque town of about 300, overlooked by hills on three sides and traversed by the Tygart Valley River, which bordered the town north and west—Porterfield's men pitched camp in the fields north of town and stayed in select buildings.[16]

No less painful for Porterfield, a graduate of VMI and veteran of the Mexican War, was the lack of military protocol of both men and officers. The few men who had military training, three young graduates from VMI who served as drill masters, were hassled by the men, who refused to take the youthful instructors seriously.

While Porterfield struggled to ready his force for combat, his Union foes were trying to trap him. Kelly's men occupied Grafton on May 30, securing the vital rail link for the Union. Additional Federals, under General Thomas A. Morris, arrived there on June 1, 1861. The next day, 3,000 Federals set out for Philippi, under Kelly's command, in two separate movements. Colonel Ebenezer Dumont, with 1,450 men and two brass six-pounders, proceeded south of Grafton to enter Philippi from the north. Meanwhile, Colonel Kelly, with 1,600 soldiers, took a more circuitous route, a turning movement to the east and south of the town, to cut off Porterfield's escape route.

Both Union columns were to arrive at Philippi on June 3 at 4:00 A.M. Kelly's force was sent eastward on the B&O line to make it appear to Southern spies that the Federals were headed for Harpers Ferry. Instead they got off at Thornton, six miles east of Grafton, and marched southward over a rough and little-used road. The march of the two columns was not easy. The hilly terrain, darkness, and a heavy rainstorm from midnight to 4:00 A.M. presented a formidable challenge to their endurance. To help with visibility, Colonel Dumont gave a large red lantern to an Indiana lieutenant, instructing him to carry it at the head of the column for the men behind him to follow. Upset by the likelihood of being the enemy's first target, the soldier protested that he did not want to be the first killed. But the colonel was unrelenting, and the soldier led the way as the companies proceeded, with 400 yards between each of them. The lieutenant made it safely to Philippi but another Indianan did not—he fell from a log while crossing a stream and accidentally shot himself in the leg. The man bled to death.

The rest of Dumont's men covered the last five miles in a little over an hour, but exhaustion took its toll. Some of the troops fainted en route and were left behind. Others threw away their haversacks and provisions to keep up.[17] Rushing his men forward as they neared Philippi, Durmont shouted, "Close up, boy! Close up! If the enemy were to fire now, they couldn't hit a one of you."

Both Federal columns were forced forward through darkness, in a downpour, and over rough ground. Thunder and lightening made the scene eerie as well as an adding occasional and momentary illumination. At any time, the men anticipated contact with the enemy. But none occurred until they reached Philippi. Southern infantry pickets who had been stationed on the roads the Federals were traveling had left their posts during the drenching rainstorm and returned to Philippi. Porterfield was not told of their leaving the roads unguarded, but the pickets felt that staying would have been futile. They had no cartridge boxes to protect their ammunition from the rain; instead, they had to carry it in their pockets, where it became wet and useless. If the enemy arrived, the pickets would have been helpless; besides—they reasoned—"no Yankee" would "venture in the conditions of that night."

Despite the inclement weather, the cavalry pickets under Captain Jenkins remained on duty throughout the night, but they were on the Clarksburg road, a route the Federals were not taking. Also, on the same road, eight miles west of Philippi, was a group of fifty civilian men. They had sent their women and children away from their neighborhoods and waited in a thicket to ambush the Yankees. They waited until midnight, when the rain convinced them to go home. Armed with only "corn cutters, scythes, pitchforks and a few flintlocks" and led by a captain with a sword, it was their good fortune not to have gotten in the path of the oncoming Federals.[18]

Colonel Porterfield and his men had been warned that Union soldiers were on their way to Philippi. Several women intrepidly rushed to Philippi, informing the colonel of a large Federal force about to descend upon him. This prompted Porterfield to meet with his staff, who unanimously recommended they leave immediately. They pointed out, accurately, their own lack of caps and the shortage of ammunition—some of the men had only two rounds. Their inferior supplies, coupled with the smallness size of their force, made staying untenable. Even fortifying the high ground around town was futile. The lack of time and artillery and the shortage of ammunition meant they would be brushed away by the enemy in mere minutes.

Porterfield still would not agree to leave, at least not until possibly the next day, and that departure was contingent on what the enemy did. His pickets had alerted him to the enemy's approach, but leaving, to him, seemed like running away in a cowardly manner. Nevertheless, vague plans were made for withdrawing the next day. The colonel informed his staff that he would investigate the disparity in the ammunition and distribute it more equitably. As a precaution, their limited supplies were immediately packed on wagons, ready to leave at a moment's notice. Porterfield and his tiny force went to sleep thinking they were relatively safe. But the next morning, around 4:20 A.M., they were rudely awakened by artillery fire.

The Federals had planned that Dumont would not fire his two artillery pieces until Kelly's men had cut off all of Porterfield's escape avenues. Luckily for the Southerners, the artillery fired prematurely while Kelly's force was just north of Philippi, not in the designated position. His captive guide had intentionally led him to the wrong road. Colonel R. H. Milroy, under Kelly, was to have gone south of Philippi, to Big Rock, to block Porterfield's retreat, but his guide also misled him. Even the initial artillery fire resulted from a mix-up.

Dumont placed the two six-pounders on Talbott Hill. Nearby lived Mrs. Humphreys.[19] Awakened by the movement of the Federals, she immediately wanted to warn the Southern force of their imminent danger. She woke her son, Oliver, and put him on a horse to ride to Philippi. This was done in full view of the Federals, who arrested Oliver. As the soldiers pulled Oliver off his horse, his mother rushed forward, inflicting blows on the Yankees with sticks, rocks, and fists until finally rescuing her son. Once he was free, Mrs. Humphreys again tried to send him to Philippi on horseback. The Federals again pulled the boy from the horse and Mrs. Humphreys again renewed her attack. This time, not content to fight with rocks, she is alleged to have "pulled a pistol from her bosom" and fired almost point-blank at the soldiers' faces. Somehow she missed her target. The soldiers, now frightened and aggravated, raised their muskets to fire, but an officer stepped in. Mrs. Humphreys and her son were able to retreat into their home.

Mrs. Humphreys' gunshot was more momentous than she had intended. The two Union artillery pieces were already in position on Talbott Hill, overlooking Philippi, and the order had been given not to fire until a pistol-shot signal was heard. Thinking that Mrs. Humphreys' pistol shot was the signal, the Federal artillery opened fire upon the cavalry tents of the Southern camp.[20] Mrs. Humphreys had inadvertently warned Porterfield and saved his men from disaster.

The diminutive form of Colonel Dumont on horseback could now be seen leading his men forward down the hill, rapidly picking up pace, to the bridge over the Tygart Valley River. One side of the bridge, according to one account, was barricaded by stones "parked in queenware crates; the other was open but guarded, though the guards ran away." As Dumont's men ran down the hill, the two guns above them "kept up a rapid fire over" their heads.

Despite the panic and bedlam, almost all of Porterfield's force was able to escape in what had been appropriately called the "Philippi Races." There was little combat, and despite that shots had been fired and several were wounded, including Colonel Kelly, no soldier was killed. In a matter of minutes the confused Southerners fled southward from town, and the Federals moved after them through the main street, terminating their pursuit just a few miles south of town. Exhausted by all-night marching and chasing Porterfield out of Philippi, the Union soldiers returned to Philippi to the Southern campsites to rest and eat breakfast.

Contrary to the meagerness of the military conflict at Philippi, the event felt monumental to the panic-stricken civilians and vulnerable men of Porterfield's command. The first artillery fire and approaching Federals caused people to flee in all directions. Many acted like startled chickens, not knowing which way to go to get out of harm's way. In confused terror, a mother ran off, forgetting she had left her baby behind in the cradle. Another woman ran for the hills, only to be confronted by the oncoming Federals. In desperation, she hoisted a pole with a white garment into the air as a gesture of surrender. A Federal officer moved by her plight attempted to reassure her of her safety.[21]

THE ENGAGEMENT AT PHILIPPI, (W.) Va., June 3, 1861. In foreground, Federal artillery firing brass six pounders from Talbott Hill, now the site of Alderson-Broaddus College. Center, left, Kelley on horseback leading his men into the town. Center, cavalry tents; Confederate cavalry leaving for Beverly. Hill in distance, Milroy's troops firing on retreating Confederates who are returning fire from the Beverly-Fairmont Pike. Center, right, Covered Bridge crossing Tygart's Valley River. (From a sketch by H. Lovie.)

Federals attack Philippi.
(Courtesy of the Library of Congress)

Some of Porterfield's men were also plagued by confusion and fright. Many marched out of town in an orderly way, while others contributed to the pandemonium. They jammed the main street, the main avenue of escape, or in befuddlement, ran to or from their quarters. Half-dressed Southerners, some without boots, hats, coats or pantaloons, ignominiously fled in what Northern observers called a "shirttail retreat." The cavalry fled from the town as an infantryman chided the horsemen for deserting them in their time of need. Riderless horses also ran through the streets with their would-be riders frantically running after them. Colonel Dumont, arriving as the enemy were fleeing, muttered, "Great on a run, if not much for a fight."[22]

George Lurty, an attorney in one of the militia companies, was upset when he learned his unit was to provide cover during the town's evacuation. Wanting no part of this, he threw his musket over a fence and talked a cavalryman who was leaving town into letting him double up on his mount. Soon the saddle loosened and turned. Both men fell off. George then jumped into a wagon, admonishing the driver to hurry and not spare the whip, as 17,000 Union soldiers were upon them. The fleeing attorney arrived at Beverly six hours ahead of his anxious comrades.

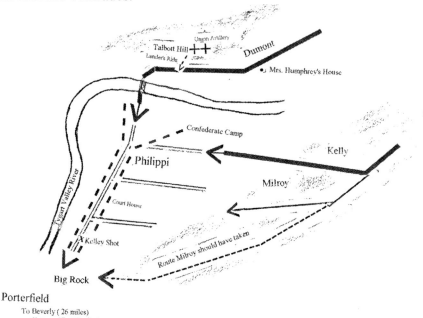

PHILIPPI "RACES"
JUNE 3, 1861

Porterfield's demeanor during all of this contrasted sharply with that of the civilians and many of his soldiers. When told the enemy was firing upon them, he calmly finished dressing, then mounted his horse and rode off looking for his men, even though his frightened mount didn't want to move. After asking where his troops were, he saw blue-clad soldiers at the northern part of town, just south of a two-lane covered bridge that stretched 312 feet over the Tygart Valley River. He rode toward them, mistakenly thinking they were his men. After coming nearer the blue-uniformed soldiers, he realized his mistake and avoided detection by turning and moving slowly southward. Soon he found his own men leaving town. The colonel's vigorous and continuous attempt to halt them was fruitless. He had no alternative but to join them in fleeing.

Shortly after Kelly led his Union soldiers into the main street, he was shot in the chest. He continued to ride forward for fifty yards before falling from his saddle. Those who saw the blood flowing from his chest were certain the wound was fatal, but Kelly survived to spend most of the war defending the Baltimore and Ohio Railroad. Soon after Kelly was wounded, Federal soldiers swarmed around a burly man who was believed to have fired the pistol shot that struck their colonel. They were going to kill the man on the spot when Colonel Frederick W. Lander rushed forward and rescued the man by insisting he was a prisoner of war. Lander had just arrived after an intrepid, risky ride from Talbott Hill down a steep grade to Philippi— some would later call it the "most hazardous ride ever seen by man."[23]

Another happy benefactor of the Federal occupation was Private Mayer in the Philippi jail. Earlier Mayer was arrested by Porterfield's men for spying, was court-martialed, and was sentenced to hang at sunrise on June 3, but with the advent of the Federals, Porterfield's men fled, leaving behind the condemned private. Less fortunate was John, an elderly African-American resident of the area. According to the story, John was spotted on the street by Private John Lott, a black Indiana soldier. Lott asked the elderly man if he was a Rebel. When John said yes, Lott gave him fifteen minutes to recant. When he did not, the private, of Company E of the Sixth Indiana, shot and killed him. Union authorities then arrested Lott for the crime.[24]

Another local resident, attorney B. F. Martin, found it prudent to retract his allegiance to the Southern cause. After the Federals chased Porterfield out of Philippi, they took down the Virginia flag at the courthouse and put up the U.S. flag. They raided the newspaper office of the *Jeffersonian,* broke the printing press into pieces, tossed the type down a well, and blew open the bank's safe, but found it empty. A few Union soldiers searched for hidden treasure in a pile of hay, poking their bayonets into the haystack. As they were doing this, the attorney crawled out from underneath the hay and proclaimed that he had just reconsidered the cause of secession and felt it was time for him to take the oath of allegiance to the United States.

Union soldiers found another man, James E. Hanger, hiding in the hayloft of a barn. Upon hearing the enemy's first artillery fire, Hanger had gone to the barn to fetch his horse. As he was preparing to get his mount out of the barn, a solid shot from one of the pair of six-pounders on Talbott Hill came crashing into the barn, horribly shattering his left leg. Unable to escape, he somehow struggled up to the hayloft. There the eighteen-year-old waited for four hours before the Yankees found him. They took Hanger to a nearby church where his leg was amputated just below the hip. He was the first amputee of the war.[25]

The early-morning military activity on June 3, 1861, would launch claims of many Civil War firsts; the most ambitious claim was that the events at Philippi made up the first land battle of the Civil War. Other claims included those of the first cannon shot and the first amputation of the war.[26] Newspaper coverage of this first clash in a small campaign early in the war was extensive and imaginative. The clash was heralded in Northern papers as the first Union victory. Bold and descriptive headlines told of "The Philippi Rout" and the "Disgraceful Conduct of the Rebels"—who were "A Band of Thieves and Robbers" and whose defeat led to the "Rejoicing of the People for their Deliverance." These accounts were refuted by Southern papers such as the Richmond *Examiner,* which called such accounts "Black Republican stories." The *Examiner* claimed that reliable sources revealed that after being kicked out of Philippi, Porterfield repulsed an attack, killing seventy of the "Abolitionist and Submission forces," compared to eight Southern deaths.[27]

The Southerners had been fortunate to escape. Their withdrawal had been afforded—and beleaguerment prevented—by the premature firing of the Federal artillery. The small number of casualties and lack of military fatalities were not only caused by Porterfield's successful escape, but by the inadequate equipment and inexperience of men on both sides. Even many of Kelly's men had no weapons and marched on Philippi armed with only sticks and clubs. Two Federals and two Southerners were wounded, and five of Porterfield's men were captured, including Hanger. Both wounded Southerners became amputees. The second was Fauntleroy P. Daingerfield, a former VMI cadet. He was wounded in the knee and was carried by Porterfield's fleeing men to Beverly, where, in a private home, Dr. Hoff amputated the limb with a borrowed butcher knife and a wood saw.

Porterfield was not a happy colonel as he retreated to Huttonsville. Humiliation gnawed at him, and for several reasons: he had been totally surprised by the enemy at Philippi after being informed that they were approaching; his force had left town without his orders to do so; and he had lost some of his wagons, in which, the night before, he had stored his meager supplies in the event of an evacuation caused by an attack. He vented his frustration at Captain Jenkins upon his arrival at Huttonsville.

Jenkins and his company had been west of Philippi at Elk City when the Federals attacked Philippi. Finding he could not return to Philippi, Jenkins took county roads to join the retreating Porterfield. A dozen or so of Jenkins' men who had strong Union sentiment deserted. When Porterfield was told, he sent for Jenkins and berated him for having such men in his company. An argument ensued. Porterfield asked for Jenkins' commission, then wrote "discharge" across it, and handed it back to the stunned captain. Porterfield also discharged Jenkins' whole company. Angered by this intemperate act, Jenkins sold his horse and returned to Philippi, where he was arrested as a spy, was tried, and was then paroled. He sat out the remainder of the war at his home, having served only fifteen days.[28]

Porterfield also expressed his frustration in his report to Lee. The colonel bitterly complained of the ignorance of "the most ordinary duties" of the officers and men sent to him. "If it had been intended to sacrifice me," he wrote, "[I could] not have expected less support than I have had." Furthermore, he told Lee that if "[at] least 5,000 well-trained troops are not immediately sent, northwestern Virginia west of the Alleghenies will be lost as that region is in a state of revolution, the law-abiding citizens being driven off by traitors assisted by northern troops. The private property of secessionists, but otherwise inoffensive citizens, their cattle, young unbroken horses and colts, and the clothing of women and children, have been seized and taken off from citizens of Philippi."

Lee expressed his regret for the colonel's problems and difficulties, but he informed Porterfield that General R. S. Garnett was replacing him as commander of Confederate forces in northwestern Virginia. Lee might have had sympathy for Porterfield's plight, but the colonel had to go. The danger of opening the back door to the Shenandoah Valley by the Federals, Porterfield's inability to complete paperwork for supplies, and what Confederate authors considered the disgraceful surprise at Philippi made Virginia authorities agree with Major M. G. Harman's report of June 6, 1861. In it he wrote, "From all the information that I have received, I am pained to have to express my conviction that Colonel Porterfield is extremely unequal to the position which he occupies." Porterfield soon requested a Court of Inquiry to clear him of any wrongdoing in the "Philippi Races." A court was convened at Beverly. It concluded that although Porterfield had displayed "coolness, courage, and energy…at the moment of attack," the court could not "exonerate him from the blame in not taking proper precautionary measures beforehand."[29]

Southern authorities hoped that the promising Garnett, a Virginian with fine military credentials, who was schooled at West Point and was also a veteran of the Mexican War, could—with additional troops—do what Porterfield could not. His appointment was intended to stay the Federal advance and again secure control of the Baltimore and Ohio through Virginia. While Garnett was sent to accomplish these goals, former Virginia Governor Wise, now a brigadier general, was sent to rally the people to arms in the rich Kanawha Valley to thwart any enemy movement there. Obtaining arms was still a problem, and recruits to Wise and Garnett were encouraged to bring their own firearms. Garnett's needs were more immediate. He faced growing numbers of the enemy.

On June 14, 1861, Virginia Governor Letcher, in an attempt to aid Garnett's effort, issued a proclamation to the people of northwestern Virginia. He hoped to counter Union sentiment and swell Southern ranks. His proclamation emphasized the long-standing ties between western and eastern Virginia, quoted from the Declaration of Independence, and concluded that the majority of the sovereign people of Virginia had exercised their right to form a new government, and it was the duty of all to defend it by bringing their good weapons to Huttonsville and joining, as "brothers," the troops already there. Letcher continued, "[the] heart that will not beat in union with Virginia's is a traitor's heart." Additional forces were sent to Garnett, but Letcher's appeal failed to rally significant a number of men or increase Confederate support in the northwestern part of the state. As Garnett found, "These people are thoroughly imbued with an ignorant and bigoted Union sentiment." Both Lee and Letcher had underestimated Union sentiment and the difficulty of defending that region.[30]

Garnett arrived at Huttonsville on June 14, 1861. He immediately organized the men he found there into two regiments and moved most of his command northward to block the approaching Federals. Part of his force was positioned at the western base of Rich

Mountain, on the Parkersburg Turnpike, seven miles west of Beverly. Garnett and the rest of the men went more than twenty miles farther north, where they took possession of Laurel Hill on June 16. The two entrenched Confederate camps were located on two vital turnpikes that led to Staunton and were on the most westerly range of the Alleghenies of the Appalachian system. Garnett strategically positioned his 4,000 men at an area that has been called the "gates to northwest Virginia." He placed a fifth of his men under Lieutenant-Colonel John Pegram at Rich Mountain, placed nearly 400 at Beverly, which became his supply base, and placed the remainder of his men, the bulk of his command, at Camp Laurel Hill, two miles south of Belington.

The topographical features of the mountains in the region of the Confederate camps formed the shape of a gigantic yawning worm. Rich Mountain formed the belly, in the middle of which was Lieutenant-Colonel John Pegram at Camp Garnett. To the north, at the opened mouth, was Garnett at Laurel Hill. To the east of Laurel Mountain, at the top of the head of the configuration, was Valley Mountain. The back was formed by Cheat Mountain. It curved southward, forming the eastern boundary of the approximately two-mile-wide, long valley. The valley was traversed north–south by a turnpike and the Tygart Valley River. On the turnpike that cut southward through the middle of the valley were three towns: in the north, Leadsville (modern-day Elkins), in the center, Beverly, and to the south, Huttonsville. Beverly was of special importance to Garnett because it was where the turnpike from Parkersburg merged with the one from Laurel Hill to Huttonsville. This made Beverly the logical place for storing Confederate supplies from Staunton. From the Beverly depot they could be moved westward to Pegram and northward to Garnett.[31]

Garnett, as urged by Lee, hoped to do more than guard the two passes. He coveted the B&O Railroad, but lacked the manpower to take it. He proposed to Richmond that, in his opinion, "General Wise's command could be of more service...by operating in the direction of Parkersburg and the Northwestern Railroad than in the Kanawha Valley." It would produce a diversion that would allow Garnett to move north from Laurel Hill to the B&O Railroad. Furthermore, it was Garnett's belief that as long "as the enemy believed there is a threat to their possession of the railroad and country in front of me they will not attempt any roads in the Kanawha Valley."

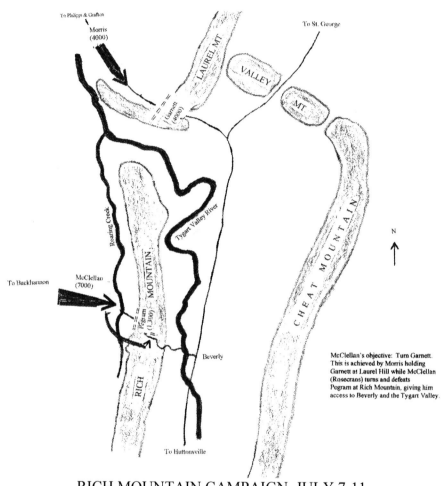

RICH MOUNTAIN CAMPAIGN, JULY 7-11
McClellan Attacks Garnett's Divided Forces at Key Gaps in the Mountains
(The Outline of These Mountains Forms an Abstract Configuration of a
"Yawning Worm")

It was too late, even in the unlikely event that Richmond would agree to move Wise. The very day—July 11, 1861—that Garnett was again proposing his plan to Richmond, Cox was launching an invasion into the Kanawha Valley, and McClellan was attacking Garnett's forces at Rich Mountain, while Morris confronted him at Laurel Hill.

McClellan had launched a two-pronged maneuver in which he hoped to trap Garnett, who, in the Union general's view, had foolishly divided his army, leaving it twenty-three miles apart. Morris' 4,000-man force from the north (at Philippi) was to amuse Garnett's 4,000 men at Laurel Hill while McClellan led a 7,000-man force from the west that would turn and defeat Pegram's 1,300 men at Rich Mountain. McClellan's enthusiasm for the execution of his plan made him annoyed with subordinates who were less eager. He brutally rebuked Thomas Morris for expressing apprehensions about facing Garnett's force, which was at least as large as his own. Morris was told, "If you cannot undertake the defense of Philippi with the force now under your control, I must find someone else who will...Do not ask for further reenforcements. If you do, I shall take it as a request to be relieved from your command and to return to Indiana."

STANDOFF AT LAUREL HILL

Admonished by his boss, Morris moved his command out of Philippi in the middle of the night of July 6 and rushed toward Garnett at Laurel Hill. He did so in such a hurry that much of the baggage and needed provisions were left behind. His adversary had taken up a position behind two hills south of the town of Belington, blocking the turnpike, which ran through the middle of his entrenchments and earthworks of rocks, cut trees, and abatis. Garnett's position was not a strong one and could be more easily turned than the Confederates' position at Rich Mountain. As Morris neared Belington on July 7, he scattered Confederate pickets with several artillery blasts, seized several hills around town, and raised a large U.S. flag from a house on Elliott's Hill. The structure was the home of Private William Elliott in Garnett's line; he was chagrined to see the enemy emblem atop his house.

For nearly a week, amid rain and sun, the two combatants were at a standoff in what some have called the Battle of Belington. Their clashes were limited and casualties were light—a dozen or so—

despite sniper fire from trees, occasional infantry and cavalry charges, and exchanges of artillery fire. Any territorial exchange of the wooded hills south of Belington was meager and temporary, as they were almost immediately re-occupied by the original possessor. On one occasion, it was unclear who was friend and foe: one evening at twilight, four companies of the newly arrived Twenty-third Virginia, atop a hill, fired on their approaching reinforcements.

Garnett had a close call during an artillery exchange. A shell that, luckily for Garnett, had not exploded, struck near where he was dining, causing him to drop his silver cup. He calmly picked up the cup, had it washed and refilled with coffee, brushed the dirt from the table, resumed the meal, and as a memento of the occasion, he kept the unexploded shell after it had been defused.

While on picket duty, an infantryman from the First Georgia found enemy artillery fire more unsettling than Garnett had. As the private walked his beat, shots from a Federal cannon that first struck fifty to 100 yards in front of him were dropping progressively closer. The concerned soldier asked an officer inspecting the area if he had been placed there as a target for the enemy. The lieutenant-colonel instructed the Georgian to take his beat in a ditch, and when he saw smoke, to duck. For two hours, until relieved, the anxious private marched back and forth, keeping a sharp vigil for smoke from the enemy's artillery piece. He soon learned that from the time he saw smoke it would take eight seconds to hear the report and four more before the shot arrived from about a mile away. In all he had twelve seconds to duck.

When not skirmishing, the men did drills. Curious civilians visited the Confederates on Sunday, wandering about Camp Laurel Hill, taking in the martial sites. Not all of the warriors were accepting of military life. Among the recent arrivals were the First Georgia Infantry, many of whom came from wealthy families, were fashionably dressed, and were attended by two body servants apiece, along with a valet and a cook. Despite this assistance, some of the Georgians became quite homesick. One took a sharp hatchet and cut off three toes and mangled his foot so he would be sent back home.

Others were better adjusted, including an Indiana soldier who thought it would be fun to harass the enemy by reading them one of Lincoln's messages. Standing on a stump, he hollered, "I say secesh, don't you want to hear old Abe's message?" He began reading from a newspaper, but stopped abruptly when the "secesh" started shooting.

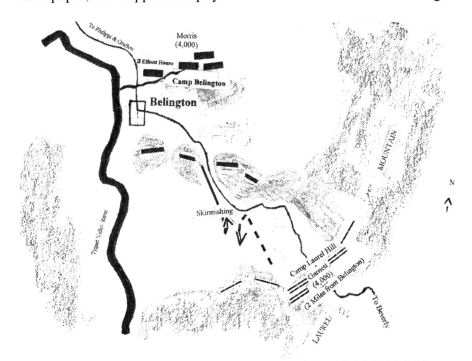

"BATTLE OF BELINGTON:" SKIRMISHING BETWEEN
MORRIS AND GARNETT, JULY 7-11, 1861

The stalemate at Laurel Hill came to an end on July 11, 1861. That morning Garnett was informed that the enemy was marching to turn Pegram at Rich Mountain. That afternoon Garnett and his men could hear the artillery and musket fire from the battle on that mountain. Later news was received that Federals had seized the top of Rich Mountain cutting, off Pegram's route of retreat to Beverly and Staunton, and imperiling Garnett's retreat route to those same sites. To buy time, Garnett ordered the Forty-fourth Virginia to hold the road, if possible, between Rich Mountain and Beverly by probing and intensely engaging the enemy to give the appearance of an imminent attack; meanwhile, Garnett would begin his withdrawal. As darkness descended, he ordered the withdrawal to commence. To continue the deception, Garnett left tents standing, fires burning, and a rear guard appearing to guard the camp as usual as his main force moved southward, forming a line two miles long. Nevertheless, Federals soon ascended upon the camp site. One Yank, seeing an abandoned ten-gallon brass kettle, carried it on his shoulder to Corrick's Ford and later to his home, where it was his prize trophy of the war, supposedly "more dear to him than his pension."

Garnett's hasty withdrawal forced him to leave behind a flock of about 100 sheep and fewer than a dozen sick and wounded. The latter were left in a local home under the care of the lady of the house. The memoirs of Isaac Hermann, a Georgia soldier, record, "An appeal for mercy for those hapless souls was made in a note left and addressed to any Federal officer who may appear."[32]

RICH MOUNTAIN

Earlier, while sending Morris to distract Garnett from the north, McClellan gathered another force, sending it south by way of Clarksburg to Weston and then eastward by the way of Buckhannon to Rich Mountain. There they set up camp near Roaring Creek, which separated them from the enemy, who were two miles away at Camp Garnett. McClellan arrived at the Federal camp on July 9, the same day the Confederate commander, Lieutenant-Colonel John Pegram, apparently unaware of the size of his opponent (seven times that of his own), was unsuccessfully seeking General Garnett's permission to attack. McClellan was more cautious than Pegram and was naturally nervous about fighting his first battle as the commander. Reconnaissance on July 10 revealed that Pegram was strongly fortified at the base of the mountain. An eyewitness recorded Pegram's position: "his right covered by an almost impenetrable laurel thicket; his left resting high up on the spur of the mountain, and his front defended by a log break-work, in front of which was abatis of fallen timber." A Union frontal assault would be too costly. That night, the Federals found a solution when a young man appeared in their camp; he was attempting to pass through Union lines to return to his home at the mountain gap on the road behind Pegram's camp.

The youth was David Hart, a Unionist returning from visiting relatives. After being closely examined by Rosecrans, Hart was taken to McClellan—along with a plan for turning the enemy. Hart agreed to guide a Federal force to his father's house over a circuitous route through the forest, around the enemy's left, to a point on the mountaintop one and a half miles from the gap. From there they could follow a rough road to his father's house. The rough terrain would forbid them from taking artillery. McClellan consented, perhaps reluctantly, to allow Hart to lead Rosecrans with 1,917 men to the mountain gap. From there, less than three miles from the enemy camp, Rosecrans could descend the western slope of the mountain on the turnpike and approach Camp Garnett from the rear. The sound of Rosecrans' attack would signal McClellan, with the bulk of the Union force, to attack the enemy from the front. Rosecrans planned to attack the rear of Pegram's works by 10:00 the next morning, July 11. A company of cavalry was taken to keep McClellan apprised of Rosecrans' progress in case something happened unexpectedly. A message, carried by a cavalryman, was to be sent every hour.[33]

Things did not go smoothly for the four infantry regiments (the Eighth, Tenth, Thirteenth, and Nineteenth Ohio) and Burdsal's seventy-five cavalrymen. They were to silently and secretly gather at 3:00 A.M., but one regiment sounded assembly and lit fires. It was daylight before the Federal force moved out; this delay, along with their fear that they might have alerted the enemy, cause them to decide it was best to climb the slope much further to the right than had planned. This lengthened the route. Intermittent rain pelted them from 6:00 to 11:00 A.M. as they made their way through what Rosecrans described as "a pathless forest, over rocks and ravines," with the added difficulty of "using no ax to clear their way to avoid discovery by the enemy." Eight hours after their start they were halted—wet, hungry and weary—for a rest as Rosecrans and Colonel Frederick W. Lander reconnoitered the terrain. The Federal force still had not reached the mountaintop. Rosecrans now sent his first and only message to McClellan, telling of his difficulties and stating that because of the roughness of the terrain and the exhaustion of the horses, no additional dispatches would be sent until there was "something of importance to communicate." Frustration led to threats against young Hart, whom Rosecrans said was so scared he was about to leave. Hart seemed to have run off, but might have returned to help guide the soldiers to his father's house by midafternoon.[34]

Rosecrans' march to the mountain gap lasted about ten to twelve hours, and in the meantime, the fear that Confederates might learn of his turning movement had become a reality. The night before Rosecrans' march, sights and sounds—lights flashing, axes chopping, and bugles sounding—alerted the Confederates to possible enemy movement. Pegram was afraid he would be attacked from the rear, so he sent two companies to the gap at Hart's house. The next morning around 9:00, a Federal courier—who had mistakenly ridden into Pegram's camp, carrying a dispatch from McClellan to Rosecrans—was wounded and captured, and it was revealed to Pegram that a Union turning movement was indeed in progress.

Pegram wrongly assumed this was taking place over a country road to his right and sent one of his force's artillery pieces and Captain Julius A. De Lagnel, Garnett's chief of artillery, to command a 310-man force at the Rich Mountain pass at Hart's residence. The force was comprised of two squads of cavalry from the Fourteenth Virginia and six companies of infantry from the Twentieth and Twenty-fifth Virginia. One company from the Twentieth, was known as the College Boys, consisting of students from Hampden-Sidney College and commanded by one of their professors, John M. P. Atkinson. To further aid in the protection of his rear, Pegram ordered Colonel Scott at Beverly to position his regiment (the Forty-fourth Virginia) at the junction of Merritt Road and the Beverly-Buckhannon Turnpike to protect his rear from the enemy's turning movement.[35]

At 2:30 P.M. on July 11, Rosecrans' force arrived on the hill to the south overlooking the mountain pass. Half a mile from the Hart farm, Confederate pickets unexpectedly fired upon his skirmishers. The pickets pulled back to their main force at the pass, shouting repeatedly, "Yanks from the south!" The Confederates were expecting an enemy attack from the north. They turned their only artillery piece to the south and opened fire on the oncoming enemy.[36] Union skirmishers fired from behind rocks and trees several hundred yards away at the Confederates, who concentrated their artillery fire of spherical shot at the rate of four per minute upon the main Union force. After a brief time the Federals withdrew. Twenty minutes later they advanced and renewed the fighting, firing from the protection of the woods. The Confederate gun was pulled a short distance northward across the road to a slope and again commenced firing.

Unable to see the enemy, the Confederates fired in the direction of rising smoke that emanated from the edge of the woods.

After an hour, the Federals suddenly withdrew, so the cheering Confederates assumed they had won. De Lagnel notified Pegram that they had twice repulsed the enemy and won the fight. This news set off an uproar of cheering at Camp Garnett that was heard by McClellan in his camp just to the west across Roaring Creek. He too assumed Rosecrans had been defeated. Earlier McClellan had moved his force closer to the enemy fort in anticipation of attacking. Now he seemed perplexed. A frontal assault without Rosecrans attacking from the rear would be costly. Finally he moved his force back to camp and armed even the teamsters in case the enemy attacked. In the meantime, a road was being cut to a rise on the enemy left where the next morning the Union artillery was to enfilade Pegram and drive him from his camp.

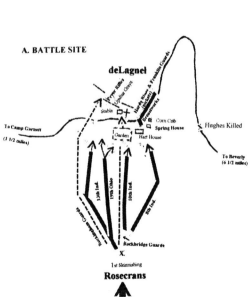

McClellan plans to turn Pegram at Camp Garnett by sending Rosecrans with 2,000 men of the 7,000 Federals to the top of Rich Mt. From there Rosecrans would descend down the mountain and attack Camp Garnett from the rear. McClellan would then attack from the front. Suspicious McClellan would attempt to turn him, Pegram sent one-third of his 900-man force under Capt. DeLagnel to the top of the mountain (Hart Farm) on the road to Beverly. After a long and difficult climb, Rosecrans makes three attacks on the hastily formed Confederation position. The third assault overwhelms and drives the Southerners from the mountain gap. Pegram unsuccessfully attempts to reinforce the gap. Defeated Southerners flee from the battlefield and Camp Garnett. A few escape, but most with Pegram surrendered at Beverly on July 13, 1861. The defeat at Rich Mt. forces Garnett to retreat from Laurel Hill, resulting in his death and a disastrous round-about retreat to Monterey.

BATTLE OF RICH MOUNTAIN

Rosecrans was far from defeated. He suffered little in the first two advances—the woods had shielded his men as the shot from the Confederates' brass six-pounder flew over their heads. Rosecrans was determined to take the enemy's six-pounder and overwhelm their

271

work with an all-out attack. Some regiments misunderstood his orders and were positioned incorrectly, which caused a delay of nearly three-quarters of an hour. Rosecrans, personally leading one of his regiments, moved his whole force forward. Some men stamped through Hart's garden near the house as the Union force converged on the Confederates. Southerners who had earlier fired with relative impunity from the windows and the chinks between logs of the Hart house were driven from the dwelling as Federals swarmed to the left, center, and especially to the right flank of the Southerners, placing De Lagnel in danger of being cut off from the road to Camp Garnett. Frightened artillery horses pulling the ammunition caisson became unmanageable and stampeded down the road, carrying away their drivers and most of the ammunition. They soon collided with a brass six-pounder being pulled from Camp Garnett, which De Lagnel had requested. Drivers were hurled from their seats, a dozen horses were injured or killed, and their mangled bodies were mixed with smashed equipment as the artillery piece careened down an embankment. (Federals would later capture it.)

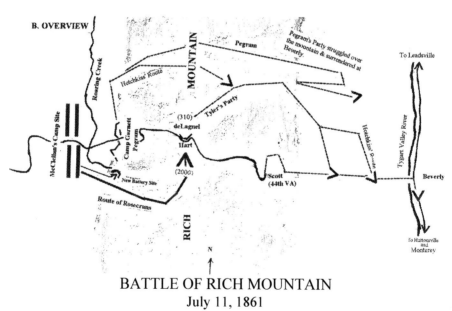

BATTLE OF RICH MOUNTAIN
July 11, 1861

Back at the battle site, the Virginians' situation was desperate. Overwhelmed by vastly greater numbers, the Southerners pulled the six-pounder behind Hart's barn just north of the road, but attempts to fire the piece were futile. There were only two artillerymen left. Captain De Lagnel—after having his horse shot from under him and before being seriously wounded—briefly helped fire the six-pounder. After De Lagnel was injured, he was pulled out of the sight of the enemy by a young artilleryman.[37] The wounded captain ordered his men to escape to Beverly if they could. Federals now swarmed over the hastily constructed log works that paralleled the road. One Federal repeatedly bayoneted a wounded Confederate. This infuriated De Lagnel, who attempted to retaliate and struggled to stand, but he lost consciousness and fell down a bank, where he lay, unconscious and undetected, for a couple of hours. The remainders of his command on the left made their way to Beverly. Those on the right returned to Camp Garnett after leaving the main road to escape the enemy's fire. They left behind thirty-three dead and thirty-nine wounded. Fourteen dead Federals and sixty wounded were also scattered over the saddle-shaped terrain of the Hart farm, where the mountain sloped downward from the back of the house to the turnpike and then rose to wooded heights.[38]

An artist depiction of
Rosecrans' men attacking Confederates at Rich Mountain
(Courtesy of the Library of Congress)

Pegram attempted to reverse his sagging fortunes. Arriving at 6:00 P.M. as the three-hour battle was ending, he saw his men fleeing the works at Hart's. He tried unsuccessfully to rally them, despite having to exert great personal effort. Finding the situation hopeless,

Pegram hurried back to camp and ordered his regiment's remaining companies toward the battle site, leaving the right side of the Camp Garnett works totally unmanned. Approximately midway up the mountain, he met the men who had fled from battle down the western slope of the mountain—under the command of Major Nat Tyler—waiting in the woods to ambush the enemy. Pegram asked them if they were willing to go back and fight. While the men were responding with a cheer, a captain interrupted, saying, "Colonel Pegram these men are completely demoralized, and will need you to lead them." Taking his place at the head of the column, Pegram led the men single-file in the rain through what he called "laurel thickets and through almost impassable brushwood" to the top of the mountain, a quarter-mile away from Rosecrans' right flank. There Pegram was about to position his men to attack when Major Tyler informed him that during the march up the mountain "one of the men in his frightened state had turned around and shot the first sergeant of one of the rear companies, which had caused nearly the whole company to run to the rear." Soon after a captain told Pegram, "the men were so intensely demoralized that he considered it madness to attempt to lead them into attack." Pegram wrote in his official report, "A mere glance at the frightened countenances around" him convinced Pegram that this distressing news was true. It was confirmed by the opinion "of the company commanders around him." They all agreed with Pegram, who stated, "there was nothing left to do but to send the command under Major Tyler" to join Garnett at Laurel Hill or to Colonel William C. Scott's regiment, which was believed to be near Beverly.

It was 6:30 P.M. when Pegram sent Tyler's men northeastward to escape off the mountain. Pegram started back to camp. He frequently lost his way and was thrown from his horse and was injured, so he did not arrive until 11:15.[39] The situation was becoming desperate. A council of war was breaking up when Pegram arrived. Heck, the second in command, had called the meeting and had restated Pegram's orders to hold the camp at all costs. Pegram immediately reconvened the officers, and they concurred it was time to leave. Heck would lead all the able-bodied men over the mountain to join Garnett, while Pegram, battered by his ordeals, would stay behind with the sick.

Totally unaware of the demoralized state of his opponent, Rosecrans feared for his own safety at the mountain gap. He called his men back after they had pursued the fleeing Southerners for only several hundred yards. Darkness was approaching, and it was too late to attack a well-fortified enemy camp almost three miles away that could only be reached by a road described by Pegram as "skirted with almost an impenetrable thicket of underbrush." Nor did he feel he could head eastward to Beverly, as he was already separated from the main Union force by an enemy whom, he believed, had 5,000 to 8,000 men. McClellan had made no attack, so no help could be assured from him. Rosecrans tried to find a cavalryman to carry a message of his plight to McClellan, but this proved to be futile. No one who would undertake such a venture could be found. Feeling vulnerable and isolated between an entrenched enemy camp to his west and another unknown force to the east, Rosecrans decided to spend the night on top of the mountain. It was a very dark, cold, and rainy summer night. The wounded of both sides were huddled together in the Hart house and on its porch, and they filled all the outbuildings to protect themselves from the inclement weather. The next morning a detail buried thirty-two Confederate dead in two trenches in or near Hart's garden.[40]

That night was an anxious one for Rosecrans, who wrote that his men were "turned out six times…on account of the picket firing on the front, expecting an attack of the enemy." At 3:00 A.M. welcome news arrived. A prisoner who was brought before Rosecrans revealed that the enemy was attempting to leave. This news led Rosecrans to move on to Camp Garnett at daylight, where he found a white flag flying.

McClellan's anxieties would also lessen. Impending combat had made him edgy and cautious, and he had been plagued with doubt about whether battle plans and order would be properly implemented. His doubts were fueled, in part, by inexperienced officers' rash acts before and during the battle; in their naive zeal for success, they made impetuous decisions. While camped at Buckhannon, Newton Schleigh, a militia general, had sent two companies from the Third Ohio to locate the enemy—without McClellan's knowledge. A skirmish had ensued at Middle Fork Bridge on July 6 and July 7, 1861, with several casualties. McClellan had been furious and had censured Schleigh for the unauthorized expedition.

275

The colonel of the Third Ohio, I. H. Morrow, who professed to have McClellan's confidence, had showed his lack of sound judgment when he called out the regiment at midnight before the battle of Rich Mountain to tell the men what they faced:

> Soldiers of the Third: The assault, on the enemy's works will be made in early morning. The Third will lead the column. The secessionists have ten thousand men and forty rifled cannon. They have more men and more cannon than we have. They will cut us to pieces. Marching to attack such an enemy, so entrenched and so armed, is marching to a butcher-shop, rather than battle. There is bloody work ahead. Many of you, boys, will go out who will never come back again.

The frightened men of the Third Ohio had spent a fearful, sleepless night. When one soldier modestly suggested to Morrow that he speak to the men in a way that inspired confidence, rather than fear, Morrow declared that they should be told the truth.

The morning of July 11 had seen a noncommissioned officer's stubbornness and eagerness preclude rational behavior and lead to foolish acts that ultimately cost him his life. McClellan was becoming more apprehensive as the morning passed. It had been more than three hours, the time he and Rosecrans had agreed it would take to reach the rear of the enemy's camp, and McClellan had heard no sounds of an attack; nor had he received any of the agreed-upon hourly progress reports from Rosecrans. Fearful that the plan had gone amiss, McClellan sent a message that is purported to have countermanded his former orders and instructed Rosecrans to wait for new ones. Regardless of the content of the message, at 9:00 A.M. the courier, Sergeant David A. Wolcott of the First Ohio Cavalry, galloped toward the enemy's earthworks. Encountering Federal pickets, Wolcott was informed he was going in the wrong direction to overtake Rosecrans and was warned that it was dangerous to proceed on the main road, as he was only a half-mile from the enemy's camp. Ignoring the caveat, Wolcott rode boldly forward. He was soon shot through both legs and captured; two months later he would die from his wounds.

McClellan's message was now in enemy hands, revealing a movement but not revealing the direction the Federals were approaching from. The intercepted message did reinforce Pegram's mistaken belief that Rosecrans was attempting to turn his right via a country road; Pegram believed no one would attempt to move over the wilderness heights to his left.[41]

RETREAT, DEATH OF GARNETT, AND DISASTER

The approximately 170 men, mostly sick and wounded, whom Pegram left behind surrendered to Rosecrans and turned over to him the two remaining artillery pieces, their wagons, the equipment, and the quartermaster's store. McClellan's force was positioned a short distance in front of Fort Garnett and was preparing to send artillery to a hill by way of the road they had cut during the night; this would enable them to enfilade the Confederate camp. Amidst their preparations, one of Rosecrans' cavalryman reported that the enemy camp had been abandoned. When McClellan sent someone to verify this report, his scout found the camp occupied by Rosecrans. McClellan soon moved out, leaving behind several companies of the Thirteenth Indiana to destroy the "Rebel" fortification and bury the dead.

By midday McClellan had moved across Rich Mountain via the gap at Hart's farm and had occupied Beverly. The most eventful part of the march occurred during a half-hour rest at the site of the previous day's battle. The soldiers' eyes were drawn, as if magnetically, to the sobering sight of the dead. Some were half-naked and scattered over the field; others had been placed in a long trench, which was still open. The bodies included Clay Jackson's, one of the first Confederate fatalities. Prior to the battle he had boasted that he would "kill a damn Yankee and cut out his heart and roast it."

Colonel Heck had left Camp Garnett at 1:00 A.M. on June 12 with most of the remaining Confederates—except for the disabled—who were west of the mountain, in order to join Garnett. Jedediah Hotchkiss, who had recently been appointed Confederate topographical engineer and was known as Professor Hotchkiss, led the way, followed by Captain R. D. Lilley's company of the Twenty-fifth Virginia. Meanwhile, Pegram, who was nicknamed Little Corporal by his men, changed his mind about staying behind. He sent word for the column to halt so he could lead it. The message never reached Hotchkiss and Lilley's company, and they proceeded forward, separating themselves from the rest of the column. Somewhere behind them was the main body, with the exhausted Pegram, who, according to one of the Hampton-Sydney boys, had a high fever and had to be conveyed over the mountain in a blanket carried by four men.

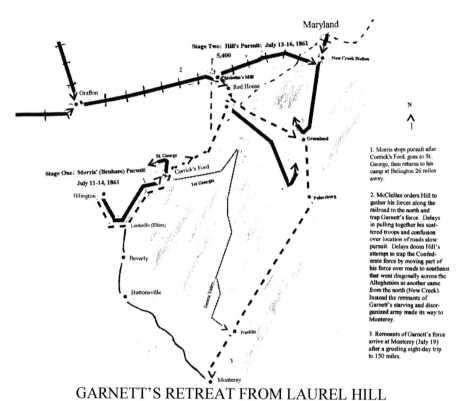

GARNETT'S RETREAT FROM LAUREL HILL

Frustration and exhaustion would only increase. Three-fourths of his men had no rations, and the rest had only enough for one meal. It took eighteen grueling hours to move twelve miles and cross the mountain to the Tygart Valley. Pegram was told that Garnett was at Leadsville, so he hired a horse and made his way near that town— only to be informed that Garnett had been there, but had fled northeastward, pursued by a large Union force. With no chance of joining Garnett, Pegram returned to his fatigued men. He found them in a state of confusion, firing randomly into the darkness, believing the enemy had surrounded them. Knowing a Federal force was above him, McClellan was below him at Beverly, and there was little in the way of food to be obtained on the back roads, their only possible route of escape, Pegram held a council of war. Most agreed with their commander that surrender was the only alternative to starvation, but forty men left during the night rather than surrender. The rest, 600 men, surrendered to McClellan at Beverly on July 13, 1861. When the hungry Confederates were marching, still fully armed, to Beverly to capitulate, they were met by several wagon loads of bread benevolently sent by McClellan.[42]

Some of the Confederates involved in the Rich Mountain battle escaped across Cheat Mountain by way of Huttonsville. They made their way to safety before McClellan seized Beverly. First was William Scott and his Forty-fourth Virginia infantry, then Nat Tyler with part of Pegram's command, followed by Jed Hotchkiss with fifty men who had led the evacuation from Camp Garnett. While crossing Rich Mountain, they encountered darkness, drenching rains, fallen trees, dense thickets, and precipices. These obstacles were burdensome for Hotchkiss and his small band, as well as for the rest of Pegram's retreating force. Hotchkiss faulted Pegram for the high-handed manner in which he had taken command of Camp Garnett away from Lieutenant-Colonel J. M. Heck before the battle, as well as for "his arbitrary and selfish direction of affairs," which, according to Hotchkiss, "enraged many" and "brought about the disasters that attended and followed the battle of Rich Mountain and led to the surrender of 600 brave men to the enemy."[43]

Scott also came under criticism for not having come to the aid of his comrades at Rich Mountain; for the rapidity of his retreat, leaving stores at Beverly unguarded and enabling local citizens to help themselves to supplies; and for the burning of the bridge at Huttonsville, which hindered the movement of later retreating forces. He filed a lengthy but belated report once the idea of holding a court of inquiry—to investigate Rich Mountain and his role there—had been abandoned. In his own defense, against charges of having failed to attack Rich Mountain, Scott cited conflicting orders he had received from Pegram and Garnett; the need to protect the Confederate supply base at Beverly, preventing the enemy from turning Pegram from the north; and the likelihood that participation in the battle would have led to friendly fire upon his men. He had moved up the eastern side of the mountain to join the fray late in the afternoon, but found that the enemy controlled the gap. Several Confederate horsemen and wounded, who were descending the eastern slope, told Scott that the volunteer messenger, Mr. John N. Hughes, whom he had sent to Pegram for instructions had been mistaken for the enemy and killed. Scott recorded that then he pulled back to Beverly and proceeded north to join Garnett. Soon he learned that Garnett had left the area and that the enemy was near Leadsville. Scott reversed his course in the direction of Cheat Mountain.

The day Pegram surrendered, McClellan moved through Huttonsville to secure the Cheat Mountain Summit. The summit, at 3,500 feet high, was dreary but pivotal in traveling to Staunton. The gap was thickly covered with pine trees, except for a three-acre cleaning, where there was an old log cabin known as Soldiers White Tavern, the only habitation for twenty miles. Finding no Confederate force in the vicinity of the mountain pass, McClellan became convinced that the retreating enemy would not stop until they reached Staunton. He moved his force back to Huttonsville. A few days later (on July 15), leaving two regiments of infantry, a battery, and a cavalry company at Huttonsville to patrol Cheat Mountain Summit, he moved the rest of his force back to Beverly. He felt he was in a better position there to move rapidly in any direction necessary.[44]

In the meantime, Garnett and his men north of Beverly were having a difficult time escaping; at Beverly on the morning of July 12, they had mistaken fleeing Confederates for the enemy. This mistake cost the Confederates a relative easy and shorter escape southward through the Tygart Valley to Cheat Mountain. (McClellan would not occupy the town until that afternoon.) Garnett instead moved northeastward toward Red House, in the panhandle of Maryland, in an attempt to escape the enemy from above and below.

It was a difficult time. Rain poured down on them, turning the road into a nearly bottomless pit of soupy mud that resisted every exhausting step. Wagons fell off narrow, winding, slippery roads and crashed into trees below. The farther they went the greater the disorganization, especially in the rear of the line, which spread out for ten miles. Many discarded their weapons. Shoeless soldiers limped along, leaving bloodstained paths. The sick crawled into whatever structures they could find, from houses to barns to pigpens, where they lay for several days until taken prisoner by Northern patrols.

Starvation forced able-bodied men away from their hiding places in the woods to give themselves up. From Red House, hungry Confederates, in disarray and panic, feared the enemy was upon. They moved south, back into Virginia, through a valley seam between the formidable mountain ranges that prevented direct eastern movement. Men became separated, including the rear guard, the First Georgia, which was compelled to climb over a steep mountain, wondering if they would ever again see those they had left at home. A father and son in this group attempted to ease the pain of hunger after going without food for four days; they shared a one-inch tallow candle found in the elder's knapsack. Finally, on July 19, after an arduous and circuitous eight-day trip of 150 miles, and after wading through rivers two dozen times, the remnants of Garnett's bedraggled army reached Monterey. Stragglers continued to arrive for the next week. They had escaped the Federals, but their weakened bodies now had to cope with outbreaks of measles and mumps.[45]

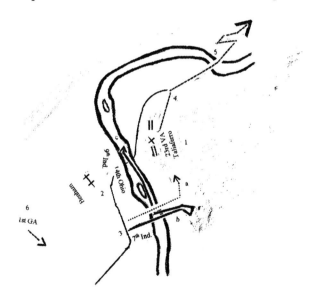

1. Taliaferro placed his 23rd VA (behind rail fence & bushes) and 3 artillery pieces on the hill commanding the ford. Twice they drove Benham's men back from the crossing.

2. Union artillery fired at Taliaferro's men as the 9th Ind. & 14th Ohio crowded together at the ford shooting at the enemy.

3. When the 7th Ind. Arrived Benham sent 6 companies to his right to get to the rear of the enemy on the hill. But they went too far to the right and turned in the wrong direction. Benham called them back and redirected them down the river in an attempt to turn Taliaferro's right.

   a. Route 7th Ind. should have taken
   b. Route 7th Ind. took
   c. Route 7th Ind. redirected down the river.

4. Fear of being turned Taliaferro withdrew leaving the wagon train stalled in the river.

5. Garnett was killed at the next crossing while attempting to delay the Federals with ten sharpshooters.

6. First GA, earlier left behind to delay the enemy from reaching Corrick's Ford, was cut off from the main Southern force and took a different route to Monterey.

CORRICK'S FORD
July 13, 1861

They had escaped, but they lost their commander early in their retreat at Corrick's Ford and had been pursued by two Federal forces in McClellan's attempt to trap them. With limited provisions, from Belington, General Morris hurriedly pursued his former West Point classmate R. S. Garnett. Leading the chase were 1,800 men under Captain H. W. Benham. Garnett moved from Leadsville to New Interest (now Kerens), then eastward toward Shavers Fork, a branch of Cheat River. The river took Garnett's force across the muddy and narrow mountain road of Pleasant Mountain and along the headwater of Pleasant Run. Garnett believed this route would make it more difficult for the enemy to attack.

Confederates felled trees in an attempt to impede pursuit over a road that was already nearly impassable from drenching rains. Eighteen or twenty trees were felled on the slopes of Pleasant Mountain in select areas to block the road for intervals from eighty to 300 yards. This only delayed the Federal pursuit briefly, as they soon removed the impediments. Travel for both forces across Pleasant Mountain was anything but pleasant. The desperate Confederates were leaving a trail. Advanced Union skirmishers frightened away some Confederate ax men, who beat a hasty retreat, often leaving their axes embedded in the trees they were cutting. Their Federal pursuers were encouraged by seeing broken wagons in gorges, roadsides littered with officers' baggage that was discarded to lighten loads, and mud thickened with discarded blankets and other items tossed away by exhausted Southerners.

Upon reaching Shavers Fork, Garnett turned north along the river. He was now more assailable. He spent the night of July 12 at Kaler's Ford, with the rear of his command several miles back on Pleasant Run. The following morning, scouts told him the enemy was close to his rear. For the protection of their vulnerable wagon, slowed by crossing Shavers Fork's many fords, the Confederates made successive halts at defensive positions until the vehicles had cleared. Then Garnett's covering force of infantry and artillery would retreat to the next fording area. Only limited firing occurred until they arrived at the two fording areas known as Corrick's Ford.

Crossing the river here involved two fords, 500 yards apart, separated by 250 acres of land, including cornfields. The first ford was a deep one, rendered deeper by rain. Here wagons were stalled and had to be abandoned. As the Union approached the ford, they came upon a Confederate train that was still crossing the river. In an attempt to protect their train, the Southerners had taken a strong position. Colonel W. B. Taliaferro, with his Twenty-third Virginia infantry and three artillery pieces, occupied a fifty- to eighty-foot-high hill that commanded the first crossing.

The Federals had the disadvantage of approaching the ford upon low land only slightly above the river. Their skirmishers arrived at 2:00 P.M. on July 13. At first the Confederates mistook them for several companies of the First Georgia that had been left behind to hold off the enemy, but were actually now cut off from the rest of Garnett's army. Soon after the first Federals arrived, the Virginians gave a loud cheer for Jefferson Davis, then fired the opening shots. Twice they drove Benham's men back from the ford, despite heavy fire from Federal infantry and artillery. The artillery fire flew over the heads of Taliaferro's men, doing little damage except to bring tree limbs down upon the troops. Federals crowded near the first fording area in an attempt to fire at the enemy. On the Union left the Ninth Indiana was compelled to fire obliquely, while pressed together thirty deep and crowded next to the Fourteenth Ohio. When the Seventh Indiana, under Colonel Dumont, arrived soon after the start of the fighting, Benham ordered six companies from this regiment to cross Shavers Fork, 300 yards above the first fording area, in an attempt to get on the heights to the rear of the enemy. A misunderstanding led to crossing at double the ordered distance and turning in the wrong direction (right instead of left). This led to a fifteen-minute delay. Benham found such a movement to the high ground on the Confederates' left impracticable, and he aborted the movement. He redirected the same men of the Seventh Indiana down the river. They moved hugging the bank on the Confederate side, which afforded some protection, but precariously placed them beneath the fire of both sides as they splashed down the river in an attempt to turn Taliaferro's right.

During the fighting, a minister of an Indiana regiment proved to be an excellent marksman. His rapid fire far exceeded the average of eleven rounds fired by other soldiers at the site. After each shot, the preacher uttered, "and may the Lord have mercy on your soul." Benham's men continued to fight until the Southerners, who were running low on ammunition and fearing the enemy was attempting to turn their flank, pulled back, ending the thirty-minute clash.

Charles P. Poland Jr.

Confederates left thirteen dead and nineteen wounded upon the field (most of whom were from the Twenty-third Virginia), along with a damaged six-pounder, which they spiked, as well as a log in the midst of the Federals containing 144 bullet holes. More than forty wagons were mired in the mud before the ford or were hung up on rocks in the river and were abandoned. Thirteen Confederates were missing, while the Union had two killed and nearly a dozen wounded. Among the wounded was a young Massachusetts lad who was shot in the leg. The youth had been visiting the South when the war started and claimed to have been "impressed" into the Rebel ranks. When the fighting started, he tried to flee down a hill and across the river to the Union side. His lieutenant saw what he was doing and shot him with his revolver.

Once Taliaferro abandoned the first ford, Garnett's next concern was to temporarily block the second one to give his army enough time to distance itself from the enemy. To accomplish this, he placed ten skirmishers behind driftwood to ambush the enemy.[46] The general and his officers sat on their mounts near the river, bending forward in an attempt to see under the tree limbs and vines to spot the oncoming Federals.[47] The general's aide, Gaines, heard the cries of a wounded Southerner left on the other side of the ford. He rescued the man, finding him shot in the face with both jaws broken and his tongue mostly destroyed. Soon after the aide returned, the enemy cautiously approached the fording area and Garnett's sharpshooters opened fire. The Federals responded by sending a hail of bullets that caused all the officers but Garnett and his young aide, Gaines, to ride to safety. The aide ducked in a desperate attempt to avoid being hit and was rebuked by Garnett. The general, wearing a black overcoat, a dress sword, and an opera glass across his shoulders, sat upright in the saddle. He turned to look down the road behind him, perhaps to order the sharpshooters to leave, when a bullet struck him in the back and went through his body. Garnett threw up his arms, then fell from his horse, landing on his back with his head near the river. Gaines dismounted and tried to lift his fallen commander back into the saddle, but heavy fire forced him to ride away on the general's horse, leaving the body to the nearing Federals.[48]

Garnett was the first general to fall in the Civil War. Benham and others, including a weeping Union major, John Love, Garnett's former roommate at West Point, recognized the slain general and gave special care to his remains and personal effects. The body of the black-haired, slightly built, five-foot-eight-inch-tall general was carried to Corrick's house, where the blue colonel's uniform with a brigadier general's star on each shoulder was removed and replaced with clean clothing taken from a captured wagon. Garnett's body was placed in a temporary, rough wooden coffin and was taken by wagon to Grafton, by rail to Washington, and finally, to Richmond. The trip's first leg was the most perilous, creeping over narrow mountain roads only inches wider than the wagon. On one occasion the back wheels slipped off the road. Only the perseverance of sure-footed mules, the skill of the driver, and good fortune prevented them from falling 1,000 feet.[49]

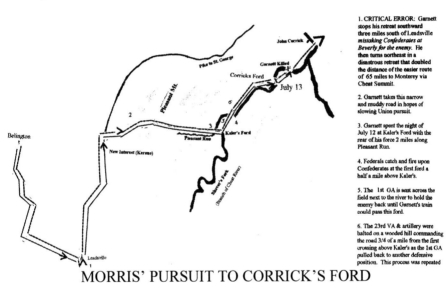

1. CRITICAL ERROR: Garnett stops his retreat southward three miles south of Leadsville *mistaking Confederates at Beverly for the enemy.* He then turns northeast in a disastrous retreat that doubled the distance of the easier route of 65 miles to Monterey via Cheat Summit.

2. Garnett takes this narrow and muddy road in hopes of slowing Union pursuit.

3. Garnett spent the night of July 12 at Kaler's Ford with the rear of his force 2 miles along Pleasant Run.

4. Federals catch and fire upon Confederates at the first ford a half a mile above Kaler's.

5. The 1st GA is sent across the field next to the river to hold the enemy back until Garnett's train could pass this ford.

6. The 23rd VA & artillery were halted on a wooded hill commanding the road 3/4 of a mile from the first crossing above Kaler's as the 1st GA pulled back to another defensive position. This process was repeated

MORRIS' PURSUIT TO CORRICK'S FORD

Back at Corrick's Ford, the reverberating sounds of a shot from the blunderbuss of a lone Confederate soldier, a scout from nearby Alum Hill Gap, were mistaken by Federals for sounds of Confederate artillery. The sounds stopped any further pursuit by Morris' army. Their only supply of food was beef sent by McClellan, and it was blamed for causing diarrhea. Many, despite their hunger, preferred to go hungry rather than risk the illness that, according to Morris, was caused by eating beef alone, without bread or salt. Despite their hunger and exhaustion, the men found ample energy to loot the $250,000 worth of supplies in captured wagons. They found clothing, tents, gold watches, and even Garnett's defused artillery shell, a souvenir from Laurel Hill.

Morris' pursuit of Garnett was over. He left Corrick's Ford on July 14 and went to Saint George, which was a soldier described as "a half-score of struggling, dilapidated houses" and a courthouse. Two days later Morris was back at his camp at Belington, twenty-six miles from St. George. The exhausted Federals had hiked a muddy and broken road and had waded—five times in one day—through thigh-to waist-high water across the Cheat River. Walking over the muddy road caused a soldier of the Fourteenth Ohio to stumble and accidentally fire his musket, killing his lieutenant. According to an Indiana soldier at the scene, William K. Kemper, "The lamentations of the poor fellow who discharged the gun were pitiful."[50] Once back at Belington, the Union destroyed the vacated Confederate fortifications.

The chase was now in the hands of Brigadier General Charles W. Hill. McClellan had ordered him to gather his scattered forces who were defending the Union rear and protecting the Baltimore and Ohio and Northwestern Virginia railroads and to trap the fleeing Confederates.[51] Hill had nearly 6,000 men spread out over 200 miles, from Parkersburg and Wheeling eastward to West Union on the Northwest Turnpike. Pulling together scattered forces, supplies, artillery, and wagons in one of the most mountainous regions in western Virginia was slow work. The process was hindered by delays, caused in part by the civilians who ran the railroads and resented military meddling.

Confusion over the location of roads also impeded Union progress. A lack of awareness of a railroad offshoot, which went from St. George to Red House, caused the first Federals to station themselves to the west (at Chisholm's Mill) of the route that the 3,000 Confederates would take. Upon discovering their error, on the morning of July 14, Colonel J. Irvine rushed his unfed force of 1,300 men to Red House, only to find that the Confederates had cleared that town three hours earlier. He proceeded southward for a time, but fatigue and not knowing the location of the enemy caused him to return to Red House.

In the meantime, General Hill was told he could trap the Confederates before they reached Petersburg. The plan was for one force to move diagonally over roads that crossed the Alleghenies, to emerge midway between Greenland and Petersburg, and to turn and trap Confederates from the south. Another force would go by rail to New Creek Station and march southward, trapping the Southerners from the north. The men were unused to marching and proceeded slowly, with many hobbling along on sore feet. Nearly one-quarter of those coming across the Alleghenies would drop out. Despite their efforts, they were too late. The Confederates had escaped to Petersburg and beyond. McClellan called off the pursuit.

Six companies, totaling 350 men, of the First Georgia were forced to take a different route to Monterey. They had been cut off from their main force at Corrick's Ford "with no avenue to escape except the pathless mountains that hemmed them in." They wandered about over mountains and stumbled through streambeds running with knee- to waist-high water made icy from gurgling through deep, mammoth gorges. For three days they had nothing to lessen their hunger except leaves, roots, and the inner bark of laurel trees. They were lucky to come upon a middle-aged, cross-eyed mountaineer and trapper named Parsons. After feeding the exhausted and famished men with beef cattle he had killed on his farm, Parsons guided the soldiers over forty miles of virtually uninhabited mountains, through Seneca Valley, and finally to Franklin. From there the Georgians proceeded to Monterey and McDowell where they were given a ten-day furlough to recuperate. The sick were taken to Staunton.

Three days lapsed before authorities in Richmond learned of the defeat at Rich Mountain and Garnett's retreat. This defeat presented them with their greatest military crises to that point in the war.[52] Staunton and the Virginia Central railroad were now vulnerable to enemy attack, and once the enemy was in the valley, they could threaten Johnston. Wise (at Charleston), Floyd (at Wytheville), and McDonald (at Romney) were notified to come to the Staunton area. In the meantime, General Henry R. Jackson, at Monterey, was put in charge of merging the remnants of Garnett's army with his own recently arrived command—forming a force of about 3,500. His job was to block the Federal advance toward the valley from Cheat Mountain. To promote better communication, the telegraph between Staunton and Richmond was kept open twenty-four hours a day. A pony express was established between Monterey and Winchester as the Southerners braced for the worst.[53]

McClellan did indeed plan to go to Staunton and proposed this plan to Scott. But when Scott approved the move, McClellan backed off. He was wrongly informed that Wise had routed and demoralized Cox's army; McClellan said he would have to go there. Furthermore, about fourteen disgruntled regiments—made up of three-month volunteers who distrusted their officers—were going home, leaving him with a weakened force with which to take on the Confederate army at Monterey and to move on Staunton. Unaware that Johnston had joined Beauregard at Manassas and had defeated McDowell McClellan telegraphed Scott from Beverly late on July 21 to suggest an alternative plan. Instead of going to Staunton, he would leave part of his army in the Tygart Valley and at Cheat Mountain and would send help to Cox, while the bulk of his force would be sent to defeat Johnston. Hours later McClellan was ordered to Washington, leaving Rosecrans in charge of the Union forces in western Virginia.[54]

Once in Washington, he invited reporters to his headquarters; many of them doubted that a man so young should be put in charge. These press events were extensively reported throughout the North and gave detailed descriptions of McClellan, including that his compact build was reminiscent of Napoleon. The characterization stuck. From then on, the youthful McClellan was often referred to as "Young Napoleon" or "Little Mac."[55]

A shaken Washington had turned to the North's first victorious military war hero. McClellan had driven the enemy beyond Cheat Mountain as well as away from the B&O and Northwestern Virginia Railroads. He was the man of the hour. Everywhere he went crowds gathered to look upon their new savior. Such popularity amazed him. After being in Washington for only days, he wrote to his wife, "I find myself in a new strange position here: President, Cabinet, Gen. Scott and all deferring to me. By some strange operation of magic I seem to have become the power of the land." Later he jokingly wrote that he could be a dictator if he wanted, but he did not. All the adulation reinforced his growing view that he alone could save the country. Like Napoleon, he talked of ending his war with one campaign. He brought with him not only administrative skills but other traits he had displayed in western Virginia: distrust, conflict with superiors, criticism of officers under him, and praise for the common soldier. He extolled his soldiers of the west for having

288

"annihilated two armies," and because of this, McClellan said to them, "you...are more than a match for our misguided brethren."

McClellan's confidence in the men was contrasted with his disdain for their commanders, Cox, Morris, and Rosecrans, who had helped make him victorious. He had not directly led any of his troops in combat. It was Rosecrans who had fought the battle of Rich Mountain. McClellan's confident and bold statements gave way to caution as the execution of battle plans grew near. Refusing to attack fortified Fort Garnett might have been prudent, but it appeared to Rosecrans and critics that the general had failed in his agreed-upon role. In person he was usually charming and likeable, but Cox noted that this contrasted sharply with the sting of McClellan's pen. He was, however, compassionate in the treatment of civilians and their property. He had offered to loan wagons to the Confederate at Monterey to aid in the exchange of prisoners and had notified General Jackson that Garnett's body had been placed on ice at Grafton until instructions were received from the fallen general's family. As head of the Army of the Potomac, and later as General-in-Chief, he believed the country's fate rested solely upon him; this belief was accompanied by a heightened distrust of civil authority over him. His conservative views on slavery and the prosecution of the war provoked his enemies to lobby for his removal. But it was his caution in combat that would force Lincoln, in November 1862, to relieve the hero of 1861 from command. He had what Lincoln called the "slows."[56]

While authorities in Washington struggled with problems resulting from the Union disaster at Bull Run Richmond continued to labor to secure the upper Shenandoah Valley and its railroads, which had been imperiled by the disaster at Rich Mountain and Garnett's retreat. On July 20, 1861, Brigadier General W. W. Loring was appointed by Lee to replace Henry R. Jackson as commander of the Northwestern Army. His immediate task was to block all mountain gaps as needed to prevent the enemy from reaching the Virginia Central Railroad by the Monterey and Huntersville roads. Once he had secured the valley, offensive action was to be taken to win back the Rich Mountain region and menace the railways to the north. But illness, rain, organizational deficiencies, and Federal resistance during the summer and fall frustrated and prevented offensive success. Failure to act soon brought Lee to the scene, much to Loring's resentment, but Lee, too, would later leave the region tainted by failure.

Unlike Loring, who was upset by Lee's unannounced appearance only weeks after he had been put in command, Henry Jackson welcomed the general. A Georgian, Yale graduate, ex-judge, former minister to Austria, and an ex-colonel in the Mexican War, the modest but able Jackson had urged Lee to come to the Monterey area and replace him with a man of greater military experience. Before Jackson was superceded by Loring, the Georgian general displayed intelligent judgment in the disposition of his limited force; his force was comprised of Garnett's debilitated command, along with Georgians he had recently brought with him from his home state. He was aware that the valley was vulnerable not only from the historic Staunton-Parkersburg Turnpike but also from lesser-known road from Huntersville to Millborough, so he divided his force and blocked both routes.[57]

Jackson was aware that the Federals had won the race for Cheat Mountain Summit, the most formidable mountain gap in the region. He countered by blocking the road on the Allegheny Mountain, twenty-five miles east of Cheat Mountain.[58] The other part of the Jackson command was sent from Millborough to Huntersville. There his advance guard failed to find an enemy. This presented the intriguing possibility of moving into Tygart Valley, attacking the Federals at Cheat Mountain from the west, and trapping them between the two Confederate forces. Lee was unenthusiastically received by Loring at Huntersville, which Loring called "a most wretched and filthy town." Loring had been there since July 30 and was planning to move northward. He had reconnoitered Cheat Mountain Summit and had concluded that attacking it was impracticable. Instead he planned to seize Huttonsville, thus turning Cheat Summit Fort and cutting it off from the main Union supply base, Beverly. But Loring would not go forward with his plan until adequate supplies had been carried to Huntersville, and the delays were extensive. It rained for twenty successive days. Supplies come slowly, as horses strained to pull loads through seemingly bottomless mud. The soldiers were plagued by wet weather, cold, ragged clothing, measles, and meager rations. Through it all, Nancy Hare endured. She was the intrepid wife of a Tennessee soldier and was equal to any man in the long marches, carrying her own supplies and cooking utensils. When she was in camp, she cooked and washed for her husband's mess. Nancy chewed tobacco, did not seem offended by others' profanity, and was greatly respected by officers and men. One Confederate described her as "plain, home spun, honest, devoted, but a misguided woman"—for accompanying her husband in the army.[59]

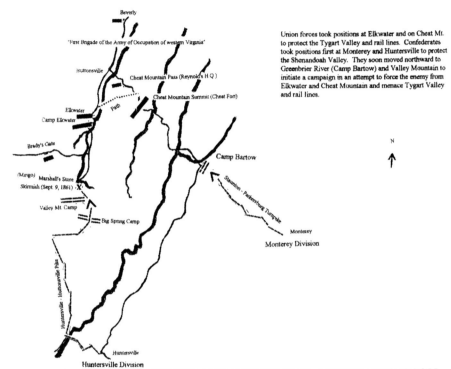

Union forces took positions at Elkwater and on Cheat Mt. to protect the Tygart Valley and rail lines. Confederates took positions first at Monterey and Huntersville to protect the Shenandoah Valley. They soon moved northward to Greenbrier River (Camp Bartow) and Valley Mountain to initiate a campaign in an attempt to force the enemy from Elkwater and Cheat Mountain and menace Tygart Valley and rail lines.

UNION AND CONFEDERATE POSITIONS AFTER THE RICH MOUNTAIN CAMPAIGN

Lee realized that time was critical; the opportunity to seize the area west of Cheat Mountain was disappearing. Federals under his old West Point friend, J. J. Reynolds, whom Rosecrans charged with commanding the Union troops in the region, was moving to block any Confederate advance. Loring was not ready to move, and Lee refused to force the issue. Instead he attempted to placate the jealous, surly Loring. Lee allowed his belief in gentlemanly ways to dominate over military objectives—a trait Lee displayed well into the war, allowing subordinates to get away with annoying behavior until, according to the famed Lee biographer Douglas S. Freeman, "his temper broke bounds." After that, said Freeman, Lee "would freeze men quickly in the cold depths of his wrath."[60] With Loring, Lee displayed only forbearance and seeking alternate ways of getting at the enemy.[61]

The enemy was positioned at Beverly and Huttonsville, with outposts at Elkwater, Cheat Mountain Summit Fort, and Cheat Mountain Pass. These outposts were on the two roads from Huttonsville that formed two sides of a triangle and led to the Shenandoah Valley. Reynolds' headquarters was at Cheat Mountain Pass, at the foot of Cheat Mountain, and was three miles from Huttonsville and nine from Cheat Mountain Summit Fort. To shorten the distance of moving troops—in the event of an enemy attack—the seventeen miles from Elkwater to Cheat Mountain Summit Fort via Huttonsville, paths were established across the Tygart Valley and Cheat Mountain. With considerable effort, the other outposts could be reached by traveling seven miles.

Defenses at Elkwater were formidable. Three infantry regiments (the Fifteenth and Seventeenth Indiana and the Third Ohio) and two artillery batteries were placed behind defensive works in the narrowing valley on both sides of Tygart Valley River, Rich Mountain on the west and a spur of Cheat Mountain on the east. Acres of land were cleared from the mountains to enhance visibility. This task was complicated by numerous rattlesnakes, copperheads, black snakes, and a seemingly endless variety of snakes everywhere. Further north at Cheat Mountain Pass, there were detachments of cavalry, a section of artillery, and the Thirteenth Indiana. South at Cheat Mountain Summit or Fort were three infantry regiments (the Fourteenth Indiana and the Twenty-fourth and Twenty-fifth Ohio), an artillery battery, and a detachment of cavalry. The position of these men under Colonel Nathan Kimbell was also formidable, but it was the least desirable place to be stationed. The men called Cheat Mountain "the country God forgot."

One soldier wrote in his diary that Cheat Mountain was appropriately named because they had been cheated in numerous ways since their arrival: they were living on half-rations; enduring horrible wet, cold weather; and lacked clothing, forcing men to wrap themselves in blankets to hide their nakedness. Others attempted to make pants out of their rubber blankets or wrote their governors in Indiana and Ohio to send clothes. The end of August saw Kimball's regiment (Fourteenth Indiana) so disgruntled that their actions bordered on mutiny. Angered by their living conditions at such inhospitable heights, the soldiers' tempers boiled over when they heard the news that Congress had approved Lincoln's call for three years of service. The thought of putting in extended service when they were only days from the end of their three-month terms led to defiant utterances. Some claimed that no one could make them stay. Officers resigned, and one company refused to elect replacements. Reynolds came to Cheat Mountain and placed the obstreperous officers and their followers in the guard house, then reorganized camp and improved conditions.

Men had originally placed their tents between the pines and the rocks on the summit, on any spot they wished. Some were on such inclines that occupants had to brace their feet against rocks to keep from rolling away. Numerous springs bubbled out of the ground, and several men had placed their tents over the springs to have water nearby. Soldiers cleared land from a farm owned by a gaunt, illiterate man named White. His was the only residence on the summit. His farm and tavern were modest. Soldiers described the farm as covering a splendid twenty acres, "averaging ten rocks to every blade of grass." Some called the tavern "Hawk Tavern," for White allegedly served hawk for dinner, disguised it as another dish.

White was suspected of having Southern sympathies and was placed under arrest. His only employee, a woman who worked at his tavern and whom the soldiers called "Maid of the Mist," held similar views. She resisted the soldiers' advances for romantic favors by responding that her price was Lincoln's scalp.

White's house was turned into a hospital, and the barn was used for storage. When the telegraph was extended to the Cheat Mountain camp, he was mystified. He exclaimed that he could understand how a written note could be attached to the wire and moved along, but how could it get past the poles without tearing? This mystery, as well as the speed of communication, convinced him it was witchcraft. He avoided the telegraph operator, believing he dealt with the devil.

The Federals were well aware of the positions of the Confederate camps, as scouting expeditions were continuously sent forward from their outposts. Scouts from Cheat Fort kept a vigilant eye on the road to Greenbrier River. Others from Elkwater reconnoitered the pike to Huntersville along with lesser roads to the west, where a picket station was established at Brady's Gate on Point Mountain Pike. Only days before Lee launched his Cheat Mountain offensive, nearly 300 Federals moved down the Huntersville Pike and engaged three companies of Confederates. A brisk encounter occurred at Marshall's Store (modern-day Mingo), very near the Confederate camp at Valley Mountain. Perhaps several dozen casualties occurred before Federals pulled back to their camp at Elkwater, eleven miles away.

Losses that were even more vexing were those inflicted by Southern irregulars, or guerrillas, called Mountain Rangers, who hid beside the road to ambush unsuspecting Union scouts. To the Union military, these were cowardly acts by unconscionable low-lifes who were neither members of a legitimate military organization nor deserving of being treated as prisoners of war upon capture. Some felt these bushwhackers should be hung or shot on the spot without the benefit of judicial niceties. The Federals refused to see guerrillas as men who were attempting to defend their communities from invaders and instead viewed them as wanton murderers. Scouting parties were sent south and west far distances over difficult mountains to try to destroy the bushwhackers.

One such scouting expedition, returning from Bulltown, stopped at a mountain home to rest. A middle-aged mother was discovered to have never seen a flag of the United States. The captain had the flag unfurled in dramatic military fashion as the mountain mother and her children watched in wonderment.

When Lee arrived at Cheat Mountain, he curtailed guerrilla activities, but the guerillas continued to shoot Union scouts around Cheat Mountain. On one occasion, the "bushwhackers" were accused of returning to the scene of an ambush and shooting—again—a helpless, already wounded Union soldier. The livid Colonel Kimball interrogated two previously captured guerrillas to learn the whereabouts of the Mountain Rangers, but they refused to tell. Finally, in frustration, Kimball drew his revolver and shot one of the prisoners, who then divulged the information. A Union physician then cared him for. Based on this newly acquired information, a party of soldiers was dispatched, and they killed or captured the offending guerrillas.[62]

CHEAT MOUNTAIN: AN AMBITIOUS PLAN GOES AWRY

General Lee worked out an elaborate new plan to attack the Federals on September 12, 1861. The key to the plan was the discovery of a path to Cheat Mountain Summit. A civil engineer who was traveling over the mountain from Jackson's command to Loring's accidentally came upon the enemy's position at Cheat Mountain. After showing Colonel Albert Rust the way and then telling Loring, the general sent both men to Lee. The enthusiastic and persuasive Rust convinced Lee to allow him to lead a column over the newfound route. Even officers who outranked Rust agreed to serve under him on this mission. Lee's decision to put Rust in charge has been called the most critical and costly choice of the campaign.

Five separate columns were to secretly and simultaneously move on the enemy located at two fortified sites, Elkwater and Cheat Mountain Summit Fort. From two Confederate camps, Mace's Farm at Valley Mountain and Big Spring Camp, the three columns of Loring's force moved out. One was to go down Tygart Valley south of Elkwater. Colonel Jesse S. Burks' brigade and cavalry were to go west of the river as Colonel Gilham's men, accompanied by Lee and Loring, were to proceed over the Hunterville pike. Another column, under General Daniel S. Donelson, was to move to the north of Elkwater, trapping the Federals there. The third column, under General S. R. Anderson, was to proceed to the western heights of Cheat Mountain. There Anderson was to cut the telegraph wires, block Union reinforcements, and assist in an attack on Cheat Mountain Summit, after which he would be in a position to assist Confederates at Elkwater. Two other columns from the Allegheny Mountains and Greenbrier River were to advance to Cheat Mountain Summit Fort. General Jackson was to proceed toward the fort over the Staunton-Parkersburg Turnpike while a 1,600-man force under Colonel Albert Rust was to move to the left, turning and capturing the works at Cheat Mountain Summit. Rust's opening shots were to signal the start of a coordinated attack by the other four columns.[63]

The Confederates started forward on September 9, 1861. Wanting all five columns to be in position by the night of September

Charles P. Poland Jr.

11, Lee staggered their starts over three days. Rust left on September 9, and Donelson's brigade left at dawn on the 10th, followed several hours later by Anderson's men. The columns going over or near the turnpikes, Rust's and Loring's, proceeded forward on the 11th. Food was limited and usually consisted of two biscuits for breakfast and two for supper. Two of Donelson's regiments left with their haversacks empty. Food for two days was supposed to have been cooked and brought to them, but their rations never arrived. Half the 15,000 Southern force was sick. Three of the columns were not traveling over roads, but often had to climb rugged mountain terrain in almost continuous rain and cold. Artillery frequently had to be left behind.

Men from Valley Mountain marched off, many without blankets, coats, and shoes. The wife of an Irish private was moved by what she saw, so she took off her shoes and gave them to a barefoot soldier. To distinguish themselves from the similarly clad enemy, each man attached a piece of white paper or cloth to the front of his hat.[64]

Most soldiers carried about thirty pounds (a musket, a cartridge, a blanket, a canteen filled with water, and a haversack that was mostly empty, except for several hard, dry biscuits). Men of Donelson's and Anderson's brigades stared at the rugged heights with frightful precipices and almost perpendicular cliffs, thinking they would be impossible to descend or ascend. To solve the problem, mountain men had been obtained as guides. They knew the formidable terrain and could move about like mountain goats. None was more effective than an elderly man named Samuel. A Confederate gave a detailed description of the mountain man in *Cheat Mountain* (author unknown): He "looked like he was just out of some dark cavern or hollow tree, and was a second cousin to the ground-squirrel family." Samuel wore an "old-fashioned bee gum hat," and "there was fully as much of the hat as there was of the guide, and each was about the same age, both relics of the Revolutionary War and both moss covered." The old-timer tied around his old hat "a white rag, which could be seen through the dense timber and on huge mountain cliffs, bobbing along like an old crippled goat." He was always in front, leading his flock. Men followed him by "meandering from point to point, swinging to limbs, leaping from cliff to cliff,

296

22

aiding each other by holding to each other's hand and forming a kind of chain made of...arms."

Moving down one mountain ridge and up another was exhausting. To assist the movement, and mainly to keep the men from falling off the mountain, a pick-and-ax company of sappers and miners followed Samuel and dug steps in the huge mountainsides, making a pathway around "monster projecting" rocks. They bent down "small trees and saplings, uniting them together in such a manner as to form a sort of hand railing by which" they could "pull up by, gradually winding at times around edges and cliffs of precipices, where a step" out of "the exact line or path" could be fatal.

The mountain-man guide was busy, but the whole exhausting affair "seemed to him to be a pleasant pass of time." Confederate officers were perplexed about what to do with their mounts, believing it impossible to take them up to the top of the mountain. Once again Samuel solved the problem. One at a time, he led each horse to the top. Unable to figure out how he did it, the soldiers jokingly explained that Samuel must have put each horse in "a deep slumber, and he took them apart and carried the pieces up, once at the top put them all in a heap." When all the parts had been carried up, said the soldiers, they must have mysteriously reassembled when he issued the command "Horses come forth."[65]

Anderson's men's march was especially difficult. One soldier stated that when he came in view of Cheat Mountain, it was "[the] roughest and wildest country that I ever beheld, and we were to traverse it for twenty miles. The mountain was cut up into peaks and crags." The men had to march single-file, and their line of the brigade was spread out over three miles. They frequently received and passed back this command: "Keep quiet, keep well closed up." The latter order was impossible over the rugged terrain. Men would be thirty feet apart, struggling over boulders or clambering up the mountain by hoisting themselves up on saplings. Mules frequently slid ten or more yards down slippery inclines. Men collapsed from exhaustion. On the night of September 11, Anderson's exhausted men were on top of one of the peaks on Cheat Mountain, a short distance west of the fortified and cleared land of the Federal camp, at the mountain fort. During the night a downpour soaked the men and turned rations of biscuits into dough. The next morning the added weight of waterlogged blankets made movement more difficult.

Rust's men would experience discomfort and exhaustion similar to what was suffered by Anderson's command. Rust's force had started their trip by leaving Camp Bartow on the Greenbrier River. Because the heather-lined banks were not traversable, they waded through Shaver's Fork of the Cheat River—some contend for five miles—at times in neck-high water. They climbed seemingly inaccessible heights covered with fog and clouds that dropped continuous drizzling to drenching rain upon them and their weapons and destroyed one Georgian's cherished still-unread letter from his wife (he had not yet had time to read it). By day the men pulled themselves up by grabbing bushes, trees, and rocks and moving through waist-high ferns as their feet sank in rain-drenched moss four to six feet deep, forcing them to use large bowie knives in a futile attempt to create a path. At night they slept on top of branches on the ground, above the running water.

Lee's campaign, by the night of September 11, held great promise. In spite of all the obstacles, the five Confederate columns were in the planned position to attack. To promote secrecy, campfires were prohibited and communication was limited to whispers. Donelson's advance guard had captured or chased away Federal pickets on Stuart Run. For security reasons, the Confederate brigade left the lowland around Becky's Creek to spend the night on the western part of a ridge behind the enemy's Elkwater camp. The night was anything but restful. A bear wandered into Donelson's camp, disrupting sleep and creating a commotion, which prompted an escape attempt by recently captured Union prisoners. They were unsuccessful. None of this foiled Lee's plans. The Union was still unaware of Anderson, Rust, and Jackson's movements and of the number of Confederates around Elkwater.[66]

The Southern forces waited during the early morning of September 12, 1861, for sounds of Rust's attack to signal the start of their own. Then random and scattered shots were heard, but from the wrong direction, from the north of Elkwater near Becky Creek, not from the direction of Cheat Mountain. Lee, who had left Loring's column the day before to join Donelson, was worried and confounded. He rode hurriedly toward the sound of gunfire, narrowly escaping capture by a Union scouting party. He found the disheartening news that Donelson's green troops had merely cleaned their rain-drenched smooth-bore and old flintlock muskets by firing them. This musket fire alerted the enemy to a large Confederate presence in the Tygart Valley. Anderson was ordered to retreat from his exposed position.

Lee and Donelson waited until midmorning for the sound of Rust's attack. When it never came, they left the ridge and moved toward Becky's Creek. There they had a brisk but brief exchange with a sixty-man Union scouting party under Captain John Coons. The captain pulled back his small force and exchanged shots with part of Anderson's line before finally getting back to Cheat Summit Fort.

Anderson's column, earlier that morning, had moved eastward on Huttonsville Road, where they captured a Federal engineer riding a magnificent horse up a bridle path that intersected with the road. The surprised lieutenant, upon hearing the command to halt, asked, "Did you men come from the clouds?" A short distance further, Anderson's men drove back a Union ambush party of ninety men from Ohio under Captain David Higgins, who had been sent from Cheat Mountain Fort (four miles to the east) to relieve Coons. At least three Confederates were killed, and eight were wounded. Later that day, Anderson received Lee's orders to pull back from Cheat Mountain to their original camp. On their way back, they carried their wounded down the mountain on stretchers made of blankets. Four men held each blanket, but they needed to switch carriers often. Even then, fingers would cramp, and the wounded men would be placed on the ground while their bearers changed hands.[67]

Implementation of Lee's five-prong attack had gone awry on the day of September 12. Loring's men were south of Elkwater and could not cross the flooded Tygart Valley River. Wet, tired, hungry men and officers had lost all interest and enthusiasm for a fight. Donelson's men had nosily cleared their weapons and later pulled back to Becky's Creek. Anderson's men withdrew from Cheat Mountain. But the most critical error of the campaign had been committed by Rust. Captured Union pickets convinced him that there were at least 4,000 Federals at the summit; the actual number was about 3,000. Rust and his officers decided it would be suicidal to attack the Cheat Mountain Fort, and they pulled back from the mountain.[68]

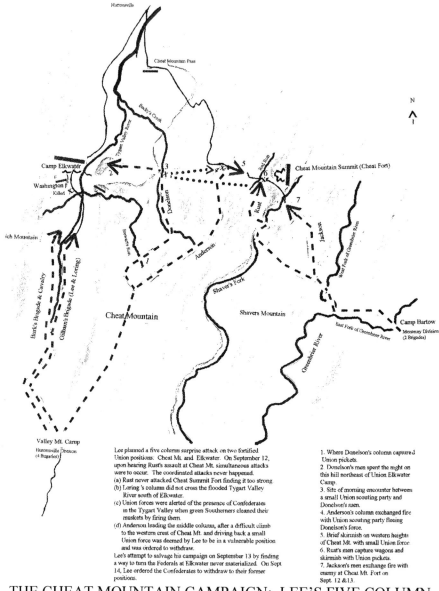

THE CHEAT MOUNTAIN CAMPAIGN: LEE'S FIVE COLUMN
ASSAULT ON SEPTEMBER 12, 1861 FAILS

The night before, the inexhaustible, golden-tongued Rust had
stood under a tree, waiting for daylight. The rain stopped at dawn as
he left 200 disabled men behind and moved the rest of his command,
single-file, a half-mile below and north of the Union fort. His

advanced men took horses from three Union wagons and exchanged shots with Union pickets. Because this occurred a half-mile down the side of the mountain in dense woods, the sounds were muffled and did not carry to Lee and the other Confederate columns. After personally scouting the area of the enemy fort, Rust gave the order to pull back. While moving back over the mountain, he found that a company of the Thirty-first Virginia, who had earlier been deployed one-third mile west of the Union fort, had been forced back a half-mile by enemy skirmishers. The hurried retreat forced the Virginians to abandon their knapsacks and other equipment. When Rust—who was usually benevolent, often walking to allow an exhausted soldier to ride his horse—discovered that the Virginians had abandoned their gear, he angrily ordered them to retrieve their items. The few who attempted to comply with the order found the enemy entertaining themselves by bayoneting the abandoned knapsacks.

Their mission unaccomplished, Rust and his men returned to their camp at Bartow wet, without food, and with sore feet and bruised bodies from repeated falls over rocks and precipices. Of the 3,000 Union troops at Cheat Mountain, only 300 had exchanged shots with Rust's men. The Federals nevertheless had desperately rallied every available man; musicians, teamsters, sutlers, commissary and quartermaster sergeants, and "all the sick that could crawl"—in a Union officer's words—grabbed a spare gun in a feeble attempt to look as formidable as possible. Rust's withdrawal left the Federals with the mistaken impression that superior fighting by a small group had driven the enemy away. An even smaller force of 100 men was sent in pursuit of what they believed to be a frightened opponent.

The physical appearance of the Federals under Kimball was anything but imposing. The men were nearly naked. Their shoddy clothing, which had been hurriedly produced by greedy manufacturers and sold to state and federal governments to send to their soldiers, rapidly deteriorated under the mountain environment. Uniforms were frequently wet, snagged, and torn from climbing over rocks and through thickets, often leaving little more than the waist of what had been pants.

On the morning of September 13, Lee still hoped to continue offensive action. He had not received news of Rust, but he planned to see if he could hold his position in the Tygart Valley and find a new way to the enemy's rear, perhaps by a turning movement in the direction of Rich Mountain. Reconnoitering parties were sent forth. Gilham's brigade started cutting a road through the forest in anticipation of moving northward and to outflank the enemy fortifications. Scattered and ineffectual shots were fired from some of the Union artillery in these works on September 13 in an attempt to discourage the new Confederate advance.

Colonel John A. Washington and Major Rooney Lee, the general's second son, went forth with a few men as part of the reconnaissance to scout the area north of Elkwater. Later that day, Rooney Lee, who was riding Washington's horse because his own had been killed, returned with the sad news that the colonel had been shot and the enemy had possession of his body. Major Lee had earlier warned Washington that it was too dangerous to proceed further, but the intrepid Washington was intent on making a thorough reconnaissance; he continued northward until enemy pickets, hidden by the roadside, fired three bullets that entered his back and exited his chest. First his assailants, and then their whole company, rapidly gathered around their prey.

Their elation was soon dampened by the pitiful sight of another human being dying, bleeding, gasping for breath, and feebly attempting to rise on his elbow. His last words were a request for a drink, which was eagerly granted. They discovered his name on his personal effects, but did not realize he was from a famous family. A litter was made from rifle muskets and accoutrements, and the body was placed on it and carried back to the picket post. From there it went by ambulance to the Union camp, where the remains were lain in a farmhouse serving as the camp hospital. There Captain Cyrus Q. Loomis of the Michigan Battery, a former acquaintance of the deceased, identified Washington. The next morning, the body was sent back to the Confederates; it was eventually buried in the Zion Churchyard at Charles Town, West Virginia.

Once the men knew they had killed the great-grandnephew of the first president, they grew curious. Washington's personal effects became prize possessions. One of the pistols was sent to Cameron, the secretary of war. The three men of the Seventeenth Indiana who had shot Washington were each given an item of his effects: a pistol, a large knife, and gauntlets with the name of the deceased inside. The colonel of the regiment and the officers of Company E took the spurs, powder flask, and a letter from Washington's shirt pocket that was damaged by one of the killing bullets.

The news of the loss of his close friend, brother-in-law, personal aide, and messmate hit Lee hard. For a time he stood, in the words of chaplain Charles T. Quintard, "with his right arm thrown over the neck of his horse" and with a "look of extreme sadness." He "seemed greatly dispirited."[69] On September 14 Lee sent forth a messenger under a flag of truce to arrange for the exchange of the colonel's remains, but Lee was desperately hoping to hear that Washington was alive. Instead, Federals met the messenger on their way to return Washington's body. In the late afternoon and night of September 14, Confederates withdrew from the Elkwater front toward their Valley Mountain Camp.

The only other shooting on September 13, the day Washington was killed, occurred at Cheat Mountain when Federals fired on Jackson's men on another ridge. Jackson had done his part to prepare to fight. The day prior before the planned five-prong Confederate attack, he sent some of his cavalry to scout the road to Cheat Mountain and sent a party of infantrymen to capture the enemy pickets. At 2:00 P.M. on September 12, with the rest of his cavalry leading his main force, Jackson left Fort Bartow, crossed the Greenbrier River over a bridge of wagons, and moved toward Shaver Mountain—just east of Cheat Mountain and parallel to it. Shavers Fork of the Cheat River separated the two ranges. A few days earlier, Kimball, fearing an attack, had had log works constructed and placed men behind them and in front of the bridge over Shavers Fork.

By dawn on September 13, Jackson was halfway up Shavers Mountain, waiting to hear Rust's attack. Instead, he heard only an occasional signal gun fired by enemy scouts and shots by his own 100-man advance force. The advanced Confederates inflicted casualties upon Federal pickets and mistakenly fired on the First Georgians of Jackson's main force, killing three and wounding several. One of the unlucky Southern victims was a man who had had a premonition that he would die. Another bled to death from a severed artery in his thigh; his blood ran fifteen feet down the road. The third died instantly when he was shot in the heart. That night, Jackson left a force to ambush any enemy pursuit and pulled the rest of his men back to Fort Bartow. The following morning, thinking Rust might still attack, Jackson returned to Cheat Mountain and learned that Rust had withdrawn. For several days, Jackson moved his men back and forth between Fort Bartow and Cheat Mountain until Lee abandoned the campaign. After this, Jackson's efforts were devoted to strengthening the fortifications of Fort Bartow and clearing the area around it of trees.[70]

After Lee wrote his condolences to Washington's daughter, he penned a confidential letter telling Virginia Governor John Letcher of the failed plan. In it he did not blame others—including Rust and the recalcitrant Loring—but instead cited the weather, tough terrain, and loss of the element of surprise. Still thinking aggressively, he told the governor, "We must try again." But it was too late. There would be no surprise attack. It had been raining for six weeks, and rain and mud stymied not only the forward movements of Lee, but also the advance of Reynolds' men. Lee's men were now out of food, and the sixty-mile trip by wagoners from Millboro to bring more provisions required the Herculean effort of dragging wagons through mud up to the axle, which took a heavy toll on horses and mules. Loads had to be lightened so they carried little more than it took to feed their teams. Confederate John L. Hill wrote in his diary that dead mules were seen lying in the road "with nothing more than their ears showing above the mud."[71]

Men marched back toward Valley Mountain feeling disenchanted and frustrated, especially with General Loring; they believed he had failed them. The profane general had lost their respect prior to the campaign when he had said that one of his regiments had been a "fine looking body" of men; however, he continued, "until they are able to sleep in the winter amidst the snow and ice without tents, they are not soldiers!" This statement swept through his command, evoking great indignation and condemnation.[72] The men were aware that the original order for the Cheat Mountain campaign (Lee's attempt to placate Loring) had been issued under his name. They scoffed at Loring's failure to cross the swollen stream south of Elkwater. They had made grueling marches under hideous conditions and had nothing positive to show for their labor. On their way back they came upon a herd of cattle on a mountain top. The starving men hastily shot every animal and used their ramrods to cook the beef over numerous small fires. Before leaving what they named "Beef Mountain" and "Jubilee Mountain," they made makeshift footwear out of hides, as half the men were barefooted. These cow skin shoes soon wore out. During the march back the men passed Loring Headquarters. The general, who had lost his left arm in the Mexican War, jumped upon a stump and stood "as erect as a cock partridge in August, and gave the passing soldiers a grand military review," one Confederate present at the scene would later write. The men had been instructed to salute him as they passed. All refused. Not a voice was raised, nor a cap lifted, as they marched "sullenly by." Once back at Valley Mountain, Lee sent Loring and part of his force south to meet the threat posed by Rosecrans.

Lee's first campaign had ended ingloriously. Critics called him Granny Lee. The Southern press was critical. Later historians would count among Lee's failings his excessive gentility in failing to push Loring; his allowing the inexperienced yet enthusiastic Rush to direct the most critical point of the attack; and his having a battle plan that was too elaborate for green troops and inexperienced officers under harsh conditions. Whatever Lee's weakness, he displayed traits he would carry throughout the war. Among them was a gentle style of command and a contrasting aggressive habit of constantly looking for offensive ways, Lee stated, "to get at those people [the enemy]."

Soon after the failure at Cheat Mountain Lee went south to meet the threat of Federals moving over the James River and the Kanawha Turnpike toward the Great Valley of Virginia. There Lee would again have to deal with problems created by rugged terrain, inclement weather, and not just one intractable Southern commander, but two: the feuding former governors of Virginia, Henry Wise and John B. Floyd.

FEDERALS PROBE CONFEDERATE POSITIONS

From the Cheat Mountain campaign to the end of the year, the only significant military action in the region consisted of two Federal probes of Confederate positions. The first took place in early October at Greenbrier River (Camp Bartow) and was followed by an attack on the main Confederate camp on top of the Allegheny Mountain (Camp Allegheny) in December. In both instances the Southern gatekeepers to the Shenandoah Valley did their jobs and turned back their attackers.

ENGAGEMENT AT GREENBRIER RIVER

After Lee's September campaign, the Federals increased their numbers and fortified their position on Cheat Mountain Summit, which some referred to as Lincoln's Gibraltar. As winter commenced, life on the desolate mountain was difficult. The only water source was melted snow. At night each man had only one blanket and an oilcloth poncho to keep him warm. Even new recruits had no opportunity to drill—except in the use of an ax. Trees had to be cut, and space needed to be cleared for tents, cabins, a hospital, and additional fortifications. A portable sawmill was brought from Zanesville, Ohio, and logs were rolled to it with handspikes over the rough and rocky mountainsides. This routine was interrupted in early October.[73] At midnight on October 2, 1861, General Reynolds left Cheat Mountain Summit with 5,000 Indiana and Ohio men (some of whom were from the camp at Elkwater) were to carry out his order to make "an armed reconnaissance of the enemy's position on the Greenbrier River twelve miles away."

Their movement over the winding road frightened deer, which could be heard running through the underbrush. In the dark, the eerie cries of cougars and wildcats and the hoots of great horned owls seem to heighten the atmosphere of uncertainty surrounding the men as they marched toward combat. By 4:00 A.M. they stopped about a mile in front of the Confederate camp. An inexperienced captain, William Douglas, with his company of the thirty-two Ohio Volunteers, was ordered to the right to prevent or detect any possible enemy flanking movement. After marching 300 yards they could see what appeared to be very large men in front of them walking around in the fog. Thinking they were the enemy, but wanting to be sure, the captain walked on wobbly legs, weakened by fear, toward the mystery figure—only to discover that he had almost had his command fire on soldiers of the Thirteenth Indiana.

The enemy was located nearby where the road to Monterey and Staunton crossed the East Fork of the Greenbrier River, which meandered through a narrow valley cutting through the mountainous terrain. The Southerners had burned the bridge over the river in August. Near the southern banks of the river was Camp Bartow, under the command of General Henry Jackson.

Around 7:00 A.M. on October 3, advanced Confederate pickets who were driven back by Milroy's Ninth Indiana reported the presence of a large enemy force. This was the opening of an engagement that lasted until 2:30 that afternoon.[74] Hoping to buy time, Jackson reinforced his pickets, increasing their numbers to 100. They were positioned to the right of the turnpike, beside a fence thickened with small trees, and in the timber on the hillside to the Federals' left. The ambush party was a mile in front of the Confederate camp located to the south and on the other side of the Greenbrier River. This small force under Colonel Edward Johnson, held the enemy in check for nearly an hour. Johnson displayed sound leadership and would later be nicknamed "Allegheny" Johnson. Flanking enemy infantry (Colonel Nathan Kimball's Fourteenth Indiana) forced the greatly outnumbered Southerners back across the river and behind their works. Accompanying their withdrawal was a artillery piece that had been sent in their support, but was unusable until a broken lanyard was replaced.

After Cheat Mountain, Jackson's force had been reduced by illness and the loss of detachments that accompanied Loring to assist Floyd. Those unfit for duty had been sent to Crab Bottom in Highland County, and those faking illness were warned that they would have charges brought against them. Jackson now had to fight the enemy with his diminished force. He believed he faced a desperate struggle. His position behind the East Fork of the Greenbrier was not a commanding one. The river offered limited protection; it was only a shallow stream twenty yards wide. He feared his force could not defend the unfinished earthworks, which were strung out over a mile, and that his men were vulnerable to being turned. He bolstered his force to 1,800 men by bringing the only regiment available, the Fifty-second Virginia, from the two brigades at Camp Allegheny. Detached service and illnesses of two-thirds of the men of the other brigade denied him additional reinforcements.

307

Jackson's greatest fear was that an enemy column would go over the mountain across the river in front of him and turn his right. He sent the few available mounted men of the Churchville Cavalry to watch his right and inform him of approaching Federals. Colonel Johnson (with the Fifth and Twelfth Georgia) was put in charge to defend his right. The center was defended by Colonel William B. Taliaferro's brigade (Twenty-third, Forty-fourth, and Twenty-fifth Virginia) and supported by Shumaker's and Rice's light batteries.

Rust (with the Third Arkansas, Twenty-first Virginia, and Hansborough's battalion of Virginians) was assigned to defend Jackson's left flank and was told not to allow Federals to turn him under any circumstances. Two pieces of artillery, under B. P. Anderson, were placed in position to enfilade the road from Cheat Mountain.

Jackson's suspicion that his opponent would attempt turning movements proved correct. The first was early in the contest. The Federals crossed the river and proceeded to climb the base of the mountain to Rust's left. When they came in range soon after 9:30 A.M., the Third Arkansas fired a volley, causing the Federals "to retire"—according to Rust—"instantly" across the river, rejoining the main enemy force. Covering the retreat, the Federals turned two pieces upon Rust's men, "pouring out canister and shell in large volume," in the words of a Union soldier, William D. Hamilton, but inflicting little damage because the woods protected the Southerners.

Federals batteries (first six and later eight pieces) assumed positions 700 yards from the Confederate entrenchments. For seven and a half hours, from 7:00 A.M. to 2:30 P.M., the Union batteries of Loomis and Howe and the five guns of Shumaker and Rice hammered away at each other. The incessant roar of artillery reverberated off the mountains as shots arched and whizzed back and forth, dropping and exploding, while solid shots slammed into the earth as "iron moles." Over the course of the day, the eight Union pieces fired 1,180 round shots, spherical cases, shells, and—occasionally—canisters on the Confederate center. Shumaker was repeatedly forced to move his three brass six-pounders and one rifled gun a few feet after about every three shots were fired from each piece. The rifled gun was difficult to fire, as balls lodged in its tube. Soon a ball became permanently stuck, and the piece was sent to the rear. Defective fuses and nonexploding shells made the other Confederate pieces less effective. In the middle of the lengthy artillery exchange—during which some Confederate pieces fired ninety or more rounds—a kitten belonging to one of the soldiers scampered playfully on top of the Confederate earthworks, seemingly unaware of the danger all around it.

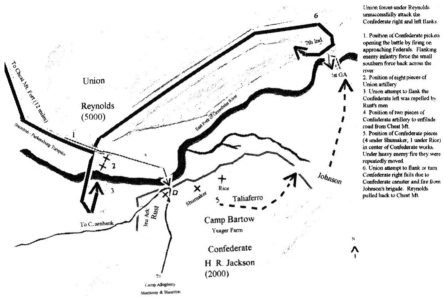

Union forces under Reynolds unsuccessfully attack the Confederate right and left flanks.

1. Position of Confederate pickets opening the battle by firing on approaching Federals. Flanking enemy infantry force the small southern force back across the river
2. Position of eight pieces of Union artillery
3. Union attempt to flank the Confederate left was repelled by Rust's men
4. Position of two pieces of Confederate artillery to enfilade road from Cheat Mt.
5. Position of Confederate pieces (4 under Shumaker, 1 under Rice) in center of Confederate works. Under heavy enemy fire they were repeatedly moved.
6. Union attempt to flank or turn Confederate right fails due to Confederate canister and fire from Johnson's brigade. Reynolds pulled back to Cheat Mt.

ENGAGEMENT AT GREENBRIER RIVER
October 3, 1861 (7:00 a.m. to 2:30 p.m.)

Across the river, at around noon a curious member of the First Ohio Cavalry in his first engagement rode to the summit of a hill where the Seventh and Ninth Indiana regiments were positioned. Wanting to see more, he tied his horse to a tree and started descending the slope when an enemy shell exploded nearby. Looking around, the cavalryman was sickened by what he saw. One man was "borne along with his head entirely severed from his body." An eyewitness recounted, "Others more or less mutilated were carried and laid by the roadside."[75] To the rear of the Federal troops were "ambulances, with the surgeons, distinguished by green sashes, waiting to perform their duty." The witness noted that "some were careful to remain out of harm's way, while others braved danger to search for the wounded."[76]

Simultaneously with the Federal movement on the Confederate left, Reynolds started another column toward the wooded hill near the Southern right. Movement there was slower because of the greater distance, more rugged terrain, and a misunderstanding of an order by Colonel William P. Richardson to move Reynolds' Twenty-fifth Ohio Infantry as part of the movement. Movement toward the Confederate right persisted throughout the conflict. After the attempt to turn the Confederate left failed, Reynolds kept some of his force to protect his artillery while sending the majority of his men to turn Jackson's right, which included men earlier repulsed by Rust. Most of Reynolds' men sent toward Jackson's right were never engaged. Only limited fighting occurred on that front, between the Seventh Indiana and Johnson's men. Confederates who had advanced by running a half-mile and crossing the waist-high water of the Greenbrier, getting within 300 yards of the Federals, were forced back. When Private J. W. Brown of the First Georgia heard the order to fall back, he shouted, "I will give them one more shot before I leave." While ramming down his twenty-ninth cartridge, he was killed by enemy fire.

In the meantime, Johnson rushed toward the approaching Federals and had two of Shumaker's guns open on the enemy. Shumaker had pulled these and other pieces back from the center of the Confederate line to cool them and to rest his men after hours of fighting. He had given orders for no firing. Angered by what he heard, Shumaker rode rapidly toward the two pieces to find out why his order was violated. His relationship with his men had been stormy and distrustful; twice they had petitioned for his removal. On this occasion, he could not condemn them for insubordinate behavior—he found that Colonels Johnson and Taliaferro had given orders to fire. Union artillery responded, inflicting heavy casualties. Captain Rice had a leg blown away, and his crew and horses were killed or wounded, leaving the piece unmanned. Shumaker, who was slightly wounded from a shell fragment that had struck his arm, had the cannon rolled away.

Confederate artillery fire was also effective. It caused the leading Federal regiment, on the Southerner's right, to break and run back into the woods. Soon all Union regiments in that area were pulled back. Confederate canisters and Johnson's brigade had Reynolds convinced that the enemy was too strong. This belief, as well the exhaustion of his artillery ammunition, caused Reynolds to break off the engagement, pull back three miles, and then head back to camp.

The Federals carried off horses and cattle from the area to prevent them from falling into enemy hands. Lieutenant-Colonel Richardson's Twenty-fifth Ohio brought up the rear, carrying the dead and the injured in ambulances, along with prisoners. They carried with them a Union artillerist who, despite losing his arm, never complained. He is said to have surveyed the bleeding remains of his arm and said, smiling, "That is pretty well done." Grizzly remains were left in a house the Union had converted into a hospital two miles from the battlefield. In it were pools of blood, bloody clothing, and amputated fingers. Also left behind was the body of a Confederate scout who had a brother in the Union army. The captured Confederate had died of his wounds prior to the end of the battle. Others were more fortunate. Colonel Nathan Kimball was one of the lucky ones returning unharmed. While leading his Fourteenth Indiana during the fight, an officer near him gestured to his men by throwing an arm in the air. His arm shielded the colonel and was struck by a canister shot that would have entered Kimball's forehead.

Ahead of the Federals marching back to their camp was a Union citizen who had accompanied Reynolds' army to watch the battle. Seeing the Federals leave without capturing the enemy camp, the Unionist assumed they were defeated. He mounted his horse, and galloped off, announcing to all he saw, including the men remaining at the Cheat Mountain Camp, that Reynolds "had been whipped and was in full retreat." This was soon repudiated.

After fighting an engagement that started at 7:00 that morning and ended at 2:30 in the afternoon, Reynolds traveled at a leisurely pace back to his camp on Cheat Mountain. He arrived there by sundown. He optimistically depicted his reconnaissance as "having fully and successfully accomplished the object of the expedition." He claimed to have confronted an enemy force about twice the size of his own and knocked out three of their artillery, inflicting at least 300 casualties while sustaining only minor loses (eight killed and thirty-five wounded). A reporter for the Cincinnati *Times,* who had been at the engagement, even concluded "that if General Reynolds deals such heavy blows in a mere reconnaissance, what will he do when he marches out for a full fight?"[77]

Jackson was also proud of his men's performance, but he was anxious to retire from military service. During the weeks after the engagement at Greenbrier River he was growing weary of seeing his undersized and unappreciated force suffering and sick on the cold heights of the Alleghenies. He was annoyed by criticism in the newspapers of his role in the Cheat Mountain campaign. In frustration, he wrote to J. P. Benjamin, the acting secretary of war, "it was necessary as well as proper that his men be shown appreciation for their meritorious service." He continued, "The command is mainly composed of the wrecks of Garnett's army, and the annals of warfare might be searched in vain to find a more pitiful picture of suffering, destitution and demoralization that they presented at the close of their memorable retreat." Despite having overcome this, he argued, fate continued to be unkind; his men were suffering miserably in obscurity on the mountains, while the sympathy and the glory were given to soldiers elsewhere. In the meantime, he said, his men were spending "most disagreeable nights" in tents that had been riddled by enemy shells and cannonballs and kept out neither cold nor rain.

Jackson's men were more upbeat immediately after the Greenbrier fight. Jackson had won the affection and confidence of his entire command. He was serenaded by the brass band and was cheered when a large U.S. flag, left by the enemy, was presented to him. His men were convinced he was responsible for a great victory that sent the enemy retreating in a demoralized terror, as evidenced by blankets and haversacks strewn on the ground for four miles. Their excitement was heightened almost to euphoria as erroneous reports swept through Camp Bartow of the burning of Washington, Beauregard in Maryland, and Lee defeating Rosecrans.

Their optimism was a fleeting emotion, as somberness and apprehension soon took over. As October waned, Confederate pickets clashed two or three times a week with enemy scouts near Camp Bartow. Each incident convinced residents of the Confederate camp that the enemy was once again attacking them. Chilling winds, falling leaves, dropping temperatures, and their shivering under blankets at night heightened Confederate concerns of the approaching winter and their inadequate winter quarters. Illness reduced their ranks. The Fourteenth Georgia Volunteers could muster only 255 men, rank and file, out of 760. Officers resigned their commissions, including one-quarter (thirteen) of the officers of the Fourteenth Georgia. The reasons given were "bad health" and "can't stand the climate." These were the same men—reported a Georgia newspaper—who, before leaving Atlanta in July, and "before the hardships and privations of a campaign were known and realized, told the men of their command: 'Boys, just vote for us, and we'll take you through right and cling to you until death.'" But as an enlisted man wrote, "Those glorious electioneering times, and promises were forgotten."

An additional annoyance were orders that prohibited the shoeless, scantily clad Georgians at Camp Bartow from wearing clothing sent by friends; it was stored at Millboro, forty miles away. Another irritant was an editorial in a Savannah paper, the *Republican*, calling for winter campaigning rather than going into winter camp. Responding in a letter to the paper, a Georgia soldier, contended that the editor's position was not only unsupportive but also ill-conceived. The editor, the soldier pointed out, sat comfortably in a warm, cozy office much farther south, criticizing military movements "which he does not understand" and dictating "a policy for the poor soldiers shivering on his guard-post in the beating rain or vainly courting sleep upon a bed of mud, or dragging his weary limbs over miles of freezing, snow-clad ground." The idea of a winter campaign, wrote the soldier, was "no doubt" full of "romance to him [the editor], but let him try the reality—let him, by turning soldier, purchase the experience of one winter's campaign in these mountains." The soldier went on to point out, "True, soldiers are machines to *act,* but they are at the same time human beings to feel, to suffer, and to die, and some of these *home* patriots will have to take the places of some of us…if the murderous policy of a winter campaign in *this* country is adopted."[78]

FEDERALS ATTACK CAMP ALLEGHENY

The second Union probe, on December 13, 1861, was an attack on the Confederate camp on top of Allegheny Mountain. New commanders Brigadier General Robert H. Milroy and Colonel Edward Johnson had replaced Reynolds and Jackson.[79] Fort Bartow had been abandoned by the Confederates after the Greenbrier fight, except for visits to the area by their scouting parties, which frequently led to skirmishing with Federal scouts from the Cheat Mountain camp. Life on Cheat Mountain had become more difficult with each passing week. Many men became severely ill, causing Colonel Thomas H. Ford to procure permission to move his regiment (the Thirty-second Ohio) down the mountain to Beverly for more hospitable accommodations. While building new quarters, his regiment was ordered on December 10 to return to Cheat Mountain; Milroy needed them.

Milroy had devised a plan for an attack on the enemy at Camp Allegheny, and he would use Fort Bartow as his staging area. Two companies of the Ninth Indiana were sent from Cheat Mountain on the morning of December 12 to secure Fort Bartow. Two miles from Fort Bartow they were fired upon by a body of 106 Confederates waiting in ambush. After sustaining minor casualties, the Federals secured the fort and forced their attackers to flee to Allegheny Mountain. That afternoon Milroy's main body left Cheat Mountain Summit, arriving at Fort Bartow soon after dark. A Federal officer was surprised to see the personal effects the Confederates had left behind. Rather than coming upon empty whiskey bottles, they encountered an inscribed Bible, religious documents, and loving letters from the soldiers' families. These discoveries changed the officer's prejudices and feelings about Southerners.

At Fort Bartow Milroy fed and rested his men for a few hours. He then divided his 1,900-man force into two groups in preparation for a surprise attack at daybreak on the enemy's left, right, and rear.[80]

Camp Allegheny, eight and a half miles southeast of Fort Bartow, straddled the Staunton-Parkersburg Turnpike, like the Union camp at Cheat Mountain. East of the turnpike the Confederates had virtually no fortifications; west of the same road they had hastily constructed entrenchments and placed their eight pieces of artillery. Cabins dotted the camp on both sides of the pike, usually on lower points behind the two hills that rose above the surrounding area. The tops of the two hills flattened out, especially on the left, near a plateau about 300 yards long. Around the plateau's irregular sides were the earthworks of the main fortification, 4,400 feet above sea level. It was at the highest altitude of any works in the eastern theater. A short distance below and in front ran the road from Green Bank that intersected the Staunton–Parkersburg turnpike a short distance to the east. This juncture was in the saddle, or lowest point, between the two hills; the lowest point in the camp was behind the left hill, which dropped sharply over 100 feet to a swell that gradually rose to higher ground to the south. All the land on top of the hills and behind the camp had been cleared.

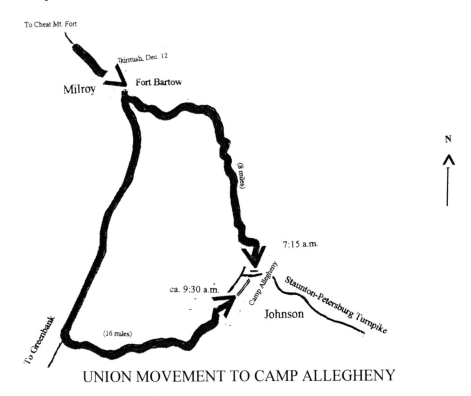

UNION MOVEMENT TO CAMP ALLEGHENY

The Federals attacked the Confederates at their highest points, the two hills at each end of their camp. To attack the left, Milroy sent Colonel Gideon C. Moody with a force of 1,025, men composed of 950 infantry from Moody's Ninth Indiana, the Second Virginia, and seventy-five weaponless artillerymen who were expecting to capture and take possession of enemy guns. Colonel J. A. Jones and 860 men—830 men from the Twenty-fifth and Thirty-second Ohio Volunteers and the Thirteenth Indiana, along with thirty of Brasken's cavalry—were to hit the Confederate right and rear. Milroy had based his plan on information gleaned from interrogating Confederates who had deserted from Hansbrough's battalion at Camp Allegheny a week earlier. Two Unionist Virginians named Shipman and Slater—called traitors by Johnson—led the two Federal groups up the dark, winding, mountainous roads toward their targets. Both knew the area well. One lived less than three miles from the Southern camp. Shipman led Jones' tired and sleepy force, turning off the turnpike for a mile before reaching the enemy camp in order to surprise the enemy on their right. Jones states in his official report that his men moved into a strip of timber, beyond which "was a field rising at an angle of about fifteen degrees up to the plateau." The Confederate camp was on the plateau.

In the meantime, Slater led Moody's men from Fort Bartow on the road to Greenbank to approach the Southerners' left flank. They had to march almost double the distance of the eight and half miles Jones and his followers had traveled. The disparity in distance thwarted any attempt at coordinating a simultaneous attack on the enemy camp.

Johnson—dressed in civilian clothing and carrying a club—and his 1,200-man command were not surprised on the morning of December 13. They had been alerted at about 4:00 A.M. by the sound of firing on their pickets in the strip of timber before the plateau, and they had rapidly formed to meet an enemy of unknown size. Some of the Southerners were placed in trenches on the left as Lieutenant-Colonel G. W. Hansbrough was sent with his battalion to protect the right. The Thirty-first Virginia was ordered to join him. Among the men of the Thirty-first were two brothers, Privates William and Henry Yeager, whose father owned the land upon which Camp Allegheny and much of Camp Bartow were located. The center was guarded by two companies of the Twelfth Georgia, located a quarter-mile in front of the camp and down the mountain. They were assisted by sixty men from the Twenty-fifth Virginia and were sent to the site of the blacksmith shop at the fork in the road.[81]

While the Federals under Jones were approaching by a path on the extreme right, they were spotted by Hansbrough's pickets. Determined to test the strength of his enemy, Hansbrough moved his 300 men within 150 yards of the Federals. Their line (the Thirty-second Ohio on the Union left, Twenty-fifth Ohio in the center, and Thirteenth Indiana on the right) appeared to the Confederate colonel to be ten times the number of his own, though the Federals were actually less than triple the size of his force. Anxious about his plight,

Hansbrough sent a message to the Thirty-first Virginia, who had earlier been ordered to join him, telling them to hurry.

In the meantime, at 7:15 A.M., while the sun rose, the engagement began. Hansbrough, who would be wounded by a pistol shot and carried from the field, ordered his men to fire and fall back until reinforcements arrived. They pulled back to the cabins in an orderly fashion as both sides fired wildly over their opponents' heads, inflicting few casualties. (This account contrasts with Federal reports of inflicting heavy casualties on Confederates who were fleeing in panic.) But even in the early stages of the fighting, the Union men on the Confederate right had been unsteady. The sight and moans of a wounded comrade injured during the conflict with Confederates pickets in the early morning unnerved them, so an order was sent to the skirmish line to keep the wounded men away from the column. During this early stage of the conflict on the plateau, with the Confederates voluntarily pulling back, pursuit was timid. Some Federals seemed confused and wavered, intimidated by the smoke and noise. To rally his men, an officer of the thirty-second Ohio shouted, "Steady boys, keep steady. Remember we are making half the noise." His men cheered and moved forward. An Ohio soldier, William Hamilton, would later write that to their right, a "big burly fellow of the Twenty-fifth Ohio moved ahead," shouting as he turned, "Come on boys, come on. Let's give 'em hell." Soon a ball struck him in the heel; he threw his musket into the air and limped across the Thirty-second Ohio line, hollering "Oh, Lordie, Oh, Lordie" in a manner so dismal it evoked laughter—and momentary relief—in those who saw him.

According to William Hamilton, at about this time, George Harvey of the Thirty-second Ohio called to his officer that something was "the matter with his gun—it would not 'go off' and had hurt his shoulder the last time he fired." He was instructed to discard it and pick up another. After the battle Harvey brought his faulty weapon for the officer to examine. The muzzle was slightly spread and cracked. They found "a Minnie ball at the bottom of the barrel with the point down." The Thirty-second used only round balls in their muskets, but the Confederates used conical balls. In the same instant that Harvey was firing at the enemy, an enemy ball had hit his gun.[82]

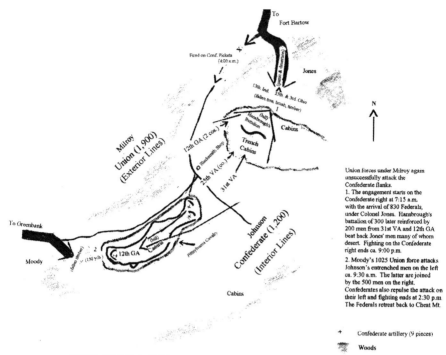

THE ENGAGEMENT AT CAMP ALLEGHENY
DECEMBER 13, 1861
(7:15 a.m. to 2:30 p.m.)

The Thirty-first Virginia soon arrived, along with other reinforcements. The reinforced Confederates, now numbering about 500, were rallied by the shouts from the Georgians and renewed the attack. They were slowed by enemy fire from behind fallen trees, brush, and timber. But the Federals were unnerved by the attack. Failing to hear any firing from Moody's men on the enemy's left, a large number of Federals panicked and broke to the rear. The fleeing Federals belonged mostly to the Twenty-fifth Ohio, though a few were from the Thirteenth Indiana and Thirty-second Ohio. Some were rallied by the vigorous efforts of their officers, but the Confederates slowly pressed forward. The fighting became uncoordinated, as Confederate units intermingled and men fired without supervision.

Accounts differ significantly about the details of the fighting at this point. Southern reports imply that after the early pullback, they slowly pressed forward without being forced back; but the Union version contends that they repeatedly beat back the men under

Hansbrough's command, including attempts to turn the Union left and right (probably referring to reinforcements' entering the fight). Confederates concentrated on the Union right and center, forcing the Federals back. As the fighting continued, so did extensive Federal desertion. Milroy reported that "many base cowards...deserted the field." He added, "They should be remembered in eternal infamy." Running out of ammunition, many Federals fired their last cartridges, while making one last desperate rally. They claimed to have driven back the enemy once again toward their cabins, which enabled the Federals to gather up their dead and wounded before leaving. Their force had dwindled to 150 men. The fighting on the Confederate right was over.

After the Federals on the right had left the battlefield and come down the mountain to the turnpike, they heard Moody's force of nearly 1,000 men firing on the enemy's left. It was around 9:30 A.M. Johnson pulled all his men from his right to the trenches on his left to meet the new threat. While men were moving from the right to join their comrades on the left, a Confederate captain, P. B. Anderson, mistook advancing Federals on his left for returning pickets. He rode toward the enemy, inviting them into the trenches and at the same time forbidding Southerners to fire. Anderson was immediately shot down by the advancing Federals.

Confederates in the hastily constructed ditches responded by opening fire, driving the enemy back into fallen timbers 150 yards from the Confederates trenches. From there, Federals kept up constant fire at the Confederates. Southern artillery fired shot and shell back at Moody's men, but like their earlier fire on the Federals on the right, it had limited impact because of the Federals' sheltered positions. Even the Confederate cavalry (the Pittsylvania cavalry) joined the fight. Cavalrymen secured their mounts behind the protecting cabins and attempted to get into the trenches. Only a dozen or so carabineers were able to do so in the already overcrowded works. The original force in the ditches had been joined by the 500 men from the right. All jockeyed for position, anxious to get a shot at a Yankee. Among them was Johnson's acting assistant adjutant-general, Captain James Deshler, who sustained wounds in both thighs. He refused to leave the trench until the fighting was over.

By 2:30 P.M., after nearly eight hours of fighting, the engagement ended. The Federals pulled back toward Cheat Mountain, having lost 137 men (twenty killed, 107 wounded, and ten missing). Confederates had similar losses, totaling 146 (twenty killed, ninety-eight wounded, and twenty-eight missing). Among the Southern wounded was Dr. H. R. Green of the Twelfth Georgia, who suffered a slight hand injury while tending to wounded soldiers. Confederates did not vigorously pursue the enemy. They moved only a short distance, gathering up a stand of 100 weapons thrown away by what seemed to be the routed and fleeing Federals. They heard rumors from prisoners that Milroy was wounded, and rumors from citizens who lived along the turnpike, they were told that a dozen ambulances carried away the Federal wounded. A few of the Union dead and wounded were left on the field. Several days later, according to a Confederate observer, six Union dead were found "with their eyes picked out by the crows."

The Federal withdrawal back to their Cheat Mountain camp was the saddest trip Captain William D. Hamilton of the Thirty-second Ohio ever made. The road over the mountains was rocky and rough. Hamilton tells of the moaning of the wounded and their "continual plea for water made the night dismal." "Water could be procured only by breaking the ice in the horses' footprints of the night before." The captain was worried about his seriously wounded younger brother, Robert. He also reflected upon the death of one of his most intrepid men, S. H. Prior, who had been killed during the Federal charge on the Confederate right. Two nights earlier, Prior had come to Hamilton and said, "Captain, I have a presentment that I will be killed in the next engagement, it troubles me and I have come to tell you and to ask if you would join me in prayer." Marshall had taken Prior's hand, and they had walked to a log, knelt, and prayed.

Upon arriving at their Cheat Mountain camp a surgeon examined Hamilton's brother and asked if they had an experienced surgeon at home. Hamilton said yes, but wondered why the surgeon had asked. He was told, "this wound is a bad one for which the books prescribe amputation and I would rather not take the responsibility." Hamilton then laid his brother on straw in "common springless wagon," He "wrapped him in blankets, and started the forty miles to Grafton." They were befriended at Beverly by Laura Jackson Arnold, the wife of the most prominent citizen of the town, and the sister of Stonewall Jackson. An avid Union supporter, she frequently took Union wounded into her home and cared for them.

From Beverly, Hamilton took his brother to Grafton, where they traveled by rail to Zanesville, Ohio. There the shattered limb was removed, but the delay would prove fatal. Blood poisoning and gangrene had begun, and Robert soon died. A hearse draped in a U.S. flag was escorted through Zanesville by two infantry companies and took the body to the Hamilton home. They arriving there at 9:00 P.M., and by that time the body was rapidly decomposing. Robert was laid to rest at midnight next to the three-month-old grave of his father and the even more recent one of his cousin—he had died from illness on Cheat Mountain as William and Robert were fighting at Camp Allegheny.

Authorities in Richmond were appreciative of "Allegheny" Johnson's victory and protection of the valley against an enemy that was assumed to have more than 5,000 men. He was rewarded with a Christmas promotion to brigadier general. At first, authorities in Washington were also pleased by what they assumed was a Union victory. On the day after the engagement, the War Department received a telegraph from an operator in Cleveland that was about as far from the truth as possible. Supposedly, Milroy and 700 men had conclusively defeated and inflicted 300 casualties on the Confederate force of 2,000, while suffering a loss of only thirty of their own men. Union accounts claim that a demoralized Johnson "burned his camp on Allegheny Mountain and retreated to Staunton."

A week later, Milroy wrote his report telling of his failure. While maintaining that the enemy had outnumbered his own force by about two to one and that the enemy had suffered 300 casualties, he surmised that victory had eluded him because of desertion—which terminated fighting on the enemy's right before Moody could attack their left—and because Confederates had learned, two days prior to the engagement, of his plan to attack. Based on the interrogation of Southern prisoners (who also told him Colonel Johnson had been killed), Milroy was convinced the enemy had learned of his plan from a deserter from his Cheat Mountain camp.

A correspondent of the Cincinnati *Commercial* presents an interesting account. It ignores the problem of widespread Union desertion and asserts, "there has not been a single fight of the war as nobly fought as the late one at Camp Allegheny." The contest on the Confederate right (where the Union desertion occurred) was, according to the *Commercial,* "fought beyond description; never did old veterans fight so bravely;" and had the other column arrived in time on the enemy left, the newspaper surmised, "one of the grandest victories of the war would have been achieved." The writer continued, "As it is, our boys did well, and are satisfied."[83]

At the time of the engagement, General Loring, who was still in command of the Army of Northwestern Virginia, was moving most of his command, 6,000 men, down the valley to join Stonewall Jackson at Winchester. Jackson was anxious to move toward Hancock, Maryland, to menace the rail line and canal used by the enemy. Loring temporarily left Johnson to block the Federals from taking Allegheny Pass and to reinforce General Kelly at Moorefield. He also left a token force of several cavalry and infantry companies at Huntersville to keep an eye on Federal movement there. On January 3, 1862, the Federals easily seized Huntersville, destroyed Confederate supplies, and created the fear that Johnson—at Allegheny Mountain—could be turned. Instead, the Federals returned to Huttonsville.

Johnson's 1,200 men would spend a miserable winter in Camp Allegheny, as would up to 5,000 Federals who were twenty-one miles to the north at Cheat Mountain Fort (also called Fort Milroy). Living 4,400 feet above sea level made camp life more difficult. The winter of 1861 was a cold, damp one that started on August 13, 1861, with snow at Cheat Mountain. In September horses froze to death. By March, brutal weather and disease had killed a substantial number of men and horses, and graves dotted the mountaintops. While many men suffered through the winter with measles, pneumonia, and other maladies, extensive effort was spent in keeping the communication and supply lines open. Soldiers gladly left these mountains in April 1862 when both sides abandoned their camps. Colonel Augustas Van Dyke of the Fourteenth Indiana expressed the common viewpoint when, as his regiment left, he wrote that he fondly hoped it would be their last look at Cheat Mountain. Neither side would spend another winter at Cheat Mountain Fort or Camp Allegheny.[84]

[1] The forty-eight counties in and west of the Allegenies had only 18,376 slaves owned by 3,605 owners. The ninety-eight counties in central and eastern Virginia had 54,601 free blacks, compared to 2,773 in western counties.

[2] Public exuberance had not waned by August. Early that month an Ohio regiment returned to Cincinnati. Newspapers reported that all business was suspended as crowds lined the streets of the city "gaily decorated with flags." Volunteers were "completely covered with the bouquets and wreaths showered upon them."

[3] Charles R. Williams, ed., *Diary and Letters of Rutherford Birchard Hayes*, (Columbus, Ohio: Ohio State Archaeological and History Society, 1922), vol. II, 30; Moore, ed., *The Rebellion Record*, vol. II, 52; T. Harry Williams, *Hayes of the Twenty-Third* (New York: Knopf, 1965), 39-40.

[4] Stephen W. Sears, *George B. McClellan: The Young Napoleon* (New York: Ticknor & Fields, 1988), 56, 8–10, 14, 24–32, 42, 60–63, 68–69. McClellan might have accepted command of the troops of his home state of Pennsylvania, but, through to no fault of Governor Curtin's, his telegraph offering the job to McClellan was sent to Chicago instead of Cincinnati. The day after accepting the Ohio appointment, McClellan received the offer from Pennsylvania and one from the governor of New York.

[5] Ibid., 70-71. McClellan's rapid rise was due in large part to the beneficence of a key Ohio politico, Salmon P. Chase.

[6] Ibid., 72-73. McClellan was unable to get Fitz John Porter and Jesse Reno but was able to get his father-in-law on his staff by going over Scott's head and appealing directly to the president. One officer he did not want was Ulysses S. Grant. The man with the reputation of being a hard drinker went to see McClellan for a position on his staff, but the chief of the Department of Ohio avoided seeing him. There was a negative side to McClellan's personality. The optimism that often abounded in youth was not as apparent in the mature adult. Under the personable outward personality of this young man of promise was a rather pessimistic and fatalistic vision of life as often unfair and consisting of little happiness and endless struggle.

[7] Stan Cohen, *The Civil War in West Virginia: A Pictorial History* (Charleston W. Va.: Pictorial Histories, 1982), 16; Hungerford, *The Story of the Baltimore and Ohio Railroad*, vol. I, 300. The hotel and railroad station were built at a narrow point in between where the two lines merged. It was a large building, "in its day regarded as an architectural triumph."

[8] Fritz Haselberger, *Yanks from the South* (Baltimore, Md.: Past Glories, 1987), 17-19, 26-27. The Fetterman postmaster later informed Porterfield of McClellan's "secret" movement of Unionist troops to Grafton.

[9] Ibid., 28. Knight had several run-ins with the law in two separate counties. One was for stealing bees and cutting a constable with a knife; the other, for shooting a cow. In both cases law officers were unable to arrest him until the sheriff of Taylor County sought Brown's help. When Brown and the sheriff rode up to Knight's house, he was sitting on his porch with a gun. He told them he would kill the person who entered his yard. At this point Brown leaped from his horse and ran forward,

capturing Knight. Knight is to have said he would kill Brown if he ever got the chance. Many make the claim—in accordance with the inscriptions on the monuments to Brown along the road marking where he was shot, and with the twelve-foot-high white marble memorial in the Grafton National Cemetery—that Brown was the "first Union soldier to be killed in the Civil War." This claim is based on the distinction that Ellsworth and the Union soldiers killed at Baltimore, who died before Brown, had their lives taken by civilians, not by Southern soldiers. In May 22, 1928, a monument was erected where Brown was killed. It was later moved a mile or so north on a spot on U.S. Route 50, just west of the bridge across the Tygart River.

[10] Ibid., 74-79.

[11] Cohen, *The Civil War in West Virginia,* 22; Haselberger, *Yanks from the South,* 28-30.

[12] George B. McClellan, *Report on the Organization and Campaign of the Army of the Potomac* (New York: Sheldon & Co., 1864), 15-16. McClellan issued two proclamations from his Cincinnati headquarters on May 26, 1861. One was to Union men of western Virginia, and one was to soldiers, telling them they were going to cross the Ohio to act in concert with Virginia Union troops.

[13] Ibid., 126-127.

[14] Haselberger, *Yanks from the South,* 34-35; *OR*, Ser. I, vol. 23, 251-52.

[15] Hu Maxwell, *History of Barbour County, West Virginia* (Morgantown, W.Va.: Acme, 1899) 241, 260.

[16] Haselberger, *Yanks from the South,* 36, 38; *OR*, Ser. I, vol. 2, 52.

[17] Haselberger, *Yanks from the South,* 67-69; Maxwell, *History of Barbour County,* 251-52; *OR*, Ser. I, vol. 2, 66-67; C. J. Rawling, *History of the First Regiment Virginia Infantry* (Philadelphia: J. B. Lippincott, 1887), 23-27.

[18] Frederick W. Fout, *The Dark Days of the Civil War* (St. Louis, Mo.: F.A. Wagenfuehr, 1904), 67; Haselberger, *Yanks From the South,* 44-45; Maxwell, *History of Barbour County,* 255; *OR*, Ser. I, vol. 2, 67; Rawling, *History of the First Virginia Infantry,* 24-25.

[19] Today this hill is also known as College Hill, or Broaddus Hill, as it is the location of Alderson-Broaddus College.

[20] Fout, *The Dark Days of the Civil War,* 67; Maxwell, *History of Barbour County,* 255-56. The Pittsburgh *Evening Chronicle,* June 3, 1861. Another version of this story is that the twelve-year-old boy successfully warned Porterfield of the approaching enemy. The boy's father was said to have been with Porterfield's force.

[21] Eva Margaret Carnes, *The Tygarts Valley Line: June–July 1861* (Parsons, W.Va.: McClain Printing, 1988), 48-59; Fout, *The Dark Days of the Civil War,* 68; Maxwell, *History of Barbour County,* 257.

[22] Catharine Merrill, *The Soldier of Indiana in the War for the Union* (Indianapolis, Ind.: Merrill & Co., 1864), 31-33. The cavalrymen known as Churchville Cavalry did set up a temporary line of defense south of Philippi.

[23] For the different accounts of how and who shot Kelly, see pages 72-73 of *Yanks from the South,* by Haselberger. Authors' account vary on the number of Union wounded at Philippi, from one to five.

[24] Ibid., 77. It had been argued that John might not have known what "rebel" meant.

[25] *AOPA Almanac*, vol. 31, No. 3, March 1982, 31-32; Haselberger, *Yanks from the South*, 77-78; Richmond *Times Dispatch*, November 28, 1954. After convalescing in several homes near Philippi and later being freed in a prisoner exchange, Hanger returned home during late summer of 1861. The inventive Hanger secluded himself in an upstairs bedroom. Three months after the start of his self-imposed isolation he walked downstairs on an artificial limb that he had shaped from barrel staves and willow wood. Soon he was renowned for making prostheses for others.

[26] Haselberger, *Yanks from the South*, 313.

[27] New York *Times*, June 7, 1861; New York *Tribune*, June 8, 1861; Richmond *Examiner*, June 7, 1861.

[28] Maxwell, *History of Barbour County*, 258-59.

[29] *OR*, Ser. I, vol. 1, 69-71. The Court of Inquiry met for three days. Garnett, a member of the court, recommended that higher authorities convene a court-martial for Porterfield, but Lee rejected this.

[30] Hotchkiss, *Virginia*, 45, 58-61; New York *Tribune*, June 8, 1861.

[31] John H. Cammack, *Personal Recollections of Private John Henry Cammack* (Huntington, W.Va.: Paragon, 1923), 24-25; Carnes, *The Tygarts Valley Line; June-July 1861*, 91; Ebenezer Hannaford, *The Story of a Regiment: A History of the Campaigns, and Associations in the Field of the Sixth Regiment Ohio Volunteer Infantry* (Cincinnati, Ohio: E. Hannaford, 1868), 69-80; Thomas M. Rankin, *Twenty-Third Virginia Infantry* (Lynchburg, Va.: H. E. Howard, 1985), 8; *OR*, Ser. I, vol. 2, 208-209, 232.

[32] Haselberger, *Yanks from the South*, 189-194; Isaac Hermann, *Memoirs of a Veteran* (Atlanta: Byrd, 1911), 16-17; *OR*, Ser. I, vol. 2, 217-218; *SHSP*, vol. 16, 88-89; Jack Zinn, *The Battle of Rich Mountain* (Parsons, W.Va.: McClain, 1971), 2-6.

[33] *OR*, Ser. I, vol. 2, 215; Zinn, *The Battle of Rich Mountain*, 10-12. Four members of Company B of the Twenty-fifth Virginia (Upshor Grays) fought behind two large rocks. Before the battle they had carved their names, which are still visible on the boulders. Only one of the four, Private George W. Dawson, survived the battle. Today the rocks he fought behind are called Dawson's Boulder.

[34] By 1:00 P.M., eleven hours after they started, a short distance from the top of the mountain, the men were "halted to rest and lunch," while Rosecrans, Hart, and Colonel Lander reconnoitered their position. Hart later joined the Tenth Indiana, one of the regiments that hiked to the top of the mountain. He died of measles and pneumonia at Nashville, Tennessee, on March 29, 1862.

[35] *SHSP*, vol. 27, 45. Soon after Scott received this order, he was ordered by Garnett to report to him. Garnett later canceled his order in favor of Pegram's.

[36] As soon as Pegram heard the firing at the gap, he sent three more infantry companies to that site. During the battle a party of Confederate cavalry from Beverly had supposedly attempted to join their brothers at the gap, but were mistaken for the enemy and were fired upon. They turned back.

[37] William H. Broyles pull back De Lagnel, who was wounded in the hip. Broyles refused to leave despite De Lagnel's orders. De Lagnel was left at a sympathetic

home, was nursed back to health, and later (August 1861) attempted to get through the Union line at Elkwater by pretending to be a local farmer. All was going well until he was betrayed by his fancy boots. He was sent to Fort McHenry, which also housed his commander at Rich Mountain, Pegram. Both were later released in a prisoner exchange.

[38] Haselberger, *Yanks from the South*, 135-38; *Joint Committee on the Conduct of the War*, pt. 3, 1-6; *OR*, Ser. I, vol. 2, 214-17; Zinn, *The Battle of Rich Mountain*, 24-25.

[39] *OR*, Ser. I, vol. 2, 265; Martin A. Fleming, "The Northwestern Virginia Campaign," *Blue and Gray Magazine*, August 1993, 54; Haselberger, *Yanks From the South*, 177.

[40] John Beatty, *The Citizen-Soldier* (Cincinnati, Ohio: Wilstach, Baldwin & Co., 1879), 22-26; Fleming, "The Northwestern Virginia Campaign," 50-51; Joseph W. Keifer, *Slavery and Four Years of War* (New York: G. P. Putnam's Sons, 1900), vol. I, 191-202. Schleigh, A general from Ohio, was in command of the second brigade of the three brigades. McClellan was moving toward Rich Mountain. Schleigh sent two companies of the Third Ohio under a Captain Lawson to reconnoiter the enemy.

[41] Several years after the battle of Rich Mountain, the Confederates dead were removed to Beverly and were reinterred in Mount Iser Cemetary. A marble shaft marks the burial site.

[42] Walter S. Griggs Jr., General John Pegram, C.S.A. (Lynchburg, Va.: H. E. Howard, 1993), 28-34; *OR*, Ser. I, vol. 2, 262-64; Zinn, *The Battle of Rich Mountain,* 524-25. The retreat from Fort Garnett by Hick's force at first went to the left, but Hotchkiss found they were near Roaring Creek, a swampy area too near the Federal camps, so they turned to the right toward Rich Mountain. Early in their march they heard a whistle. Hotchkiss whistled back and later learned a Union regiment was parallel to the Confederate line of march, and answering the whistle might have prevented their being fired upon by many.
The night of July 12, Pegram wrote McClellan that because of "the reduced and almost famished conditions" of his force, he was compelled "to offer to surrender." The message was sent to McClellan early the next morning and was accepted. During the night before the surrender, about forty of Pegram's men left and successfully escaped. Pegram later returned to Confederate service after being exchanged in January 1862 for an artillery leader, James B. Ricketts, who had been wounded four times and captured at First Bull Run

[43] *OR*, Ser. I, vol. 2, 262-64.

[44] Ibid., 262, 273-85. Upon arriving at Beverly Hotchkiss found the people helping themselves to a supply of crackers and other goods from the store. From Beverly he proceeded toward Huttonsville.

[45] Cammack, *Personal Recollections, 28; OR*, Ser. I, vol. 2, 204-13. At Monterey what remained of Garnett's force under Colonel Douglas Ramsey joined General Henry R. Jackson's command. Strangely Ramsey never filed a report of the retreat.

[46] During the retreat along Shavers Fork, Garnett had the Twenty-third Virginia under Colonel W. B. Taliaferro formed in the rear of the Confederates. This was to

buy time for several companies of Colonel J. N. Ramsey's First Georgia to take a position that would delay the enemy until the wagons passed the river. Then the Georgians would retreat behind the Virginians and take up another favorable position selected by Garnett's adjutant-general, Captain James L. Corley. This was successfully repeated, with only limited firing and no casualties until Corrick's Ford. At Corrick's Ford Garnett had Taliaferro post three companies on a high bluff overlooking the crossing. Finding that the undergrowth prevented them from seeing any Federal crossing he ordered them to move rapidly and rejoin the main force. There Taliaferro's right was protected by a fence, and his left, by low bushes.

[47] W. Hunter Lesser, *Battle at Corrick's Ford: Confederate Disaster and Loss of a Leader* (Parsons, W.Va.: McClain, 1993), 9, 11, 13, 15; Hu Maxwell, *History of Tucker County* (Parsons, W.Va.: McClain, 1993), 327-31; *OR*, Ser. I, vol. 2, 222-25, 285-88. Corrick's Ford in the *OR* is usually spelled Carrock's Ford.

[48] *Daily* (Wheeling) *Intellegeneer*, July 24, 1861. Sergeant Burlingame of Company E of the Seventh Indiana is credited with killing Garnett. In Garnett's pockets were a topographical map of Virginia and a "pocket-book containing sixty-one dollars in Virginia currency."

[49] Haselberger, *Yanks from the South*, 195-200, 234-40; Lesser, *Battle at Corrick's Ford*, 19; *OR*, Ser. I, vol. 2, 218-22, 285-88. Garnett's sword, gold watch, and wallet containing $61 in Virginia currency were saved. The body was taken by wagon to Rowlesburg. A train was chartered at Rowlesburg that took the remains to Grafton, arriving there on July 15, 1861.

[50] William H. Kemper, *The Seventh Regiment Indiana Volunteers, Three Months Enlistment* (Muncie, Ind.: R. H. Cowan, 1903). Hill was brigadier-general of the Ohio Militia.

[51] Walter A. Clark, *Under the Stars and Bars* (Augusta, La.: Chronicle, 1900), 15-16; Hermann, *Memoirs of a Veteran*, 11, 19-39; *OR*, Ser. I, vol. 2, 224-27. On July 12 and 13 McClellan ordered Hill to start gathering his troops to cut off Garnett, who was being pursued by Morris. Later McClellan told Hill of the rout and of Garnett's death, pointing out, "You may never have such another opportunity again. Do not throw it away." McClellan had recommended Hill use Rowlesburg as his base for pulling together his army.

[52] Lee and Davis were notified by Major M. G. Harmon, who commanded a small Confederate force at Staunton, of the Confederate disaster and the need to protect the valley.

[53] Haselberger, *Yanks from the South*, 247-60; Savannah *Republicans*, July 30, 1861, *Southern Confederacy* (Atlanta), July 28, August 2 & 3, 1861.

[54] *OR*, Ser. I, vol. 2, 752-55; Sears, *Civil War Papers of George B. McClellan*, 66-67. McClellan was going to bring three or four regiments with him to Washington but was later instructed by Scott to come alone.

[55] Andrews, *The North Reports the Civil War*, 150.

[56] Once relieved of command, McClellan went to his home in Trenton, New Jersey, to await a new assignment. It never came. He was nominated for president by the Democratic Party in 1864 and resigned his army commission on election day.

[57] Fifty miles further south, the valley and railroad were vulnerable to Federal attack

from the James River and the Kanawha Turnpike. They were defended by the forces of Wise and Floyd. Today the spelling for Millborough is Millboro.

[58] All the mountains west of the Shenandoah were part of the Allegheny chain, but each range had its own name, such as Rich Mountain, Valley Mountain, Cheat Mountain, Greenbrier Mountain, and Allegheny Mountain.

[59] Joseph G. Carrigan, *Cheat Mountain* (Nashville, Tenn.: Albert B. Tavel, 1885), 46 (author unknown). On September 8, 1861, General Loring issued an order brigading the Army of the Northwest. Six brigades were created and divided into two divisions, the Hunterville Division under Loring and the Monterey Divison under H. R. Jackson.

[60] Freeman, *R. E. Lee*, vol. I, 546-58.

[61] In contrast to Confederate inactivity, Southern newspaper stated that Lee was on the verge of driving the enemy from western Virginia. When eyewitnesses arrived in Richmond and gave realistic assessments of the situation, press accounts turned pessimistic. Lee was confirmed as a full general on August 31, along with four others. This might have made Loring more receptive to Lee, who by early September had decided to attack the enemy. Hoping to avoid angering Loring, Lee had the order issued in the name of the touchy subordinate.

[62] Nancy N. Baxter, *Gallant Fourteenth: The Story of an Indiana Civil War Regiment* (Traverse City, Mich.: Pioneer Study Center, 1980), 49, 60-61; The Evansville *Daily Journal*, September 17, 1861; Hannaford, *The Story of a Regiment,* 104-10; Jack Zinn, *R. E. Lee's Cheat Mountain Campaign* (Parsons, W.Va.: McClain, 1974), 14-17, 23-31, 36-39, 49, 51-53, 127; *West Virginia History* (1984) vol. XLV, 165. Big Spring was three miles south of Lee's Valley Mountain camp. Old Elkwater was on the south bank of Hamilton Run and about a mile south of present-day Elkwater.

[63] Zinn, *Cheat Mountain Campaign*, 83-84, 125-27, 129.

[64] Thomas A. Head, *Campaigns and Battles of the Sixteenth Regiment, Tennessee Volunteers* (Nashville, Tenn.: Cumberland Presbyterian, 1885), 34-35. It is claimed that the "badge of white cloth prevented Anderson's brigade from attacking Donelson's at one time on the march."

[65] *Cheat Mountain*, 65-67.

[66] Marcus B. Toney, *The Privations of a Private* (Nashville, Tenn.: Printed for the author, 1905), 22-24; Zinn, *Cheat Mountain*, 65-67. The first pickets captured were four men in a small log cabin known as the Matthew house. A second stand of four pickets were captured (two tried to escape and were killed). From there Colonel John Savage led two companies to capture a company of pickets at the Simmons house.

[67] Head, *Sixteenth Regiment*, 36-40. General Donelson was informed by one of his guides that enemy pickets were on the road south of Old Elkwater, so he sent forth an advance guard. Led by a physician guide, Dr. Butcher, they captured the pickets and were told by a frightened prisoner that the rest of his company was in a nearby house. Upon approaching the house, Colonel John H. Savage of the Sixteenth Tennessee Volunteers shouted in a shrill voice to the enemy who were at the windows ready to fire: "Down with your arms or you will die! I'll blow out the last

man's brains who attempts to fire." (The actual wording differs among those who have written about the event.) In all, fifty-six prisoners were captured.

[68] *Daily Constitutionalist*, (Augusta, Ga.); August 24, 1801; Evansville *Daily Journal*, October 2, 1861; National Archives, Officer of the Adjutant-General, Volunteer Organizations of the Civil War Muster Rolls of Returns, Regimental Papers Record Group 94, Entry Box 862, 3642, 3645; Zinn, *Cheat Mountain Campaign*, 148-153, 173. Zinn points out that previous authors misinterpreted Kimball's report of 300 Federals engaging Rust as the total size of the Union force.

[69] Mills Lane, ed., *"Dear Mother: Don't Grieve about Me if I Get Killed; I'll Only Be Dead"* (Savannah, Ga.: Beehive, 1990), 53-56. John Levering, *Lee's Advance and Retreat in the Cheat Mountain Campaign* (Chicago, 1907), 29-34A. H. Noll, ed., *Doctor Quintard, Chaplain C.S.A. and Second Bishop of Tennessee* (Sewanee, Tenn.: University, 1905), 19-20; Zinn, *Cheat Mountain Campaign*, 187-92. The three shots that killed Washington were fired by Sergeant John J. Weiler (not Leiber as first reported), Corporal W. L. Brimly, and Private William F. Johnson. All were from Company E of the Seventeenth Indiana.

[70] Freeman, *R. E. Lee*, vol. I., 575; Zinn, *Cheat Mountain Campaign*, 167. When Confederates were firing upon each other, Ed Johnson, who commanded the Twelfth Georgia, at first did not believe their plea: "We are Georgians; stop firing." Johnson, riding toward the front of the column, yelled: "They are liars, boys. Pop it to 'em! Pop it to 'em!"

[71] John Lyon Hill, "Diary," Manuscript Div., Library of Congress, September 12-19, 1861; Clayton R. Newell, *Lee vs. McClellan: the First Campaign* (Washington, D.C.: Regnery Publishing, 1996), 174. Loring was wounded at Chapultepec during the Mexican War. When told the mangled arm would have to be removed, he is said to have taken the cigar out of his mouth, sat in a chair without any painkillers, and uttered not a sound as the limb was cut off.

[72] John W. Worsham, *One of Jackson's Foot Cavalry* (New York: Neale, 1912), 41.

[73] William D. Hamilton, *Recollections of a Cavalryman of the Civil War After Fifty Years* (Columbus, Ohio: F. J. Heer, 1923), 14-15.

[74] Ibid, 17-19; *OR*, Ser. I, vol. 5, 221-22. Reynolds' force consisted of Virginia Volunteers, 24th, 25th, 32nd, and Ohio regiments, the 7th, 9th, 13th, 14th, 15th, and 17th Ohio. About two and a half artillery batteries—Howe's, Loomis', and part of Down's—plus cavalry. The Union batteries fired over 1,500 shots and shells.

[75] Samuel Gillespie, comp., *A History of Company A, First Ohio Cavalry* (Washington C. H., Ohio, 1898), 22-23; Robert H. Moore II, *The Danville Eight Star New Market and Dixie Artillery* (Lynchburg, Va.: H. E. Howard, 1989), 6-8.

[76] Moore, *Rebellion Record*, vol. III, 162-165.

[77] Richmond *Dispatch*, October 12, 1861; *OR*, Ser. I, vol. 5, 220-36; New York *Tribune*, October 5, 1861; Savannah *Republican*, October 12, 31, November 1, 1861. Jackson sent a private letter to President Davis about the concerns stated to Benjamin. Benjamin responded that he, Davis, and Lee were satisfied with the performance of Jackson and his men. He added that the general should not be so thin-skinned about criticism.

[78] Joseph J. Reynolds would resign early in 1862 because of the death of his brother

and business partner. Henry R. Jackson resigned in early December to accept the command of a division of Georgia state troops.

[79] *OR*, Ser. I, vol. LI, 51. Milroy's command was comprised of the 9th Indiana Regiment (700); 25th Ohio (400); 2nd Virginia (250); 13th Indiana (300); 32nd Ohio (130); Bracken's Cavalry (30); and Rigby's artillerymen, who lacked weapons (75).

[80] Newell, *Lee vs. McClellan*, 258; *OR*, Ser. I, vol. 5, 463. Johnson's command consisted of the Twelfth Georgia, Fifty-second Virginia, Ross', Hansbrough's and Ryer's battalions, Lee and Miller's batteries, plus a detachment of the Pittsylvania cavalry.

[81] Hamilton, *Recollections of a Cavalryman of the Civil War After Fifty Years*, 23-25. Reinforcements to the Confederate right included four companies of the Twelfth Georgia and sixty-two men from the Twenty-fifth Virginia. Two of the Georgia companies and the Virginias were moving down the mountain from the crossroads when the fighting commenced. They were ordered to go to the right. The two other Georgia companies enforcing the right came from the trenches on Johnson's left.

[82] Hamilton, *Recollections of a Cavalryman of the Civil War After Fifty Years*, 13, 26-30; Robertson, *Stonewall Jackson*, 90, 233.

[83] Moore, *The Rebellion Record*, vol. III, 466-71.

[84] *OR*, Ser. I, vol. 5, 456-68; vol. LI, pt. 1, 51-54. Some Union regiments were transferred elsewhere, but they still outnumbered their opponents. Huntersville, with a large and relatively unprotected store, was an inviting target. A 750-man Union force took Huntersville (January 3, 1862) and burned the building that housed 350 barrels of flour, 150,000 pounds of salted beef from 300 cattle recently slaughtered, 30,000 pounds of salt, large amounts of sugar, coffee, rice, bacon, and clothing. The Federals were unable to carry off these items; their wagons had to be left behind because felled trees blocked the road to Huntersville. The 250 Confederates guarding the supplies at Huntersville fled to Monterey. There it was feared the enemy might come and cut the supply line to Camp Allegheny. When Monterey and Camp Allegheny were not attacked, Johnson sent several regiments to Greenbrier to check the rumor of large enemy forces there. They found no Federals, but rather fires that might have been lit as a ruse, several burned houses, and the fortifications at Camp Bartow that had been built by Confederates during late summer and were destroyed in fall of 1861.

CHAPTER VIII

WISE'S "RETROGRADE" AND FLOYD'S BLUSTER: THE UNION TAKES THE KANAWHA VALLEY

While McClellan was moving toward Garnett's divided forces at Laurel Hill and Rich Mountain, he ordered Jacob Cox to launch an invasion to the south in western Virginia through the Kanawha Valley. By traversing the James River and Kanawha Turnpike through the Allegheny Mountains, the Great Valley of Virginia could be reached, and the security of Staunton, Lexington, and the Virginia Central Railroad could be imperiled. Confederate authorities wanted to make sure this did not happen. Their top priority in Virginia—after keeping the Shenandoah Valley secure—was to secure the rich Kanawha Valley. This fertile agricultural region was also endowed with coal, lead, and salt. The latter was found on the Kanawha River three miles from Charleston. When the war started, the Kanawha region had been producing 2.5 million bushels of salt a year.[1]

Military leadership in the contest for the Kanawha Valley in 1861 primarily revolved around three political generals, Jacob D. Cox of the Union and two former governors of Virginia, Henry Wise and John Floyd. All three were strong-willed, but Cox would prove to be the most able military leader. The two Virginia politicos had huge egos and a dislike for each other that greatly contributed to their loss of the Kanawha Valley. Their feud, arrogance, and military incompetence made Cox's task easier and would taint Robert E. Lee's early reputation. Despite the Southern press's praise of Floyd, no genuine early war heroes for the South would emerge from the Kanawha campaign.

Only Southern frustration would ultimately emerge, as their three attempts in 1861 to secure the Kanawha Valley would lead to retreats.

THE FEDERALS TAKE THE KANAWHA VALLEY

The population of the region was divided. Many opposed secession and war, but some had strong loyalty to Virginia. They, like forty-three-year-old Christopher Quarles Tompkins, had reservations about secession, but they felt the war would be brief, and they cast their lot with the South. A graduate of West Point, Tompkins had spent more than a decade in the U.S. Army, fighting in the Mexican War before resigning to pursue business interests—first in Richmond and then in the region of Gauley Bridge. Several miles from the bridge, Tompkins built the most palatial home in the region, "Gauley Mount." The home sat on top of the mountain with a spectacular view of the confluence of the New and Gauley Rivers. Because of its location Gauley Mount would become a Union camp during 1861.[2]

Two residents of the Kanawha region, Lieutenant-Colonel John McCausland and Colonel C. Q. Tompkins, led the early mobilization in the region. In late April Lee sent McCausland—a graduate of Virginia Military Institute and one of the institute's cadets present at the hanging of John Brown—to take command of the volunteers and defend the region. A few days later, Tompkins was appointed colonel and was assigned this task, much to McCausland's displeasure. Tompkins found only five companies, totaling some 350 ill-equipped and poorly armed men. In early June, after a month of working to increase his numbers and after issuing a call to arms to the men of the Kanawha Valley and beyond, Tompkins was superceded by General Henry Wise.

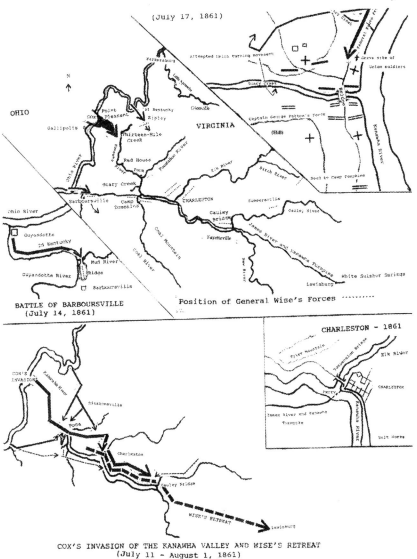

BATTLE OF BARBOURSVILLE
(July 14, 1861)

Position of General Wise's Forces

COX'S INVASION OF THE KANAWHA VALLEY AND WISE'S RETREAT
(July 11 – August 1, 1861)

TOP CENTER: THE START OF THE UNION THREE-PRONG INVASION OF THE KANAWHA VALLEY
(JULY – 1861)

The former governor was ordered to the Kanawha Valley with his small force, known as Wise's Legion. Upon arriving in the Kanawha region, Wise assumed command over the small force that was already there. Recruiting continued in the area; authorities hoped the recruiting effort would be greatly aided by Wise's enormous popularity in that region. Wise prepared to defend the region from a Union invasion. This preparation was a formidable task, in light of the troops' inexperience and insufficient arms; their only weapons were those they had carried with them. Despite calls in Charleston's *Kanawha Valley Star* for 12,000 men, by early June Wise had fewer than 3,000 men, mainly infantry.

Wise had limitations, but he also had ambitious goals. He planned to keep control of not only the Kanawha Valley but also the Little Kanawha. To this end, he made his headquarters at Charleston and concentrated two-thirds of his force in that area. The rest he scattered over a vast region. Some were spread out over a crescent-shaped line to the south and northeast from Gauley Bridge, Summersville, and the Birch River. Others were sent in three directions toward the Ohio River: Point Pleasant, Ripley, and Barboursville, all potential points of Union invasion and routes leading to Charleston. To lay claim to the Little Kanawha River valley and to protect his rear from Federals coming south to Gauley Bridge, some of Wise's army was sent to Glenville on the Little Kanawha and to Birch River, an Elk River tributary that flows toward Charleston. This led McCausland to grumble that Wise's "eyes were bigger than his stomach." By spreading his men, many of whom were ill-equipped and poorly trained, to cover a hundred miles, he had bitten off far more than he could reasonably defend.

The Kanawha River divided Wise's Charleston force. Nine hundred men under Captain George S. "Frenchy" Patton, the grandfather of George Patton of World War II fame, were west of the Kanawha near a tributary, the Coal River.[3] Patton's Camp Tompkins, on the James and Kanawha Turnpike, was ten miles from Charleston. This town and the turnpike that skirted the western banks of the Kanawha to Gauley Bridge were both accessible by a ferry.

Patton's force was positioned to meet any threat on the western forty-mile segment of the turnpike that extended from the southern bank of the Kanawha across from Charleston to the southern bank of the Ohio River at Guyandotte. East of the Kanawha River, around another tributary, the Elk River, sat Wise and about 1,600 men—of these he called only half of them "efficient."[4]

On June 29, Wise started shifting 800 of his men northward in an attempt to secure the area at Ripley. Federals had sent the Seventeenth Ohio Volunteer Infantry to the Ripley area to counter Confederate guerrillas. The men Wise sent were led by his son, Captain O. Jennings Wise, commanding the Richmond Blues, and Captain George S. Patton, who was in charge of the Kanawha Riflemen.[5] They encountered the Unionist militia of Cottageville, northwest of Ripley and near the Ohio River. The militia, led by a stuttering blacksmith in his late fifties, Captain James T. Hopkins, lay in wait on top of a hill to ambush the Confederates.

Hopkins' men fired an ineffectual volley, and when the enemy immediately returned fire, the home guards dropped to their hands and knees and crawled down the hill in the opposite direction. When they came to a rail fence, they refused to stand up for fear of being shot, so they butted the bottom rail out and continued down the hill, not standing up until shortly before they reached the Ohio River. The meager clash alerted McClellan of enemy movement in the Ripley region. He countered by ordering the 1,200 men of the Twenty-first Ohio Volunteer Infantry, under Colonel Jesse S. Norton, to go by a steamer from Gallipolis to Ravensworth to support the Union force, the Seventeenth Ohio, already there.

The Confederates responded by retreating southward toward Charleston and they were joined by General Wise at Sissonville. Wise marched his men back to Ripley to do combat. While again moving northward, Confederates spent a night lying on wet ground, being bitten by fleas and catching only a couple of hours of rest. Meanwhile, a frantic Colonel Tompkins, who Wise had left in charge of Charleston, wrote numerous communications pleading with Wise to return as Federals were posed to move from Gallipolis. But Wise was bent on defending Ripley and issued a proclamation to rally Southern supporters in the region. Finally, on July 8, Wise concluded that it would be prudent to heed Tompkins' pleas. He returned with his force after marching under boiling sun and intermittent drenching rain, stopping to spend the night in a field of fennel.[6]

Confederates fared no better in their excursion to Glenville. After driving in Union pickets, the Federal force drew up a line for battle at the courthouse, which enabled them to easily repel the Confederates, who then returned to Charleston

Brigadier-General Jacob D. Cox
He commands Union troops invading and forcing
Confederates under General Wise from the Kanawha Valley.
(Courtesy of the Library of Congress)

Only a small force remained at Birch River to keep an eye on Federals who could have moved south toward Gauley Bridge at Wise's rear.[7] Wise realized that his ambitious plans to defend western Virginia were unrealistic. He nervously waited as Cox launched his invasion of the Kanawha Valley on July 11. As the Federals approached his forces in this valley, Wise asked for more men and complained of Richmond's neglect. He lamented that not only was he facing a superior invading force, but he charged with a local Southern militia that needed so much help that he felt it was an impediment. He claimed the area he was defending was full of "snakes." "Copperhead traitors," Wise reported, filled the "grass of the soil" he was defending. He explained: "They invite the enemy, feed, and he arms and drills them…A spy is on every hilltop, at every cabin, and from Charleston to Point Pleasant they swarm. We will fight hard, retire slowly if we must, and make a last stand at Gauley." Wise continued, "[but] if we advance to meet the enemy at the north of the Kanawha he will," he predicted, come down "behind us from the north." Therefore any advance by Wise would enable the enemy to turn him either from the east or west.[8]

Wise's fears of being turned were valid. McClellan, in one of his early schemes, planned to do just that. Originally "Little Mac" had ordered Cox only to proceed up the Kanawha River and to hold Wise at Charleston until McClellan could take care of Garnett and then get behind the Confederates in the Kanawha Valley. A few days later Cox was ordered to secure positions along a 100-mile line on the Ohio River. From there, his force of over 3,000 men—five regiments from Ohio and Kentucky—was to move into western Virginia along three lines. The main column, made up of the Eleventh, Twelfth, and Twenty-first Ohio, crossed the Ohio River from Gallipolis to Point Pleasant and moved to Charleston and Gauley Bridge to reconnoiter the Wytheville area.[9] The northern column, the First Kentucky, crossed the Ohio to secure Ripley, which lay forty miles north of Charleston on the road that connected that town with Parkersburg.

More than forty miles south of Gallipolis, a third Union column, the Second Kentucky, moved from Guyandotte toward Charleston in a flanking movement to clear out any Rebels along the way. Both Kentucky regiments were filled mainly with Ohio longshoremen who were out of work because of the wartime end of river commerce. Although intrepid and not afraid to fight, they were a rowdy bunch and were difficult for their officers to control.

The three Union columns were to trap the Confederates and, in McClellan's words, "punish" the areas where Confederates were. McClellan told Cox, "drive Wise out and catch him if you can. If you do catch him, send him to [the] Columbus penitentiary."

Spies were sent ahead of Cox's soldiers to ferret out the enemy's location and plans. Lacking a Federal intelligence service, McClellan hired a famous private detective, Allan Pinkerton, to head the information gathering. Pinkerton sent one of his employees, Price Lewis, a British citizen in his late twenties, into the Confederate lines. The Southern pickets picked up Lewis and took him to Captain George Patton, who wined and dined him at Camp Tompkins (near present-day St. Albans). Patton eagerly revealed the details of what he claimed was his strong position, totally unsuspecting he was confiding in a Union spy.[10]

COX MOVES NEAR CHARLESTON

It was about seventy miles from Point Pleasant up the Kanawha River to Charleston. All but the last ten or so miles were navigable. It was over this route that Cox launched his invasion of the Kanawha Valley on July 11. His trip was facilitated by the use of river steamboats, which were abundant after having been put out of work by the war. Detached columns (two companies) marched along the roads near and on both sides of the river as protection for the boats moving up the Kanawha. Most of the troops were in the boats, behind the marching columns, but near enough to reinforce either bank in case of attack.[11]

The start of Cox's move from Ohio into Virginia at first seemed like a pleasure cruise. It was, in the general's words, "the very romance of campaigning." He took a position on "top of the pilothouse of the leading boat" so that, reported Cox, he "might see over the banks of the stream and across the bottom land to the hills which bounded the valley." It was a beautiful afternoon. Clouds drifted lazily above the picturesque scenery and the boats "dressed in their colors and swarmed with the men like bees." Cox wrote: "The band played national tunes and as" the boats upon the winding river "passed the houses of Union citizens the inmates would wave their handkerchiefs" and were answered by "cheers from the troups." All their senses were heightened and the "vividness of every sensation" was doubled from the danger of being in enemy country. "The landscape seemed more beautiful, the sunshine more bright, and the exhilaration of outdoors life more joyous than any" they had known.

Movement continued with relative ease the first five days. Leisurely travel was punctuated by brief stops at Thirteen-Mile Creek, Red House, and Pocataligo River.[12] At first hindrances were limited. As they moved toward Charleston low water and objects placed in the river by the enemy slowed progress at times, and Cox fretted over not receiving four additional artillery pieces, more cavalry, and more equipment, including wagons for land travel. All were badly needed. Many of his men had no tents; only thirty-eight of his horsemen had saddles.

On the fifth day, movement was slowed by constant skirmishing. Small bodies of enemy riflemen occupied the hills and did not leave until driven out by Federal skirmishers, who were armed only with altered muskets with limited range.[13] Wise's men were the worst equipped; many were armed only with old-fashioned flintlock muskets. By this point, only one Federal had been wounded in the skirmishing, and they suffered more casualties from their own men than from the enemy. Two deaths and one serious wounding took place in what Cox called an accident. Half the First Kentucky had joined Cox at Red House because Wise's threat to Ripley and the region around it seemed to be very slight. During the early night of July 15, Cox sent these men to meet the enemy, rumored to be nearby. The captain of the rear guard attempted to correct irregularities in marching by commanding, "Steady!" The men mistook his command for "Ready!" When someone in the rear—out of nervousness or carelessness—fired, some Federals assumed they were attached. Without waiting for orders, they fired toward the shot, inflicting casualties by friendly fire.[14]

THE "BATTLE" OF MUD RIVER BRIDGE OR BARBOURSVILLE

About thirty-five miles away, while Cox was moving toward the mouth of the Pocataligo, the five companies of the Second Kentucky under Lieutenant-Colonel George W. Neff started eastward from Guyandotte, or modern-day Huntington. After marching five miles to Barboursville, the 400 Union men engaged a larger enemy force in a lively skirmish at the Mud River Bridge.[15] Federals left their camp at Guyandotte at midnight on July 13.[16] The plan was for them to march through the night and, at dawn, surprise the enemy at Barboursville, but the five-mile trek took longer than anticipated. Movement was cautious, slowed when scouts were sent forward and the column was halted. The men were anxious to move forward, and so was their pro-Union physician guide from Barboursville. A few weeks earlier Dr. Litch had been rudely forced from his home by pro-Confederates. Now he was in a position to return the favor.

News that the Federals were coming alarmed the citizens of Barboursville. Wise had taken every opportunity to warn them and others in western Virginia to expect the worst from "murdering Yankees." Afraid of what might happen, the women and children of Barboursville fled to the nearby home of a benevolent elderly woman, Grandmother Blake. Certainly the leader of the approaching Federals, Colonel Neff, was not in a forgiving mood. Prior to the expedition he informed the wife of Captain Albert Gallatin Jenkins—the leaders of the Border Rangers, formed by men from Guyandotte and the farms on the southern banks of the Ohio—that if he caught her husband, he would hang him from a nearby tree. Mrs. Jenkins resolutely and calmly replied that if her captain caught Neff, he would treat him with civility and as a gentleman.[17]

Two hours after sunrise, the Union men neared the northern entrance to the covered bridge over the Mud River, very close to the confluence of the Mud and Guyandotte Rivers. What these Kentuckians saw was an intimidating sight. The enemy foot soldiers were perched on the end of a ridge that came up near the southern opening of the bridge. In the road near the hill, their horsemen scurried about, readying themselves for battle. The Confederate position seemed formidable.

Intrepidly—or foolishly—the Unionists continued forward. As they started into the bridge, the Southerners pulled the triggers of a variety of motley weapons: old flintlocks and blunderbusses, squirrel rifles, double-barrel pistols, and muskets, the latter firing buck and ball. The storm of lead killed one Federal and wounded a number of others. The whole Union column ran forward, seeking protection in the covered bridge—only to find that their foe had removed the floor planks at one end. Leading the group was their physician guide, who was soon clinging to a wooden support, barely escaping the fate of his mule, which had fallen to its demise through the opening.

Unable to continue into the bridge or to charge their enemy, the Federals were thrown into confusion, disorder, and panic. The unshielded Kentuckians frantically sought shelter under the bridge, behind the riverbanks, and behind some nearby brick kilns. The

Southerners, now convinced they were on the verge of a victorious routing of the invaders, screamed and cheered loudly; a few ran into the entrance of the bridge for a better shot at those seemingly trapped inside.

Then the unexpected happened. The Union men answered the rebels' yells with their own, some running to the openings of the bridge to fire at their foe, while the rest, wrote a Cincinnati *Commercial* correspondent who accompanied Cox's division, "made a dash in single file across the bare stringers and rafters of the bridge until the whole Federal force had crossed." As they ran from the bridge, they were met by a volley from the Confederates attempting to flank them, from those charging the bridge entrance, and from others on the road that "encircled the base of the hill." The Confederates' shots had been aimed too high. The Union men stormed on, relatively unharmed and brandishing a weapon that many of the untrained Southerners had never seen—the bayonet. Some mistook the sight of shining blades gleaming from the Yankee's muskets for an attempt to fire knives at them. One Southerner later remarked that he did not mind fighting with bullets, but when it came to "shooting butcher knives," he did not have anything similar to load in his weapon.

The Federals cleared the bridge as a disorganized and excited mass, "yelling and leaping like madmen." Soon they charged up the ridge with their bayonets, at times pulling themselves up by grabbing shrubs and bits of hillside. As the Confederates fell back up the ridge, the Union fired their last volley, and with effect: the Southerners fled. Panic gripped them. Most were only there to defend their homes as minutemen, and indeed, some of them fought for no longer than a minute. They ran southward and off the hill. Before the fighting one farmer had tied his horse to a tree in back of the ridge. After running off the hill and jumping on his mount, he beat his horse nearly to death in his frantic escape, forgetting that the horse was tied. While the Southerners fled, wrote the Cincinnati *Commercial* reporter, the Union men remained on top of the hill, too "breathless for pursuit, but cheering and immediately planting the Stars and Stripes on the summit of the hill."

Nearby a sixteen-year-old, Billy Miller, heard the firing. He had remained at home because his father had said he was too young to be a soldier. The sound of gunfire was more than he could endure. He grabbed his double-barreled pistol and ran for the ridge, thinking he would be the best armed of the combatants. Youthful enthusiasm, heightened by the passions of the moment, fueled a naivete that convinced him that he would put an end to the war with a weapon. He carried a weapon that, on occasion, when one trigger was pulled, would fire both barrels—at other times, both triggers were squeezed but neither barrel would discharge.

Nearing the hill, he saw Southerners fleeing, and without firing a shot, he was forced to retreat. Among the retreating men was another youth, Absolom Ballenger, who hobbled along, using his shotgun as a crutch. Ballenger had broken his leg during the retreat when he fell into the railroad tracks cut through the ridge. Billy asked Absolom if he had shot any Yankees. The limping youth said he doubted it because of the limited range of his small muzzle-loading shotgun. It fired only fine birdshot and had an effective range of perhaps only fifty feet. The able-bodied teenager helped the injured young man to Grandmother Blake's place. That night she took Absolom several miles by horseback to be ferried across the Guyandotte River. Once across, he hobbled to safety.

The Virginians had been fortunate to suffer only light casualties, with one man killed and three to five wounded. The fatality, recorded the Cincinnati *Commercial,* was an "old gray-haired man," James Reynolds. The Union was eager to believe that Reynolds and his companions in combat had been pressed into "service." The gravely wounded man had been left on the battlefield. He was taken to Barbourville and cared for by the Union, but he died there the day after the battle. Colonel J. J. Mansfield, the leader of the ill-prepared militia, was more fortunate. He was struck by enemy fire and fell from his horse during the retreat. Like most of the other wounded Virginians, he was carried to safety as most of the militiamen returned to their homes.

The victorious Federals, who had been less lucky in casualties suffering five deaths and eighteen wounded, occupied Barboursville soon after the fighting. They "marched through the town with their banners flying and the band playing" songs that were unwelcome to the ears of the remaining inhabitants, wrote the Cincinnati correspondent. One company "planted" its flag on top of the courthouse and happily mused that only two months ago it was presented to them and now "it was stream from a spire in one of the hotbeds of secession."

The Kentuckians soon left town and moved eastward in pursuit of the Confederate Rangers, who—unlike the militia—planned to fight again by taking up a position on Coal Mountain. The Union pursuit ended when they learned at Hurricane Bridge that their adversaries were planning to ambush them. The Union force marched northward to Winfield, then crossed the Kanawha to join Cox late on July 16.[18]

THE BATTLE OF SCARY CREEK

THE BATTLE OF SCARY CREEK
July 17, 1861

MAP A
UNION MOVE TO SCARY CREEK

A Union force under Col. Lowe travels five miles from Poca to Scary Creek. In the process they cross the Kanawha and move over two roads, driving back the Confederate pickets.

THE BATTLE OF SCARY CREEK
JULY 17, 1861:MAP A

The bad day at Barboursville was temporarily offset by meager and short-lived Confederate victories elsewhere. On the same day as the conflict at Barboursville, an outpost of Wise's men at Scary Creek fired upon and scared away a probing Union expedition that had been sent to the mouth the creek.[19] Two days later, on July 16, Wise had another minor victory over a small advance force of Cox's men near the Pocataligo, or Poca, River. During the Poca River skirmish, a Confederate force, numbering about 120 cavalrymen, routed several hundred Union infantrymen, driving them up mountainside.[20]

Shortly after the Poca skirmish Cox moved most of his force to Poca, (half the First Kentucky remained at Ripley and would not join Cox at Charleston until a week later). But Cox could not move forward until he cleared the enemy in front of him along both banks of the Kanawha and received the wagons he was constantly requesting. Wise was a dozen miles upstream on Tyler Mountain, five miles north of Charleston, on an eminence that commanded the Kanawha. West of the river and only three miles away at Scary Creek, there was a Confederate detachment.[21]

Cox sent a reconnoitering party on the morning of July 17 to size up the enemy on the western bank of the Kanawha. While moving through a cornfield near Little Scary Creek, the Federals fired upon and scared off two Confederate pickets. One fled in such haste that he lost his hat and false teeth. Both escaped unharmed to warn the small force at the Scary Creek Bridge and a larger body, under Captain Patton at Camp Tompkins, that the Yankees were coming.[22]

In the meantime, the reconnoitering Federals returned across the Kanawha and told General Cox that the enemy was strongly entrenched on the southern bank of Scary Creek near the bridge, very near to where the creek emptied into the Kanawha. They told him that the creek was not fordable at that site, but it was a little further up, offering the possibility that the Union might turn the Confederate force.

The Confederate position at the mouth of Scary Creek was virtually on the southern bank of the Kanawha River and, in normal times, was not as frightening as its name implied.[23] The steeply banked creek separated two hills. North of the stream lay fewer than a dozen log structures, including a church. Running through the small hamlet were two roads that merged into one in front of the northern end of an old wooden bridge and continued across the creek southward to the Kanawha River. These roads were scenic and not foreboding.

This was the scene for the three-hour battle of Scary Creek on July 17. On this hot, humid day, the Federals approached from the north and drove the advanced Confederates back across the creek to their main and entrenched position on the southern bank. After repeatedly firing at each other across the Scary, a failed Union attempt to take the bridge, and an unsuccessful flanking movement on the Southerners' left, the Federals nevertheless seemed close to victory when many Southerners panicked and fled. But the Confederates rallied, and their attacks—along with fatigue, shortage of ammunition, and failure to receive reinforcements—forced the Federals to withdraw from the field in the late afternoon. Even more surprising, the Confederates responded by doing the same, but soon returned to the battle site to claim victory.

THE BATTLE OF SCARY CREEK: MAP B

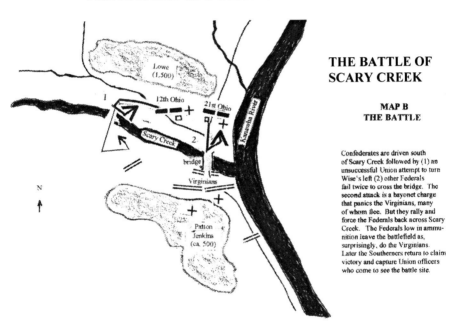

THE BATTLE OF SCARY CREEK

MAP B
THE BATTLE

Confederates are driven south of Scary Creek followed by (1) an unsuccessful Union attempt to turn Wise's left (2) other Federals fail twice to cross the bridge. The second attack is a bayonet charge that panics the Virginians, many of whom flee. But they rally and force the Federals back across Scary Creek. The Federals low in ammunition leave the battlefield as, surprisingly, do the Virginians. Later the Southerners return to claim victory and capture Union officers who come to see the battle site.

The battle began after troops moved to the battle site in the late morning and early afternoon. Southerners south of the Kanawha came from several directions to join the three companies of 200 men at Scary.[24] Their numbers were increased to about 500 with the arrival of Captains Patton and Albert Jenkins, the Kanawha artillery with two iron six-pounders, and three cavalry companies. Many of the cavalry were armed mainly with shotguns. Jenkins and one of the cavalry companies arrived late.[25] He had been detained by local ladies who had stopped him to give him a flag. The captain graciously accepted the banner and made brief remarks. He then took the only Southern flag to the battlefield, where it would be torn to pieces by enemy fire.

Before noon Colonel John W. Lowe and a force totaling 1,500 men, including his Twelfth Ohio regiment, two companies of the Twenty-first Ohio under Colonel Jesse S. Norton, a cavalry company, and two artillery pieces were ferried across the Kanawha to dislodge the enemy at Scary Creek.[26] Once across, they moved southward. Lowe and most of his men took a little-used inland road, Bill Creek Road, and the rest followed River Road along the banks of the Kanawha. Around 1:30 A.M. preliminary contact occurred.

Confederate pickets were driven from a log house at Little Scary Creek, and soon, Union cavalry did the same to pickets farther south at Scary Creek. While this was happening, Patton arrived from Camp Tompkins and deployed his men. He sent a couple of companies northward across Scary Creek. One company occupied the log structures that comprised the town of Scary and knocked out the clinking to make "loopholes" through which to fire.[27] Another company, the Kanawha Rifles, deployed as skirmishers in front of the oncoming Yankees. Around 2:00 the battle started in earnest as each side unlimbered their iron six-pounders and opened fire.[28] Both sides fired high at first. The Federal shots clipped off treetops as Confederates overshot the enemy but struck a woodpile behind a house, sending wood and splinters in all directions and convincing the Virginians that their opponents had breastworks. Artillerymen on both sides were soon killed. Such was the fate of the young and likeable John Haven, who had his thigh torn away by a Confederate solid shot as he was passing a ball to load one of the Union pieces.

When the artillery duel opened, all but one of the Union infantrymen fell to the ground. A member of the Twelfth Ohio, he hated to drill and habitually fell down, blaming his clumsiness on his toes. For some reason, he now remained standing as the rest of his company hugged the ground, grousing that this was what came of drilling: everyone was "killed dead" and he was the only one remaining to tell about it. After only fifteen to thirty minutes of firing, the Union artillery silenced the two Confederate pieces. One was put out of commission, and the other was moved to a safer place.

The primary objective of the Ohio troops after the silencing of the Virginians' artillery was to drive the Confederates from their position north of Scary Creek. The Union artillery then turned on the

346

log buildings to dislodge their inhabitants. Soon all Confederates north of the creek fled. The two sides now fired at each other from across the creek. Some of the Federals rolled over on their backs to reload, fighting in what they called "Indian style." A frustrated captain of the Twelfth Ohio, Ferdinand Gunkle, a Dutchman who always had difficulties in correctly issuing orders, yelled disjointed commands to his men. Finally, in desperation, he screamed, "do something quick." On the Southern side of Scary an elderly man with a double-barreled shotgun joined the Virginians. He would fire one barrel of his weapon and cheer Jefferson Davis and then, after discharging the other barrel, he would curse Abraham Lincoln. He continued this routine throughout the battle, but when asked afterward why he did it, he said he did not know.[29]

Once the Virginians had been cleared from the north of Scary, at 3:00 P.M. the Federals made their first of two attempts to take the bridge. The Southerners waited until the Ohio men, Colonel Norton's Twenty-first Ohio, were near the bridge, then poured a volley into them that made the Yankees take flight. The Federal officers conferred and decided that because of their shortage of ammunition, their second charge on the bridge would be with bayonets. This movement was to be complemented by a flanking movement. A detachment was ordered to cross upstream and hit the enemy's left.

Lieutenant-Colonel Carr B. White led two companies on the second assault on the bridge, assisted by the rest of the Twenty-first Ohio under Norton, firing from the houses. Some of the Ohioans in the frontal assault crossed the knee-deep stream near the bridge, where they were met by the Virginians in hand-to-hand combat. A small number of Union men were able to start attacking the Southern earthworks, which led to panic and flight in the majority of the Confederates who were not engaged. It now appeared the Federals were near victory. Patton rode to the front, attempting to rally his men, but his horse's unruliness caused many to misinterpret the movement as a signal to retreat. A few Virginians rallied, but after only fifteen minutes on the field, Patton was hit and was knocked from his horse, seriously wounding his left shoulder. Again the Confederates fled. The Union seemed close to victory once more.

Fortune soon changed. Captain Jenkins took command of the Southerners and rallied the men, who were being joined by new infantry and cavalry—many of whom rode mules. Despite the extreme-left Virginians' mistaking the new arrivals for the enemy and firing into them (wounding several), for the Confederates, desperation was being replaced by optimism.[30]

The new arrivals had brought a much-needed artillery piece called the Peacemaker. But even more fortunate for the Virginians was the stalling of Lowe's flanking movement. At least three companies were to cross under Major Jonathan Hines of the Twelfth Ohio, but only one did. Of the two captains and their companies who did not assist Hines, one captain hid behind a corncrib north of the creek while the other and his company got entangled in the heavy undergrowth and trees. They searched unsuccessfully for a fording place while the enemy fired upon them from the hill across the creek.[31]

Hines' lone crossing company posed no significant threat to the reinforced Southerners. The flanking movement had failed. The log church was now being turned into a hospital for the wounded Federals. Other Union soldiers were driven by extreme thirst from the heat and risked enemy fire to go to the creek for water. Also risking enemy fire was an English cook of one Union company, whom the men called Spider.[32] Known for his foraging ability, Spider noticed a flock of geese in between the Union and Confederate lines. The temptation got the better of his judgment, and he darted about after the geese while 100 Southerners fired at him. Onlookers were amazed to see him catch and carry off the geese he had wanted, unscathed by enemy fire.[33]

Lowe and his men looked anxiously for boats to bring help, but none came. The Union was short of ammunition and was discouraged by their inability to take the bridge or to find a crossing to turn their opponent. Of Union troops, fourteen had been killed, thirty were wounded, and twenty-one were missing, having retreated from the battlefield. Assuming that the Federals had merely pulled back before making perhaps an even stronger attack, Captain Jenkins pulled the Confederates from the field, leaving the battlefield unclaimed. Colonel F. Anderson, who had led the reinforcements from Camp Tompkins who had helped scare off the Federals, realized what had happened and re-occupied the field, claiming victory for the South. Wise's modest and short-lived victory would prove to be his most significant of the Kanawha Campaign, leaving five Southerners dead and twenty-six wounded.[34] It could have been a more substantial victory if he had not waited until late in the day to attack Cox's divided force at Poca.[35]

While the battle of Scary Creek was being fought, Levi Welch, a member of the Kanawha Riflemen (volunteers from the Charleston area), was on the rise on the Confederate left. The glittering steel of the enemy weapons across the creek and the effects and noise of those weapons were discomforting to him, and he sought refuge behind a large beech tree. As the fighting continued, the tree seemed to shrink. Welch, nevertheless, stayed behind it until Captain Albert Jenkins appeared, rallying the Virginians. The Captain's hat was off and blood ran down his hair and neck as he shouted for someone to get his horse tied behind the artillery. Welch left his tree and found the mount. When Levi rode forward, he came upon the dismounted Southern six-pounder. He immediately asked, "Where is my brother, Lieutenant Welch?" Soldiers pointed to a body with its head nearly severed. Shortly after the battle had begun, a piece of metal had flown into Levi's brother from the cannon he had been sighting after it was hit by an enemy shell.[36] As Levi stared at his lifeless brother, lying on the ground in the shape of a cross, he thought of the crucified Christ. One gave his life for humanity; the other, for his state.

Then remembering his duty, Levi took Captain Jenkins his horse. Embarrassingly for Welch, he was unable to remove one of his feet from its stirrup. Life-threatening bullets whizzed past him. Finally he cut the stirrup leather and rejoined his friend—the beech tree. Soon Welch heard a new sound: another Confederate gun, "the Peacemaker," had arrived and was belching scrap iron, chains, and broken horseshoes at the buildings across the creek from which the enemy was firing. Levi Welch survived the battle and was granted permission to return to his Coal River home to tell his mother the sad news of her son's death.[37]

The morning after the battle, as the Southerners started their day, Jenkins' Rangers walked to the bank of the Kanawha to splash water on their faces and wash their hands for breakfast. There they discovered a frightened Federal soldier hiding in a hollow tree. After breakfast, some of the Virginians started the unenviable task of burying the Union dead. Near the Kanawha River and Scary Creek they dug a pit six feet wide and twenty feet long, covered the bottom with straw, laid the bodies side by side, covered them with straw, and then covered the grave with the loose dirt they had dug from the hole. One Confederate summed up the job, calling it "rough…business."[38]

Cox was disappointed by the Federal retreat from Scary Creek, and he anticipated McClellan's wrath. Cox mused that if they had just "held on and asked for assistance" they "could have won." But, continued Cox, "as was common with new troops, they pass from confidence to discouragement as soon as they were checked and they retreated."[39]

The disappointing results were due in part to confusion during the battle. A messenger from Lowe's force had arrived at Poca with a request for more ammunition. But soon after Cox ordered reinforcements to be sent, a second messenger informed the general that a Union victory had been won. The premature news caused the response to the request for help to be canceled. Further, Cox was humiliated by three blundering colonels, William E. Woodruff, George W. Neff, and Charles A. DeVilliers, along with two captains. These officers were eager to see the battle site where they believed their side was victorious, and without first asking for permission, they were ferried across the Kanawha. Arriving after the combat was over, they rode up to some soldiers and congratulated them on whipping the rebels. To their surprise they were talking to the rebels. The officers were sent to Libby prison.[40]

The five officers were led to their capture by DeVilliers, a drill master in the Ohio regiment who was elected colonel of the Eleventh Ohio. He was a small Frenchman with quick movements. Cox at first had great expectations for DeVilliers. He was soon disappointed, referring to DeVilliers as "hare brained." The Frenchman's command had the same opinion, and they would regret his release from a Richmond prison and his return to their regiment. They resented his harsh discipline and vengefulness, as well as tendency to act like a conceited braggart, endlessly recounting his alleged superhuman military exploits. In combat he proved to be anything but bold, and was even cowardly. Finally, in 1862, his incompetence and the discovery that he had stolen goods and money led to his court martial, and he was cashiered from the army.[41]

The aftermath of Scary Creek left Colonel John Lowe embittered and anguished. He became the main scapegoat for the loss. Unnamed soldiers returning from the battlefield circulated allegations that Lowe was guilty of hiding behind a house during the battle and refusing to leave despite pleas from fellow officers. The story was printed in Ohio newspapers, but it proved to be untrue. Lowe was not guilty of cowardice—only of extreme caution. He had pulled his men back instead of waiting on the battlefield for ammunition to be brought to replenish his dwindling supply. But damage inflicted on the sensitive Lowe and his reputation could not be undone. He rode away from the Scary Creek battlefield looking for redemption of his sullied reputation. His risky opportunities in future combat would likely lead to his death.[42]

Cox's failure at Scary Creek, coupled with the capture of three colonels, did not sit well with McClellan. He fumed: "Cox checked on the Kanawha. Has fought something between a victory and a defeat…Lost two colonels, and a lieutenant colonel, who amused themselves by a reconnaissance behind the pickets…In Heaven's name, give me some general officers who understand their profession. I give orders and find some who cannot execute them unless I stand by them. Unless I command every picket and lead every column, I cannot be sure of success."

CONFEDERATES FLEE THE KANAWHA VALLEY

The disgruntled McClellan ordered Cox to stay put at Poca until Cox moved to Wise's rear and made everything right. Nevertheless, on July 24, Cox decided to renew his advance toward Charleston. Having received the much-needed wagons and teams, he could now move forward. Leaving one regiment to protect the steamboats at Poca, the rest of Cox's column headed north in a turning movement to get behind Wise's reported camp on Tyler Mountain. When the Federals were driving in Wise's pickets, the main camp became what Cox called a "panic-stricken force running off, leaving their camp in confusion, and their supper which they were cooking but did not stay to eat." From Tyler Mountain Cox's men went to the Kanawha River and found wheat sheaves being loaded on a steamboat, the *Moffet*. Cox recorded the events: Uniformed men on both sides of the river shouted to each other, "Who are you?" Cox's men replied, "United States troops," and from the other bank came, "Hurrah for Jeff Davis," followed by "a rattling fire from both banks." A shot fired from a Union cannon struck the steamboat, setting fire to it and sending Confederates scurrying from the vessel.[43]

In the meantime, Wise fled from the area. He knew the enemy was around him at Charleston and feared Garnett's defeat would enable McClellan to get behind him. Hoping to impede Cox's pursuit, the ex-governor had the cables cut of a suspension bridge that spanned the Elk River to Charleston. This slowed the Federals for only a brief time. They used the many empty coal barges that lay about to fashion a floating bridge and crossed the Elk into Charleston.

Events swirled around Cox as he entered Charleston. He received the following news: of Bull Run; of McClellan's promotion; of his new immediate boss, William S. Rosecrans; a telegram from the Ohio governor ordering him to send back the men of the Twenty-first Ohio, whose three-month enlistment was ending; and finally, that Wise was hastily retreating. After spending one day at Charleston establishing a supply depot and leaving the Twenty-first Ohio there until they could be relieved, he took off after Wise with his remaining four regiments. This act was in violation of both McClellan's and Rosecrans' orders for him to stay at Charleston. Cox later claimed he had received the latter order after he had already left Charleston. He claimed to have been acting on his belief that secretly both McClellan and Rosecrans really wanted him to seize Gauley Bridge. Even stronger was the motivation to save his reputation. To stay put would make him appear to be a failure.

The problems Cox faced while he moved toward Gauley Bridge were internal and did not come from the enemy. After eating supper and marching eleven miles on the first day, he was greeted at his tent by three regimental commanders, who, Cox wrote, informed him "they had concluded that it was foolhardy to follow the Confederates into the gorge . . . and unless...[Cox]could show them satisfactory reasons for changing their opinion they would not lead their commands" any further. They went on to say they meant no disrespect, but since Cox's military experience "was about as extensive" as their own, "they thought...[Cox] ought to make no movements but on consultation with them and by their consent." The green officers were shocked and were quickly subdued by Cox's response. He informed them that their lack of understanding of military protocol prevented them from realizing that "their actions were mutinous." Cox continued: "If they apologized for their conduct and showed earnestness in military obedience to orders, what they had now said would be overlooked," but any such recurrence would lead to their arrest and court-martial.

Several newspapermen were subdued less easily. Two correspondents from prominent eastern newspapers joined Cox at Charleston. They requested that the army supply them with tents and transportation and make them Cox's volunteer aides, with military rank. When they were told that any stories they wrote would have to be approved to prevent information from being revealed to the enemy, they declared that unsatisfactory. Apparently even less pleasing to them was being told Cox did not have the authority to grant them military rank. They renewed their request as the Union force neared Gauley Bridge and were again rejected. Angered, they replied "Very well, General Cox thinks he can get along without us, and we will show him. We will write him down." The two men immediately left camp and wrote their papers, describing Cox's army as "demoralized, drunken" looters of civilians, "without discipline, in a state of insubordination," and with a commander who was "totally incompetent." Cox was greatly vexed by what he saw as unfair and "baseless slander" of his men and feared it would put his military career in jeopardy. His term of service "as a brigadier-general of the Ohio troops had ended," he wrote. Unless the U.S. Senate confirmed his appointment as a U.S. officer, his military career would be over, and embarrassingly so, but this fear was averted: his appointment was confirmed. Cox was greatly helped by the praise he received from McClellan and Rosecrans, both of whom praised Cox for having taken control of Gauley Bridge.[44]

Once Cox arrived at what was called the gateway to southwestern Virginia, his internal problems were far from over. Men of the Second Kentucky mutinied by refusing to dig earthworks. When an officer of the Second Kentucky, a Lieutenant Gibbs, shot and killed their leader, a Sergeant Joyce, the remaining protesters ran for their muskets to kill the lieutenant. When Cox intervened, they pointed their weapons at him and threatened to shoot. Luckily for Cox, the incident ended with his gaining the upper hand. Lieutenant Gibbs was later acquitted of murder in a military court headed by Rutherford B. Hayes.

Cox felt fortunate to take Gauley Bridge on July 29 without resistance. He covered the thirty-six miles from Charleston at the rate of twelve to fifteen miles a day. Wise had not taken advantage of the rough, overgrown terrain the turnpike ran through during the last twenty miles; it could have been used to bring the Union advance to a standstill. Fearing that Federal troops from the north could get behind him by the road through Summersville to Gauley Bridge, Wise continued his hasty retreat until he reached White Sulfur Springs.

To hinder enemy pursuit, Wise decided to burn the covered bridge over the Gauley River.[45] Before the bridge had burned, he ordered his men to move their camp and supplies across the river to the east bank. As they traveled over the 190-yard structure, they could see several men tarring the sides to make it burn rapidly. Soon a heavy rainstorm struck, soaking their baggage and muddying their tents, forcing some to seek refuge under the rocky ledges by the road south of the bridge. Among those under the cliffs were A. B. Roler and the University Volunteers, students from the University of Virginia who had left school on Independence Day to fight for their state. What noble thoughts about war Roler and his college friends might have had were now being tested. Roler felt the confusion and disorder could not have been worse if the enemy had been upon them.

Two days before Cox reached Gauley Bridge, Wise moved southward. There were few wagons to evacuate supplies. Most baggage was abandoned. For half a mile, the side of the road east of the bridge was strewn with pots, coffee pots, and tents. Soldiers took only what they could carry on their backs. Large sides of bacon were thrown in the mud and trod upon. The ends of molasses and whiskey barrels were bashed in to prevent the contents from falling into enemy hands. Wise's men helped themselves, however, before pouring the contents of the barrels into the river. Fifteen hundred stands of arms and a considerable store of ammunition would find their way into Union hands. At least one company—and possibly two—went home. Another scattered on the march like frightened animals, leaving their captain to march alone. Finally the captain broke his saber in disgust and thereafter would not wear his bars.

Soon after leaving Gauley Bridge, Wise told a captain to halt his company. The general granted furloughs to any man who wanted to retreat by way of his home. The captain later entered Lewisburg with only ten men out of a company of ninety. Many of the men were from the Kanawha region and had joined only to protect and fight in that valley.[46]

The departing troops left behind the stone abutments that had once supported Gauley Bridge, an elegant structure of weatherboard with a shingled roof. At about 11:00 on the damp Saturday night of July 27, the bridge was torched. In a matter of minutes it was engulfed in flames as the sounds of marching men echoed in a darkness so extreme that it was hard to see the road. In the dark night, the glow of the flames could soon be seen for miles. The southeast wind forced the smoke both underneath and over the roof of the structure before it bellowed skyward. Onlookers thought it was a beautiful or eerie sight. One witness, Roler, reflected upon the waste of war. The bridge, which had been constructed in 1850 for the costly sum of at least $30,000, had been a vital link connecting the Kanawha and the Shenandoah Valleys; this link was being sacrificed to war.[47]

The sixty-four-mile march to Lewisburg from Gauley Bridge, and then on to White Sulphur Springs, nine miles more, was not an easy one. Wise's legion frequently faced food shortages, and men sickened with measles. Both problems began while they were in the Charleston area. The weary men were poorly clad and were fatigued by the march, but they doggedly moved toward Lewisburg. Their discomfort was intensified by the elements: they were covered in dust and were, alternately, soaked to the skin by drenching rains that forced them to sleep in wet blankets. Roler had expected his war experiences to be difficult at times. But this was worse then he imagined, and he had yet to be in combat.

Roler and others in Wise's legion had their spirits lifted by the announcement that once they arrived in Lewisburg they would finally be paid and uniformed. When they arrived in Lewisburg on August 1, it was raining once again. The men were quartered in the fairgrounds. Many slept, disagreeably, in stalls that horses had recently left. Nevertheless, they found the area of Lewisburg and nearby White Sulphur Springs beautiful, enhanced no doubt by their recent travels through rough mountainous terrain. It pleased them men to see relatively flat and rolling land.

The men of Wise's command started retreating from Charleston on July 24 and continued Wise's so-called retrograde until the first of August. They had tramped over 110 wearisome and footsore miles, ending the Confederate failure in their first and rather feeble attempt to secure the Kanawha Valley. The sensitive Wise was extremely touchy about hearing his "retrograde" being called a "retreat." Upon overhearing one of his men talking about Wise's retreat from Gauley, the fiery general exploded, shouting at the private: "Retreat!! Never dare call it a *'retreat'* again sir. It was only a *'retrograde'* movement, sir." Unflustered, the soldier responded, "I don't know nothin' about your retrogrades, General, but I do know we did some damn tall walking."[48]

The rugged terrain of western (West) Virginia
is shown in this sketch of the 12th Ohio climbing Gauley Mountain.
(Courtesy of the Library of Congress)

Wise's men had only a two-week respite. But during that time they enjoyed themselves. William C. Reynolds of the Kanawha Rifles and men of other companies, such as college student Roler, spent days seeing the local sights and "rolling tenpin." After a week at White Sulphur Springs, Reynolds finally got around to unloading the rifle-musket he had carried, loaded, since the battle of Scary Creek on July 17. It was not all fun. After several days upon arriving at White Sulphur Springs, they had to adhere to some of the military regimen of the day. Recreational activities had to be pursued in between military duties such as drills, inspections, and dress parades.[49]

Brigadier-General Henry A. Wise
He deeply resents Floyd's being given command of the Confederate forces
in southwest Virginia. Wise's defiance and feud with Floyd leads to his
removal at Sewell Mountain. (Courtesy of the Library of Congress)

Brigadier-General John Buchanan Floyd
His lack of military competence, feud with Wise, and retreats (despite
boastful threats of soundly defeating the enemy) are significant factors in
Confederate failures in southwest (West) Virginia.
(Courtesy of the Library of Congress)

SQUABBLING GENERALS AND THE FIRST SOUTHERN ATTEMPT TO REGAIN THE KANAWHA VALLEY

The Confederates made two attempts to regain the Kanawha Valley. This resulted in military action around the tributaries of the Kanawha River: Gauley River, Meadow River (which flows into the Gauley), and New River. Their meandering beds cut through mountainous terrain, forming the outline of a hooded and humpbacked man. At the man's forehead was Gauley Bridge, the main Federal base, where the confluence of the Gauley and New Rivers formed the Kanawha River. The Confederates' first attempt to regain the Kanawha Valley was contested on land forming the man's hump to his waist. The second attempt consisted of military action to the west, in front of the torso and face. For example, Floyd's first attempt ended with a small victory at Cross Lanes, followed by a retreat from Carnifex Ferry, both near the hump, to the Sewell Mountain region, or the waist of the man. There the terrain, rain, mud, and cold reduced combat to sputtering skirmishes and made supply lines extremely difficult to maintain. These conditions forced Rosecrans to pull back through the torso to the head of the configuration to Gauley Bridge and the vicinity. Floyd responded by making an unsuccessful second attempt to kick the Federals out by moving northward, west of New River, and in early November, occupying Cotton Hill, which faced the head of the figure of the hooded man. Despite sporadic harassment of the Federals by Confederate artillery and some sniper activity, Floyd soon beat a hasty retreat, fearing entrapment. No major battles had been fought, only skirmishes on Cotton Hill, Laurel Creek, and McCoy's Mill.

The Southerners' first attempt to gain back the Kanawha Valley was a short-lived endeavor during the latter half of August and the first half of September. Their attempt fell far short of penetrating the valley or of even taking back Gauley Bridge. The attempt to turn Cox's key position at the bridge would fail, with the Confederates again retreating, this time to Sewell Mountain. Their defeat was only partially the result of Rosecrans' coming to Cox's aid. A major factor was the recalcitrant Wise's refusal to cooperate with Floyd, the man who had assumed command over him and their united forces.[50] The bickering between the two, coupled with their lack of military acumen, would doom any chance of military success.

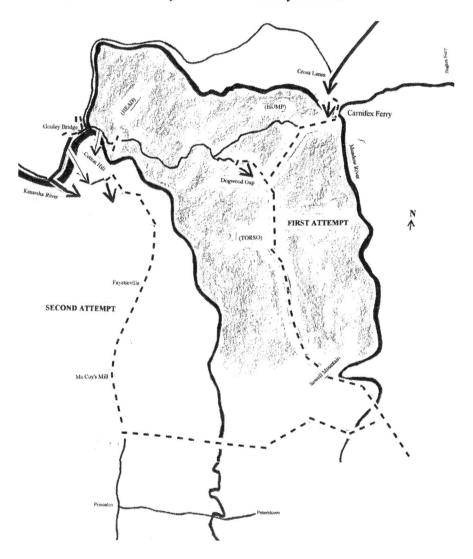

THEATER OF FLOYD'S TWO UNSUCCESSFUL
ATTEMPTS TO REGAIN THE KANAWHA VALLEY
(SEPTEMBER TO NOVEMBER 1861):
The Hooded Humpback Man Configuration

Floyd's reputation had been severely sullied by his less-than-prudent acts as secretary of war in the Buchanan administration. He sold government property for far less than its true value, approved padded bills of contracting friends who used them as collateral for bank loans and negotiable bonds from the government's Indians Trust Fund, and attempted to transfer over 100 cannons from the North to the South. When Floyd's financial indiscretions became known in December 1860, at the start of the secession crisis, Buchanan allowed him to resign. Floyd had strongly opposed secession until after his resignation. Whether Floyd was just inept or whether he was part of a planned conspiracy has been debated.[51]

Critics contend that Floyd only became governor of Virginia in 1849 because his father had preceded him in that office. One point was clear: John Buchanan Floyd lacked both sound judgment and administrative ability. Combine these flaws with his sluggish work habits, and he was hardly the man to save the Kanawha Valley or to deal with the dissentious Wise, whom he only outranked because he was commissioned three days earlier than the more recently former governor.

Floyd and Wise, long political rivals, detested each other and found it offensive to be near the other. Early in the war Floyd became livid when he learned that Wise had been sent to western Virginia. The former U.S. Secretary of War daily spewed profane denouncements of Wise: "G-- d--- him, why does he come to my country? Why does he not stay in the east and defend his own country…. I don't want the d--- rascal here; I will not stand it."[52]

As Wise was completing his retrograde on August 1, John Floyd wrote Jefferson Davis, lamenting the loss of the Kanawha Valley and the threat this loss posed to the whole southwestern part of the state. The enemy must be driven out of the Kanawha, and then, he continued, "a foray of 80 or 100 miles into Ohio could be successfully made." This, he went on, could be "speedily done" if his forces were united with Wise's.

Lee was also concerned about Wise's pullback and the possibility of any further retreat. He told the general, "Uniting with General Floyd was for the protection of Virginia Central Railroad." "Are there any strong positions in front of Lewisburg," Lee asked, "where you and Floyd can stop any enemy advance?" Wise responded that he pulled back not to protect the railroad, but to save his force.

He left to keep from being trapped. He claimed that he could not have remained in a region where, he said, "the treasonable population are worse than the invaders." According to Wise, there were several strong positions in front of Lewisburg, but before any movement could be undertaken, a week or ten days was needed for reorganization. His force had been lessened by desertion, had been racked by sickness, especially measles, and desperately needed "1,000 stand of good percussion smooth-bore muskets," portable forges to make shoes for his horses, and many other items.[53]

Unlike Floyd, Wise was anxious to move and take back the Kanawha Valley. On August 8, while preparing to move, Floyd asked Wise the numbers of men, wagons, arms, and ammunition he could supply. Wise said he would need ten more days before moving and elaborated on the problems he had earlier stated to Lee.[54]

Soon after the end of his "retrograde," Wise asked Floyd to come to see him. Floyd came and was treated to a long historical lecture. Wise stood, placed his hands on the back of a chair, and for two hours traced the history of the United States from its origin through the Revolutionary War, the Mexican War, and the causes of the war that had started in 1861. He also included his march to the Kanawha Valley, the Battle of Scary Creek, and his retrograde to White Sulphur Springs. Finally Wise asked Floyd, who had listened patiently, where he was going. Floyd pointed to the road over which Wise had retreated and said, "Down that road." Wise then asked, "What are you going to do Floyd?" "Fight," came the response, implying that Floyd was about to do what Wise had failed to do. "If a look could kill," said Henry Heth, who was present at the meeting, "Floyd would have been annihilated, for I never saw greater hatred condensed in a look before or since." Floyd then rose from his seat, bowed, and left.[55]

Wise's primary concern was not getting back Gauley Bridge and the land beyond it, but preventing his command from being united with Floyd's 1,200-man force. Repeated and lengthy requests, one of which was 2,500 words long, were made to Lee, complaining of Floyd's disrespectful treatment and his attempts to destroy Wise's force by trying to detach units with his own. But Wise's ultimate plea was for Lee to separate the two commands. Lee politely rejected each request, stating that separate commands would greatly diminish their chance of success. In turn, Wise demanded that all orders from Floyd to any member of his command must first come through him. Because Wise was forty miles away, Floyd ordered Wise to revoke the order, as it would only lead to what he called "embarrassment." Efficiency demanded that he be able to communicate with the officers of Wise's command who were nearer and working with him. Wise fired back that the order was "not revoked."[56]

As the two bickering generals moved their force of about 3,200 men and eleven artillery pieces in an attempt to trap isolated Union forces in the Gauley Bridge area, Jacob Cox took steps to defend himself.[57] He spread his force over a wide area, blocking the three main roads to Gauley Bridge to prevent his force from being turned and, at the same time, to look formidable. "Small bodies of horse" were also sent to scour the country for fifty miles or more to the front of his camps and outposts.

Cox placed half his force, two regiments, at Gauley Bridge, which he called the "gate to both the Kanawha Valley and southwestern Virginia and the Virginia and Tennessee Railroad." A small settlement hugged the northern side, where the Gauley and New Rivers met at right angles to form the Kanawha. The hamlet, wrote Cox, consisted of "a cluster of two or three dwellings, a country store, a little tavern, and a church irregularly scattered along the base of the mountain facing the road" that led to Charleston. The merging rivers that cut through the mountains walled in the village. Behind the houses, on the slopes where Cox placed his camp, were cultivated and pasture fields separated by hedgerows. Behind the camp, the gentle slopes gave way to precipitously rising "wooded steeps" punctuated by rocky precipices. "Nothing could be more romantically beautiful," Cox wrote, "than the situation" of the Gauley Bridge post.

The other two regiments of Cox's command were put in outposts in three directions on the roads to Gauley Bridge. Men were placed along the road that ran from the Gauley River to Cross Lanes and Carnifex Ferry, more than twenty miles away. This road continued northward, reaching Summersville and Weston. It was nearly the only line of communication between Cox and the Union command in the northwest, especially with Huttonsville, detachments at Cheat Mountain pass, and Elkwater pass.

A mile south of Gauley Bridge, at scenic Kanawha Falls, where mills were constructed on each bank, Cox placed men at the sawmill on the south bank, at the base of Cotton Mountain (Cotton

Hill), on the road that led to Fayette Court House. A ferry connected the outpost at Kanawha Falls with the main force at Gauley Bridge.

The remainder of Cox's men were positioned several miles from Gauley Bridge at Gauley Mount, Devil's Elbow, and Hawk's Nest, along the New River on the road that eventually led to Lewisburg. These outposts were connected with Gauley Bridge by a ferry that was guided by a cable stretched along the burned bridge's piers. From Gauley Bridge for miles eastward, the New River was walled in by Gauley Mountain to the east and Cotton Hill to the west. From Gauley Bridge for several miles there was hardly room for the road that meandered between the wall of rock and the New River. After several miles the road finally reached what Cox called "rolling uplands." Here Colonel Tompkins built his palatial home, Gauley Mount, with large porches and a huge, well-cared-for lawn that sloped from the house to the barns, stables, and slave quarters.[58]

Tompkins' wife, Ellen, and his children remained when the Federals occupied his home. Tomkins was anxious about his family's fate, and on the day after Gauley Bridge was burned, he wrote to General Cox, asking him to protect his family. Cox did so in the most gentlemanly manner. He placed twenty men to guard the house and protected the livestock and crops from pillage, despite repeated threats by men of the Second Kentucky. Ellen Tompkins described these rowdy riverboat men as villainous cutthroats, an apt description of the men who had threatened to burn her house, destroyed her property, and sadistically described her husband's horse to her and boasted that shots from 100 guns would soon kill the Southern colonel. The bright, charming, and quick-witted woman remained poised through all of this. Cox liked to stop at Gauley Mount to exchange pleasantries with its mistress. Rutherford B. Hayes, a judge advocate and future president, was far less impressed, however; he later came to the Tompkins house to hold court-martials. He was angered and appalled to see Federals guarding and protecting the property of a former U.S. soldier, now an officer in the enemy's army. Soldiers in the tents outside the main house were convinced that Ellen Tompkins was spying for the Confederates. Cox felt this was highly unlikely.

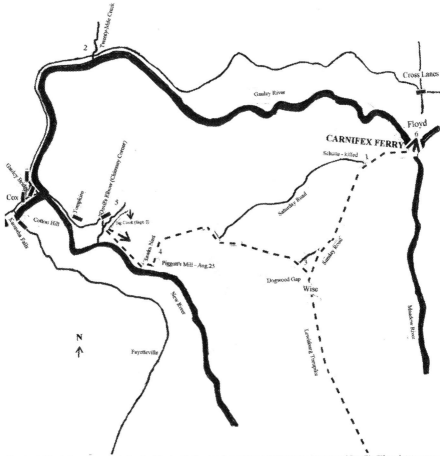

Floyd and Wise believe Cox, who is dug in at Gauley Bridge, the foot of Cotton Hill, Gauley Mount, and Devil's Elbow is too strong to attack. The Confederates plan to turn him by way of Carnifex Ferry. Watching Cross Lane and the ferry is the 7th Ohio (Tyler). (1) A reconnaissance party goes south of Gauley River on August 20, and are ambushed and their leader (Captain Schutte) is killed. (2) The same day Cox orders the 7th Ohio to pull back to Twenty-Mile Creek (They return to Cross Corners four days later). Bickering between Wise and Floyd contributes to confusion and disjointed movements. Both Wise and Floyd move toward Carnifex Ferry, leaving their rear in Dogwood Gap unprotected. (3) Wise hurries back to the gap to correct the error. (4) Without telling Wise, Floyd sends cavalry in front of Wise that is routed in a skirmish at Piggott's Mill on August 25. (5) On November 2, Wise attacks the Union camp at Big Creek (Devil's Elbow), but withdraws after his flanking party gets lost and returns. (6) Wise has strongly disapproved of Floyd crossing the Carnifex Ferry (August 20) and setting up camp (Camp Gauley). Cox now fears a dual attack by both Confederate forces. Instead Floyd fails to move toward Gauley Bridge after his victory at Cross Lanes (August 20) as Rosecrans with a sizeable force marches from Clarksburg to rescue Cox.

CONFEDERATES MOVE AGAINST COX TO REGAIN KANAWHA VALLEY
August and September 1861

Ellen Tompkins was not only intelligent, but also plucky. She was intrepid in protecting her property, with Cox's help, while informing a Federal officer that the Union force was like Moses: it would be able to glaze into the promised land from a distance, but Cox and his men would never be allowed to enter into eastern Virginia. Later in December, General Rosecrans, who also befriended her and was sympathetic to Ellen's plight, felt that her security demanded that he send her away to Richmond, as Floyd was using artillery to fire upon Gauley Mount. After Ellen departed, the house was looted and was later burned, just as she had feared.[59]

To protect the Federals at Gauley Mount, Cox placed his advance guard at Devil's Elbow and placed pickets at Hawk's Nest. Devil's Elbow (Chimney Corner) is only a mile or so from Gauley Mount where the turnpike bends around a high peak to the right. With a defile on the left created by Big Creek, it was a strong defensive position.[60] Several miles further at Hawk's Nest, overlooking the New River, walled in by vertical mountain cliffs many hundreds of feet high, a few Union soldiers watched for approaching enemy.[61] The grandeur of the view caused prisoners of war to request that their captors take them there for a quick visit.[62]

The rugged terrain presented a logistical nightmare. For almost sixty miles from Gauley Bridge southward, the land lacked sufficient cultivation of crops to sustain significant bodies of troops. The Union had to bring supplies from Charleston, and the Confederates brought theirs from Lewisburg, over steep roads muddied by fall rains. The trip was exhausting to both horse and man, with the former only able to pull half-filled wagons. Political loyalties were divided in this region, giving rise to extensive guerrilla warfare. Parts of the area were so isolated and remote that Cox's scouts found families in the hollows who had never seen the U.S. flag or traveled more than a few miles from their homes in their entire lives—and that was to go to a store or church .[63] Cox's position was a difficult one. Isolated at Gauley Bridge and nearby areas (the front of Cotton Hill, Gauley Mount, and Devil's Elbow), he fortified his position with earthworks and his few artillery pieces while eight companies vigorously patrolled at Sewell Mountain to make it seem to the approaching enemy that they faced a formidable force.[64]

He was successful in bluffing off his enemies. Floyd and Wise were convinced that Cox was too strong to be attacked in front of Gauley Bridge. They decided the best plan would be to turn him by moving northward to Carnifex Ferry. Who exactly was to do this was unclear. Wise contends that they agreed that he would move on

Carnifex Ferry over Sunday Road, which branched northeast off the turnpike about five miles before Hawk's Nest. Wise was to surprise and remove any Federal force in the vicinity of Carnifex Ferry.[65]

If the opportunity presented itself, Wise was to cross the Gauley River but to proceed no further without Floyd's permission. In the meantime, Floyd was to remain at Dogwood Gap to check any move by Cox's men, who could threaten their rear along with the turnpike to Lewisburg. Wise proceeded toward Carnifex Ferry, making sure his men did not light fires for cooking, for fear of alerting the enemy. Their trip was unpleasant, with little to eat and with inclement weather endured by men already weakened from measles.[66] The men marched seventeen miles in ankle-deep mud and through incessant rains before reaching Carnifex Ferry. There they were preparing fires to cook their meals when General Floyd, who had taken another road, arrived with his entire brigade. A livid Wise blamed Floyd's unexpected move for alerting the enemy force at the ferry, who retreated after they had destroyed the boats. What was worse, all the Confederates were now at Carnifex Ferry, leaving the main turnpike in their rear vulnerable to the enemy, men who could now cut Wise and Floyd entirely off from Lewisburg as well as seize the baggage and artillery that had been left behind.

After Wise was ordered to leave much of his artillery and cavalry with Floyd, he marched the rest of his command back to Dogwood Gap over Sunday Road to where it intersected with the turnpike, about fifteen miles west of Gauley Bridge. The next day Colonel Tompkins' two regiments arrived from Lewisburg and joined Floyd at Carnifex Ferry. Floyd raised one of the sunken boats and crossed the rope ferry to the other side of Gauley River. But in doing so the flatboat sank, drowning four of his men and leaving him, as Wise contemptuously pointed out, exposed and stranded across the river.[67]

The relationship between the two ex-governors of Virginia continued to deteriorate. Wise was preparing to send another regiment and additional artillery, as requested by Floyd, when he heard firing. Investigating the situation, Wise found 150 or more of Floyd's cavalry under Colonel Jenkins, who, without alerting Wise of his movement, had wandered over Saturday Road into an enemy ambush near Piggott's Mill, near Hawk's Nest. Fortunately for Jenkins' men, the Federals started firing prematurely; they had not totally enveloped the Southern horsemen. At least one of the Confederates was killed, and a dozen or so were wounded. Three horses were lost, along with some equipment and twenty hats. Many of the hats had been thrown away while the panic-stricken cavalrymen were fleeing eastward; there they ran into Wise and his men, who were approaching from four miles from the battle site. The general shouted at the fleeing horsemen to stop. Even threats to shoot them with his pistol had no effect. The enemy, however, withdrew back to their strong position at Devil's Elbow. Wise considered the episode another insult by Floyd: how dare Floyd take Wise's cavalry while sending his own cavalry back into the area commanded by Wise, without notifying him?[68]

The saga of confusion and misadventure continued. Cox felt isolated and vulnerable. What artillery he had was now manned by an infantryman, as the regular artillerists had been called back to Ohio. Rosecrans told Cox to hold on until he could arrive to "crush" the enemy. In the meantime, Rosy (Rosecrans' nickname) sent the Seventh Ohio to Cross Lanes (Kesler's Cross Lanes), where the road from Summersville to Gauley Bridge intersected with the roads to Carnifex Ferry. Colonel E. B. Tyler's Seventh Ohio troops were to protect and warn Cox of any attempt by the enemy to turn him.

The Seventh arrived at Cross Lanes on August 15 and camped on a rise just east of the intersection called Malcolm Heights. Company K was sent more than four miles south to guard Carnifex Ferry. To locate the approaching enemy, the captain of Company K, John F. Schutte—dressed in civilian clothes of a black coat and hat and black-and-white-checked trousers tucked into his boots—and a dozen and a half of his men went on a reconnaissance on August 20. After crossing the Gauley, Schutte and his men proceeded several miles down the Sunday to Saturday Road, where their probe ended. They ran into a Confederate ambush. Captain Schutte and several men tried to escape by running back down the road they had traveled down when a bullet struck Schutte in his back, exiting near his navel. Several men helped their captain to a nearby log cabin, where he pleaded, prayed, and ordered all to leave him, as his wound was mortal. All but Edward Bohn and Schutte escaped by the back door. When the Confederate cavalry neared the cabin, Bohn, who would not leave his captain, told them they could enter safely as he and the wounded captain were the lone occupants. The Southerners rushed in with their weapons raised, and one private bashed his pistol against

Bohn's forehead. The captors followed a trail of blood to the attic, where they found Schutte on a pile of cornhusks. He was dying.[69]

FLOYD'S ONLY VICTORY: CROSS LANES

On the same day as Schutte's misfortune, Tyler received orders from Cox, who had been given discretionary power by Rosecrans to move Tyler. Cox ordered the Seventh to pull back to Twenty-Mile Creek, which lay approximately seven miles from Gauley Bridge and about nine miles from Cross Lanes. Four days later, Cox was aware that Confederates were near Carnifex Ferry as the result of the Schutte affair, and he believed that a small force might have crossed the river, so he sent Tyler back to Cross Lanes to find and drive away the enemy.

Some had boasted early in the war that Erastus Barnard Tyler, who had been in the fur trade business in Ohio before the war and had spent years roaming the mountains of western Virginia (now West Virginia) hunting for fur-bearing animals, was sent back in western Virginia when the war started to "skin the rebels." His second return to Cross Lanes seemed to offer such an opportunity, but the inexperienced Tyler was not up to the task. Neither he nor his superiors were aware that on August 20 Floyd crossed with a significant force and started digging in just three miles from the crossroads. Tyler was unaware of the much larger force, and upon returning to the crossroads, he incorrectly posted his pickets too close to his own camp to properly alert the Union camp in the advent of a sizable enemy attack. This is especially curious in light of the fact that upon arriving back at Cross Lanes at 5:00 P.M. on August 25, Tyler knew that Confederates were in the area, as he had driven back their pickets.[70]

The nine companies of the Seventh Ohio encamped for the night without tents and blankets. Tyler ordered them not to light fires to cook or warm themselves, as this might have alerted the enemy, though some were said to have started fires for warmth at around midnight. The chilled men were scattered along the roads, where many slept on bundles of hay. Others found a house near the

369

intersection and the Zoar Church, Tyler's headquarters, on the high ground 200 yards to the west. The morning of August 26, 1861, was misty and cold. Soon fires were started, and ears of green corn gathered from nearby fields were roasted.

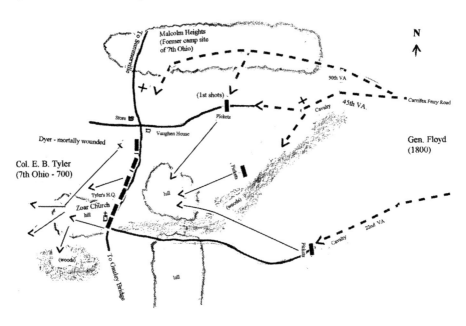

At 5:00 a.m. Floyd's force (infantry, cavalry,& artillery) arrive at Cross Lanes over two roads from Camp Gauley, two miles away. There the Confederate force spread out, surprising and overwhelming the smaller Union force eating breakfast (the origin of the "Battle of Knives and Forks"). By 5:30 to 5:45 a. m. the routed Union force scatters and flees.

"BATTLE OF KNIVES AND FORKS" (CROSS LANES)
AUGUST 26, 1861

Suddenly at 5:00 A.M., while the Union men were preparing breakfast, their pickets from Company K, who were posted around the ferry road to the south, fired at Confederate forces that had suddenly appeared. The men of the Seventh Ohio would soon learn that they were being attacked from three directions. Three enemy regiments, under Heth, McCausland, and Tompkins, with a company of cavalry and several pieces of artillery, had traveled unnoticed in the fog from the south over two separate roads. They were spreading out to the east and west, and they threatened to engulf the smaller Federal force. At first the Seventh Ohio was only aware of the enemy's approach from Carnifex Ferry Road to the south, and from the east, on a slight rise known as Malcolm Heights. Men dropped everything and would eventually run to the hills and woods to the west, where, in the middle of the high ground, sat the Zoar Church, on the road to Gauley Bridge.[71] Most would ascend to the peak just north of the Zoar Church and the graveyard. In the meantime, two companies, A and C (the latter of which ran from the country store and the Vaughan house that sat, respectively, northwest and southwest of the crossroads), reached the hill about a mile to the south.

It was a formidable task for these two companies. To reach the hill, they had to run toward the enemy on the ferry road, climb over a rail fence, and scamper 200 yards up the hill. While crossing the fence, the men of Companies A and C came under heavy fire, which splintered the rails of the fence and inflicted casualties. Once atop the hill, the two Union companies fought hard, especially Captain Giles W. Shurtleff, a former Latin professor at Oberlin College, and his former students. Their brave action put an end to the verbal harassment they had endured from others of their regiment. The Oberlin men who comprised Company C had been called the "Praying Company" and were chided for their excessive praying and reading. These acts, in the minds of the critics, showed a lack of the rough manliness necessary for soldiering. The Oberlin youths not only held their ground for a while against great odds but also suffered the heaviest casualties at Cross Lanes. The Oberlin boys, members of Company A, and part of Company K could only stay on the hill south of the Zoar Church for ten minutes. Confederates were now behind them on their left and were about to engulf the Union right.

The rest of the Union regiment had retreated behind the church. This included the two companies whom Tyler had earlier sent toward the crossroads. They were led by John N. Dyer of Company D. They provided the only other Federal resistance. After a brief stand behind a rail fence, they were driven away. As they were withdrawing across a field, Dyer was mortally wounded.

The Union position was now untenable. Confederates were about to flank them as artillery at the crossroads fired canisters at Tyler's men behind the church. The beleaguered men, in an attempt to escape, fled to nearby woods behind the church. On a nearby road four sutler wagons hastily ran away. Sitting on the rear of one of the bouncing conveyances was an employee clutching a sack containing $15,000—money earned selling items to soldiers.[72]

While this was happening, Tyler sat on his horse on top of the hill in back of the church, overlooking the battlefield and witnessing the apparent destruction of his regiment. When Chaplain Brown approached him, the dejected colonel said, "All is lost. Is there no way by which we can escape?" Brown, who was familiar with the area, led Tyler and the remnants of the regiment into the woods near the church. This was the start of an exhausting trip back to Gauley Bridge, where Cox was told that most of the Seventh Ohio had been captured.[73]

After thirty to forty-five minutes of minor combat, the rout was complete. Tyler's force had two men killed, twenty-nine wounded, and 110 captured. The remaining men were separated and scattered, lost for days. They slept under cliffs and begged food from nearby residents before finding their way to Gauley Bridge and Charleston. The chagrined Tyler, embarrassed at having been totally surprised, believed he had lost more than 500 of his force of about 750 men. He and only 200 men had reached Gauley Bridge. When 400 more, hungry and exhausted from traveling over mountainous terrain, eventually found their way back to Charleston, Tyler filed an amended report in hopes he would not look so inept.

Floyd had five killed and fifteen wounded in what Wise later called the "Battle of Knives and Forks." The scattering of a Union regiment as it prepared to eat breakfast was Floyd's only decisive victory of the war. And that was a small one.

Confederate cavalry scoured the region, capturing some of the isolated and fleeing Yankees, including a Federal soldier who had climbed to the top of a large tree when the attack started. He waited until he thought everyone had left the field, then climbed down, only to be captured. He joined the other captured members of his regiment, who were taken back to Camp Gauley, placed in a rail pen, and taunted by Floyd's soldiers, who called them their "Ohio pets." Wounded Union soldiers were taken to the Zoar Church and to three homes near the battle site. On the porch of one of the houses, the Vaughan house, lay a dying Captain Dyer. Local ladies tried in vain to help the officer, who was wounded in the side. Blood flowed from his wounds to the porch, leaving stains on the boards, stains that would remain long after his life had ended and his body was removed.[74] The Union dead were buried at Cross Lanes. A correspondent of the Lynchburg *Republican* rode past the freshly made graves while examining the battlefield. He found a piece of white paper attached to a marker at the head of one of the graves. On it some wag had written:

The Yankees come in serviced bands
To take possession of our land,
But this very small, contracted spot,
Shows all the land these Yankees got.[75]

At times the Southerners displayed compassion for the prisoners and their plight. They allowed Tyler to send a chaplain and a surgeon, under a flag of truce, to find out about their wounded and the others who were held captive.[76] The officers were restricted in what they were allowed to see and were blindfolded at times, but they found themselves and the Union prisoners well cared for. They were also told that the body of Captain Dyer, the highest-ranking Union fatality at Cross Lanes, had been "salted" to preserve the remains and would be forwarded to Union lines for return to his family.

On August 28, one of Floyd's men escorted a Federal captain, the prisoner Giles Shurleff, from Camp Gauley to a nearby house—perhaps the Vaughan house—that was being used as a hospital. The captain would have one last visit with some of his wounded men. The Confederate guard was moved by the captain's affectionate reunion with his men. Shaking their hands, Captain Shurleff told them he was happy to see them "under any circumstances." Among the most wounded were four of the Latin professor's former students. One young man died before Shurleff left, and others would soon meet the same fate. The guard noticed that all but two of the wounded were shot above the legs, which he assumed was evidence of the excellence of Southern marksmanship. According to an eyewitness, one poor fellow was shot in the "forehead, the ball passing obliquely out near the back of the right ear, and remarkable to say, he" was "still living and rational." Occasionally he was "delirious and when so," he was heard to frequently remark: "Oh, I wish I were in Cleveland." The Confederate guard later recorded, "I reckon a good many of his more fortunate companions wish the same thing. The suffering of these men is a most painful sight, and is calculated to soften even the hearts of those who most hate them, their race, and their unholy invasion. Our surgeons are as attentive to their necessities as they are to those of our own men."

The next day the Union captain, along with 103 other prisoners, whose hands were tied together with rope, like a slave coffle, started on the long march to the Richmond prisons. The Confederate who had escorted the captain for a last visit to his wounded men found the Yankee prisoners to be "the most intelligent and best looking set of prisoners" he had "yet seen in Richmond or elsewhere"—according to an eyewitness account published in the Memphis *Daily Appeal.* The Confederate escort observed: "Some of them seem to have enlisted for a frolic, some to vindicate the stars and stripes, and some from pure hatred of our people and institutions. Some are polite and communicative, some educated and well bred, and some sullen and insolent." Among the prisoners was a large "negro body servant" of a Union major recently captured eight miles from Cross Lanes. He "was frightened out of his wits." He told his captors "he was a servant" of a major "who was to pay him fifty dollars per month, which he thought was" much better than he could make at home, although he had not been paid. "He started to retreat" from Cross Lanes "with his master, but before going far, he passed one of his regiment, shot in the leg, who asked him for water. He [servant] jumped from his horse" and ran "off to search" for water to "fill his canteen. While engaged in this errand of mercy, a fleeing column of his Yankee friends passed, one of whom, in his anxiety to escape, mounted the horse" and dashed off, to the great dismay of the African-American, who was now left stranded and having "to foot it the best he could. But for the theft of his horse, he could have escaped." Once captured, he was extremely solicitous about his fate. "He had heard that some six or seven of his color were taken at Manassas, and had been hung or sold, and wanted to know if it was so. He got no consolation upon the subject" of his fate. A Confederate wrote that the man left Camp Gauley "in handcuffs, under the impression that Jeff Davis will sell him to some cotton planter of the South—which," the writer continued, "I hope he will do."[77]

In the meantime, the Richmond *Dispatch* cheered the news of the battle of Cross Lanes in headlines and predicted benevolent results for the South. Tyler's command was, according to the paper, "one of the very best" of the enemy, but it had been "defeated, routed and disgraced, with all its prestige gone." The press claimed that the people of that region would again have confidence in the Southern forces: "[They] will rally to her banner." It would come as no surprise, the editor surmised, if General Cox at Gauley Bridge were so alarmed that he would "beat a hasty retreat to the Ohio River."[78] This was bold praise, considering the apparent confusion in Floyd's mind prior to the attack. Floyd appeared to have been uncertain about what to do about Tyler's Federal troops' proximity to Camp Gauley. And if Colonel Henry Heth of the Forty-fifth Virginia is to be believed, the Southerners' attack came only after a befuddled Floyd asked Heth what to do. "Do," replied Heth, "There is but one thing for you to do, attack them at daylight tomorrow morning." Heth had—months earlier—lost all confidence in Floyd. The colonel had assumed "that a man who had been Secretary of War knew everything pertaining to military matters." Heth reported that he was soon disillusioned to find that his chief "was as incapacitated for the work he had undertaken" as Heth believed he would have been "to lead an Italian opera."[79]

BATTLE OF CARNIFEX FERRY AND THE CONFEDERATES' SECOND FAILURE TO SECURE THE KANAWHA VALLEY

After Cross Lanes, General Cox expected that the Confederates would follow the route that many of Tyler's men had taken and then capture Charleston, cutting off Cox's supply route and trapping him between two forces. It seemed imperative that Rosecrans would arrive soon. Before long, Cox became puzzled by Floyd's inaction and by his only making an entrenched camp two miles east of Cross Lanes at Carnifex Ferry with outposts in the direction of Summersville.[80]

John Floyd, while not moving, boasted of soundly thrashing any Yankee force that dared confront him. Furthermore—he claimed, and Robert E. Lee recorded—if he hadn't been detained for a week after Cross Lanes, "for the want of flour," he "would have been in Kanawha Valley," a goal he implied that he would soon fulfill. Lee suggested that because of the difficulty of finding him and getting salt to him, if Floyd controlled the roads north of Summersville then "salt might be obtained from the works near Bulltown, eighteen or twenty miles north of Suttonsville." Floyd was less optimistic, and he gave numerous reasons why this could not be done. Among them were the lack of flour, illness that reduced his own regiment to one-third, and the need for reinforcements—his own regiments had only 1,200 men, while those of Tompkins and McCausland together numbered only 600. Additionally, scouts had informed Floyd that three enemy regiments were in possession of Suttonsville and were mistreating civilians. Tales were told of captures and shootings of many rural people for crimes for which they were never tried or convicted, and of threats against the alarmed residents that if they did not stop firing on Union scouts, Union troops would be turned loose "to plunder, murder all ages and sexes, and to lay waste to the country with fire," claimed the potential victims.[81]

So Floyd stayed and dug in at a site 450 feet above the Gauley River, which curved around the back of Camp Gauley. It was a strong position, with earthworks on the highest ground within the horseshoe-shaped bend in the river. Floyd's position, however, had a major weakness. He was isolated across the Gauley River, with very limited facilities to recross or to be reinforced. In an attempt to remedy this situation a bit, a new flatboat and a rickety pontoon footbridge were being constructed. In the meantime, Floyd continued to order Wise to send him more men, and Wise continued to resist.

Floyd was annoyed at Wise's failure to join him at Carnifex Ferry, and he asked Henry Heth what he should do. Heth replied, "When a junior refuses to obey the orders of his superior, there is but one course, to pursue, arrest him and order him to Richmond." "Oh no," replied Floyd, "that would never do; I would get both of his newspapers down on me." Wise and Floyd were acutely aware of promoting a positive public image, and each kept two newspaper editors on their staffs to trumpet their military feats.[82]

Floyd claimed the enemy had abandoned Gauley Bridge and was moving on Carnifex Ferry. Finally, on August 29, several days after Cross Lanes, Wise complied with Floyd's order to send reinforcements. Old Wise took two of his regiments and trudged over the muddy road to the ferry. As he was descending to the ferry on Gauley River, he was handed another order from Floyd. It stated that the enemy threat did not require the union of the two forces, and it ordered Wise back to Dogwood Gap. Again Wise was infuriated by orders that, according to him, had been changed four times in twenty-four hours. The general marched his tired men back over the same road they had just traveled.[83]

Wise was now determined to take Hawk's Nest, seize a nearby mill to grind wheat and corn for his men, and take Cotton Hill, on the south side of New River. Toward the first objective, he forced Cox's pickets back from Hawk's Nest. On the next day, September 2, with about 1,200 men, he attacked an enemy force of similar size at Big Creek and Devil's Elbow. Wise chased the Union pickets over the bridge across Big Creek and, with artillery fire, cleared the hill to the left, despite return artillery fire by the Federals. In the meantime Wise sent one-third of his infantry, about 300, to the north to turn the Union left and expose their camp on the western bend, in the section of the turnpike known as Devil's Elbow. The turning movement was necessary to get around the Union's formidable position along the defile of Big Creek.[84] But the turning force got lost in the rugged terrain and returned. Wise then called off the attack and pulled back beyond Hawk's Nest. Few casualties were sustained by either side. Cox had feared that while Wise was attacking, Floyd would move on Gauley Bridge, but this was not the case. The rivalry between the two Confederate generals precluded such astute and aggressive action. Wise again wrote to Lee, pleading that he be "defended from the vexatious orders of General Floyd" by being ordered to the south of New River as a separate command.

Rosecrans left Clarksburg with three brigades for an arduous march of about 100 miles to come to the aid of Cox. He left General Kelly in charge of protecting the region of the upper Potomac and left General J. J. Reynolds to check Lee and Loring in the Cheat Mountain region. During the early days of September, Rosecrans' men struggled over winding mountain roads, at times stumbling over rough sections in the dark and wading through rivers, including the Big Birch. A tired correspondent believed they had crossed the "uncomfortable deep waters" of the Big Birch "a dozen times in two hours." He said it "followed the eccentric deviations of the mountain." After a week of travel, according to the New York *Times,* the weary men rested in the Big Birch River valley on Sunday, September 8, as their scouts "scoured the mountains and glens in pursuit of rebels," and drove in their pickets. The next day Rosecrans' men left the valley and "immediately began to climb the mountain," which seemed to block their way. For six miles they "climbed in tortuous windings, pausing on the way to bury a rebel, who had been killed attempting a guerrilla shot" at a Union colonel "the evening before, and whose corpse had lain in its gore by the roadside till morning." At last they "reached the summit of Powell Mountain."

At the summit a correspondent with a flare for the dramatic described his experience. Once they were on top of this mountain, he claimed, "There burst upon the eye a view that Switzerland might be challenged to surpass." The country he and the army had traveled through "was but a succession of spurs and outlying ranges." The men had been unable, the writer continued, "to see more than the foliage-masked sides and forest-top summit lines of the nearest hills on the other side." They were "on a point that overlooked the whole country westward to the borders" of Ohio. He wrote on: "The eye reached from range to range of tree-covered hills that rose and fell in the magnificent panorama spread out before us, like the billows of the ocean, growing smaller as they receded, till at last in the dim, hazy shoreline of blue that bounded our vision."[85] The Ohio and Indiana boys had not seen such mountains as the ones they encountered in western Virginia. They were impressed, but probably few were more impressed than Rutherford Hayes. He wrote home, letter after letter, until he finally wrote, "You will think me insane, writing so often and always with the same story: pleasant excitement.... I never enjoyed any business or mode of life as much as I do this. I really feel badly when I think of several of my intimate friends who are compelled to stay at home." Hayes even found the rigorous trip to Summersville exciting and enjoyable.[86]

Hardly had the Federal column begun to climb down the mountain when their advance squad of cavalry ran into the enemy. They ran off some enemy cavalry (under Colonel Jenkins) from their fires and the site they had planned to be their camp during the approaching night. As the fog engulfed them, Rosecrans' men reached Muddlety Bottoms. They camped there for the night, about seven miles above Summersville. Hours after the soldiers had gone to bed, wrapped in blankets and lying on the hay they had found in the fields, Colonel Robert L. McCook of the Ninth Ohio traveled around the whole line of pickets to make sure there were no breaks in the line surrounding the camp. Precautions were necessary, as they had earlier passed a small enemy camp, and rumors had gone through the three brigades that the enemy lay before them.

On the next morning, September 10, wrote a reporter for the Cincinnati *Gazette,* "the clammy fog was still clinging around the faces of the sleepers" when they were aroused shortly after 3:00 A.M. By dawn they were on their way in search of the enemy. The exact location of Floyd and the nature of the terrain were the two unknowns that Rosecrans assiduously worked to resolve. As he approached Summersville, McCausland's regiment hurriedly retreated from the area to join Floyd at Carnifex Ferry. Jenkins' cavalry also pulled back, minus a couple of captured troopers. The uniforms of this militia cavalry unit bemused the Federals. The *Gazette* reported that they found the "green shirt-fashion blouse and white muslin rag over" their caps quaint. The two prisoners had been at Cross Lanes; one was "relieved of the sword of Captain Dyer," which he had taken from the corpse of the Union officer on the battlefield. The Federals found one of the troopers impudent and thought that both were "loudmouths" who revealed little valuable information, except the threat that Floyd would soon "pepper" them.

Rosecrans' knowledge about the location of local roads was greatly enhanced by procuring "the official map" of Nicholas County from a court clerk in Summersville. More information was needed, so the advance guard was ordered to round up "the more intelligent of the citizens, and question them about the roads, byways," and all the topographical features of the country, according to the Cincinnati *Gazette.*

"Every woman or child of sufficient intelligence to answer a plain question, was interrogated," continued the newspaper report. Most of the mountain men had fled at the approach of the Federals, and it was difficult to "find a guide, who knew anything about the country a mile from the highways." The few "ignorami who were occasionally picked up" by Union scouts "appeared utterly impotent to satisfy" Rosecrans' inquiries, and "were usually dismissed with benevolent injunctions to refrain" from telling the enemy of the movement of the approaching army. A talkative older woman at a cabin on the mountain told the Union men that "Floyd had boasted of his ability" to turn back any enemy attack. She tried to impress upon them that Floyd was in a "might strong, ugly place." A New York

Times reporter later wrote that the "old crone spoke upon hearsay testimony, but she was right, our inferences from reports that Floyd had five to six thousand men and strongly entrenched batteries were justified."

Wherever Union forces went in western Virginia, they had to contend with what the Union called bushwhackers, or guerrillas, within range. Squads were continually being sent forward to hunt down the transgressors, capturing or killing them. An example that inspired such a policy was a July raid of Summersville led by a guerrilla's girlfriend, Nancy Hart. Most of Federal soldiers were captured, and much of the town was burned. Nancy was later captured as a Confederate spy and was put in the Summersville jail. Her youth and beauty led to lenient treatment, and her guard allowed her to examine his pistol. She killed him and escaped. [87]

The secessionists were the "wealthy and educated who did nothing openly," and the meaner sort, whom Hayes called the "vagabonds, criminals, and ignorant barbarians of the country." It was the latter class that continually took potshots at the Union. A Federal squad returned one day with the body of a man from this rougher class, a "wild man of the mountains." He had followed the men of the Tenth Ohio regiment, taking shots at them until, near Bulltown, they killed him. Witnesses described him as a shoeless, hatless, beast: "of gigantic size—weighing—two hundred and thirty pounds; had long hooked toes, fitted to climb—a very monster." Hayes surmised that they "probably killed him after taking him prisoner in cold blood—perhaps after a sort of trial." They claimed he was attempting to escape.[88]

While the local enemy was comprised of the upper and lower class, Hayes claimed that "the Union men are the middle classes—the law-and-order, well-behaved folks" who were often abused because of their opinions (especially the many informers who aided the Union in their expeditions). Hayes said that persecutions were "common, killing not rare; robberies an everyday occurrence." The "war brings out the good and evil of Virginia," Hayes wrote to his mother. He called the people he had encountered "some of the best and some of the worst characters I have ever heard of."[89] Not all Unionists were as upbeat as Hayes. After months of being in western Virginia, many Union soldiers and accompanying members of the press developed feelings of contempt for all residents.

Homesickness, the rigors of marches, and their revulsion for a lifestyle that was drastically different from life on the farms of Ohio and Indiana contributed to Federal soldiers' distaste for all western Virginians. None of the locals were more different or held in more contempt than the poor, uneducated mountain folk, who had been deprived of all contact with the world beyond their mountain residences. A Union soldier who spent a night in a meager mountain cabin, where everyone slept in the same room, reported that western Virginians ate and slept like hogs.

Even when local people tried to commit acts of kindness—and inadvertently blundered—Federals found them most irritating. One seriously wounded Federal soldier sought refuge in a mountain cabin, where a woman willingly took him in and cared for him the best way she knew how. Part of the soldier's skull had been shot away, and the wound was infected and infested with vermin. She poured a liberal amount of turpentine on the wound. It was the only remedy she could think of. When friends of the wounded man found him, he had virtually lost all of his mental faculties. Federals had few qualms about cheating and taking advantage of simple residents; they paid one poor woman for food by giving her a counterfeit Confederate $20 bill after she refused to take Yankee greenbacks. This poor honest soul gave her swindlers $16 in change.

Sheep that grazed in the mountain farms were favorite targets for Union confiscation. Soldiers justified such acts by upholding their flimsy claim that the creatures were hostile, menacingly shaking their heads and baring their teeth to bite, so they had to be shot in self defense.[90]

Hayes did not approve of such behavior. He was chagrined to learn that part of his regiment, the Twenty-third Ohio, had ransacked the courthouse at Sutton, destroying many records and causing the old clerk to cry when he saw what was done. "Disgraceful!" wrote Hayes. "What a stigma on our regiment if true! We have had and deserved to have a good name for our orderly conduct...[and] respect for the rights of citizens.... I hope nothing has been done to forfeit our place." Such behavior was unexpected in his regiment, although he admitted that others might have "troubles." Indeed, Hayes recorded, the ninth Ohio had "one man shot resisting a corporal, two men in irons for rape, and one man arrested for sleeping on post." The penalty for his third offense was death.[91]

In the meantime Rosecrans' force continued southward, but they were now advancing with caution. Rosecrans had no definite information concerning Floyd's position, and he believed his Union force would likely run into an enemy ambush or masked battery. According to a Cincinnati *Gazette* reporter, skirmishers from Benham's brigade "flanked the road on either side, sweeping every foot of ground, and scouts were sent forward to scour" the countryside. They found the enemy had tried to obstruct the road with fallen trees and found enemy scouts watching them.

Five or six miles below Summersville Rosecrans' men found a ferryboat at Hughes Ferry, a crossing on the Gauley River several miles north of Carnifex Ferry. They did not want to leave a river crossing for the enemy to gain access to the rear of Rosecrans, so Colonel Robert L. McCook and a squad of his cavalry (Schambeck's men from Chicago) were sent to the ferry to destroy the boat. At the river, they found the boat on the opposite shore. Several men were ordered to strip and swim across to get it. Once they were in the river, Confederates appeared on the opposite bank and fired at the small Union force, seriously wounding one trouper in the thigh. The Federals returned fire, but it was of no use; the enemy was out of range of their carbines stock-horse pistol. McCook immediately sent a man back requesting that ten infantrymen be sent to his aid. Somehow the request was interpreted to mean the Tenth Regiment, and this regiment was sent to the river. The Irishmen arrived anxious to fire at the enemy and soon peppered the opposite hillside, driving off the few Confederates. The Cincinnati reporter wrote: "The swimmers then brought the boat over. It was a new one, just finished, and the tools [used]…in its construction were still in it. These were used to cut it in two, and the separate halves were then loaded with stone, and sent, sinking as they went, over the falls below."[92]

After destroying the small vessel in the waning morning hours of September 10, Rosecrans' column continued probing the region south of Summersville. They knew the enemy was near, but where, exactly? Most felt Floyd was entrenched below Cross Lanes. This belief was confirmed by what reporters called "ignorant or treacherous inhabitants." According to the Cincinnati *Gazette,* around noon "an intelligent mountaineer lad, who had been in the rebel camp," arrived and informed Rosecrans that Floyd "was on the cliffs overlooking Carnifex Ferry."[93] He also told Rosecrans that two miles before the Confederate camp was Cross Lanes, which, the youth astutely added, was of military importance in light of the current situation and required thorough reconnaissance. Rosecrans briefly halted his movement, but he soon resumed his march toward Cross Lanes, arriving there at 2:00 P.M. Heeding the advice of his young informant, he sent Benham's men to clear the region. McCook's men were sent to explore the hills and found them clear of the enemy. Colonel Lytle's Tenth Ohio (of Benham's brigade) moved over the road toward the ferry in search of Floyd. The rest of Rosecrans' force waited at Cross Lanes. One man observed that around the crossing, there "spread…a variety of hills and dales, pasture and cornfields, dotted" with several "snug-looking little farmhouses, with orchards attached, backed by lofty heights that skirt the Gauley.

As the Union troops waited to be sent into combat, they were still uncertain about both the topography and position of their enemy. They would later discover that they would be moving through not only thick woods and entangling undergrowth, but also an area whose major features were in the configuration of a horseshoe, an S, or a question mark. The land in front of them lay within the horseshoe bend of the Gauley River, whose steep banks were well over 130 yards high. At the top of the horseshoe were two severe ravines running inland. Above their mouths were the eastern and western ends of Floyd's main fortification. It traversed across the top of the land for a mile in a zigzag fashion, in the shape of a somewhat flattened S. The flattened S shape was dictated by the high ground that formed this configuration across the land between the two river bends. The ridge was narrow, a mere twenty to thirty feet wide or narrower, before dropping sharply downward both in front and back of the works—except for the land immediately along the ferry road, where it intersected with Floyd's fortifications. There the land gradually declined. A secondary works of 200 or so yards in length was built just off the main fortification, on the left, to protect the left flank. It occupied the high ground above a hollow in front of the left center of the main works. The area was covered with woods except around the works, some of which had been cleared by the Confederates. The largest clearing was a 300-yard space in front of the main fortification along the ferry road where a small farm existed. In this opening and on the west side of the ferry road was the small Patteson house and several other outbuildings. They were now vacant. Henry Patteson and his wife, acting upon Floyd's admonishment, had vacated their home before the battle. They carried what they could in a wagon a mile and a half to the Carnifex house, at the ferry crossing on the southern bank of the Gauley.[94] A cornfield enveloped by woods sat to the north of the vacant home.[95]

The road to Carnifex Ferry traversed the area. The road meandered southward, with its bed forming the shape of a question mark. The approach from Cross Lanes to the Patteson farm in front of Floyd's works formed the base of this configuration. Over a stretch of this road, for half a mile, before reaching the Patteson farm, were a series of paths that shot off to the left and right through the woods. Those paths on the Union right led to farms and cleared land to the west, which would play no part in the battle. The paths, however, would be used by Federals to position their forces to the right of the ferry road. This road turned eastward nearing the cornfield, forming the start of the top curve of the question mark. In its eastward bend, the road bisected the right of Floyd's main works (at the top half of the S configuration), and for a mile and a half continued first southward then westward while rapidly descending from the heights to the ferry site. Just west of the road where it cut through the Confederate works was located their heaviest concentration of artillery. Most of these features would gradually be learned by Rosecrans' men as they moved forward during September 10 and made limited and ineffective attacks, first against Floyd's center, and then against his right.

That afternoon, the glowing sun revealed lines of men anxiously awaiting combat. As Lytle's Irishmen pushed toward the ferry, the soldiers waiting at the crossroads heard nothing but the sounds of nature, of birdsong and gentle breeze. Suddenly those at Cross Lanes heard a musket shot from the direction of Lytle's regiment. The shot was followed by others, and then quiet returned. All this, it was later learned, was the result of Confederates being dislodged from a small camp a mile from Cross Lanes. When the news was received back at the crossroads, the men cheered.

The men of the Tenth Ohio pushed on. The scene was later described by a correspondent for the Cincinnati *Gazette*. Soon they arrived where the road to the ferry "plunged into a dense forest filled with undergrowth, almost impassable for infantry, and entirely so for cavalry." Yet the road was passable, muddy but not deep, and nearly level, "more so than one would expect on such heights—but very narrow, and shut in, up to the very wagon tracks with the jungle of the underbrush." Less than a mile from the enemy camp, neither Lytle's men nor others in Rosecrans' force knew the exact location of the main enemy force or the nature of their entrenchments, though they knew it was near the cliffs. The suspense became more intense, and emotions were heightened. When would Benham contact the enemy? He had been ordered by Rosecrans to move cautiously forward for the purpose of reconnoitering. Rosecrans told him "to be very careful to feel the enemy closely, but not to engage him unless he saw…an opening." A reporter wrote that almost half an hour after leaving the small abandoned camp of the Fiftieth Virginia Infantry, where the earlier skirmishing had occurred, Lytle's four advanced companies peered through the bushes "that skirted a short curve in the road" and found themselves about two to 300 yards in front of "some sort of fortification; exactly what" it was difficult to tell. Soon they were noticed by the enemy, and there started a sharp but scattered firing, followed, suddenly, by loud musket fire. They had found the enemy, and the enemy opened fire along much of their front.

The rest of Benham's brigade rushed forward while a messenger rode to Rosecrans, requesting help. The Thirteenth Ohio, under Colonel W. S. Smith, moved up the ferry road as the Twelfth Ohio, under Colonel John W. Lowe, came along a path from the abandoned Confederate camp left of the ferry road and almost parallel to it. As Lowe's men burst forward, they abandoned their excess gear and ran toward the path leading to the woods. "Old Rosy" hurried to the front and ordered his other two brigades to move up. A howitzer battery and two field pieces stormed up the main road, followed more slowly by wagons heavy with ammunition. Soldiers and officers scurried around, creating, according to the New York *Times* correspondent, "a splendid spectacle of excitement and eager haste to dash into battle."

The two-rifle cannon, under Captain William Schneider, fired from near the left of the road at the enemy works 400 yards away. The captain then found a better position 100 paces to the right. He cut a path to the new position using his sword and a hatchet. Now in full view of the enemy's battery, in the center of their works, Schneider remained in the second position for the rest of the afternoon, firing 75 rounds of solid shot and 15 shells. He was soon joined in the firing by

Captain James McMullin's four howitzers, which had turned off the main road and had traveled over a side road 250 yards to the right of Schneider's two pieces. From these two positions the six Union pieces exchanged artillery fire with the enemy.

The scene was a dramatic one. A reporter found the "angry peals of musketry…[as] sharp as peals of heavy thunder, [which] grew fiercer, till the sound became one tremendous, incessant roar; while speedily, at least one full battery of heavy field pieces sent in their swelling, deep-toned notes to mingle with the crashing rattle of the small arms."

Lytle's men of the Tenth held their ground, although they were in a tenuous position. Fortunately for them, they were partially protected by the trees. This shelter, along with the lack of accuracy from enemy muskets and artillery, kept them from sustaining worse casualties. The Thirteenth was now nearby and to the left of Lytle's men, where they fanned out toward Floyd's right flank, as the "Rebels" continued to spray their heavy musket and artillery fire. Lytle was in the thickest of their fire. An hour after the start of the battle, he dashed forward up or near the ferry road toward the front of the enemy works. He led several companies of his men, intending to storm the Confederate entrenchments. As they left the cover of the woods, the enemy concentrated their fire upon the charging men. A short distance in front of the works and near the road, Colonel Lytle was severely wounded in the leg. The shot passed through his limb, fatally wounding his mount, named Faugh-A-ballah, who threw his wounded rider to the ground. Then the sleek black charger leaped over the breastwork and plummeted into the enemy entrenchments. (Some say the horse died in front of the breastworks).

The wounded colonel found no safe haven. He was taken to a small deserted building, probably the Patteson house, 100 or so yards from where he was wounded, in the middle of the fire. There he lay during the battle, as described by one eyewitness: "with cannon balls crashing through and around the frail building which constituted his only shelter." His men, who had fought bravely, now became "somewhat scattered in the woods" though they held their position there and continued "an incessant firing."[96]

1

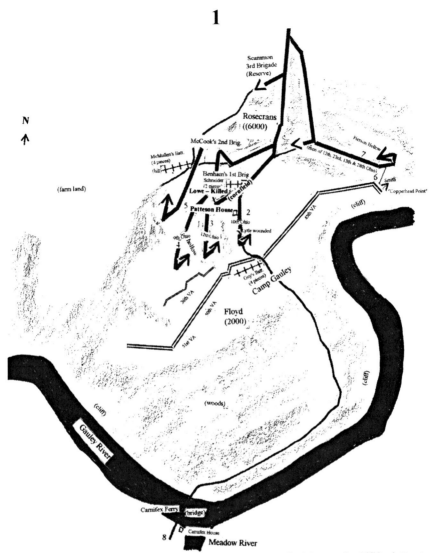

The Union makes three piecemeal, uncoordinated and unsuccessful attacks on the Confederate works. Additional attempts fail to materialize. Lytle's 10th Ohio of Benham's First Brigade leads Union troops into battle, opening the fighting by (1) capturing a Confederate picket camp and (2) attacking the center of Floyd's earthworks (Lytle is wounded). (3) A second charge is made by four companies of 12th Ohio under Lowe (killed) that moves through the cornfield and hollow to the right of Lytle's earlier attack. (4) After the arrival of McCook's Second Brigade a third charge, further to the Union right is made by three companies of the 9th Ohio that fails to hear the order to attack has been countermanded. (5) A later attempt by McCook's brigade to attack is slowed by the 13th Ohio's mistakenly firing upon the 28th Ohio and is terminated by darkness (only the 9th and 28th Ohio come under fire). (6) Col. Smith finds Floyd is vulnerable on his extreme right, but exhaustion and darkness abort an attack via Pierson Hollow. (7) While withdrawing in darkness from the hollow, Union troops fire on each other. Rosecrans pulls his three brigades back toward Cross Lanes. (8) During the night Floyd withdraws south of Gauley River by way of Carnifex Ferry.

BATTLE OF CARNIFEX FERRY: SEPTEMBER 10, 1861
(3:15 p.m. to 7:15 p.m.)

Michael Fitzgibbons, a color sergeant who was behind Lytle when the colonel fell, had his right hand shot off. According to the New York *Times,* the color bearer continued to wave the flag "until his body was torn to pieces by a round shot." Sergeant Daniel O'Connor then gathered up the Stars and Stripes, only to be struck in his left hand. He dropped behind a log but kept the colors flying until weakness forced him to drop the flag. His captain, Stephen McGroarty, soon picked up the flag and, while rolling it up, ordered his men to retire to cover. One of the last men to leave, McGroarty was struck in the chest, and the bullet passed through him. Somehow he got off of the field with the flag. Another captain was wounded in the foot, but he seized two sticks and used them as crutches as he continued to command his company.

Lytle's Irishmen had fought with determination and had earned the nickname the "Bloody Tenth," suffering the highest casualties of the day, with nine men killed and fifty wounded. During their ordeal, their chaplain, Father William O'Higgins, was constantly with them. He courageously crawled between the lines amidst enemy fire to bring water from a spring to help soothe the parched throats of the wounded Tenth Ohioans, including Colonel Lytle. Watching all of this was a boy of nine or ten, a member of the Tenth Ohio known as the "little corporal," who sat on a rail fence while bullets whizzed by him until one hit the rail between his legs. He then made a sagacious and a rapid retreat.

When Lowe's Twelfth Ohio neared the battlefield, part of the regiment veered to the left, and the rest moved to the right, apparently separating out of confusion and because of the terrain. The four companies who moved to the right crossed over the ferry road in front of the two Union field pieces, over a fence and into the cornfield, and through the field toward the Patteson house to assault the enemy works. But Colonel Lowe had only gone a few feet into the cornfield when he was instantly killed by a musket shot that struck him close to the center of his forehead. An instant later, as the body was lying on the ground, enemy fire "mangled both of his legs," according to witnesses.[97]

Was the loss of Lowe's life in combat the fate that he strangely sought? Many suggest it was. Among them were newspaper correspondents and Lowe's son, Tom, who went to his grave believing his father had intrepidly and, in his son's words, "unnecessarily exposed himself to danger to refute allegations of cowardice."

A correspondent of the New York *Times,* in an account that eulogized Lowe's death, wrote that he was not surprised that Lowe had been killed, as the colonel had anticipated his own death. He had believed he was going to die, and, according to the correspondent, "had said the sacrifice of his life was necessary to redeem his reputation." While on the way to Carnifex Ferry, Lowe had asked his regiment's chaplain to take care of his property should his presentiment come true. "He died where a soldier loves to die, in the thickest of the fight," wrote the correspondent.[98]

It was a bleak way to obtain the honor and success that had eluded John Lowe throughout his somber life. His parents' death had left him with awesome responsibilities as a youth, a lifestyle he had described as "destitution, poverty, and labor...without friends— without education—without necessary food and clothing." For years he had struggled to feed, clothe, and house himself and his younger brothers and sisters. In manhood success escaped him. He was rejected at the polls when he ran for political office in Ohio, and his law practice was insufficient to sustain his wife and children and to pay his creditors. Lowe heeded the advice of his friend Ulysses Grant and joined the army to fight in the Mexican War. The war also proved disappointing. Beset by disease, he spent most of his time coping with personal illness as well as illness of his men, while martial glory eluded him. He returned home to again practice law, but was forced to move to different Ohio towns in a vain search for clients. Desperation forced him into the humiliating situation of having to accept financial support from his grown son Tom. The final blow to Lowe's ego came early in the Civil War after he had again turned to the military in search of honor and success only to have his reputation besmirched, seemingly beyond repair, at Scary Creek.

As Lowe's broken body lay in a cornfield, his forehead covered with blood, with crimson streaks mingled with his graying hair, a poem he had written a couple of months earlier proved to be prophetic.

My day of life is over,
and here I lay me down
In the hot, red field of battle
In the arms of high renown

By the shaft of death I'm stricken
In my upward flight to fame.
And I give my life to nothingness
To win a warrior's name.[99]

The battle went on. Captain James D. Wallace assumed command of the right wing of the Twelfth Ohio after Colonel Lowe's death. He moved his men toward the enemy works, sheltering them the best way he could while waiting for orders from Rosecrans. Wallace later reported that the general ordered him to advance "to the right and front of the enemy breastworks." Wallace responded by moving over "a by-road" and stopping at the edge of the woods, within "easy musket-shot" of the enemy. There he ordered his men to fire whenever the enemy exposed themselves, but the enemy was safely sheltered behind their works. Wallace again asked Rosecrans for orders and was sent even farther to the right. The Twelfth went through woods that included thick underbrush, over a hollow, and up to the top of a hill about fifty yards from their opponents. There the Ohioans lay on the ground to fire, but their fire was again ineffective. After the second Confederate volley, Wallace found his unit without support and pulled back under the hill until ordered by a staff officer to move behind the artillery on the ferry road.[100]

In the meantime Colonel Robert L. McCook was ordered to move his Second Brigade, made up of German immigrants, forward to storm the works west of the cornfield. Upon arriving on the battlefield, Rosecrans countermanded the order to attack. McCook then positioned his men behind a hill on his right, with the wooded ferry road on his left in an attempt to protect his men from enemy fire.[101] Three companies of the Ninth Ohio had not heard that the order to attack had been canceled, and they moved west of the cornfield. Two companies engaged the enemy fifty yards from the outer works as the other got within 100 yards of the main works in front of the cornfield before they heard the signal to retire.

The sun was now rapidly sinking (around 7:00 P.M.), but the din of the firing was still terrific. McCook was again ordered to prepare to storm Floyd's works. Dressed in civilian clothes—according to the *Times* correspondent who was watching—he stood up in "his stirrups, and snatching his slouched hat from his head, roared out, 'Forward, my bully Dutch! We'll go over their dammed entrenchment if every man dies on the other side.'" The correspondent was also caught up in the frenzy and found it most moving. He wrote: "The usually phlegmatic Teutons, inflamed with passionate excitement, exploded with terrific cheers. Old, graybeard fellows threw up their hats with frenzied violence, and the gallant brigade shot forward at double-quick, shaking the road with their ponderous steps. The scene was magnificently exciting. Not a man witnessed it whose very soul was not inflamed, and as the gallant McCook dashed furiously up and down his lines, shouting to his solid Dutchmen, no man doubted [that if they got the order to storm the enemy works]...they would go over the parapet with resistless power." Several thousand "Dutchmen" again shouted loudly when Captain George Hartsuff said he would lead the column.[102]

The brigade did not storm the enemy works. The brigade moved 200 yards forward, but during this movement, the Thirteenth Ohio mistakenly fired into the Twenty-eighth Ohio, inflicting unfortunate casualties.[103] Only the lead regiments, the Ninth and the Twenty-eighth Ohio, came under enemy fire before darkness made an attack impossible. McCook was ordered to cover the artillery and ambulances as Rosecrans' whole force pulled back a mile to the abandoned Confederate picket camp and beyond.

The Federals made three very limited and uncoordinated assaults on Floyd's center and left.[104] But Floyd's main weakness was his extreme right. The Federals discovered but never exploited this weakness. When Benham ordered Smith's regiment to the left of the ferry road, Smith reconnoitered the area. He led his men down the ravine (Pierson's Hollow) to his left that ran virtually parallel with the enemy's front, then up the slope to his right until he could see the enemy works. He continued to move forward along the skirt of the woods in front to the enemy line until 100 yards from their breastworks of logs and rails from which the Confederates opened fire. Smith immediately ordered his men to fall to the ground and crawl up the hill. There they opened fire, driving the enemy from their extreme right toward their center.[105]

Smith was near what is now called Copperhead Point. It offers a spectacular view of the Gauley River far below as it bends around the steep cliffs behind the eastern half of the land that was occupied by Heth's Fourth Virginia. This narrow meandering ridge, varying in width from thirty to sixty feet, was a precarious position for the few numbers of Heth's command on the extreme right. In front of them was the protective steep drop to Pierson's Hollow, but behind them was an even steeper drop, 143 yards, almost straight down to the Gauley River. If the Federals somehow miraculously breached their line, their only chance of retreat would be eastward for hundreds of yards along the narrow ridge. Fortunately for Heth, Smith had only been ordered to probe that area, not to attack. Smith had his men cease firing and lay in their position until the return of an officer who had been sent to Benham and Rosecrans for orders. Smith waited long enough for the officer to have returned, and fearing he had gotten lost in the thick underbrush, pulled his eight companies back down into the ravine and to the ferry road to report to his commanders in person. Colonel Smith and others reported on what he called "the practicability of reaching the rebels' extreme right, if not turning it."

Floyd's works went near the cliffs over the Gauley River, but not completely. There was also a wooded area covering a narrow strip of land that led to the exposed right flank. Rosecrans, who was encouraged by what he heard, sent an extemporized brigade, consisting of the Twenty-eighth Ohio, eight companies of the Thirteenth Ohio, three companies of the Twenty-third Ohio (which included Major Rutherford B. Hayes), and two companies of the Twelfth Ohio, to attack Floyd's extreme right. Smith had asked for a brigadier to lead them, but Rosecrans put the colonel in charge; he had been over the terrain and the proposed attack site.

It was 5:00 P.M. when Smith started moving his new command into the ravine. Once there, Rosecrans ordered him to stop and await further orders. An hour and twenty minutes later, the general ordered him to attack. It was now dusk. The Twenty-eighth Ohio, under Colonel Augustus Moor, commenced what Smith called "the ascent in two ranks over very steep and slippery rocks, through undergrowth" of laurel and thorns. After a half-hour of climbing, Colonel Smith, Colonel Moor, a captain, and about thirty of the most skillful climbers from the Twenty-eighth reached the top huffing and puffing. They had to crawl on their knees, grabbing at small trees and bushes to pull themselves up. As soon as they reached the top, the adjutant arrived and informed them that "it would take until 2 o'clock in the morning" to bring up two companies of Moor's regiment.

It was now pitch dark in the dense laurel thicket. The men had been on their feet since 3:00 A.M. and were now out of water and very tired. Colonels Smith and Moor concluded that it would be best to descend again and pull back into the ravine to make the assault at dawn. Smith ordered the whole column, "Face about and quietly march out." The head of the column turned and moved up the ravine to near the rear of the men at the end of the line. This doubled the whole column into the shape of a U. While in this position a peculiar kind of whistling was heard, followed by one or two shots, either from the enemy skirmishers or from an accidental shot from Smith's column. This spooked the Federals, who, in the darkness, opened fire upon each other, killing two and wounding about thirty. The mistake was soon discovered, and the force was taken out of the ravine and marched back to the ferry road. During this movement, Colonel Moor and Lieutenant-Colonel Becker were disabled after falling down a steep cliff; they had to temporarily relinquish their commands as their men made their way back through the ravine. Finally they camped for the night, a mile north on the ferry road.[106]

Darkness had brought the curtain down on the battle without a major attack on Floyd's works. The Virginia troops stretched across the land in the horseshoe bend, which they held behind incomplete earthen works that were fronted with logs, dirt, and brush. They were safe, but this safety was temporary, as the breastwork was insecure and offered limited protection on the Confederate left.[107] In this S-shaped works, Floyd positioned Tompkins' Twenty-second Virginia Infantry on the left (it arrived less than an hour before the battle).[108]

The Fiftieth and Fifty-first Virginia Infantry occupied the center of the works, along with Guy's battery of four six-pounders just west of the ferry road, while to the east of the road, on the right, was Heth's Forty-fifth Virginia Infantry. These troops, plus the men of McCausland's Thirty-sixth Virginia Infantry in the outer works to the left, totaled around 1,800 to 2,000 men and had held off a Federal force of nearly 6,000, though about one-third of the Federals had been actively engaged.[109]

Floyd's men, protected by their works, had escaped from the battle, which lasted about four hours, from 3:15 P.M. to 7:15 P.M., without anyone being killed. Only twenty of Floyd's men were wounded, and they killed seventeen and wounded 141 Federals. Floyd himself was wounded only fifteen minutes into the battle. He was struck in the right arm, but it was not life threatening. A correspondent for the Lynchburg *Republican* wrote that Surgeon Gleaves dressed the wound, and in ten minutes the general was again moving along his lines, "encouraging the men by his presence and his voice." Many were unaware of his wound, which he later described in a letter to his wife as "writhing painful" but only a "little hurt."

Later that afternoon a "Minnie ball tore through the lapel of his coat and another through the cantle of his saddle." Fate had been kind; Floyd was not killed. If the story is true that he was standing atop a five-foot-high chestnut tree stump with steps hewn into its side in order to get a better view of the emerging battle, it is little wonder that he was struck by enemy fire.[110]

Both young and old had fought behind the Confederate works. John W. Blizzard, a sixteen-year-old, was perhaps the youngest. He was sent by his mother on the morning of the battle day to take food to his father nearby at Hughes Ferry. Once he accomplished his mission, a Confederate officer would not allow him to return home because he was fearful the youth would be captured by the enemy. Young Blizzard was given a musket and accompanied his dad's regiment to Camp Gauley, where his father tried to send his son home. But John did not want to return home, and his wish prevailed. He stayed, fought honorably while overcoming great fright, and experienced what he claimed was a maturing process that psychologically stripped away his youth and innocence and plunged him into manhood in one afternoon.

One of the oldest, if not the most elderly man to fight at Carnifex Ferry, was a poorly armed militiaman who accompanied the Local Wildcats to Floyd's camp. Like young Blizzard, he refused to leave. After being given an old flintlock musket and four rounds of ammunition and placed at the end of the line, he readied himself for combat by chewing off the ends of the cartridges and placing them on a nearby log. The anxious old man fired prematurely, but he helped repel the Union attack.[111]

The marksmanship of both sides was often inaccurate, wrote the Lynchburg *Republican* correspondent. Confederates contended that the Union's fire at first was "very bad." Their cannons were especially errant. The shots from the six Union pieces cut off tops of trees and split open oak trees in the Confederate's encampment as the Federal shells—with few exceptions—burst high in the air and at least fifty yards to the rear of Floyd's men. But late in the battle Union artillery balls started plowing into and damaging the embankments, while their shells "broke directly over" Southern heads "with terrible furry." The flag that floated over Floyd's tent was "completely riddled" by "the balls of the enemy." Confederate accuracy was also questioned. The Southerners admitted that at times they had fired too soon when the enemy was out of range. Often unable to see the Union, they took aim at bushes and fired in the direction where they thought the enemy must have been. Floyd's six artillery pieces also frequently missed their mark, with shots sailing into the tops of trees and, as one observer remarked, endangering only the squirrels.[112]

Southern musket fire was better, but like the Federals, they often fired too high or too low. The majority of the Union wounds were in the leg.

The battle had been only slightly safer for Northern reporters than for Union soldiers. Among the wounded was John H. Green, a reporter for the Cincinnati *Enquirer.* He had been assisting Colonel Lytle as his private secretary. Two other correspondents for Cincinnati papers, J. Whitelaw Reid of the *Gazette,* whose pen name was "Agate," and William D. Bickham of the *Commercial,* worked as volunteer aides to General Rosecrans. On the day of the battle the two were in the saddle from 4:00 in the morning and had virtually nothing to eat or drink except for a swallow of coffee and a cold, hard biscuit. By night, hungry and near collapse, they desperately hunted for food and a place to sleep. No food could be found and only a couple of light blankets were taken from the Confederate picket camp and were given to them by a Union officer to help them in their slumber. The two fatigued reporters soon chose a spot to rest. It happened to be in between the Union and Confederate lines. A Union sentry soon made them move to a safer spot.

Reid and Bickham led their tired horses northward, stumbling in the darkness over sleeping soldiers, who immediately responded with unflattering oaths. Eventually the two men took shelter beneath ambulances along the edge of the woods. But soon horses hitched to one of the ambulances started moving forward, as General Rosecrans was riding by. Surprised to see the two men, whom he recognized as his volunteer aides, under the ambulances, Rosecrans called out, asking what they were doing. They responded that they were there to sleep. The general replied that they had selected a dangerous spot and told them he was pulling his men back to Cross Lanes, which would leave them in an area he would expect the enemy to make a night sortie into. Soon the correspondents were headed farther north, to a log stable that was being used as a hospital. They spent the rest of the night in the rear of the barn, behind a fence. When awakened by the sun the next morning, they discovered that the hard spot in the ground that Reid had complained was a large stiff-bit bridle, the site they had selected in the dark, turned out to be an unappealing mattress: a pile of manure from the stable.[113]

The night after the battle, exhausted men slept with their weapons—the Union near Cross Lanes, and the Confederates within their works. Early in the night Floyd decided to leave. He and his staff had learned from prisoners that Rosecrans had nine regiments, a half-dozen artillery pieces, and a total force they believed to be 8,000 to 9,000 men that would be reinforced by Cox in the morning. Floyd, at sunset, said he would never retreat, but he soon felt vulnerable. This feeling was magnified because Wise had refused to join him during the battle as ordered, claiming he was in imminent danger of attack from Cox. The news from couriers whom Floyd had sent to determine the whereabouts of new reinforcements was not encouraging. The North Carolina and Georgia regiments who were being sent numbered about 1,600 men, but they would not arrive in time, so Floyd and his force left during the night. They were preceded by the servants, who had been frightened during the battle and had crossed the river before everyone else. From 10:00 P.M. to 4:00 A.M. Floyd's men ascended the winding, dangerous road in the dark, crossing the Gauley River by two small flatboats and a footbridge that had just been completed on the day of the battle. Once across, the bridge and boats were destroyed.[114]

A correspondent from the Lynchburg *Republican,* who had served as one of Floyd's couriers to Wise, returned after the Confederates had completed their crossing to find he had lost his horse, all baggage, clothing, and other items. This did not daunt the reporter's praise for Floyd. He wrote what Floyd must have been pleased to hear "that the public and all military men will agree that both the fight and our fall back to the side of the river are among the most remarkable incidents in the history of war." After all, he continued, "several hundred men with six inferior pieces of artillery, fought back four times their numbers…for more than four long hours, repulsing them three times" (though Floyd contended it was five) "…and remaining masters of the ground." The correspondent recounted that Floyd had also succeeded in moving the men, baggage, stores, and more than 200 sick and wounded across the road by the Gauley, which was, he wrote, "along one of the steepest and worst single track roads that ever horses hoof trod or man ever saw." The writer continued, claiming that 4:00 A.M. "found these men three miles from the enemy," with the recently constructed bridge destroyed and crossing with "boats sunk behind us." The Lynchburg reporter concluded: "[These] facts show a generalship seldom exhibited anywhere."[115]

Although Floyd did not describe his achievements in such heroic terms, he stated what he had done in the most positive terms. "We repulsed them [Federals] in five distinct and successive assaults, and at nightfall had crippled them to an extent that they were in no condition whatever to molest us in our passage across the river." The latter he claimed was "accomplished without the loss of a gun or any accident whatever." The Richmond *Dispatch,* while lamenting the slowness of obtaining information, found Floyd's actions laudatory against a repugnant force made up nearly all of foreigners. The paper's writers claimed that "Irish" and "German Brigades," had engaged "our band of heroes" but were forced back amidst furious fire. The Federals claimed to have returned the same. How can this be, scoffed the *Dispatch*? They killed no one. Their claim of having returned fire, held the *Dispatch,* was "an attempt to hide the disgrace of what we conjecture is a repulse, almost tantamount to the defeat, of an overwhelming force by a small body of brave men."[116]

Federal officer Rutherford Hayes found Floyd's men less impressive. He wrote his wife, describing the young men of the "upperclass": "kind hearted, good-natured fellows, who are [as] unfit as possible for the business they are in." He continued, "They have courage but no endurance, enterprise, or energy. The lower class are cowardly, cunning, and lazy. The height of their ambition is to shoot a Yankee from some place of safety."[117]

The Confederate press' description of Floyd's "brilliant retreat" is also contrasted with accounts by participants, telling of confusion and lack of coordination. Exhausted by the activities and excitement of the day, the men were asleep behind their works. Nothing disturbed their slumber, except for the eerie and unsettling groans of wounded men who were not far from the fortification. The troops were awakened early in the night and ordered to quietly prepare to leave. Floyd and his men were the first to go, followed by McCausland's Thirty-sixth Virginia, and finally Tompkins and his Twenty-second Virginia, which served as the rear guard. Before Tompkins could leave, the artillery had to precede him. It was a long and anxious wait. For two and a half hours, he waited for the artillery to leave, and with each passing moment the fear heightened as it became more and more likely that he and his regiment would be trapped and captured. The steep and treacherous road to the ferry, which required quiet and slow movement, might well have prevented Tompkins' men from reaching the ferry until long after daylight. Floyd might have considered McCausland as somewhat of a favorite, but he did not have such warm feelings for Tompkins. The colonel, a knowledgeable military man who worked well with Wise and disliked Floyd deeply, resented the general's treatment of his regiment. He felt that the useless and exhaustive marches back and forth over mountain terrain could only be the product of incompetence. Floyd was aware of the colonel's views, leading some to conclude that he left Tompkins as the last to leave so that if any mishap occurred in the retreat, it could be blamed on him.

While Tompkins waited and anxiety heightened, Major Isaac Smith was given permission to see what was delaying the artillery. Smith found people setting around and horses unhitched from their artillery pieces or limbers. The officer he talked with claimed that he had received no orders to leave, and he was unaware of his perilous predicament. When informed of the situation, Tompkins sent Smith back with orders for the artillery to leave immediately. Smith personally went to each piece in an attempt to hurry up the process. All this took valuable time. It was well past midnight before Tompkins' men started to leave. The trip a mile and a half down the precipitous ferry road, which was barely wide enough for a wagon, required the artillery to move at painfully slow pace, forcing Tompkins' men to frequently stop and wait. Smith and others found the road even worse than the one at Poca. Its decline was between tall mountains, with shade from trees that made the darkness even more intense. Anxiously they inched their way toward the river, feeling fortunate in losing only one caisson and a lot of baggage, which fell off the cliff.

Once at the bottom at the ferry site, where smooth but swift waters ran between treacherous rocks, with rapids above and below, none felt safe until they were on the other side. If it had not been for the frail and narrow pontoon bridge above the water, many a foot soldier would have failed to escape. But crossing to safety had its own perils. The bridge was poorly lit, with only a few lights. There was no railing. Before Tompkins' men arrived, stories circulated that four or five men had fallen off the bridge into the river and had drowned, but others claimed they had been rescued. At daylight the Twenty-second Virginia started over the footbridge, single-file, and about five feet apart. After thirty minutes Tompkins' men were safely across. What a relief—they now felt safe. To the Twenty-second Virginia and others, their retreat to safety was a great achievement, regardless of the confusion and lack of orders from their commander, Floyd. What they had to overcome during the retreat was, in some ways, more menacing than the Federal attack.[118]

True prospective of this very limited fight was not to be found amidst the excitement of combat. The men on each side had displayed considerable effort, especially the Union soldiers, but the inconclusive results hardly brought long-lasting glory to either Floyd or Rosecrans. For Floyd, at least, the short-term effect was a brief moment of glory. It was his only one of the war. His proclivity for retreat continued: his actions at Cotton Mountain and Fort Donelson in late 1861 and early 1862 would doom his military reputation. In retrospect, if he was not going to move upon Cox, it would have been smart to dig in the mountains south of Carnifex Ferry. On the other hand, the Federals were unable to get their act together for an all-out attack before dark, though it was not due to any failure of the men. They had been marching since 3:00 A.M. over 17 miles before the battle. Rosecrans referred to his orders calling for a "strong reconnaissance," implying that he did not mean for a piecemeal attack to occur. The lack of coordination fell heavily on Benham, who was better at building fortifications than attacking them. He had fallen out of favor with Rosecrans, who later in the war would charge Benham with drunkenness during the battle of Carnifex Ferry.[119]

Benham, in turn, blamed Lytle. He contended that Lytle had acted on his own in the early attack on the enemy works. In his official report, Benham emphatically claimed that he had not ordered this attack. This is in contrast with Benham's eagerness to attack after flushing Confederates out of their advance camp. He had incorrectly assumed that Floyd was on the run.[120] Benham referred to Lytle's charge, praised in the Northern press, as "the ridiculous assault by the hare brained colonel."[121]

As indecisive as Rosecrans' battle results might have been, he had reopened the line of communication between Suttonsville and Gauley Bridge and had stopped (due to Floyd's proclivity for retreating) the second Confederate movement toward the Kanawha Valley. This proved to be but one of several Union successes of 1861, which gave Unionist politicians the opportunity to take actions that would later culminate in the formation of the new state of West Virginia.

In contrast to the military politics and recriminations, there was abundant praise heaped on Union warriors for their efforts at Carnifex Ferry. As expected, the Union papers, like the Confederate press, reported that their side fought bravely and inflicted heavy casualties on the enemy. For example, Union accounts held that Federal soldiers displayed great courage and coolness. This bravery was exemplified in the story of Lieutenant-Colonel Mason, of the Thirteenth Ohio, who, said the press, "had his forefinger shot off, but enveloped it in a handkerchief and remained on the field." He and others of Rosecrans' men bravely confronted the formidably entrenched enemy, who were so frightened that they marched away in the dead of night, leaving behind what a reporter described as "camp equipage, large quantities of forage, and subsistence, muskets, ammunition, lead, wagons, and horses, and even blankets of the privates, swords and the personal baggage of Floyd, of his colonels and other officers—besides sixty head of beef cattle."[122]

As day broke on September 11, Colonel Hugh Ewing and his Thirtieth Ohio Infantry, who had been held in reserve during the battle but were assigned to guard the Federal force during the night, found a slave, a body servant of a Confederate soldier from Tazewell

County, Virginia, on the road leading from the enemy works. The slave informed them that the Southerners had left during the night. Ewing immediately awakened and informed General Rosecrans, who had been asleep in a mow in a nearby barn. Rosecrans directed Ewing to verify the claim that the enemy was gone, so a company of the Thirtieth Ohio was marched to the entrance of the fort. There, according to Colonel Ewing, they encountered "a picket of fifteen men," who had just entered the fort, "ignorant of the retreat of their army." They immediately surrendered, and Ewing and his regiment occupied the fort. Ewing took down and gave to Rosecrans "the rebel colors that bore" the inscription "Floyd's Brigade The Price Of Liberty Is The Blood Of The Brave." Rosecrans displayed the enemy flag "to the troops then in line of battle, who received them with cheers."[123]

This was the start of a cheerful few hours for the Union. By 6:00 A.M. the stars and stripes were floating over the former Confederate camp. In jest they flew the captured stars and bars of the rebels underneath the flag of the United States. Along with the abandoned supplies, the Union men found twenty-five wounded Federal soldiers captured at Cross Lanes. Eagerly, gleefully, Rosecrans' men divided among themselves the spoils they found within the works. Hayes and other found "Bowie knives, awful to look at, but no account for war" were found, and Hayes took one as a souvenir. One of the wagons contained family stuff, what Hayes described as "spinning, leaving rolls of wool, knitting, and [the] making [of] bed quilts." All this was abandoned by a family fleeing the advance of the Federals. Among the debris were letters. One was in a perfumed white envelope written by a young lady, a Miss Becky, to a preacher in Floyd's army. In it she vehemently informs the predicant, her boyfriend, that the rumor that she had used tobacco was totally false. She wanted him to know that she eschewed such a vile habit.[124]

Union men took mementos, such as a photo of a Confederate, to send back home to curious family members and friends who wanted to know what a "Rebel" looked like. Finally order was restored, and fifty wagons of abandoned stuff were hauled off. What was not removed was burned.

Union soldiers went about their tasks. Later in the day Mrs. Patteson and her family, returned to her home, apparently without her husband, who would go to Ohio. They found the walls perforated with bullet holes and damaged from artillery shells, and the top of the chimney destroyed, along with the corn crop just north of the house. Twisted and scarred trees both north and south of the dwelling greeted them on their return. But nothing could compare with the gruesome sight on the roof of the front porch. There, just outside an upper window, lay the severed head of a man with brilliant red hair. Apparently the fellow had sought protection inside the house, went up the stairs and stuck his head out the window to see how the battle was going when a cannonball severed his head from his body. While the Pattesons were approaching their home, two barefooted and curious neighborhood boys of ten years of age, Clark Fitzwater and Thomas C. Brown, who had wanted to see what the battle site looked like, were gazing at the morbid, unforgettable sight on the porch roof.[125]

The day after the battle, the Federals captured a dozen Southern stragglers wandering about trying to cross the river. They, like the exhausted Union soldiers, found the more-than-120-yard-wide river—without any ferry boats or bridge—too formidable to cross. This made any pursuit of Floyd impossible, though much desired. As a precaution, Floyd left some skirmishers on the 100-yard-high cliffs along the Meadow River, which empties into the southern side of the Gauley near the ferry site. Any movement of the Federals across the river until they reached the rolling and partially cultivated land would make them an easy mark for snipers. Lacking a way to cross, Rosecrans encamped his fatigued men, occupied the banks north of the river crossing, and fired several "rifle cannon shots after the enemy to produce a moral effect." It would be two days before the Federals under McCook would cross the Gauley in pursuit of Floyd—who had, on the day after the battle, retreated south of Dogwood Gap, which Wise held as well as Hawk's Nest. On September 11, the day after the battle, just south of Dogwood Gap, according to General Wise, Floyd was "prostrate" and suffering from his wound and exhaustion. Wise asked him for orders, and he replied that he "did not know what orders to give."[126]

The Confederates would pull back to Sewell Mountain, where the feud between Wise and Floyd would again erupt to new heights.

[1] Ella Lonn, *Salt as a Factor in the Confederacy* (University, Ala.: University of Alabama, 1965), 19-20. When the war started there were three ways of producing salt; "Extracting the salt from saline artesian wells, boiling down sea water of water from inland salt lakes, and mining deposits of rock salt." Since the Federals controlled the Charleston region soon after the start of the war, Saltville, in southwestern Virginia, became the key source of salt for Confederates.

[2] Tompkins moved to Gauley to supervise the coal mines and iron manufacturing.

[3] Terry Lowry, *The Battle of Scary Creek: Military Operations in the Kanawha Valley April–July 1861* (Charleston W.Va.: Pictorial Histories, 1982), 4-9. Like Colonel Tompkins, Patton had family roots in Richmond. He had studied law there in his father's office after graduating from VMI. George often gazed out the window of his father's office, silently admiring the drilling of Virginia's premier and oldest militia unit, the Richmond Light Infantry Blues. The same year Patton moved to Charleston to practice law, he formed what would become one of the area's most illustrious militia units, the Kanawha Riflemen. Like the unit it was patterned after, the Richmond Blues, it was comprised of the area's socially elite. Patton first called his organization the Kanawha Minutemen, a name that was soon changed to Kanawha Rifles, which in 1859 became the Kanawha Riflemen. The Riflemen, like many of the other militia units of the Kanawha Valley during the Civil War, became part of the Twenty-second Regiment of Virginia Volunteers. Other militia units formed before or at the advent of war were the Border Guards from Hurricane Bridge, the Buffalo Guards (also known as Blues), and the Coal River Rifle Company.

[4] Cohen, *The Civil War In West Virginia*, 34; Hotchkiss, *Virginia*, 59-60; *OR*, Ser. I, vol. 2, 290-291. Also during the month of June another ex-governor faced the same problems obtaining weapons that Wise had. John B. Floyd was appointed brigadier-general and sent to the southwestern part of the Great Valley, adjacent to the Kanawha Valley. Floyd was born in southwestern Virginia and was very popular in that region. The former U.S. Secretary of War was charged with raising a large force and protecting the Virginia & Tennessee railroad. So lacking were the Virginians in weapons, Floyd sent a special messenger to the governors of South Carolina and Georgia for 1,600 guns, "giving as his excuse that neither the Confederate government nor the State of Virginia could furnish arms for his troops."

[5] Jay C. Mullen, "Dear Brother...I send you a brief account of 'the action at Scary Creek...' George S. Patton's Baptism of Fire," *West Virginia History* (Oct. 1971), 55. Patton was the son of a former Virginia governor, a graduate of VMI, and nicknamed "Frenchy" for his pointed beard.

[6] Jacob D. Cox, *Military Reminiscences of the Civil War* (New York, C. Scribner Sons, 1900), vol. I, 62-65; *OR*, Ser. I, vol. 51, pt. 2, 416-18; John A. Cutchins, *A Famous Command: The Richmond Light Infantry Blues* (Richmond, Va.: Garrett & Massie, 1934), 79-80; David L. Phillips, ed., and Rebecca L. Hill, chief researcher, *War Stories: Civil War in West Virginia* (Leesburg, Va., McClain, 1991), 89; Lowry, *The Battle of Scary Creek*, 77-81. Union and Confederate troop movement

in the Ripley region is not clearly explained by primary sources.

[7] Lowry, *The Battle of Scary Creek*, 81-82. The Confederate force consisted of a cavalry force of 160 of the Mounted Rangers of Bierne's Sharpshooters under Captain Robert A. Caskie.

[8] *OR*, Ser. I, vol. 2, 291.

[9] Before the war, Gallipolis, nicknamed "Negropolis" because runaway slaves from the Kanawha Valley settled there. The town was also the depository of supplies for the Kanawha Valley.

[10] Cohen, *The Civil War in West Virginia,* 34, 36. Price Lewis changed his mind as he landed at Guyandotte about posing as the son of an English nobleman. After Wise refused to grant him a pass to Richmond, Lewis is said to have gone to his friend Colonel Tompkins, who told him he didn't need a pass; the road was open to Richmond. Instead Lewis returned to the north.

[11] Hotchkiss, *Virginia*, 60.

[12] Cox reports that he planned to send half of the Second Kentucky to Ripley if they were ready twenty-four hours after his arrival at Thirteen-Mile Creek. At Pocataligo, he was waiting for the Second Kentucky from Guyandotte and half of the First Kentucky from Riley and Sissonville.

[13] Cox claimed Wise had 4,000 men, and Wise felt his adversary numbered 6,000.

[14] *B & L*, vol. I, 137-39; Hotchkiss, *Virginia*, 60-61; *OR*, Ser. I, vol. 2, 198-99; 2 vol. 51, pt. 1, 418-21; Cox, *Military Reminiscences of the Civil War*, vol. I, 59-69; Wise, *The Life of Henry Wise of Virginia*, 287.

[15] Today this skirmish is referred to as the "Battle of Barboursville." Several days before this encounter, Confederates attacked a Union ship at Guyandotte.

[16] Lowry, *The Battle of Scary Creek*, 92; Moore, ed., *Record of the Rebellion*, vol. II, 285. Companies A, B, D, F, and K of the Second Kentucky were commanded by Colonel William E. Woodruff. He gave the men a rousing pep talk before turning command over to Lieutenant-Colonel George Neff, who was to lead the Federals to Barboursville.

[17] Lowry, *The Battle of Scary Creek*, 92. Captain Jenkins' place was a large plantation with numerous slaves and was located north of Guyandotte on the southern banks of the Ohio River. It was at this estate, "Greenbottom," that Colonel Neff had his conversation with Mrs. Jenkins. Captain Jenkins was not at the battle of Barboursville; some of the Rangers were, but he would play a key role a few days later in the battle of Scary Creek.

[18] Lowry, in *The Battle of Scary Creek*, 96-98; Moore, ed., *Record of the Rebellion*, vol. II, 285-86.

[19] Lowry, *The Battle of Scary Creek*, 98-100. Cox sent Colonel Jesse Norton and three companies of the Twenty-first Ohio to make a reconnaissance of the enemy's position in the Scary Creek region on July 14. The skirmish has also been called the "First Battle of Scary Creek."

[20] Ibid., 102. Wise ordered Colonel John Clarkson with Captain John Brock's and Albert J. Beckett's cavalry to attack the Union at Poca. Lowry, in *The Battle of Scary Creek,* pointed out that until recent discovery of new evidence, it was believed that Wise's claim of victory at the Poca skirmish was a fabrication.

[21] Poca (called "Pokey" by residents) was a small settlement at the mouth of the Pocotaligo River, where the latter empties into the Kanawha.

[22] Lieutenant-Colonel Carr B. White of the Twelfth Ohio, with a detachment, crossed the Kanawha around 9:00 A.M. to probe the enemy's position.

[23] Lowry, *The Battle of Scary Creek*, 109-113. The origins of the name Scary Creek are shrouded in the mysteries of legends that tell of unfortunate happenings to Native Americans and early settlers.

[24] The three original companies at Scary were the Putnam County Border Riflemen, led by a physician from Putnam County, Captain Andrew R. Barbee; an infantry company from Wheeling under Captain James W. Sweeney; and the Kanawha Riflemen under Second Lieutenant Nicholas Fitzhugh. Wise had advised Patton at Camp Tompkins to pull back and take a stand further southeast, if practical. Patton felt Scary Creek would be a stronger position to make a stand.

[25] *B & L*, vol. I, 148-49; John M. Belohavek, "John B. Floyd and the West Virginia Campaign of 1866," *West Virginia History*, July 1968, 283-91; Frank Klement, "General John B. Floyd, and the West Virginia Campaign of R61," *West Virginia History*, April 1997, 319-31. The cavalry companies were the Border Rangers under Captain Albert Jenkins and the Kanawha Rangers, under Captain Charles I. Lewis. The total Confederates south of the Kanawha were fewer than 900.

[26] Lowry, *The Battle of Scary Creek*, 117, 119-21; Phillips, ed., *War Stories*, 50-51. Captain Charles S. Cotter was in command of the Independent Ohio Volunteer Artillery, which accompanied Lowe, along with Captain John S. George's Independent Company of Ohio Volunteer Cavalry. Cox's adjutant, Charles Whittlesey, a graduate of West Point and the Black Hawk War, suggested Cox send Colonel Jesse S. Norton along with Lowe, as Norton was familiar with the area. Once across the Kanawha, they stopped at the John Morgan farm north of Scary Creek. There it was decided most of the Union were to go by a little-used road further inland that merged with Teays Valley Road near the mouth of Scary Creek. The rest of the Union force went by River Road along the Kanawha River.

[27] This company was Captain Sweeney's infantry from Wheeling.

[28] The Union piece was north of the bridge across Scary Creek and near the Kanawha River, and the other was near the Scary Creek and Teays Valley Road. The Virginians had one piece south of the bridge near the river and another to the west on a hill.

[29] Lowry, *The Battle of Scary Creek*, 122-23.

[30] The new arrivals were Captain Corn's Sandy Rangers from Coal Mountain and Colonel Anderson, part of Wise's legion, B. S. Thompson's Kanawha Militia.

[31] Scary is much wider in this area than at its mouth.

[32] "Spider" was the cook of Company A of the Twelfth Ohio.

[33] Lowry, *The Battle of Scary Creek*, 125-27.

[34] Cohen, *The Civil War in West Virginia*; Stan Cohen, *A Pictorial Guide to West Virginia's Civil War Sites and Related Information* (Charleston, W. Va.: Pictorial Histories, 1990), 88-89; Cox, *Military Reminiscences*, 69-70; Phillips, ed., *War Stories*, 50; Lowry, *The Battle of Scary Creek*, 132-33; *OR*, Ser. I, vol. 2, 288-91.

[35] While the battle of Scary was being fought, Wise ordered Colonels John

McCausland and Christopher Q. Tompkins to lead 800 men north of the Kanawha to attack Cox at Poca. By the time the Confederates got to Cox's camp, the Union commander was waiting, well entrenched and with artillery, including twelve-pound howitzers, pointed at the Confederates. McCausland realized an attack would be foolish and returned to Two Mile Camp near Charleston The number of casualties and the details of the battle of Scary Creek, like other battles, vary greatly in source materials. See Lowry, pages 136-137.

[36] Welch was killed by the third shot fired by the Union artillery.

[37] Phillips, ed., *War Stories*, 44-49, 50-51, 90. Another Confederate at Scary Creek, James D. Sedinger of the "Border Rangers," writes that the only flag their side had on the battlefield was one given to them the morning before the battle. It had been made by local women who had stopped the Rangers while on their way to Scary Creek. The flag was carried by the Rangers until the Confederates adopted a battle flag. It was given to a young lady to keep until after the war, when it was turned over to one of the veteran Rangers. The flag remained in his house for twenty years until his wife, who was looking for red fabric for a rug she was making, tore the flag apart.

[38] James H. Mays, *Four Years for Old Virginia* (Los Angeles: Swordsman, 1970), 13; Lowry, *The Battle of Scary Creek*, 135; "War-Time Reminiscences of James D. Sedinger," Boyd B. Stutler Collection, West Virginia State Archives, Charleston, West Virginia, 3. There are several versions of the capture of the soldier in the hollow tree. Confederates buried the Union dead 100 yards from Scary Creek and thirty yards from the road that ran to the north paralleling the Kanawha.

[39] Cox later lamented that he should have paid more attention to events at Scary Creek.

[40] Neff was a lieutenant-colonel; the other two were full colonels. The captains were George Austin and John R. Herd.

[41] Cox, *Military Reminiscences*, vol. I, 70; David L. Phillips, ed., and Rebecca L. Hill, chief researcher, *War Diaries: The 1861 Kanawha Valley Campaigns* (Leesburg, Va.: Gauley Mount, 1990), 13-14; Phillips, ed., *War Stories*, 325-381. There is another—albeit improbable—account of Colonel Neff's capture: He was allegedly found the morning after the battle, wounded and hiding in a hollow tree. Captain Jenkins, the commander of Neff's capturers, is said to have treated him with great kindness, fulfilling a promise to his wife to behave like a gentleman. This was lenient treatment, considering Neff's earlier behavior while in Cox's army. He had gone to Jenkins' farm, driven off cattle, and taken many items from the house, informing Jenkins' wife that if he caught her husband, he would hang him.

[42] Carl M. Becker, "John Williams Lowe: Failure in Inner-Direction," *Ohio History* (July 1964), 84-85.

[43] Roy B. Cook, "The Civil War Comes to Charleston," *West Virginia History*, January 1962, 153-67; Cox, *Military Reminiscences*, vol. I, 71-74; Lowry, *The Battle of Scary Creek*, 140-48; *OR*, Ser. I, vol. 2, 288. For various accounts of the sinking of the *Julia Moffitt,* see Lowry, 141-145. Tompkins had his commissary stores placed on the ship as he was getting ready to evacuate Fort Tompkins and the Scary Creek area when the Federals appeared at Charleston and fired across the

river at the boat. After this, the Federals crossed the river in a small boat to capture the *Julia Moffitt*. A Confederate, claimed to be Phil Doddridge, ran back on the boat, gathered mattresses, doused them with oil taken from the engine room, and started a fire that destroyed the *Julia Moffitt* and her Confederate cargo worth $100,000. Doddridge is said to have barely escaped, hurriedly scampering from the burning boat to shore, where he covered himself with dry leaves. Union soldiers soon trod all around him, but could not find him in the dark. During the Confederate retreat, they had to leave behind the seriously wounded George Patton, who had been wounded at Scary Creek. Federal surgeons tried to amputate the Virginian's arm, but when he pointed a loaded pistol at them, they changed their minds. One of the Union doctors came up with an alternate solution to the amputation. He devised a sling attached to a bucket "with a hole in it which dripped water" onto the wounded arm; he is credited with saving the limb. Patton was soon exchanged for Colonel Jesse S. Norton, captured at Scary Creek. Although Patton would be out of the Kanawha campaign, he would later return to service until killed at the third battle of Winchester (1864).

[44] Cox, *Military Reminiscences*, vol. I, 76-77, 79. McClellan sent a telegraph from Washington congratulating Cox. Rosecrans was also greatly satisfied and made Cox think he had achieved more than his new commander had expected.

[45] Covered bridges were common in that era, used primarily to protect the wood from the weather. This new, and many felt elegant, structure had replaced an old and run-down bridge. It rested, according to one of the retreating Confederates, on four stone abutments, two of which were in the river. The others were next to the banks. The sides, according to one of Wise's men, were covered with weatherboard, with four windows on each side. Wooden shingles covered the roof, and the whole structure was painted white. A painting in Cohen's *West Virginia Civil War Sites*, page 15, of this covered bridge, shows no windows but shows unboarded space several feet down from the eaves and running the length of the bridge. The picture also shows a divider on the bridge that separated traffic.

[46] Terry D. Lowry, *Twenty-Second Virginia Infantry* (Lynchburg, Va.: H.E. Howard, 1988; Second ed.), 16; *OR*, Ser. 1, vol. 5, 770-75. Wise lamented that since leaving the Valley, 500 men had deserted. He was unaware that many were on leave granted by other officers.

[47] Lyle M. Blackwell, *Gauley Bridge: The Town and Its First Church* (Parsons, W. Va.: McClain, 1980), 35-37; Phillips, ed., *War Stories*, 148-50. Cox's men used a rope ferry at Gauley Bridge until a new bridge was constructed on the piers of the former covered bridge. The new structure was a suspension bridge with one-and-one-quarter-inch cables. It was in service from February until September 1862, when it was burned. Who was responsible, Confederate or Union? This has been debated. The demise of the suspension bridge left the region without a bridge over the Gauley River for sixty-three years. In 1925 a bridge was built to carry traffic on U.S. Route 60. In all there have been six bridges at Gauley Bridge, starting with first in 1822 and followed by new bridges in 1828, 1850, 1862, 1925, and 1952.

[48] Beuhring H. Jones, "My First Thirty Days Experience as a Captain," *Southern Literary Messenger*, vol. 37, no. 2, 1883.

[49] Phillips, ed., *War Stories*, 91-92, 150-53, 156. Reveille was supposed to be at 5:00 A.M., inspection of quarters a half-hour later, breakfast at 7:00, drill at 9:00, dinner at 1:00 P.M., drill at 4:00, retreat at sundown, dress parade at 6:30, supper at 7:00, and taps at 9:00. Reynolds records that they renewed drilling on August 5, and on the same day he performed the even more disagreeable task of washing his own clothes.

[50] The force Floyd recruited was from his home country of Montgomery and the surrounding region.

[51] See James M. McPherson, *Battle Cry of Freedom* (New York: Oxford University, 1988), 226; Nevins, *The Emergence of Lincoln*, vol. II, 196-200, 372-75; Roy Nichols, *Disruption of American Democracy*, (New York: MacMillan, 1948), 190, 553-54; Randall and Donald, *Civil War and Reconstruction*, 310-11.

[52] Henry Heth, *The Memoirs of Henry Heth*, ed. James L. Morrison Jr. (Westport, Conn.: Greenwood, 1974), 152. Reproduced with permission of Greenwood Publishing Group, Inc., Westport, Conn.

[53] *OR*, Ser. I, vol. 5, 766.

[54] Wise said the delay was needed because of desertion, improperly supplied men with insufficient clothing, "camp equipage, arms, or ammunition." Many were "destitute of blankets, shoes, tents and clothing, knapsacks, cartridge and cap boxes, mess-pans, and camp-kettles." They had only half the wagons needed and lacked every kind of medical stores. Over 300 men were in hospitals.

[55] Heth, *Memoirs*, 153.

[56] *OR*, I, vol. 5, 766, 778-89, 784, 792-95, 804-5, 813-16, 822-23.

[57] Ibid., 787. Floyd moved about 2,500 men forward; Wise's 1,200-man force was left behind in the Lewisburg area. The artillery pieces were all six-pounders, except for a twelve-pound howitzer. Wise lamented he rarely had ammunition for the twelve-pounder.

[58] On the north bank at Kanawha Falls was a flour mill. Today Cotton Mountain is called Cotton Hill.

[59] Blackwell, *Gauley Bridge*, 34; Cox, *Military Reminiscences*, 80-87; Phillips, ed., *War Diaries*, 293-94, 369-71; Williams, *Hayes of the Twenty-third*, 91-92. It is not known if the Union or Confederates burned the house, perhaps in 1862. The site of the Tompkins house and farm is now the Hawks Nest Golf Course.

[60] Cox in his *Reminiscences*, on page 14, calls Big Creek "Pig Creek."

[61] Cox also sent cavalrymen to scout the area fifty miles east of Hawks Nest. To get to the overlook at Hawks Nest required traveling several hundred feet from the turnpike.

[62] J. T. Peters and H. B. Carden, *History of Fayette County, West Virginia* (Charleston, W. Va.: Jarrett, 1926), 9-10, 27-32. About three and a half miles east of Hawks Nest is another 500-foot cliff known as Lover's Leap. The site is named for a legend involving ill-fated young lovers, Indian and white, who met their deaths while accidentally falling or intentionally leaping to their death while fleeing their disapproving families.

[63] Cox, *Military Reminiscences of the Civil War*, vol. I, 85.

[64] Cox, *Military Reminiscences of the Civil War*, vol. I, 90-91; Phillips, ed., *War*

Diaries, 106. Patrols were also sent to Summersville and thirty to forty miles up on the left bank of the Kanawha River. Guerrillas often fired upon Federal supply steamboats in the Charleston area. At Gauley Cox placed two cannons "high up on the hillside covering the ferry and the road up New River." Other works included "an infantry trench, with parapet of barrels filled with earth" along the banks of the Gauley, a blockhouse made of logs with "loopholes for musketry" below Kanawha Falls, and the cut timber along Gauley Mountain that would entangle any enemy who tried to move through it.

[65] The nineteenth-century spelling of Carnifex Ferry includes Carnifax Ferry and Carnifix Ferry.

[66] Wise's cavalry was exhausted from scouting, and he lacked the horses needed to pull the artillery pieces. He had to leave two of the pieces at Dogwood Gap.

[67] Wise was urged by Floyd to hurriedly build another flatboat. Some say two boats were used. The crossing was slow because only one wagon at a time could cross.

[68] *OR*, Ser. I, vol. 5, 813-16.

[69] Lawrence Wilson, ed., *Itinerary of the Seventh Ohio Volunteer Infantry, 1861-1864* (New York: Neale, 1907), 60-63. Three Federals, counting Schutte, had been mortally wounded or killed. Three were slightly wounded, three captured. Bohn was captured. Before his capture, as he was running down the road, Bohn's canteen fell off when the string was cut by a bullet. A bullet also went through his hat.

[70] Terry Lowry, *September Blood* (CharlestonW. Va.: Pictorial Histories, 1985), 13, 17; Wilson, *Itinerary of Seventh Ohio*, 69, 71.

[71] The hill upon which the Zoar Church is located is much higher than Malcolm Heights.

[72] Cincinnati *Daily Commercial*, September 4, 1861; Detroit *Tri-Weekly Tribune*, September 6, 1861. The sutlers were fortunate to have escaped. Captain John P. Boggs, the leader of the Snake Hunters, a group of independent Union partisan Rangers, saw the overwhelming Southern force and rushed back to save the wagons. Boggs warned the sutlers' department, four wagons owned by Samuel Hatch of Cincinnati. An employee, Edward Halsted, heeded Boggs' alarm by moving the wagons away from the battle scene and "seizing a carpet sack containing $15,000.00 in government orders, from one of the chests." He rode "twenty miles on the tail of a wagon, anticipating the enemy, and awaiting an opportunity to disappear into the woods upon their approach."

[73] Lowry, *September Blood*, 17, 25, 27; Wilson, *Itinerary of Seventh Ohio*, 70-83; Letters to General J. D. Cox from Colonel E. B. Tyler, August 27, 1861, National Archives, Record Group 94, Entry 329, Box 119. At the time Tyler ordered the retreat, six of the companies were north of the road to Gauley Bridge, and three were on the other side of the road to the south. Members of Company C tried to escape to Gauley Bridge through a mountain pass, but found Colonel Tompkins and his Twenty-second Virginia Infantry waiting. Before firing, Tompkins gave the Oberlin men a chance to surrender, which their captain and a dozen and a half did.

[74] Lowry, *September Blood*, 21, 28-29; Wilson, *Itinerary of Seventh Ohio*, 78-79.

[75] Richmond *Whig*, September 13, 1861.

[76] The day after the Cross Lanes fight, Tyler sent chaplain Brown and surgeon

Cushing to check on Union wounded and prisoners.

[77] Memphis *Daily Appeal*, September 11, 1861. Some contend Dyer's body was temporarily buried near one of the outbuildings.

[78] Richmond *Dispatch*, September 7, 1861.

[79] Heth, *Memoirs*, 151-53. Heth's contempt of Floyd arose during the early mobilization of Floyd's forces. Heth received little or no help from Floyd in mustering men into service. Night schools for officers in which tactics were given to them to study had to be abandoned; some could not read.

[80] Cox, *Military Reminiscences of the Civil War*, vol. I, 97.

[81] *OR*, Ser. I, vol. 51, pt. 2, 271-72.

[82] Cox, *Military Reminiscences of the Civil War,* vol. I, 97; OR, Ser. I, vol. 5, 124-26, 819-23; Heth, Memoirs, 154.

[83] Wise was also greatly annoyed by what he considered Floyd's "sneering order" belittling Colonel Henningsen in Wise's command for sending a report to headquarters signed only with his name and not his rank.

[84] Big Creek was also called Pig Creek.

[85] *B & L*, vol. I, 145; Frank Moore, ed., *The Rebellion Record* (New York: G.P. Putnam, 1862), vol. III, 49, 50, 55-56; *OR*, Ser. I, vol. 5, 129; Baltimore *Sun*, September 19, 1861.

[86] Hayes, *Diary*, 76, 79. Hayes spent much of his first few months (end of July to end of September) traveling to Beverly and finally to Carnifex Ferry.

[87] Cohen, *West Virginia Civil War Sites*, 27. The Federals sent daily parties from ten to 100 on expeditions from ten to forty miles to hunt down the menacing partisans. Union soldiers were also kept busy escorting and protecting their wagons, especially in the mountains, where they were constantly met by attacking parties.

[88] Ibid., 63.

[89] Ibid., 66-69.

[90] Joshua Horton and Solomon Teverbaugh, *History of the Eleventh Regiment Ohio Volunteer Infantry* (Dayton, Ohio: W.J. Shuey, 1866), 33; Williams, *Hayes of the Twenty-Third*, 63-64. Company H of the Eleventh Ohio, with Cox's army near Poca, used such an excuse when interrogated about why they always had "a good supply of fresh meat" The captain creatively explained, "I heard something cautiously approaching the post. Receiving no answer to my hail I fired, and upon examination found I had killed a fine fat SHEEP. My boys were hungry, and *mutton is very healthy meat in summer time*. After this I noticed that the comrades of the animal *accidentally* killed seem to entertain malice toward my company; they would congregate around us, shake their heads, and made such hostile demonstrations that I was fearful some of my boys might be *bitten*, so I thought it best to shoot a sheep occasionally in order to prevent any such catastrophe!"

[91] Hayes, *Diary*, 62-63, 83.

[92] Confederate scouts had been hanging around Rosecrans' force since the Federals arrived at Birch River. Floyd had long been aware the enemy was coming.

[93] Moore, ed., *Rebellion Record*, vol. III, 44-50.

[94] Lowry, *September Blood*, 69. Mrs. Patteson remained in the area while her husband traveled to Ohio, where he is believed to have stayed for three years.

[95] *The Official Atlas of the Civil War* (New York: T. Yoseloff, 1958), plate IX, 1. The Confederates cleared the woods around their works to build fortifications and clear their line of fire to the north.

[96] Lowry, *September Blood*, 83-84; *OR*, Ser. I, vol. 5, 130; Moore, ed., *Rebellion Record*, vol. III, 47-50. Estimates of where Lytle was wounded range from thirty to 150 yards from the Confederate works. Lytle's reputation for boldness had permeated Floyd's camp. Supposedly a dozen or more of the Southerner's best marksmen were given the task of shooting him.

[97] Lowry, *September Blood*, 87; Moore, ed., *Rebellion Record*, vol. III, 52-53; *OR*, Ser. I, vol. 3, 138; Whitelaw Reid, *Ohio in the War* (New York: Wilstach & Baldwin, 1868), vol. II, 78. Reid reported that Lowe's back was on the ground and his face, toward the enemy, wore a smile of satisfaction.

[98] Becker, "John Williams Lowe," 87; Moore, ed., *Rebellion Record*, vol. III, 52-53. Lowe's remains were sent to his family. The colonel had not received a military education, but was a longtime, respected citizen of Xenia, Ohio.

[99] Becker, "John Williams Lowe," 76-87.

[100] *OR*, Ser. I, vol. 5, 138-39. Lieutenant-Colonel Carr B. White first ordered Wallace to leave his far right position and join the rest of the regiment on the left in an attempt to reunite the unit. When Wallace arrived at the ferry road, he was ordered by a staff officer to halt and await further orders. As a result, the regiment was not united until after the battle. In his report Wallace states, "nor do I personally know how or why the regiment was separated."

[101] Ibid., 141. To protect his brigade, especially from Confederate artillery fire, McCook moved seven companies of the Ninth Ohio and the Twenty-eighth Ohio over a path to the right of the ferry road to the back of the crest of a hill occupied by McMullin's battery. When enemy projectiles started falling among his men, McCook pulled them further back. The rest of his brigade, the Forty-seventh Ohio remained back on the ferry road, protected by woods.

[102] Moore, ed., *Rebellion Record*, vol. III, 51.

[103] Most of McCook's brigade proceeded toward the Confederate works by moving on the western side of the ferry road. Only the Ninth Ohio was on the eastern side of the road.

[104] Only three or four Federal companies made the assault on Floyd's center and left.

[105] After the battle a prisoner informed Smith that this was what had happened. At the time Smith was not aware that he had driven away Confederates on the extreme left.

[106] *OR*, Ser. I, vol. 5, 139-40; 143-44.

[107] William Childers, ed., "A Virginian's Dilemma" (The Civil War Diary of Isaac Noyes Smith), *West Virginia History* (April 1966) (hereafter cited as Smith, "Diary"). Most of the fortification was in the center of the line, where earthen redoubt, which included a parapet battery, protected in the front by a trench. The log breastworks on the left, three-quarters of a mile long, consisted of a double line. Floyd's right was more easily defended because of a steep slope in front that descended to a ravine.

[108] Lowry, *September Blood*, 69-71. Colonel Gabriel Wharton's Fifty-first Virginia infantry, placed originally on Floyd's far left flank, seemed to have been pulled to the left of Guy's battery upon the arrival of the Twenty-second and Thirty-sixth Virginia infantry regiments. The Fiftieth Virginia, upon evacuating its camp a mile in advance of Camp Gauley, took up positions at 2:30 P.M. on both the right and left of the artillery. The artillery consisted of Guy's four pieces and supposedly two pieces of Captain S. A. Adams' Company of Virginia Light Infantry. There is little documentation to support the position of Adams' two pieces.

[109] *OR*, Ser. I, vol. 5, 147-57. The exact numbers and the disposition of Confederate units at Carnifex Ferry are difficult to determine because of the lack of official reports by the participants. Only Floyd and Wise—who was not at the site—filed reports. Floyd stated he had only 1,800 men. Wise claimed he had more: 2,400 infantrymen; Corn's and Beckett's cavalry, numbering 100; the 40 men of the "State Volunteer Artillery" and their two pieces; plus the three pieces and 61 men of Wise's artillery; and Tompkins' and McCausland's regiments of just under 800 men, making the grand total of 2,600 men minus the number sick and on furlough. McCausland's men, like Tompkins, arrived shortly before the battle, around 12:30. They ate lunch and went to the outer works.

[110] James A. Davis, *Fifty-First Virginia Infantry* (Lynchburg, Va.: H.E. Howard, 1984), 5; Lowry, *September Blood*, 81; Moore, ed., *Rebellion Record*, vol. III, 56-57.

[111] Lowry, *September Blood*, 80-81.

[112] Moore, ed., *Rebellion Record*, vol. III, 56-57. Federal accounts contend Floyd had sixteen artillery pieces, Wise said five, and another reliable account gives the number as six.

[113] Andrews, *The North Reports The Civil War*, 109-11.

[114] Wise said Floyd had only one flatboat; other accounts list two, the Union, more. During the crossing, Surgeon Gleaves, who had cared for Floyd, carried with him the pistol of Colonel Lytle and a saddle and bridle taken from the colonel's black horse, who had died within their works.

[115] Moore, ed., *The Rebellion Record*, vol. III, 56-57.

[116] Richmond *Dispatch*, September 14, 1861.

[117] Hayes, *Diary*, 93.

[118] Phillips, ed., *War Diaries*, 212-15; Thomas J. Riddle, "Reminiscences of Floyd's Operation in West Virginia in 1861," *SHSP*, vol. XI, 92-95.

[119] Benham responded to the charge of drunkenness by making the same charge against Rosecrans. Neither accusation was proven.

[120] Lowry, *September Blood*, 76.

[121] Henry W. Benham Papers, National Archives, Washington, D.C.

[122] Moore, ed., *Rebellion Record*, vol. III, 54; *The Baltimore Sun*, September 19, 1861. One of the "runaway negroes" told the Federals that Floyd had fifty killed and many wounded. The Union wounded had been taken during the battle to a barn and house immediately to the rear of Rosecrans' battle lines, except for several who fell near Floyd's works. They were not found until the next day.

[123] Hugh Ewing, *U.S. Army General's Report of Civil War Service*, 1864-1887, Roll

3, vols. IV & V, 5 & 6. Rosecrans stated that he "would deposit the banner at Washington, inscribed with the name of the 30th (Ohio) regiment."

[124] Hayes, *Diary*, 91; Phillips, ed., *War Stories*, 21.

[125] Lowry, *September Blood*, 129. Clark Fitzwater's home was a short distance north of the battlefield and apparently was one of the area homes used as a hospital. The postwar years saw the Patteson family dig out the large chestnut stump where Floyd had stood and directed his troops during the battle. They removed and burned the log breastworks for firewood. Repairs and additions were made to the house. In 1931 the state of West Virginia created the Carnifax Ferry Battlefield Park Commission. In 1935 the Patteson farm, 218.8 acres of land, was purchased, and a state park was established. The park was constructed on the area of the Confederate right flank. Numerous celebrations of the battle have been held, starting with the seventieth anniversary of the battle on September 10, 1931, attended by 5,000 people.

[126] *OR*, Ser. I, vol. 5, 129, 130-34, 161. Wise claims he rode up and found Floyd upon the ground and received that reply to his question.

CHAPTER IX

RAIN, MUD, MOUNTAINS, AND ENDLESS MARCHES: THE UNION KEEPS THE KANAWHA VALLEY

The march back to Sewell Mountain completed the Confederates' second failed attempt to secure the Kanawha Valley. Floyd and Wise did not even reach the edge of the Kanawha Valley, much less drive the enemy from it. Now the enemy pursued them to Sewell Mountain, where the terrain and inclement weather stalemated combat and forced the Federals to fall back nearer their Gauley Bridge base. Spurred on by Lee, Floyd followed in what was the Confederates' third attempt to secure the Kanawha Valley. He got no nearer than Cotton Hill. From there he harassed the enemy across the river with scattered artillery fire before retreating when the Federals advanced. The year ended with the Kanawha Valley firmly in Union hands.

WISE MUST GO

Wise's time as part of Floyd's command was numbered. Two days after Carnifex Ferry, Floyd wrote in his report to the Confederate secretary of war that he was "very confident" that he could have defeated Rosecrans and retaken the Kanawha Valley if Wise had reinforced him as he had been ordered to do and if the regiments from North Carolina and Georgia had reached him before his withdrawal. Any chance of success was doomed by the lack of unity of command, which had to be remedied if the Kanawha Valley was to be secured.[1]

Five days after the battle at Carnifex Ferry, Floyd wrote President Davis, asking that Wise and his command be transferred elsewhere, as, he wrote, "his presence…is almost as injurious as if we were in the camp of the enemy." Floyd explained that the transfer of Henry Wise and his legion, all enemies of Floyd, to Beauregard's or McGruder's command would save Wise "from the pains and penalties from being cashiered." The real reason, however, was not to spare Wise's feelings, but to save Floyd from attacks from pro-Wise newspapers in Richmond. Much of Floyd's long letter to Davis was nevertheless filled with embittered denunciation of his rival.[2]

Pressure to do something also came from the citizens of Lewisburg and the surrounding region. They were fearful that their town and communities were in imminent danger of being seized by the Federals, a danger that was increased by the bickering of the generals, Wise and Floyd. Citizens wrote letters to Davis, pleading for help.[3] This was all the Confederate authorities needed to hear. On September 20, Acting Secretary of War J. P. Benjamin sent two dispatches from President Davis. One was sent to Floyd, congratulating him on his "brilliant affair" at Carnifex Ferry, and the other went to Wise, instructing him to immediately turn over all his troops to Floyd and to return to Richmond. Before Wise was informed of his removal, he and the rest of the tired and often rain-soaked Confederates had pulled back to Sewell Mountain, where Wise— unaware of his impending departure—countered Floyd's wishes one more time.

SEWELL MOUNTAIN

The rugged terrain of Sewell Mountain, also know as Big Sewell, sits halfway between Gauley Bridge and Lewisburg, about thirty miles between the two. Its two summits are located to the east and west, about a mile apart from each other, and are interrupted by steep gorges and ravines. A mile and a half east of Big Sewell, separated by a valley, is Little Sewell Mountain.

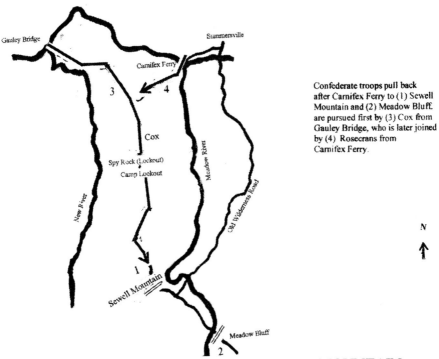

Confederate troops pull back after Carnifex Ferry to (1) Sewell Mountain and (2) Meadow Bluff are pursued first by (3) Cox from Gauley Bridge, who is later joined by (4) Rosecrans from Carnifex Ferry.

CONFEDERATE RETREAT TO SEWELL MOUNTAIN

Fourteen miles east of Big Sewell is Meadow Bluff, where the Old Wilderness Road from the north intersects with the James and the Kanawha Turnpike. This region was where the saga of the aftermath of Carnifex Ferry would be played out during the last half of September and the early days of October.[4]

Floyd's retreat was a miserable one. Unremitting rain, mud, cold, hunger, and illness plagued both Confederates and their Federal pursuers. Hundreds on both sides were disabled by measles, diarrhea, typhoid, and other maladies.[5] For the Virginians, the march back to Sewell Mountain was made harder by their loss of sleep from three difficult night marches. All found the weather, marching, and camp life very unpleasant and fatiguing. Some found their situation dismaying. Rations were limited and sporadically served, often consisting of a shrunken piece of burned beef with a small piece of bread. Horses were broken by disease, overwork, bottomless roads, and insufficient forage. It was difficult to find mounts to scout the whereabouts of the enemy. At Sewell Mountain Floyd's diminished horses forced him to ask Wise to send out twenty cavalrymen to scout the turnpike to the west. Wise sent only twelve cavalrymen, and they soon returned without locating the enemy.

Bleak conditions hurt morale. Major Smith along with others of Tompkins' Twenty-second Virginia, had experienced great anxiety before evacuating Camp Gauley, but once he was south of the river, Smith felt the greatest relief of his life. He believed the worst was behind him. He was wrong. After enduring the conditions of a miserable march to Sewell Mountain and later to Meadow Bluff, he became despondent. He feared for the life of his Unionist father back home and saw little hope for the future as the war dragged on, growing harder every day, while hopes for peace dwindled. A religious man, Smith was dismayed by the unchristian behavior of "everybody bent on the shedding of blood." The division of loyalties and opposing armies, he feared, would turn western Virginia red before the war ended.[6]

While Smith and others lamented, their plight darkened more each time they had to bury the body of a dead comrade who was carried back after being killed by an enemy picket. In the meantime, Wise and Floyd's feud intensified. While on Sewell Mountain, on September 16, Floyd received information that Union troops were coming and might attempt to turn him by moving to the east and south over the Wilderness Road to Meadow Bluff. This would put the enemy fourteen miles southeast of Sewell Mountain and behind the Confederates.[7] A greatly alarmed Floyd sent a small force to block or retard any enemy movement on the Wilderness Road. At 5:00 that afternoon he called a council of war to decide what else they should do. Wise was unaware that Floyd had the day before sent a letter to Richmond, a letter that Floyd hoped would remove him; and Wise had the answer. He claimed that Floyd's current position on the western summit of Big Swell Mountain "indefensible." Wise argued that his own position on the eastern summit was "impregnable." Therefore, he said, Floyd should pull back to Wise's camp to wait and see what the enemy was going to do. Since the latter position could easily be defended, Wise proposed that he be allowed to take part of his own infantry and move along the left bank of the Kanawha River toward Charleston to support his cavalry, who had just won a battle twelve miles from Charleston.[8]

Wise left the council claiming that Floyd would examine the eastern summit, located a mile and a half in back of Floyd by road, or about a half-mile straight back, as the crow flies. Wise believed that if Floyd found it a strong position, he would defend the eastern summit. But Floyd either changed his mind or deceived Wise, knowing it was likely that any day Richmond would act upon his request and remove Wise, the thorn in his side. Soon after the meeting, Floyd left to fall back to what he called "the most defensible point between Meadow Bluff and Lewisburg" and "ordered Wise to prepare to do the same."[9]

Major Tyler broke the news to Wise. Upon leaving the meeting, Tyler told Wise that Floyd's camp was preparing to move and had been intending to retreat since before the council of war took place.[10] Infuriated, General Wise got on his horse and rode to his command. As he rode near his first encamped men, Wise stood up on his stirrups and called out loudly, "Who is retreating now? Who is retreating now?" The general repeated the question as he rode slowly among his men. Soon his whole command gathered around him, and Wise exclaimed, "Men, who is retreating now? John B. Floyd, G-d--- him, the bullet-hit son of a bitch, he is retreating now."[11]

DEFIANCE AND OBSTINACY: WISE STAYS ON SEWELL MOUNTAIN

Wise refused to leave Big Sewell and naming where he stayed, appropriately, Camp Defiance. Even the diplomatic Robert E. Lee could not talk Wise into uniting with Floyd at Meadow Bluff. When Lee arrived at Meadow Bluff on September 21, after failing to dislodge the enemy from Cheat Mountain, he found a mess. Lee was still mourning the loss of his friend and aide-de-camp Colonel John A. Washington, who had been killed at Elkwater during the Cheat Mountain campaign, and he had to deal with pressing military problems. The forces of the bickering Wise and Floyd were divided.

Many were sick. There was a shortage of wagons to bring supplies to the rugged terrain, which was pelted with ceaseless rain. Coupled with these problems was the question of which road the enemy might use to attack. No matter the attack route, Confederate weapons were inadequate. Many men were armed with flintlock muskets, while others had percussion muskets. While Wise was digging in at Camp Defiance, Floyd was doing the same along the eastern bank of the Meadow River, a position of limited worth; an enemy seizing the surrounding heights could make the position untenable. Entrenching was hampered by the lack of adequate tools. One company who worked on the breastworks had only one axe and two butcher knives.[12]

Lee felt that a united force back at Meadow Bluff was superior to a divided one and immediately wrote Wise: "I beg therefore, if not too late that the troops be united, and we conquer or die together." A united force at Meadow Bluff would not only reduce the distance in taking supplies to the men, but would put the Confederates in a better position to counter Federal movement over the Old Wilderness Road as well as over the James River and the Kanawha Turnpike. Wise not only was unswayed by Lee's request, but also managed to read insult in the letter. He insisted his position at Sewell Mountain was stronger and superior to that of Meadow Bluff. The unsubmissive Wise, in defense of his honor, responded by saying that he deeply resented any "imputation" of his "motives," but he continued, saying, "I will delight to obey you, sir, even when rebuked.... I am ready to do, suffer, and die for [the Confederate cause]."[13]

Lee's position was a difficult one. Inclement weather, insufficient information about the enemy, plus his previous relationship with Floyd and Wise hindered decision making. His relationship with the two Virginia politicians complicated matters that went back to 1859 and the capture of John Brown at Harpers Ferry. Wise, then Virginia's governor, had received Brown and other prisoners from Lee. Floyd had been Buchanan's Secretary of War and had ordered Lee and the small detachment of marines to Harpers Ferry. Now the two were Lee's subordinates; Lee required delicacy when exercising authority over these two huge egos.[14]

On the day after Lee's arrival at Meadow Bluff, he went to Sewell Mountain to examine Wise's camps and fortifications. He found Wise's claim of being in a strong location was true. But Lee still remained skeptical about letting Wise stay there. He could be flanked by several secondary roads and trails, and the disparate forces of Wise and Floyd made the latter vulnerable to attack over the Old Wilderness Road. Lee returned to Meadow Bluff without directly ordering Wise to pull back.[15]

The next day, September 23, Lee received two dispatches from Wise, who said that a strong enemy force of 3,000 had appeared on Sewell Mountain. "We are expecting an attack," he wrote, "[and] are compelled to stand here and fight as long as I can endure and ammunition lasts." He also wrote that a scout from Nicholls Mill reported seeing 7,000 enemy soldiers there. A few sentences later in the same dispatch, Wise wrote, "I get reports from Nicholls Mill and there have not been seen any but a few stragglers there. The idea of the enemy passing from Sunday Road to the Wilderness Road by Nicholls Mill is simply absurd. There is hardly a trail there."

Lee responded, "It is difficult, without knowing more of the facts in the case, to suggest what is your best course." However, he repeatedly told Wise that if the enemy was too strong, Wise should leave. Concerned that Wise might be turned, Lee cautioned him that the enemy may have been making "a feint to keep you in position" while attacking Floyd on the Old Wilderness Road. In any event, wrote Lee, "send to the rear all your encumbrances." That night Lee decided the main enemy threat was at Sewell Mountain and ordered much of Floyd's brigade to reinforce Wise. Floyd was left at Meadow Bluff with about 1,000 men.[16]

A CAUTIOUS PURSUIT: THE FEDERALS MOVE TO SEWELL MOUNTAIN

The enemy force who faced the Confederates at Sewell Mountain also had their problems, many of which paralleled those of the Southerners and caused the Federals' slow and cautious pursuit of Floyd. Five days after the battle of Carnifex Ferry, Rosecrans met with Cox and others at Cross Lanes to plan their pursuit of the Confederates. Rosecrans was still stranded north of the Gauley River with no adequate means of crossing, only a little flatboat that had been raised and repaired. His supply line from Clarksburg went over the mountain roads and could not be stretched any further. So Rosecrans, on Cox's recommendation, later transferred his line of communication from Gallipolis, via Gauley Bridge, to Spy Rock (present-day Lookout), about fourteen miles from Sewell Mountain.[17] Spy Rock was halfway between Gauley Bridge and Big Sewell. Union movement to Spy Rock, where they established a camp, was the first stage in what would turn out to be a two-phase movement to Sewell Mountain.

Rosecrans triggered the second phase of movement by ordering Cox to Sewell Mountain. This precipitated lively skirmishing, but no battle; inclement weather and logistical problems caused the Federals to pull back.

Lee's fear of being turned proved to be unfounded. Rosecrans made no attempt to use the Old Wilderness Road to turn the Confederates. Cox and McCook's brigades, totaling about 5,000 men, reached Spy Rock on September 16 and established Camp Lookout. There they wiped out seventy-year-old George Alderson, who operated an inn known as De Kelb, a tollgate and stagecoach stop. Alderson, a known Virginia militia colonel, was a Southern sympathizer with a son active in the Confederate government in Richmond. This prompted the Federals to demolish seven acres of his wheat and twenty acres of corn, and to take his books, household supplies, and his furniture, putting him out of the inn business, with a loss totaling nearly $5,000.[18]

Cox sent half a regiment to scout the enemy at Sewell Mountain while he and the rest of his force remained at Camp Lookout. Soon reports came in of an encampment of an enemy regiment between Cox's camp and the New River, somewhat in the Union rear. Most said this news could not be true, but excitement prevailed, and Lieutenant Bontecou, a very capable scout, was sent forward to check it out. On his return, he verified the reports: there was an enemy camp among them. Cox then sent McCook to drive the enemy away. When they arrived at the location of the enemy camp, they recognized it as the rear of their own camp. The combination of woods and curving roads had confused the scouts, who had believed that they were miles away and that the tents were the enemy's. At first McCook's men, who had marched through rain and mud, were furious at the erring scouts. But anger soon gave way to laughter, and the expedition was dubbed the "Battle of Bontecou." Lieutenant Bontecou was ribbed about his mistake for a long time.

After a week at Camp Lookout, Cox advanced twelve miles toward the Confederates at Sewell Mountain, forewarned by Rosecrans to "remain upon the defensive there and to avoid bringing on any engagement" until he arrived with the rest of the column. Upon arriving at Sewell Mountain, Cox concluded he must go two miles further for the best position, which was at the mountaintop. This position put him near Wise—and in danger of being seen—which led to a lively skirmish on September 23. This annoyed Rosecrans, who thought Cox had gotten too close to a reinforced enemy.[19]

On the day of the skirmishing, Rosecrans wrote Cox: "You have by mistake got too near for anything but fighting.... Nevertheless you will take every precaution not to be drawn in a fight. Remember if the [enemy] have made a stand they have been reinforced. They will at least teach you the lesson of precaution." The sparring between the two forces on separate ridges included exchanging artillery fire and probing, counter-probing, and skirmishing in rugged terrain that hindered movement. Wise ordered an officer to fire his artillery piece, and the man protested that he was unable to see the enemy, and if he fired, he would "do no execution." "Damn the execution, sir," snapped Wise. "It's the noise that we want."[20]

The next day skirmishing continued, with Lee strengthening his left by sending a Georgia regiment to dig in on a conspicuous large bald hill (Buster's Knob) about a third of a mile from the Confederate left flank, and a mile from Lee's headquarters and main camp in Myles Knob. The latter covered thirty-five acres on the highest site in the area (3460 feet), commanding the road and area to the west. The knob was narrow on top and only fifty yards wide where a west-facing trench was dug. In front, the land sloped down at a forty-five-degree angle, mild in comparison to the almost straight drop on the northern and southern sides. Hugging the southern side was the turnpike. The broken terrain forced the Confederates to spread out, making it appear as if their numbers were much larger.[21]

Late in the afternoon a courier handed Wise a most unwanted message from President Davis. It informed Wise he was immediately relieved of command and was to return to Richmond. A frustrated Henry Wise wrote Lee questioning how he could leave when they were under enemy fire; what should he do? Lee's thoughts remain unknown; he could have been afraid that the strong-willed Wise would disobey the order. In a tactful yet firm reply, Lee told Wise to obey the president's order. Wise drafted a farewell to his men, and the next day he left for Richmond.[22]

In addition to dealing with Wise, Lee found other aspects of the situation at Sewell that displeased him. Now that the enemy seemed on the verge of an attack, Lee became edgy. He vented some of his frustration during his second visit to Camp Defiance as Wise's men were skirmishing with the enemy. A lieutenant who was looking and asking for the ordnance train was told by a passing soldier, "Yonder is General Lee, he can tell you." According to an observer, Captain T. C. Morton, of Virginia, the green lieutenant "saw, not far away, a martial figure, standing in the rain by a log fire before a small tent, with his breeches tucked in his high cavalry boots, his hands behind his back, a high, broad-brimmed black hat, with a gilt cord around it on his head, which was bowed as if in deep thought." Boldly, the young officer walked up, saluted, introduced himself, "and asked the general to favor him with information as to who was the ordnance officer and where was the train? Lee "quietly eyed his intruder" in a way the lieutenant later claimed he would "never forget those eyes," then the general said, "I think it very strange Lieutenant, that any officer of this command, which has been here a week, should come to me, who has just arrived, to ask who his ordnance officer is, and where to find his ammunition. This is in keeping with everything else I find here—no order, no organization. Nobody knows where anything is, no one understands his duty, officers and men are especially ignorant. This will not do." Lee then pointed to some wagons and a tent on a knoll several hundred yards away. "There you will find what you are looking for, sir, and I hope you will not have to come to me again on such an errand."[23]

Lee was more sympathetic to a later request, but he was unable to grant it for a time because the needs of war came first. While Union and Confederate faced each other on Sewell, fifty-year-old Sergeant Shaggs, a Virginian who had volunteered out of a sense of duty, received a distressing letter from his wife. Diphtheria was raging though his family. T. C. Morton recorded: "One child was dead or dying and the others were stricken and the poor-wife begged piteously for her husband to come home." The old sergeant went to his captain, had him read the letter and "begged him to go to General Lee and get him a furlough." The captain refused, saying that it would be useless to try. The sergeant was desperate. With tears in his eyes, he approached his lieutenant, T. C. Morton, who was deeply moved. Morton found Lee" sitting on a campstool at the door of his tent. The general read the letter and upon handing it back to Morton, said, "I wish, Lieutenant, I could send your man home to his sick children, but, my dear sir, we all went into the struggle expecting to make sacrifices for our country. We are all making sacrifices; your Sergeant must make his. He cannot go now, every man is wanted at his post. Tell him as soon as the emergencies of this occasion will admit he shall have his leave." Twenty-four hours later, Rosecrans left Big Sewell and Sergeant Shaggs got temporary leave to go home to his stricken family.[24]

RAIN AND MUD ARE THE VICTORS

On September 26, the day Wise left for Richmond, Rosecrans joined Cox on Sewell Mountain with Scammon's brigade within supporting distance. Like Lee, Rosecrans found major problems on the Union side, including illness and a supply shortage, but the weather was his most formidable immediate foe. What barriers the mountainous terrain presented for a major attack on the Confederates were compounded by a three-day downpour, amid intermittent sleet. It was the worst rainstorm residents in the area had seen. In all, during the Federals' nearly two-week stay at Sewell Mountain, from September 23 to October 5, there would be eleven days of cold rainstorms. Roads were washed away and reduced to mire. Horses pulling supply wagons struggled mightily to pull half-loads the thirty-two miles from Gauley Bridge or about half that distance from White Sulphur Springs to the Confederates on Sewell. During the latter trip, a wagon was washed away and was lost during the three-day storm. At Charleston the Kanawha River, which normally flows forty to fifty feet below the town's plateau, rose above those banks, sending four to five feet of water into houses that had not been flooded before. The inundation almost put an end to communication among the forces. For the Union it was very difficult to protect their food and other supplies, with no protection but lengths of canvas spread over the bags, boxes, and barrels of food. Much was lost, though the Union kept their men in better—if more limited—rations than the Confederates.

The torrential downpour took its toll on the men, who frequently lacked tents. Animals also suffered. In one night Rosecrans lost eighteen horses. Rosecrans' four brigades, of 8,000 men, were reduced—by sickness and the sending away of men on other assignments—to 5,200 effectives. The Eleventh Ohio lost almost sixty percent of their 717 members to illness. Floyd later claimed that the week and half of storms at Sewell Mountain had "cost more men, sick and dead, than the battle of Manassas Plains." The Twentieth Mississippi infantry saw more than sixty percent of their regiment become sick from the torrential rains and cold at Sewell Mountain. The Fourteenth North Carolina saw illness reduce their numbers by sixty-three percent, shrinking their 750-man force to only 277 who were able to carry on their duties. One member of the regiment wrote home that an epidemic of sickness swept through his regiment, hitting almost everyone and causing many men to die in their tents. They were buried along the side of the road.[25]

In a letter to his wife, Lee reported that the Southerners on Sewell Mountain were all exposed and without tents. Even Lee had to spend two nights covered only by his overcoat before his tent arrived.

In the words of Major Isaac Smith of the Twenty-second Virginia Infantry, "A more merciless, cheerless rain, and more miserable" time "could scarcely have been experienced by anyone— the poor half frozen, half-starved men" who subsisted on an occasional meal of "some bread with salt in it, and some potatoes," had to endure "shivering in the wet and cold" while their blankets remained in wagons back at Meadow Bluff. At one point they were without food for two days. Isaac Smith recorded, "We can get no provisions here—the bridges along the meadows have been washed away, and the road overflown…. Our last barrel of flour goes today. The poor horses are starving. In two days mine have had six ears of corn, and a small armful of hay. Chestnut leaves is all they get…. I have little hope (indeed none) that the troops will reach Kanawha this fall.[26]

Amid the monotony of the rains, and in their isolation in the wet mountains, men forgot the day of the week. Even the optimistic

Hayes, who had been given the duty of judge-advocate, court-martialing offenders, ceased writing of the joys of military life and the beauty of western Virginia. He found the isolation of the mountains "out of reach of mail," and he called the leaky tents, worn-out blankets, insufficient socks and shoes, and lack of overcoats "taxing." He wrote home, "this is no joke."[27]

So bad was the plight of the Confederates that Lee informed Floyd that newly arrived reinforcements might have to be sent back to Meadow Bluff because they arrived without provisions and there were none at Sewell Mountain. The problem of shortages was not only due to inclement weather, but also to Wise's failure to rescind an order issued on September 18, prohibiting provisions being sent to Camp Defiance. The order was not rescinded for eight days.[28]

While Confederates struggled to get supplies to Sewell, privates in Rosecrans' force found things to grouse about. While at Sewell Mountain, Major S. Sleminer, of Fort Pickens notoriety, joined Rosecrans's staff as Inspector General of the Department. On a Sunday in late September it became the turn of the Eleventh Ohio to be inspected by the major. According to an Ohio soldier on the scene, the men of the Eleventh expected to find Slemmer "an officer and a gentleman, but *were disappointed.*" "Allowing nothing for long marches and severe duty in rain and mud, without changes of clothing nor opportunities for washing, this officer treated the men as if they were *dogs,* and evidently considered *volunteer* officers but little better." So strong was the men's indignation that after the war one soldier wrote, "We bear no malice toward Major S., but his unwarranted abuse of better men than himself, although they were but *privates* in a volunteer regiment, ought not be passed over in silence."

Union officers had their own problems. When Rosecrans was preparing to pull back on the night of October 5, he heard a Colonel Frizell ranting and raving in what a witness called "very *emphatic language.*" When Rosecrans rode up and asked about the problem, the colonel lamented, "I have the ague, General, and don't feel like lying around in the mud all night." Rosecrans responded, "Oh, a little quinine and whiskey will sit you all right." "I have plenty of quinine, but how do you expect a man to get whiskey in this Godforsaken country," growled Frizell. "Well, Colonel," answered Rosecrans, "just get a tin cup, put your quinine in it and I will furnish the whiskey." The general took a small "pocket pistol" from the breast of his coat and poured a liberal amount of whisky into the colonel's cup. A witness wrote that Frizell thanked Rosecrans "for his kindness, and assured him that the *medicine* would undoubtedly prove beneficial."[29]

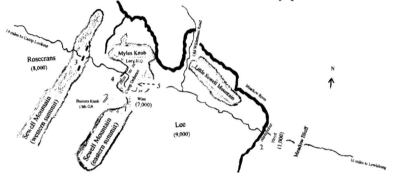

STALEMATE AT SEWELL MOUNTAIN
The crisis of Confederates pulling back toward the Shenandoah Valley brings Lee to the scene. He finds the Confederate force divided with (1) Wise refusing to leave Sewell Mountain and (2) Floyd digging in behind Meadow River (near Meadow Bluff). Fearing Wise might be turned by the enemy if they move over the Old Wilderness Road, Lee unsuccessfully attempts to unite the feuding generals at Meadow Bluff. When sporadic fighting breaks out between (3) Union forces on the western summit of Sewell Mountain and (4) Wise's men on the eastern summit. Lee sends help. He moves (5) the recently arrived men under Loring and Floyd's men to increase Wise's force to 7,000 (Lee had 9,000 men in the region) to counter the Federal force of about equal numbers of 8,000. Rain, mud, and cold causes sickness, dramatically reduces the effectiveness of both sides, makes getting supplies all but impossible, mutes combat to sporadic skirmishing and ultimately causes Rosecrans to pull back to Gauley Bridge.

SEWELL MOUNTAIN: SEPTEMBER 23 TO OCTOBER 5, 1861

Rosecrans's personal plight was better than that of his men, if not good. He did not have to sleep out in the rain, and instead bunked with Cox. Other officers were less fortunate. Another general under Rosecrans' command, Robert Schenck, arrived too late in the stormy weather for construction of a resting place, and, in Cox's words, "he was obliged to content himself with a bed made of three or four campstools set in a row" in Cox's tent. "Anything was better," said Cox, "than lying on the damp ground" in a storm. Schenck long remembered "the aching weariness of that night," as he precariously balanced himself "upon the narrow and unstable supports which threatened to tumble him upon the ground at the least effort to change the position of stiffened body and limbs."[30]

Cox, who was earlier relieved that Rosecrans assumed direct control over the pursuit of the enemy after Carnifex Ferry, found "Rosy" delightful and thoroughly enjoyed his commander's stay in his tent during the horrible storm. Cox thought Rosecrans's physical appearance seemed to exude an image of leadership. Rosecrans was said to have an aquiline nose and alert, impulsive manner. He expressed his emotions freely, especially when he was annoyed or pleased. When discussing military questions, he would cite maxims of war and would compare the problem before him to analogous cases in military history. But Rosecrans also reveled in lighter moments and loved to joke around with his staff. An anecdote told after the war by a preacher reveals Rosecrans' engaging personality. As the story goes, later in the war, when Rosecrans was in the western theater, he was in the presence of several prominent Catholic priests when a staff officer informed him that a spy had been caught within the Union lines. Excitedly, Rosecrans shouted orders that were spiced with profanity. Suddenly realizing he was in the presence of clerics, he turned toward them, apologizing: "Gentlemen, I sometimes swear, but I never blaspheme!"

Rosecrans, said Cox, was "altogether an attractive and companionable man, with intellectual activity enough to make his society stimulating and full of lively discussion." It is easily understood why Garfield later wrote that he "loved every bone in the man's body."[31]

The jocularity in Cox's tent was but a brief respite from a difficult situation. Weather and terrain discouraged offensive action as Rosecrans, Lee, and 16,000 men—on the two ridges of Big Sewell, separated by a large ravine—looked at each other, waiting for the other to attack. Lulls in the rain provided opportunities for fortifying, scouting, and sporadic skirmishing.[32]

One of the more somber event took place when an intoxicated lieutenant-colonel, James W. Spalding, of the Sixtieth Virginia Infantry, decided on his own to take a company of men to scout beyond the Confederate pickets, which were posted only 300 yards from the enemy. Spalding carelessly rode ahead of his escort, ascending the mountain, and rounding a curve, suddenly came upon enemy pickets. The drunken colonel fired, and missed, but the enemy fire soon hit him in the chest, causing his mount to turn back and run down the mountain. After going 150 feet, Spalding's body was thrown to the ground. His party took the body back to camp, where a body servant was given the sad task of washing the blood from the saddle and from Spalding's horse. Back at the spot where he had fallen, his adversaries found a small pool of blood, a picture of his wife, a bloodied pocket book, and papers perforated by the bullets that had killed him. The news did not sit well with Hayes, a Union officer. He wrote: "Our pickets killed a colonel or lieutenant colonel of the enemy who rode among them. All wrong and cruel. This is too much like murder. Shooting pickets, etc., etc., ought to be put down."[33] The news of the fate of the likeable colonel soon spread throughout the Confederate camps at Sewell Mountain.

During the same time period, Henry Hutchison had a humiliating—though not life-threatening—experience at the hands of his comrades. Hutchison lacked good hygiene and would not take off his boots once he had put them on his feet, until they were worn out. This practice created a malodorous condition that the other soldiers could not tolerate. Finally some of his compatriots threw him to the ground, and while some held his hands, others tugged at his footwear. Unable to remove the smelly boots, they split the leather and peeled them off as the strong-voiced victim set records for profanity.[34]

Rain, terrain, supply problems, and an exaggeration of Lee's numbers finally convinced the Federals to pull back on the night of October 5. Rosecrans, at Sewell Mountain, was sixty miles from the head of steamboat navigation. The wagon trains were too small to sustain his army any further away unless good weather set in and the roads became dry. This did not happen. So desperate for meat were Union and Confederate parties that they fired on each other as they chased a herd of cattle in the gorge that separated their respective camps. Reports to Rosecrans told of formidable earthworks and a line of camps five miles long protecting 30,000 of the enemy.[35] The Federals believed that the reason for Lee's extended lines was their great numbers, rather than the wild terrain of Sewell Mountain, which forced Lee's troops to spread out.[36]

Before Rosecrans left Sewell Mountain, Lee waited for the Federals to attack. But as the month of September drew to a close, Lee wrote Floyd, "I begin to fear the enemy will not attack us. We shall therefore have to attack him. If we could get a week's provisions we could...move against his rear and thus break up his position. Please see what arrangement can be made for provisions."[37] Adequate provisions would not be forthcoming, but during the night of October 5, Lee's hopes were raised; it looked as if he would not have to attack the enemy. Lee and his men heard noises emanating from Union camps. The Confederates assumed that this movement was part of the Union's preparation to attack them the next day. Instead after dawn they found that the site that had been occupied by their enemy was abandoned. There would be no battle at Sewell Mountain. The weather and rugged terrain had forbidden it. There was nothing to be gained by a battle.

General William E. Starke, who, as colonel of the Sixtieth Virginia Infantry, served under Floyd and Wise in western Virginia in 1861, would later ask Lee why he had not attacked Rosecrans at Sewell Mountain. General Lee, having had time to reflect, replied that it would have failed to produce "substantial results." He added they were "seventy miles from the railroad, their base of supplies; the roads were almost impassable; and it would have been difficult to obtain two days' rations." "Furthermore, he continued, "if the Confederates had attacked and won the Federals would have retreated. The Southerners would not have been able to pursue them, and would have to pull back to the source of their supplies." "But," responded Starke, "your reputation was suffering, the press was denouncing you, your own state was losing confidence in you, and the army needed a victory to add to its enthusiasm." Lee smiled and answered, "I could not afford to sacrifice the lives of five or six hundred of my people to silence public clamor."[38]

Rosecrans had pulled back under the cover of darkness. His tents were struck at 10:00 P.M., and the men pulled out after midnight. In leaving Sewell Mountain, tens of thousands of dollars' worth of supplies were destroyed. Wagonloads of pork and beef were sent tumbling down the mountain toward deep valleys. Union soldiers walked ankle deep in flour poured from broken barrels for a hundred yards. The Confederates found a large quantity of abandoned cooking utensils, as well as chairs, tables, and destroyed medicines in the former Union campsite.[39]

Mud prevented an easy retreat. Troops tramped through mud nearly knee deep as they traversed down the winding roads of Sewell Mountain. It was slow going. Men were halted after going only ten or twenty yards, until a stalled tram could get moving or some broken-down wagon "was turned over out of the way and set fire," recalled Cox. The trains were in the front, and they moved slowly. General Rosecrans rode among the wagons, choosing wagons full of supplies and officers' personal items to be burned and thrown away. Members of the Eleventh Ohio found their general's behavior odd.[40] But apprehension had set in that enemy might be following them in the dark and that the Federal force would not reach a strong position by sunrise. At dawn the rear of Rosecrans army was only four miles from where it had camped the evening before, but they had reached an easily defended position. There was no immediate Confederate pursuit, with the exception of feeble attempts made by a detachment of Confederate cavalrymen to see what the enemy was doing and an occasional brief exchange of fire. This continued until Rosecrans had encamped his troops between Hawk's Nest and the Tompkins farm. There they were near their supplies.[41]

COTTON HILL: FLOYD RETREATS AGAIN

On October 6, the day Lee discovered that Rosecrans had left Sewell Mountain, he formed plans for what would prove to be the last attempt to drive the enemy from the Kanawha in 1861. The horrible condition of the roads precluded any infantry movement until the turnpike was repaired. Lee recorded that he ordered the troops under Loring and Floyd and the militia under A. A. Chapman to "thoroughly drain the roads and lay timber over all soft and muddy portions, to form a flooring."[42] As soon as the road was traversable, Floyd was to take a brigade to the south side of the Kanawha by moving up the south side of the New River.

Colonel Heth was adamantly opposed to sending Floyd on another attempt to seize the Kanawha, and he told Lee so in a long talk. Amid the rain Heth argued that if Floyd were to attempt Lee's plan, he would be captured. On the following morning, Heth met General Lee at breakfast. Lee said, "Well, Colonel, I hope on this bright day you take a less gloomy view of matters than you did last night when we parted." Heth responded, "No, General, I am of the same opinion still; I have seen too much incompetency in General Floyd during the past four months to cause me to change my views."[43]

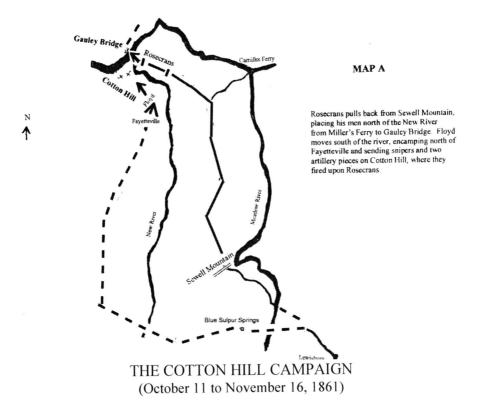

Rosecrans pulls back from Sewell Mountain, placing his men north of the New River from Miller's Ferry to Gauley Bridge. Floyd moves south of the river, encamping north of Fayetteville and sending snipers and two artillery pieces on Cotton Hill, where they fired upon Rosecrans.

THE COTTON HILL CAMPAIGN
(October 11 to November 16, 1861)

Floyd left for Cotton Hill on October 11, by way of Green Sulphur Springs, crossing the New River at Richmond's Ferry. By the night of October 19, Confederates reached Raleigh Court House (modern-day Beckley). From there they turned north, going through Fayetteville to Dickerson's farm, arriving at the latter on October 21, 1861.

Lee had originally hoped to move on the north side of the New River toward Gauley Bridge, in a coordinated move with Floyd to defeat Rosecrans. But only three days after Floyd had left to move south of the New River, Lee was forced to change his mind. Disease, bad weather, untraversably muddy roads, and difficulty obtaining supplies were formidable obstacles. But the most foreboding was the threat of the Federal movement toward Staunton from Cheat Mountain, necessitating Loring's return to that region after which Lee returned to Richmond.[44]

433

On October 21, Lee left Sewell Mountain and pulled back to Meadow Bluff, as General Floyd—after a ten-day march—moved to Fayetteville, less than a dozen miles from Rosecrans. The day before, Lee had informed Floyd why he could not move north of the New River and why Loring was leaving, but Floyd falsely claimed he had not been told. In a duplicitous letter to the secretary of war, written October 27, 1861, Floyd tried to have Confederate authorities pressure Lee to move toward Gauley Bridge. Floyd claimed:

> I shall be unable to do anything with [the enemy] unless the Department can prevail on General Lee to make a movement against his front. My march to this point is only part of a larger plan. But if General Lee, with his large army on Sewell Mountains, should have operated on the front of the enemy, while I made my way through a desert to attack his flank. I have done my part of this work, but I have not heard of General Lee's movements, and unless he should make them speedily, I fear that this campaign must end without any decisive results, and that all the force lately assembled around Sewell Mountain will be of no profit to the war.[45]

The day after writing to the secretary of war, Floyd wrote to Lee, "I have possession of Cotton Hill.... If you will now make a decided movement in advance with the Army at Sewell Mountain, it is nearly certain that we will capture the whole Northern Army, or drive it entirely from the valley." Lee, with great restraint, responded, "I advised you in my letter of the 20th of the necessity of the return of the troops under General Loring to the Huntersville line, and of the withdrawal of the Wise Legion to [Meadow Bluff]." He then explained that he would be leaving Meadow Bluff that day, October 29. After visiting the hospitals at Lewisburg and White Sulphur Springs, Lee proceeded to Richmond.[46]

Lee left with very few favorable memories of his western Virginia experiences. One of the few favorable ones was the sighting of a sixteen-hands-high dark gray four-year-old colt named Jeff Davis, ridden by a young Confederate soldier.[47] The spirited horse, who had a small head, a rapid, short, bouncy walk, and a high trot that fatigued most riders, had won two first prizes at the Greenbrier County Fair. Lee often saw the horse and became an admirer of the animal, whom he spoke of as "my colt." After leaving western Virginia, Lee was sent to North Carolina, where he again saw the colt, ridden by an officer also transferred there. While in North Carolina,

Lee purchased the colt, who would become his favorite mount, for $200 in Confederate currency. After calling his colt Greenbrier for a short time, he changed the name to Traveller.[48]

In the meantime, Lee's former adversary, Rosecrans, concluded his pull-back from Sewell Mountain by dispersing his men at or near Gauley Bridge to Miller's Ferry. Some were placed at the Federal supply base six miles from Gauley Bridge, others, at Gauley Bridge and Tompkins's farm (Rosecrans' headquarters), while the majority of the men were in echelon north of the New River and just north of Miller's Ferry. The latter group could guard the New River and meet the anticipating attack from the enemy from the east over the James River and Kanawha Turnpike. Across from this force on the south side of the New River and Miller's Ferry, the bulk of Floyd's men would congregate.[49] Once the Union soldiers were placed in the different locations, they were paid and received much-needed new clothing. Rosecrans had written of this need, "The troops were so naked that in one regiment I counted one hundred and thirty-five men without pantaloons on parade."[50]

Brigadier-General William Starke Rosecrans
He plays a key role in the Union victory at Rich Mountain and succeeds
McClellan as the commander of the Union forces in western (West)
Virginia. (Courtesy of the Library of Congress)

At this time Rosecrans attempted to get his command to strive for excellence through a not-altogether-appreciated micromanagement style. He insisted that his brigadiers and staff cooperate vigorously to obtain this goal. Cox, who greatly admired Rosecrans, was eager to observe the commander. He found Rosecrans's impulsiveness led him into "personal efforts at discipline" that bordered on meddling and were better left to subordinate officers. "Rosey" would at times go through the camp at evening after taps, and if he saw a tent lighted or heard talking or singing, Cox claimed, he would "strike loudly on the canvas with the flat of his saber" and "command silence or the extinguishment of the light." Cox recorded: "in good-humored mischief," the men found ways of getting even. One of the most popular ways was to pretend their wagon master was "playing a practical joke on them and to shout back [at the general]...all sorts of rough camp chaff." When the exasperated Rosecrans "appeared at the door of the tent," wrote Cox, they pretended "the most innocent astonishment, and explained that" their "wagonmaster was in the habit of annoying them, and that they had really not heard the 'taps'."[51]

Rosecrans' more pressing problem was the advancing enemy south of the New River. He ordered a preemptive strike south of the river. Around October 18, before Floyd reached Fayetteville Court House, Rosecrans directed McCook to take part of his brigade and disperse or capture rebel militia that were believed to be assembling in Fayetteville. McCook passed over the New River at Miller's Ferry, and in the words of Rosecrans, "had a slight skirmish with a small militia force, occupied Fayetteville, reconnoitered the roads in the vicinity, satisfied himself there was no force there except bushwhacking militia" and secessionist residents. He retired north of New River without leaving a company south of the river to guard Miller's Ferry.

Although Rosecrans had not specifically ordered McCook to leave a force south of Miller's Ferry, he was upset that it was not done.[52] He had wanted at least a foothold on the other side of New River at Miller's Ferry. When Rosecrans later attempted to place a detachment there, around October 25, he found the shore and cliffs held by enemy sharpshooters. This left the area south of New River to Gauley Bridge virtually unoccupied by Federals, which exposed their supply base and ferry to future fire by the enemy on the rugged heights known as Cotton Hill.[53]

CONFEDERATE MOVEMENT TOWARD THE KANAWHA AND ALIENATION

Floyd's army's movement toward Fayetteville and beyond was difficult. Men sloughed through mud, and horses strained to pull wagons over mired roads and steep mountains.[54] Weakened horses forced Southerners to hitch twelve horses to one artillery piece. Even this effort was not enough, so soldiers had to help by putting their shoulders to the wheel.

The Twenty-second Virginia had it especially tough. Floyd, who disliked two of their officers, Colonel Tompkins and Major Isaac Smith, exacerbated their difficulties. Early in the march toward Fayetteville, Tompkins left for a few days to go to Lewisburg to see his wife, leaving the Twenty-second under Smith's command. Soon after Floyd's force crossed the New River, they were rushed forward. Following orders, Smith pushed his men and teams for seventeen miles along terrible roads to within one mile of Raleigh Court House. Reporting for orders, Smith was told to keep his camp. He found this strange, since the rest of Floyd's force had received orders to march at 6:00 the next morning with two days' worth of cooked rations. At about 9:30 the next morning, Floyd rode up, thinking that the enemy was at Fayetteville, and ordered the Twenty-second Virginia to move at once. They marched sixteen miles, nearly catching up with troops with three- and four-hour head starts. The march had thoroughly fatigued the Twenty-second Virginia. I "never saw them so used up," said Smith. "They could scarcely stand up long enough for orders for the night."

That night Floyd camped across a creek, about 150 yards away from Smith's regiment's camp, and yet, orders to cook and march did not reach the Smith's men until 11:00 that night. Smith decided not to awaken the exhausted men, but he had them up early the next day. He needed time for the men to complete their cooking and requested an hour's delay in starting the march. Floyd denied the request and ordered the men forward at once, but said that they could march at a leisurely rate, as he had found out that the enemy was not at Fayetteville. The men of the Twenty-second Virginia protested, declaring that they were unable to march any distance. But on they went. When they were outside Fayetteville, where they thought they would camp, they failed to receive any orders to do so. Thinking that the enemy must be nearby, Smith left the wagons and cooks behind and pushed his men beyond Fayetteville. There he received orders from Colonel McCausland to rush the men forward. Smith rode up and down the line, cheering on the weary men, who astonished him with their agreeable manner and their speed. The men hurried on, without eating or even halting for a moment's rest, passing well-rested and well-fed men, until they were on Big Fall's Creek, only a mile and a quarter from the Kanawha River, and only hundreds of yards from enemy pickets. As a cold rain fell on their ranks—which were thinned from having marched twenty-one miles in a day and from having gone without food for twenty-four hours—the men of the Twenty-second Virginia set up camp at Huddleston's residence. It was near the southern banks of the Kanawha, seven miles from reinforcements. Smith felt that the top of Cotton Hill would have been a safer place to camp; he believed their position was a trap.[55]

It was a difficult time for Smith. He fumed with righteous indignation over an incident that occurred during the difficult march. Four or five miles out of Fayetteville, while Smith was moving his tired men rapidly forward, McCausland rode up, and without a word to Smith, he gave orders and assumed command of the Twenty-second. Smith was mortified by the snub, but he knew that McCausland was second in command of Tompkins' brigade (consisting of the Twenty-second and the Thirty-sixth Virginia). Soon Smith asked McCausland if he had assumed command under Tompkins. The colonel replied that he had been sent by Floyd to aid him. This greatly distressed Smith, who saw it as another insult from Floyd; McCausland was merely following orders. Smith decided that he must resign.

A few days later, Tompkins returned and was greatly upset by events. He encouraged Smith to demand a review by a military court. But that would take up to half a year, and Smith refused to serve under Floyd that much longer. So while on Cotton Mountain, in early November, Smith sent his resignation to Floyd, who immediately

439

forwarded it to Richmond. Smith requested leave, and it was granted, but he planned to stay on the mountain until he could sell a horse he had just purchased for $200, along with a saddle and bridle that cost him $60, a new uniform, at $85, and another military saddle for $35. While selling off his unneeded property, and thinking his dilemma with his demeaning commander was over, Smith received another in a series of humiliating emotional traumas. Friends of Smith's arrived in camp with the startling news that his father had been identified as belonging to the Pierpont (Unionist) government. Those around Smith cursed his "Pa" for being a traitor, causing Smith to lament: "Why my dear father had chosen to place me in this terrible situation is beyond my comprehension. I have been shocked beyond description in contemplating the awful consequences to the peace and safety and happiness of both of us."

The situation deteriorated even more. A day or so after receiving the news about his father, Isaac Smith had just sold his horse when the adjutant handed him orders revoking Smith's furlough. An astonished Smith went to Floyd for an explanation. At first Floyd insinuated that it was because Smith had resigned because battle was expected. Smith, knowing Floyd was aware that it was his insult that had led to the resignation, which was originally approved by Floyd, asked for an explanation. Floyd exploded in a profanity-filled tirade of verbal abuse that, according to Smith, "evinced the coarsest brutality, the most outrageous tyranny, injustice and meanness." Floyd bellowed that Smith's father was fighting against the Confederacy, making him a traitor. Therefore, Floyd proclaimed that he intended to keep Smith in the Confederate Army for as long as he could. Smith, said Floyd, "should stand in the front of the battle and meet [his] father face to face." The general also told Smith that he would immediately write to the War Department asking them to reject the resignation and to keep Smith in the army. Feeling awful, like a captive in his own army, Smith commanded his regiment until the end of the Cotton Hill campaign. While accompanying Floyd's retreat, Smith received the news that the Confederate War Department had accepted his resignation. The day Floyd had revoked his furlough, Smith had sent two friends to Richmond, and they secured his resignation. A now-jubilant Smith felt he had been liberated from Floyd's abuse and bondage. He excitedly wrote in his diary, "Free at last...restored to civilization once more."[56]

AN ANNOYED ROSECRANS PLANS TO TRAP FLOYD

Prior to Smith's resignation, while he was camped on the Huddleston farm in front of enemy pickets near the Kanawha, Floyd and the bulk of his force arrived near Cotton Hill Mountain and went into camp between Fayetteville and Miller's Ferry.[57] Union pickets were chased away from the road from Fayetteville to Montgomery Ferry on the Kanawha River at Big Spring Creek. A few artillery pieces were placed on Cotton Hill, some at heights overlooking Montgomery Ferry; others were placed to the north so they could annoy Rosecrans' headquarters at Tompkins Farm and threaten his base and the ferry at Gauley Bridge. Artillery was also placed several hundred yards in front of main camp, facing the road from Miller's Ferry. Rumor had it that the Federals were going to cross there. Floyd started fortifying his main camp with great difficulty; men struggled to convey the artillery pieces to the top of Cotton Mountain, overlooking the almost-straight drop of 1,000 feet to the New River. Finally, after cutting a path, using ropes and pulleys, and hanging onto bushes and trees, they got the artillery pieces in a position to fire upon Tompkins Farm and Gauley Bridge. A similar struggle was required to get artillery pieces that could fire at the Union at Montgomery Ferry.

On the first day of November, fog lay in the gorge of the New River, and Rosecrans and Cox and their men had just finished breakfast. Cox's records state that suddenly "the report and echo of a cannon-shot, down the gorge in the direction of Gauley Bridge" was heard. Cox, who was attending to the usual morning clerical work, wondered what it meant, but he passed it off as Union target practice. Soon an orderly hurriedly arrived and told Cox that General Rosecrans wanted to see him at his tent, 100 yards from Cox's. As Cox approached, he saw Rosecrans standing in front of his tent, acting very excited. The general said to Cox in what Cox recalls was a "rapid, half-stammering way peculiar to him at such times, 'The enemy has got a battery on Cotton Mountain opposite our post is shelling it! What d' ye think of that?'" Rosecrans had expected Lee to attack on the James River and Kanawha Turnpike, and he was aware McCook was exchanging shots across New River with the enemy at

Miller's Ferry. But to be attacked in his rear from a point where enemy artillery had fired directly into his depot of supplies, telegraph, and commanded his only road to Gauley Bridge had been so startling as to throw Rosecrans "decidedly off his balance," in Cox's words. The error in the Union's failure to occupy Cotton Hill was now all too plain, and the consequences were most unpleasant to contemplate. Rosecrans's nervous mannerisms—normally displayed in all of his movements, from dictating a dispatch to the constant chewing and tearing of his cigar—were intensified.

Cox was more concerned about Rosecrans' state of mind than the enemy fire, and he tried to calm his commander. He engaged Rosecrans in a drawn-out conversation about the situation to try to help the general recover.

Soon the brigades farthest up, across from Miller's Ferry and beyond, were notified of the attack. Schenck, whose brigade was the farthest out, was to send scouting parties to check for an enemy advance from Sewell Mountain while Benham, whose brigade was nearer, was ordered to send a detachment to Gauley Bridge. A battery of mountain howitzers was ordered to heights on the Gauley cliffs where they could drop shells on enemy skirmishers on opposite banks of New River. Additional orders were to secure telegraph, ordnance stores, and the ferry at Gauley Bridge. An hour or two after the first shot, the Thirteenth Ohio from Benham's brigade arrived at headquarters for instruction. Still excited, Rosecrans rattled off orders, confusing the colonel, and when he asked for further clarification, Rosecrans became more agitated. The colonel then bowed and rode off with a confused expression. Cox, seeing this, walked rapidly along the bushes until he was out of Rosecrans' sight. He then beckoned the officer to him, saying, "Colonel, I thought you looked as if you did not fully understand the general's wishes." The colonel responded that he did not, and said he had been afraid of irritating Rosecrans with further questions. Cox explained that was "a wrong principle to act on," and then he explained what Rosecrans had meant.[58]

While Cox was talking with Rosecrans, Colonel Charles DeVilliers rode up. Despite the enemy artillery fire, he ran past the skirmishers, whom, he reported, were on the other side of the New River and opposite the road connecting Tompkins Farm and Gauley Bridge. He had recently reported to his regiment, claiming he had made a spectacular escape from Libby Prison at Richmond. The

442

Confederates asserted that DeVilliers had been allowed to work as a hospital attendant on parole and he violated this by escaping. At any rate, he was the senior officer at Gauley at the time of the enemy's first artillery fire from Cotton Hill. But as Cox stated, "in his [DeVilliers'] light-headed way, instead of taking steps to protect his post and reestablish the telegraph communications, he had dashed off to report in person at headquarters." Willing to race back on the same road, he was allowed to return after being given specific instructions to set up a telegraph office in a ravine out of range of enemy artillery and to move the ferryboat and ordnance store out of danger.

The thought of having DeVilliers in charge at Gauley Bridge heightened Cox's desire to return there to resume command. An agitated Rosecrans had rejected an earlier request, wanting Cox nearby for consultation. Later he agreed to let Cox go.

The trip to Gauley was rough, mountainous climbing, as Cox avoided the road out of fear of enemy fire. Cox describes his trips as toilsome work that included sliding over "great wet trunks, climbing through and under branches of trees Cox's men fell during August" to prevent the enemy's easy approach to Gauley River. After finding no crevices to climb down, Cox and his few companions were forced to retrace their steps, stopping several times out of exhaustion. Finally, with "clothes heavy from rain on the outside and perspiration on the inside," they reached the bank of the Gauley and followed the river downstream until opposite the guard post above the camp. They hailed a skiff and crossed as darkness approached.

The following morning Cox was annoyed to discover that the ordnance store "had not been loaded upon the waiting wagons till nearly daylight." The wagons were moving toward safety, but were brought to a standstill by balky mules. The enemy took advantage of the lifting fog to enfilade the wagon train. Cox wrote that "Negro wagon drivers crouched over their mules" and cracked their whips as solid shot fell nearby. A fresh team of mules replaced the obstinate ones, enabling the wagons and the explosive loads to be pulled to safer ground.[59]

The exchange of artillery fire across the rivers continued for ten days, with minimal damage to either side. The distance was too great for much efficiency, although the Union forces were unable to use their ferry at Gauley and the road to the south, except at night.[60]

The Confederate artillery firing made the Confederate Colonel Tompkins very anxious. One of the primary targets of the Confederates was his home, Rosecrans' headquarters, where Tompkins' wife and children still lived. The colonel asked for permission to visit his home and to check on his family. Floyd denied the request, adding an insulting accusation that Tompkins was disloyal and intimate with the enemy, including General Rosecrans. This insult added to previous ones: his men had been depleted by earlier marches back and forth between Wise and Floyd, which Tompkins denounced, claiming his men had been treated like "coach-horses." Tompkins' disillusionment with the war caused him to follow the same course of action taken by his good friend Isaac Smith. He resigned and left the army.[61]

In retrospect, the enemy shelling of Rosecrans' headquarters and supply base could have been prevented by a little vigilance. Upon Rosecrans' withdrawal back to Gauley Bridge and the vicinity, he had left unattended the rugged region of Cotton Mountain west of the New River. Major reasons for this oversight were the fear that Lee would lead a force against him east of the New River, along with the preoccupation with paying and clothing the troops.[62] A solution was needed to solve the problem of Floyd's occupation of the land west of the New River, which threatened Gauley Bridge and the surrounding area. The excitable Rosecrans calmly asserted at the end of November, after the Cotton Hill campaign had ended, that he had devised a plan after hearing the rumor of Floyd's advance. Rosecrans stated that he was "determined to draw them in and capture them."[63]

The plan was to trap Floyd by sending Union contingents across the New and Kanawha Rivers. McCook's brigade was to remain opposite Miller's Ferry, threatening a crossing there and checking any Confederate movement east of the New River on Lewisburg Road. Schenck's men were to cross the New River much further south, at Bowyer's Ferry or some other site (possibly Townsend's Ferry, in between Miller's Ferry and Bowyer's Ferry). Crucial for the plan's success was the movement of Benham's brigade across the river at Gauley Bridge to below Kanawha Falls; it was to be made at night to avoid Confederate guns. From there he would cross over the Kanawha River at or near Loop Creek. With reinforcements from Charleston, Benham could flank the enemy, or, in a turning movement, get in the rear of the enemy. Cox's forces were to clear Cotton Hill and proceed from the north to Dickerson, Floyd's main camp.

Rosecrans' original plan had options, but as time passed, it became even more fluid with a myriad of choices. The only constant goal was to trap Floyd by getting Federal troops on the Fayetteville Turnpike in front of and behind the Confederates. The decision about which routes to take was to be determined after receiving reconnaissance reports.[64] In his testimony before the Joint Committee on the Conduct of the War later in the war, Rosecrans contended that he also had a corollary plan to counter an attack by Lee. Once Floyd had been defeated by Benham's force, then Schenck's men could cross the New River six miles south of Fayetteville at Bowyer's Ferry, placing 6,000 men on the Lewisburg road behind the rear of Lee.[65]

This plan, and variations thereof, greatly pleased Rosecrans; he eagerly expected and anticipated that it would lead to the demise of Floyd and his army. The plan looked relatively easy to carry out on a flat map, but this map failed to convey the many impediments to success. The sovereigns of the campaign proved to be the terrain and the inclement weather. The New River ran through a narrow chasm of several hundred to 1,000 feet deep, cutting through rock. The water whirled and foamed through this channel, leaving only three places twenty miles south of Gauley where Union forces could cross in great numbers.[66]

Flooded banks and rapid currents would make crossing difficult even at these sites. Not knowing Lee had left the area, Rosecrans took valid precautions east of the New River. It was not his caution that hindered the execution of his plan as much as the dilatory behavior of one of his own generals, Henry W. Benham.

Within a seven-day period, November 3 to 10, Rosecrans bombarded Benham with twenty-three telegraphs and one written dispatch. Benham was told he must cross at Loop Creek and reconnoiter the roads from Loop Creek that intersect with Raleigh Road south of Fayetteville—especially the one by Cassidy Mill, which was the crucial route in turning and trapping the enemy.[67] Benham was informed that his brigade would be reinforced by detachments from three regiments (the Seventh, Thirty-seventh, and Forty-seventh Ohio) and that everyone under his command should be supplied with rations for three to five days.[68]

Finally, on November 6, 1861, Benham crossed the Kanawha River to the mouth of Loop Creek. But Henry Benham still failed to comply with most of the many orders he had received.[69] His timidity was caused in part by his not wanting to get heavily engaged with Floyd until Schenck had crossed the New River. For this or whatever reason, he seemed to ignore Rosecrans' constant request to scout all the roads and report his findings.

In the meantime, Schenck was attempting to cross the New River somewhere behind Floyd's main camp at Dickerson to strike at his rear. Efforts were thwarted by swollen and rapid currents as well as rugged terrain. The task of solving these major impediments was given to a special aide-de-camp assigned to Brigadier-General Schenck, Major Samuel W. Crawford of the Thirteenth U.S. Infantry. The site selected for the crossing was as the little-used Townshend's Ferry.[70]

To effect a means of crossing the 80 to 90 yards of turbulent water, four skiffs were carried by wagon on the Lewisburg Road from Gauley, as were materials to build two ferries. One was to be formed from two wagon-boxes fastened together by poles and rope, and covered by canvas. The other, called a bull boat (bull boats were covered with skins in the west), was covered with canvas.[71]

Major Crawford's first task was to secretly move his potential crossing vessels from the mountain—with its steep perpendicular cliffs—to the river. After a laborious search, the best solution he could find was a point where the cliff opened. Even this presented formidable obstacles. In places, wrote an eyewitness, trees had to be cut and all the structures had to be "carried over rocks to the heads of steep ravines over which the skiffs and wagon beds were sent by means of ropes." It took from November 7 until November 9 to get the skiffs and wagon beds a short distance from the river, where they were concealed. The men performed this taxing labor in heavy rain that continued for seventy-two hours. A dozen men were left at night to guard the boats and were instructed to light no fires and to remain silent.

The day after the boats were placed and hidden near the New River, secrecy was threatened by the enemy, who appeared on the opposite shore and launched a small craft made of rough planks. The meager vessel could only carry two of the men. They made their way to the eastern shore, where they were captured, while their comrade on the opposite shore tried to escape while he was being fired upon.

This potential crisis averted, Crawford's men continued their work, and by late on Monday, November 11, after dark, the bullboats and two wagon-beds were fastened together and floated, and the skiffs were launched. All that remained was to get a rope across the river. Three experienced oarsmen in one of the skiffs attempted to cross, towing a small rope. The days of incessant rains had flooded the river. When the three men got to the middle of the river, the rapid currents seized their vessel and hastily propelled it downstream toward the rapids. Only by the utmost effort and good fortune were they able to return safely to shore. Orders were later received that there would be no crossing that night. The crafts were withdrawn from the water and were again hidden. On November 13, Schenck's men, the Third Brigade, in accordance with contingency plans, were ordered back to Gauley Bridge. They crossed the Kanawha a short distance from the falls to join Benham's movement against Floyd.[72]

PRELIMINARY ACTION: DIFFICULT CROSSINGS AND COX'S MEN TAKE COTTON MOUNTAIN

While Rosecrans waited for his grand plan to be executed, Confederates continued to harass the Federals with sporadic gunfire from across the New and Kanawha Rivers. They knew the ferries at Gauley Bridge and nearby Montgomery were being used by the Union at night, and they would fire an occasional shot in the dark that did no harm. The Confederate guns were so masked that the Union limited their response, finding it a waste of ammunition to fire except when fired upon.[73]

Confederate sharpshooters firing from shorter ranges also harassed the Federals by killing and wounding a few men and a number of mules and horses. Union picket duty was especially dangerous at Miller's Ferry. From later October into early November, men often fired across the river at each other. The Confederate skirmishers, who had hidden on numerous places on the cliffs and under the cover of rocks and trees, were so annoying that a Union regiment was sent to drive them away. A spirited skirmish on October 21 occurred across the New River until the Confederates "broke and fled," according to a Union account. But they soon returned. A few days after the skirmish, concealed Confederate shooters fired across the river, hitting a member of the Fourth Ohio Volunteers Infantry while he was carrying dinner to the picket post. The Ohio man ran for a nearby house and was hit again, this time in the abdomen as he fell in the doorway.[74]

Cox, with Rosecrans' blessings, decided to end the annoyance of the Confederate sharpshooters and the menace of the two guns on top of Cotton Hill, which impeded daytime use of the ferries. On November 10, 200 men were sent across the New River, and 200 crossed the Kanawha below the falls. They were to scurry up both ridges of Cotton Hill and chase away the Confederate sharpshooters, especially those manning the artillery. Lieutenant-Colonel David A. Enyart and the men of the First Kentucky Volunteers crossed the Kanawha and were to occupy the mountain, take the mills in the area, and reconnoiter the Fayetteville road. In the meantime the bombastic little Frenchman, Colonel Charles DeVilliers, took his men of the Eleventh Ohio Volunteers across the New River, a short distance upstream from where it emptied into the Kanawha.[75]

A scouting expedition by one of DeVilliers' Company K, under Captain Philander P. Lane, was ahead of both movements. The captain received an order during the night of November 9 that he was, at 3:00 A.M., to take his company by boat from the Gauley to the mouth of the New River and up a short distance to the base of Cotton Hill. Lane was ready at the appointed time, but only thirty-seven of his men were fit for duty.[76]

As they attempted to cross to the appointed destination, the swift currents of the flooded rivers swept the two boats, carrying the thirty-seven men down the Kanawha River toward the falls. The men were in great danger. Only after desperate efforts were their boats able to reach the northern banks of the Kanawha. Once ashore, the resolute Lane, intent on carrying out orders, had the boats hauled up to the Gauley on the left bank. Once again he launched the vessels. This time they carefully worked their way into the water and up the New River a short distance. There the two boats were pulled ashore.

DeVilliers, the colonel over Lane, had the company move in two directions. Half the men moved along the bank of the Kanawha in front of Gauley Bridge then straight up the formidable face of Cotton Hill. It was no easy task, pulling up over rocks and clinging to laurel bushes to keep from falling—which some did, suffering cuts and contusions.[77]

The other half of the advance party, according to official reports based on DeVilliers' version of events, was led by DeVilliers. They had an easier ascent. He led them along a path near the river and under the cliffs to a ravine, which led them to the Blake farm on top of the mountain, about a mile up New River. There he engaged one of the enemy outposts until Union reinforcement arrived and forced the Confederates back.

Official reports differ with the version of events told by Lane. In the captain's version, he contends that he was the first to cross, and he led the men to the Blake farm. According to Lane, DeVilliers crossed the New River later in a rowboat with three men, with two manning the oars and one steering. DeVilliers left four men, taking one from the several men left by Lane to guard the two rowboats so they would be ready to use. A sergeant was left in charge of the four, along with instructions from the colonel to shoot any of the four who attempted to leave. Then DeVilliers told the sergeant that if he failed in any of his duty, then he would cut off his head. The story was wild, but the threatened men told it. Furthermore, it was true to DeVilliers' erratic and bullying nature to have done such a thing, or at least to have threatened to do it.

While DeVilliers was threatening the men at the river, Captain Lane, after exchanging fire with enemy pickets, took up a defensive position at the edge of the Blake farm. He sent a man back to the river to report the situation to DeVilliers.[78] The colonel sent the messenger back to Lane, telling him to immediately report to DeVilliers at the river. Lane found the order astonishing under the circumstances, as it took him away from his small force in front of the enemy, for at least an hour. The captain, however, had no choice but to hurriedly report to his colonel at the riverbank.

Upon Lane's arrival, DeVilliers, without asking for a report of the situation on the mountaintop, immediately began to berate Lane for not crossing the river earlier. The truculent little colonel, according to Lane, "filled the air with violent and vulgar abuse and epithets." Lane was told he was unfit to command and was a coward. During his bellowing tirade, DeVilliers, who carried a cavalry saber instead of the appropriate infantry officer's sword, waved the weapon as "wildly as a madman," claimed Lane. Lane tried to speak, but DeVilliers had worked himself into such a state that he would listen to no one. Lane, upset, stood silently and endured the beratement while keeping his hand on his revolver in case DeVilliers attempted to strike him with the saber.[79]

Soon after DeVilliers' tantrum, he and Lane went to the mountaintop, where Lane's small company had remained under Major A. H. Coleman. Shortly after dark, Cox sent six companies of the Eleventh Ohio to reinforce DeVilliers. By 9:00, the Confederates, who had been reinforced with more than 200 men, drove the Union left under Coleman back a quarter-mile from the Blake farm. In turn, Coleman, who was reinforced by two companies of the Second Kentucky, drove the enemy back and occupied their former position on the Blake farm. In the meantime, the Confederates made a succession of attacks upon the remainder of the Union force, which was pushing up the mountain to Blake's farm from the Kanawha River. This push to the mountaintop included fighting with the First Kentucky, who had, during daylight, crossed the Kanawha and occupied part of the Fayetteville road and the western part of Cotton Hill. Brisk skirmishing between the two forces continued until after midnight.[80] At dawn the next day, November 11, following Cox's order, DeVilliers pushed the enemy further back to the southern end of the mountain referred to in 1861 as Cotton Hill.[81] While DeVilliers pushed southward, the enemy kept up scattered skirmishing as they pulled back, taking the two artillery pieces they had used to annoy the Federals.

Angered and annoyed by being fired upon, Rosecrans planned to trap Floyd by sending Schenck's brigade across the New River and Benham's across the Kanawha. The details and implementation of the plan changed because of rugged terrain, raging currents, inclement weather, and Benham's defiance in following orders.

ROSECRANS' PLAN TO TRAP FLOYD
Schenck from the east: Crossing the New River (Boyer's or Townsend Ferry to the Fayetteville-Raleigh Turnpike
Benham from the west: Crossing the Kanawha River to the Fayetteville-Raleigh Turnpike by one of four routes or combinations thereof: Kincaid Route, Settle-Cassidy's Mill Route, Laurel Creek Route, Nugent's Path

THE COTTON HILL CAMPAIGN
MAP B

As DeVilliers' men pushed back the small advanced Confederate force of several hundred, Southern men were positioned in advanced camps on the Raleigh Turnpike. One such camp had been located at the Huddleston house, to the west of the mountain. It had come under attack, probably several days earlier, and had to be evacuated. The attack had occurred when Isaac Smith and his men had just finished dinner and were lounging inside and outside the house without their weapons. Smith had long felt that this position was insecure, but the Yankee pickets down the road seemed to ignore them. Then suddenly the unsuspecting Confederates heard musket fire crashing all around them, causing confusion, terror, and panic. Smith ran upstairs in the house to get his sword and pistol but could not get down the stairs, which were jammed with men rushing up for their weapons. Others, attempting to get out with what Isaac Smith described as bayonets "bristling above their heads," inadvertently threatened to impale Smith and anyone else attempting a rapid descent of the stairs. Finally Smith was able to escape the house, only to see his men running in every direction. After seeing the confusion, Smith determined the enemy were firing from the hill in front of the house, and not, as he had feared, also from the rear of the dwelling.

Smith jumped on top of a stone wall and urged his men to follow him from the rear of the house. Smith's act was a brave but dangerous one. A minnie ball struck at the feet of the major, throwing dirt in the eyes of soldiers attempting to follow him.

From behind the wall, they drove off the enemy attackers, who left a trail of blood from their wounded: one fellow was dead, shot in the center of his forehead, and one was mortally wounded. The wounded man was taken to Huddleston's house, which now had a number of bullet holes in it. Smith talked compassionately to the wounded enemy, who said he would soon die. Smith wrote that he "felt great pity for the poor wounded man, about twenty and fine-looking, fair skin, dark hair, and intelligent face, who was in great agony." The Confederates' casualties were minor; two men suffered minor wounds, one in his hand and one in his foot.

McCausland, who had not been present during the attack, arrived and finally agreed with Smith that their position, only a mile and a half from the Kanawha River, was no longer tenable. They moved to the top of the hill, where they felt more secure, but without tents and with few fires in the bitter cold, they had far less comfort.[82]

On November 11 (while DeVilliers' men were pushing southward on top of the mountain) their new position was reinforced by a Union force from the west. One hundred fifty men of the First Kentucky under Major B. G. Leiper were moving along the Fayetteville road. They followed the Confederates under McCausland and Smith, who retired from their camp on the hill behind the Huddleston house. The Federals moved up the Fayetteville turnpike, crossed Cotton Hill, and took up a position at Laurel Creek during the afternoon. There, Leiper's men remained until evening, when they pulled back a half-mile to join the rest of Cox's force on the southern edge of Cotton Hill. This ended the first phase of the fighting. Rosecrans called it "a vigorous and brilliant skirmish," which lasted thirty hours. He reports that during that time, "700 men of General Cox's brigade drove the rebels from the front of Cotton Hill and their camp at Huddleston's and held the entire ground for nearly three miles between the Fayetteville road and New River, with a loss of two killed, one wounded, and six missing."[83]

DELAYS ALLOW FLOYD TO ESCAPE

All this time, Benham waited for Schenck to cross the New River. On the afternoon of November 11, 1861, he was told that Cox had taken Cotton Hill. Despite the urging by Rosecrans to move immediately by sending 1,000 of his 3,000 men to Cassidy's Mill to cut off Floyd's retreat and sending the rest to join Cox, Benham did not reach those positions until twenty-four hours later.[84]

About 3:00 P.M. of November 12, Benham's main force reached the eastern end of Cotton Hill, eight miles away from his camp on Loop Creek. A slight skirmish soon ensued between a few advanced companies of the brigade who were making a reconnaissance of the Laurel Creek ravine. Upon entering the ravine, men of the Twelfth and Thirteenth Ohio regiments were fired upon by an outpost of Confederates. The Federals took cover and a brisk exchange occurred at close range. The Union soldiers were driving the Southerners back when Benham ordered the skirmishers to retire. This ended the skirmish at Laurel Creek; each side had at least one killed and several wounded.[85]

Benham sent a courier to Rosecrans with a message stating his position and complaining, in Benham's words, of "the weakness of his main force compared with the supposed force of the enemy (4,000 to 6,000 men) and asking for reenforcements" so he might attack them. The enemy was entrenched at Dickerson's two and a half miles away. At 9:00 P.M. of November 12, 1861, Floyd started his retreat. General Benham did not find out about the enemy's retreat, according to his reports, until 4:30 the next afternoon. A Union company at Cassidy's Mill entered Fayetteville at 9:00 A.M. on November 13, and immediately messages were sent back to Cassidy's Mill and to Benham. He had been only two and a half miles away from the enemy and had been unaware of their retreat for almost a day. After discovering that Floyd had left, Benham moved cautiously and did not reach Fayetteville until late night, around midnight, of the thirteenth, twenty-seven hours after had Floyd commenced his retreat.[86]

Rosecrans' grand plan was unraveling, as the chance of trapping Floyd was eluding him. If Floyd retreated, as he was doing, the plan called for Schenck to cross the New River and attack him in the front while Benham cut off his escape and attacked him on the rear. But Schenck could not cross the swollen New River, and Benham's slowness allowed the enemy to escape.

General Schenck was unable to cross the New River, so he crossed the Kanawha on November 13 at Montgomery Ferry and set up headquarters at Huddleston's. He sent a messenger to inform Benham of his position and that he was now in command. Schenck's messenger was Major Samuel Crawford, who had worked so hard for the aborted crossing at Townsend Ferry. In his search for Benham, Crawford found the road muddy and difficult to pass, especially for the wagons. Soldiers of Benham's command were found straggling, separated from their regiments, and some of them had even abandoned the chase in favor of camping for the night.

At 9:00 P.M. Crawford found General Benham at Dickerson's farmhouse, where Floyd's troops had been prior to their retreat. Crawford told Benham that Schenck's troops had crossed the Kanawha and that General Schenck was now in command, which Benham was unhappy to hear. Schenck told Benham not to advance unless there was an immediate prospect of overtaking the enemy. Henry Benham responded that he was very near Floyd's wagon train and was resting his men for an hour at Dickerson before moving on to Fayetteville. Benham also told Crawford that the enemy was rapidly retreating, leaving baggage and other items behind. Crawford then asked if the men at Cassidy's Mill had definite instructions. He was told Benham had sent his aide-de-camp to that location with discretionary orders as to what route to take. Benham said that the aides had withdrawn the troops to the rear, and he was waiting for these troops to join him. Crawford then showed Benham a map with the positions marked on it and told the general: "the importance of the position at Cassidy's Mill could not be overestimated, and both General Rosecrans and General Schenck regarded it as the most important point in the whole position, as it threatened the enemy's rear, and the force there could fall upon the enemy's flank in a short march of 3 1/2 miles." Benham replied that he "had no maps, but he was confident that he would overtake the train anyhow, and that he hoped General Schenck would come at once." At 9:15, Crawford left to return to General Schenck's headquarters at Huddleston's. On his way back, he found a large number of stragglers of Benham's command heading toward Dickerson's with some confusion about their whereabouts and destination.[87]

After Crawford left, Benham nervously and hastily scribbled a badly written—and at times contradictory—message to Rosecrans: "I push forward now with the chance of catching Floyd's trains, do not let me be interfered with although he [Floyd] has a long start, two great blunders made by my two best officers have put me 12 hours behind Floyd. I should have been only 12 hours late but for this." Benham concluded, "I intend to take his train. It is safe for all to come on as I am pushing to Raleigh."[88]

At midnight Schenck sent his Third Brigade toward Dickerson. They arrived there at daylight. After a short halt, the Third Brigade moved to Fayetteville, where they were told the enemy was far in advance and Benham had left Fayetteville in pursuit nine hours before. This information—coupled with heavy rain, the exhaustion of the men, who were tired from the night's march and a lack of rations, tents, and blankets because the provision train had not been able to pass over the roads—all led to the decision to send the brigade no farther.[89]

While frustration was mounting in the Rosecrans camp, trepidation was building in Floyd's prior to evacuating from the base of Cotton Hill. On November 4, officers under Floyd, led by Henry Heth, requested that they pull back to Newborn, Dublin, or some point near the railroads.[90] This request was made both in person and in writing to Floyd. Fifteen officers signed the written request.

Floyd's officers worried that their location put them in a position to be trapped in what Heth called "a cul-de-sac as man or nature could have constructed." Heth also feared the command would be unable to survive because provisions had to be hauled 100 miles. To Heth's warning that Rosecrans could drive the Confederates away anytime he chose, Floyd replied, "Let him dare cross the river and not a damned Yankee will ever re-cross it. I will never yield a foot of *my country* to the rascals." Heth then objected, "General Rosecrans will capture you and your entire command." But Floyd insisted, "No sir, I will die before I will be captured. Do you know what they say they will do with me if captured? They say they will put me in an iron cage, haul me around their damned country and exhibit me as if I were a wild beast."

Floyd's retreat from his entrenched position at Dickerson occurred shortly after the end of the skirmish at Laurel Creek. Union artillery shots started falling in his camp, and Confederates were unable to get their wagons and horses out of harm's way. Around dusk, Floyd called another council of war, like the one preceding his retreat from Carnifex Ferry. News had reached the Confederate camps that the enemy had gotten behind them. The retreat started immediately. The man who boasted he would never "yield a foot" of his country was now in a hurried retreat. Again he seemed to come unraveled when confronted by his opponents. Before the retreat, during the skirmishing at Laurel Creek an extremely excited—if not panicky—Floyd rode up to Hill and said that "a country girl had just ridden in and informed him of the approach" of Benham's force. He exclaimed, "By God, they will get in my rear; I shall be attacked in front and rear; what must I do?" Floyd was now more than willing to leave, as had been recommended to him on November 4. Heth later remarked, "I think visions of the iron cage were very vivid then."[91]

A number of Floyd's regiments had no transportation and were forced to burn most of their belongings. On the night of November 11, according to Isaac Smith, they burned "about three hundred tents, several bales of new blankets and overcoats, and a number of mess chests, camp equipage of all kinds, and flour barrels were burst, contents scattered on the ground and all kinds of provisions were wasted and scattered, all to prevent the enemy from getting them." Even wagons that could have been used to carry off needed supplies saw wagoners unhitch the horses and ride them quickly to safety.[92]

Isaac Smith's men again brought up the rear of the retreat and saw piles of discarded items. As they marched through the night for fifteen miles in mud and cold, they saw where flour had been thrown away, as well as blankets, overcoats, and sundry other items. Smith's needy men picked up some of the discarded items. During the march to Raleigh, which lasted several days, the road and roadside were strewn with tents, boxes, weapons, clothes, food, and dishes. Full wagons were left stuck in the mud. At one location twelve wagons were abandoned, most of them turned upside down. At this site a number of horses became mired down and could not get out of the mud. They were shot. Matters were made worse by the quartermaster-general's drunkenness.

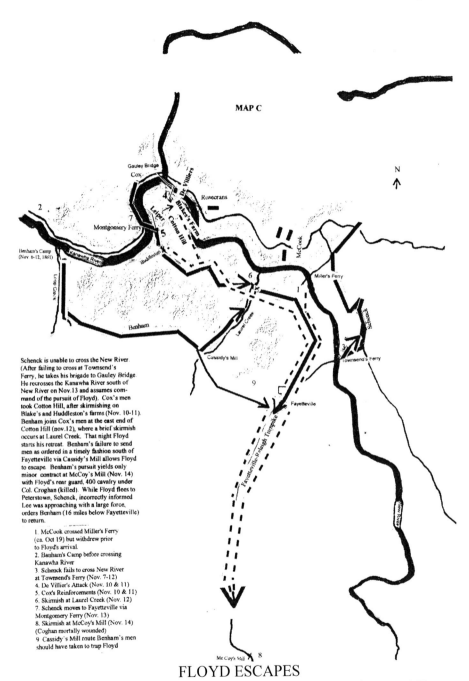

MAP C

N
↑

Gauley Bridge
Cox
De Villiers
Rosecrans
Leiper
Blake's Farm
Cotton Hill
Montgomery Ferry
Benham's Camp
(Nov. 6-12, 1861)
Kanawha River
Long Creek
Huddleston
McCook
Miller's Ferry
Benham
Laurel Creek
Schenck
Cassidy's Mill
Townsend's Ferry
Fayetteville
Fayetteville-Raleigh Turnpike
New River
Mc Coy's Mill

Schenck is unable to cross the New River.
(After failing to cross at Townsend's
Ferry, he takes his brigade to Gauley Bridge.
He recrosses the Kanawha River south of
New River on Nov.13 and assumes command of the pursuit of Floyd). Cox's men
took Cotton Hill, after skirmishing on
Blake's and Huddleston's farms (Nov. 10-11).
Benham joins Cox's men at the east end of
Cotton Hill (nov.12), where a brief skirmish
occurs at Laurel Creek. That night Floyd
starts his retreat. Benham's failure to send
men as ordered in a timely fashion south of
Fayetteville via Cassidy's Mill allows Floyd
to escape. Benham's pursuit yields only
minor contract at McCoy's Mill (Nov. 14)
with Floyd's rear guard, 400 cavalry under
Col. Croghan (killed). While Floyd flees to
Peterstown, Schenck, incorrectly informed
Lee was approaching with a large force,
orders Benham (16 miles below Fayetteville)
to return.

1. McCook crossed Miller's Ferry
(ca. Oct 19) but withdrew prior
to Floyd's arrival.
2. Banham's Camp before crossing
Kanawha River
3. Schenck fails to cross New River
at Townsend's Ferry (Nov. 7-12)
4. De Villier's Attack (Nov. 10 & 11)
5. Cox's Reinforcements (Nov. 10 & 11)
6. Skirmish at Laurel Creek (Nov. 12)
7. Schenck moves to Fayetteville via
Montgomery Ferry (Nov. 13)
8. Skirmish at McCoy's Mill (Nov. 14)
(Coghan mortally wounded)
9 Cassidy's Mill route Benham's men
should have taken to trap Floyd

FLOYD ESCAPES
Rosecrans' Plan Improperly Executed as Federals Fail to Cut Off Confederate Retreat

One night Smith laid down on some straw and covered himself from head to toe with his old shaggy blanket as the rain poured down in torrents. Sleep was impossible, wrote Smith, as "vivid lightening and tremendous peals of thunder were seen and heard every few minutes."

The rainstorm, the drunk quartermaster, the mud, the cold, the apprehension of a potentially fatal contest with the enemy, and the "tyranny of Floyd," wrote Smith, combined to make him feel that it was the most unfortunate night of his life. It seemed that God was against him. A day later they camped outside of Raleigh Court House, when a heavy snow fell during the night. Many of the Virginia soldiers were barefoot or wore shoes that were so worn out, wearing them was an encumbrance rather than a benefit. Smith had to beg from a Georgia colonel four pairs of shoes for those he described as "poor fellows who had been marching entirely barefoot, with their feet bleeding almost as they walked."[93]

Floyd and his army feared being attacked every day of their retreat. He incorrectly believed that 5,000 additional troops had recently joined the other Federals who were chasing him. Though his official reports claimed he was always in control, Heth reported a story to the contrary. Around midnight during the disorderly retreat Heth reported to Floyd, and they began discussing their present condition. Floyd said, "this is fast becoming a rout. I tell you what I will do: I will have the command assembled and make them a speech and tell them that reinforcements are coming to join me." Heth responded, "General, I would not disturb the men. They have had a hard day's march. Let them sleep. And especially I would not tell them that reinforcements were coming to assist you. They would soon find out that it was not true, and their confidence in you would be destroyed." "But they like to hear me speak." said Floyd. "Yes, but now I think they would prefer sleeping," answered Heth. If Heth's account is accurate, which it seemed to be, then Floyd was unable to distinguish the differences between a political rally and military necessities.[94]

In the meantime, Benham was having problems catching Floyd. On the morning of November 14, he had his last clash with the former Virginia governor. Again, it was only a skirmish. Floyd's men had left their camp at McCoy's Mill and had gone two miles when it was reported that the enemy was nearby and was approaching quickly. The small Confederate cavalry force of about 400, under Colonel St. George Croghan, was sent to the rear. Upon rounding a bend in the road two miles north of McCoy's Mill, the cavalrymen were fired upon by the Thirteenth Ohio, who had hidden in the woods surrounding the road. Several of the horsemen were wounded, and the rest panicked. Colonel Croghan spurred his mount to the center of the road, and while he stayed in plain view of the enemy, he had his men dismount as he remained the lone inviting target in the saddle.

Suddenly Croghan noticed the Federals were spreading out in a V shape, on one side of the road in an open field a couple of hundred yards away, to flank the cavalrymen. Croghan began shouting to his men to fall back. Suddenly, while still mounted, he reeled in the saddle, grabbed his horse's mane, and slowly fell from his mount. But his foot was caught in the stirrup. His frightened charger leaped and ran, dragging his rider into the weeds on the side of the road. There somehow the foot became dislodged and Croghan lay, profusely bleeding from wounds in his wrist and his upper abdomen, where a ball had passed through his body. Four of his men rushed to him and carried him to a house in the field. Ignoring the bullets flying around them and the scared screams of the inhabitants of the house, they laid their mortally wounded colonel on a bed. Soon one of the cavalrymen looked out the window and hollered, "They are flanking us. We will be captured!" The wounded colonel raised himself on his elbow, pointed to the door, and, struggling to breathe, told his men to go because he was dying.[95] They left their colonel and, with some difficulty, ran off into the woods.[96]

The Confederate cavalry left on the field were swept back, and they narrowly escaped capture. Their retreat was hastened by Union artillery shots falling among them. Soon the Confederate cavalry had retreated to the rear of the Confederate infantry, informing them of the Union's rapid pursuit. Upon hearing this, panic set in and the foot soldiers in the immediate area retreated haphazardly, with some soldiers leaving their belongings behind. It required great effort by the officers to restore order and calm.[97]

The Confederates were in no real danger of being captured. The road that was so aptly described as a "perfect mire, about half a leg deep," had to be waded through by both sides, hindering the movement of both. The skirmish at McCoy's Mill was an unsuccessful attempt by Benham to capture Floyd's wagon train. He had not come close to capturing Floyd and his force, as the skirmish consisted of the simple rearguard action of the Confederate cavalry suddenly running into Union infantry who waited around a bend in the road. It was amazing that there was only one fatality, Colonel St. George Croghan, but he was notable. His death got considerable coverage in the press and official reports on both sides. Croghan came from a prominent Irish-American military family. His father had fought in the American Revolution, and his uncle William Clark was the partner of Meriwether Lewis in the historic trip across the continent. Another uncle, George Rogers Clark, was a Revolutionary War hero, on the American side, for his exploits in the Northwest Territory.[98]

St. George Croghan was wounded at McCoy's Mill at 9:30 A.M. on November 14 and lived in agonizing pain until 2:30 that afternoon. Shortly after he was taken to a nearby farmhouse, the dwelling came under the control of Federal troops. Their commander, General Benham, entered the house. Before the war, Benham had been a friend of the father of the wounded Confederate. Croghan recognized Benham, who was in pain but still conversed easily and shook the Union general's hand. Before leaving the dying man, a saddened Benham left a regimental surgeon and other medical personnel to look after Croghan. Benham later wrote that when he was leaving the dying man, Croghan requested that the general "state that he died the death of a brave soldier." In a moving and sensitive letter to General Floyd, the usually overbearing Benham later wrote that Croghan had died "in every way worthy of his gallant and noble father."[99]

Benham informed Floyd that Croghan's remains would be taken to Fayetteville, where, he explained, "they will be interred if we are not able to take them to Gauley; though I will if possible, place the body there in a box with salt to preserve it for his friends."

A private citizen sent the letter to Floyd from Benham. In it Benham concluded by stating that this was the third time he had had the opportunity of "extending courtesies somewhat of this character to your officers." The first was returning the baggage and uniform of Colonel Porterfield at Philippi; the second, wrote Benham, was "preserving the sword, effects, and body of General Garnett at Carrick's Ford." "I trust," concluded Benham, "your officers will appreciate the desire thus exhibited of mitigating in every way the horrors of this fratricidal strife."[100]

Brigadier-General Henry Washington Benham
A fine engineer, Benham has a violent temper and profane rebukes, which makes him ill suited for line command. His slowness to act, which allows Floyd to escape from Cotton Hill brings the wrath of Rosecrans upon him.
(Courtesy of the Library of Congress)

McCoy's Mill was the last whimper in the Federals' pursuit of Floyd. It was the last exchange of fire. Benham's men continued to follow the Southerners southward, going as far as Ketron's farm (also called Blake's farm) fifteen miles from Fayetteville. There Benham stopped for the night. His men were too weary to continue. But the

461

stop provided little rest as nine-tenths of his men were without tents and blankets after having thrown them away in the chase. They could only stand around their fires, unable to sleep on the ground in the drenching rain during a succession of violent thunderstorms.

Benham sent a dispatch to Schenck telling of this situation, but stating that he wanted to continue to pursue. He told Schenck that if he could send troops, they might "drive the enemy through Raleigh." He also told of a scouting report of an enemy wagon train coming on Bowyer's Ferry Road, and of information given at McCoy's Mill by a major that indicated that Lee was coming down with a force of 5,000 to reinforce Floyd and to attack. Schenck ordered Benham to return to Fayetteville as soon as practicable to defeat Lee. Benham's men left at 1:00 A.M. on November 15 and arrived at McCoy's at 4:00 A.M.[101] They rested until 6:00 A.M. and then continued their march back.[102]

FAILURES, FRUSTRATIONS, AND CONTROVERSIAL CHARACTERS: FLOYD, BENHAM, AND DEVILLIERS

Lee never came, having long ago left the region. No battles had been fought in the Cotton Hill campaign, only a few skirmishes.[103] As in the Sewell Mountain campaign, the weather and terrain proved to be sovereign. Cold weather, steep mountain ranges, and traveling in continuous rain exhausted the men and sickened them with camp fever, typhus, and typhoid. Battle plans were thwarted.[104]

These conditions were aided, however, by human error. Rosecrans blamed Benham. Benham responded that he could have caught Floyd had he not been called back by Schenck. Benham also blamed his subordinates for the delays in carrying out Rosecrans' plan. At the start of the pursuit scouts were not sent out to see if Floyd was retreating because the usually reliable Colonel W. S. Smith of the Thirteenth Ohio thought that Benham's directions were merely suggestions. According to Benham, later, troops were withdrawn at a critical time from Cassidy's Mill because an aide also misunderstood Benham's order. And finally, at McCoy's Mill, for half an hour

Colonel Edward Siber of the Thirtieth Ohio refused to carry out Benham's order for a flanking attack.[105]

The tenor of Floyd's official reports was very similar to Benham's. Both claimed to have been robbed of success because of their superiors' decisions and a lack of reinforcements. Floyd's scenario had the hyperbole of a politician's campaign speech. On November 7, 1861, from his headquarters at Dickerson, just east of Cotton Hills in a strong fortified position in a gap between two mountain ranges, he boasted that he could hold off an army five times the size of his own. Furthermore, in getting to Dickerson, he claimed to have "driven the enemy across the Kanawha," removing their penetration to "within 70 miles of the Virginia and Tennessee Railroad." He claimed to have restored the "feeling of confidence and security in all the country in our rear." He would claim his artillery on Cotton Hill had severely harassed the enemy, closed their ferry, killed many horses, "and not less than 50 men."

Apparently Floyd had boasted, in response to a local lady who said she hoped he would not leave Cotton Hill, "I assure you, madam, I'll not leave Cotton Hill until compelled by death or the order of the Secretary of War."[106] He had made a similar promise a couple of months earlier, on the high bluffs overlooking the Gauley River at Carnifex Ferry. All bluster aside, Floyd preferred retreat to battle. He claimed victory was denied him and he had had to withdraw, not because of the fear of being flanked or being turned by the enemy, but because Lee had not moved to Gauley east of the New River.[107]

Floyd also complained that Confederate authorities in Richmond had aided his pursuers by having recently released from confinement two men who guided the enemy "along obscure and unused paths." He strongly recommended, "under no circumstances should a traitor be let loose"—especially one who had been arrested and sent to Richmond, unless the person be proven innocent beyond all doubt. In spite of the guides, Floyd claimed the "enemy followed, but with great timidity." At Loop Mountain, said Floyd, the "enemy declined to attack me, but retreated to Gauley in a very disorderly manner." Floyd claimed that Loop Mountain was of no "strategic value," so, he continued, "I thought it best to fall back." He added proudly that during his retreat, on November 10, a cavalry raid he had ordered in the direction of the Ohio River had "annihilated...a force of the enemy about 300 strong" at Guyandotte, who, the general wrote, "[took] 95 prisoners, killed or drowned the remainder, and captured about 300 Enfield rifles."[108]

Floyd pulled back to the New River, east of Princeton, to the Peterstown area, but on December 2 he was ordered to move his command further south to Dublin Station, on the Virginia and Tennessee Railroad.[109] On December 16 he received orders that split up and sent his command to three different locations. He was told it was unnecessary for him to go into winter camp at Dublin because, in the words of Judah Benjamin, the Confederate secretary of war, "the enemy are pressing superior force on columns of General Lee in South Carolina and General Johnston in Kentucky." Several regiments were sent to Lee, but the bulk of his command, including Floyd, was ordered to join Johnston at Bowling Green, Kentucky. One regiment of Floyd's troops who were accustomed to the rigors of the winter climate among the mountains was to be sent to the Lewisburg area. This was to allay fears of agitated residents who had petitioned for protection after Floyd's retreat from Cotton Hill, as well as to block the enemy from moving uncontested into the Valley of Virginia.[110]

Floyd's supporters continued their chant of his greatness. Even his retreat from Cotton Hill was cited as proof of his superior military tactics. The Richmond *Examiner* lauded him as "the hero of thirty engagements." But other Virginia papers, the Richmond *Whig,* and Lynchburg *Virginian,* proclaimed Floyd's retreat from Cotton Hill as "the most disgraceful rout that our armies have suffered during the war. This unfortunate affair eclipses all the rising fame of General Floyd and ends the ill-fated campaign in Western Virginia in a blaze of glory for the Yankees." Knowledge of Floyd's fate would have certainly given Virginians and other Confederates cause to pray when President Jefferson Davis proclaimed November 15, 1861, a day of fasting, humiliation, and prayer. Floyd had failed in his second attempt to regain the Kanawha Valley. This time he had been forced back without even fighting a battle.

Benham also had his reviewers. The New York *World* claimed it was Benham and not Rosecrans who came up with the plan to trap Floyd. Even his defenders described Benham as "a *brusque,* imperative and rather overbearing man with his equals and superiors," but they also contended that his rapidity of movement, fertility of resource, and consummate military capacity were recognized by the rank and file, with whom he was wonderfully popular.[111]

Certainly William A. West, a cavalry captain, did not deem Benham so wonderfully popular. In early December at the Huddleston house, Benham called West "a God damned Son of bitch." He also threatened to shoot one of the men in West's company and called him "a damned son of a bitch."[112]

Later J. D. Hines wrote to Cox regarding the pending prosecution of Benham for the "use of offensive words" as charged by Captain George L. Hartsuff. Hines stated it was commonplace behavior by the general and should not be taken seriously. Hines wrote, "General Benham was so often in ill humor, and so often used abusive language to officers and men that it excited but little attention and less surprise. It came rather as a matter of course." Hines himself was chided by the general at the camp of the Twelfth Ohio at Huddleston's, regarding the efforts to police the camp: "God damn you, there is nothing done," denounced the general.[113]

Certainly Captain Jonathan S. Devenny of the U.S. steamer *Silver Lake* did not concur in tolerating Benham's harsh tongue. On the evening of November 6 the ship's captain took Benham's brigade from his Camp Huddleston—a different Huddleston than the one east of the river—on the northern bank of the Kanawha a mile and a half away, to the mouth of Loop Creek. The next morning at 3:00, the steamer waited to take Benham, his staff, and some twenty cavalry horses across. The last horse to be loaded was the general's. His German servant had great difficulty getting the steed on board. The animal got off the loading platform into the mud and water. In the words of Devenny, "After a great deal of trouble, in fact after putting lines around the Horse and pulling him," they finally "succeeded in getting him on Board." Benham then came aboard, and, seeing his mount muddy and wet, began a tirade of profanity, yelling for the captain, who was inside the cabin sitting by the stove because he was suffering from the effects of a severe cold. The captain was unaware of what had happened to the general's horse, but on hearing an angry, loud voice, he went to investigate. He was greeted by the general, who shouted, "God damn you Captain, I will shoot you. God damn you, you ought to be shot." Benham "got his pistols and had one in each hand repeating the expression, 'God damn you, I will Shoot you.'" He added, "God damn you, Captain, this might be the means of breaking up this expedition," and finally he threatened, "God damn you, I will have you discharged." The stunned captain could not imagine the reason for Benham's outrage. It was only later did he learn the cause: according to the captain, the "Stage was not lying *Exactly* Square with the Boat which," the captain knew, "did not make a particle of difference in regard to taking on the Horses." Benham even followed Devenny, whose hoarseness from a cold prevented him from speaking above a whisper, back into the cabin, where the general continued cursing him and stated, according to Devenny, "any God damn Steam Boat Captain that would let his Horse get in the River ought to be Shot."[114]

Besides annoying those of lesser rank, Benham—who had talent as an engineer but was totally ill-suited for a line command—had so angered Rosecrans for letting Floyd escape that he had Benham arrested on November 24. Counsel for Benham argued in mid-December that according to the law, Benham must be released, since "some twenty days had elapsed since his arrest" and he had not been charged. The judge-advocate general, with Lincoln's endorsement, ruled "there was just cause for delaying the trial," but he recommended Benham's release and return to duty. On November 29, Rosecrans reported to his superiors, "I found it necessary to arrest Brig. Gen. H. W. Benham for unofficer-like neglect of duty...The arrest had been ordered because Benham failed to cut off the retreat of General John B. Floyd in West Virginia."[115] George McClellan, now the general-in-chief, notified Rosecrans in early January 1862: "the charges filed by you against Brig. Gen. Benham cannot be sent to trial until the state of military operations will permit a court martial to be convened...The delay is unavoidable, but as the charges are too grave to be dismissed they must be reserved for trial when the convenience of the times will permit."[116]

During Benham's arrest after the Cotton Hill campaign, he applied for medical leave. Rosecrans granted him permission to go to New York. Benham's brigade surgeon no doubt greatly helped in granting him medical leave. The doctor urged Benham to go and be properly fitted with a truss to replace the worn-out and unfit one he had. Benham's hernia was severe; the protrusion was increasing and demanded immediate attention. This condition certainly did not help make Benham more agreeable.[117]

Benham was involved in controversy even during his medical leave: claims were made that he continued to wear his sword after his arrest. This, Benham denied.[118] Most of his time on medical leave was spent on his defense. The day after his arrest, and before he left Camp Huddleston, Benham was in favor of convening a court of inquiry. He wanted not only an investigation of the Cotton Hill campaign, but also what Benham claimed were lies sanctioned by General Rosecrans and published in Cincinnati newspapers.[119]

Benham resented two of Rosecrans' statements. The first was "While Benham's columns laid upon their arms, waiting for morning, the rebels began to retreat from their entrenched camp and before our troops discovered the movements, they were well on their way to Raleigh." The other offending statement was "Gen. Benham, on learning of their retreat pursued them [the enemy] for twenty-five miles—amidst a drenching rain, over muddy roads, when finding there was but little chance of overtaking them turned back from the pursuit." Overall these statements were correct, except for the omission of General Schenck's ordering Benham back, but Benham decried this omission. Furthermore, Benham claimed these statements ignored the fact that he begged Rosecrans that he "not be interfered with." Benham objected to Rosecrans' failure to mention his bravery. Benham claimed,"[I] had not said or thought one word of failing or returning from the chase—though with a command reduced by stragglers and guards left behind—to less than 2,400—and though we had passed in the pursuit on the two previous days *within cannon range of not less than nine* regiments of Gen. Rosecrans's command not one man of whom had joined to aid in the pursuit." Benham thought he had every right to feel "aggrieved." Furthermore, Benham argued, it was Schenck who caused Benham's troops to be detained for a week with his failure to cross the New River.[120]

After his arrest, Benham personally appealed to McClellan and Lincoln. In January 1862, Benham went to see the ill general-in-chief, but he would not see Benham. Instead he wrote to McClellan, "I cannot but greatly regret that you were not able to hear me for a few minutes, suffering as I am under the most foul and undeserved wrongs, as I believe that have ever happened to any officer of our army, and for the most meritorious conduct of my whole life." Benham went on to charge "[I am] as sure—as of my Existence that I should not have been arrested, if I had not asked for a Court of

Inquiry which must have shown the errors of Gen. Rosecrans and others that prevented my capture of Floyd's forces."[121] When McClellan advised Benham to be patient, Benham wrote Lincoln on February 11, 1862, "The 'patience' that Gen. McClellan wrote you that I 'must have' I have had, not only for these three weeks, but for *nearly three months,* that this prosecution has existed."[122]

The Benham case got more newspaper coverage than the Cotton Hill campaign. The New York *Tribune* concluded, with a fair degree of accuracy, "we fear it is true there are serious dissensions and unworthy jealousies among our Generals in Western Virginia; and it has been intimated that more than one of them are anxious to receive a Major-General's commission." Not all the press was critical of Benham; one writer asserted that "General Benham's plans were laid with skill and carried out with his usual promptness and energy." But the Cincinnati *Gazette* responded, "We are painfully curious to know what those plans were?" As a correspondent for the *Gazette* stated, "General Benham was, from the beginning to the end, unnecessarily excited." When he passed Gauley Bridge at midnight on early November, wrote the correspondent, "he publicly stated that General Cox's position was untenable, and that his entire brigade would be shelled out the next day." Benham told the skirmishers who were poised to cross the Kanawha River that Rosecrans' order—said the correspondent—"was madness, and they all would be murdered." The writer continued: "he wound up saying that he must push on and get his brigade out of that slaughter pen."[123]

The case dragged on without resolution. Benham was finally ordered to report for duty on March 17, 1862, and was soon transferred to Major General David Hunter's command at Port Royal, South Carolina. It did not take him long to get in trouble there. In June 1862 he was relieved of his command, arrested, and later stripped of his appointment as brigadier general by Lincoln for his failure at Secessionville and for disobedience of orders.[124]

Benham was disliked by his men and by Rosecrans, but Charles A. DeVilliers, Colonel of the Sixteenth Ohio, was also despised by many who knew him. Those who suffered under his command held him in great disdain. His high-handedness, arrogance, and self-centeredness were manifested in insensitive and demeaning treatment of those under him. In December 1861, finally, Captain Philander Lane could take no more. He filed many charges against his colonel. Two incidents, at the base of Cotton Hill, were cited among the violation of articles of war. In the presence of others, DeVilliers said to one officer, "You, Lieutenant McCabe, are a coward. You have more shit in your breeches than in your guts." To Lane, whom he called down from the top of Cotton Hill, he said, "Captain Lane, you are not fit to command a company, you are a coward. Your company are all cowards. I will take off your shoulder straps."[125]

According to a member of the Second Kentucky, on the same day, November 11, when reinforcements came, DeVilliers said to them in German: "Gentlemen, I am glad you came; the officers and men of the Eleventh regiment are cowards." After Cotton Hill, the Eleventh Ohio went into winter quarters at Point Pleasant. There on December 20 DeVilliers entered the quarters of Company B at about the time of reveille and stated, "If I ever enter your quarters again and if every man does not rise and salute me, I will shoot you down like dogs, so help me God." A few days earlier he had humiliated the lieutenant-colonel, Frizell, in front of the command and townspeople at a dress parade where DeVilliers was given a horse. He was hoarse from a cold and was unable to speak, so he told the lieutenant-colonel to address the crowd. After he had spoken for about five minutes, "DeVilliers drew his sword, stepped in front" of Frizell and demanded that he should say no more," claimed Frizell. When Frizell requested that he might "close by saying a few words more… DeVilliers rudely and ungentlemanly pushed him back and demanded" Frizell dismiss the parade. The day after the incident, December 18, 1861, M. W. Frizell wrote to General Cox, making him aware of what the lieutenant-colonel complained was "a gross unmitigated, ungentlemanly, and dastardly insult." A few days later, DeVilliers wrote a rambling, and at times disjointed letter to headquarters, stating his version of the incident. His letter contends that he apologized to Frizell in front of other officers and believed the matter had ended. The continued resentment, claimed DeVilliers, was the result of men not being allowed to go to hotels to drink. Harmony would never exist "as long as whiskey is allowed among them," wrote DeVilliers to Cox. "When you come here you will see…the Stuff itself. I have Six (6) *Bottles* of *meanest* Kind and 12 Decks of cards which I shall Keep for you to See, when you come down, which I hope you will soon come down."

469

DeVilliers' popularity was diminished even further among the other officers by the incident, so he turned to threats once again. "If you expect to get along with me," DeVilliers told them, "you must not love Lieut.-Col. Frizell. I would find out who these Frizell men are and I will fix them."[126]

DeVilliers was also charged with stealing. Among the charges were misappropriating funds, with selling seven head of cattle and pocketing the money. The most blatant crime was the confiscation of a citizen's property at Point Pleasant. Kenny J. Fisher's house was stripped of all of its contents, from beds to silverware. DeVilliers also emptied the safe, which included $280 in currency belonging to an old black woman and several thousand dollars more, including bonds, notes, and mortgages, which, along with other property taken from Fisher, was valued at about $40,000. DeVilliers used the silverware, table linens, and many of the items at his mess table. Other objects were boxed and shipped to his home. Later, military authorities found confiscated items when inventorying DeVilliers' property. They seized and opened a trunk and found $450 in treasury notes and $500 in gold, an unusually large amount of money for someone to have in camp.[127]

Soon after charges were filed against him, DeVilliers started defending himself through numerous letters to headquarters, including letters to Rosecrans and Cox, a citizen petition, and attacks on Lane. DeVilliers argued that the whole case was "nothing but a conspiracy," fueled by whiskey and vindictiveness, that treated him unfairly and undermined his health.

Apparently citizens of the Point Pleasant area signed a petition demanding the removal of DeVilliers; a counter-petition was sent to Rosecrans on December 17, 1861, signed by twenty-three—no doubt Unionist—residents.[128]

The petition against removal lauded DeVilliers' "energetic measures...adopted for the security and protection of all good and law-abiding citizens." It continued: "His untiring vigilance, his strict enforcement of judicious regulations, his fearless administration of justice deserve our warmest commendation." Several days later, DeVilliers wrote Cox that "[my] office is full most all the time by Soldiers asking me not to resign." Also shortly after charges were filed by Captain Lane and attested to by a large percentage of officers of the Eleventh Ohio, on December 27, 1861, DeVilliers had Lane arrested on the parade grounds in front of the captain's company. In two days Lane was released, was given back his sword, and was told by DeVilliers to resume command of Company K. He refused to tell Lane why he had been placed under arrest.[129]

DeVilliers seems to have been placed under arrest on January 14, 1862. The next day he wrote headquarters, protesting that it was "[more Lane's] *vindictiveness* than anything else that had induced him to prefer charges against me." DeVilliers claimed to be anxious to refute the charges at a court-martial. He also informed headquarters that he had "preferred charges against Capt. Lane" of "False Assertions," "Unofficer-like and ungentlemanly conduct, Disobedience to Orders, & etc. & etc." Regarding a citizen's complaint, DeVilliers dismissed it as coming from "as rank a secessionist at heart as it is possible for a man to be."[130]

Finally, on February 11, 1862, DeVilliers again wrote Rosecrans saying he wanted to be released or else stand trial immediately. Rosecrans responded by ordering both Lane and DeVilliers to be tried by the court that was in session. After hearing dozens of witnesses, both military and civilian, Charles DeVilliers was dismissed from service on April 23, 1862. Lane was acquitted and resumed his military duties.[131]

Soon after the termination of the Cotton Hill campaign, Rosecrans' forces went into winter camp as he established his headquarters at Wheeling. His command was scattered throughout western Virginia, but the bulk was concentrated, to hold what Rosecrans considered three vital areas: the Kanawha Valley, Cheat Mountain Summit, and Romney.

Rosecrans hoped to get rid of dead wood and shape up his forces during the winter. He planned for a winter campaign to seize Winchester. Neither plan came to fruition because McClellan was opposed to them and Rosecrans' forces were transferred to the west.

Schenck suffered from typhoid and had to leave his men, who were in winter camp at Fayetteville and the Gauley Bridge region. Their presence enabled Rosecrans to protect the Kanawha Valley and his crucial supply base at Gauley Bridge as well as the outlets toward Sewell and Raleigh.[132]

The roads were so decrepit by late November that the bodies of dead horses littered the way between Meadow Bluff and Sewell. South on the Lewisburg Pike, below Gauley Bridge, Captain

Philander Lane described seeing a "wagon sunk in the road until the bed reached the mire, with its four mules hitched to it" and the more they struggled, the more they sank, "like a man caught in quicksand, until their heads were above the half-fluid mass, and there of course they died."[133] Rosecrans formed a pack-mule train in a hopeful attempt to supply his own camps that were not accessible by water.

Winter activities shifted from attempting to engage the enemy to scouting, drilling, building breastworks and blockhouses, and getting artillery into position. The least enjoyable task was standing guard or having picket duty in the mountains. One soldier of the Forty-seventh Ohio stationed at Camp Gauley on Gauley Mountain described such duty. "Without fire [it] is awful in the extreme, the cold penetrating every joint until the whole body is benumbed." The original tents at Camp Gauley often gave little protection against the cold. Sibley tents arrived; they were round and shaped like large tepees and were an improvement. Installation included digging a round ditch the circumference of the tent, putting boards upright in the ditch three to four feet in height, and forming a bank of dirt as high as the wooden slabs. The Sibley was fastened to the boards with wooden pins. Once the tent was erect, an iron stove would be set up inside, its stovepipe reaching out the top; fires were common. Around the stove were built bunks to accommodate three to fifteen men.[134] The floors were covered with boards taken from abandoned houses and barns.

Rutherford B. Hayes was among those stationed at Fayetteville. Rosecrans had learned his lesson, not to leave the region west of the New River unprotected. Hayes greatly enjoyed his rides to Gauley and back, even despite the cold and the hard day's ride. He wrote in late November after making this trip in the rain and snow: "How I enjoy these rides, this scenery, and all!" He wrote of seeing a "teamster with a spike team [three horses] stuck" and Hayes tried, unsuccessfully, to help. He had to give up, giving a pair of his socks from the load as his only recompense.[135] On November 29, 1861, road conditions prompted Hayes to write his niece, Miss Laura Pratt:

> We are in no immediate danger here of anything except starvation.... All our supplies come from the head of navigation on the Kanawha over a road remarkable for the beauty and sublimity which bound it on either side.... Yesterday one of our bread wagons with driver and four

horses missed the road four or six inches and landed in the top of a tree ninety feet high after a fall of about seventy feet. The miracle is that the driver is here to explain that one of his leaders [horse in the front] hawed [went left] when he ought to have geed [gone right]."[136]

He continued in his letter to his niece, saying that road conditions had forced the use of pack mules to bring in supplies. "They [mules] do well among the scenery," Hayes wrote, "but unfortunately part of the road is a Serbonian Bog where …armies… might sink if they haven't, and the poor mules have a time of it. The distance [from Fayetteville] luckily is only sixteen to twenty miles. If, however, the water gets low…the distance will increase thirty to forty miles…then we shall all be looking for the next thaw for victuals."[137]

Ruddy, as friends and family members called Hayes, found very few male residents in the area. He pitied the plight of the local women. He felt sorry for them because of their conditions. Hayes wrote his mother: "A great share of the calamities of war fall on the women. I see women, unused to hard labor, gathering corn to keep starvation from the door." Much of Hayes' time, once he was assigned command of the post at Fayetteville, after Schenck left, was occupied in "hearing stories of distress and trying to soften the ills the armies have brought on this country." Whenever possible, Hayes tried to pay for the Union soldiers' destroying corn, hay, and other property; he distributed a small amount of salt, sugar, coffee, rice, and bacon to local residents. An enterprising young man from the county came to Fayetteville with apples, pies, bread, and tobacco. He attempted to sell the apples for ten cents a dozen and the pies for twenty cents each. The soldiers thought the prices were outlandish, got mad, and robbed the apple cart. Hayes became angry when he heard what had happened and, along with several other officers, made recompense with money from his own pockets.

At the end of November the weather moderated, and Hayes wrote that the people in and around Fayetteville were "crowding in to take the oath of allegiance." Ruddy wrote to wife: "Dearest, [the locals are]…a narrow-chested, weakly, poverty-stricken, ignorant set. I don't wonder they refuse to meet our hardy fellows on fair terms. Captain Sperry says: 'They are too ignorant to have good health.'" They continued to come for paroles in December from as far away as twenty-five miles. Hayes contemplated their reasons. "How much is due to a returning sense of loyalty and how much to the want of coffee and salt, is more than I know. They are sick of war, ready for peace and a return to the old Union. Many of them have been Secessionists, some of them soldiers."

A week later, on December 15, 1861, Hayes wrote that the weather continued to be lovely. Repatriation continued, and he described many of those taking the oath as "fresh from the Rebel armies...and [they] really behave as if they were sick [of war]." "Nothing but ill luck," the optimistic Hayes continued, "will prevent our wiping out the Rebellion. The common people of this region want to get back to coffee and salt and sugar, etc., etc., none of which articles can now be got through whole extensive districts of country."

Contrabands also came to Fayetteville. Hayes said that they "gave themselves up" to him, and he let them go to Ohio. He believed, "The rule is...that slaves coming to our lines, especially if owned by Rebels, are free." Hayes alerted his uncle in Fremont, Ohio, that the contrabands would likely go there, and he should look for one family that was "one in a thousand—faithful, intelligent, and industrious," who would make excellent household servants.[138]

On December 29 five Union companies started a march to occupy Raleigh, twenty-five miles south of their Fayetteville camp, Camp Union. The plan was to go beyond Raleigh to Princeton to capture the enemy there and to burn the railroad bridges near Newbern. The enemy was believed to consist of 600 sick men with a guard of only 100, along with arms and stores, and maybe even Floyd, who was rumored to be unguarded.[139] The year ended with the Federals occupying Raleigh.

UNION SUCCESS AND THE EMERGENCE OF A NEW STATE

The end of December saw the Federals in firm control of the Kanawha Valley. Thomas (Stonewall) Jackson's earlier warning to Confederate authorities that to fight in the rugged terrain of western Virginia would lead to failure was proven correct. The three attempts by the Confederates to hold or regain this region had failed. No major battles rivaling the size of First Bull Run had been fought. Cox's invasion had forced Wise's retrograde from the Ohio River to Lewisburg, with only a fraction of the Union army meeting resistance. This occurred with sporadic skirmishing, the small battle of Scary Creek, and the even smaller battle—really an engagement—fought earlier at Barboursville. Gauley Bridge, the salient crossing point on Lewisburg Road, which crossed the Allegheny, now became a crucial Federal base.

The rest of the year was spent in two enfeebled Confederate attempts to regain what they had lost. The first of these attempts was severely hampered by bickering between Wise and the man now placed over him, John B. Floyd. After winning a small victory at Cross Lanes, and after the battle of Carnifex Ferry, Floyd pulled back to Sewell Mountain and beyond. There the rain, mud, and cold limited combat to skirmishing and made supply lines almost impossible to maintain. For the sake of supply lines, Rosecrans pulled back to Gauley Bridge and the vicinity. This enabled Floyd to counter by occupying Cotton Hill in what would be his second and final attempt to kick out the unwanted Yankees. Despite sporadic harassment of the Union by two Confederate six-pounders and some sniping, Floyd fled when Rosecrans attempted to flank or turn him. There would be no major battles—only small attacks and skirmishing—on Cotton Hill (also referred to as skirmishes at Blake's farm), Laurel Creek, and McCoy's Mill.

The Kanawha campaign of 1861 not only was one of limited combat and extensive marching over difficult terrain in difficult weather, but also involved self-inflicted destruction of supplies and stores that far exceed the amounts destroyed by the enemy. These were caused by virtually impassable roads over rugged mountains, long supply lines, and numerous retreats.

The hero who emerged from Floyd's defeat was Rosecrans. The Confederates considered him one of the best generals the Yankees had. Tributes that claimed he had clearly out-generaled Robert E. Lee came from the North and from as far away as London.[140] His future looked promising, but as with his successes at Rich Mountain, Carnifex Ferry, and Cotton Hill, which were far less than what they might have been, so was his career after 1861. McClellan disliked him and thwarted his military plans. And despite military success in 1862 and 1863 in Tennessee, his crushing defeat at

Chickamauga denied him the chance for military greatness and relegated him to what his biographer called "the edge of glory."

By securing control of the land west of the Alleghenies, Rosecrans and his army of blue enabled the creation of a Union government of Virginia, followed by the creation of a separate state. The formation of a new state was the result of what renowned historian J. G. Randall called "irregular and illegal processes." The roots for the political division were in long-standing divergences and sectional conflict between the eastern and western portions of Virginia. A convention at Wheeling (in June through August 1861), dominated by delegates from only the most northern and western counties, many bordering the Ohio River, created a Unionist government of Virginia and set in motion the creation of a new state. It was to be called Kanawha and was to be made up of forty-eight counties from the 150 counties that traditionally made up Virginia.

In accordance with the convention's directions, delegates were elected to a constitutional convention, which met in Wheeling in November and drew up a constitution for the state of "West Virginia." The picturesque name Kanawha was dropped, and two more counties were added so the new state would have fifty counties. The new document, which, incidentally, did not abolish slavery, was ratified in an election held on April 3, 1862, in which the anti-separatists refused to vote. On May 13, 1862, the "restored," or Unionist, government at Wheeling, agreed to the creation of the new state. On the last day of December 1862, Lincoln reluctantly signed a bill creating West Virginia.[141] West Virginia was admitted into the Union on June 20, 1863. This left the Unionist government of Virginia at Wheeling under Francis H. Pierpoint high and dry. It moved to Alexandria, Virginia, the place where Elmer Ellsworth lost his life at the start of the war. Pierpoint, recognized by his contemporaries as the father of West Virginia, rejected a leadership position in the new state government. He continued as the governor of the Union's Virginia and remained dedicated to promoting Unionism and ending slavery in what remained Virginia, despite the fact that most of the Old Dominion remained under the control of the Confederate state government in Richmond.[142]

1 *OR*, Ser. I, vol. 5, 147-49.

2 Ibid., vol. 51, pt. 2, 296-97. Floyd certainly spared no words in rebuking his rival to Davis. Floyd charged that Wise "perpetually attempted to justify his own former blunder by inducing me" to repeat the same. He claimed Wise was bitterly opposed to Floyd's crossing "the Gauley at Carnifex Ferry and declared even to my teamsters that I would be cut all to pieces." Wise not only refused to "come to my [Floyd's] assistance; but worst of all," "his mean spiritedness" had attempted to turn his officers and his men against Floyd's command. Finally, Floyd promised the Confederate president that if he replaced Wise's Legion with the same number of men, he "felt extremely confident" he could regain the Kanawha Valley before winter.

3 Ibid., vol. 5, 265-66, 270.

4 Peters & Carden, *History of Fayette County, West Virginia*, 615; Otis K. Rice, *West Virginia: The State and Its People*, (Parsons, W.Va.: McClain, 1972), 33. Sewell Mountain was named after one of the first settlers to cross the Allegheny Mountains, Stephen Sewell. Sewell and his companion, Jacob Marlin, settled along the Greenbriar River in 1749. They built a crude cabin isolated in the vast forest, but religious differences soon threatened their friendship. One was Catholic, and the other, Protestant. After quarreling over religion, Sewell is said to have abandoned the cabin and moved to a nearby hollow tree, where the only verbal exchange between the two was a salutation to the other after they rose each morning.

5 Tim McKinney, *Robert E. Lee of Sewell Mountain: The West Virginia Campaign* (Charleston W.Va.: Pictorial Histories, 1990), 22, 59; Smith, *Diary*, 182. Floyd turned Allegheny College at Blue Sulphur Springs into a hospital for the sick and wounded of his Army of the Kanawha.

6 Smith, *Diary*, 186-87.

7 The Wilderness Road crossed the Gauley River a few miles east of Carnifex Ferry at Hughes Ferry. From there the road ran southwest to Meadow Bluff.

8 *OR*, Ser. I, vol. 5, 854. Wise argued that going toward the "left bank of the Kanawha" would secure Bowyer's Ford across the New River, and the Old State Road that ran from east of Meadow Bluff to Charleston

9 McKinney, *Robert E. Lee at Sewell Mountain*, 29; *OR*, Ser. I, vol. 5, 854-55.

10 It took Floyd thirteen hours to travel fourteen miles to Meadow Bluff. He left behind many sick men to be cared for by Wise.

11 Heth, *Memoirs*, 155; *OR*, Ser. I, vol. 5, 855-56. On September 16, Floyd wrote Wise, demanding as explanation for his failure to comply with the order to pull back to Meadow Bluff. Wise replied that he had received "no order to move"—only one to get ready to do so. Wise continued: "After a verbal conference with you, at your request, in which I understood you distinctly as determining to hold, for a time at least, the almost impregnable position which I now occupy. I deem it essential to protect your rear. Your use of the road to Meadow Bluff and additional rain has

made it impassable. Illness of my men, and surplus which I cannot transport and the loss of control of Bowyer's Ford and the Old State Road are factors for staying at Big Sewell. I respectfully and earnestly therefore ask to be permitted to remain in position here until I see [what the enemy is going to do]." In *Robert E. Lee at Sewell Mountain,* McKinney maintains that while Wise was openly defying Floyd, he was making plans to withdraw from Sewell Mountain (see page 31).

[12] McKinney, *Robert E. Lee at Sewell Mountain,* 33.

[13] *OR,* Ser. I, vol. 5, 868-69. Wise's response to Lee maintained that he and Floyd were as "united...as much" as they ever had been, and their separate position was "the most effectual for co-operation." Wise contended he was in position to stop Cox on the James River and Kanawha Turnpike, and Floyd was in position to stop any enemy force that ventured over the Old Wilderness Road.

[14] Cox, *Reminiscences,* vol. I, 118; *OR,* Ser. I, vol. 5, 848. The suggested command style used by Lee in this situation was not an isolated incident. He continued it when dealing with subordination throughout the war. President Davis, on September 12, had authorized Lee to transfer Wise and his command elsewhere and replace them with other troops. Lee apparently felt this would be dangerous when facing a possible enemy attack.

[15] McKinney, *Robert E. Lee at Sewell Mountain,* 41.

[16] John A. Cutchins, *A Famous Command, The Richmond Light Infantry Blues,* 94; McKinney, *Robert E. Lee at Sewell Mountain,* 46-47; OR, Ser. I, vol. 5, 873-74, 878. On the morning of September 24 Lee called for additional reinforcements by ordering General William Loring at Marlings Bottom (Marlington) to immediately send regiments forward to Meadow Bluff.

[17] Cox, *Reminiscences,* 109-28; *OR,* Ser. I, vol. 5, 602-6. Cox was proud of his ferry ("a very large flat boat running along a hawser stretched from bank to bank") at Gauley Bridge and was confident it could easily move needed supplies for Rosecrans and himself. Rosecrans was not so confident; he ordered a pontoon bridge to be constructed.

[18] McKinney, *Robert E. Lee at Sewell Mountain,* 25-26. Floyd got a number of supplies from Alderson on the way to Sewell Mountain, but he paid the innkeeper for them.

[19] Cox, *Reminiscences,* vol. I, 114-117; *OR,* Ser. I, vol. 51, pt. 1, 484-87. McKinney, *Robert E. Lee at Sewell Mountain,* 42-43; Cox was fortunate as he started for Big Sewell that his movement wasn't discovered by a Confederate party sent under a flag of truce by Wise to return to Cox mail taken from Union prisoners in the skirmishes before Carnifex Ferry. The Confederates ran into Cox's advance guard, mistaking it for an isolated picket. After returning the Union mail and returning to Wise, the Confederate party, unaware of an approaching larger Federal force, told their commander that they believed Rosecrans and Cox were not together as their Union "pickets" only talked of General Cox.

[20] Walter H. Taylor, *General Lee: His Campaigns in Virginia, 1861-1865*

(Brooklyn, N.Y.: Braunworth, 1906), 34.

[21] McKinney, *Robert E. Lee at Sewell Mountain*, 53-54. The regiment Lee sent to the Bald Hill was the Thirteenth Georgia.

[22] *OR*, Ser. I, vol. 5, 879. Wise took five officers to Richmond, including his son, Captain Wise.

[23] T.C. Morton, "Anecdotes of General R.E. Lee," *SHSP*, vol. 11, 518-19.

[24] Ibid., 519-20. McKinney, *Robert E. Lee at Sewell Mountain*, (pages 75-76) cites another incident in which a private directly approached General Lee and asked him to change a Confederate $5 bill. The private, a giant of a man with a horribly disfigured hand that had been mangled by a hog, unabashedly stuck out his hand to the general, who shook it as the private made his request. Although Lee did not have change, others of his staff did. The private and his friends wanted change so they could buy a quart of flour.

[25] Cox, *Reminiscence*, vol. I, 120-21; McKinney, *Robert E. Lee at Sewell Mountain*, 61, 71, 74, 85, 109.

[26] Smith, *Diary*, 186-87.

[27] Hayes, *Diary*, 102-3, 105.

[28] McKinney, *Robert E. Lee at Sewell Mountain*, 63, 67. Colonel St. George Croghan, sent by Floyd to White Sulpher Springs to speed up sending supplies to Sewell Mountain, discovered the problem and rescinded Wise's order.

[29] Horton & Teverbaugh, *History of the Eleventh Regiment Ohio Volunteer Infantry*, 47-48.

[30] Cox, *Reminiscence*, vol. I, 119.

[31] Ibid., 111-12, 120-21.

[32] There was a three-day lull in the rain from September 29 through October 1. Confederate numbers were increased when Loring's men and other reinforcements arrived.

[33] Hayes, *Diary*, 104.

[34] McKinney, *Robert E. Lee at Sewell Mountain*, 65-66, 82-83.

[35] The Confederates also greatly exaggerated Rosecrans' strength, believing it to be 12,000 to 15,000.

[36] McKinney, *Robert E. Lee at Sewell Mountain*, 68, 77, 78-79, 82, 86. By early October Lee reinforced his army to around 9,000 and twenty artillery pieces. Reinforcements included Loring commanding Forty-second and Forty-eighth Regiments of Virginia Infantry and First, Seventh, and Sixteenth Regiments of Tennessee Infantry under General Samuel R. Anderson (Loring was in command of all five regiments). Phillips Legion of Georgia Cavalry and Rifleman also joined Lee.

[37] *OR*, Ser. I, vol. 52, pt. 2, 325-326.

[38] A. L. Long, *Memoirs of Robert E. Lee* (New York: J.M. Stoddard, 1886), 493-94. Cox later wrote that prior to Rosecrans' pullback, both sides discussed possible movements to turn the other's flank, "but the physical condition of the country was

an imperative veto upon aggressive action."

[39] McKinney, *Robert E. Lee at Sewell Mountain*, 92-93.

[40] Horton & Teverbaugh, History of the Eleventh Regiment Ohio Volunteer Infantry, 49. Rosecrans personally supervised the movement of the wagons and artillery. Cox brought up the rear during the withdrawal. Once the Eleventh Ohio got to or near Gauley Bridge, it, along with other regiments, was ordered by headquarters "to send in the morning reports and other reports equally impossible to furnish correctly." Cox said, "Here was a fine state of affairs!" Rosecrans had destroyed many of the books and papers needed to make the reports. All that could be done was to guess, and this took a full week of arduous work by adjutants, orderly sergeants, and other officers of the Eleventh. For their efforts they were "censured" by headquarters "for being remiss in the discharge of their duty."

[41] Cox, *Reminiscences*, vol. I, 123-24; *OR*, Ser. I, vol. 5, 252. Once the Federals pulled back to Tompkins Farm and Gauley Bridge, the men were clothed, equipped, and paid.

[42] They were to repair the road west and east of Sewell Creek.

[43] Heth, *Memoirs*, 156-57.

[44] McKinney, *Robert E. Lee at Sewell Mountain*, 107-8; *OR*, Ser. I, vol. 51, pt. 2, 335, 337-38. Lee had only fifty-four wagons to carry supplies from the railroad depot at Jackson River to Sewell Mountain. On October 15 he sent back to Meadow Bluff the Fourteenth Regiment of North Carolina infantry, decimated by illness. Three months earlier the regiment had 750 men, but now there were fewer than 300.

[45] *OR*, Ser. I, vol. 5, 925. Floyd wrote a number of letters to the secretary of war.

[46] Ibid., vol. 51, pt. II, 360, 361-62.

[47] The soldier was J. W. Johnston. The colt had been raised by his father near Blue Sulpher Springs and given to his son. Johnston sold Jeff Davis to Captain Joseph M. Brown, who gave the horse to his brother, Major Thomas L. Brown. Both brothers rode Jeff Davis at different times at Sewell Mountain.

[48] Sue Cottrell, *Hoof Beats North and South* (Hicksville, N.Y.: Exposition, 1975), 35-36; Freeman, *R. E. Lee*, vol. I, 644-47; Long, *Memoirs of Robert E. Lee*, 131-33; *SHSP*, vol. 35, 99-101. Lee left the Confederate capital on a horse called Richmond, a troublesome mount who disliked being around strange horses. The mountains of western Virginia necessitated Lee's purchase of an additional horse he called Roan or Brown-Roan. Later at Sewell Mountain Lee talked about buying a third horse (Traveller), but did not do so until in North Carolina. Captain Brown, transferred to North Carolina, brought Jeff Davis (Traveller) with him. The captain volunteered to give the horse to Lee, who refused, saying he would only accept the horse by purchase. Brown then sent the colt to Lee to ride, which Lee greatly enjoyed, but after a time he returned the colt, saying he could not use such a valuable horse in dangerous times unless he owned him. Captain Brown contacted his brother, Major Brown, who was ill back in western Virginia, and who replied that if Lee would not accept the horse as a gift, he could have him for what they had paid, $175 in gold.

Lee paid $200 in Confederate money. Traveller survived both the war and his famous owner. The famous horse died from lockjaw caused by a nail that had penetrated his hoof.

[49] *OR,* Atlas, plate IX. At Gauley Bridge Rosecrans stationed part of Cox's Kanawha Brigade, comprised of the 1st and part of the 2nd Kentucky and the 11th Ohio; at his headquarters on the Tompkins farm, the remainder of the 2nd Kentucky; while placing the 1st Brigade (10th, 12th, 13th Ohio), the 2nd Brigade (9th, 20th, 47th Ohio), and the 3rd Brigade (23rd, 26th, and 30th Ohio) on the James River and Kanawha Turnpike north of New River at Miller's Ferry. Schenck's Brigade (3rd brigade) was ten miles from Gauley Bridge; McCook's (2nd brigade), eight miles; Benham's (1st brigade), six miles. Cox's Brigade guarded Gauley Bridge and Rosecrans' headquarters at Tompkins.

[50] Granville D. Hall, *Lee's Invasion of Northwest Virginia in 1861* (Chicago: Mayer & Miller, 1911), 135.

[51] Cox, *Reminiscences*, vol. I, 127. Cox also felt that Rosecrans—who at times "hotly lectured" a sentinel who was ignorant or inattentive to his duties—could have handled situations better, such as by going to the responsible officer and privately making him understand it was his duty to have proper instruction and discipline among his men.

[52] *OR*, Ser. I, vol. 5, 252-53.

[53] There were a few Union pickets across the Kanawha River on the Fayetteville road near the mouth of Big Falls Creek, or Great Falls Creek.

[54] Fayetteville was also referred to as Fayette and Fayette Court House.

[55] Smith, *Diary*, 190-93.

[56] Ibid., 194-97.

[57] Phillips, ed., *War Stories*, 164-65.

[58] Cox, *Reminiscences*, vol. I, 129-36. Rosecrans' headquarters was connected by telegraph to Gauley Bridge, where the operator came under fire and had to move the telegraph office.

[59] Ibid., 135-136. Cox felt Rosecrans' ordnance officer, an intemperate man, should have moved the ordnance during the night. Cox also felt they were fortunate the enemy used only solid shot instead of shells, as exploding fragments could have ignited the ordnance stores without making a direct hit.

[60] Phillips, ed., *War Stories*, 165.

[61] National Archives, Record Group 109, letter from Tompkins to Wise; Phillips, ed., *War Diaries*, 379, 384. Tompkins and Smith both disliked Floyd, and both received less than favorable treatment from the general. Wise came to like and respect both Tompkins and Smith. Once Wise was ordered from the region, he urged Confederate authorities to replace Floyd as the commander in western Virginia with Tompkins.

[62] *OR*, Ser. I, vol. 5, 251-57.

[63] Ibid., 254. Rosecrans set forth a contingency to his plan. If a Union scouting

expedition deemed it feasible, Benham's brigade, along with Cox's men, might cross at Kanawha Falls. The scouting report was unfavorable, so Benham crossed the river at the mouth of Loop's Creek.

[64] *OR*, Ser. I, vol. 5, 255. The original plan for Schenck to cross at either Bowyer's or Townsend's Ferry soon shifted to crossing at Townsend's. Benham at first had the option of two routes to Fayetteville Turnpike, one by Kincaid's to below Fayetteville or by Cassidy's Mill to Fayetteville. Rosecrans' ordered that if Schenck crossed at Townsend's Ferry and got behind Floyd, then he was to attack Floyd "on the flank or by the front and flank." If Schenck could not cross the New River, he would cross the Kanawha and join Benham in a combined attack on the "front flank and rear," or Schenck's troops could be sent to Fayetteville by way of Cassidy's Mill. In his dispatch number 23, November 9, 1861, Rosecrans was still hoping for Schenck, crossing the New River, he ordered Benham to take "the Laurel Creek route only or by the Nugent path only, or by both, as may be determined by the nature of the ground, which you will learn from your scouts, and communicate to me your opinion thereon when they come in as soon as practicable."

[65] *Report on the Conduct of the War*, pt. 3, 12-14. The committee also asked Rosecrans why he refused to exchange prisoners with Lee after Sewell Mountain. Although Lee proposed the exchange on "grounds of humanity," Rosecrans rejected the offer because he saw it as an attempt by Lee "to get to his available strength in exchange for men captured at Bull Run which would add nothing to my strength, and, in fact could not even serve with my command."

[66] There were three crossable sites south of Miller's Ferry (which was approximately six miles from the Union base at Gauley Bridge): Townsend's Ferry; (five and a half miles from Miller's); Boyer's Ferry (seventeen and a half miles above Miller's); and Claypoole's Hole, between Townsend's and Miller's ferries.

[67] *OR*, Ser. I, vol. 5, 255, 260-70. Rosecrans' numerous dispatches to Benham repeatedly instructed the latter to scout out the best way to get behind Floyd then report the findings. Benham did neither. Rosecrans pointed out there were several possible routes that could be used to turn Floyd. The southern and longer route was by Kincaid's farm, and it intersected the Raleigh road five miles below Fayetteville, whereas the more direct route by Settle's and Cassidy's Mill led directly into Fayetteville. As events unfolded, the latter route became most feasible. Cassidy's Mill was a crucial crossroads that gave the option of going to Fayetteville on the Raleigh road or going north along Laurel Creek to the same road at the base of Cotton Hill and a mile or more in front of Floyd's main and entrenched camp at Dickerson.

[68] Five hundred men of the Seventh Ohio left Charleston by boat on November 4, 1861, to join General Benham. They arrived that night with only one mishap. Corporal John D. Dicks of Company I fell overboard and was "never again heard from."

[69] Rosecrans gave Benham some discretion in carrying out the attack. If Schenck

crossed the New River in the rear of the enemy, then it would be Benham's task to attack Floyd's front, either by taking Cotton Hill on the Raleigh Road or by flanking him via Cassidy's Mill. If Schenck's 3,000 men were unable to cross the New River, he would cross the Gauley and join Benham in a combined frontal and flanking attack.

[70] *OR*, Ser. I, vol. 5, 275; *Report of the Committee on Conduct of the War*, pt. 3, 11-12. A successful reconnaissance of the opposite shore near the town of Fayetteville, one and a quarter miles from the ferry, convinced the Union to attempt to cross at Townsend's. Rosecrans described Townsend's Ferry as a small pool with a "descent by a small foot path and a small ascend leading from the opposite side of the plateau southeast at Fayetteville." However, it was not easily assessable.

[71] Ibid. A bull-boat is made of hides over a light wooden frame. The floats were constructed of two wagon beds "9 1/4 by 4 feet placed upon frames a distance of 3 1/2 feet apart, and secured by wedges and pins, tightly drawn around the beds and secured with duck paulin." "Light planks were then laid over the wagon beds and the whole secured by ropes," which not only held the structure together but also could be used to "control and guide it."

[72] Ibid., 276. Upon crossing the Kanawha, Schenck took the on-site command from Benham.

[73] Cox, *Reminiscences*, vol. I, 138-39. For the first week of November, enemy artillery on Cotton Mountain had prevented the Union ferry at Gauley from being used except at night. During the day the ferry was hidden from view and enemy fire. The ferry boat was hidden at day behind the projection of mountain, called Gauley Mountain (also the name used for Tompkins' farm, then Rosecrans' headquarters), east of the confluence of the Gauley and New Rivers. The hawser was not removed, so at night the boat "would be maned, dropped down to its place, made fast to the hawser by a snatch-block, and commence its regular trips passing over wagons" and supplies. About three miles down the Kanawha River from Gauley Bridge and below Kanawha Falls was another ferry, known as Montgomery's Ferry, which was also used by the Union. The boats used at both ferry sites were three or four times larger than normally used for civilian purposes. Cox's men found lumber brought to the river by lumbermen for use as gunwales on flatboats to be constructed for the coal trade. The larger timbers, sixty or eighty feet long, two or three feet wide, and averaging six inches thick, were used by Federal mechanics to form the sides of the commodious ferries.

[74] Joseph A. Saunier, ed., *A History of the Forty-Seventh Regiment, Ohio Veteran Volunteer Infantry* (Hillsboro, Ohio: Lyle, 1903), 31-34.

[75] Ibid., 138. Cox had several small flatboats constructed to move detachments across New River.

[76] William F. Scott, *Philander P. Lane* (Privately Printed, 1920), 61-62. The Eleventh Ohio regiment had also been much reduced by sickness; fewer than 300 men mustered for duty.

[77] Cox, *Reminiscences*, vol. I, 142; *OR*, Ser. I, vol. 5, 272-73. Cox later went up the mountain by the same route. He found the climb more exhausting and found that he and the other officers were accustomed to movement on horseback and were less fit than footsoldiers.

[78] *OR*, Ser. I, vol. 5, 272.

[79] At the Blake farm Lane's men discovered and attacked fifty to sixty Confederates guarding the guns overlooking New River. The surprised Southerners went back into the woods dragging their casualties with them. There they were reinforced with the additional 200 men kept in the area for the security of their artillery overlooking the rivers. The small Union advance party fell back to the end of the Blake farm "behind a fence at the edge of a ravine." There they were able to hold their enemy in check until most of the Eleventh Ohio arrived. The Federals then drove the enemy back up the hill from the Blake house to a crest above.

[80] *OR*, Ser. I, vol. 5, 272-73; Scott, *Philander P. Lane*, 64-66.

[81] In 1861, Cotton Hill did not include the whole mountain, which is a mile and a half of hogback ridge (a ridge with steep sides) running from the banks of the Kanawha and New Rivers. This is typical of the area today known as Cotton Mountain. At the northern end, steep rocky cliffs, standing hundreds of feet above the river, are inaccessible except through narrow gorges. Behind the "head" the land falls away into what has been called a "saddle" large enough for a small farm. This was the location of the Blake farm. Southeast of Blake's farm, the land rises to heights higher in the northern part and was then covered with trees.

[82] Smith, *Diary*, 193-95.

[83] *OR*, Ser. I, vol. 5, 256. Not reported were those Union injuries resulting from falls while attempting to climb the face of Cotton Hill.

[84] Ibid., 257. Actually 1,300 instead of 1,000 men went to Cassidy's Mill. This also angered Rosecrans.

[85] Ibid., 257, 283-84. The next day the Union found a dead Confederate who had been dragged a long distance from the skirmish site.

[86] The last Confederates left Fayetteville on the morning of November 13, 1861.

[87] Ibid., 258, 275-77. At a point known as Widow Stauridge's, where the road from Cassidy's Mill joined the Fayetteville turnpike, Major Crawford found a large body of Benham's men had stopped.

[88] "Benham's letter to Rosecrans," National Archives, Record Group 94, Entry 159, General Papers, Box 3, Benham Papers—File 1.

[89] Ibid., 277. Schenck's brigade would stay at Fayetteville and communicate with the forces under Benham.

[90] *OR*, Ser. I, vol. 51, 368-69.

[91] Heth, *Memoirs*, 17; Scott, *Philander P. Lane*, 59-60. This concerned the controversial, if not illegal, actions of Floyd at the end of his tenure as Buchanan's secretary of war.

[92] Moore, *Rebellion Record*, vol. III, 388-89.

[93] Smith, *Diary,* 194-98. Smith complained that officers from other states hogged all the supplies for their men, leaving little or nothing for Virginia soldiers.

[94] Heth, *Memoirs*, 18. Heth recommended, "get the men up at three o'clock (it was midnight) and make your speech before the march or while on the march."

[95] Forrest Hull, "Death of Colonel Croghan," *The West Virginia Review*, vol. XXIV, No. 1, 20-21; Moore, *Rebellion Record*, vol. III, 389; Phillips, ed., *War Diaries*, 179-82.

[96] Moore, *Rebellion Record*, vol. III, 384-86, 389.

[97] Phillips, ed., *War Diaries*, 178.

[98] Moore, *Rebellion Record*, vol. III, 385. Benham found out Croghan's family was living in Newburgh, New York, and planned to write them and send the dead colonel's personal effects. Unfortunately someone had taken most of them from the body and they could not be located.

[99] Benham also stated that what he wanted to do with Croghan's body was subject to approval by General Rosecrans.

[100] Moore, *Rebellion Record*, vol. III, 385-86.

[101] *OR*, Ser. I, vol. 5, 258, 279-81. The usual reason stated by the Union for Schenck's recall of Benham was that the condition of his men and the chance of catching Floyd seemed to have passed. Rosecrans' account of what Benham said in his dispatch from Ketron's differs greatly in the tone and content. Benham's report made no mention of his having told Schenck of reports of Lee's coming. Furthermore, Benham's report stated that he and his men were eager to continue the chase, and if Schenck had only moved up to Ketron's to support him as asked, then they could have moved to Raleigh to "capture that place and depot with their train, and certainly [would have] routed, if not captured, the whole of Floyd's force." Benham also claimed that in Schenck's first dispatch to him on the night of November 14, 1861, he said he was sending the Twenty-sixth regiment and mounted men, but in a second dispatch, Schenck said they had been ordered back and so had Benham's command.

[102] Cox's men were called back to their camp across the Kanawha after fighting ended on Cotton Mountain. These men, from this limited vantage, felt good about their achievement, thinking they had won a significant battle.

[103] General Schenck suffered from typhoid during the Cotton Hill campaign, and at its end he was advised to recuperate at his Dayton home. Instead he continued his military duties.

[104] *OR,* Ser. I, vol. 5, 258-59. Benham's command consisted of the 7th, 10th, 12th, 13th, and 44th Ohio regiments, plus McMullen's battery of mountain howitzers (also called the "Ass Battery,") Schneider's battery of rifled cannon, and a small detachment of cavalry.

[105] Hayes, *Diary*, 148.

[106] *OR*, Ser. I, vol. 5, 285-88. Floyd also claimed that the Federals had "laid waste the village of Fayetteville and the country upon their lines of march." "He added if

he had larger caliber artillery (instead of six-pounders,) it would have been impossible for the enemy to hold his position."

[107] *OR*, Ser. I, vol. 5, 287-88.

[108] Ibid., 1000. He also instructed enough men be left to gather up the sick and bring them east.

[109] Ibid., 1000-1001. Reinforcements originally intended to be sent to Floyd (Anderson's brigade and Starke's regiment) were now sent to Lee, along with the 20th Mississippi and the 13th Georgia, Phillip's legion, and Waddell's battalion from Floyd's command. Floyd and his remaining command, 22nd, 36th, 45th, 50th, 51st Virginia infantry, 8th Virginia cavalry, and three artillery batteries, minus the infantry regiments to be sent to Lewisburg, were sent to join Johnston.

[110] Moore, *Rebellion Record*, vol. III, 388-89.

[111] "Letter by William W. West," National Archives, Record Group 94, Entry 159, General Papers, Box 3, File 1, Benham.

[112] "Letter by J.D. Hines," National Archives, Record Group 94, Entry 159, General Papers, Box 3, Benham—File 1.

[113] "Letter to Major Darr, Provost Marshall from Jonathan S. Devenny," December 18, 1861, National Archives, Record Group 94, Entry 159, Box 3, General Papers, Benham—File 1.

[114] Basler, ed., *The Collected Works of Abraham Lincoln*, vol. V, 69-70.

[115] "Letter to Rosecrans," National Archives, Record Group 94, Entry 159, Box 3, General Papers, Benham—File 1.

[116] "George G. Shumard, Brigade Surgeon Letter to Benham," National Archives, Record Group 94, Entry 159, Box 3, General Papers, Benham—File 2. Shumard's letter of November 24, 1861, stated that he had repeatedly urged Benham to get a new truss and recommended having several made. The surgeon went on to say that no army trusses were adequate for Benham's need.

[117] Ibid. While at Wheeling, Benham demanded the name of the field officer who said "he wore his sword when leaving Camp Huddleston."

[118] The Cincinnati newspapers were the *Commercial* and *Gazette*.

[119] Benham also claimed Schenck told him upon his return that he had done a fine job.

[120] It seems Benham called for a Court of Inquiry the day after Rosecrans issued an order for his arrest.

[121] Basler, ed., *The Collected Works of Abraham Lincoln*, vol. V, 106.

[122] One of Benham's defenders wrote that the general only had 1,700 against Floyd's 5,000 or more. Furthermore, to think Benham did not vigorously pursue Floyd is contrary to his behavior in chasing General Garnett for fifty hours, the last six of which were in violation of orders to return.

[123] Basler, ed., *The Collected Works of Abraham Lincoln*, vol. VI, 35; Boatner, *The Civil War Dictionary*, 58-59; *OR*, Ser. I, vol. 14, 979-83. Benham was reduced to the rank of major but was restored to the rank of brigadier-general on February 6,

1863. For the rest of the war he distinguished himself as an engineer, constructing pontoon bridges for Hooker's retreat across the Rappahanock and the Federal crossing of the Potomac at Edward's Ferry on their way to Gettysburg.

[124] On at least one other occasion, DeVilliers said, "Captain Lane is a damned coward."

[125] Frizell's resignation was sent to Cox, who wrote DeVilliers that the resignation was forwarded contrary to Frizell's wishes. DeVilliers wrote back that it was not contrary to Frizell's wishes, and he wished it would be accepted so Frizell could go. "I could do better," added DeVilliers.

[126] DeVilliers wrote asking for clothing and a horse to be sent to him as seizing an officer's trunk was an unfair thing to do. DeVilliers also interfered with the work of J. W. E. Wetzel, the Deputy Marshall at Point Pleasant. On January 6, 1862, Wetzel seized property of L. G. Mampin. who had joined the Confederate army. January 11, 1861, DeVilliers took the confiscated property by force from the marshal, telling him, "there is no law but military law, and he being the Commander of the Post he will do as he pleases." Wetzel also complained the property taken from him was placed in the hands of a secessionist. Wetzel took his complaints to authorities in Wheeling. A former cook for DeVilliers, Barbara Weiss, swore to the Provost Marshall that DeVilliers told her he took the key and opened the safe in Fisher's home, took silverware from it, and had some of it boxed up and sent to his brother-in-law. Part of Fisher's property taken by DeVilliers was ordered to be returned to Fisher's partner, a Mr. English, prior to the court-martial. The court later ordered boxes of confiscated property that DeVilliers had shipped north to be returned.

[127] The citizen petition for DeVilliers' removal has not been found in the National Archives but is referred to in the counter-petition. It might have been lost or never sent, or else mere rumors of a petition sent to headquarters for DeVilliers' removal prompted the counter-petition that the colonel himself might have masterminded.

[128] Angered even more, Lane wrote directly to Rosecrans on January 2, 1862, sending him the charges on the grounds that the earlier ones might not have been forwarded. To the second list of charges was added the arrest of Lane, "disgracing him and not treating him as a gentleman."

[129] One of DeVilliers' letters to Cox, February 5, 1862, was written in French. All of the others were in English, although they were occasionally sprinkled with French terms.

[130] Scott, *Philander P. Lane*, 78-105. When Fremont replaced Rosecrans, DeVilliers wrote to the former, asking permission to come to Wheeling. The matter was referred to Cox. He said he had no objections to DeVilliers' coming, but anything the colonel would say on his behalf could not be trusted, nor would it counter the testimony against him. Cox also called DeVilliers' relationships with his regiment "most lamentable," continuing, "his return to it would undoubtedly distract its efficiency."

[131] *OR*, Ser. I, vol. 5, 657. General J. J. Reynold's men were at Philippi, Elkwater,

and Huttonville to protect Cheat Mountain Pass; General B. F. Kelley was in charge of forces at Romney, and Schenck's brigade was left in the Gauley region.

[132] Scott, *Philander P. Lane*, 76.

[133] Saunier, ed., *A History of the Forty-Seventh Regiment Ohio Veteran Volunteer Infantry*, 84.

[134] Hayes, *Diary*, 150.

[135] Ibid., 153. "Gee" and "haw" were commands horses, oxen, and mules were trained to respond to when the teamster or farmer wanted them to move to the right or left.

[136] Ibid., A telegraph line was completed to Fayetteville from Gauley Bridge on November 30, 1861. Daily mail service was also established but was frequently interrupted by weather and road conditions. Hayes heard by telegraph on December 23 of the birth of his fourth son. "In these times," Hayes wrote "boys are preferred to girls."

[137] Ibid., 156, 159, 163.

[138] The original plan was to mount one-half the Union men on the expedition on pack miles so they could surprise the enemy.

[139] The weather during the month of December was better than in November. Hayes records twenty-six fine December days, though a few were cold.

[140] William M. Lamers, *The Edge of Glory* (New York: Harcourt, Brace, 1961), 61-64. Henry Adams, secretary to his father, the U.S. Minister to England, Charles Francis Adams, praised Rosecrans' double-victory over Lee and Floyd.

[141] The law creating West Virginia also required the gradual abolition of slavery.

[142] Among the sources to check for additional information on the formation of West Virginia, see J. G. Randall's *Constitutional Problems Under Lincoln* (New York: D. Appleton, 1926), 433-76, and his *Civil War and Reconstruction*, 236-42. The controversy over West Virginia's refusal to assume its share of Virginia's prewar debt dragged on until 1920. Randall argues that formation of West Virginia was the result of processes that were irregular and illegal. Additional information on Pierpoint can be found in Charles H. Ambler's *Frances H. Pierpont: Union War Governor of Virginia and Father of West Virginia.* (In 1881 Francis changed the spelling of his name to Pierpont.) Ambler maintains that ambition and determination were Pierpoint's salient characteristics. An example: As a young adult, Pierpoint walked 180 miles from his home in western Pennsylvania to attend Allegheny College, in Meadville, Pennsylvania.

PART IV

THE NORTHERN INVASION CORRIDOR

CHAPTER X

FROM POMPOUSNESS TO WINTER CAMPAIGN: THE FALL OF HARPERS FERRY TO THE START OF JACKSON'S ROMNEY CAMPAIGN

The end of spring of 1861 saw the Federals target Virginia for invasion from the west, east, south, and north. Potomac crossings from western Maryland provided a northern invasion corridor into the Shenandoah Valley. The Great Valley of Virginia is shaped like a gigantic gun barrel pointing southwest into the heart of the Old Dominion. This was an inviting target for an invading force wishing to menace Harpers Ferry, Winchester, or the agriculturally rich valley or to turn east across mountain gaps in the Blue Ridge to threaten Southern forces at Manassas Junction. The Shenandoah Valley also points northeast into Maryland and Pennsylvania; later in the war, this corridor would be used by Confederates invading the North.

At the very start of the war Southern forces seized Harpers Ferry and went through a type of "play" war before a degree of organization was imposed by Thomas Jackson and his successor, Joe Johnston. Johnston had grave concerns about the defensibility of Harpers Ferry. When Robert Patterson mobilized troops to the north in Pennsylvania, the Confederate general moved to Winchester. But Patterson's failure to keep him there would prove to be the crucial determinant in the outcome of the most important battle of 1861. Both before and after Bull Run, Winchester and the lower valley were vulnerable from invasion from northern crossings of the Potomac at Williamsport, Hancock, Cumberland, and Piedmont. By crossing at the latter two sites and moving to Romney, Federals could threaten Winchester from the west. Three times in 1861 Federals attacked and twice seized the Confederate outpost at Romney, mainly to stop raids on the B&O along the Northern Branch of the Potomac River. In November, Jackson assumed command at Winchester and planned a campaign to establish a buffer at Romney and to cut Union communications at Hancock. Delays prevented him from launching his campaign until the last days of the year. Most of the action took place during the new year in inclement weather and with limited results and was controversial.

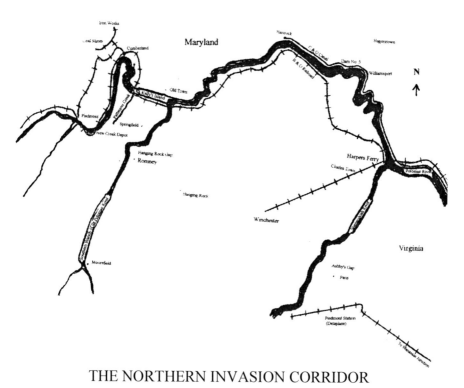

THE NORTHERN INVASION CORRIDOR

HARPERS FERRY AND THE PLAY WAR

Harpers Ferry was a key Union target because the Virginia militia had occupied, since late April, what was left of the Federal arms facilities and menaced the Baltimore and Ohio Railroad, a vital link between the Northeast and the East. The Virginia plan to seize the Ferry started a day before the Virginia Convention voted for secession and one and a half months before the Federals took Alexandria. The restive former governor of the state, Henry Wise, took steps to protect his state and originally headed an impromptu scheme to seize Harpers Ferry. A few militia heads, such as John D. Imboden of Staunton, who happened to be in Richmond, were told to round up their men under the ruse of telling them they were going to protect the Portsmouth Navy Yard[1]

In reality, most of the infantry and artillery would move by rail to Manassas Junction then west on the Manassas Gap line to Strasburg. Then they would go by foot down the Valley Turnpike to Winchester. From there they would go by rail to near Harpers Ferry. Meanwhile, cavalry units under Turner Ashby, his brother Richard Ashby, John Scott, and others would also gather near the targeted town. All this was contingent upon obtaining the approval of the current governor, John Letcher. He approved the plan contingent upon the state convention's approval of secession. Soon after the convention's April 17 vote for secession, Letcher ordered the militia units into service of the state. Anxiety was heightened when Wise was told by a Washington physician that a "Massachusetts regiment, one thousand strong, had been ordered to Harpers Ferry." Rapid movement to Harpers Ferry became urgent—as was the need for deception.

Militiamen left the cars at Strasburg at midmorning of April 18 and hurried toward Winchester. Because the artillery had no draft animals, Imboden searched for horses to pull his arms. He found farmers working their cornfields. Some agreed to hire out their horses to pull the wagons the eighteen miles to Winchester, but others refused. The situation was urgent, and Imboden took additional horses by force. Indignant farmers responded by shouting that the militiamen would be indicted for thievery, yelled the protestors, by "the next grand jury of the county." As the artillery was pulled down the Valley turnpike, the people from Strasburg to Winchester received them coldly. Imboden observed, "The war spirit that bore [the people]…throughout four years of trial and privation had not been aroused." At Winchester the farmers were given back their horses as the militiamen and artillery set out by rail for Halltown. There they left the train and prepared to move the artillery by hand to Bolivar Heights, several miles west, overlooking Harpers Ferry. From there they were poised for attack, if needed.[2]

No attack was necessary. Before dawn the next day, April 18, while the militiamen, under the command of Major-General Kenton Harper, were preparing to attack what they believed to be a Union regiment, the Virginians watched as a glow lit up the sky from near where the Shenandoah met the Potomac. The enemy, who were rumored to be 1,000 men, though they were only a force of 45, had set fire to the two arsenal buildings and fled. Piles of powder had been placed in all the buildings in straw, and the small Federal force set fire to the works after pickets signaled to them that the enemy was coming. Thousands of weapons were burned—20,000, by one estimate. The workshops in the armory had been spared by friends of Southern sympathizers, who had added water to the gunpowder overnight before Union troops could set fire to the armory shops. This enabled the Southerners who soon occupied the area to send the remaining machinery and unassembled weapons to Richmond, Columbia, and Fayetteville, accompanied by some of the armory employees. It was asserted in the Richmond *Enquirer* in a short time the machines would be operational in the South and producing a variety of weapons "to cleave and perforate the beastly skulls of…Yankee invaders."[3]

The arsenals were destroyed and the shops were saved because of the action of Alford Barbour, former superintendent of the Federal works at the Ferry. In an attempt to save the facilities for the South, he had blown the cover of secrecy for the advancing Virginia militia. On April 17, Barbour, who had been a part of Wise's meeting the previous day to plan the seizure of Harpers Ferry, hurried to the town. There he went from mechanic to mechanic, informing them that the Virginia troops would be capturing the armory within a day and asking them to help protect the shops for the South.[4] Many of the armory workers were from the North and were angered by Barbour's pro-Southern remarks. Fighting broke out between men of different loyalties, and according to one resident, the town was on the verge of a riot, requiring citizens to help guard key places. Town Unionists were riled up when they saw a Southern soldier guarding the telegraph. Not fifty yards away was a huge pro-Union Irishman, Jeremiah Donovan, standing guard at the armory with his musket. Legend contends that after the Virginia militia had seized the town, local Southern supporters placed a rope around Donovan's neck planning to end his life. But calmer heads prevailed and allowed the Irishman to leave for the North. Several other Unionists were also threatened with "hemp justice."[5]

Within a week 1,300 Virginia militia—in an almost endless variety of attire, some in fancy dress uniforms, others in civilian dress—arrived at Harpers Ferry. Additional Virginians continued to arrive, but nowhere near the exaggerated numbers reported by the Northern press. Among the new recruits were the "Grayson Dare Devils" and a detachment of the "Virginia Mountain Boys." During their trip, the latter group was temporarily stranded for several hours in the interior of Virginia, where their train broke down. The hungry men spotted a cow in a nearby field, and in thirty minutes they had killed and quartered the cow and were roasting the beef over a dozen campfires. Fearing that the train would be repaired and would move before they were finished with their repast, one of the Mountain Boys was said to have "removed the coupling between the engine and the forward car." A correspondent and others were impressed by the Mountain Boys' resourcefulness, a trait no doubt not appreciated by the owner of the cow.[6]

In May, Marylanders, Mississippians, Alabamians, and Kentuckians joined the Virginia troops in and around Harpers Ferry. Among the arrivals was a detachment of Cherokee Indians from North Carolina.[7] Most traveled by way of Manassas Junction, a vital link, but an unimposing site in the South's railway system. At that time its junction, described in the Charleston South Carolina, *Daily Courier,* consisted of a "hotel, two barns, a country residence built by an absquatulated Yankee, and a deformed wagon. Add to that a few clumps of woods, and a good deal of meadow, an undulating surface, a small amount of excruciating dirt, and you have Manassas."[8]

Troops continued daily to travel through Manassas on their way to Strasburg. From Strasburg, like the men before them, they had to walk the eighteen miles to Winchester. This was depicted in the press as an intrepid achievement. Flowery press accounts state that a few got fatigued during the "journey through the dust, without the inspiration of even a drum." The men were said to have "had to take their baggage wagons, but the majority walked it bravely and found their reward in the approval of the fair ladies of Winchester," who, accounts stated, received "them with almost 'open arms.'" A number of the Winchester citizens, said the press, "[threw] open their houses and offered to take them in for the night, in numbers varying from five to twenty, but most of the noble fellows prefer going to Hotels." The soldiers responded, "We've plenty of money, and as Winchester is the last stopping place before we get into camp [at Harpers Ferry], might as well spend it here as anywhere else."[9]

Confederate supporters viewed the men and their conditions in a positive light. An Alabama regiment of 1,063 men was described: "[They are] a fine set of men, and the small hands and feet and delicate features of hundreds among them mark them as the blood stock of the Southern race. Two hundred servants attend the regiment, all [soldiers] well armed." A Virginian correspondent contended that the "finest looking men" at Harpers Ferry were from southwestern Virginia: large, muscular men, almost all of who were six feet tall. Another newspaperman described the Mississippians as "gallant and noble looking." Still another pronounced the Kentucky soldiers from the western part of that state and from Louisville the most desirable warriors: "better material for good soldiers...could not be desired, [they are] superb physical specimens and excellent marksmen armed with 'Minnie rifles.'" The troops were depicted as aware of the dangers of their position at Maryland Heights, but eager for a fight.

This description is in sharp contrast to reports by Northern sympathizers, who contended that the men from Kentucky were "low lifes" and "dregs of Louisville" who fled from Maryland Heights in a cowardly fashion. Mississippians, Alabamians, and men of other Confederate states were described as "hard looking, poorly clad and dirty." Critical accounts also tell of soldiers plagued with problems, sick of camp life, and wanting to return home. It was reported that at the end of May the average daily desertion rate of Southerners at Harpers Ferry was twenty-five. Fights and occasional shooting and killing broke out among the disgruntled men. Virginia soldiers' clothing was described as being "so worn out...that they are obliged to wear blankets during the day to conceal their deficiency." Conditions were reported of extreme shortages of provisions, and according to the New York *Herald*, predictions were made that Southern men within a week would "be in a starving condition." An outbreak of smallpox and numerous cases of diarrhea also plagued the Southerners, who, according to the Northern press, harassed Unionists despite their problems and destroyed their property and livestock, thus causing a continuous stream of people to flee northward.[10]

The arrival of troops did dislocate civilians and disrupt their lives. At first soldiers made barracks out of the larger buildings in the armory as well as individual homes. (Later they and the new arrivals occupied Camp Hill and Bolivar Heights.) One soldier at Harpers Ferry wrote: "There had been h--l to pay here. The citizens who occupied the Government houses had all to vacate them...There were no exceptions; everyone had to leave. Troops helped themselves to whatever they want in barns or houses, and the people are powerless to resist, receive 'Virginia script' in the hope that some day it will be the means of reimbursing them for the losses they sustain." But in early May, Virginia script "wasn't worth a d--n." The dismantling of the armory ended the arms manufacturing and disrupted the work life for town workers. Travel on the Chesapeake and Ohio Canal also suffered.[11]

To compensate for the loss of jobs, civilians sought other ways of making money. Smuggling whiskey and baking pies" became profitable despite the military's prohibition of liquor smuggling.[12]

At the site where less than two years earlier John Brown's raid had occurred, many of the newly arriving militia were bloated with militia generals and excessive staff who were dedicated to the pomp and circumstances of war. Every afternoon, weather permitting, there were martial displays of "fuss and feathers," while serious problems, such as the shortage of weapons, ammunition, equipment, horses, and proper uniforms, were not addressed.[13] An exception was Captain John Imboden of the Staunton Artillery Company. He was one of the first to address the needs of his men. He used his private credit to order harnesses from Baltimore, and from Richmond, he ordered flannel shirts and other practical clothing to replace the fancy uniforms that were too delicate for the wear and tear of daily work.[14] Young mechanics in Imboden's company ingeniously solved the shortage of caissons. They used the wheels and axles of the many strong horse carts found at the armory to construct caissons that were used until after the First Battle of Bull Run.

The pomp and ceremony of the militia's play war soon came to an end. Authorities in Richmond realized that to improve mobilization, changes were necessary. To help bring this about, the governor placed Robert E. Lee in command of all Virginia forces while an ordinance was enacted that vacated all positions in the Old Dominion's militia above the rank of captain. This was a devastating blow to the play war. Former militia generals and their staff left in a huff. Some would return appointed to a lesser rank by the governor and his military council, who had recently been given the task of filling the vacancies created by the reform. One of their new appointments made Colonel Thomas J. Jackson the new commander of the troops at Harpers Ferry. Jackson was the antithesis of the superficiality that had preceded him. Even his mount, which was one of the two horses he purchased from those seized on the B & O Line, was described as a "plebeian-looking beast" that was anything but fancy in his appearance. Originally Jackson had planned to send the small, stocky courser—whom he named Fancy—to his wife. But soon the animal the men would call Little Sorrel, because of his appearance, became Jackson's mount. The little, muscular, plain-looking stead had great endurance and, in the next couple of years, would help to carry his new owner to immortal fame.[15]

Jackson's personal appearance and demeanor were as ordinary as his horse's. Once he had arrived at Harpers Ferry, he worked without the ostentatious martial display. He wore the well-worn uniform he had worn as a professor at VMI, where students had considered him ill-suited for the classroom and as dull and unimaginative as his uniform. They referred to him unflatteringly as "Tom Fool Jackson," an appellation that would prove to be inaccurate. In a no-nonsense manner, Jackson brought discipline and order to the forces at Harpers Ferry. He procured horses for the artillery by sending men to buy or impress draft animals from the agriculturally abundant Quaker settlements in Loudoun Valley. He also concocted a shrewd plan to trap locomotives on the B & O line and send them south. Jackson complained to John W. Garrett, president of the Baltimore and Ohio Railroad. The continuous coal traffic from Cumberland by rail to the east was disruptive to the sleep of his men. It was subsequently agreed that all eastbound traffic would pass through Harpers Ferry between 11:00 A.M. and 1:00 P.M. Soon after this was implemented, Jackson requested that the same be done for the empty cars returning westward to the coalfields. Garrett, well aware of Jackson's ability to harm his rail line, concurred. Jackson had men block the road at Martinsburg and Point of Rocks when both the eastbound and westbound traffic were between these two points. They trapped 300 cars and 56 locomotives. Unfortunately for the South, Jackson was unable to move most of the rolling stock southward. Four small locomotives were all that could be taken over the rickety spur line to Winchester. From there horses pulled them over the Valley Turnpike the eighteen miles to the Manassas Gap Railroad at Strasburg.[16]

At the end of May, Jackson was superseded in command by Brigadier-General Joseph E. Johnston. The new commander immediately began what a Confederate officer called the "organization of the men on a larger scale than Jackson had attempted." Johnston organized the several thousand men, representing nearly all the seceded states, into brigades. Jackson was assigned to command the Virginian citizen-soldiers who would soon be known by their renowned combat reputation as the Stonewall Brigade. Johnston felt vulnerable at Harpers Ferry and asked for more men. When Federals assembled at Chambersburg under General Robert Patterson in response to the Southerners' occupation of Harpers Ferry, Johnston would pull back toward Winchester.

PATTERSON FAILS

Sixty-nine-year-old Robert Patterson was born in Ireland and rose to fame during the Mexican War. He was ushered from civilian life into emergency service in late April as the head of the Department of Pennsylvania. From his headquarters in Philadelphia he was to oversee the forming of an army. Almost immediately, he received repeated requests by Winfield Scott to prepare to help secure Baltimore. Problems in outfitting his men led to delays. Finally a mix-up in communication caused Patterson to send unwanted troops to the wrong place, evoking Scott's wrath.

When the Baltimore crisis abated, Patterson turned his attention to the Confederate occupation of Harpers Ferry. He moved to Chambersburg in early June, optimistically setting forth a plan to cross the Potomac and turn Johnston at Harpers Ferry. He planned to go to Hagerstown, cross the river at Williamsport, and move toward Winchester by way of Martinsburg. To protect his troops from being attacked from his right he sent Colonel Lewis (Lew) Wallace and his Eleventh Indianans to Cumberland, Maryland, another crossing site on the Potomac. Wallace was to gather information and capture or rout enemy forces forming in that area. The enthusiastic Wallace, who pleaded with Patterson not to be left out of any battle, chased a newly formed force of several hundred Confederates from Romney on June 13, and then returned to Cumberland. This was the first of three raids by Union forces from Cumberland and nearby areas on that site during 1861.[17]

Scott approved Patterson's turning plan for Harpers Ferry and sent him reinforcements. As a secondary and diversionary movement, Scott ordered Stone, with 2,500 men from Washington, to Edwards Ferry. The elderly and grumpy commander warned Patterson that anything less than a victory would be unacceptable. Scott emphasized, "There must be no reverse, check or draw as it would be a victory to the enemy, filling his heart with joy, his ranks with men, and his magazines with voluntary contributions."[18]

Things did not go smoothly for Patterson in preparing for his invasion. In early June Patterson ordered New York regiments in Harrisburg to join him at Chambersburg, but their colonels refused to allow these regiments to comply. Other reinforcements would, however, join him at a time when Johnston's numbers were also increasing. But the opportunity for Patterson to turn Johnston soon slipped away. On June 15, 1861, Johnston evacuated Harpers Ferry after burning the railroad bridge and took a position between Martinsburg and Winchester at Bunker Hill, in a direct line south of a Federal crossing at Williamsport. On June 18, his main force was camped around Winchester, where they were welcomed by secessionist flags hanging from every house. In the meantime, in Patterson's camp north of the Potomac, a rumor circulated that the women of Martinsburg were prepared to fight to defend their land.

The evacuation of Harpers Ferry created great excitement and movement. Businesses were closed, and families loaded their possessions onto wagons. Every street was crowded with loaded wagons belonging to both civilians and the military. Soldiers moved about in an attempt to stock up on bread and sugar. Vast amounts of military provisions that could not be transported were dumped into the river.

Harpers Ferry was no longer the primary Federal target. Johnston's evacuation and the push to continue on to Richmond now made Manassas Junction the center of Federal attention. Troops, including the U.S. Regulars and Rhode Island Battery, were taken from Patterson. This loss of manpower took place two weeks before Patterson crossed the Potomac, and it left him with three-month volunteers whose terms would expire in only a matter of weeks. He was relegated to the secondary but important role of keeping Johnston from joining Beauregard.

Johnston had left Harpers Ferry, with Jefferson Davis' reluctant blessing, out of fear of being cut off by Patterson from the north and by men from McClellan's command in the west. The threat from the west was more imagined than real. Scott had ordered McClellan to send nothing across the mountain to support Patterson. But Lew Wallace's June 13 raid at Romney—forty-three miles west of Winchester—which had chased away a small, recently formed Confederate force, vividly illustrated to Johnston his vulnerability from the west, as well as Romney's importance. So he sent Colonel A. P. Hill with two regiments to regain the town. From Romney, Hill sent four companies to the New Creek Depot, eighteen miles southwest of Cumberland. There, on June 19, they routed several hundred Federals and burned the railroad bridge.[19] This unnerved Wallace, who feared 3,000 Confederates were approaching. He asked for help and packed his baggage to make a hasty retreat. He received no reinforcements, and 3,000 Confederates did not attack.

Encouraged by the New Creek Depot raid and news that McClellan was involved elsewhere in western Virginia, Johnston pulled Hill back from Romney and devoted his attention to Patterson. Twenty-five hundred militiamen were called out, earthworks were constructed outside Winchester, and Jackson and his brigade moved northward to assist the watchful Stuart's cavalrymen. Across the river anxious civilian refugees, who had been driven from their homes south of the Potomac and were eager to return to harvest their crops, gathered around Patterson's army. Support for the Union was not, however, universal. One observer noticed a significant difference between the people around Williamsport compared to Chambersburg. "Reports say," stated a Northern paper, "they are all true for the Union, but they do not speak out with the warmth of feeling as in Pennsylvania. You see a coldness. They desire guards around their property...while in Pennsylvania they desire none."

A contrasting view is presented by a member of the First Virginia cavalry. News came to his camp, just north of Martinsburg, that the Yankee invaders were "plundering houses, stealing negroes and stock of all kinds." "Several families" passed the cavalryman's camp, going southward, and, the soldier recounted, "a great many persons 'passed' in vehicles of all kinds fleeing from the fiends."

Troop movement, according to a Northern reporter, resembled "the swarming of bees—regiments coming" into camp at Williamsport as others left. On July 2, Patterson's men waded across the two-and-a-half-foot-deep water of the Potomac at Williamsport. It took about fifteen minutes to cross. Some took off their shoes and pants, creating a comical—or even ludicrous, some contend—scene by holding them on their heads, along with their knapsacks, haversacks, and guns. A young soldier of German descent, in an attempt to avoid getting wet, climbed on top of one of the wagons only to be thrown into the water when a wheel struck a large stone in midstream. Shouts of laughter greeted him as he surfaced.[20]

From Williamsport they proceeded to Falling Waters, four miles south of the crossing. There they engaged Stuart's cavalry and some of Jackson's men. A little farther south, near Hainesville, on the Porterfield farm, the Federals destroyed a barn and a carriage house in order to make a charge upon the enemy. Confederates stood up from hiding in a wheat field, behind logs and trees, and engaged in a brisk but brief exchange of gunfire. After occupying wooded terrain, the Southerners momentarily slowed the Union advance during an hour of fighting that saw relatively light casualties. But to Porterfield and other local farmers, what had happened near Hainesville, resulting in several dozen casualties, was not a minor occurrence. In their woods they found the horribly mutilated bodies of two Confederates, killed by exploding shells from Union howitzers.

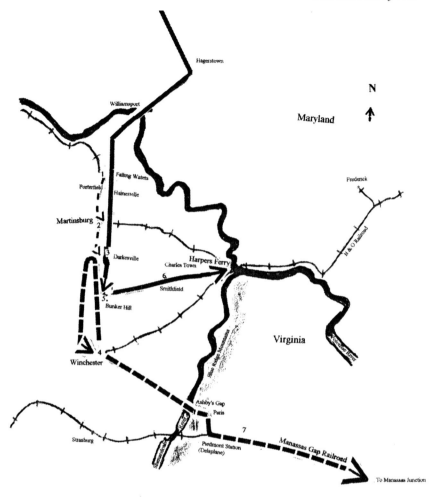

Johnston prevents Patterson from turning him by withdrawing from Harpers Ferry to Bunker Hill (June 15) and then to Winchester.
1. After Patterson crosses the Potomac at Williamsport the men of Stuart and Jackson briefly engage the oncoming Federals at Falling Waters (July 2) and
2. Martinsburg (July 3)
3. In the meantime Johnston moves the rest of his force to Darkesville where Stuart and Jackson join him.
4. When Patterson moves to Martinsburg, but fails to attack, Johnston pulls back to Winchester.
5. Patterson then furthers his southern penetration by moving to Bunker Hill.
6. But on July 14, Patterson moves eastward (to Smithfield and Charles Town) away from Winchester.
7. This presents Johnston with the opportunity to slip through Ashby's Gap (july 18) and ride the rails from Piedmont Station to Manassas Junction.

PATTERSON'S FAILED CAMPAIGN OF JULY 1861

A slave became a local hero in this fight by capturing and disarming a Union lieutenant of the Fifteenth Pennsylvania Infantry and by marching his prisoner of war to Winchester. Forty other members of the same regiment were captured two miles from Falling Waters when they mistook about 100 Confederate horsemen for Union cavalry. Their uniforms were very similar, so many of the Pennsylvanians laid their arms on the ground to take down a fence so the cavalry could pass. To their surprise, they were suddenly attacked. One man was killed and forty were separated and captured as the rest of the command withdrew. The prisoners' hands were tied behind them, and they were quickly marched to the Winchester jail, eighteen miles away, protesting along the way. Similar protests were evoked from Union prisoners who were captured elsewhere and were made to walk, tied behind their wagons, to the same destination.[21]

After the fight near Hainesville, the Confederates pulled back to the outskirts of Martinsburg; Stuart was to the north of the town, and Jackson's men were to the south, at Big Spring. The next day Johnston ordered them southward, and by noon the Federals entered Martinsburg. At one point, two Southern officers mistook Federal artillery for their own. They rode up to a Federal officer, greeting him cordially and asking how far "the boys" were behind. Suddenly realizing their error, they dashed away as the enemy artillery—who had no small arms—could only fire spherical shot, belatedly and harmlessly.

Earlier that morning Johnston was marching forward from Winchester when he met Jackson's brigade seven miles south of Martinsburg, at Darkesville. There the 10,000-man force waited for Patterson to attack. Instead Patterson and his 15,000 men stayed at Martinsburg, where their position was deemed unassailable. Confederates became convinced that the Yankees would not fight. After expressing this feeling to his colonel, Samuel Buck, of the Thirteenth Virginia, requested permission to go to Winchester to get a tooth filled. He was told to wait until the next day; an officer told him, "You may have it filled with lead by night."[22]

Finally, after four days, Johnston grew tired of waiting and returned to Winchester, disappointing those of his force who were eager to fight. The Federals finally moved from Martinsburg on July 15, 1861, and advanced to Bunker Hill, where they stayed until the July 17. On that day, Patterson moved to his left to Smithfield and

Charles Town. To Confederates, it appeared that he was planning to go to Berryville and get between Johnston's and Beauregard's forces. The next day, July 18, things became more urgent for the Confederates. Beauregard had been attacked. Richmond immediately telegraphed Johnston, telling him to join Beauregard. Johnston pondered whether he should try to fight Patterson or slip past his forces. Certainly the latter was preferable.

Once Stuart found that the Federals had not advanced from Smithfield and were too far away to stop an immediate move eastward, Johnston decided to elude his adversary. Seventeen hundred sick men, who were plagued with measles, mumps, and other ailments, were left behind. The local militia was assigned the task of defending Winchester, while Stuart's cavalry was to screen the movement. Johnston was closer to Manassas than Patterson was, and he hoped to slip away undetected, taking advantage of the Confederates' interior lines. This advantage was enhanced by a rail line that Johnston hoped would enable the two Confederate forces to rapidly unite.

By midday of July 18, Johnston's puzzled men, who had at first thought that they were retreating until they were told otherwise, started moving east to join Beauregard. The first third of the trip was by foot. Johnston's advanced infantry splashed through the Shenandoah River with their cartridge boxes on their bayonets, then over the Blue Ridge through Ashby's Gap to the small hamlet of Paris on the eastern base of the mountain. Jackson's men spent the night there while the rest of Johnston's army slumbered at the western base of the Blue Ridge. Hundreds of infantry, states William W. Blackford, a Confederate cavalryman, "slipped out of the road to sleep," and "were scattered about everywhere" requiring Stuart's men, who followed after dark, "to be on the lookout to keep from riding over them." The following day Jackson's foot soldiers walked the six miles to Piedmont Station (Delaplane) of the Manassas Gap Railroad. There was a shortage of cars, and the conductor refused to run the train during the night, which delayed the last of Johnston's men from arriving at Manassas Junction until July 21. It was an enjoyable delay. Citizens from miles around flocked to Piedmont Station to see the soldiers, bringing them food and providing sumptuous fare. It was an enormous picnic for the soldiers, with plenty to eat, lemonade to drink, and beautiful ladies to chat with.[23]

Travel by rail was meant to save both time and energy, but it took a series of eight-hour trips over three days to move Johnston's army the thirty-six miles from Piedmont Station to Manassas Junction—about the time it would have taken to march there. All this was despite the assurances of Edward C. Marshall, the president of the Manassas Gap Railroad and son of famed Chief Justice John Marshall; he had said that Johnston's entire force could be transported in twenty-four hours. The ride might have been less taxing than marching would have been, but it was still taxing and unpleasant. Inside the cars were hot sweaty bodies pressed tightly together and jostling about, reminding one passenger of the "black hole of Calcutta." Those on top of the train were beset by hot metal and boards, cinders, and choking smoke. The snail's pace of travel, slower than five miles an hour, afforded some the opportunity to jump from the slow-moving train to pick blackberries. They incurred the wrath of General Kirby Smith, who bellowed, "If I had a sword I would cut you down where you stand."

Further reasons given for the delay include some intriguing but vague references by a few Confederate soldiers, who told of sabotage by Unionist railroad employees. A rail collision or crash that resulted from tracks being torn up was said to have occurred on Saturday evening, July 27. A conductor was said to have been blamed by Confederate officers, hastily court-martialed, convicted of bribery and of causing the crash, and shot.[24]

For two days Patterson was oblivious to the fact that Johnston had left. Scott's repeated pleas to Patterson to make sure the Confederates did not slip away had been useless. The general-in-chief telegraphed Patterson at Charles Town on July 18, "Has he [Johnston] not stolen a march and sent reinforcements toward Manassas Junction?" Patterson wired back, "The enemy has stolen no march upon me. I have kept him actively employed, and by threats and reconnaissances in force caused him to be re-enforced. I have accomplished in this respect more than the General-in-Chief asked or could well be expected, in face of an enemy far superior in numbers, with no line of communication to protect." Patterson simply had no grasp of the situation. Scott wanted Patterson to do one of three things: "either to attack Johnston and best him, or to detain him or if he left, to follow him." Patterson did none of the three.

His furthest penetration was to Bunker Hill, halfway between Martinsburg and Winchester. There on Thursday, July 18, he skirmished with some of Johnston's men who had blocked the road to Winchester with trees and fence rails. Two days later, Patterson withdrew back to Charles Town, doubling his distance from Winchester, and eventually moved even further away, to Harpers Ferry. The last move caused Scott to wire Patterson, telling him he must not cross the Potomac again.[25] Patterson gave sundry reasons for leaving Bunker Hill, including that he lacked supplies, which had, in his words, "crippled" his "movements." He imagined he faced a much larger force of "42,000 men at Winchester with sixty-three pieces of artillery." He argued that eighteen of his twenty-six regiments' term of service would expire within seven days; he believed they would not re-enlist, and he wanted to secure Harpers Ferry.

Patterson's force was not well supplied. Many wore tattered uniforms, patched with material from the flaps of their tents, and were without shoes. Patterson also wrote that the feet of some soldiers "were so cut and injured by the flinty roads over which they had marched some had to be carried in wagons." But what weakened their resolve was not their bedraggled condition. By moving to Charles Town, Patterson was allowing Johnston to escape, but it angered the Union men, who were eager for a fight. Instead they had retreated. One of the Union soldiers wrote that he and his comrades "declared that they had no deposition to be bamboozled any longer in that way, and as their time was up they would go home, unless [Patterson]...was disposed to go out and attack the enemy."

Scott also was agitated with Patterson's failures and contemplated his immediate removal. Instead Patterson was notified on July 19 that when his tour of duty expired on July 27, Major-General Nathaniel P. Banks would replace him. Patterson went into retirement railing against Scott, claiming that he had "suffered...injustices at the hands of the general-in-chief." He charged Scott with failing to provide direct, specific orders and proper manpower, and with having ordered Patterson to attack a superior force that would have annihilated his army. He added that Scott had misinformed him that the battle of Manassas was to be fought on July 16—when Patterson claimed he had been directed to keep the enemy in Winchester. Patterson further claimed that he made the demonstration as ordered on July 16, but that Scott "did not avail himself of the fruits of that movement." Patterson audaciously added, "All that was demanded of me, and more, was effected."

Secretary Cameron rejected Patterson's demand for a court of inquiry. Cameron responded that there was no precedent to grant a court of inquiry to someone who had been honorably discharged from the service.

Patterson continued what he called his "pursuit of justice" into 1862 before the Joint Committee on the Conduct of the War; he defended his actions and attacked Scott in a 148-page statement. The committee was unconvinced, and they accepted Scott's brief rebuttal by concluding that "the principal cause of the defeat" on July 21 at Bull Run "was the failure of General Patterson to hold the forces of Johnston in the Valley of the Shenandoah."[26]

ROMNEY AND THE DEFENSE OF WINCHESTER AND THE LOWER SHENANDOAH VALLEY

During the second half of 1861, the area along the Potomac from Harpers Ferry westward witnessed a pattern of activity similar to that found to the east. Both sides feared enemy crossings and attacks. Federals were vulnerable to forays on the B&O Railroad on the southern banks of the Potomac, and the on C&O Canal on the northern banks. Confederates were concerned about the threat of Federal penetration into the Shenandoah Valley to their main base in Winchester from northern crossings (Harpers Ferry, Shepherdstown, Willliamsport, Hancock, and Cumberland) and from the west, across the southern branch of the Potomac, at Romney. The military activity to the west consisted of sparring and probing that resulted in minor clashes, usually with inconsequential results. While Winchester continued to be the key supply base for Confederates in the lower valley through 1861, the Federals would use Frederick, Maryland, for the latter half of 1861.

Almost immediately upon succeeding Patterson, with Scott's approval, Banks withdrew from Harpers Ferry into Maryland. He felt unsafe despite the fact that the enemy at Winchester had no more men than 5,000 to 6,000 men—the same number he had at Harpers Ferry. Banks nevertheless maintained that it would take 20,000 men to defend Harpers Ferry. There were three points that must be held, he believed: the heights of Loudoun, Maryland, and Bolivar. Banks thought that if they fell, the enemy would command the town. At the end of July, as he moved his troops north of the Potomac, Banks also moved his supply base, which had been used by Patterson, from Hagerstown to the more centrally located Frederick. The new location was far enough from the river to be safe from marauding enemy parties, and it had the best railroad facilities and sufficient buildings for storage.[27]

When Johnston evacuated Winchester, defending the vicinity was left to local militiamen and horsemen under the leadership of an aged cavalry leader, a sixty-two-year-old native of Winchester who was an attorney and a graduate of West Point, Colonel Angus W. McDonald. When Johnston left for Manassas on July 18, McDonald was positioned at Romney on the Northwest Turnpike. The same day Richmond ordered Angus McDonald to Staunton to cover the "disastrous retreat of Garnett's command" to Monterey. Southern leaders were concerned that McClellan's pursuit would threaten the Central Railroad and possibly Staunton, thus penetrating the Allegheny barrier and the upper Shenandoah Valley. Soon it was realized that the immediate Federal threat to this region was more imagined than real. McDonald returned to Romney, where he stayed into the fall.

The previous June McDonald had formed an independent regiment later known as the Seventh Regiment of Virginia Cavalry, for border service. After Johnston's departure from Winchester, it became the duty of the Seventh Virginia Cavalry to guard the Confederate frontier from Harpers Ferry to the headwaters of the Potomac, a distance of 125 miles. Romney became McDonald's headquarters because it was a critical point from which to watch Union movements and conduct destructive raids on the B&O Railroad. These raids could be done in the sixty miles extending from the Piedmont to the Big Cacapon River. So thoroughly were bridges, culverts, and water stations destroyed, Federals would retaliate with repeated attacks on Romney.

View of Romney (West) Virginia
from the east by Alfred R. Ward, 1861.
(Courtesy of the Library of Congress)

Federal troops approach the bridge over the
southern branch of the Potomac River in 1861.
Romney is located on the high ground in the center above the bridge.
Confederates placed artillery on the cleared land west of the town.
(Courtesy of the Library of Congress)

510

While McDonald was stationed at Romney, where he had lived before moving to Winchester, with most of the Seventh Virginia Cavalry and militia units, he left the rest of his command at Charles Town, along with other local militiamen to protect the Potomac border north of Winchester. They were commanded by an able young partisan from Fauquier County, Virginia, Lieutenant-Colonel Turner Ashby. Ashby's fame started early in the war. At the end of June he attacked and drove off a superior number of Federals at Kelly's Island on the Potomac to avenge their harsh treatment of his younger brother, Richard. The Federals had ambushed the younger Ashby and mangled his body with eight wounds, the last from a bayonet being jabbed into his stomach, as he lay prostrate on the ground. Richard had died after seven agonizing days of intense suffering.[28]

This incident might have been a factor in the treatment of the remains of four Union dead during the skirmish at Bolivar Heights near Harpers Ferry on October 16, 1861 (reported in papers as the "Battle of Bolivar Heights). Several days before the skirmish, Banks sent Colonel John W. Geary and a Union force of 600 men and two cannons to Sandy Hook. Most crossed the Potomac at Harpers Ferry and removed 24,000 bushels of wheat to the Maryland shore. To stop what Confederate Colonel Turner Ashby called the enemy "depredations," he approached Harpers Ferry with 300 militia armed with flintlock muskets, and two companies of cavalry, "one rifled four pounder gun" and a "24-pounder gun." He placed his artillery on Bolivar Heights. At 7:30 in the morning, with the help of supporting artillery fire and sharpshooters on Loudoun Heights, Ashby drove in Federal pickets on Bolivar Heights. This touched off a skirmish that lasted until the early afternoon. Geary beat back three Confederate charges, silenced their force on Loudoun Heights with artillery fire from Maryland Heights, and forced Ashby to retreat to School House Hill, near Halltown.

Ashby lost ten men, one killed and nine wounded; Geary had thirteen casualties, four killed, seven wounded, and two captured. Federal troops viewing the four Union fatalities were convinced that after their men were killed, the bodies were victims of barbaric treatment at the hands of Ashby's cavalry. The remains had been stabbed through, stripped of all clothing, and left naked. One was laid in the form of a crucifixion, with his hands spread out, and cut through the palms with a dull knife. Geary reported, "This inhuman treatment incensed my troops exceedingly, and I fear its consequences may be shown in retaliatory acts hereafter."

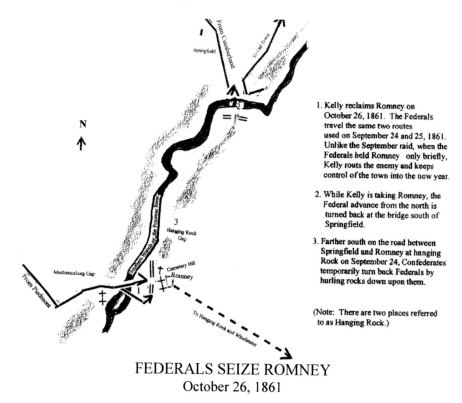

1. Kelly reclaims Romney on October 26, 1861. The Federals travel the same two routes used on September 24 and 25, 1861. Unlike the September raid, when the Federals held Romney only briefly, Kelly routs the enemy and keeps control of the town into the new year.

2. While Kelly is taking Romney, the Federal advance from the north is turned back at the bridge south of Springfield.

3. Farther south on the road between Springfield and Romney at hanging Rock on September 24, Confederates temporarily turn back Federals by hurling rocks down upon them.

(Note: There are two places referred to as Hanging Rock.)

FEDERALS SEIZE ROMNEY
October 26, 1861

The morning after the skirmish, wrote Colonel John Geary in his official report, a "few of the enemy Confederates in citizen dress came secretly to Harpers Ferry, by way of the Shenandoah road, burned Herr's Mill, from which a great portion of the wheat had been taken, and immediately retired." That night the Union force crossed back into Maryland, and many returned to Frederick.[29]

During the fall, Ashby's small force limited Federals incursions into the lower Shenandoah Valley as well as they could. Several attempts were made by the Union to evict McDonald's men from Romney and end their annoying raids on the B&O Railroad. Romney sits on a 150-foot plateau overlooking the South Branch of the Potomac to the west, and is surrounded by mountain ranges, which seemed to be major barriers to any Federal attack. But the town was accessible through mountain passes in the north and west, and by a bridge and three fords across the South Branch.

Late in September, Federals tried to surprise McDonald by night marches from Cumberland, through Springfield and Hanging Rock Gap, in the north and from Piedmont, through the Mechanicsburg Gap, in the west. Aware of the approaching enemy, McDonald's men beat them back at both gaps, Mechanicsburg Pass (three and a half miles southwest of Romney) and Hanging Rock Pass (two and a half miles north of the town). The repulse at Hanging Rock Pass was accomplished in an unconventional manner. At that site is a narrow pass, with the river on one side and a steep cliff on the other. On the foggy morning of September 24, after emptying their firearms, a dozen or so local militiamen threw rocks down onto the Federals below. Panicking Federal cavalry (a company of the Ringgold Cavalry) ran over their own infantrymen, forcing many into the river, where at least five drowned. The Confederates were unaware— because of fog and a false report that claimed the Union was advancing— that the Federals had retreated, and the Confederates left Hanging Rock Gap, pulling back to Romney. The following day, reports that the enemy was moving toward the Winchester road east of town caused McDonald to pull back as well. After he left, the Federals occupied the town. Upon learning that the enemy was pillaging, McDonald attacked, driving the Federals from the town. He pursued them westward for fifteen miles before returning to Romney.[30]

A month later, on October 26, 1861, the Federals under General Benjamin F. Kelly successfully seized Romney and held it until January 10, 1862. McDonald was overwhelmed by a vastly superior force of more than three times his own 400. Federals came from the same two directions and routes in night marches as they had in their September attack. Kelly approached Romney from the west and ordered the Maryland Home Brigade Militia to come from the north and enter the town from the east, trapping McDonald's men and preventing their escape to Winchester. But the 600 Maryland militiamen failed to reach Romney because of the stubborn resistance of the 114th Virginia militia, who blocked the crossing of the bridge over the South Branch, one and a half miles south of Springfield. The Virginians removed more than 150 feet of planking from the suspension bridge and strongly positioning themselves in nearby earthworks and on top of the 150-foot perpendicular wall of rock to the south of the crossing. After a futile attempt to cross the bridge, the Marylanders climbed the rock cliff on the north side of the river and shot at the Virginians on the heights 250 to 300 feet away. After two hours, the Union militia withdrew northward into Maryland. Their commander, Colonel Thomas John, later reported that the retreat occurred after he had heard firing to the south and had assumed Kelly had taken Romney.

Colonel John's assumption proved correct. McDonald resisted as well as he could. First he confronted the invading column six miles west of Romney then fell back through Mechanicsburg Gap to the South Branch bridge near the town. There McDonald decided to make a stand on the Romney side of the bridge by positioning his force and his artillery pieces on the formidable high ground, especially Cemetery Hill (the site of an Indian burial mound), which commanded the bridge and road to Romney. A severe cannonade took place between the artillery of both sides for an hour. Finding he could not silence the Southern guns, Kelly ordered his infantrymen to charge across the bridge and ordered the cavalry to cross under it and through a nearby ford. The Southerners were overwhelmed by the enemy, and finding a Federal squadron on their flank, they abandoned their works and retreated. They tried unsuccessfully to rally east of town as the retreat became a rout. Infantrymen abandoned their weapons and ran for woods and mountains while pursued by enemy cavalry. The wagon train and two artillery pieces two miles east of town were captured reached by the Federal cavalry. Upon learning of the rout, the commander of the 114th Virginia Militia, at South Bridge, withdrew eastward to North River Mills.

The loss of Romney created a crisis in the protection of the lower Shenandoah Valley and was a major factor in sending Jackson to Winchester on November 4, 1861, to defend that region. Immediately Jackson ordered the 114th Militia, which had pulled eastward from South Bridge, to go to Hanging Rock, six miles east of Romney, to block the main road to Winchester.[31] McDonald was embarrassed at having lost Romney, and he was also crippled by rheumatism. He retired to limited duty, turning his command over to the young man he had praised in reports, Turner Ashby.

The Federals were content to thresh grain and carry off livestock around Romney. They were confident that their occupation of the town protected the B&O Railroad west and east of Cumberland and saw no need to move eastward toward Winchester. Jackson was less content. The enemy presence at Romney made Winchester vulnerable. He planned to get Romney back and to cut Union communications around Hancock, Maryland. This plan became known as the Romney Campaign and lasted most of the winter of 1861. By mid-December Jackson had Dam No. 5 breached, in an attempt to make the C&O Canal inoperable. On New Year's Day, after obtaining reinforcements, he moved toward Hancock, but he was plagued by ice, snow, and illness. He damaged the B&O Railroad, shelled Hancock in retaliation for what he considered the Federals' wanton and repeated shelling of undefended Shepherdstown, and by mid-January had reoccupied Romney. But several weeks later a disgruntled Brigadier-General W. W. Loring, whom Jackson had brought court-martial charges against for his failure in the recent campaign, went above Jackson to get permission from Richmond to evacuate Romney. The evacuation set off a series of Confederate reversals, including Romney's reoccupation by the Federals. Angered and frustrated, Jackson resigned, but he was later persuaded to stay in charge of the defense of the valley.[32] The changing occupation of Romney continued, and the town of seventy to eighty houses changed hands more than fifty-six times during the war, second only in the region to Winchester's number of changes: more than seventy.

[1] The ruse was to prevent their plan from being leaked to the Federal authorities.
[2] *B & L*, vol. I, 111-17.
[3] Richmond *Enquirer*, June 18, 1861; Charleston (S.C.) *Daily Courier*, May 20, 1861; New York *Times*, April 21, 1861.
[4] Ibid., 117-23. Roger Jones was in charge of the Federal force at Harpers Ferry. Upon learning that Virginia was about to seize the plant, he made the necessary plans to fire the Federal arms works.
[5] Barry, *The Strange Story of Harper's Ferry*, 97-100.
[6] *Daily Courier*, May 20, 1861.
[7] The New York *Times*, May 25, 26, & 27, 1861, gave the total number of Southern troops at Harpers Ferry at between 7,000 and 11,000; 2,000 being from Mississippi, 1,000 from Alabama, 800 from Kentucky, and 800 from Maryland, principally from Baltimore.
[8] *Daily Courier*, May 20, 1861.
[9] Ibid.
[10] New York *Herald*, May 21, 1861; New York *Times*, May 11, 19, 21, 25, 26, & 27, June 2 & 5, 1861. By the end of May several militiamen had died of smallpox. Those who were sick with the disease were isolated in a camp along the Shenandoah River.
[11] New York *Herald*, May 22 & 25, 1861. During one week in mid-May Southern forces at Harpers Ferry seized from the B&O Railroad "upward to two thousand bushels of corn."
[12] Barry, *The Strange Story of Harper's Ferry*, 101-2; New York *Times*, May 17, 1861; Richmond *Examiner*, June 18, 1861.
[13] *B & L*, vol. I, 111-23; New York *Times*, May 17, 1861. An additional problem of the Virginia militia at Harpers Ferry was the difficulty of communicating with Richmond. The state capital was "out of telegraphic reach," and since members of the seceded state could not travel by rail through Washington and Baltimore, it was a two-day trip to Richmond.
[14] The governor of Virginia subsequently ordered the state to pay for Imboden's purchases.
[15] Lenoir Chambers, *Stonewall Jackson* (New York: William Morrow & Co., 1959), vol. I, 339-40; Douglas, *I Rode With Stonewall*, 202. The soldiers also called Jackson's horse "Old Sorrel" or "Sorrel." The horse had the unusual habit of "lying down like a dog when the command halted for a rest." Sorrel was sent to Mrs. Jackson after her husband's death. The horse lived until 1886. He died at the Soldier's Home in Richmond, where he had been a pet of the aged warriors. The body of the famous charger was mounted and displayed behind a glass case. The mounted remains were sent in 1950 to VMI.
[16] Chambers, *Stonewall Jackson*, vol. I, 339; Hungerford, *Story of the Baltimore and Ohio Railroad*, vol. II, 7.
[17] *OR*, Ser. I, vol. 2, 123-124, 660, 670-72. Wallace, the future author of *Ben Hur*, returned to Cumberland after the June raid. While at Romney one of the assignments was to prevent local Confederate supporters from forming military

units. For more details, see Fritz Haselberger, "Wallace's Raid on Romney in 1861," *West Virginia History,* January 1866, 97-110.

[18] Ibid., 671.

[19] Ibid., 130-132. Hill took with him the Thirteenth Virginia infantry and the Third Tennessee infantry under Colonel John C. Vaughn.

[20] New York *Tribune,* July 6, 1861; Pittsburgh *Chronicle,* June 22 & 24, 1861; VMI Archives, John H. Ervine Letter, Manuscript No. 331. Most of the horses that Ervine's company rode were valued at $175 to $200.

[21] Pittsburgh *Evening Chronicle,* July 8-10, 1861.

[22] Charles T. Harrell, "Too Few Trains," 1999. http://nps-vip.net/history/too_few_trains1.htm (August 6, 2001); New York *Weekly Journal,* June 4, 7 & 25, 1861; *OR,* Ser. I, vol. 2, 181-86. A post office was established after Union occupation of Martinsburg that facilitated communications with the North.

[23] Blackford, *War Years with Jeb Stuart,* 19; Casler, *Four Years in the Stonewall Brigade,* 22; Johnston, *Narrative,* 29-35. The Federal cavalry of Patterson outnumbered Stuart, but would not leave the cover of their infantry. This enabled Stuart to move about at will.

[24] Harrell, *Too Few Trains,* 6-12.

[25] Skirmishing also occurred at Charles Town on July 21, 1861.

[26] *Joint Committee on the Conduct of the War,* pt. II, 5, 59, 88-89, 103, 105, 226, 231, 233; *OR,* Ser. I, vol. 2, 156-87.

[27] *OR,* Ser. I, vol. 2, 364, 367-368, 970.

[28] C.M. Ambler, "Romney in the Civil War," *West Virginia History,* April 1944, 151-60; *Daily Chronicle and Sentinel* (August, Ga.), July 11, 1862; William N. McDonald, *A History of the Laurel Brigade,* (Baltimore, Md.: Sun Job, 1907), 22-24. On June 21, 1861, Turner Ashby ordered his brother to take a few men (eleven went) and "arrest a certain obnoxious (Union) citizen," who was believed to be a spy. Richard did not find the citizen but proceeded toward Federal lines along the B&O Railroad. He was ambushed near Kelly's Island, where Patterson Creek empties into the North Branch of the Potomac River. Some authorities believe Kelly's Island has been washed away by floods. There are other islands in the vicinity today.

[29] *OR,* Ser. I, vol. 5, 239-49; Pittsburgh *Evening Chronicle,* October 23, 1861. Turner's twenty-four-pound cannon broke an axle and had to be spiked. It later fell into Union hands.

[30] Samuel C. Farrar, *The Twenty-Second Pennslyvania Cavalry and the Ringgold Battalion* (Pittsburgh, Pa.: New Werner, 1911), 17; McDonald, *A History of the Laurel Brigade,* 26; *Or,* Ser. I, vol. 5, 200-14. McDonald had 300 mounted men and an infantry of about 350 militiamen. He estimated the enemy force (no official reports were made by the Federals) at 1,500, which included about seventy-five cavalry. Confederate losses were remarkably small: five wounded (two by their own men) and five horses killed. Five Federals were captured, but the number killed or wounded is unknown.

[31] B. F. Kelley, "U.S. Army General's Report of Civil War Service," National

Archives, Microfilm Publications M1098, Roll 1, vol. 2. Note there are two Hanging Rocks: Hanging Rock Gap, two and a half miles north of Romney; and Hanging Rock, east of town. On August 3, 1861, Rosecrans put B. F. Kelly in command of the newly formed special military district called the District of Grafton, to protect the rail lines in northwestern Virginia. This district included all rail lines, stations, and depots from Wheeling to Cumberland.

[32] McDonald, *History of the Laurel Brigade,* 20, 28-29; *OR,* Ser. I, vol. 5, 378-83, 1055. McDonald was given limited duty by Jackson in the defense of Winchester. After Winchester fell into Federal hands, McDonald went to Lexington. Later in the war, he was captured and imprisoned (1864). His health ruined, he died two weeks after being released from prison. He was buried in Hollywood Cemetery near a son, Captain C. W. McDonald, who was killed at Cold Harbor. The senior McDonald had five more sons fight for the Confederacy.

PART V

CONCLUSION

CHAPTER XI

IT ISN'T WHAT WE EXPECTED: 1861 IN REVIEW

The first year of the war proved to be far different than envisioned by most political and military leaders, soldiers, and those left at home. Grand military plans were difficult to implement and failed to achieve the hoped-for victories that would terminate the war. Mobilization proved a formidable task, complicated by many factors. Among them were the logistical problems of obtaining proper arms, uniforms, and other supplies; molding farm lads and boys from urban areas into soldiers often under officers selected or elected because of civilian prominence, which often failed to translate into military acumen. The division of power between state and central authority in the war effort was neither clearly defined nor accepted. Governors retained a paternalistic interest in regiments formed and equipped by their state, even after the units were incorporated into centralized service. Lincoln's nationalistic policies would ultimately win out over states' rights in the North; Davis' would not in the South.

A romantic view of war, plus the excitement and fanfare that accompanied the seductive idea of going to war with friends and neighbors for a noble cause, created unrealistic expectations. Excitement was fueled by the anticipation of captivating, glorious, and dangerous experiences. No doubt some felt they had better get in the war before it ended because it might be a short one.

UNFULFILLED GRAND PLANS

It was up to the Federals to take the offensive and maintain the union through force. In 1861 an important Union strategy to accomplish this objective was to invade Virginia from four directions. Only one, the western invasion, produced significant and positive results. In the east, south, and north, Union penetration into the Old Dominion was limited. After major Union offensives failed in each of these areas—in the east at Bull Run, in the south at Big Bethel, and in the north, Patterson's failure to hold Johnston in the valley—the rest of the year was spent in vigilant defensive posturing, reconnoitering, skirmishing, and keeping occupied territories. If, by maneuvering and limited combat, one side could get the opponent, mainly Confederates, to abandon an outpost, that was a bonus. The primary objective of both sides was to prevent the fulfillment of their continual fear of a major enemy offensive.

Union forces seemed content to occupy the southern tip of the peninsula, while in northern Virginia the primary objective was to secure Washington, D.C. A protective ring of forts was constructed around the city. It was further hoped that the Southerners could be forced back from their outposts near the Potomac. This would lessen the chance of an enemy attack on the Federal capital from Munson's Hill or the chance that Southern forces would cross the Potomac from Leesburg and menace Washington from the northwest. When Johnston pulled Southern forces back from outposts such as Munson Hill, the encouraged Federals hoped to intimidate the Confederates into abandoning Leesburg. Instead this pullback led to the disaster at Ball's Bluff, a demoralizing Federal defeat second only to the one at Bull Run. Despite Unionists' claims of vindication by their victory at Dranesville, as the year waned, the scars of Bull Run and Ball's Bluff remained. In the meantime, in the northern invasion corridor, Union penetration south of the Potomac was transitory. Patterson withdrew back into Maryland after Bull Run, as did forces who later forayed into Harpers Ferry and Romney.

The defensive posturing throughout much of 1861 in the eastern, southern, and northern invasion corridors resulted not only from the South's defense of Virginia, but also from caution by Union military leaders after the failures of the first major offensives. The most influential factor of all was the lack of preparedness on both sides. Throughout the year, both Federals and Confederates continued to mobilize, reorganize, amass supplies, get and drill new troops, and search for competent officers.

While Southerners kept the enemy at bay to the north, east, and south, they failed to keep control of western Virginia. Dual Union invasions from Ohio into the northwest and the southwest of Virginia would drive back Southern forces. The Southerners were hampered by logistical problems and limited recruiting in a predominantly Unionist region and were forced back into and beyond the Alleghenies. To protect the valuable rail lines that ran through northwestern Virginia, Federal troops occupied Grafton and then, drove the Southerners, under Porterfield, from Philippi. Union forces under McClellan moved from the north and west in an attempt to trap the divided army of R. S. Garnett, who had replaced the overwhelmed Porterfield. Defeat at Rich Mountain caused the collapse of Confederate opposition. Pegram, after an unsuccessful attempt to escape from Rick Mountain, surrendered most of his force. Garnett retreated from Laurel Hill, but shifted from moving southward to moving toward the northeast after mistaking Confederate soldiers for the enemy at Beverly. This fateful decision would cost Garnett his life at Corrick's Ford and would send the remnants of his command on a circuitous route over rugged terrain, in one of the most harrowing retreats of the war.

Their retreat to Monterey and beyond left the Great Valley of Virginia vulnerable to enemy penetration from roads through Cheat and Valley Mountains. This was addressed by three Confederate commanders after each arrived at Monterey: first by H. R. Jackson, then by his successor, William W. Loring, and finally, by Robert E. Lee. To win control of Cheat Mountain and push the enemy back, in mid-September Lee launched an ambitious movement of five columns, some moving over what seemed to be impassable terrain. His plan never reached fruition, even though the columns reached their destinations. After sporadic exchanges of gunfire, Lee's columns withdrew; the plan was aborted because of Rust's failure to attack Cheat Summit Fort, which would have ignited a coordinated attack. The Confederates had lost the northwestern Virginia and were forced to find consolation in their subsequent turning back of Union attacks on their camps at Bartow and Camp Allegheny.

A similar fate had befallen the Confederates in southwestern Virginia. Jacob Cox's invasion from Ohio up the Kanawha River, as well as secondary movements to the north and south, drove Henry A. Wise and his Southern forces from the Kanawha Valley. Southern resistance was brushed aside at Barboursville, and despite Wise's momentary small victory at Scary Creek, Charleston was soon abandoned. The former governor of Virginia left the Kanawha Valley by way of Gauley Bridge, which he burned, in his "retrograde" to White Sulphur Springs.

Two Confederate attempts were made to regain the Kanawha Valley. Both failed. Inclement weather and rugged terrain greatly lessened the chances of success. So did the feud between the Confederate commanders, John B. Floyd and Henry Wise, in their first attempt to gain back lost territory. Floyd won a small victory over a greatly outnumbered Federal outpost at Cross Lanes. Days later, when attacked at Carnifex Ferry by William Rosecrans' substantial force, Floyd abandoned his camp and retreated—an act he later repeated—to Meadow Bluff. The stubborn Wise refused to withdraw beyond Sewell Mountain as pursuing Federals gathered on another ridge of the same mountain. Lee's arrival failed to ameliorate the bickering, as the rain, mud, and the distance from the supply bases created a logistical nightmare, preventing a major offensive by either side. Finally, Rosecrans was forced to pull his force back near his Gauley Bridge base. Wise was relieved of his command, and Lee left, appointing Floyd in charge of any pursuit. Floyd moved south of the New River to Fayetteville and Cotton Hill. From Cotton Hill he annoyed Federals across the New and Kanawha Rivers with intermittent and limited artillery fire until Rosecrans tried to trap him. Floyd escaped with limited encounters on Cotton Hill and McCoy's Mill and limited Union pursuit.

The only other attempt by the Confederates to gain control of the Kanawha Valley was in the fall of 1862. The transfer of 5,000 Federal troops to the east enabled 4,000 Confederates, under General Loring, to seize Charleston. But after seven weeks Loring was driven from the Kanawha Valley. Despite later Confederate cavalry raids and guerrilla activities, Union control of trans-Allegheny Virginia was never again seriously threatened.

Union troops, by gaining control of western Virginia in 1861, legitimated the Unionist civilian government and provided a springboard for the creation of the state of West Virginia in 1863. The conquest of western Virginia was the major Union military achievement of 1861. The victory, however, was incomplete. Federal troops had not broken the Allegheny barrier, which would have enabled them to enter the Shenandoah Valley and threaten the rail lines, military stores, and vast agricultural riches.

THE NOBLE CAUSE AGAINST AN EVIL AND UNSAVORY ENEMY

Although men had diverse motives for and attitudes about going to war, including those who joined up because it just seemed the thing to do, there were some common reasons to join: out of duty and honor, as an expression of manhood and patriotism, to seek adventure, out of a quest for glory, and out of pride for one's state.[1]

In nationalistic terms, going to war meant risking life and limb and enduring the discomforts of military life for one's country. For the Union soldier, this meant fighting to subdue Southern rebels in order to keep the country united—the country that George Washington helped create. For the Confederate soldier, it meant protecting his home and defending his way of life from an invading enemy. Southerners also invoked the revered name of George Washington for their cause by pointing out that he was the first great American "rebel." The articulate argued that not only was it their legal right to secede, and in effect de-ratify the constitution of 1787, but important progress in the world had been brought about by rebels. They found ideological support and comfort in the old proverb "Rebellion, if successful, is sacred; if not, is treason."[2]

Both sides sought support for their respective noble causes from the supernatural. Each believed God was on their side and prayed for divine help. Victories were viewed as God's approval of the cause and actions. Defeats were seen as divine punishment for sins. As the level of hardship mounted, soldiers looked for solace in religion.[3]

Lofty words in support of the noble cause contrasted sharply with those used in vilifying the enemy, soldier, or civilian. Economic and cultural differences spawned emotional and political events leading to war. After 1861, the fighting and killing to deny what the other deemed important made it easy to hate the enemy. Each believed that the other's despotic leaders had duped the ignorant and often vicious masses and were now dedicated to the destruction of the other's liberty. Northerners viewed Southerners as not only enslaving blacks, but also trying to destroy a democratic nation and Northern liberty by not playing by the constitutional rules. This was being done, claimed Northerners, by rejecting Lincoln's election and secession and by waging traitorous war. Southerners, on the other hand, felt like victims. They believed they had the constitutional right to leave the union, but Lincoln's minions were invading Southern soil to divest the people of their freedom, their country, and their lives.[4] For many in the North and South, the war was a case of right versus wrong, of good versus evil. Many were seen as villains: first the opposing chief executives, Lincoln and Davis, then the soldiers and civilian supporters. Political and military leaders gave speeches and issued proclamations to rally support for mobilization and to intensify the war effort; their rhetoric sharply delineated the purity and grandeur of their purpose as opposed to that of the enemy.

A congratulatory proclamation to their soldiers by Johnston and Beauregard was filled with the sentiments of a righteous cause and the glory of war. It was issued during the euphoric days following their routing of an army they believed trebled their own:

> One week ago a countless host of men, organized into an army...invaded the soil of Virginia. Their people sounded their approach with triumphant displays of anticipated victory. Their generals came in almost royal state; their great ministers, senators, and women came to witness the immolation of our army and the subjugation of our people, and to celebrate the result with wild revelry.

> It is with the profound emotions of gratitude to an overruling God, whose hand is manifest in protecting our homes and our liberties, that we, your generals commanding, are enabled, in the name of our whole country, to thank you for that patriotic courage, that heroic gallantry, that devoted

daring, exhibited by in the actions of the 18th and 21st, by which the hosts of the enemy were scattered and a signal and glorious victory obtained.

Soldiers, we congratulate you in an event which insures the liberty of our country. We congratulate every man of you whose glorious privilege it was to participate in this triumph of courage and truth—to fight in the battle of Manassas. You have created an epoch in the history of liberty, and unborn nations will call you blessed. Continue this noble devotion, looking always to the protection of a just God, and before the time grows much older we will be hailed as the deliverers of a nation of ten million people.

Comrades, our brothers who have fallen have earned undying renown upon earth, and their blood, shed in our holy cause, is a precious and acceptable sacrifice to the Father of Truth and Right. Their graves are beside the tomb of Washington; their spirits have joined with his in eternal communion. We will hold fast to the soil dust of our brothers. We will transmit this land free to our children, or we will fall into the fresh graves of our brothers in arms. We drop one tear on their laurels and move forward to avenge them.

Soldiers, we congratulate you on a glorious, triumphant, and complete victory, and we thank you for doing your whole duty in the service of your country.[5]

At times, Northern and Southern press coverage of the military events of 1861 approached fiction. Even firsthand accounts by those at battle sites reported as hard fact what witnesses thought they heard or believed they saw. Often these accounts were rumors or exaggerations, spawned by the emotions of war and heightened by the drama and trauma of combat. Certain universals emerged in the reporting of military conflicts of 1861. The enemy always outnumbered the side reporting the event, regardless of whether a report was written by a military official or partisan reporter. In cases of indecisive action, the side reporting the incident claimed conclusive victory, often over a foe who lacked morality and the warrior qualities of courage, bravery, and pride; in contrast, the winning side displayed these virtues. Reports of enemy casualties were always far greater than on the reporter's side.

All this hyperbole was a part of the psychology of war and, in part, stemmed from the desire to believe not only that the cause was superior to that of the enemy, but that the quality and capabilities of the armed forces were too. To the writers, these traits indicated, if not an invincibility, at least a likelihood of winning the war. The realities on the battlefield, however, were less lofty and were not played out in such stark contrast.

Soldiers, civilians, and, especially, the press painted a picture of an evil and depraved enemy who was responsible for barbaric acts. Confederates decried wanton acts by Federals, such as the way Richard Ashby was bayoneted in the abdomen as he lay prostate on the ground, suffering from eight wounds. Northern readers were roused to righteous indignation after Bull Run, when rumors of atrocities by the enemy were printed as fact. There were reports that helpless, wounded men, in a church and still on the battlefield, were killed after the battle had ended. The New York *Post* reported an eyewitness who, while fleeing the field, claimed a Southern soldier came upon a defenseless wounded Fire Zouave lying on the ground and "deliberately," said the *Post,* cut the victim's throat "from ear to ear, almost severing his head from his body." The Baltimore *American* tells of another Zouave, who was taken prisoner, but escaped, and reported that "he was treated with Indian barbarity by the rebels and that *many prisoners were pinioned to trees and tortured with bayonets thrown at them.*" There were stories of sadistic mutilation of Union soldiers being wounded by unqualified persons performing amputations. Several months later a wounded lieutenant who was angered by being wounded by the enemy in another engagement was reported by the press to have claimed that he "would have Congress pass a law compelling every [Confederate]...to be branded with the word 'traitor' on the forehead."[6]

Many Union soldiers found little that was favorable in western Virginia. "The country is wild and romantic, but good for little or nothing for farming," stated one soldier. Members of the Fourth Ohio Infantry questioned the wisdom of building a fort on the northwestern peak of the Alleghenies. "No rebel," argued one soldier, "would think of marching through such a forsaken country where the laurel was thick as hair on a dog's back," and infested "with bears and wildcats." One asked, "How in creation did the Government ever find out that God had such a country?" The response was, "This isn't God's country." Rebel guerrillas in western Virginia received special denunciation in both military reports and in the press. They were blamed for a reign of terror of "barbarous outrages" on loyal citizens, "burning their buildings, carrying off their property," and killing the men.

William Kepler, of the Fourth Ohio Volunteer Infantry, described the inhabitants of western Virginia as "lazy and ignorant," as begrimed and ugly, and as people who lived in "mere huts of logs." They raised "hardly enough to keep starvation from their doors." The soldier claimed, "Only one in ten of the population can read or write." They know just enough, Kepler went on, to "make them *dangerous.*" The few who were literate read in their "country newspapers that Vice-President Hamlin is a negro, and that Lincoln is waging" war "for the purpose of liberating slaves and killing their masters. This they believe and any amount of reasoning cannot convince them to the contrary. It seems enough for them to know that they are *Virginians*; upon this, and this alone they live and have their being. They are by far the most wretched and degraded people in America." The females "are worse than the men." They are "dressed in a loose, uncouth manner, barefooted and bareheaded; their principal occupation is chewing tobacco and plundering Union troops by getting ten prices for their eggs, butter, and cornbread." And these are the people, wrote one Federal, "our children—and their fathers before them—have been taught to regard as the true *chivalry* of America! The people of the United States are beginning to see that Virginia and her sons have been greatly overestimated."[7]

WHERE IS THE GLORY?

People involved in something as horrible as war have to have an ideological justification for the destruction, sacrifice, suffering, and loss of life that are involved. One justification was found in the concept of admirably performing one's duty for the noble cause under difficulty and life-threatening conditions. Those who were recognized for notable performance of their duty received praise in battle reports, newspaper accounts, speeches, and poetry. The highest praise usually went to those who were killed. They were described as having selflessly given their lives while performing brave deeds in a manner that brought honor and glory to their name. This is amplified in *The*

Fallen Brave, published in 1861. Flowery prose heaps praise upon select officers who had fallen during the first year. These men were eulogized in a manner depicting virtually flawless character, unflagging devotion, and a commitment that considered it an honor to die for the cause. One of the many men eulogized in this book is Lieutenant-Colonel James Haggerty of the Sixty-ninth New York Infantry. The writer sets the scene with "On Sunday, the twenty-first of July, a day never to be forgotten in American annals," and continues on to tell the tale of the Sixty-ninth New York, the lead regiment on Sherman's brigade, who crossed Bull Run on that day. Haggerty had left in the early afternoon, leading a charge against the enemy, who retreated into the pine trees. The book calls Haggerty "the first of his regiment to meet glorious death on that day of gallant deeds." The eulogy continues, "He died ready and devoted: as a patriot and as a Christian soldier, with his soul prepared to meet his creator, with the blessings of his Church upon him. He died foremost in the fight."

The expression of idealistic motives and acts was not limited to tributes of the slain. Soldiers of all levels could not help but think about their own demise and what would happen to their widowed wives and fatherless children. Many, like Captain Elisha N. Jones, of the Second Maine Volunteers, attempted to prepare his family, especially his spouse, for his death. The day before the Battle of Bull Run, Jones wrote his wife: "We have not fired a gun at an enemy yet, but we mean to if we can get near enough. Now don't worry; if it is God's will that I should fall in battle in defending the flag of my country, it would be wrong for you to repine. I could wish for no more honorable death, nor could you wish for a more honorable one for your husband." Jones went on to tell her he did not anticipate being killed and should see her soon. According to *The Fallen Brave,* he was mortally wounded, "while exhibiting great courage in rallying his men to the charge" at the Robinson house. Edwin Greble, killed at Big Bethel, wrote a similar letter to his wife, concluding with the statement: "If I die, let me be as a brave and honorable man; let no stain of dishonor hang over me or you."

Soldiers often entered the war with a romantic view of combat and a desire for glory. They seem to believe one soldier's words: "the paths of glory lead but to the grave." Major Theodore Winthrop, like Greble, was killed at Big Bethel. He wrote a poem stating, "Of deadly conflict may I nobly die, / In my first battle perish gloriously." Did he seek his own death by conspicuously standing in front of the fortified enemy? Did Colonel John W. Lowe, who was killed at Carnifex Ferry, seek his death—as was rumored—to redeem his besmirched reputation after the defeat at Scary Creek? Despite the uncertainty of guessing what was in another's mind in a bygone era, it seems overwhelmingly unlikely that Lowe and others would have died to improve a reputation. Lowe's attitude, and the attitude of many, was reflective of society's view of war based on heroic martyrs of the American Revolution and earlier wars. Heroic glory was the justification for loss of life in pursuit of a noble cause. It gave purposefulness to the deaths of those killed in combat and gave meaning to the grief of mourners. Although Colonel Lowe, who was weary of long marches and was suffering from poor health, did not seek his own death, he had a premonition that he would be killed. In his last letter to his wife, he wrote: "I feel as though my life's journey is nearly ended. The chances of war render it very probable that this is so, but still, you must not despond. God has given us many, very many happy hours together, and if it be his will that we meet no more on this earth, you must thank him, as I do, for the happiness he has already granted us, and submit with resignation to his holy will." A fair number of others also had premonitions of being killed and then were killed. These visions usually occurred before a battle. Examples include from Elmer Ellsworth, just prior to invading Alexandria, to Confederate Private S. H. Prior, before the battle at Camp Allegheny.[8]

Those who lost their lives early in the war, like Ellsworth, received more press as martyred heroes than those who were killed later. As the war continued and fighting increased, events competed for space in print, and the novelty of battle deaths lessened. The stardom of most of the important living heroes of 1861—such as McClellan, Beauregard, Johnston, and Rosecrans—would not have lasting luster. None of their reputations would reach the sustained height of Jackson's, and none would be resurrected to icon status, like Lee—whose name, as 1861 ended, was associated more with failure than with heroism.

Enticing visions of enjoying an adventurous, exciting, and dramatic life permeated the thoughts of nascent warriors, but these dreams were rapidly dashed by the realities of military life. The unsettling aspects of the soldier's new life included the tedium of camp life; homesickness; drills; seemingly endless and exhaustive marches; shortages of food, clothing, and proper arms; slowness of receiving pay; an awareness that life could end at any time from a bullet or disease; the sights and sounds of combat; and worries about those left at home. These problems tested soldiers' resolve. Many three-month Union volunteers had enough by the end of their term and gladly went home, although few had been in combat. These three-month volunteers made up numerous regiments from Patterson's army, and some from McDowell's, who left on the eve of what would be the largest battle of 1861.

Disaffection threatened control in the eastern invasion corridor after the battle, causing McClellan to subdue rebellious dissenters with arrests and threats of firing upon them. In the western invasion corridor, Kimball was forced to resort to similar means to quell the unrest at Cheat Mountain. Others continued their service, claiming that honor and the noble nature of the cause demanded their sacrifice. Most would endure the tedium and hardships with humor and perseverance, while some were slackers who schemingly and creatively avoided danger the best they could. Their counterparts were the stay-at-home men who were prevalent in Ohio towns. These pretend soldiers never joined up, but wore soldiers' uniforms, often parading the streets to attract attention and solicit adulation.

The bulk of the men who made up the armies of both sides lacked a military background. They were civilians, and they brought with them civilian values and ways. These were not easily put aside for the conformity demanded by military life. Humor and jesting were a part of their life. Such was the case with a private in the Third Ohio in western Virginia; he falsely wrote home that he had killed two of the enemy. His letter was published in the local paper and was read by members of his company. As the camp looked on, several men grabbed shovels and visited the embarrassed private, graciously offering to bury his dead. Sometimes officers played practical jokes. One September night, according to a newspaper account, a Seventh Louisiana major removed all the "fifth wheels" from the caissons and "rolled them noiselessly through the main street" of their Centreville camp and "piled them up in front of headquarters." The next morning the unamused colonel gave the major hell and placed him under arrest for a week.

On at least one occasion—recorded Rutherford B. Hayes—a civilian tried to impose a mother's standards on the military. While visiting her son in a Union camp in western Virginia, a mother saw another lad in the hot sun "walking up and down on his sentinel's beat." She "took pity on him" and sent him "a glass of wine and a piece of cake with a stool to sit on while he ate and drank." She also told him not to keep walking, but "sit down and rest! She also advised him to resign!"

More recent standards suggest that young boys and dogs should have been kept at home, not in military camps. In western Virginia, a number of youths had run away from Ohio and attached themselves to a Union regiment they liked. When they found one that pleased them more than the others, they became a "boy" in that regiment and a curiosity in their new camp. Amused soldiers would watch such a youth "drill, play soldier, officer, and run errands if needed." Hayes records that not only were juveniles joining their forces, but "dogs too, some fine ones."[9]

Nonconformity by soldiers could lead to serious and chilling punishments. Such was the case with the executions of two Louisiana Tigers whose regiments' uncivil ways earned them the nickname "wharf rats from New Orleans." The two offenders were shot for insubordination and attacking one of their officers at a guardhouse at Centreville in an attempt to free some of their buddies who had attempted to leave camp without orders.[10]

Private Michael Lanahan, of Company A of the Second United States Infantry, shot his sergeant, John Brennan, at Georgetown at 2:30 A.M. on October 29, 1861. Lanahan was angered when Brennan struck him in the side of the head and told him, "Doggone you, you ought to have been on post a quarter of an hour ago," so Lanahan killed Brennan. Lanahan was found guilty by the court and was hung January 6, 1862.[11]

Occasionally a life was ended for misdeeds without a trial. On one occasion an officer shot a man who refused to obey an order. At another time, four Pittsburgh volunteers of the Fireman's Legion left their camp near Baltimore, Maryland, without permission, went to town, and got drunk. Twice soldiers were sent to bring them back and twice the intoxicated four refused. They also took a musket from one of the soldiers sent to force them to return. Exasperated, their captain sent a third squad with orders to bring the miscreants back dead or alive. This party of five was greeted by musket and pistol fire, but the squad subdued the malcontents by shooting and killing the most notorious of the group, Robert (alias "Loafer"). Robert had an extensive police record for drunkenness and violence prior to joining the military.[12]

Officers as well as privates ran afoul of military regulations and were court-martialed and frequently dismissed from service. Court-martial records show that a common charge was "conduct unbecoming an officer and a gentleman due to appearing drunk in public and using foul language." Others such as Captain William F. Tully had their services terminated for "contempt and disrespect toward his commanding officer." Near his colonel's tent, Tully had shouted, "He would not go on picket now if Colonel Pickell or even Jesus Christ would order him to do so." Tully was arrested and confined to his tent, but he violated that order by leaving. He was kicked out of the army.[13]

Private Lewis Stanley of the Twelfth Ohio Volunteers also had his services terminated. He ran away as his regiment was marching into battle at Carnifex Ferry. His trial at the Tompkins farm, headed by Cox and Hayes, resulted in a punishment of twenty days of fatigue while attached to a ball and chain. After this, his head was shaved and he was drummed out of the service.[14]

Officers were released from service with more decorum. Colonel James E. Kerrigan of the Twenty-fifth New York Volunteers was tried for sundry charges, varying from neglect of duty, intoxication, "shameful" abandonment of his post, and communicating with the enemy. After listening to 250 pages of testimony, the court concluded that he was just plain incompetent and allowed Kerrigan to resign.[15]

Officers as well as privates left camp without permission. Lieutenant-Colonel Samuel N. Bailey, of the Twelfth Pennsylvania Reserves, habitually and without permission of his commanding officer, left his quarters in Camp Pierpoint at Prospect Hill in northern Virginia, probably for romantic forays into the nearby community. He was warned that if he continued his nocturnal absences, he would be reprimanded. On the night of November 15, 1861, Bailey was assigned to be the Field officer of the picket lines and was ordered to report to Brigadier-General Meade for instruction. The lieutenant-colonel could not be found, and he did not return to camp until morning. For his transgression he was court-martialed, found guilty of neglect of duty, and reprimanded.

Other officers from Camp Pierpoint—including Major Richard H. Woolworth of the Third Pennsylvania Reserves—were tried for violating military regulations. The arrest of four men who attempted to return after going hunting set off a chain reaction that implicated the Major Woolworth. He was charged with having run afoul of military regulations by ordering the four men on a foray beyond the picket line to hunt wild turkeys. The court seemed to buy Woolworth's explanation that his orders had been misunderstood; they found him not guilty of disobeying orders and neglecting his duty.[16]

Discipline was needed on both sides. At times men resented, protested, and even refused to comply with orders. Some balked at orders that were counter to what they believed their role should be. Some found it hard to conform. Others were reluctant to give up their individualistic ways as the early days, full of their playing soldier and the hype of glorious patriotism, were being replaced by the rigors of army life and war. The Fifteenth Massachusetts' band members found their orders unacceptable when they were told to perform duties to prepare them for medical service during combat. When they were first ordered to perform these drills, the band members refused. They were then placed under arrest and were not allowed to have food or drink until they complied with the order. They claimed they would die first, but they complied within a day. At the behest of Colonel William R. Lee, the Andrew Sharpshooters were detached from the Twentieth Massachusetts because they refused to follow his orders. They had enlisted as a separate company and believed they were mere sharpshooters who did not have to follow his orders.

A company of men of the Seventeenth Mississippi had a meeting and drew up resolutions in an attempt to persuade their captain to reverse his order to have all body servants in camp cook for the company. The men who brought slaves with them said they would send their body servants back home first before forcing them to cook for the entire company. The following day, the captain refused to drill his men, stating that he would not have anything more to do with drilling them because they would not obey his order to consolidate the cooking. Later, the same captain again angered his men. On August 26, 1861, they were paid $12.80 for their services through July 1, as well as a clothing allowance of $21. The captain put the clothing money aside for the purchase of winter uniforms. Several men became very angry and refused to accept their wages because they did not get the clothing payment.

Several weeks later, a man from the same regiment, the Seventeenth Mississippi, was among several who were court-martialed. When the sentence was read at dress parade, the man walked out before the regiment and threw down his sword and musket, swearing he would never obey the sentence. He was placed under arrest and was given only enough bread and water for four days. In the same regiment, the drum major cashiered his fife player, who did not follow his orders. A less serious offence was the refusal of some Seventeenth Mississippi men to do their own washing. On washing days, which were usually once a month, the men found washing and cleaning up beneath them, despite the lack of drilling on that day. Those who had body servants had their slaves perform the task. Those who did not usually hired someone else to do it for them.[17]

Soldiers of both sides committed numerous inglorious acts. Civilians were often the victims; food, crops, and livestock were sometimes taken out of need, but more often they destroyed by acts of vandalism. Civilian supporters of the side opposite the invaders frequently abandoned their homes and farms. Those who remained received, in the eyes of the enemy troops, punishment for backing the side that caused the war. In western Virginia, soldiers pulled up a farmer's corn crop because he was suspected of being pro-Confederate. Store owners' and farmers' property was vandalized by some Union troops on their way to Bull Run. When Confederates pulled back from their outer lines in northern Virginia in September 1861, Federal troops occupying the vacated area burned property, including untenanted houses and their contents, regardless of the homeowners' political convictions. Even the New York *Weekly Journal of Commerce* condemned "these wanton acts," claiming that they would "doubtless undergo investigation by the military authorities, as they were strongly condemned by Gen. McClellan." The wanton destruction of property continued. "With a view to check these outrages the commanding officers…issued verbal orders to shoot down any man who may be caught in the incendiary act." A few days later, across the river near Poolesville, "an unprincipled speculator smuggled a hogshead of liquor into the 5th Connecticut Camp. "Before detected by officers, enough of the poisonous compound had been dispensed...During the reign of its influence an affair occurred in which one citizen was killed, two or three wounded, and several horses and cattle shot." General Banks then ordered "all liquor within the limits of Union pickets to be immediately destroyed and those selling it to be arrested." Booze was the bane of discipline and proper behavior. A corporal of the guard of the Fifth Ohio Infantry, while making his rounds on December 8, 1861, at Romney, was, in the words of a soldier present at the scene, "shot in cold blood...and without provocation," by a drunken sentinel.

There were other inglorious incidents, including some accidents that took people's lives. One such occasion occurred in September when the Federals were attempting to penetrate further into northern Virginia. It was night and the Federals mistakenly fired on each other. During the confusion, two Union soldiers probably lost their lives by being run over by cavalry horses and weapon-bearing carriages.[18] Unfortunately, friendly fire resulted in deaths in most of the 1861 battles. Accidental shootings in camp frequently claimed the lives of innocent bystanders and led to inconsolable remorse by those responsible. Such incidents occurred in a variety of settings: Men were sitting around in camp when someone carelessly and unintentionally discharged his musket. Another soldier was shot when a soldier was wading in a stream while returning to his Union camp at Elkwater. Frightened by a snake in the water near him, the soldier shot at the reptile, but instead hit a comrade. A Union sergeant lost his life by going around after dark at Cheat Mountain Summit to see if the guards would shoot. They did. They mistook him for the enemy and told the sergeant to halt. When he did not halt, they shot him.[19]

Both civilians and soldiers possessed a naivete about war. Civilian behavior during the Bull Run campaign amply illustrates the point. Reporters were oblivious about the dangers of being in a combat area, and they stood out in the open within enemy range at Blackburn Ford on July 18, 1861. Three days later, men and women came with picnic lunches and baskets of champagne to watch the fighting at Bull Run; they never got close enough to see the battle. The casual and festive atmosphere soon changed for both reporters and other civilian spectators. An assistant to one of the three reporters at Blackburn's Ford became so unnerved when a bullet passed close to his ear that he rode rapidly back to Washington, reporting, in his hysteria, that 500 men had been killed. At the same site, reporter Edward H. House was enticed by ripe cherries and climbed a tree—only to draw Confederate fire. House immediately dropped to the ground and joined the other reporters in a house. One of his colleagues, Charles Coffin, a correspondent for the Boston *Journal,* was soon traumatized by seeing the torn body of a wounded Federal being carried back to Centreville. Horrified, Coffin dropped to his knees and muttered, "If this is war, let it stop right here. Let the Southern States go. Let them have their Confederacy. Anything rather than this."

Washingtonians went to bed on July 21, 1861, thinking that Union forces had won the battle at Bull Run. The joyful feelings from earlier reports of victory were cruelly destroyed during the night when those fleeing the battle site brought terrorizing tales back to the city. Despite government censorship by restricting use of the telegraph by reporters, the news of the Union disaster spread northward.

Seeing the wounded certainly did not increase a feeling of security. One soldier walked the twenty-five miles to the city with an amputated arm. Another made it with bullet holes shot through his cheeks, tongue, thighs, and scrotum, as well as a broken jaw.[20] These injuries were a testimony to unbelievable persistence, courage, and endurance, but also to the frightening results of war. Once again people fled from Washington, as they had done when they had feared the Confederate army's approach.

Some civilians were disillusioned prior to the Bull Run campaign. A young preacher, W. G. Hammond, in northern Virginia, frequently visited the Southern forces gathered at Manassas Junction. At first he saw all soldiers as noble knights and gentlemen. That soon changed. He wrote in his diary on June 18, 1861: "Went to Manassas Junction—felt sad to see as much wickedness as there seems to be in camp, and so few restraining influences…May the Lord remember mercifully those who may soon bite the dust in death."[21]

Soldiers were also ill prepared for their new life, so many were dissatisfied and disillusioned. A Confederate at Winchester wrote in early July 1861 that dissatisfied men could be found in all companies. He attributed this to the way men left home unaware of the nature of a soldier's life. These novice warriors assumed that war would be similar to the first couple of days after they volunteered.

They had read and thought little about war, so, according to the Confederate soldier in Winchester, when the "first fun had worn away and the realities of their situation hit them, they became disappointed and disillusioned."[22]

Some would write home telling a younger brother to stay home and not to join up, as it was no life for him. Camp life, marches, illness, and combat were among the major causes of disenchantment. One Confederate soldier wrote, "It was the day after day, morning and afternoon, drill, drill, drill...This monotonous life was occasionally broken by alarms of the enemy's appearance."[23] A Confederate from Tennessee wrote the Fayetteville *Observer* in August 1861, "I have read a great deal about the romantic scenery of northwestern Virginia, and I have come to the conclusion that the individual who wrote such stuff never had the extraordinary pleasure of wearing their feet out to their ankles walking over the mountains to see the romantic scenery, as I did." Many others would agree. A Union colonel, John Lowe, wrote his wife before reaching Carnifex Ferry, "We are marched almost to death. We have met with one unending succession of hills. They roll like the billows of the ocean, or, rather, seem as though they were waves of a great ocean, which, at the moment of their greatest agitation, had suddenly become solid." Another Confederate wrote, "I am yet among the living. We are now encamped on the top of Big Sewell Mountain in the roughest and poorest county in Virginia. I have been in service six weeks, have had the measles, marched 305 miles and am now retreating from the blame Yankees." An Indiana soldier marching to Cheat Mountain wrote a female friend, stating that they "were pretty badly fatigued" as many had dropped out. The only thing that kept him going was the fear of being ridiculed as a dropout. He concluded, "[a man] must think a d--n sight of his country to suffer this way to defend it." Another way to view it, he wrote, is to blame the damn Rebels for "bringing all this upon us."[24]

Sickness sapped men's strength, morale, and life. Near Sewell Mountain in the fall of 1861 a Southern soldier wrote, "I have seen good soldiers, good true—men [who] would be a honor to any nation, parched and burning up with fevers, lying in wet tents without bedding supplied." If a sick man were to send for a doctor, the writer continued, and if *"perchance he saw fit in the majesty of his exalted position"* to come at all, he wrote, "it would be to ask a few crabbed questions...and without one word of sympathy or encouragement, turn upon his high heeled boots and proudly strut off." The soldier wrote, "I have seen worse sufferings if possible than this...I have seen wagons crowded with sick men with no bedding but a knapsack and an old blanket and conveyed over miserably rough roads....I have seen the same men put out of wagons when they could be hauled no further to drag themselves over the mountains best they could—staggering from weakness and disease, after they had been literally jolted to death—or try to walk until their last expiring breath...and then buried in some unknown spot, far away from home and loved ones."[25]

At about the same time, in mid-September, disease was also the worst enemy for the Confederates at Manassas. Because of the lack of "proper enforcement of hygienic regulations," wrote one soldier, "the past month has been one in which there has been a reckless waste of life in the army in consequences of which our camp is now suffering." Major contributors to the suffering and death included flies, lice, fleas, and mosquitoes, which bit and crawled over men's bodies, annoying the living and transmitting diseases such as dysentery and malaria. Insects contributed to the ungodly sights on the battlefield. Flies swarmed over swollen and darkened corpses, emitting stomach-turning stench from bodies covered with large masses of wiggling maggots that feasted upon the corpses' eyes, nose, mouth, and other body parts.[26]

Every battlefield, especially Bull Run, was "an awful looking place," wrote a Southern soldier. Yet this and other sites of combat had almost a hypnotic attraction. More than one Confederate soldier who was camped at Centreville near the Bull Run battlefield would state, "If we do not go away from here soon, I think I shall go up and take a look at it." What they saw were about a dozen abandoned houses in different areas of the battlefield where families had previously lived happily. The Henry house had been riddled by a dozen cannonballs and numerous bullets. Others had bloodstained floors, where wounded men had been carried. Fence rails were strewn about everywhere, and fields of corn had been trampled down, presenting a sight far worse than most had imagined. The evidence of the battle remained: clothing, old shoes, and human bones were scattered in every direction. Several hundred yards east of the Henry house stood a small monument marking the spot where Bartow had fallen. Every tree around the Henry house that was large enough for a walking stick had been cut down and taken away; large cherry trees' branches had been stripped to make pipe stems. The ground around the Henry house was strewn with dead horses and the graves of Union soldiers. Those who fell on the Southern side were buried respectfully; the Yankees received less care and were tossed in gullies and mass graves, where dirt covering them had washed away. Arms and legs could be seen sticking out of the ground.

The graves of New York Zouaves were a popular visitation site of Confederates camped at Centreville. The Southerners used fence rails to pry up their bodies to get buttons off their clothes. One Confederate sent his wife samples of hair from a Zouave's head and a tooth from a Union artillery horse. In early December, Confederates dug up a Federal artilleryman and were amazed to find that from the waist down, the flesh was firm and well preserved. Finding this difficult to believe, all who passed by took a rail and turned the body over to get a complete look. This and other sights caused the soldier who sent his wife the Zouave's hair to tell her that it was "shocking to look over such a place, but a soldier's heart soon gets hard and he can look at much [of] anything." Nevertheless, men on both sides would agree with the Federal soldier who, after campaigning in western Virginia, wrote, "I *think* I have discovered that the martial road to glory 'is a hard road to travel.'"[27]

The gods of war would demand even more.

[1] For an analysis of why men fought in the Civil War, see James M. McPherson, *For Cause and Comrades* (New York: Oxford University, 1997). Men fought not just for patriotic reasons but also because of pride in one's unit (especially regiments) and concern for comrades.

[2] E. Merton Coulter, *The Confederate States of America, 1861-1865* (Baton Rouge, La.: Louisiana State University, 1950), 59, 309; McPherson, *For Cause and Comrades*, 5, 24, 78, 82, 86, 94-95, 103; Reid Mitchell, *Civil War Soldiers: Their Expectations and Their Experiences* (New York: Viking, 1988), 4-11, 17-18, 31-32; James I. Robertson Jr., *Soldiers Blue and Gray* (Columbia, S.C.: University of South Carolina, 1988), 3-15; Bell I. Wiley, *The Life of Billy Yank* (Indianapolis, Ind.: Bobbs-Merrill, 1952), 37-40; Bell I. Wiley, *The Life of Johnny Reb* (Indianapolis, Ind.: Bobbs-Merrill, 1943), 17-19.

[3] Richard E. Beringer, Herman Hattaway, Archer Jones, and William N. Still Jr., *Why The South Lost The Civil War* (Athens, Ga.: University of Georgia, 1986), 272.

[4] *Daily* (Wheeling) *Intelligencer*, July 31, 1861; Mitchell, *Civil War Soldier*, 31-36.

[5] *OR*, Ser. I, vol. 2, 574.

[6] *Daily* (Wheeling) *Intelligencer*, July 31 and October 10, 1861.

[7] *The Continental Monthly*, March 1862, 338; Kepler, *History of Three Months and Three Years Service*, 38.

[8] Owen, *In Camp and Battle*, 53; Moore, *A Life for the Confederacy*, 52-55; *OR*, Ser. I, vol. 2, 354; John G. Shea, ed., *The Fallen Brave* (New York: C.B. Richardson, 1861), 107, 112-13, 120-21, 137, 139, 173; Winthrop, *Life in the Open Air and Other Papers*, front page. There is little information on those who might have had premonitions that they would be killed and were not. Those who died after telling others of their premonitions made a far greater impact.

[9] Hayes, *Diary*, 60, 86-87; Zinn, *Cheat Mountain*, 22.

[10] Terry L. Jones, *Lee's Tigers* (Baton Rouge, La.: Louisiana State University, 1987), 40-42. At times tempers flared in camps and fistfights occurred. Drinking was also a problem. More acceptable leisure-hour activities included lounging, smoking, cards, checkers, chess, dominoes, reading, or writing letters. Even the men with meager education and knowledge of grammar possessed the ability to express their thoughts and opinions with an uncanny clarity, brevity, and, at times, eloquence.

[11] National Archives, Records of the Office of the Judge Advocate General (Army), Court Martial Case Files, 1809-1938 (hereafter cited as Court Martial Files), Record Group 153, Box 289, File No. II2924.

[12] New York *Weekly Journal of Commerce*, September 26, 1861.

[13] Court Martial Files, Record Group 153, Box 288, File No. II506.

[14] Ibid., Box 289, File No. II53.

[15] Ibid., Box 320, File No. II680.

[16] Ibid., Box 300, File No. II660.

[17] Bruce, *Twentieth Massachusetts*, 20; Ford, *Fifteenth Massachusetts*, 63; Moore, ed., *A Life for the Confederacy*, 54, 55, 58, 61, 63-64.

[18] New York *Weekly Journal of Commerce*, September 26, October 3 & 17, 1861; John M. Paver, *What I Saw from 1861 to 1864*, (Indianapolis, Ind.: Scott-Miller, 1906), 24-25.

[19] Nancy N. Boxter, ed., *Hoosier Farm Boy in Lincoln's Army: The Civil War Letters of Pvt. John R. McClure* (N.P., Privately published, 1971), 17.

[20] Andrews, *The North Reports the Civil War*, 89-100; Rich Britton, "Rush to Glory," *Civil War Times Illustrated*, June 1996, 52; Charles C. Coffin, *The Boys of '61 or Four Years of Fighting*, (Boston: Estes & Lauriat, 1896), 42; Cunningham, *Field Medical Services at the Battles of Manassas*, 18. The most complete story of the battle of Bull Run was published in the Richmond *Dispatch*. Their correspondent was one of the civilians allowed to watch the battle from the Confederate side.

[21] Poland, *Dunbarton*, 52.

[22] Harlan R. Jessup, ed., *The Painful News I Have to Write*, (Baltimore, Md.: Butternut & Blue, 1998), 11.

[23] Rawling, *History of the First Regiment Virginia Infantry*, 42-43.

[24] Carrington, *Cheat Mountain*, 40; James I. Robertson, Jr., ed. "An Indiana Soldier in Love and War: The Civil War Letters of John V. Handley," *Indiana Magazine of History*, September 1963, 197; Shea, ed., *The Fallen Brave*, 173; Atlanta *Southern Confederacy*, October 3, 1861.

[25] *Southern Confederacy*, November 1861.

[26] Gary L. Miller, "Historical Natural History: Insects and the Civil War," *American Entomologist*, Winter 1997, 227-44; *Southern Confederacy*, September 22, 1861.

[27] *Continental Monthly*, March 1862, 338; Letter, John Carter to Mollie Carter, December 10, 1861, Section 11, MSS1C2468B163-183, Virginia Historical Society; Union Miscellany, Eyeler Letter, Box No. Union Miscellany no. 99, item 2, The Robert W. Woodruff Library, Emory University; Letter, T. T. Fogle to Dr. J. Fogle, September 14, 1861, Box No. 1, The Robert W. Woodruff Library, Emory University, Savannah, Georgia.

BIBLIOGRAPHICAL COMMENT

Materials used in preparing this volume are cited in detail in the Notes. They include a wide range of sources, from the *Official Records of the Union and Confederate Armies* to Northern and Southern newspapers and unpublished materials. Those mentioned below are select materials that are generally more accessible reading.

Herman Hattaway's *Shades of Blue and Gray* (1997) is an excellent overview of the military history of the Civil War with superb suggestions for further reading. A more detailed military history can be found in Hattaway and Archer Jones' *How the North Won* (1983). Also see Archer Jones' *Civil War Command and Strategy* (1992). A fine overview of the war in Virginia is *Virginia* (1899), by Jed Hotchkiss, vol. III in his *Confederate Military History;* also useful are articles by participants in the war, in vol. I of *Battles and Leaders of the Civil War* (1887), edited by Robert U. Johnson and Clarence C. Buel. Valuable overviews are vol. I of D. S. Freeman's *Lee's Lieutenants* (1950), and vol. I of Freeman's *R. E. Lee* (1934).

The life of Ellsworth can be traced in Ruth Randell's *Colonel Elmer Ellsworth* (1960), and the life of Jackson in the difficult-to-find *Life of James W. Jackson* (1862). The background history of Alexandria is ably presented by William F. Smith and T. Michael Miller in *A Seaport Portrait of Old Alexandria, Virginia* (1989). For the defense of Washington, D.C., consult *Symbol, Sword, and Shield* (1975), by Benjamin F. Cooling III, and *Mr. Lincoln's Forts* (1988), by Benjamin F. Cooling III and Walton H. Owen II.

The largest battle of 1861, Bull Run is covered by R. M. Johnston in *Bull Run: Its Strategy and Tactics* (1913) and by William C. Davis in the readable *Battle of Bull Run* (1977). The best military coverage of the battle is *The First Battle of Bull Run* (1989), by John Hennessy. More recent studies include *"We Shall Meet Again"* (2000), by Joanna M. McDonald, and *A Single Grand Victory* (2002), by Ethan Rafuse. Rafuse provides a superb overview of the first Manassas campaign. Additional information is presented by Horace H. Cummingham's *Field and Medical Services at the Battle of*

Manassas (1968); Joe E. Johnston's *Narrative of Military Operations* (1874); T. Harry Williams' *P. T. G. Beauregard: Napoleon in Gray* (1954); and James Longstreet's *From Manassas to Appomattox* (1896).

Information dealing with the second-most-famous conflict of 1861, Ball's Bluff, by participants and earlier writers can be found in Eppa Hunton's *Autobiography of Eppa Hunton* (1933); George A. Bruce's *Twentieth Regiment of Massachusetts Volunteer Infantry* (1906); Andrew E. Ford's *Fifteenth Massachusetts Volunteer Infantry in the Civil War* (1908); Robert A. Moore's *A Life for the Confederacy* (1959); Francis W. Palfry's *Memoirs of William Francis Barlett* (1881); and Isaac J. Wistar's *The Autobiography of Isaac Jones Wistar* (1937). The most complete recent study is the *Battle of Ball's Bluff,* (1985) by Kim Holien. Other useful books dealing with this topic are Joseph Dorst Patch's *The Battle of Ball's Bluff* (1958); Bryon Farwell's *Ball's Bluff: A Small Battle and Its Long Shadow* (1990); William F. Howard's *The Battle of Ball's Bluff* (1994); and John E. Divine's *Eighth Virginia Infantry* (1983).

Serveral works deal with the lesser-known conflicts at Dranesville and Big Bethel. For Dranesville, see William S. Hammond's "The Battle of Dranesville," *Southern Historical Society Papers* (1907), vol. 35; O. R. Howard and William H. Rauck's *History of the "Bucktails"* (1906); Edwin A. Glover's *Bucktail Wildcats* (1960); E. M. Woodward's *History of the Third Pennsylvania Reserves* (1883); and Charles P. Poland Jr.'s *Dunbarton, Dranesville, Virginia* (1974). *Histories of the Several Regiments from North Carolina in the Great War*, vol. I (1901), by Walter Clark; *Lee's Maverick General* (1961), by Hal Bridges; *Butler's Book* (1892), by Benjamin F. Butler; and *Defenders of the Chesapeake* (1989), by Richard P. Weinert Jr. and Robert Arthur, cover Big Bethel.

Recommended overviews of military activity in West Virginia are presented by Otis K. Rice, in *West Virginia: A History* (1985); Stan Cohen, in *The Civil War in West Virginia: A Pictorial History* (1976) and in *A Pictorial Guide to West Virginia's Civil War Sites* (1990); Richard Andre, Stan Cohen, and Bill Wintz, in *Bullets and*

Steel: The Fight for the Great Kanawha Valley (1995); Clayton R. Newell, in *Lee vs. McClellan: The First Campaign* (1996); George E. Moore, in *A Banner in the Hills: West Virginia's Statehood* (1963); and David L. Phillips, in *War Diaries: The 1861 Kanawha Valley Campaign* (1990). Phillips also edited *Civil War Stories: Civil War in West Virginia* (1901).

A number of useful articles can be found in the magazine *West Virginia History*. Among them are C. H. Ambler's "General R. E. Lee's Northwest Campaign" (October 1943); Clarice L. Barles' "Jacob Dolson Cox in West Virginia," (October 1944); John M. Belohavek's "John B. Flood and the West Virginia Campaign of 1861," (July 1988); Robert B. Boehm's "The Battle of Rich Mountain, July 11, 1861," (October 1958); Frank Klement's "John B. Floyd and the West Virginia Campaign of 1861," (July 1947); and Joseph W. Thomas' "Campaigns of Generals McClellan and Rosecrans in Western Virginia," (July 1944).

Select biographies and related material about significant players in western Virginia include Warren W. Hassler Jr.'s *General George B. McClellan* (1957); Stephen W. Sears' *George B. McClellan* (1988) and, edited by Sears, *The Civil War Papers of George B. McClellan* (1989); George B. McClellan's *McClellan's Own Story* (1887); Rutherford B. Hayes' *Diary and Letters of Rutherford Birchard Hayes* (1922); T. Harry Williams' *Hayes of the Twenty-third* (1965); Jacob D. Cox's *Military Reminiscences of the Civil War,* vol. I (1900); Henry Heth's *The Memories of Henry Heth* (1974); William M. Lamers' *The Edge of Glory: A Biography of William S. Rosecrans* (1961); Walter S. Griggs, Jr., *General John Pegram, C.S.A.* (1993); Barton Wise's *The Life of Henry A. Wise of Virginia* (1899); Craig M. Simpson's *A Good Southerner: The Life of Henry A. Wise of Virginia* (1985); D. S. Freeman's *R. E. Lee* (1934); and James W. Raab and W. W. Loring's *Florida's Forgotten General* (1996).

Military events from Cox's invasion from Ohio to Carnifex Ferry are ably covered by Terry Lowry in *The Battle of Scary Creek* (1982) and *September Blood: The Battle of Carnifex Ferry* (1985). For the Sewell Mountain Campaign, see Jim McKinney's *Robert E.*

Lee At Sewell Mountain (1990). McKinney also gives an overview of events from Carnifex Ferry to Camp Allegheny in *Robert E. Lee and the Thirty-fifth Star* (1993). Martin K. Fleming's "The Northwestern Virginia Campaign of 1861," *Blue and Gray* (August 1993) is a fine overview of military activity in northwestern Virginia. Detailed information about aspects of this campaign can be found in Fritz Haselberger's *Yanks from the South, the First Land Campaign of the Civil War: Rich Mountain, West Virginia* (1987); Jack Zinn's *The Battle of Rich Mountain* (1971) and *R. E. Lee's Cheat Mountain Campaign* (1974); John Ashcraft's *Thirty-third Virginia Infantry* (1988); and W. Hunter Lesser's *Battle at Corrick's Ford* (1993). The more illuminating of the accounts by participants in western Virginia include Ebenezer Hannaford's *The Story of a Regiment: A History of the Campaigns...of the Sixth Regiment Ohio Volunteer Infantry* (1968); John Beatty's *The Citizen-Soldier* (1879); John H. Cammack's *Personal Recollections of Private John Henry Cammack, a Soldier of the Confederacy* (1923); and *Hanging Rock Rebel: Lt. John Blue's War in West Virginia and the Shenandoah Valley*(1994), edited by Dan Oates.

INDEX

Seventh New York .. 209, 214, 216, 237, 238

Seventh Ohio....368, 369, 370, 372, 409, 482

Seventy-first Pennsylvania 105, 167

Seventy-ninth New York... 87, 100

Seward, William H............. 92

Sewell Mountain 357, 359, 366, 402, 415, 416, 417, 418, 419, 420, 421, 422, 423, 425, 426, 427, 430, 431, 432, 434, 435, 442, 462, 475, 477, 478, 479, 480, 482, 524, 539

Shavers Fork 282, 283, 303, 326

Shavers Mountain............. 303

Shenandoah Valley 4, 48, 244, 261, 289, 292, 306, 331, 355, 491, 508, 509, 512, 514, 525

Sherman, William T.... 55, 67, 73, 76, 87, 115, 530

Shipman (Virgina unionist) 315

Silver Lake 465

Simonds, George B. 132

Sissonville, VA* 335, 404

Sixth South Carolina 178, 181, 186, 194

Sixtieth Virginia....... 429, 431

Sixty-ninth New York . 30, 73, 87, 530

Sixty-ninth Pennsylvania.. 137

Skirmish.... xvii, 3, 35, 39, 40, 41, 42, 43, 44, 47, 52, 53, 60, 67, 82, 83, 84, 89, 95, 96, 99, 101, 103, 105, 106, 108, 127, 128, 130, 131, 132, 135, 137, 138, 139, 140, 141, 143, 151, 154, 159, 160, 168, 173, 175, 178, 182, 183, 184, 192, 193, 216, 217, 218, 228, 234, 247, 266, 270, 275, 282, 283, 284, 301, 314, 317, 339, 343, 344, 346, 359, 382, 385, 393, 402, 404, 422, 423, 424, 429, 437, 442, 448, 450, 452, 453, 456, 458, 459, 462, 468, 475, 478, 484, 511, 512, 522

Smith, G.W. 91, 118

Smith, William (Extra Billy) ...29, 30, 36, 39, 40, 42, 53, 82, 83, 87, 105, 167

Smith, William S...... 385, 462

Soldiers White Tavern...... 280

South Bridge 514

South Carolina24, 62, 87, 111, 178, 186, 403, 464, 468, 495, 542

Spafford, Caroline (Carrie) 18, 22, 27

Spies...................... 253, 337

Sprague, William ... 56, 62, 69

St. George, VA* 286, 459, 460, 479

Staunton Artillery Company 497

Staunton, VA....247, 263, 267, 280, 287, 288, 290, 295, 307, 314, 321, 327, 331, 433, 493, 497, 509

CPSIA information can be obtained at www.ICGtesting.com
Printed in the USA
BVOW010220160212

283083BV00001B/14/A